Power and
Organizations

FOUNDATIONS FOR ORGANIZATIONAL SCIENCE

A SAGE Publications Series

Series Editor

David Whetten, *Brigham Young University*

Editors

Anne S. Huff, *University of Colorado* and *Cranfield University* (UK)
Benjamin Schneider, *University of Maryland*
M. Susan Taylor, *University of Maryland*

The FOUNDATIONS FOR ORGANIZATIONAL SCIENCE series supports the development of students, faculty, and prospective organizational science professionals through the publication of texts authored by leading organizational scientists. Each volume provides a highly personal, hands-on introduction to a core topic or theory and challenges the reader to explore promising avenues for future theory development and empirical application.

Stewart R. Clegg • David Courpasson • Nelson Phillips

Power and Organizations

Foundations for
Organizational
Science
A SAGE Publications Series

SAGE Publications

London • Thousand Oaks • New Delhi

First published 2006

SAGE Publications Ltd
1 Oliver's Yard
55 City Road
London EC1Y 1SP

SAGE Publications Inc.
2455 Teller Road
Thousand Oaks, California 91320

SAGE Publications India Pvt Ltd
B-42, Panchsheel Enclave
Post Box 4109
New Delhi 110 017

British Library Cataloguing in Publication data

A catalogue record for this book is available from
the British Library

ISBN-10 0-7619-4391-9   ISBN-13 978-0-7619-4391-4
ISBN-10 0-7619-4392-7   ISBN-10 978-0-7619-4392-1 (pbk)

Library of Congress Control Number: 2005935973

Typeset by C&M Digitals (P) Ltd., Chennai, India

Printed on paper from sustainable resources

Knowledge works as a tool of power ... the measure of the desire
for knowledge depends upon the measure to which the will to power
grows in a species: a species grasps a certain amount of reality in order to
become master of it, in order to press it into service.

Frederick Nietzsche, from *A will to power,*
Book Three: Principles of a new evaluation,
I: The will to power as knowledge,
Aphorism 480 (March–June 1888)

About the Authors

Stewart R. Clegg is Professor at the University of Technology, Sydney, Australia and Aston Business School, UK, as well as the Director of ICAN Research (www.ican. uts.edu.au). He is Visiting Professor of Organizational Change Management at the Maastricht University Faculty of Business; Visiting Professor at both EM-Lyon Business School, France, as well as the Vrije University of Amsterdam, Netherlands, where he is also International Fellow in Discourse and Management Theory, Centre of Comparative Social Studies.

David Courpasson is Associate Dean for Research and Professor in Organizational Sociology at EM Lyon Business School (France). He is Visiting Professor at Lancaster University Management School, UK. He is also co-editor of *Organization Studies*.

Nelson Phillips is Professor of Strategy and Organizational Behaviour and the Head of the Organization and Management Group at the Tanaka Business School, Imperial College London.

Contents

Acknowledgements

As the project began a small number of people contributed significantly to the clarification, refinement and extension of the ideas herein; in particular, we would like to thank Tyrone Pitsis and John Gray for asking smart questions at an early stage of the project's development. As the project gathered pace, we were fortunate to have many more occasions for gratitude. In particular, we owe thanks to Eduardo Ibarra-Colado who made incisive, extended scholarly comments on a great deal of the manuscript; Jacqueline Kenney for her deep engagement and commentary on the evolving text; Chris Carter who was a wonderful supporter of the project, giving freely of his time to provide frequent, supportive and thoughtful commentaries, good friendship, and shared experiences (not to mention Cobras and eggplant curries at Mosley's K2); Tim Ray for his insights into knowledge management; John Sillince for many acts of considerate criticism of the text as it evolved; Mark Haugaard for his engagement with some of the central questions concerning power, his commitment to debate and exchange, and his doggedness in ensuring that we got some important things right; David Silverman for his guidance on some matters of ethnomethodological and Goffman interpretation, as well as some details related to the Holocaust; and Richard Badham for his comments on our general approach, as well as for reminding us of Isaiah Berlin.

A number of people helped in small but significant ways: Delia With advised us about the state of Romania under the Ceauşescus; Brian Torode offered some comments on total institutions; Hugh Willmott sought some clarification from Stewart of a cryptic response to a discussion site posting, which reflections were then incorporated and expanded in the final chapter; Suzanne Benn gave us feedback on our treatment of Ulrich Beck's work; Jean-François Chanlat offered comments on the dissemination of management in France in the early years of the last century; Peter Meijby offered some thoughts on Foucault and on Danish politics; Peter Clarke made suggestions concerning time; Julie Gustavs contributed some comments on the 'politics of truth'; Dirk Bunzel provided advice on German language, history and Luhmann; Tor Hernes also offered advice on Luhmann; Sonya Pearce provided guidance on the Stolen Generation; Margaret Grieco suggested inclusion of the Magdalene Laundries and gave us some advice on the gendering of total institutions; Ray Gordon looked over our criticisms of Foucault; Paula Jarzabkowski suggested, early in the manuscript's development, the necessity of restructuring the early chapters through the use of more subheadings, a suggestion which led to considerably enhanced clarity; Saku Mantere also made some good suggestions about clarity and restructuring. We'd like to acknowledge Malcolm Warner for alerting us to Kafka's critique of Taylorism; Halleh Ghorashi for her insights into matters of Islamic identity; and finally, Julie Gustavs and David Bubna-Litic for drawing our attention to the website maintained by Phillip Zimbardo.

More generally, Arie Lewin and Bill McKelvey stimulated thought about meta-routines, while Ralph Stablein and J.C. Spender provided insightful comments about the ways in which these meta-routines have been conceptualized in the mainstream, all of which occurred at the 2005 Organization Science Winter Conference (for which Stewart would like to thank Arie Lewin for the invitation to participate); Martin Kornberger, Alexandra Pitsis, George Ritzer, and Carl Rhodes all offered some feedback on different aspects of the manuscript, and we also wish to acknowledge Jean-Claude Thoenig's insightful comments on the elite dimension of power studies. In addition, Kevin Foley has been a constant source of enthusiasm and support for this and other projects, which Stewart appreciates greatly.

We would also wish to thank Chris Carter and Martin Kornberger for allowing us to draw on a small section of their joint work with Stewart Clegg, to frame the discussion of negative and positive power, deconstruction and translation in Chapter 10 (the paper in question, 'Rethinking the polyphonic organization: managing as discursive practice', was published in the *Scandinavian Journal of Management* in 2006). We also wish to thank Steve Little for ideas on the Internet economy in Chapter 13 (which, together with Stewart Clegg, were first explored at greater length in 'Recovering experience, confirming identity, voicing resistance: the Braceros, the Internet and counter-coordination', published in *Critical Perspectives on International Business* in 2005).

In addition to people, institutions should be acknowledged. Stewart wishes to thank the following universities and research centers that have supported this endeavor in some way or another: first, the University of Technology, Sydney and its Key Research Center, ICAN (Innovative Collaborations Alliances and Networks) Research, and especially the support received from Rob Lynch, Ian Palmer, Anne Ross-Smith and Siggi Gudergan in the Faculty of Business, as well as to acknowledge the stimulation he receives from his good colleagues Tyrone, Martin, Carl, Ray, Julie, and from the team at ICAN Research; second, the University of Aston, especially the Aston Research Centre and Work and Organizational Psychology Group, and, in particular, Michael West, John Saunders, John Sillince, and Debbie Evans; third, the Strategy and Organization Studies Department of the University of Maastricht, especially Robert Roe and Ad van Iterson; fourth, the Centre of Comparative Social Studies, Vrije Universiteit of Amsterdam, especially Heidi Dahles, Bert Klannermans, Ismintha Waldring, and all the good colleagues and support staff whom he has encountered and enjoyed working with there; fifth, Arne Lindseth Bygdås, Kjersti Bjørkeng, Arne Carlsen, Erlend Dehlin, Morten Hatling, Roger Klev, Emil Røyrvik and all the other researchers at SINTEF KUNNE, in Trondheim, Norway, who hosted him as he completed the penultimate phase of revising the manuscript, after being 'First Opponent' at Arne Carlsen's successful PhD defense in the Department of Interdisciplinary Studies of Culture at the Norwegian University of Science and Technology. David wishes to thank EM Lyon Business School and the Fuqua Business School at Duke University; Nelson wishes to acknowledge the support of the Judge Institute of Management at

Cambridge University and the Tanaka Business School at Imperial College, London. Both Nelson and Stewart wish to thank David and EM Lyon Business School for providing facilities for two days in July 2005 when we completed a great deal of the final work for the preparation of the manuscript.

As the project drew to its conclusion and Stewart worked on the final manuscript, Cleo Lester assisted in preparing it for submission. As ever, she was invaluable, and we want to record our appreciation of her efforts. Olga Bruyaka and Alan Johnson helped David finish off the bibliography, and we appreciate their assistance greatly. Without a couple of special people the book would never have happened. David Whetten was a cheerful and efficient series editor, who first commissioned the book, accepted Stewart's idea of having co-authors, and then tolerated our initial delays, due to other projects, with good humor. Kiren Shoman, as ever, was an exemplary editor at Sage, although occasionally inclined to worry. Of course, the writing buck stops with the names on the title page – despite all this fantastic friendship and exemplary editorial support.

Finally, all books have very special acknowledgements as their production definitely takes it toll on those loving and intimate relationships that sustain us as the people we strive to be; Stewart's, as ever, are to Lynne, Jonathan, and William; David's to Françoise, Salome and Eleana; and Nelson's to Neri for her love and support (and whose turn it is to write a book now).

Stewart R. Clegg

David Courpasson

Nelson Phillips

 1   Fixing the Institutionalization
of Theory and Practice

Chapter outline

In this chapter we will:

- Outline the approach and the intention behind the book.
- Provide some background information on how power has been discussed in organizational theory.
- Explain our approach to power and how it differs from more traditional views of power in organizational theory.
- Introduce the chapters and elaborate their main themes, present a roadmap of the chapters that are to follow, and elaborate the logic of the book.

Taking our bearings

Three ways of fixing things

The book that you have in your hands will fix some aspects of the terms 'power' and 'organizations', and we consider that fixing in three ways. First, we use 'fixing' as in *fixing a hole where the rain gets in*, that is *repairing the fabric of a construction*. With this book we aim to repair the construction of the problematic of power in organization analysis, and thus, by extension, that sphere of analysis itself, because we will argue that power is the most central concept in the analysis of organization(s) and organizing.

Second, we use 'fixing' as it is deployed in the context of *developing an image*, as in the pre-digital use of fixing fluid in a photographic darkroom. The image, its properties, what is exposed and what is not, are a matter of aesthetic judgment and technical know-how by the persons doing the developing. Thus, we develop different images of power in this book, some familiar, others more challenging in their representation and imagery. (By extension, some may think some images are too underdeveloped, and some perhaps too overdeveloped: the aesthetic dimension is important, as we have said, and the readers are as entitled to their aesthetic sense as are the authors.)

Third, we use 'fixing' in the sense that one of us used it previously in designing a model of circuits of power (Clegg 1989). Here, the idea was that *one could exercise power by fixing or refixing its relations, thus making them necessary nodal points, obligatory points of passage through which exchange, intercourse or discourse, must pass.* Power resides in the routing. Using this notation to make sense, we may say that in this work we seek to refix the institutionalization of power and organizations in both theory and practice, in the analysis and even the experience of being in organizations, as well as of organizing. We wish to reroute these terms and change their circuitry, transforming their currency, terms of trade, and meanings.

While some books, somewhat immodestly, claim to change lives, we want merely to change the orientation of a discipline and field of research. We believe that after this book makes its appearance it will be impossible for organization theorists, in their discussion of power and organizations, to marginalize certain things that should not have been marginalized; to disdain to mention certain scholars and researchers who should not have been slighted; and to confine speculation within a straitjacket of narrow concerns that should never have been so restricted. Thus, our ambition is to signal a way to reinscribe a field of analysis and to provide some tools with which to do so.

What is power and why is it important?

What is organization but the collective bending of individual wills to a common purpose? If, once upon a time, it could be said that man was born free but is everywhere in chains, today we would have to conclude that the links in those chains, binding both men and women, are overwhelmingly organizational, often fashioned from the finest things money can buy. With organization almost anything can be attempted: wars waged, empires challenged, worlds conquered, space explored, and good fortune built. Positive, wonderful things may be achieved with power: tyrannies defeated, democracies created, relationships forged, and freedoms established. Equally however, as we learn from the daily news, the power to achieve each of these good things may entail violence being unleashed, domination being enforced, and manipulation being employed.

When words such as manipulation, violence, and domination are so often associated with power, it is not surprising that power is often seen as something bad, something ignoble, indeed, as famously remarked by Lord Acton, something corrupting.[1] Yet, power is not necessarily constraining, negative or antagonistic. Power can be creative, empowering and positive. The organizational media that form, condense, and distribute social relations shape power and they can shape it *either way*.

We cannot enquire into power without an enquiry into its organization. Equally, we cannot make serious enquiry into organizations without an enquiry into power. Power is inscribed in the core of organizational achievement. If it were not, there would be nothing to remark on because, *whether for good or evil,* the social relations that constitute organization, the collecting together and coordinating of individual wills, endeavors, and energies, would not occur.

Organization requires power and, while not all power requires organization, most does. Power is to organization as oxygen is to breathing.[2] Politics are at the core of public life and their expression is invariably dependent on organization, be it in government, business, administration, religion, education, or whatever. Formal politics are organized and all organizations are themselves crucibles of political life. The term 'organizational politics' is not a part of the lexicon of every-day speech without good reason. Usually it has negative connotations, as if there were an organizational life *without* politics which was somehow more technically rational. We doubt that very much, but we do not think that organizational life and politics are *necessarily* nasty and backstabbing. They often are, but power – the central concept of the social sciences – need not always be regarded as something to be avoided. Power can be a positive force; it can achieve great things.

Positive power

Nothing has quite captured what power can do positively so well in recent years as the Live8 Make Poverty History events held globally on July 2, 2005. It was a movement organized from scratch in a matter of a few months by a small group of high-profile entertainers and socially engaged activists. The point of the event was to demonstrate the importance of new modes of politicking, organizing and educating, in order to make a difference to the conditions of everyday life and death in contemporary Africa.

Popular music cannot change the world but it can help make complex issues of power, ethics and inequality relevant and understandable for mass audiences who might not otherwise be moved. And, in democracies, the elected leaders are ultimately responsible to those who elect them and no political party in any country could have captured the imagination to the extent that occurred that day. The message was simple, but simple messages are much more likely to be understood widely than complex ones. And not only did the message reach an estimated 5.5 billion people globally, but the fact that it had done so, and that the stars involved used the celebrity that their status bestows on them to repeat the simple message widely and often, had some effect in shaping the views of the eight world leaders and their advisors who attended the Gleneagles G8 meeting, convened shortly after the concert.[3]

Power concerns the ways that social relations shape capabilities, decisions, change; these social relations can do things and they can block things unfolding. Power is ultimately about the choices that we make, the actions we take, the evils we tolerate, the goods we define, the privileges we bestow, the rights we claim, and the wrongs we do. Power means finding the most effective leverage for particular relations, such as those that *The Economist* argued for with respect to the Make Poverty History campaign, including an end to agricultural subsidies in the developed economies in order to open them to imports from the developing economies.[4] To do so would encourage economic growth in the poorest sectors of African countries as well as trade liberalization, improving infrastructure, and access to capital, all of which can hasten improvement in the lives of the continent's poor. The leaders who met in Gleneagles began the slow job of putting in place globally agreed policies that might serve to deliver on some of the aims of the Make Poverty History movement. These leaders are able to do so because they occupy the *relational spaces* from which a difference might be made. However, it is how the local contexts of power unravel in specific countries that will ultimately make – or not make – a difference. And making a difference is what power does.

Notice that, in this introductory discussion of power, we have stressed not the outcomes achieved but the process. The reason is that these outcomes will always be indeterminate and subject to revision from the many here-and-now moments from which what is temporally defined as an outcome will be viewed, both retrospectively and prospectively. If we were to determine power by its outcomes we would be in a state of constant revision as to the meaning and interpretation of these; even the definition of what they are taken to be would constantly change as the relevancies and priorities of the here-and-now change. Everything depends on the here-and-now and the relevancies one uses in making connections. For instance, in the week that these words were written the capillaries of power linked two highly disparate events, the 2012 Olympics and 2005 G8 meeting, to explosions on the streets of free London and occupied Baghdad. Power unleashed from the backpack of a suicide bomber, wreaking death and destruction, is clearly not positive for those whose lives are ruined and whose security is threatened.

One of the last major concentrations of people in London before Live8 was the many tens of thousands who had gathered, on its eve, to protest against the Iraq war. There were huge marches globally against that war being waged and they had no success whatsoever in stopping it. Judged in terms of outcomes the protests were impotent, despite the war being widely seen as both 'immoral and counterproductive', sanctioning 'the use of state terror – bombing raids, torture, countless civilian deaths … against Islamo-anarchists whose numbers are small, but whose reach is deadly' (Ali 2005a).

Negative power

As power politics the Iraq war appears to have been a bad calculation, at least in the short term. Judged by its outcomes at the time of writing it has been worse than impotent because it seems to have been counterproductive. The most optimistic scenario is that from some time in the future we may be able to look back and see that the 'domino theory' of democracy, implicit in the longer-term objectives of the war, has been achieved.[5] Maybe then we will see that it was better power politics than it now appears. At present, it is overwhelmingly negative: continuing resistance to occupation, escalating deaths, much more expensive oil, and increased insecurity in the major cities of the combatants. As we will discuss in Chapter 7, is it paradoxical to think that it is in people's real interests to liberate them by invading and occupying their space? The ultimate arbiter of what such interests are is not some external agency but the selves whose interests are at issue, suggest some theorists (Benton 1981). Of course, as Habermas (1979) has constantly stressed, the conditions for interest formation require a degree of non-distorted communication and reflection, both of which are inimical to a state of terror, political spin, military propaganda, or religious fundamentalism.

Leaving the contentious issues of Iraq and US foreign policy to one side, and returning once more to the issues that Live8 was designed to articulate, consider the parlous state that many of the countries in the continent of Africa find themselves in. These states were, rather like modern day Iraq, an effect of power being imposed on peoples rather than an expression of some sense of linguistic, religious or ethnic solidarity.[6] Colonial lines were arbitrarily imposed on tribal territories irrespective of ethnic, linguistic or traditional cleavages.[7] When decolonization occurred in the post Second World War era, the states that were created had very few indigenous administrative resources on which to draw for state building, because these had largely been controlled by colonial European elites. The absence of indigenous elites, particularly in those countries most hastily decolonized, such as the territories previously controlled by Portugal and Belgium, which had been the most violently and corruptly plundered, was another factor hastening the descent into anarchy. What elites there were, or those who managed to claw their way in to office, increasingly relied on royalties and aid for income. Many states were ruled and managed by despots who were spectacularly malfeasant: they made themselves presidents for life, rigged elections, or seized power through military coups. It is not surprising that having gained office through one or other of undemocratically malfeasant means, rulers typically pursued ruinous civil wars, implemented disastrous economic policies, and practiced systematic kleptocracy, looting, and corruption on a grand scale.[8]

In African states power is highly concentrated rather than democratically dispersed. Because of this, powers external to these African states, mainly European and US multinationals and governments, deal with their rulers to get things that they desire, such as oil or arms sales, precious minerals or metals. These external organizations deal with the power concentrated in the elites. Dealing with the regimes invests external legitimacy in them; in order to make deals the incumbent elites often demand concessions and favors from organizations and governments in transactions, which often amount either to outright bribery, blackmail and corruption or to canalization of inward investment into opportunities for profligate personal gain at the expense of the general population and for the benefit of the elite.[9] Whether or not they intend to, these external authorities feed both avarice and legitimacy, in a mutually dysfunctional loop. Of course, there are great differences between states – democratic and responsible power exists in an increasing number of African countries – but a large number remain hostage to forms of governance that are unaccountable to their people and whose vicious circle of power is multiplied and accelerated by state and business organizations more globally.

Power in organization and social theory

Investigating power

In this book we will investigate various conceptions of power, focusing particularly on the intersection of these conceptions with that of organization in both theory and practice. Power is a difficult idea to pin down and has been very widely ignored, marginalized and trivialized in many discussions of organizations, for a number of reasons that we shall elaborate in this book. We aim to make it impossible to claim good faith and still continue to ignore, marginalize or trivialize power in future. Of course, we are not naive, so we do not expect intellectual capital to be liquidated and assets trounced immediately, but we do see ourselves as building the *foundations* for future generations who want to design both different theoretical understandings of power in organizations and, informed by these, better practices of power in organizations. It is in this way that we interpret the series brief – to provide foundations of organization science.

The broad literature on power is diverse and complex and its ramifications for the study of organizations have remained largely unexplored. In organization studies, discussions of power have remained muted at best. Simplified application of ahistorical formulas serves to confound this understanding. Power is not only contingently situational but also historically formed. Power is not merely a crosssectional causal variable in a field of instantaneous coterminous correlations. Power can be reduced to a block diagram but there is far more to it than the mere attribution of putatively causal cross-sectional relations will allow for. Power defines, constitutes and shapes the moment. Power is inseparable from interaction and thus all social institutions potentially are imbued with power.

Situating power in organization theory

The *Administrative Science Quarterly* (*ASQ*) published a forum on power to which one of the present authors contributed (Clegg 2002). In this forum Greenwood and Hinings (2002: 411) noted that enquiry into the consequences of the existence of organizations traditionally defined organization sociology. Such sociological enquiry was deeply embedded in the work of a major founder of the organization theory discipline, Max Weber. As is typical of classical academic work in the social sciences, Weber drew on an Enlightenment tradition. However, despite these impeccable Enlightenment origins, it was utilitarian claims that came to dominate the most powerful branch of organization theory knowledge, that of the United States. Here organization theory found lucrative sponsorship in the gilded cages of the world's leading business schools from where it disseminated globally.

In much of the work on organizations that became globally disseminated, the dynamics of power are not at the forefront of analysis. That is not to say, however, that power was entirely absent. For those works that did explicitly focus on power, simplified and undertheorized conceptualizations were often used. Our intention here is to broaden and deepen discussion and provide an overview of the varied and nuanced theories of power that are available to organizational scholars.

Greenwood and Hinings (2002: 411) see the key questions concerning organizations to be how they pattern privilege and disadvantage in society. In retrospect, they look back to the 1950s as a golden age extending Weberian enlightenment when scholars such as Selznick (1949), Gouldner (1954), Etzioni (1961) and Blau and Scott (1963), amongst others, still asked important questions. At this time, they suggest, the sociology of organizations had not been wholly incorporated into an apolitical organization theory oriented to efficiency. Thus, they define the central concern of the *sociology of organizations* to be *power* while the central concern of *management theory* they define as *efficiency*: power and efficiency are seen as the central terms of two opposing and antithetical discourses.

> We would characterize a sociological approach to studying organizations as being concerned with *who controls and the consequences of that control*. The central question emanating from a business school, in contrast, leans more to understanding *how to understand and thus design efficient and effective organizations*. The perspective is that of the senior manager. (Greenwood and Hinings 2002: 411)

The separation between power and efficiency serves a rhetorical purpose in their essay. Power marks the center of gravity of the world we have lost while efficiency is the fulcrum of the world we have gained. Generally, a concern with power marks the sociology department while a fixation on efficiency characterizes the business school scholar. The terms mark antithetical discourses between which scholars must choose. It appears as if one must be either for enlightenment and against efficiency or for efficiency and against power as the analytic through which bearings are pursued.

Greenwood and Hinings' (2002) argument juxtaposing power and efficiency as central and opposed problematics is an argument that is intriguing. But it is also wrong. The origins of power in organization theory are deeper than the golden age of the 1950s. To oppose efficiency to power as totally distinct and separate terms is to miss, entirely, that it was a concern with efficiency that gave birth to power in management and organizations, as we shall elaborate. Thus, we mark an initial distinction from contemporary accounts, even those as well informed and intentioned as Greenwood and Hinings. We do not understand the relation between efficiency and power as one of opposition. We will argue that efficiency and power are inextricably linked and understanding their relationship is the key to understanding power in organizations.

In their *ASQ* piece, Greenwood and Hinings (2002) cite Aldrich approvingly when he argues that 'The concentration of power in organizations contributes not only to the attainment of large scale goals, but also to some of the most troublesome actions affecting us ... We might view the growth of organizational society as a record of people enslaved and dominated by organizations' (1999: 7). We agree with Aldrich in so far as we do 'view the growth of organizational society as a record of people enslaved and dominated by organizations', but we do not think that we can arrive at an appropriate understanding of this enslavement and domination other than through a wholesale revision of existing ways of conceptualizing power in organizations. If we were to rely on the central organization theory accounts of power we would find few, if any, pointers to enslavement or domination. Sure, there would be much on managing uncertainty, or controlling resources, but these hardly seem to get us very far in terms of understanding enslavement and domination. For this, we need to investigate the relations between rationality and efficiency in more detail.

Efficiency may be defined as achieving some predetermined end at the highest output in terms of the least input of resources. The concept of efficiency, defined in this way, is constructed in such a way as to slice off the value dimension. It tends to still discussion by making the goals served by any particular efficiency out of bounds. It displaces any serious concern with ends, which are given in terms of the need for efficiency. Consideration of differential means for the achievement of the given ends accompanies the focus on efficiency.

The institutionalization of organization theory may be said to have resulted in the rationalization of rationality without a moral dimension (see also Clegg et al. 2000). Truth is seen as something outside of social practices, located in an autonomous sphere of science. In this way, theorists can absolve themselves from moral responsibility. The institution of science will legitimize whatever analytical action they attend to and engage in. They are not the actions of interpretive subjects making sense with the tools that are available to them (tools often taught, picked up, or reinforced in business school, with all its mobilization of bias toward shareholder values), but the workings of the market, natural selection, structural adjustment, or some other grand and abstracted narrative. The consequence of these tendencies is to gradually obliterate cultural and social differences through the institutionalization of a general project of organizational modernity shaped by efficiency requisites.

In any process of institutionalization, meaningfulness is never 'given' but has to be struggled for, has to be secured, even against the resistance of others. Systematic thinking rationalizes the image of the world through the theoretical mastery of reality by increasingly precise and abstract concepts. It was this aspect that Weber sometimes called the de-enchantment of the world. It is the process by which all forms of magical, mystical, traditional explanation are stripped away from interpretation. The world laid bare is open and amenable to the calculation of technical reason. Calculable means are connected to given ends.

Uncertainty threatens calculability because it both defines and limits freedom. Where there is a rule there is no freedom other than to obey or not obey, which is really no freedom at all. Uncertainty has the ontological and metaphysical status that it has in organization theory because rationality is a central assumption of the discipline. With rationality, however bounded it may be, the organization theorist will ward off evil, defend the faith of theory, and keep at bay the ever-threatening tide of chaos, undecidability, and indetermination that uncertainty represents. In organization theory freedom is usually defined through posing the existential and environmental conditions under which rational action is possible. These conditions limit freedom by imposing an ethic of calculation, as totally objective rationality, upon a freedom to act.

Modernity entails a loss of freedom to the constraints of rationality; it also entails a loss of faith because, as one becomes free of the old dogmas, any authoritative basis for one's life, other than rationality itself, disappears. Of course, modernity is a variable condition, even in a modern world full of modern, rational, organizations. When such rationality is working properly it will be in dominance – perhaps having to accommodate itself to some split rationalities. One sphere, the dominant one, will belong to commerce, a second to the state, and a third to whatever transcendent forces are institutionalized and legitimated as those to which one pays homage.

Although the process of rationalization unyokes new possibilities for cultural construction in all spheres of knowledge, rationality modeled on efficiency has become dominant, become an ultimate value in its own right. Opposition to it appears as nothing other than irrationality. Of course, in a truly modern world there would be no such opposition to rationality defined as efficiency because such irrationality would have been rationalized out of existence. Yet, as we shall see in the concluding chapter, modernity has never been so established that it corrals and drives out all those pre-modern elements whose construction preceded it.

It might be expected that the pre-modern would become modern and rationalized, much as the Protestant ethic (Weber 1976). However, not every set of medieval or ancient beliefs has been so rationalized. Surprisingly, as Chapter 13 will establish, the irruption of a modern remaking of pre-modern ideas has produced a heightened state of insecurity threatening modern organizations. Presciently, as Dumm suggests, we need always to be on guard against 'the possibilities that our own institutional arrangements will encourage the rise of new destructive forces inimical to the possibilities of our being free' (1996: 153).

Situating power in social theory

Outside the increasingly autonomous discipline being defined by organization theory, the broad power theory agenda was being shaped by a continuing debate with major nineteenth-century theorists. Lukes (1974; 2005) drew on Marx's legacy, as it had been interpreted by Gramsci, using the concept of hegemony. If Marx offered one coordinate for social theory then Nietzsche provided another. Nietzsche's (1967) influence could be seen in the work of Michel Foucault (1977), who introduced a mode of analysis that linked power with knowledge. Foucault conceived of power as operating not only in a prohibitive way, by telling people what they cannot do, but also through knowledge. In a permissive, positive manner, power can be good, thus constructing *the normalcy of the normal*, through everyday ways of sensemaking that are more or less institutionalized in disciplinary knowledge.

When Üsdiken and Pasadeos (1995) made a comparison of co-citation networks in European and North American organization studies, they identified Foucault as the seventh most cited researcher in the European journal *Organization Studies*, just behind Weber, who was fifth. Neither Weber nor Foucault, nor many others influential in the European list, made the top 10 in the comparable North American journal *Administrative Science Quarterly* based lists; Weber just snuck in at the bottom of the 'hot 100', but Foucault didn't rate a mention. Marx languished in obscurity, out of sight and off the lists. While our book has little to add to the many discussions of Marx elsewhere, including some by one of the present authors (Clegg and Dunkerley 1980; Clegg et al. 1983), it does add to the discussion of both Weber and Foucault.

Weber is recognized as a founding father of institutional theory, and Foucault has been seen as someone with a largely neglected contribution in what has been referred to as the adolescence of institutional theory (Scott 1987b).[10] While this book is intended to be a guide not to institutional theory *per se* but to the literature of power and organizations, it will draw on and add to the classical heritage of institutional theory in order to enable it to become more powerful.

We simultaneously address organization theories of power while breaking with many of the assumptions that frame their current interpretation. The break is organized around a genealogical analysis of power and organizations for which we take our bearings from Michel Foucault (1980), a point of reference becoming increasingly known to organization theorists (Burrell 1988). Genealogical theory seeks to understand how what is taken for granted as the truth of one time can be transformed at another without analytic recourse either to a teleological theory or to one which relies on the role of great individuals as the 'switchmen' of history (Weber 1976).

Foucault makes a theory of power central to the dynamics of change and development because it is through the dominant regimes of power in place at a certain point in time that particular conceptions of truth and rationality are established (Foucault 1980: 112) while others are marginalized. What is taken to be true 'is linked in a circular relation with systems of power which produce and sustain it, and to effects of power which induce and which extend it' (1980: 133). Thus, power has no essential qualities because *power is not a thing but a relation between things and people as they struggle to secure 'truthfully' embedded meanings.* Hence, for Foucault, power is not just something that is prohibitory and negative but it also has a positive side that makes things possible – as well as impossible. As Haugaard argues:

> The formation of truth does not simply happen. Rather, the truth of any discourse formation is the consequence of the struggles and tactics of power. This means the disqualification of certain knowledges as idiocy and a fight for others as truth. In the modern period one important tactic for giving discourse formation the status of truth is to argue that it is a science. (1997: 68)

Modern organization theory as a science

Sketching the field

The epitome of modern rational organization theory was the program institutionalized as contingency theory. One reason why functionalist contingency theory became so widely debated was because the Aston Research Programme was so successful. Its findings dominated the pages of the journals, especially the *Administrative Science Quarterly,* during the 1960s and early 1970s. Ostensibly it said nothing directly about power *per se*, although its variables could be seen as very much an effect of power: routinization, standardization, centralization and so on. Although, subsequently, some of these same contingency theorists were to address power (Hickson et al. 1971; Hinings et al. 1974), as were some resource dependence theorists (Pfeffer and Salancik 1974), they did so mostly through concepts of power that remained marginal and somewhat quirky in terms of the broader evolution of social theory. Oddly, they addressed power without once ever addressing its hierarchical qualities.[11]

Power was placed center field in contingency theory when Child (1972) published his influential article on 'strategic choice', in which he drew deeply on debates that Silverman (1970) had sparked in Britain among organization sociologists, drawing on influential sources such as Berger and Luckmann (1967) to rekindle an interpretive account of organizations. Silverman (1970) counterpoised an 'action frame of reference' to the open systems contingency perspective that was by now dominant in organization analysis. His key point was that organizations were neither natural nor rational systems *per se* but were socially constructed phenomena. Silverman was an important, but outside Britain largely neglected, early institutional theorist (Clegg 1994). The key point that Child and Silverman were making was that organizations were a result of choices, particularly by those whom Selznick (1957) had referred to as the 'dominant coalition' (see Colignon 1997).

Institutional theory quickly lost its focus on power after Meyer and Rowan (1977) and DiMaggio and Powell (1983) initiated its renaissance by asking why there are so few types of organizations. Organizations, they suggested, are as they are not for efficiency reasons (as contingency functionalist theorists had argued) but for reasons of social construction. Hence, it is the cultural stock of knowledge rather than functional necessity that determines how and why organizations are as they are. Strangely, given Weber's pre-eminent role as both a cultural theorist (Clegg 1995) and an analyst of power and domination (Clegg 1975), these latter terms seemed somewhat underdone in the new institutionalism. As Mizruchi and Fein (1999) suggested, research programs applying DiMaggio and Powell left out power by concentrating on mimetic isomorphism whilst downplaying the coercive and normative.

The neglect of power in much institutional theory was made more evident through the work of other contributors, especially the European Aix School (Maurice et al. 1980), who had arrived at similar conclusions to those of the North American institutional scholars, but with a stronger focus on power. They did so through the process of comparative cross-national research, in which they compared the organization structures of different countries, seeing the differences not only in terms of contingency factors but also as a 'societal effect' (Sorge 1991): different relations of power were differently valued in different countries (Whitley 1994). The reason that different institutional structures were valued differently in different countries was that different national elites had formed around different constellations of values and interests, giving rise to quite distinct patterns of elite formation, recruitment and reproduction. To make the connection between institutions and power evident, we can contrast the role of the party in Eastern European states for much of the twentieth century with the role of the market in the United States, or we might look at the way in which Margaret Thatcher's project in the United Kingdom sought to defeat not only the institutionalized unions but also the institutionalized ethos of aristocratic disdain for commerce. Of course, as the case of the Eastern European states demonstrates, an interest in the stabilizing effects of institutions has to be balanced with a fascination with the process of institutional change. Newer forms of 'neo-institutional' theory (Greenwood and Hinings 1996), with its focus on the 'institutional entrepreneur', have an explicit interest in power and agency, as we shall see.

As organization theory became increasingly institutionalized, especially in business schools, it began to develop the traits that we would expect of any institutionalized body of knowledge. Rival camps with competing claims to territory emerged. Definitions of the field became contested. What was regarded as holy writ differed within each citation cartel, centered on different fulcra, whether journals, theories or theorists.[12]

What do organization theories do?

Theories of organizations reflect, systematically, on what occurs organizationally. We can make a distinction between those objects they construct through their concepts, methods, and models, and the 'naturally' occurring phenomena that these reflect. The latter would exist irrespective of their theorization or non-theorization as practices – what people do. Hence, any account of power in organizations has to operate on at least two planes: first, the phenomena of changing organization practices; and second, changes in the ways in which organization scientists have theorized these practices.

Theory inhabits its own specialist realm and has its own terms. There is always a gap between theory and the practice it reflects on, which will be an effect of the social constructions, conventions, and grammars of analysis within which translation between them is made. Translations from practice to theory that achieve systematicity and institutionalization can become objects of analysis in their own right, creating their own truths. Theories of organizations – and theories of organization power – are just these sorts of translations. The important question, however, is not so much to identify what it is that they construct as *true* (on this one should, properly, be agnostic rather than faithful) but to enquire what are the *functions* of the truths that they posit. What is important is to analyze the machinery of truth production. Truth claims that are granted and respected perform an essential function in ordering membership and normalcy in the social contexts in which they pertain, such as business schools and other organizations. They specify the conditions of existence for possibilities and impossibilities; they legitimate relations of domination and subordination. In this sense, what is (taken to be) true is a social fact, as Durkheim (1983: 67) puts it.

Haugaard (1997: 69) suggests that those who benefit from extant machineries of truth production will be least keen to see its mechanisms exposed. Truth is typically taken to be that knowledge indubitably standing as provisional after exposure to robust skeptical procedures of conjecture and refutation (Popper 1965). Thus, the essence of science is to be protected from power at all costs. Rather than conjecturing and refuting the truths posited within specific ensembles of truth claims, we are interested in demonstrating how these ensembles of truth come to be taken for granted. What the objects of knowledge are, and what they are not; how they are constituted, and how they are not; these are the consequences of power experienced as choice and non-choice, decision and non-decision, action and non-action, expressed through relations of knowledge. Hence, at the center of our analysis of power there resides power. We are nothing if not reflexive.

All of the preceding has a direct bearing on the way in which we have constituted the project of this book. We have not dwelt on the minutiae of the various variables constructed in numerous empirical studies, being disinclined to accept their self-evidence as such; rather we have always asked the key sociological question of *how is the phenomenon of power, that is being constructed in theory and in practice, possible.* And the theory/practice distinction is important – indeed it is essential – because power was inscribed in practice long before it was reflected in theory.

Sharpening the focus on power in organization theory

Fixing a focus

Power is something that only came into sharp focus for much organization theory in the post Second World War era, when a hypothesis, that control over uncertainty bestowed power in otherwise rationalized systems, was widely elaborated. Organization science developed this way of addressing power in the 1950s; organization power seemed barely to exist in *theory* prior to this address. The new theoretical representation of power as related to uncertainty relied on a whole machinery of truth production. The machinery in question was the integration of the formal organization and the informal organization in the model of the open system. Until the system model had been produced, power, as it was to be represented, seemed invisible to most commentators. Hence, as we shall see, certain historic silences were evident; lacking the machinery to produce the truth of power, the discourse on power remained mute. Thus, organization theory as it is ordinarily understood appears to be ignorant of how its prehistory is characterized in terms of power.

We see power at work in the production of both organization theories and practices, even when the topic under address by these theories is not explicitly that of power. For instance, while F. W. Taylor was a designer of managerial practices that accomplished the outcomes of power, he was not a theorist of power. This may sound paradoxical but it is not. Taylor did not explicitly develop an analytical theory of power but, nonetheless, the practice that he helped to shape began to reform the way power works in organizations, and continues to do so. He produced a whole positivity of power at work through the new truths of work study, truths which made each worker individually much more visible and potentially normalizable in terms of their efficiency than had previously been the case. One of the major techniques of power, according to Foucault (1979), is the creation of 'docile bodies'. Taylor's zeal for changing the relation between men and machines focused on the body of the worker and its drilling in what he believed, scientifically, was the one best way of working. Taylor and his colleagues produced exacting procedures that workers had to follow and did so in the name of efficiency. It was this that became installed as rationality. Thus, the machinery of organization theory creates rationality.

Even beautiful scientific machines do best that which they were designed for. After the Second World War, the dominant machine of the system was designed to aid the extension of conceptualizations of organizations as rational open systems (Scott 1987a). Our task is to bring some small fraction of those practices outside the remit and gaze of the rational system into view, both historically and more or less contemporaneously.

Before rational theory developed, a practice of power could, nonetheless, be observed in modern organizations, in the creation of a new type of human subject as an object of knowledge. The subject in question is one constituted by a political economy of the body. Inscribed in this subject we find early traces of power. Through a process of individualization and subjectification a program for a new type of person is created. The program is oriented first towards the efficient worker and second to the docile employee. Any individual can be laid bare for analysis in terms of their normalcy and potential for normalization. That we can speak of normal and normalization suggests a range of conduct, not all of which will fit the categories being constructed. These latter cases, the exceptions, are important, because they justify further attempts at normalization, and become the ground for the refinement of power practices. The spectrum of categories stipulates ways of measuring human worth in their contribution to the dreams and visions of the organizational elites.

Elites have always defined the terms on which the others are measured. In pre-industrial society the problems of deviance were dealt with in summary and severe ways, largely related to problems of security of life and property. No life or property was more valuable than that of the elites and no one was more elite than the monarch. Thus, in Foucault's (1977) *Discipline and punish*, the gruesome process of drawing, quartering, and burning in execution of Damiens on March 2, 1757 for the crime of attempted regicide on the French monarch is contrasted with the rules of a model prison written a mere 80 years later. Here, there is deadening bureaucracy, rules for everything, an existence as calibrated as that of any novitiate in a religious institution (Keiser 2002).

Despite the fact that these regimes of power had long been known in religious orders, Foucault argues that they constitute a new secular regime of knowledge and truth. The point of application of power shifted from marking and punishing the body to 'a whole new system of truth and a mass of roles hitherto unknown … A corpus of knowledges, techniques, "scientific" discourse is formed and becomes entangled with the practice of … power' (1977: 22–3). Foucault traces these changes in criminal justice from a marking of the body to a reform of the soul. According to Foucault (1977: 136), the turn to discipline was widespread and general in nineteenth-century schools, armies, prisons and factories. In terms of any individual biography, regular habits of work practice were first encountered in the school, then demanded in the army, imposed in the prison, and trained in the factory. All were based on systematic discipline, the uniform application of obligatory regulation. Discipline creates an order into which the individual is inscribed, an order that is artificial, explicit, codified, programmatic, and regulated by inspection (1977: 179; Haugaard 1997: 80). As Haugaard (1997: 80) remarks, 'Order and discipline go together' by making their subjects both visible and examinable. 'By assessing acts with precision, discipline judges individuals' says Foucault (1977: 181), adding that it does so 'in truth'. By this he means that each discipline imposes its own rules and norms on the hierarchy of competent subjects that its practices arrange through judgment.

When we apply these ideas to organization theory their import is clear. The truth of scientific management's discipline was to make each individual worker visible and responsible for his or her own efficiency, a truth conditioned by the power of piece-rate wage systems. Maximize one's own efficiency as a worker and one maximizes one's happiness through maximizing the means for its achievement – wage payments. Each solitary individual employee had to come to know this truth, and to know that it was to be accomplished by the 'transformation' of individual irregularity by self-correction (Foucault 1979: 239–40).

The mechanisms for the achievement of mutually compatible utilitarian ends were simple, using examination and individualization. Examination is mediated by making individuals visible as individual subjects; individualization is achieved by making the individual a case that can be traced through various documents and statistical records, and classified as a specific case through precise performance measurement (Foucault 1977: 187–92). Scientific management fits the model effortlessly. Scientific management promised to make any body a machine that could move exactly and precisely – a body fixed in time and space by organization, anywhere, as something essentially biddable, plastic and routine.[13]

In the remainder of the book we will trace the history of the development of the knowledge of organizational power from these humble beginnings addressed to the body as a machine for productive efficiency. We will trace the shifting regimes of knowledge and truth that produce different and incommensurable ideas of power and organization. Next, we will explain the overall logic of our particular translation of the history of power and organizations and provide a brief overview of each chapter.

Programmatics and analytics

The logic of the book is constructed according to two principles: first, a principle of programmatics, and second, a principle of analytics. Where we address programmatics we are focused on *practices* of power, rather more than their extant theorization. We justify this logic in terms of the fact that the practices in question have been either undertheorized or not theorized at all by organization analysts. Where we address analytics we are focused on *theories* of power. Because we seek to reframe the understanding of power in organizations we do not focus merely on that which has been constituted as part of the canon of organization theories of power. Instead, we cast our net wider, to incorporate social theories of power. We do this because we see organization and management theory as branches of the social sciences. As such, we do not believe that they can be hermetically sealed or cut off from wider analytic developments in these social sciences.

Although organization and management theories have developed their own traditions of analysis, we argue that these have been inadequate in terms of what they address and more especially what they do not address – the programmatics of power – as well as inadequate in the means through which they have constructed their understanding – the analytics of power. Hence, our book is addressed to both the programmatics and the analytics of power, to both theory and practice, and to the practice and theory of both broader social theory and more restricted organization and management theories.

When we were given the brief for this book by the series editor, David Whetten, he explained that the book should be the next best thing for the graduate students and researchers who use it to taking a seminar with the authors. We have borne this injunction in mind throughout the book and have used as many devices as we could think of – including writing style, diagrams, and tables – to make the materials we provide as effortless as a large and complex field, interpreted in a radically different way, will allow.

Dialog stands at the heart of the book. There is, first, a dialog between the authors, two of whom must have despaired at times at the capacity of one of them to engage in endless conversations, expressed in redrafting, not only with himself but with the many others credited in the acknowledgements to the book; second, a dialog with the previous texts and traditions of research that are captured momentarily herein; third, a dialog with unfolding events that were shaping our sense of being in the world; fourth, a dialog with past accounts of power and organizations which we recovered through reflective glances, retrospective gazes, and half-remembered fragments that drifted into cognition; and fifth, a dialog between our conception of what an analysis of organizations could aspire to and the actuality of so much of what it has achieved. Furthermore, we have realized that power is a constant attempt to impose different modes of being on disparate ways of becoming – which is why we have consistently stressed the importance of power *relations* in this book, and why we have stressed the action as well as the structuring aspects of power, because the process can only be grasped through an understanding of the constant dialectic between the two. We have understood that good conversations take place in a context in which there are, like it or not, barriers to agential creativeness and structural determination, just as in life. We have tried to maintain a degree of openness, while at the same time making clear our points of difference and dispute with other positions. And, as we conclude, what is essential to the whole conception of science that is articulated in this book is that the dialog is ultimately with you, the reader and user, of the text produced. As one of us said a very long time ago, 'The possibilities of your reading have been an ever present feature of my writing' (Clegg 1975: 157). And that goes for this collective enterprise as much as it did for earlier singular ones.

Our book is designed to be different and to make a difference; hence in writing about power we seek to exercise power. We propose to change not only the knowledge of power relations in the field of organization studies but also the power relations in the field itself. We want to reorient thinking from the present axes of concern to a new axis of power – not the axis of resource dependency theory or other orthodoxies that serve as much as ways of *avoiding* discussion of certain key elements of power, but a new genealogical axis reaching from bureaucracy to polyarchy (Dahl 1971). In accordance with the differences we have pinpointed in this introductory chapter, we suggest a framework that can function as a guiding thread to the book.

We emphasize five major differences with the orthodoxy of mainstream or simple organizational approaches:

1 Power and efficiency are not two opposite sides of a continuum constituting the core problematic in organization studies. On the contrary, we claim power and efficiency should be simultaneously analyzed as fundamentally tangled up in the social fabric of power as both a concept and a set of practices.

2 Power and discourses are equally intermingled in so far as they constitute the political structure of organizations through diverse circuits of power. Discourses shape structures and provide the means for ordering the political structure. Thus, organizations and individuals use discourses purposefully to shape the political situations in and through which they can act and perform.

3 To understand power means deciphering various forms of political economy in organizations; that is, the means that organizational leaders use to perpetuate power and the structures of dominance they strive to create and legitimize. Only though the use of power can elites steer organizations through upheaval and turmoil as well as structure what gets taken for granted as normal. Only through the use of power can others resist and challenge this steering. Organizations, above all, are means of constituting relations between people, ideas, and things that would not otherwise occur. Organizations are performances of various kinds and power relations constitute the essence of these performances.

4 A very definite idea of sovereignty passed into organization theory from political theory. In political theory, sovereignty is 'the highest power of command'. Of course, in political theory, as Foucault so famously expressed it (see the discussion in Clegg 1989), the head has been chopped from this concept of sovereignty. Rule based on popular will expressed through democratic systems, rather than *solely* and merely on elite preferences, is instilled as the normalcy of political theory. Increasingly, organizations are witness to the emergence of notions of *popular* rather than *singular* sovereignty. Hence, a subtheme of the book is the emergence of challenges to hierarchy as a guiding principle for organizations.

5 Finally, we shall argue that power must be seen in its contemporary political context; it cannot be conceptualized as wholly abstracted from those contexts in which it is embedded. Thus, it is not only political economy which frames organizations but also the changing global context of politics, as we shall explore in the final chapter.

Running through these five major features of our approach is a stress on the combination of the idea of power and the idea of performance. Power is the major factor in organizational performance over the last century. Power accounts for most of the reasons why organizations embark upon programs of organization change. When new CEOs are appointed they invariably institute a change program.

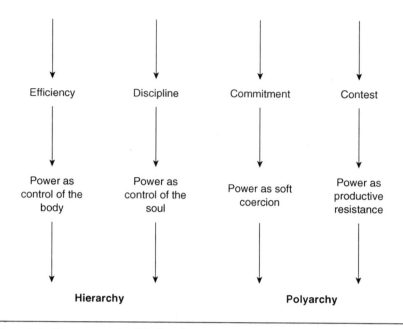

Figure 1.1   Four types of political performance

The old regime's schemes and favorites will languish; new elites will strive to be inducted. Whether the elites succeed or not in their relentless attempts to change, and keep up with, changes occurring everywhere in their relevant environments, will also be a matter of power. Power should be viewed as the basic ingredient reconciling the economic realm of performance and the social world of people's actions, decisions and those fates they have to endure. Let us synthesize this framework in the diagram of power in Figure 1.1 – the first of many that will be used in the book.

While we would not want to go as far as to suggest a unilinear or evolutionary logic to this schema, we argue that over the last one hundred or so years there has been a gradual movement of the cutting edge points of contestation in theory and practice from the left to the right side of the schema. Looked at in this way, it reveals a shift from organizational forms premised on the singular rule of hierarchies towards a realization of polyarchy. However, the histories of the present never eclipse or write over the histories of the past; thus, we should not see any one of these organization forms as an essential or universal principle of social formation, for there are no such essential verities in matters of social construction, no essences that recurrently move history in deep but mysterious ways. The sediments of history sludge around in the detritus of every present day, as we shall explore. A road map of our exploration is provided in Table 1.1.

Table 1.1 Reading the book

Chapter	Title	Focus	Themes	Main theorists and schools
1	Fixing the Institutionalization of Theory and Practice	Overview	A roadmap and synopsis of the main themes and an explication of theoretical approach and methods	
2	Power and Efficiency	How power became embedded in routines in organizations and how social programs evolved to buttress power at work	The political economy of the body as the locus of efficiency	Jeremy Bentham F. W. Taylor and systematic time and motion
3	Body, Soul, and Mind	How the analysis of organizations shifted from the formal design of work to a concern with the consciousness of the employee at work	The moral economy of the soul as a locus of legitimacy	Ford's Sociological Department Mary Parker Follett Elton Mayo and the Human Relations School Chester Barnard and leadership Knowledge management Social capital
4	The Curious Case of Max Weber	How, unbeknownst to American theorists, a sophisticated analysis of power in organizations was being constructed in German in Max Weber's work	The transformation of the topic referenced by the German term *Herrschaft* from a concern with domination to a concern with legitimate authority	Max Weber Talcott Parsons Georg Simmel

(Continued)

Table 1.1 (Continued)

Chapter	Title	Focus	Themes	Main theorists and schools
5	The Rational System and Its Irrational Other	How power became the systemic enemy of the incorporation of formal and informal organization in one frame: power was the source of irrationality in an otherwise rational system, and invariably came from disenfranchised lower-order employee objections	Power as resource based and the futility of prescriptive lists of what these resources might be	The Pareto Circle J. D. Thompson Michel Crozier David Hickson Jeffrey Pfeffer and Gerald Salancik Gerard Fairtlough
6	The Heart of Darkness	How disenfranchising, marginalizing and simplifying power in organization theory obscured the ample evidence of the consequences of total institutions, such as the Holocaust and other horrors of modernity – the heart of darkness at the core of organized modernity	The ways in which total institutions are a concentration and condensation of normal techniques of power; how extreme cases serve a vital function in alerting us to the dangers inherent in the structures of normalcy, and how that which divides what we take to be good from that which we take to be evil is a very thin and porous membrane, as well as one that makes situational rather than transcendent sense	Erving Goffman Michel Foucault Zygmunt Bauman Stanley Milgram Philip Zimbardo Hannah Arendt Winton Higgins Pierre Macherey

Table 1.1 (Continued)

Chapter	Title	Focus	Themes	Main theorists and schools
7	Power To and Power Over	How there have been two dominant tendencies in modern conceptions of power and how one of them, the positive conception associated with Talcott Parsons, has been relatively neglected by organization theorists – even though it has deep roots in the work of Mary Parker Follett	Exploring the sophisticated debates in social theory that, with few exceptions, have hardly informed organization theory. Establishing organization theory as something of a backwater in terms of the relative lack of sophistication of its theorizing in social science terms	Ralf Dahrendorf Talcott Parsons Jürgen Habermas Anthony Giddens Niklas Luhmann Michael Mann Thomas Hobbes Robert Dahl Peter Bachrach and Morton Baratz Steven Lukes John Gaventa Mark Haugaard Cynthia Hardy Slavoj Žižek Ernesto Laclau and Chantal Mouffe John Allen

(Continued)

Table 1.1 (Continued)

Chapter	Title	Focus	Themes	Main theorists and schools
8	The Foucault Effect	How the assumptions of the power debate that stretched from Hobbes through Locke to Steven Lukes' work were to be radically questioned by Michel Foucault's evolving analytics of power	The different emphases in Foucault's evolving thought and its major criticisms from the point of view of power in organizations, as well as the extension of his ideas into a workable research practice for organization theory	Michel Foucault
				Stewart Clegg
				Mark Haugaard
				Bent Flyvbjerg
				Sally Davenport and Shirley Leitch
				Michel Callon, Bruno Latour and actor network theory
				Arturo Escobar
				Gilles Deleuze and Félix Guattari
				Pierre Bourdieu
				Steven Lukes
				Torsten Hägerstrand and life-path analysis
				Rom Harré and Edward Madden

Table 1.1 (Continued)

Chapter	Title	Focus	Themes	Main theorists and schools
9	Critical Theories of Organizational Power	How management scholars built on ideas from Critical Theory in sociology to challenge taken-for-granted assumptions about the nature of the corporation, modern management, and management knowledge	The development of a critical moment in management studies, focused on explicating the structures of power and control that characterize the modern corporation and on challenging the notions of performativity, naturalness, and non-reflexivity that characterize mainstream management thought	Frankfurt School Antonio Gramsci Jürgen Habermas Karl Marx C. Wright Mills Michel Foucault Stewart Clegg and David Dunkerley Mats Alvesson and Hugh Willmott Valerie Fournier and Chris Grey
10	Discursive Theories of Organizational Power	How the linguistic turn in philosophy led to an increasing interest in linguistic approaches in social science and organization studies, ending in the development of a discursive analytic in organization studies	Philosophical approaches to discourse analysis as an approach to studying power in organizations Sociological approaches to discourse analysis as an approach to studying power in organizations	Ludwig Wittgenstein Michel Foucault Norman Fairclough Dennis Mumby

(Continued)

Table 1.1 (Continued)

Chapter	Title	Focus	Themes	Main theorists and schools
				Nelson Phillips and Cynthia Hardy
				Mats Alvesson and Dan Kärreman
			Organizational discourse as a field of study	Stewart Clegg
				Deidre Boden
			Gender, power and discourse	Karen Lee Ashcraft
			Identity and power	Nelson Phillips and Cynthia Hardy
11	Power and Organizational Forms	How the endless debates on bureaucracy relate to fundamental dynamics of underlying structures of power, stretching from democratic to oligarchic forms	The hybrid capacities of power regimes	Robert Dahl
			Exploring the notion of political performance as the basis of political dynamics	Alexis de Tocqueville
				Robert Michels
				Harry Eckstein
				Chantal Mouffe
12	Corporate Power Elites	How power is shaped by the question 'Who governs?'	Investigating the elitist/pluralist debate as shaping the way scholars analyze the roles and dynamics of elite bodies	Robert Dahl
				Robert Putnam
				C. Wright Mills

Table 1.1 (Continued)

Chapter	Title	Focus	Themes	Main theorists and schools
			The contemporary dynamics of corporate elites and how they influence the deep political structures of organizations, particularly the forms of subordination	Philip Selznick
				Michael Useem
				Gerald Davis
				Georg Simmel
13	The Futures of Power?	How current societal and social tendencies might affect power as a concept and as a practice in the near future	Exploring the new dynamics and relationships between power and the production of resistance	Ulrich Beck
				Émile Durkheim
		How the wheel of power has come full circle: back to the issue of (productive) resistance	The emergence of new types of 'social movement' within organizations	Jim March and Johan Olsen
				Max Weber
				Michel Foucault
			The ongoing paradox between the rejuvenation of systems of domination and the social fabric of resistance	Georg Simmel
				Charles Tilly
				Robert Nisbet

The themes, figures and theories of the following chapters

Chapter 2: Power and Efficiency

In the second chapter we begin to address how certain aspects of the way management and organizations were conceptualized first emerged, concentrating especially on how power became embedded in routines in organizations and how social programs evolved to buttress power at work. We begin by examining mundane understandings of management as they are embedded in the language that we habitually use to discuss it. Some of this language bears etymological analysis in historical terms and we endeavor, as non-specialists, to make such an analysis. Where does a concern with the management of work as an object of scientific reform begin? We locate it in utilitarianism, which flowered in England in the eighteenth and nineteenth centuries under the particular tutelage of Jeremy Bentham and J. S. Mill. They were interested in using work to reform indigence, and in Bentham's case, he was interested in framing the conditions in which work was done to maximize individual utility. However, as fascinating as these famous philosophers were, it was not them but a Philadelphian Quaker who was most responsible for bringing utilitarianism into organizations, and he did so by focusing on reform of the body of the worker, instituting a political economy of the body as the locus of efficiency. Frederick William Taylor, we argue, produced the first modern technology of power, one that is oriented to constituting a political economy of the body. In this respect, we find some parallels with Foucault, albeit with the periodicity being historically time-lagged.

In an ideal organization, constructed according to the principles that Taylor advocated, and as they were to be developed subsequently, uncertainty would have been eliminated, because people did exactly what they were supposed to do. Innovation was not favored; instead, strict obedience to the plan was rewarded. As we shall see, it is perhaps not surprising that in a world prepared by Taylorist thinking, when organization theorists did start to conceptualize power, they sought its sources not in the certainties that Taylorism prescribed as normal but in those uncertainties that escaped its normalizing discipline. It is this development of a practice of efficiency that we will explore in Chapter 2.

In the early years of the twentieth century there was an expansion of management's remit from the focus on the separate individual's bodily movements by Taylor to the person's social and family life by Ford. The reason for the shift in focus was the impact of routinization that was paced by the speed of the moving production line and its impact on labor turnover, which necessitated a second expansion of management's remit in the form of a new type of employment contract over a whole day rather than over a piece of work. While political economy addressed to the body was an effective means of disciplining European peasants and turning them into American workers, in the post First World War era a new type of industrial worker appeared on the scene, the descendants of slaves who were fleeing the sharecropper society of the southern states to work in the factories of the northeast United States. We argue that these workers gave rise to a series of moral panics about the contagion of hitherto largely white society by black bodies, which led to the development of new technologies of power, oriented far more to regulation of the soul of the worker than merely to the body. The body gained a consciousness.

Chapter 3: Body, Soul, and Mind

The chapter begins by looking at how reform of the economy spread rapidly and globally, eventually becoming the basis for a reform project of society as a whole. We also explore how the analysis of organizations shifted from the formal design of work to a concern with the consciousness of the employee at work. The body was set to acquire a soul at work, which, in turn, would be disciplined further, so that new conceptions could supplement a wholly embodied concept of the person in a cascading quantum of efficiency. Such an innovation meant mounting a project opposing individualism. Not surprisingly, when we seek opposition to individualism, we find it located in community, which is where Mary Parker Follett fixed it. The moral economy of the soul as a locus of legitimacy emerged as a key topic. Neither the theme of the political economy of the body nor that of the regulation of the soul disappeared subsequently; in fact, there are periodic recurrences in subsequent waves of intervention (Abrahamson 1997). Nonetheless, neither the focus on the body nor that on the soul provides a point of application for subsequent theorizing on power in organizations. Indubitably, each is a fulcrum for its practice but neither becomes a conduit for its theorization within mainstream organization science. In fact, power as such was rarely discussed. In the third chapter we demonstrate why this marginalization of power in favor of authority, even in those discourses that were framing it in practice, was an analytical as well as a practical mistake.

Where subaltern or lower ranks cannot countenance any range of alternatives to change the mechanisms of rule, then this implies a considerable resource for those who would seek to occupy the existing higher ranks. It is a kind of legitimacy by default, as that which exists is taken for granted as defining and exhausting the range of possible legitimacies. What is taken for granted as authority is not merely defined by the ruling authorities that sustain it but, ultimately, depends on the consent of those who are ruled. That this is an important point will be evident to anyone that has the faintest inkling of how politics works. Neither tyrants nor democrats can secure the legitimacy of their rule by declaring their full confidence in it, if that rule lacks legitimacy in the perceptions of those subject to it, and if those subject to it have access to means that enable an alternative rule to be established and legitimated.

The foundations of early organization and management theory, as they were laid in the first 50 years or so of the twentieth century, echo into the present era. Scientific management has been reborn many times since; the latest incarnation is knowledge management. Follett's ideas, although never so well received in her time, contained the seeds of contemporary thinking about social capital. The combination of social capital and knowledge management is one of the dominant trends in contemporary approaches, focusing on appropriating the brain rather than the body.

Positions of sovereign power, where a certain figure, office or institution stands at the apex and center of a net of power relations, are not easily achieved, especially when a new order is being born. We deconstruct the ways in which claims to legitimacy have been established, by noting the ways in which management's focus shifted quite rapidly from a political to a moral economy of the body in the early twentieth century.

Chapter 4: The Curious Case of Max Weber

In this chapter we investigate how a sophisticated analysis of power in organizations was being constructed in German in Max Weber's work in the early years of the twentieth century. Early in the twentieth century some German scholars had given great thought to the dynamics of power, the business of rule, and how domination might become authority. Chief amongst these were Max Weber and Georg Simmel. While organization theorists rarely mention Simmel, Weber is frequently claimed as a founding father of rational classical administrative theory. Of particular importance in the process is the transformation of the topic referenced by the German term *Herrschaft* from a concern with domination to a concern with legitimate authority. In this chapter we shall demonstrate how such a translation is wrong and inadequate and misrepresents Weberian analytics. We shall provide a more adequate account, and we shall show how the work of Weber's friend, Simmel, also contributes to a better understanding of power.

Chapter 5: The Rational System and Its Irrational Other

We examine how power became the systemic enemy of the incorporation of formal and informal organization in one frame. Power was the source of irrationality in an otherwise rational system, and invariably came from self-interested lower-order employee objections. The constitution of power in modern organization and management theory was accomplished in the inter-war years between 1918 and 1939. Of particular interest here is the role of the Fatigue Laboratory at Harvard University, and another key Harvard institution, the Pareto Circle, an institution that became central to the production of what would be taken to be compelling truths about modern management, as well as providing an analytical framework in which to embed them. The most famous member of the Pareto Circle was Talcott Parsons, who had first introduced the work of Weber to English-speaking audiences.

Parsons was the grand theorist of functionalist theory. Functionalism honored normalcy, and socialization into it, and saw deviance from the norm as a case for reform. The condition of normalcy was to be found in routine and certainty, in that which was predictable. Functionalist postwar organization theory sought to construct uncertainty as the central ontology of its analysis. Uncertainty played a metaphysical role, linking theory to practice. Organizations sought for certainty but did so in an uncertain world. Some organizations, those least able to standardize, centralize, routinize and formalize their actions, were most hostage to the misfortunes of an uncertain world. Mostly, the sources of these uncertainties were to be found outside organizations, in their environments, or in the technologies they used, but sometimes there were sources of uncertainty to be found in the organization system itself. It was these sources of uncertainty that became the locus of deviance – which is where power was to be located – as that which was antithetical to the perfect rationalization of the system. Thus, organization theory did not seek power in the normal. Authority defined the normal; indeed, it was coterminous with it. Hence, it was in the abnormal, the uncertain, and the non-routine that it sought to find power as a deviation from authority.

If Parsons was the great mid-century synthesizer then a considered nemesis was Erving Goffman, the major miniaturist of social theory in the same era. Goffman established that there were other ways of thinking about the relations of power and identity in organizations. These did not see identity wholly in terms of an all-pervasive central value system instilling its norms in the person, nor did they see anything other than the wholesale acceptance of the corporate message as a failure of socialization and a problem of deviance. Thus, a different basis for analysis of organizations was on offer at this time, formulated by Erving Goffman's (1961) institutional theory, but, by and large, the invitation to a different way of thinking about power, deviance and identity that Goffman offered was not widely taken up. In Goffman, the active, resistant agency of the person was the locus of identity rather than merely its deviant expression.

One strange consequence of the identification of functionalist power with deviance was that power only became addressed in the margins of organization life rather than being seen as its centerpiece. While modern management was in fact a practice of an increasingly more sophisticated power, it was practiced in a form of analytic silence, without explicit recognition discursively. It was a knowledge that dare not speak its name other than as authority and its deviations. It is only relatively recently that attention has been drawn back to the fundamental question of hierarchy and its necessity, most successfully by Gerard Fairtlough (2005), who counterpoises heterarchy and responsible autonomy to hierarchy as alternative ways of getting things done.

Thus, in this chapter we deal with the normalization of power as a deviant part of an otherwise rational system, an interpretation already prepared by the strategies of translation followed by Parsons in respect of Weber's work. A strange alchemy occurs whereby power is ever more discussed but the discussion serves to cover it in confusion rather than to clarify it. That is to say, the form of its discussion, as deviant, as other to authority, occludes any deep-seated understanding. It is a conception of power without ownership and control; it is a conception of power without bodies; it is a conception of power confined to system irregularity. It is a conception of power that is so relatively powerless that understanding it could threaten few authorities and resistance to it would achieve little. It is a conception of power as resource based, in which lists of critical resources are endlessly rehearsed, despite the futility of constructing prescriptive lists of what these resources might be, in the face of the indeterminacy of contexts and events.[14]

Chapter 6: The Heart of Darkness

At the core of modern organizations there is a *heart of darkness,* one which stains not only history but also present realities.[15] We argue that the heart of organization is power and at the heart of power is a darkness that has been bleached out of contemporary accounts of power in organizations. Rather than be stain removers, we wish to draw attention to what turns the heart black.

Certain small but essential studies alert us to the importance of the mechanism of total institutions for the proliferation of the worst kinds of power, that which was banal, total, and evil (Milgram 1974; Haney et al. 1973). Little from these studies seemed able to cross the great divide that systems theory had developed as insulation from other discourses. A great deal could and should have been translated. Had it been so, then it might have been more apparent how disenfranchising and marginalizing a concern with power in organization theory obscured the ample evidence of the consequences of total institutions – such as the Holocaust – and some other horrors of modernity – constituting the heart of darkness at the core of organized modernity.

We gain insight into this heart of darkness through retrieving the work of Erving Goffman on total institutions. Erving Goffman's work never became lodged as a major contribution in the pantheon of organization analysis. Of course, the fate of marginalization that he suffered was hardly unique. While the stress on domination was written out of the received wisdom of Weber, at least his work entered into the everyday lexicon of organization science, albeit in a bastardized form. Goffman is undoubtedly the most important institutional theorist to have written on organizations but his work on total institutions is rarely cited. Had it been discussed more then it is possible that the bizarre fact that the theory of power in organizations has had little to say about some of the most horrendous organizational events of world history in the twentieth century – the Holocaust – would not have to be remarked on. In other areas of inquiry, in political theory (Arendt 1970), these events have been a central concern. In organization theory little if anything was written about how organization could be used for the purpose of systematic extermination, even when the horror was fresh in the minds of the postwar generation who first addressed power systematically. It was as if the extremes of organizational behavior were of little or no interest, even in the world so freshly marked by their horror, a horror that had been planned, produced, and delivered by the finest mechanics of organization theory's preferred methods of efficiency.

The truth of the Holocaust showed what organization could really achieve. Here, where spatial control, disciplinary practice and industrial methods conspired with a visionary purpose, power asserted its might. In Chapter 6 we address the Holocaust as an instance of what Goffman (1961) termed the power of total institutions; we do so initially through the work of Bauman (1989), who, to widespread indifference amongst the ranks of organization scientists, has provided significant social theory implicating future organization analysis. We also draw on important work by Winton Higgins (2004).

We go on to address a range of more recent attempts at constructing total institutions: the Magdalene Laundries, the mission schools and reserves of the Australian Aboriginal Protectorate, the East German Democratic Republic, and Abu Ghraib. We argue that the heart of darkness, while it may have been expressed in throughputs of different types, such as the organization of death, the washing away of sin, the cleansing and blending of race, and the interrogation of guilt, is marked by exactly the same practices of rationality as conventional organizations, with the difference between them being a matter of relative intensification.

The Holocaust and other forms of organized horror in total institutions prefigure how space, when it is precisely configured, can be conquered by power, as writers such as Higgins (2004) have elaborated. Organization theory has not attended much to some of the most significant of recent uses of organizational power, particularly as it relates to issues of space. Lacking an account of excess, it cannot see the extremes that may be incipient in the normal. The chapter will reveal the ways in which total institutions are a concentration and condensation of normal techniques of power; how extreme cases serve a vital function in alerting us to the dangers inherent in normalcy; and how that which divides what we take to be good from what we take to be evil is a very thin and porous membrane as well as situational rather than transcendent.

Chapter 7: Power To and Power Over

There have been two dominant tendencies in modern conceptions of power, and one of them, the positive conception associated with Talcott Parsons, has been relatively neglected by organization theorists, even though it has deep roots in the work of Mary Parker Follett. We explore sophisticated debates in social theory that, with few exceptions, have hardly informed organization theory, thus establishing organization theory as something of a backwater in terms of the relative lack of sophistication of its theorizing in social science terms. We look at the development of contrasting views that stress 'power to' and 'power over'. We consider the contributions of scholars such as Talcott Parsons (1964), Michael Mann (1986), Niklas Luhmann (1979), Pierre Bourdieu (1984) and Steven Lukes (1974; 2005) and the debates that arose around these works. There is no doubt that these debates were significant sociologically and in political science and generated reflection about many of the issues that we now take for granted in the contemporary lexicon of power. They were broad and interdisciplinary in scope, so this chapter will involve us in addressing debates in political philosophy, political science, and political sociology, as well as studies of power *per se*. These contributions were primarily oriented to an exploration of the links between power and consciousness – debates to which the contributions of Ernesto Laclau and Chantal Mouffe (1985) have been central, work that has recently been significantly addressed by Žižek (2005a).

Parsons created the space in which a positive concept of power could flourish in the postwar era. Other functionalist-oriented theorists, such as Niklas Luhmann and Michael Mann, also built theories of systemic power. Other contributions were more concerned with the power of capital or, as we might say, after Pierre Bourdieu (1986), capitals. Marxist theory was an important anchor of late-twentieth-century analytical programmatics, either as an absent presence in functionalist writers such as Parsons, or explicitly in later theorists such as Lukes. A radical view of power, with its stress on the importance of 'ruling consciousness' through 'ruling culture', as opposed to structural accounts that dwelt on relations of production in a case of

structuralism versus humanism, Marxism versus liberalism: these were the significant themes that Lukes (1974; 2005) addressed.

Chapter 8: The Foucault Effect

The assumptions of the power debate that stretched from Hobbes through Locke
to Steven Lukes' work were to be radically questioned by Michel Foucault's evolving
analytics of power. It is often the case that, just as it seems that a debate is about to
be resolved, it is reopened from a space that no one was expecting. Michel Foucault
opened up such a space that offers a case in point. The different emphases in
Foucault's thought, and its major criticisms from the point of view of power in organizations, as well as the extension of his ideas into a workable research practice for
organization theory, will be examined. According to Foucault, discourse constitutes
both the subjects and the objects of knowledge, linked via generic practices of observation and documentation. Thus, a discourse constitutes a field of objects and legit-
imizes the specific kind of observer associated with a type of knowledge (Foucault
1972; 1977; D'Amico 1982). Legitimacy is profoundly embedded in discourse.

Foucault's work has been very influential; no one has put it to better use empirically than Bent Flyvbjerg (1998) in his *Rationality and power: democracy in practice,* a marvelous ethnographic account of urban planning, politics and
construction in the Danish city of Aalborg. In theoretical terms, Foucault was a
major influence on the work of Stewart Clegg (1989) in developing his influential
'circuits of power' framework. In this chapter we use the latter to give an account
of Flyvbjerg's work. We also look at a fascinating case study from Sally Davenport
and Shirley Leitch (2005), which also uses the circuits' framework.

Foucault has many critics and we consider some of the more significant critiques
towards the end of the chapter. First, it has been argued that Foucault maintained
too singular a focus on surveillance and that is certainly true of his reception in
organization studies. Second, we consider the criticism that Foucault is insufficiently attuned to essential elements of the human condition such as gender in his
theorizations. Third, Deleuze (1988) argues that power is mainly negative for
Foucault in his institutional analyses. Fourth, Foucault has been criticized for being
too Eurocentric. Fifth, Foucault has been criticized for being too structuralist.
Sixth, he is so promiscuous in his definition of what is power that it ends up being
a meaningless construct, one that cannot be everywhere and everything. Seventh,
his definition of power has been criticized for being impractical, amoral, and not
usefully evaluative. Eighth, his work is empirically dubious because he concentrates
on the design of practices rather than the actual practices. Finally, in this chapter
we use the idea of life-paths, drawn from social geography, to suggest some ways
that one might apply Foucault's ideas in practice, and consider the implications of
Harré and Madden's (1975) thinking about causal powers.

Chapter 9: Critical Theories of Organizational Power

Management scholars built on ideas from Critical Theory in sociology to challenge
taken-for-granted assumptions about the nature of the corporation, modern

management, and management knowledge. We consider the development of a critical moment in management studies focused on explicating the structures of power and control that characterize the modern corporation and on challenging the notions of performativity, naturalness, and non-reflexivity that characterize mainstream management thought.

While there is a broad divergence in definitions and understandings of what constitutes critical management, at its most fundamental it means 'to say that there is something wrong with management, as a practice and as a body of knowledge, and that it should be changed' (Fournier and Grey 2000: 16). Critical management concerns questioning the nature and underlying assumptions of management practice, management knowledge, and the underlying belief in the usefulness of efficiency as a measure of value. Scholars working in this tradition generally eschew the quantitative methods that are the mainstay of management research and instead use more interpretive methods or, as is most common, employ various forms of theoretical critique to highlight the shortcomings of current approaches. The focus of work in this area is directly on questions of power and advantage and scholars work, at least implicitly, towards some idea of emancipation (e.g. Alvesson and Willmott 1992b), believing that social science should engage with the world and make it more just rather than just more efficient (Mills 1967).

In Chapter 9 we consider this stream of work and explore the motivation and approach of critical management scholars (or 'critters' as they have embarrassingly taken to calling themselves). We examine traditional streams of work in the area inspired primarily by Marx and the Frankfurt School and then discuss later post-structural approaches that draw on Foucault, Derrida, and Lyotard among others. A split has arisen between the more traditional stream of work drawing on Critical Theory from sociology and this newer poststructuralist stream. Foucault (1977) has been especially influential, leading to a concentration on the 'disciplinary gaze' of surveillance in work that was important for organization theory (Barker 1993; Sewell 1998). We will discuss some of the key areas of examination that occupy critical management scholars, including surveillance, gender, colonialism, and race.

One question that we will also consider is the rather subdued reception that this work has received in North America. Even a cursory look at critical management as a body of work shows an almost complete absence of the large American business schools where most management research originates, as well as a marked under-representation in more prestigious journals. Critical management research is largely conducted in Europe and Australasia and published in either specialist journals or journals based in Europe (or published in books, another variance from traditional management research). An important aspect of understanding critical management research is therefore to understand the dynamics of the relationship of the community of scholars engaged in critical management research to the more traditional management research community.

Chapter 10: Discursive Theories of Organizational Power

Largely neglected by organization theory were sociological models that located organization members as essentially discursive (i.e. speaking) subjects. Given that much management and organization may be seen as discursive work, this was surprising. As Clegg (1975) recognized, much of what is done in organizations is done discursively, through words and other signs in both text and talk, an insight that has gathered pace with the popularity of Foucault's work, at least in Europe and Australasia. The insights available from schools such as ethnomethodology and conversational analysis (CA) have rarely been referred to in the business school literature (Garfinkel 1967; Sacks 1972; Lynch 1982; Molotch and Boden 1985). The ethnomethodological and CA focus was on situated *rationalities in practices*. To see rationality as situated, plural and practical is to see it as an index of power working discursively through constituting what it is normal to say and do in specific contexts. Thus, we mark a further significant difference with the account provided by Greenwood and Hinings (2002), where discourse does not figure at all, let alone in the mainstream. The linguistic turn in philosophy led to an increasing interest in linguistic approaches in social science and organization studies, ending in the development of a discursive analytic in organization studies. In this chapter we will consider philosophical and sociological approaches to discourse analysis as an approach to studying power in organizations, and the creation of organizational discourse as a field of study. We focus on gender, power and discourse; identity and power; and deconstruction as areas in which these accounts have developed.

The increasing interest in philosophy in the nature and role of language in the early part of the last century led to a fundamental shift in how language specifically, and meaningful action more generally, were understood. Starting with work in hermeneutics and semiotics, the idea that language was in some one-to-one correspondence with reality became increasingly untenable. The work of Wittgenstein and others created the possibility in Anglo-American philosophy, and subsequently social science, for a new approach to the study of social phenomena. These approaches all share an interest in the role of language in the active construction of social reality (Berger and Luckmann 1967).

One of the most important of these approaches can be broadly described as discourse analysis. While this term covers a broad terrain, our interest in power and organizations makes the more explicitly critical approaches of more relevance. We therefore focus on critical discourse analysis (CDA), beginning with its roots in Foucault and other social theorists and following its development first in sociology and then in organization studies. The resulting organizational CDA provides one of the most explicit treatments of power in organizations in organization studies. We will then explore the range of topics in organization studies to which CDA has been applied and examine the usefulness of a discursive analytics in organization studies.

Chapter 11: Power and Organizational Forms

Debates on bureaucracy relate to fundamental dynamics of underlying structures of power, stretching from democratic to oligarchic forms. The hybrid capacities of power regimes will be explored to uncover the notion of political performance as the basis of political dynamics. Thus, in Chapter 11 we look at the complex intricacies between power and the underlying political forms that have shaped the agenda of organization scholars for decades. An endless debate has concerned bureaucracy and power in relation to the issue of democracy. In other words, since at least Weber, the connections between power and organizational forms constantly confirm the political nature of bureaucracy, and the great flexibility of bureaucratic political structures. We borrow insights from political science (Dahl, Tocqueville, Eckstein and Mouffe, amongst others) to feed the debate about the current hybridization of organizational forms. We suggest the social fabric of *polyarchic* forms comes from the very malleability of the concept of power, its inherent diversity, and the relative fuzziness of its frontiers. Chapter 11 inquires into the processes through which specific forms of political performance are built and maintained, all processes in which power exerts the role of both an enabling and a constraining force.

Chapter 12: Corporate Power Elites

Analysis of power has been shaped by the question 'Who governs?' We investigate the elitist/pluralist debate as it has shaped the way scholars analyze the roles and dynamics of elite bodies, and the contemporary dynamics of corporate elites and how they influence the deep political structures of organizations, particularly the forms of subordination. From the early years of the twentieth century, when the discourse of the managerial revolution first took hold, and the idea that there had been a separation of the powers of ownership and control caught on, the issues of governance and control have been center stage – issues whose contemporary manifestation we explore through some classic resources in Chapter 12. Issues of governance and control return reflection to one of the earliest concerns of European theorists of power, such as Pareto, whom we encountered in Chapter 3, and that is the nature of elite rule in societies. In modernity, these elites are overwhelmingly corporate elites. In Chapter 12 we consider the debates surrounding analysis of these corporate elites. Largely, these debates have to do with the question of fragmentation and cohesion of elite bodies. Behind these classic issues the nature of the perpetuation of the contemporary corporate elite is of particular interest, because it focuses attention on how power holders use different forms of power (cohesive class, small world phenomenon, organizational endogenous mechanisms) in order to produce new forms of legitimacy, as a Weberian strategy, so to speak.

Chapter 13: The Futures of Power?

Chapter 13 suggests new problems, new perspectives, and new avenues for political and organizational scholars interested in the broad issue of power. New problems arise from the further extension of what Beck has termed a risk society into one that we refer to as a heightened state of insecurity. New perspectives are needed to incorporate such concerns within the remit of organization studies. In consequence, new issues materialize, especially around issues of identity and the ways in which these are increasingly scanned, simulated, and structured in action. New technologies are involved but these are not the necessary and sufficient causal agencies shaping identity; the extension of surveillance into hypersurveillance through simulation has been associated with many different technologies.

New ways of thinking about emergent and continuingly important issues confirm that power might well be the broadest issue in the social sciences, stretching its tentacles almost everywhere, for very good reason. We ask how current societal and social tendencies might affect power as a concept and as a practice in the near future and see how the wheel of power has come full circle to the issue of what constitutes productive resistance. The new dynamics and relationships between power and the production of resistance are developed, and we consider the emergence of new types of 'social movement' within organizations, as well as identify the ongoing paradox between the rejuvenation of systems of domination and the social fabric of resistance.

Among the many suggestions we put forward in this last chapter, of utmost importance is rethinking both the issues of resistance and the issues of oppression in the light of current transformations of the relationships between business organizations and the societal context. How can the (post) Weberian, (post) Foucauldian, and (post) Durkheimian stances that we have adopted along the journey be reconciled, so as to enable fresh thinking about some of the most fundamental issues for organizations and their members, including democratic forms, new social movements, the circulation and stability of elites, the reality of organizations as political 'subjects', and, especially, what it is that organization/s bring to the overall structuration of societies?

Notes

1   In a famous letter of April 3, 1887 to Bishop Mandell Creighton, Lord Acton reflected that 'Power tends to corrupt, and absolute power corrupts absolutely. Great men are almost always bad men.' It is, perhaps, the most widely quoted statement concerning power in the modern world.

2   To allude to something that Bernard Crick (1982) once remarked with respect to the role of politics in public life.

3   Of course, in power, putative or pronounced intentions are not the same things as achieved outcomes, something that should be clear from the outset.

4   See: http://www.economist.com/agenda/displaystory.cfm?story_id=4126793 andfsrc=nwl.

5   The domino theory was a justification for foreign policy that the US Eisenhower government established in 1954. The theory said that if any part of Indo-China fell to communist insurrection, then the neighboring states would fall as if they were a line of dominoes. One push could topple the whole set. In Iraq a similar theory seems to be at work. Create a democracy in one state, with a freely elected government, and the others in the region will fall into line. It is interesting that in 50 years, although the ends may have changed from defeating communism to promoting democracy, the means remain the same: the end can only be achieved by the force of US arms invading sovereign states on a pretext.

6   Iraq was carved out of the Ottoman Empire by the British after the collapse of that empire as a result of the First World War. On November 11, 1920 it became a mandated protectorate of the British Empire under the imprimatur of the League of Nations with the name 'State of Iraq'. The British government laid out the political and constitutional framework for Iraq's government, one consequence of which was that the new political system lacked legitimacy, because it was seen as an alien imposition. Britain imposed a monarchy on Iraq and defined its territorial limits with little regard for natural frontiers and traditional tribal and ethnic settlements. It was, to all intents and purposes, an artificial and puppet state in which British Petroleum interests were paramount.

7 Africa prior to colonization was 80 percent controlled locally by indigenous people. At the Berlin Conference of 1884–5, called by Bismarck, the European powers created geometric boundaries that divided Africa into 50 irregular countries. The new map of the continent was superimposed over 1,000 indigenous cultures and regions. The new countries divided coherent groups of people and merged together disparate groups who really did not get along. Nearly all of Africa's contemporary problems can be seen to have their roots in this initial map making (see http://geography.about.com/cs/politicalgeog/a/berlinconferenc.htm).

8 Nugent's (2004) comparative history of Africa since independence is a superb guide.

9 The interested reader might wish to consult Transparency International's website and look up some of the material in the Corruption Perceptions Index (http://www.transparency.org/surveys/index.html#cpi). Interestingly, there is no parallel index for the many organizations that symbiotically sustain these corrupt regimes and their elites. If the latter are bribed there have to be bribers, such as Lockheed International and BAE, both documented as corrupt. These are not isolated cases; there are many, many more. Unfortunately, there seems to be a marked reluctance to name and shame, especially on the part of political elites and administrations.

10 For Weber to have been a founder, the adolescence was either extremely protracted or the time reckoning system somewhat askew. On balance, we favor the latter explanation. All time reckoning systems that seem to be predicated on a knowledge of a future maturation yet to occur seem inherently faulty, whether that future be projected as one of 'late capitalism' or an 'institutional adolescence'.

11 In the later 1970s and into the 1980s, in the period when population ecology and its focus on organizational dynamics bloomed (Hannan and Freeman 1977; 1984), changes *in* organizations were seen to take place primarily through the change *of* organizations. Change was likely to take the shape of punctuated equilibrium in which long periods of stability in organizational populations and forms would be disrupted by short bursts of innovation and creativity, as new forms were innovated and either selected in or out. While asking about such matters seems to be a sociological question, the way in which it was posed, applied through the much-trod path of adopting biological models, tended to screen out the possibility of human agency: it wasn't individuals that made a difference but natural forces over which individuals had no control. Once the capacity to make a difference was marginalized, so was power, by definition.

12 Theories became increasingly hermetic within their assumptions. Most impressive in this regard were economic theories of organizations. It was the economists who did most to abandon questions of power. The classic landmark in this genre of work was Coase (1937), on whose work, together with the concept of bounded rationality, Williamson (1981) built the transaction cost approach. Perrow's (1986b) trenchant critique of the resulting economic theories of organizations strikes to the heart of what is so unsatisfactory in these approaches: their sociological disinterest, shown by their derivation of theory from market auspices and their resolute blindness to empirical matters of power and politics in organizational structuring. Their central question was how organizations could be better tools. The nature and needs of individuals who worked in organizations and the communities and social formations on which they had an impact were regarded as inconsequential and the concept of power as unnecessary. Increasingly, as differences were consciously organized, using Kuhn's (1962) work on paradigms as ways of seeing and ordering impressions, to make sense systematically, the subsequent differentiation came under attack from Pfeffer (1993). The project of moral rearmament represented by the Pfefferdigm has been discussed elsewhere (see Clegg and Kornberger 2003). Burrell and Morgan's (1979) work, using Kuhn, sparked a shift in the appreciation of organization studies as a multiparadigm enterprise and created both more spaces and a stronger sense of what was core and what was periphery (Pfeffer 1995). One positive outcome of the paradigm wars (Pfeffer 1993; van Maanen 1995) is that today, apart from one or two fundamentalists, few philosophically informed scholars insist on the need for epistemological orthodoxy around a functionalist, correspondence model of reality. However, much organization theory is remarkably ignorant of contemporary debates in the

philosophy of social science, or has only a narrow grasp of them, and still seems to cling to a correspondence model of truth long after its abandonment by most contemporary philosophers. Such a constipated conception of science is in itself a particular type of power that has become widespread in contemporary organization theory, often used to justify restricted and limited research programs because they offer a correspondence with putative states of affairs. Such studies proliferate and populate the leading journals. However, it is not necessarily the most robust research programs that flourish but the better-resourced and publicized programs located in elite institutions, which are taken to be the most robust. Being consecrated by the most powerful patrons they benefit from broader circuits of symbolic capital. Armed with these resources, the powerful can then play the incommensurability card by constituting those who do not agree with their 'paradigm' as, at best, saying the same things, only making them more difficult – being marginal, not people like us – or, at worst, belonging to a dangerously separate or even lunatic fringe. Some players are avid dealers of this hand (Donaldson 1985; 1995; 1996).

13   The ideas spread rapidly and widely. In 1915 we find Robert Moses, architect of much of modern New York, preparing a 'detailed report on the efficiency of civil service employees, excepting members of the uniformed forces in the police and fire services and in the lower ranks of the street cleansing service', which is indistinguishable in its language of report cards, classifications, and standardization from the work of the scientific managers. The report was not adopted and it is instructive to see the ways in which those whose power and organizations would have been adversely affected by it were able to resist, as Robert Caro (1974: 75–88) analyzes.

14   When a young journalist asked British Prime Minister Harold Macmillan, whilst still in office, what can most easily steer a government off course, he answered 'Events, dear boy. Events.'

15   The reference, of course, is to Joseph Conrad's (1998[1902]) 'Heart of darkness', the classical critique of European imperialism in Africa which became the basis for the equally compelling critique of US imperialism in Vietnam, in the film *Apocalypse now* (of which the best version is the director's cut by Coppola 2002). We shall revisit the heart of darkness in Chapter 6.

2 Power and Efficiency

Chapter outline

In this chapter we will:

- Establish the emergence of a distinct concern with management and explore the historic connections between the principles of modern management and liberal utilitarianism.
- Elaborate the precise historic constitution of modernity's arrival at a conceptualization of efficient and effective management that sought ways to reform and control the individual employee.
- Articulate the context, aims and ideas of Taylor as the main contributor developing a science of management as a political project and introduce some of his key ideas about efficiency and the political economy of the body.
- Demonstrate how Taylor's ideas about the individual body were superseded by the development of the Sociological Department in the Ford Motor Company. Consequently, the focus shifted from the political economy of the individual body to a bio-power that was oriented to the collective body politic of the organization membership.
- Establish the normalization of a scientific management approach to work study in the early years of the twentieth century, showing how these ideas were widely disseminated internationally in the economy and society, not just organizations.

Introduction

In this chapter we will focus on the beginnings of management as a 'science' and the correlative instrumentalization of power via routines. We will discuss the work of Taylor, seeing it as an extension of earlier utilitarian projects that were oriented to making the expectation of work normal. We will explore how Taylor took utilitarianism inside the factory and addressed it to the actual conditions of work, reconstituting it in the process.

Taylor's theory of management can equally be seen as a theory of power in modern organizations. By focusing on efficiency as the uncontestable object of management, Taylor developed a theory of management and organization that both prescribed the modern organization and legitimated the complex system of power it constituted. Taylor's novel conception of power and the body at work provides us with the opportunity for theorizing differently. Hence, it should be evident that where others might see the foundations of scientific management we see the foundations of a practice of power.

Recovering an appreciation of Taylor and the early science of management is only the first step in the prehistory of power and organizations. We will go on to discuss how the theory and practice of management soon shifted their focus from the body and began to consider the soul. The Sociological Department at Ford was the first and most striking extension of management from a focus on the body to the management of the soul, legitimated by the uncontestable discourse of efficiency. The concern for the soul in management was supported and strengthened by a range of societal trends that focused attention more broadly on this issue. We conclude with a discussion of the complex interrelationship between developments in management theory and these broad societal trends.

Management and modernity

It is a truth universally acknowledged that an organization not in possession of good fortune must be in want of a good manager.[1] What managers do has traditionally been defined in terms of relations of handling, supervision and control.[2] The precise unfolding of these relations, in part, is a charting of the forms that power in organizations has assumed. There are different degrees of sophistication related historically to different strategies of management and managing. Generally, management as a practice of power involving the imposition of will is directed at framing the conduct not only of others but also of oneself. It is a form of government linking 'how to mandate' with 'how to obey'. Managing implies power because it involves governing the conduct of oneself and others.

Managing in any epoch will be a particular skill that involves execution and doing. It will be active, a practice. Moreover, it will be not merely a practice of the self – one doesn't just learn how to be a manager – but also a practice of the many others who are to be managed. Others must learn to be managed just as those who will manage them must learn that which constitutes managing in any given place and time. While managers originally were constituted as the delegated 'servants' of 'masters', and indeed various Masters and Servants Acts still frame employment relations, modernity saw servants become employees.[3] What is distinctive about being an employee is that one is presumed, as someone in receipt of a wage, to be an *obedient subject,* who in return for an income is expected to be responsible to the control of another higher in a chain of command, one of the key concepts of early management theory. But there was management before there was management theory.

Pre-modern management theory

Forced labor and pre-modern management

Cooke (2003) suggests that many of the ideas developed in the plantation economy of the US southern states as a means of disciplining the bodies and coordinating the large numbers of people at work there entered into modern factory management. In particular, given that slaves were assumed to be untrustworthy and unreliable, they were expected to work strictly according to rules, under close surveillance through extensive supervision designed for routine enforcement of these rules. (When rules were breached there was exemplary and spectacular punishment of those who transgressed, through public floggings.) [4]

The use of close supervision of people was very much an engrained habit of pre-modern society, if only because practices of rule were invariably tightly coupled spatially, as the vast majority of people were, literally, placed in a specific locality in a here-and-now that they rarely transgressed or moved away from. For the majority of people life was lived in and around the limits of a walk that might take a day or so to undertake. Being settled they were subject to frequent informal as well as occasional formal scrutiny. Interruptions to settled life would most likely be because of being pressed into military service of some kind, often literally, as the press-gangs roamed the streets of ports seeking to press available young men into the service of the navy, or recruiting sergeants sought out young village laborers for a life of adventure. Once pressed into service they would meet much more formal management than in the fields or village. They entered an institutional space.

On board ship what they entered was more or less a total institution (Goffman 1961) where they could not escape a particular fusion of power and knowledge, oversight and insight, embodied in the person of the bo'sun. The bo'sun was a boatswain, or petty officer, who controlled the work of other seamen. He knew what was to be done and how it should be done and would ensure that whatever was to be done would be done his way, often using harsh punishment, if necessary, to discipline the recruits. The recruits could not escape. That is what it means to say that they were in a total institution: it was an organizational space that wholly contained them. Their time was enveloped by a single space, that of the ship. Whilst on board they were contained within a disciplinary framework of shifts, work, punishments, and provisions that were totally outside their control. The insights of those who managed and handled sailors enabled them to learn skills that they needed for survival in a harsh and dangerous environment. There would be gaps: for instance, when the ship docked, those seamen allowed shore leave would gain a temporary degree of freedom. (Of course some were forbidden leave; others might go ashore only under supervision.)

Those who were pressed into military service on land were barely more fortunate. Admittedly, the environment was slightly less total, in the way that a garrison affords more freedom than a ship. Yet, they were more regimented. Being regimented not only meant assuming a regimental identity and the uniform that went with it; it also meant learning a uniform mode of behavior, taught through drill (on which see Foucault 1977). There are some scholars who suggest that the main basis for early management ideas came from the lessons learned in such garrisons, especially as it pertained to the assembly and disassembly of muskets and the drilling of soldiers in the use of these and other weapons on the parade ground (Dandeker 1990). These methods were first applied to muskets by French gunsmiths, and brought from France to the United States at the time of the American Revolution, where they led, in a way mediated by Charles Davies' position at the West Point Military Academy, to the 'disciplining' of America through the new science of engineering.[5]

Managing formally free labor

Slaves and indentured laborers were not formally free. Nor were serfs or other forms of feudal laborer. Free men and women were those who were owned by no one, to whom no one had any obligations, whose number swelled in Europe after the Black Death of 1348, which tipped the balance of power in favor of the diminished supply of labor and against the feudal serf-owners (Anderson 1974). Serfs could more easily defy their masters and flee to the towns and become free men and women. But not all could find economic opportunity there, and as common land was privatized increasingly from the sixteenth century onwards, their life chances narrowed. If they were not in employed labor, they formed the dangerous, unruly pauper class, the vagabonds and ruffians who roamed the countryside, unattached to land or masters, widely regarded by most of polite society and the respectable poor as being without skills other than those of thievery and trickery. Their crimes and misdemeanors saw them become felons in Britain's overcrowded jails and prison hulks or dispatched to the penal colonies of New South Wales and other antipodean destinations (Hughes 1987).

The indigent poor became an object of moral scrutiny for the simple reason that their propensity to form a dangerous mob was the major source of domestic moral panic in Britain, and had been since at least the sixteenth century and the development of land enclosures. Such enclosures made the poor wandering and dispossessed rather than able to scrape a subsistence living from 'the commons', that is, communally accessible land. As the supply of commons disappeared, vagabondage became *the* British social problem from the seventeenth century onwards, and the Poor Laws – subject to frequent reform and attempts at improvement – were the instruments designed to handle and manage the problem.

Much politics surrounded the administration of the Poor Laws, their repeal and reform (Court 1962), which hinged on who should pay, in which borough relief should be dispensed, who was eligible to receive it and where, what the tests of eligibility should be, and how those who were subject to these Poor Laws might be reformed so that they no longer fell under their sway. In fact, minimizing the number of the latter was the disciplinary intent of these laws. Poovey notes that the New Poor Law of 1834 succeeded where its predecessors had failed 'because it incited in the poor the fear that all freedoms would be abrogated if one acknowledged the need for relief' (1995: 111). The workhouse became the chief instrument of policy. To receive poor relief the vagabond had to renounce wandering ways and accept the discipline of the workhouse where, in return for work, they might receive public assistance.

Spurring the reform of the Poor Laws were robust debates between different philosophies (discussed in Ryan 2004). The principal architect of utilitarian philosophy, which won the day, was Jeremy Bentham (1843). Utilitarian philosophers argued that the overall utility or benefit produced by an action ought to be the standard by which we judge the worth or goodness of moral and legal action and that the principle of usefulness must be elevated above all else in order to minimize human misery and maximize human happiness.[6] They reasoned that assistance to the indigent few was justified by the needs of the many for an orderly life. Such order was to be founded on principles of economic competition.

Bentham was absolutely sure that it was necessary to 'sequester certain classes of subject within an enclosed space which is cut out of the wider society, a controlled space where they could be subjected to techniques of training and character-formation' (Ryan 2004: 134). What Bentham proposed was a program for distilling a certain mode of rationality into widespread consciousness and use. He wanted to produce individuals who would think as liberal subjects, as people capable of calculating their best interests and acting on them, and he devised and categorized a specific means to achieve this end. In this way, he sought to abolish the mentality of the pauper through reforming character and creating individual effort in work. Honest laborers should see the poverty relief as an abomination. It not only rewarded indigence but also taught vice (2004: 133–4).

What was required, thought Bentham, was a system that would produce administrative certainty and perfection for society as a whole by categorizing and reforming the classes of vagrancy and vagabondage. The classes needed to be differentiated and categorized because pauperism had many different causes and each cause should be subject to a different program. The underlying genus that was being classified was the disinclination of indigent paupers to be managed and, thus, to be a hand. The problem was one of management. Why did poverty not act as a spur to productivity amongst certain classes of the poor (Dean 1991; 1992)? The reason, Bentham suggested, was that work was not the most attractive option. Certain classes of indigent people would prefer to live at the expense of others, from the fruits of others' labors, rather than live off the fruit of their own labor. They were poor *and* feckless. In this era, to be designated as a pauper was to be judged as lacking in moral fiber; thus it was warranted that the state could and should make intervention, correction and rehabilitation.

Bentham thought that there was no singular cause of indigence, and so there could not be a simple or singular answer to the question of how to combat it. To demonstrate the many causes of pauperism, Bentham (1843) devised a Pauper Population Table (reported in Ryan 2004), which classified certain categories of unproductive hands by a complex of causes, their duration, and the degree of uncertainty attached to them.[7] Bentham's aim was to create a universal labor theory of value which, through considering the efficient causes of indigence, the nature, degree, and duration of the inability to work, and the mode of relief, would place the whole economy on a sound workmanlike basis. These systematic classifications expressed a centralized power that fixed the social, cultural and moral grounds for economic management of those on the margins of society.

All types of indigent hands could be confined in the poorhouse and, once there, be subject to employment in a widespread division of labor. Exposing vagabonds to institutionalized moral and productive correction was intended to induce workmanlike ideals.

O'Neill notes that as the supply of surplus labor grew, and grew more disaffected, 'houses of correction became even more punitive' and work in them was 'limited to intimidating and useless tasks so that no one would ever enter them voluntarily' (1986: 51). Once put to work, the poor would stay in the workhouse until they earned sufficient funds to cover the costs of their relief in the institution. It was a self-liberation principle, showing that the individual subject was capable, responsible and worthy. They would not receive relief unless they had met the daily requirement of their labor, showing that they could fulfill the essential duties of a liberal subject to work and earn productively. Bentham's philosophy elevated the principle of usefulness above all else, and used it to provide a new meaning for efficiency, as an 'efficient cause', a predicate for causes that will shape a desired effect.[8]

The Panopticon as an 'efficient cause' of compliance

The Poor Laws said little about how work should be done – only that it should be. Bentham turned his attention to how one might design a rational enterprise so that the utility of oversight could be maximized, and came up with a design for something that he called a Panopticon. The Panopticon was designed as an efficient cause.[9] It was a complex architectural design for a workplace, adapted from his brother's factory in Russia. It consisted of a central observation tower from which any supervisor, without themselves being seen, could see the bodies arranged in the various cells of the building. In each cell, the occupants were backlit by natural light, isolated from one another by walls and subject to scrutiny by the observer in the tower. Control was to be maintained by the constant sense that unseen eyes might be watching those under surveillance. You had nowhere to hide, nowhere to be private, and no way of knowing if you were being watched at any particular time.

The principles embodied in the Panopticon had widespread influence. The key principle was inspection by an all-seeing but unseen being – rather like a secular version of God. And it did not matter if the inmates were actually being watched at any specific time: they would never know, but they did know that they were always at risk of being watched. The principle of inspection or surveillance instilled itself in the moral conscience of those who were being overseen. The aim of the Panopticon was to produce a self-disciplining person subject to an asymmetrical experience of knowing you were possibly being watched, but not when or if you were. It was designed to produce employees socialized into submitting their will to the task at hand; the alternative to imposed self-adjustment was the fear of being corrected and disciplined.

The ingenuity of the Panopticon resided in the economy of effort required to administer it, once it was designed and built. Literally, it was a means for making work as visible as it could be, by virtue of the supervisor seeing as much as possible. It was the particular relation between the overseer and the seen that was significant in the Panopticon. Those who were being seen were scrutinized in ways that did not enable them to see that they were under surveillance (see Hannah 1997 for a good account; also see Ignatieff 1978). The situation was structured such that obedience in and through productive activity seemed the worker's only rational option, not knowing whether or not they were being watched but obliged to assume that they were.

Bentham designed the Panopticon as a progressive phenomenon. Moreover, as a pioneering 'best practice', the Panopticon could equally be applied to schools, hospitals, and factories, as well as poorhouses. It was a project to be applied to everything. Not only was it panoptical but it also had wide applications (explored in McKinley and Starkey 1997).[10] The Panopticon was not just a system of surveillance but also a system of records and rules, comprising disciplinary power. The authorities would have a complete file on the behavior of each inmate. There would be rules governing timetables, the nature of work, and the authority to exercise surveillance. Disciplinary power was embedded in the small things of everyday working life, the routines, the tiny details, especially as these were regulated through training and practices of examination that sought to constrain human action into useful aptitudes, framed through what Foucault (1977) termed 'normalizing judgments' established through the establishment of limits of accepted behavior and the standards to be achieved.[11] The pre-modern world of civil organization was largely characterized by discretion concerning freedoms and exploitation; Bentham's Panopticon program began to think about the organization of work as something more systematic.[12]

The emergence of modern management theory

Modern management

As far as one is concerned with management, the maturation of modernity is marked, programmatically, by the work of F. W. Taylor, for he was responsible for creating the individual and responsible employee not just as a creature of religious imperatives such as the Protestant ethic – or habit – but as a consciously designed utilitarian project.[13] Taylor's (1911) preface to *The principles of scientific management* makes this quite clear when he stresses the need for national efficiency. His utilitarianism can be seen in a number of characteristics of his thought. First, it is teleological in its orientation to means. What is important is securing the desired consequences. Second, in Taylor's philosophy, actions can be judged only by their consequences, such that a dogged empiricism is allied to an unquestioned grasp of the ends to be served. Third, ends are defined in terms of efficiency (primarily for the factory owners) but are represented as the common good. Taylor took utilitarianism from a program for dealing with the marginal and abnormal, the other, and transposed it into a program for dealing with the everyday and the normal, the worker.[14]

Taylor's concern with productivity and performativity shifted the focus on hands from the margins of society, from indigent trash, to the key centers of employment relations constructed in the market economy. It was this that provided the intellectual and social context within which management was first defined. It was a context riddled with power at every turn. Assumptions about the natural order of things underlay Taylor's idea that some were born to manage and direct, while the fate of others was to be managed and directed. Efficient management was based on reforming power/knowledge relations, taking them out of the hands of the workers and systematically refashioning them so that they could be placed in the hands of management. Efficient management should obey the precepts of science and respect a liberal mentality, much as should efficient employees in general. Once the one best way was devised, any deviation from it should be regarded with anathema. The purity of power consisted in its eternal return as repetition, as the same routine.

Power – getting others to do what one wanted them to do, even against their will – was inscribed as the normalcy of the new system of scientific management. In this system one should always do just as one was told; one should never be where one does not belong; and what one should do and where one should be were not to be left to chance but should be determined, authoritatively, by the science of productive efficiency and management. Through the alchemy of science the new system of rule could be denoted as a regime of impersonal authority which served no interest other than the general interest in utilitarian efficiency, an interest from which all, with the exception of lazy people who refused to change their behavior, might prosper. The poor but honest laborer could enrich himself through the dignity of his own exertions in a system designed to maximize the rewards that flowed. So could the employer in the counting house, amassing profits from the same principles. In principle, all would be for the best in the best of all possible worlds.

F. W. Taylor: the father of modern management as power shaping efficiency

Although born to a wealthy Quaker professional family, and despite passing the entrance exam for the Harvard Law School, Taylor decided to become apprenticed as a pattern maker and machinist at the Enterprise Hydraulic Works, a valve making firm owned by a friend of the family. Following that, in 1878 he joined the Midvale Steel Co., first as a laborer and then rapidly climbing the ladder to machinist, gang boss and shop supervisor, and eventually becoming chief engineer. One consequence of this biography was that he had a unique degree of practical shop floor knowledge for a man of his class and time. Whereas Bentham was concerned with bringing idle hands to work, Taylor's utilitarian calculus was oriented to the problem of making hands already at work even more productive, for the greatest good of national efficiency and for the better reward of both hands and the businesses that employed them. To this end he assembled a disciplinary apparatus to achieve efficient scientific management.

After Taylor, the individual workman need not exist merely as a creature of habit, tradition or craft but could become an *object* of scientific knowledge and a *subject* produced by the application of that knowledge. The worker became a utilitarian subject. Taylor marks a significant break not because he was some unique innovator or discoverer of truths previously unknown but because he popularized ideas that, although they had been practiced previously, had not been collected, synthesized, documented, and marketed as specific ways of intervening into the everyday organization of work. They had not been 'made up' into a bundled program, designed to regulate conduct and to order the spaces within which things are thinkable, utterable, and doable. It was the achievement of this that marks the emergence of modern management as the application of rational means to everyday practice and measurable ends.

Taylor was oriented to the problem of making employed, rather than idle, hands busier in the service of the greatest good of national efficiency and for the better reward of both hands and the businesses that employed them. In fact, one of Taylor's biographers, Kanigel (1997), suggests that efficiency became iconic for almost all American organizations, and increasingly those of other industrialized nations. It had to be worshipped, feted, and widely represented in cultural artifacts of the age. Taylor's (1911) *Principles of scientific management* was such an artifact. It helped persuade people that efficiency was desirable as an end in itself and that all legitimate means should be oriented towards it.

From the point of view of Nelson and Winter (1982), efficiency became a meta-routine that shaped the future of power. Meta-routines have a direct impact on the complementarity of other routines for which they serve as a pattern maker. Pattern making in meta-routines is provided in an application model for the spread of new solutions to old problems and in generating new problems that had not been constituted under the regime of earlier solutions. In organizations, meta-routines organize the modernization or transformation of existing practices, products, processes, and industries. Meta-routines define the nature of the normalcy within which problems appear. Defining normalcy and establishing it as such are two separate activities and it can be argued, in fact, that a measure of slackness in the former, a measure of indeterminacy, and a lack of total success, are essential to the success of the latter – in a paradoxical way – because success requires failure to further stimulate the development of its own programmatics. Where definitional deficiency and opaqueness exist there is always an expectancy of more output, more efficiency, more productivity. Thus, it is important not to mistake programmatics for accomplished practices; however, although they differ, they are inherently related, for every program requires its exceptions to continue expanding.[15]

Measuring time and motion

A key feature of Taylor's work was use of a stopwatch to time his observations of work – in a less than perfect attempt to impose exactness – whose accuracy was later to be improved greatly by the use of film by some of his associates. In many respects, Taylor was an acute, if somewhat one-dimensional, ethnographer. Taylor was a detailed chronicler of life in the factory. He wanted to know exactly how workmen did what they did when they worked, which entailed detailed ethnographic observation, for which he developed a system of denoting and coding. However, it was an ethnographic method devoid of understanding and of input from the subject it objectified.

Taylor's ethnographic interests were not anthropological; he did not wish merely to describe accurately the customs and rituals of those whom he encountered in work but sought to reform the nature of that work. And his reforms were guided by a concern only with increasing efficiency. He sought to redesign work so that it was conducted in the most efficient way that he could imagine, based on his detailed empirical ethnographies and timings of how it was actually done, as well as how it might be done differently, according to his redesign. The approach constituted management as a science premised on the dangerous conviction that a single view, based on efficient ends, was to be esteemed above any grasp of interpretive understandings that might be found in the context being studied.

Taylor stressed three techniques in the design of work. Empirical examination, division of labor, and individual competition were his themes for the analysis of work in the factory. Examination was conducted through the detailed observation, note taking and timekeeping of the methods engineer. The redesigned work that would flow from this close inspection and examination was premised on a radical division of labor, with a strict separation between the mental labor of oversight, intended to see the strict dictates of the system were followed, and the manual labor of the production worker, which followed the formalized plan of the engineer. Finally, each individual employee competed against all other employees to maximize the pieces that they could make and thus the piece-rate that they could earn such that they could become a 'high-priced man' (Taylor 1911: 60).

Timing and redesign were the panoptical mechanisms that Taylor designed. All work practices were subject to hundreds of observations and timings, through which he sought to establish what he thought of as the one best way in which to do any given task. Taylor's primary objective in doing a time study was to ascertain an appropriate production rate to use as a basis for an incentive payment. What he sought was the fastest rate, and then he wanted to be able to decompose its elements so that he could understand how it was possible, and how it could become the standard for all operatives.

Expensive measurement and observation instruments and preprinted notepads were used to develop the standards. Observations were made with care for precision, up to a thousandth of a minute in some cases. Taylor compartmentalized productive activities into elements. For each job, elements were defined in such a way that activity within the element could not easily be interrupted. They were the micro-components of work, the smallest unit of task time complete in themselves.

Taylor's procedure made time study much easier, making it possible to produce detailed descriptions for production planning, using the central notion of standard data. If elements were properly designed, according to Taylor's rules, it became possible to determine a standard for the process by describing the process in terms of its pre-rated elements. A lack of task variability and the repetitive nature of the tasks involved in the occupations studied extended the usefulness of the approach.

Against systematic soldiering

Taylor uncovered a whole underground of practices that rendered employed hands as idle, imperfect, superseded, suspect, and so on. Indeed, Taylor was quite clear about his purpose. He believed that the employee is paid by the employer for his time but that time is systematically wasted and squandered by the employed man, which he saw as a moral outrage. The time that is wasted is not the person's but the employer's because, as Taylor notes, the employer is paying for it.

The workers were able to get away with a great deal partly because management was so unsystematic, Taylor thought. The employer and his overseers, or managers, often did not know when time was being wasted. They lacked both sufficient insight and oversight of working practices. Taylor had been a working man and knew the tricks of the shop floor, such as 'soldiering', a term derived from the practice of workers agreeing on a common work pace, like soldiers on parade. The pace was arbitrary and, Taylor believed, often yielded about half the production rate that was achievable. It occurred when workers made a 'show' of 'working hard' in order to escape detection whilst idling on the job, using work already produced but released more slowly than the time taken to make it to cover up the deception.

Taylor also knew that, with the invention of electricity, the balance of power between worker and employer was changing. Standardized inputs of energy which were not under the craft control of the workman meant that, in principle, there was no reason why more standardized outputs, in terms of quantity and quality, should not be possible. Taylor took the battle against lazy, imperfect, and other malfunctioning hands into the workshop. What was required was reform that would mean that the value of a thing or an action would be determined by its utility. How useful labor was depended on how well engineered it was. And that was a task whose terms could not be set by those happy to soldier and steal the employer's time but could only be established, *authoritatively*, to determine the best way in which work should be designed and accomplished.

Power and knowledge would come together to produce an authoritative discourse of 'scientific management', which would establish the norms of work not on the basis of custom and tradition – pre-modern conceptions – but on the basis of modern empirical observation, design and timing. And, in order to obtain the greatest happiness of the greatest number involved in the program, the employee should be rewarded more generously in line with the greater rewards flowing to the employers in the way of increased profits. The working man should receive income through piece-rates. The more they produced (and they would produce more because of scientific management) the more they should earn and know that they would earn.

Taylor thought it a fair trade, such that as workers became more productive bodies when reformed by scientific management into better machines for making things, their powers were enhanced. Now, they would be accountable, which entitled them to an enhanced capacity to earn income. A worker could make significantly more money with the piece-rate system because the company would pay 150 percent or more of the day rate on the entire day's production. The organization could do even better. Since actual production would be more than doubled and labor costs were only a small portion of total costs for a piece, the company would do very well indeed.

The distribution of power in relations of production was mediated through transferring larger financial reward to workers whilst at the same time nullifying the intrinsic worth of an individual's task-related knowledge and experience. Anyone could be trained to undertake tasks using Taylorist methods. Thus, scientific method stripped down and supplanted practice-based knowledge with a science that induced the worker to see their own power in terms of their monetary gain. A new more productive regime and higher earnings were gained, and a regimented and authoritarian managerial regime was introduced which now *collectively* prioritized economic benefit on the part of owners as the dominant social value shaping management and work.

Psychologically, the system offered incentive only for a sustained high-level performance for an entire day. If employees worked hard and consistently all would be happy. Workers' happiness was delivered through piece-rates; the employers' through greater profits. The utilitarian auspices could not be clearer. Scientific management replaced old rule-of-thumb methods with a utilitarian calculus. The selection and training of workers was to be a specific focus, so that, particularly as Münsterberg (1913) developed these techniques, they represented simple but effective technologies of power. Selection was a mechanism of fitness for purpose; those men who were deemed unfit for the Taylor system were not selected. Fitness might be expressed in any terms; it could refer to rude bodily health as much as dispositions, such as being docile and willing to follow instructions. Training represented an equally humble modality of power; it functioned in terms of a standard that men fit for purpose ought to be able to achieve. It represented a way of constructing the concrete person in relation to the abstracted standard – abstracted, that is, from the detailed process of observation, ethnography and timing that created it. Training consisted, primarily, in gaining absolute obedience to the prescribed methods, as Taylor's account of Schmidt makes clear.

Schmidt: exemplar of a technology for the melting pot

Schmidt was a worker whom Taylor reports having interviewed. He was a 'Pennsylvanian Dutchman', whom Taylor represents as 'phlegmatic'. Whether he was or not is debatable, but what is evident is that he did not have great fluency and finesse in the use of the English language. Schmidt's voice is represented as heavily accented and as one that deploys a limited vocabulary. Jacques (1996) notes in passing that the fact that Schmidt was 'Pennsylvanian Dutch' need not necessarily indicate that he was an immigrant so much as his ethnic origin. Nonetheless, his lack of linguistic fluency points to an important aspect of the field of social relations within which Taylor was intervening.

The melting pot was running at full pressure in the late-nineteenth-century United States. European peasants from diverse ethnicities went into Ellis Island and came out as Americans, to enter the mills of the northeast industrial machine. No assumptions either of English-language competency or of scientific rationality could be made about such pre-industrial subjects. One reason why a degree of indeterminacy had flourished in the control of workshop practices was a lack of ability to communicate effectively, so that much remained unsaid. Hence, Taylor produced instructional cards that communicated through images, which had great representational power.

Taylor and the college graduates he employed to set the standards were all educated men. And when they had finished designing a job the worker didn't need much functional literacy to be able to do it, but just did what he was shown to do and did nothing else. In fact, as Taylor once said, famously, a 'trained gorilla' would be able to do a job once he had redesigned it, and he was also reported as saying that people with intellectual disabilities might make better employees in the Taylor system because they would be less likely to become bored by the conditions of the job.

Handling materials

Taylor studied the handling of pig iron in terms of the design of work, especially tools and human movement, with variable results (see Banta 1993; Wrege and Hodgetts 2000; Wrege and Greenwood 1991; Stark 2002; Palmer 1975; Cutler 1978). Research on incentive schemes followed, as did observations on piece-rate systems and their impact on production. Henceforth, management became simple, Taylor thought, as it simply became a task of determining the one best way that had been derived from the systematic observations of 'scientific management' (the name that he gave to his practice) and, by applying it to practice, furthering subservience. As long as managers and the managed did not deviate from this path then efficiency and productivity would be ensured, he argued. The greatest amount could be produced with the least effort. Scientific method, he advocated, could be applied to all problems and applied just as much to managers as to workers.

Taylor turned his attention to shoveling coal. By experimenting with different designs of shovel for use with different materials, he was able to design shovels that would permit the worker to shovel for the whole day. In so doing, he reduced the number of people shoveling at the Bethlehem Steel Works from 500 to 140. He introduced shovels of different sizes for handling different materials (21½ pounds was the most efficient load in a US Steel company study) and saved the company $78,000 per year, which was a great deal of money if translated into contemporary values. As a result of all of these changes, the cost per ton for handling materials dropped from 7 to 8 cents per ton to 3 to 4 cents per ton. The average number of tons shoveled per worker increased from 16 to 59. Average worker pay per day increased from $1.15 per day to $1.88 per day.

Previously, each of the workers supplied their shovel and performed their job in a slightly different way. Taylor told the workers that their pay would be doubled while he made some investigations into how they worked. Taylor and his associates used stopwatches to time the laborers as they performed various tasks. That process also counted the number of shovel-loads they each moved. Based upon his studies, Taylor discovered that the load could vary from 4 to 38 pounds. Starting at 38 pounds per shovel-load, Taylor counted the number of shovel-loads and tons carried per day. Then Taylor had the laborers use short shovels that carried 34 pounds and found that more tons were moved. Experimentation with larger shovels and shovel-loads continued until the optimum shovel-load was determined to be a standard. Also, Taylor suggested that different types of shovels be used for different types of materials. Methods for better scheduling and assignment of workers to shoveling jobs were recommended. Some training was done with the laborers on efficient shoveling techniques.

Sometimes inscribing the design of work meant taking matters literally out of the workers' hands. It was the custom for workers to supply their own tools, and a good workman would have a special sense of the fitness of the tools they were accustomed to using. Taylor stipulated that, instead of the workman supplying his tools, they would be supplied and maintained by the organization. The best tools that could be had would be used at every level, and machines would be kept fully operational by engineers. Hands were to become operatives whose operations would be decided elsewhere. The traditional value of the craftsmen's tool ownership disappeared with the need for his knowledge and expertise. Scientific management required empty hands and minds to flourish because its success was dependent on depersonalization, contrived practices and a sterile, fabricated environment. In the past, at least as Taylor constituted it, employees had too much freedom to do as they would and not as they should. He fixed this problem. But he also had to fix the overseers.

Instead of allowing workers to choose their own tasks and train themselves as best they could, management reformed by the Taylor system should take responsibility for workers' formation as laboring subjects. These managers were to develop a spirit of hearty cooperation with workers to ensure that all work would be carried out in accordance with the scientifically devised procedures. The work was to be divided between workers and management, in such a way that each group took over the work for which it was best fitted, rather than inheriting a system where management oversight was dependent on worker insight into how responsibilities were distributed. Management was to be based on knowledge of scientifically designed routines so that their *exercise* of power would be restricted to exceptions. The everyday business of power – getting others to do what one willed them to do – would be handled by the routines.

The political economy of the body

Efficiency at work

The innovation with which Taylor is most associated is *the linking of efficiency to power through the medium of the human body*. At the core of the new meta-routines that systematic or scientific management ushered in was the efficient use of the human body. The program sought to drill efficiency into the nature of being, starting with the individual body (anatomical politics), moving to the collective body of/in the organization (bio-politics), and generally percolating into the societal body by economizing society (social politics), all in the name of efficiency.

Efficiency, as an engineering term, means getting the most for the least, 'the biggest bang for the smallest buck', as it is often put colloquially. Efficiency means achieving desired effects or results with minimum waste of time and effort, through minimizing the ratio of effective or useful output to the total input in any system. It was Taylor's practical experience, rather than theoretical knowledge gained from engineering, that enabled him to begin the enquiries for which he became famous. These started with a practical problem of how workmen might best use lathes to cut metal when they were powered by the new invention of electricity. As Jacques (1996: 105–6) notes, Taylor's innovations with the lathe were a result of applying mathematics, creating quantitative tables, and using slide rules to shape new practices.

The central focus of Taylor's system was the body of the individual laborer and its relation not only to other bodies but also to the material artifacts that formed the laborer's immediate work environment. What Taylor produced may be characterized as a political economy of the body.[16] As such, Taylor was the symbolic icon and the visible point of an epoch and a mentality. In this way, the overall contribution was made by a broad movement in which several individuals made an important contribution to building this management of bodies (Taylor, of course, but also the Gilbreths, Münsterberg, Gantt, and others who responded to the structural conditions provided by the new factory system powered by electricity, by producing new mechanisms for managing bodies in the factory and beyond: see Nelson 1975; Watts 1991).

Canguilhem (1992: 63) points out that Taylorism established a mode of work premised on the subjection of the worker's body not only to the superior intelligence of the manager's mind, but also to industrial machinery. The human body was measured as if it functioned like a machine. For the former, Taylorism represented a working out of Cartesian dualism – the split between mind and body – as a social relation, as Braverman (1974) was to argue. But it is how this was done that interests us, as it was through new disciplines focused on the individual human body that Taylor's (1911) practice sought to produce its effects. The new disciplines, the subjection of the body to new rigors, were clearly justified by productive economic practices. Foucault defined a discipline as a 'unitary technique by which the body is reduced as a "political" force at the least cost and maximized as a useful force' (1977: 221). It was in this context that Foucault introduced the idea of anatomical politics, related to the disciplinary regime of the individual body. It was in this sphere that Taylor's major contributions were made. Taylor was the founder of the discipline dealing with the design of machines and equipment for human use, and the determination of the appropriate human behaviors for the efficient operation of the machines, which has subsequently and variously been called human factors, human engineering, and ergonomics. (The last of these could, in fact, be seen as an example of what Foucault 1977 refers to as 'bio-power' – the government of the social body – while Taylor was more concerned with the management of individual actions than with the use of knowledge and categorizations to manage populations.) Discipline targeted the human body, with the goal of simultaneously exploiting it and rendering it docile and cooperative. For instance, in his experiments with shovels at Bethlehem Steel, Taylor focused on the body of the men; he told a worker that the most efficient method of shoveling was to put the right arm down by the right hip, hold the shovel on the left leg, and throw the weight of the body forward when digging the shovel into a pile, instead of using the arms and just pushing the shovel into a pile.

From Taylor's point of view, the working body should be maximally productive and minimally fatigued to become more efficient, a frame which very much defined the legacy that he bequeathed to important followers such as the Gilbreths, who developed his practice to innovative heights through the use of time-lapsed

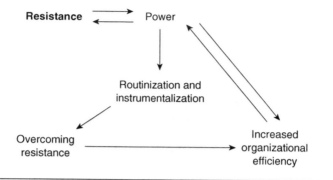

Figure 2.1   The dynamics of Taylor's programmatics of power – and resistance

photography, in a form of industrial futurism (Mandel 1989). Although often critiqued it is possible to provide a humanist gloss on Taylor as a reformer who aimed to eliminate inefficient and excessively debilitating practices in industry, by laying the foundations for a sophisticated disciplinary apparatus for productive technological bodies (see, for example, Amar 1920). In short, we might say that Taylor produces a political economy of technologies for the body. The political aspect is the deliberate, reformist intervention into the body politic of the factory or steel works; the economic aspect is the achievement of efficiency as an overarching aim; while the reference to technologies applies to a whole new system of notation, measurement and representation of the body.

What Taylor did was to routinize power. Management intervention, in terms of an explicit exercise of power, was designed to handle situations where routines were not working.[17] Management knowledge was designed to order and control what was known, protecting and insuring it against the uncertainty of the unknown, to the greatest extent possible (Yates 1989; Brown and Duguid 2000). The less that management had to exercise power, the better power was embedded in the routines. We can diagrammatically represent Taylor's analytics as in Figure 2.1.

Taylor's whole program began from his observation of systematic resistance on the shop floor, in the form of soldiering and like practices.[18] His response to such systematic resistance was the famous systematic of scientific management. It was this that was his design to overcome resistance. Once resistance was overcome, then efficiencies would be enhanced. But of course, enhanced organizational efficiency would in turn lead to a greater application of power as management systematically developed further ways of making employees do what they would not otherwise have done, which, in turn, would ratchet up resistance as new impositions were experienced.

Representing power and the body

At the end of the nineteenth century the conditions of possibility for building new practices and knowledge with which to discipline bodies had produced, as we have seen, a new economy of the body. Now, while this was newly applied to factory work, it was not a new occurrence. Foucault (1977: 28) discussed the development of a political anatomy where 'power seeps into the very grain of individuals, reaches right into their bodies, permeates their gestures, their posture, what they say, how they learn to live and work with other people', in relation to earlier forms of drill observed in the bodies of marching soldiers and the posture of schoolchildren. With Taylor, their non-institutionalized parents, if they worked in the factory, could also be reformed through an inspectorial urge.

The most important of these new graphic technologies were developed to record previously unrecorded physical processes like heart rate, muscular contraction, and, most importantly, movement. Some of Taylor's associates took his interest in body measurement to great extremes. One of these was a fellow engineer, Frank Gilbreth, who became a lecturer at Purdue University. From 1911, after the publication of Taylor's *Principles of scientific management,* he left his construction business to devote himself entirely to scientific management, to which he made a number of important contributions. Gilbreth's (1972) technique of micro-motion study permitted calculation of a standard from a description of the process constructed at the level of a movement of a single body part – a finger or a hand. Taylor never became as detailed in his study of the body as did these subsequent motion experts, for example, Gilbreth and Gilbreth (1916) and Price (1992), who were associates of Taylor but also competitors, fighting over the paternity of time and motion studies.

Power and the moving line

The slaughterhouse

One thing that Taylor did not develop but which lifted the applicability of some elements of his system to new heights, whilst seeing the abandonment of much that he held dear, was the moving production line. In 1913, 30 years after Taylor installed his first system, a revolution in manufacturing occurred when Henry Ford introduced the assembly line as a new way of producing automobiles, modeled on the Chicago slaughterhouses. There is a remarkable account of these slaughterhouses in Upton Sinclair's (1906) ethnographic novel, *The jungle.* Sinclair spent two months in 1904 observing and recording what he saw in the Chicago stockyards and discussed with the immigrant workers who provided the labor. It is evident from Sinclair's text that the jobs in the slaughterhouse were designed on Taylor's lines. In the abattoirs each job was separated into a series of simple repetitive actions as the carcasses moved down the line to be progressively dismembered.[19] Sinclair wrote about the extensive division of labor and the use of piecework, as well as the speed of the line. To relate the full terror of this work it is worth quoting Sinclair, who demonstrates both the extensive division of labor and the occupational risks that were entailed:

> There were the men in the pickle rooms, for instance … scarce a one of these that had not some spot of horror on his person. Let a man so much as scrape his finger pushing a truck in the pickle rooms, and he might have a sore that would put him out of the world; all the joints in his fingers would be eaten by the acid one by one. Of the butchers and

floorsmen, the beef boners and trimmers, and all those who used knives, you could scarcely find a person who had the use of his thumb; time and time again the base of it had been slashed, till it was a mere lump of flesh against which the man pressed the knife to hold it ... There were men who had worked in the cooking rooms, in the midst of steam and sickening odors, by artificial light; in these rooms the germs of tuberculosis might live for two years, but the supply was renewed every hour. There were the beef luggers, who carried two-hundred-pound quarters into the refrigerator cars, a fearful kind of work, that began at four o'clock in the morning, and that wore out the most powerful men in two years. There were those who worked in the chilling rooms, and whose special disease was rheumatism, the time limit that a man could work in the chilling rooms was said to be five years. There were the wool pluckers, whose hands went to pieces even sooner than the hands of the pickle men; for the pelts of sheep had to be painted with acid to loosen the wool, and then the pluckers had to pull out this wool with their bare hands, till the acid had eaten their fingers off ... and as for the other men, who worked in the tank rooms full of steam, and in some of which there were open vats near the level of the floor, their peculiar trouble was that they fell into the vats; and when they were fished out, there was never enough of them left to be worth exhibiting – sometimes they would be overlooked for days, till all but the bones of them had gone out to the world as Dunham's Pure Beef Lard! (1906: 100–2).

Indeed, as a more contemporary observer notes:

Since its inception, the 'meat' industry has employed the same formal rationality, the same language of calculation, measurement and efficiency and the same bureaucratic, accounting and scientific techniques that Max Weber deemed indicative of modernity in general. The analytic division of tasks and the rational ordering of production are designed to manage and control both working lives and animal deaths, to regulate the bodies that labor and are belabored. The irrational elements of sweat and blood are subjugated within a scheme of things that, from its own instrumentalist perspective, is entirely reasonable. (Smith 2002: 51)

The assembly line of production borrowed heavily from that of death. It vastly simplified production through running at a constant speed by which the workman must measure his pace, so that products are delivered at a constant production rate. Each job on the line had to be completed in an amount of time commensurate with this production rate. Each job became known by a precise description of the task it comprised; however, there were many thousands more jobs involved in the making of a car compared to the killing and butchering of a pig, with the job description manuals coming to resemble telephone directories.

The relations of power in these organizations were shaped by ever more elaborated definitions of routines, embedded less in traditional craft and practice and more in the creation and specification of new workplace relations and routines. They reached their zenith in the new workshops and factories of the automobile industry, especially the Ford Motor Company, which in the 1920s was seen as the very harbinger of what modernity was all about. The power of mass production was seen as the greatest productive power that had been unleashed by the modern world. But behind the glittering automobiles, behind the assembly lines of modern times, there was another more complex and subtle moral machinery of power at work.

While it is important to know how much time each element requires to be accomplished, other aspects of time study techniques were not appropriate for assembly line manufacturing. Individual incentives were not appropriate because every operator was tied to the speed of the line and they were not needed because of the discipline the line imposed. What remained from the Taylor system was the elemental decomposition of jobs. Jobs were small, repetitive and routine. In fact, routine became such a problem among Ford's workers that, in the first year of full assembly line operation, the company experienced about 900 percent turnover (see Williams et al. 1992). Between October 1912 and October 1913, Ford hired 54,000 workers in order to maintain a workforce of 13,000. The annual turnover rate settled at around 400 percent and daily absenteeism ran between 10 and 20 percent. It was for this reason that on January 5, 1914, the Ford Motor Company announced the five-dollar, eight-hour day for all production workers, irrespective of pieces produced (which was determined by the speed of the line anyway, not individual effort). What the company announced was not a plan to pay workers an hourly rate equivalent to five dollars a day but a plan that allowed workers to share in the company profits, which, in principle, would amount to a five-dollar day. This represented a considerable sum of money for production work in contemporary terms, doubling incomes; and, with the possibilities afforded by hire purchase, a new innovation, it meant that having consumer goods such as cars became something to whose ownership it was feasible to aspire. Ford's innovation reflects the relentlessly upbeat, optimistic culture of consumption, premised on the five-dollar day, which became a significant feature of American life and American world-wide culture.

Ford and the Sociological Department

Hitherto, the regulation of work had stayed within the organization and its disciplinary practices. It soon expanded outside, into the streets, the homes, the bars, and the savings accounts of industrial workers. The stimulus was an attempt to ensure that only deserving workers received the high wages that Ford's factories were paying. In 1914 Ford established the Sociological Department to investigate the home lives of workers (Marcus and Segal 1989: 236–8). It was a remarkable example of an ultimately failed attempt to institute meta-routines governing societal politics. The five-dollar day was designed to include only those who were 'worthy' and who would 'not debauch the additional money'. The rules governing eligibility were demonstrating that, if one were a man, one lived a clean, sober, industrious and thrifty life, while women had to be 'deserving' and have some relatives solely dependent upon them. After a probationary period, subject to a recommendation from their supervisor, worker eligibility would be investigated. About 60 percent were found to be eligible. Investigators from the Sociological Department visited workers' homes and suggested ways to achieve the company's standards for 'better morals', sanitary living conditions, and 'habits of thrift and saving'. Employees who lapsed were removed from the system and given a chance to redeem themselves. Long-term failure to meet Ford Motor Company standards resulted in dismissal from the company.

Meyer (1981) reports a 1917 Sociological Department study. Fifty-two investigators visited 77 districts throughout Detroit and its suburbs. Each district contained an average of 523 workers. Each investigator had an average caseload of 727 workers, making 5.35 regular investigations each day, 5 'absentee calls' and 15 'outside calls'. For each investigation Ford maintained a record consisting of every available source of information from churches, civic organizations, and the government. The company wanted to know whether or not the worker was purchasing a home, whether he had a savings account and whether he had debt. It required the bank account number, name of the bank and balance of any accounts; for debts, the company needed to know the holder of the debt, its reason and the balance (1981: 130).

Highway 61, urban blues, and moral panics

There was a degree of racism at work in these sociological investigations, paralleling Ford's well-documented anti-Semitism (Lee 1980). After the Civil War, black people had been leaving the sharecropper society of the deep south in droves, fleeing a culture rooted in slavery. And, after hitting Highway 61, they headed for the burgeoning factories of the north, in Chicago and Detroit, in the latter of which Ford began hiring African Americans in large numbers in 1915, paying them the same wages as his white employees. The material basis of the jazz age for the many black people who headed north was work in the factories and assembly plants. By 1923, Ford employed 5,000 Detroit-area black men, far more than in other plants.

The influx of black people into northern cities and jobs was the occasion for middle-class white anxieties. Indeed, at the time they were a source of what Stanley Cohen has referred to as a 'moral panic' (1972: 9). A moral panic occurs when some 'episode, condition, person or group of persons' is 'defined as a threat to societal values and interests'. Such moral panics are based on the perception that some individual or group, frequently a minority, is dangerously deviant, and poses a menace to society. They often occur as a result of a fear of a loss of control when adapting to significant changes. Typically, as Cohen suggests, authorities create 'stylized and stereotypical' representations, raise moral fears, and 'pronounce judgment'.

Moral panic fed into the work of Ford's Sociological Department. They wanted to ensure that Ford employees were sober, disciplined men, whose energies would be conserved and minds wholly focused on the necessity of being excellent five-dollar-a-day men. Workers who wasted money on booze, dope, and vice were not welcome as Ford employees, as members of the Ford family. Decent Protestant white folk knew the type of person most likely to be wasteful of their energies: anybody not like them, especially European Catholic immigrants and black economic migrants from the south.[20] They also knew the kinds of excesses in which they would be wasted. Bars and clubs sprouted in the black areas of the cities, featuring the new music of jazz, selling liquor to its *aficionados*, turning night into day, as the poet Langston Hughes remarked. African Americans, jazz, and intoxication of various kinds became inexorably intertwined in the popular imagination of, as well as some of the experience in, black culture. The scapegoating of black cultures, such as jazz, was emblematic of a deep-seated paranoia.

Jazz received a fair amount of negative press in the late 1910s and then became the object of a moral panic during the 1920s. Some whites feared jazz because it was rooted in black culture, because it played a role in facilitating interracial contact, and because it symbolized, in racially coded terms, the intrusion of popular tastes into the national culture. (Porter 2002: 9)

The moral panics that grew in the 1920s and 1930s around 'jazz' were barely coded concerns for the contagion of white society by black bodies and black culture. As Lopes suggests, from the Jazz Age of the 1920s 'the sordid world of jazz and the deviant jazz musician became a common trope in the popular press, pulp fiction, and Hollywood film. Jazz in general served as a trope for the darker side of the American urban experience' (2005: 1468). For Ford, establishing a Sociological Department (as well as employing Pinkerton's to spy on potential troublemakers and unionists and to break up union meetings) to ensure the moral probity of these new employees seemed a small investment to make to ensure an efficient, reliable and certain workforce, untroubled by an inability to save, invest and consume. Such irrationalities were to be expected of people who made jazz their culture.

It is not surprising that jazz played this role; first, it was associated by respectable white society with unrespectable black society; second, it infused the body with passion, rhythm, movement, and a lack of disciplined sobriety. It was wild dance music and its main feature was its exuberant ability to move its fans and musicians to shake their bodies, dance, and beat the rhythm. As Appelrouth suggests, 'manners of the body share the potential for becoming a stage on which the struggle for social legitimacy and control is dramatized' (2005: 1497). In the body may be seen the larger social order and its struggles to impose good order, taste and discipline on nature. Pollution of the body is a metaphor for the disruption of the boundaries that shape 'legitimate' society, as Douglas (1996) suggests. Thus, following Appelrouth 'we should not be surprised to find anxieties concerning social disruptions expressed through a body-centered discourse. During periods in which challenges are posed to existing social divisions and schemes of classification, attempts to define the body publicly take on heightened significance' (2005: 1497). As the *Ladies Home Journal* saw it,

> Jazz disorganizes all regular laws and order; it stimulates to extreme deeds, to a breaking away from all rules and conventions; it is harmful and dangerous, and its influence is wholly bad ... The effect of jazz on the normal brain produces an atrophied condition on the brain cells of conception, until very frequently those under the demoralizing influence of the persistent use of syncopation, combined with inharmonic partial tones, are actually incapable of distinguishing between good and evil, right and wrong. (Faulkner 1921: 16; from Appelrouth 2005: 1503)

Degenerate brains, an inability to follow rules, and a general lack of moral qualities were not what Mr Ford required in his employees, so the Sociological Department had much to do as a private moral police for the Jazz Age and, even though the department did not last long, it hardly mattered.[21] After 1921 it was discontinued and rolled into the notorious Service Department, run by ex-boxer and security chief Harry Bennett, who formed it into a private army of thugs and gangsters to terrorize workers and prevent unionization. Ford's Service Department would grow to be the largest private police force in the world at that time. Its major work was spying such that no one who worked for Ford was safe from spies, intent on seeing that the five dollars was not being wasted, both literally and metaphorically.

There was increasing societal support for Ford's 'sociological' and 'service' projects. First in the ranks was the project of Prohibition, the doomed attempt to ban alcohol consumption from a number of US states, which started in 1920, and which Ford had long supported and promoted. It also intensified a prohibitory gaze that sought to ensure that employees could resist temptations to vice. In fact, the struggle against liquor was also a struggle against the jazz with which it was associated in licentiousness. Gramsci explicitly made the connection to moral panics:

> The struggle against alcohol, the most dangerous agent of destruction of laboring power, becomes a function of the state. It is possible for other 'puritanical' struggles as well to become functions of the state if private initiatives of the industrialist prove insufficient or if a moral crisis breaks out among the working masses. (1971: 303–4)

Power in the organization was now effectively buttressed by power in the wider society; in order to ensure the most efficient routines at work, some control over the type of person that was employed was required. Initially, the new power of surveillance over private life was vested in and an extension of the organization; latterly, as Fordist modernity became characteristic of modernity in general, in workshops large and small, the state took over the functions that private capital had hitherto assumed.[22] Small employers or those new to business could not develop their own sociological departments, but the state, as an ideal total moralist, supplemented the work of surveillance over those in whom the churches and associated temperance movements had not succeeded in instilling a governmental soul. Power shifted its focus from the individual to the collective.

Conclusion

The earliest formal management theory, developed by Taylor, emerged from a prior tradition of liberal utilitarianism (Jordan 1994). We see this best in the work of Bentham, not so much in his celebrated work on the Panopticon but more in his reformist zeal applied to the Poor Laws. Bentham was concerned to make idle hands industrious rather than looking at how to improve the efficiency of hands that were already employed. Primary conceptualizations of management discourse stressed managing as handling, controlling, directing, acting, and doing. Management barely existed at the beginning of the twentieth century in the sense that is now taken for granted, although counting houses, clerks, and typewriters, the origins of bureaucracy both public and private, were all evident.

To look inside the factory and to imagine new ways of disciplining work was a great extension of utilitarianism, one that is seen in the figure of F. W. Taylor, who stands as a representative example of the forms of disciplinary power that shaped modern management. His innovation was to extend reform from a concern with non-work to a concern with work itself. Taylor's way of framing scientific management normalized hierarchy and the functioning of rules and inscribed power as a less central concept, something not implicated in hierarchy or rules in use. In fact, its 'science' legitimated the normalcy of these to such an extent that power came to be seen only as a category of irrationality because to resist science, by definition, was to oppose reason. Managers exerted power in every factory but, as they did so, few who wrote about management talked about the power they wielded. Practices of power became more or less invisible even as knowledge about 'management' became increasingly normalized and legitimated.

There was an expansion of management's remit from a focus on the separate individual's bodily movements by Taylor to the person's social and family life by Ford. The reason for the shift in focus was the impact of routinization paced by the speed of the moving production line and its impact on labor turnover, which necessitated a second expansion of management's remit in the form of a new type of employment contract over a whole day rather than over a piece of work. On the back of this new focus developed a new moral economy of the subject. We should understand Ford's innovations as extensions of a panoptical complex. They lacked the specificity of Taylor's targeting of the body and were more oriented to what Foucault (1977) referred to as bio-power – power oriented to the collective body politic. In accord with Gramsci (1971) we can see these new managerial techniques of Taylorism and Fordism seeking to suppress 'the "animality" of man, training him', as Turner (1984: 100) suggests, 'for the regular disciplines of factory life', in an anatomical politics. Even as the state supplemented 'the private initiatives of the industrialist' in framing the political morality of work (in an era before random drug testing of employees had become widespread), newer, more specifically targeted practices were being shaped in opposition to Taylor's political economy of the body, the private initiatives by industrialists, and the state's regulatory bio-power.

A decisive shift was under way. The body had been on the front line of power and the new disciplines of management at the inception of its modernity. As modernity and its management were consolidated the emphasis was to shift from the physical to the moral shaping of the body. New sources of automated routinization were increasingly able to do what once had been done by bodies. Correlatively, the embodied person fades into the background and the foreground increasingly is filled by the moral body as being – as soul, or in more secular vein, (un)consciousness. These shifts will be reviewed in the next chapter.

Notes

1   Although acknowledgement is barely needed for an allusion which is so evident, the reference is to Jane Austen (1982: 1).

2   Indeed, etymologically, the notion of handling, as in one who handles horses, is the origin of the term 'management' in contemporary usage. It is derived, some sources suggest (Mant 1983; Jacques 1996: 88), from the Italian verb *maneggiare*, a word with a Latin root in *manus*, meaning hand. Such a handler disciplined the horse, trained it, and made it obedient and safe for those functions designed for it (Jackson and Carter 1998). The introduction of the term 'management' into English seems to have come from the French *ménager*, a word applied to domestic management which entered common currency in England by 1847. Scarborough and Burrell (1996: 174) note the self-description by Mrs Fairfax, the housekeeper of Mr Rochester's house

Thornfield, in *Jane Eyre* (Brontë 1847/2000), that she is 'a mere manager' when Jane mistakes her for the owner of the house. In grand houses, such as Thornfield, there were many under-servants to manage as a part of the household. The essence of the French meaning was carried over into later usage, applied to the disciplining not of horses but of hands. A 'hand' was the common term for an employee, in widespread use across most industries. Hands were subject to supervision or overseeing by the lower echelons of management on behalf of owners. House managers do the will of the master, for it is not their house; horses are subservient to the tasks we require of them; hands are the pliable, directed tools of the mind and will. Supervision means just what it says: it is super(ordinate)vision, the practice of one who is structurally superordinate to another and who, by virtue of this superordinacy, is able to exercise vision *vis à vis* the other; that is, to make the other visible by bringing them into relief and focus as a distinct entity.

3   In US English, Jacques (1996: 68) tells us that the term 'employee' first occurs in the context of a discussion of the railways, in which context it stays until the 1870s, when it started to be used more generally. By the early years of the twentieth century 'employee' had become the accepted and most commonly used term, carrying a weight of semantic meaning: being a permanent worker belonging to an organization; being subordinated; being assigned to tasks to which one is fitted and for which one is paid a wage; being subject to the expertise of a managerial specialist and the panoply of management knowledge; all of which, finally, enables one to become a specialist producer and consumer (1996: 70–86). The employee was one half of an emerging binary division, of which the other half was the manager: a specialist in obedience was overseen by a specialist in authority. The division is significant because together they constitute a systemic unity. The worker is power (energy to work), the manager is knowledge (authority by science to conduct behaviors); they comprise the essential unity between power and knowledge, the base of modernity (Ibarra-Colado 2001a).

4   Slaves in plantation economies in the subtropics of the Americas and the Caribbean, as with those in other parts of the world, were forcibly removed from their families and places of residence and sold as commodities into the ownership of plantation owners. Violently removed from one place by slave traders they were, not surprisingly, in an essentially European-dominated society, assumed to be culturally alien and lacking in loyalty – much as were convicts, a similar cargo to other places, at much the same time.

5   Hoskin and Macve (1988) note that from 1817 up to the 1840s, West Point was the prime conduit from France to the US through which the emergent disciplines of mathematics and engineering were introduced to US practice. It was, throughout that period, America's leading engineering and scientific school, and both the material taught, and the pedagogy used to deliver the material, derived initially from the French model of education developed in the late eighteenth century at the École Polytechnique. French techniques, in turn, have their roots in the methods pioneered by the masters of the Venetian Arsenal in warship building and crossbow manufacture.

6   The most notable utilitarians were the English philosophers Jeremy Bentham and John Stuart Mill, the former spanning the late eighteenth century and early nineteenth, the latter the first three-quarters of the nineteenth century. Mill died in 1873 shortly before F. W. Taylor's industrial version of the utilitarian project was first developed in the US, as we shall discuss presently.

7   In short, the categories of indigence amounted to the following: Insane hands, through mental deficiency; Imperfect hands, through infirmity; Unripe hands (children), through the gradualness of evanescence; Sick hands, occasioning an inability to work; Child-burdened hands, through procreation; Lazy hands; Superseded hands; Out-of-place (or unemployed) hands, due to temporary loss of work ; Stigmatized hands, whose inability to obtain work are due to badness of character, such as thieves, forgers, and smugglers; Suspected hands (those who might be guilty of something but whose guilt is unproven); Unavowed-employment hands, such as gypsies and deserters; Strange hands, such as foreigners and travelers; and Past-prosperity hands, including Decayed-gentility hands, whose loss of property has thrown them onto a labor market of which they have no prior experience, having lived off property previously.

8   After Bentham, the notion of efficiency developed additional utilitarian meaning: it denoted
     being cost-effective. In his writings on political economy, Mill was concerned with the great-
     est efficiency of labor (Plamenatz 1949) to be attained best by a division of labor, sophisti-
     cated use of machines, and, only as necessary, skilled people, because of their greater costs in
     the labor market. Efficiency was not an end in itself so much as a means to maximizing public
     welfare: an efficient society would be a happier society.

9   Michel Foucault (1977) is responsible for the contemporary interest in Bentham's Panopticon
     as a unique instrument of reform and governance.

10   The *idea* of the Panopticon, as a system of surveillance, flourished subsequently as new tech-
     nologies enabled it to extend its visual sway. Thus, it implies not just an architectural design
     but rather a principle of surveillance imposing a specific mode of rationality. Extended to
     modern times, new technologies continue to proliferate, offering new potentialities for sur-
     veillance. Panoptical possibilities have been extended to more sophisticated forms, creating a
     condition characterized by Deleuze (1992) as the society of control.

11   It was not just in and through the Panopticon that normalization occurred: in the early twen-
     tieth century in Japan, as Littler (1982) describes, coerced labor was kept in factory dormito-
     ries. Indeed, as the occasional news story demonstrates, tragic fires kill workers in Chinese
     factory dormitories, demonstrating that the practice still persists in China. Xinhua News
     Agency reported an incident in which a serious fire broke out in a factory in Zhangzhou city
     in east China's Fujian province on Saturday March 14, 2005, killing six people and injuring two
     others. The fire broke out in a paper products factory in Beixitou village and soon engulfed the
     factory dormitories in which dozens of people were housed (see http://news.surfwax.com/
     worldcities/files/Zhangzhou_China.html, retrieved March 5, 2005).

12   The concept of the Panopticon was more a program than a widely accomplished practice.
     Albeit that it was indubitably a liberal political program, it was thought largely unnecessary
     for government to intervene directly into the economic machinery of production and
     exchange; that was why the issue most discussed in substantive detail in Marx's (1976[1887])
     Capital was the regulation of organizations by various Factory Acts: they were a novel fron-
     tier of control and intervention. But these were a frontier; the main battlefields of liberal
     political economy were phenomena such as the Corn Laws and the Poor Laws, for it was
     through these instruments of regulation that the costs and the necessity of labor, respectively,
     were administered. The Poor Laws 'played a key role in establishing the conditions under
     which the laws of political economy might operate to best effect' (Rose 1999: 70). They cre-
     ated a threshold of necessity for work through the principles of eligibility in such a way that,
     literally, only work could make one free. But within work freedom was not explicitly regu-
     lated, except as the various nineteenth-century Factory Acts (most of which were ineffective
     as the Inspectorate was so limited) were implemented. Other than the gross limits of these on
     the age, gender and hours of employees that might be employed in various activities, the lim-
     its to exploitation or freedom in the workplace were, on the whole, at the discretion of indi-
     vidual masters of capital or their delegates. It was enough that work should prevail, be made
     necessary; how it was conducted was of less explicit concern. In the earliest days of the new
     factory organizations of the nineteenth century, contemporary observers noted that the
     'manufacturing population ... new in its habits of thoughts and action' was 'formed by the
     circumstances of its condition, with little instruction, and less guidance from external sources'
     (Thompson 1968: 209). During the nineteenth century, as recorded by Weber (1976) and
     Thompson (1968), owners and managers sought workers who were instructed and guided
     spiritually by religious, often Protestant, ethics. Sometimes, as Spybey (1984) recounts, the
     moral machinery was supported by a social organization of the built environment that facil-
     itated its surveillance, such as factory estates of workers' houses – a domestically ordered
     Panopticon. But rarely did the state intervene systematically in relations between master and
     employee, other than through the Factory Acts; that was a project of modernity yet to unfold.

13   Taking etymology as a guide, it seems that there is something distinctive in the emergence of
     management as a characteristic of the modern era, an era that literally means 'of our time'.

The literal meaning is too imprecise, however. More specifically, one can think of modernity as a quality that first emerged in Western civilization (Sayer 1991). In general, it is a period of time and a quality of culture that the world has been experiencing for at least the last two centuries. While there are many different ways of dating, defining, and characterizing modernity, we will take the modern world as being born at the point where the individual emerges as a conscious reflecting and reflected subject opposed to the 'universal, social body of customs and laws' (Kolb 1986: 67). Bauman (1997: 1) characterizes modernity as an obsession with order. Modernity, among other things, represents the cutting off of the individual from traditional ways of life; it inscribes the use of reason to govern and limit uncertainty.

14   Individual actions were conceptualized as entailing a whole within which comparison and differentiations must be made. Individuals were differentiated from one another; their attributes were to be measured in quantitative terms, their abilities were to be hierarchically arranged. The expected range of normal output at work was to be codified and then used as a mechanism of feedback, enforcement and further normalization. Through fusing an economic function with one that is social, the organizational workplace became a huge laboratory for the perfection of techniques of management. Disciplinary programs were created with the power to shape people, to shape work, and to shape the organization's technical and human systems. Of course, programs are not projects that are perfectly accomplished: they are always situated in the future perfect, designs for a world that would be made if there were no obstacles to its unfolding as such. Yet there are always such obstacles, always resistances to the projects of power, always unanticipated consequences of social action. In many ways these resistances, these imperfections in specific power projects, only serve to heighten the resolve and the perception of need for the failed project to try again. The problems that it was designed to address are evidently still there and so the project needs to be revised, perfected and enacted again ... and again. It is this recurrence that comprises the specific nature of management knowledge, a set of *savoirs* produced by everyday practices of power. The power that is at work in programs of management, a pragmatic science of immediate practical consequence shaping the existence of people in their everyday life, is highly specific. It is not merely a repressive or prohibitory power; it does not just involve the possibility of imposing one's will upon the behavior of other persons through prohibiting behavior that they would otherwise normally be disposed to. Rather, it works in a more positive way by shaping the dispositions that define what we take, normally, to be true. The calculations subjects make about effort, disposition, and demeanor, for instance, are both subject to, and resources for, this pragmatic science. Managing means constituting central aspects of identity through relations of power; thus, when one is managing this implies that one is exercising power – over both other people and things. Managing means making things happen through the exercise of initiative and agency – and that means power. To address management is to address power in all its historical variation.

15   Although Taylor's employment in the Bethlehem Steel Works, owned by Wharton, paralleled the founding of the Wharton Business School, there is no evidence that he taught there, although he was an occasional lecturer at the Harvard Business School. Taylor also gave regular lectures on management to a paying audience at his mansion in Philadelphia (Wrege 1995). The Wharton School adapted many ideas into its curriculum from the engineering community associated with institutions such as West Point and with the extensive civilian contracting its graduates did in the railways. Other famous engineering schools did the same, such as Rennselauer, Rochester, MIT, and the Stevens Institute of Technology, where Taylor gained his part-time degree. In the restricted 'society' of Philadelphia's upper-class circles, Taylor may have shared professional and social circles with academic pioneers hired by the Wharton School. He might also have learnt about the formal theories of administration that were being imported there from Prussia – which Max Weber (1978) was later to systematize as the theory of bureaucracy – but there is no evidence to suggest that he did. In fact, Taylor's *Principles* were rather homespun and firmly rooted in the observations and prejudices that he brought to the Midvale and Bethlehem organizations, rather than conventionally academic,

in the way that they divided up labor and space and related men to machines (see Crossley 1996: 107; Bahnisch 2000: 62; also the *Transactions* bulletins of the American Society of Mechanical Engineers; Litterer 1959) and time and motion. The language and treatment addressed to workers in Taylor's book suggest a science born from an apparent frustration with the practices of contemporary work, in terms of both worker identities and those of supervisors.

16   Even perceptive observers of the body, such as Dale (2001) and Turner (1984), fail to recognize Taylor's contribution in terms of a political economy of the body.

17   These routines were premised on a hierarchy: organizations should be arranged in a hierarchy, based upon systems of abstract rules and impersonal relationships between different categories of employees. Taylor's framework for organization thus created a seemingly scientific basis for a clear delineation of authority and responsibility, based on a separation of planning from operations, a high degree of task specialization (although this was subsequently to be developed to new heights by Henry Ford), and a system of incentive schemes for workers.

18   In the overall US population of organizations, the program that Taylor proposed was not widely adopted (Nelson 1980). The Taylor system was more programmatic than widely practiced. Programmatically, it has been suggested that 90 percent of what subsequently developed as management theory, especially in the areas of knowledge management, hardly deviated much from or added a great deal to the corpus of Taylor's program (Spender and Kijne 1996). If these claims are correct, then management theory's foundations are indeed suspect. The Taylor system was hardly scientific. It was not based on a scientific methodology and it was highly normative in its assumptions about the distribution of moral qualities in a population.

19   Even today, many job titles in meat works are given by the piece of carcass worked on, such as First Legger, Knuckle Dropper, Navel Boner, and Splitter Top/Bottom (Schlosser 2001).

20   The prohibition of alcoholic drink became interwined with black disenfranchisement and subordination, initially in the southern states in the aftermath of the Civil War, as the *New Georgia encyclopedia* notes (http://www.georgiaencyclopedia.org/neg/Article.jsp?id=h-828). Temperance began as a rural movement against the emancipations and freedoms afforded by the sinful northern cities.

21   The Jazz Age viewed through 'respectable' white eyes was characterized by anxieties about the association of blackness, jazz, booze, and dope. The last was a particularly significant trope, as was alcohol. Despite the fact that, as its name suggests, marijuana first came into the US from Mexico, jazz and marijuana became inextricably linked with black people and black music in the popular imagination. The first recorded use of marijuana in the US was in Storyville in 1909 (Abel 1980), which was the red light district of the port of New Orleans and the birthplace of jazz. Foundational jazz musicians, such as Jelly Roll Morton, honing their craft in the bordellos, created incidental accompaniments to the central commerce conducted there. Rather than drink, dope was the preferred drug. Marijuana didn't slow down the reflexes and improvisation the way that alcohol could; also it seemed to heighten the creative impulse. Jazz and dope were not exactly the stuff of a rationalizing impulse.

22   Prohibition dealt with drink, at least until its failure and its creation of a criminal economy were acknowledged by its repeal in 1933. In consequence, the moral panic shifted from alcohol to dope during the 1930s, enacted by the banning of cannabis in 17 states. The Federal Bureau of Narcotics was established in 1930. In 1937 the Marijuana Tax Act effectively banned cannabis throughout the United States. One presumes that the new intensification of work was a significant reason for the panic, in addition to its association with the moral corruption of white society from black culture. Taylorized and Fordized workers could hardly be both intoxicated by recreational drug use and aspiring to become the new men of the industrial age, eager to earn their five dollars a day.

3 Body, Soul, and Mind

Chapter outline

In this chapter we will:

- Reflect on how to read a history of management ideas seeking to reform the worker socially, morally and culturally through redefining and normalizing efficiency into obedience.
- Situate Follett as an authentic voice of democracy in her political analysis of organizations against the tide of technocracy and the stress on efficiency.
- Examine the work of Mayo and the Human Fatigue Laboratory at Harvard, and Barnard on leadership, as a bridge between the political economy of the body and the moral economy of the soul, a term first used by Follett.
- Elaborate the 'soft power' practices associated with the new moral economy of the soul.
- See how the shift from political and moral economy, from scientific management and human relations, to knowledge management and social capital, sought to create conditions in which coactive power could operate.

Introduction

In the previous chapter we saw the ways in which the analytics of power, focused on a political economy of the body, sought to create workers as precision instruments through the use of meta-routines. We noted the importance of task decomposition, the reformation of tasks and their physical undertaking according to methods, and the use of imposed sequences. However, as time passed it became increasingly evident that the body alone was not what was employed at work: the worker's body, to be truly disciplined at work, required disciplining in life. The body, though always individuated, houses a social being – one with a culture and an identity, as well as passions and interests transcending the working week. The conceptualization of this managerial problem was a natural progression of the moral projects that sought to reform the employee through political economy aimed at the body. If projects of power were to overcome the limited efficacy of their efficiency concerns to date, then they had to address both body and soul; they had to recognize the place of the *being* in the body as a social subject.

The realization that the body sustains a soulful life with communities of others that may undercut individual efficiency was to have some bizarre disciplinary effects, not least Ford's spin on sociology, which we encountered in Chapter 2. More important, in intellectual terms, were several theorists who were representative of these new concerns, including Mary Parker Follett, the most innovative in many ways, as well as better-known figures such as Elton Mayo and Chester Barnard. Eventually, as they brought the emergent idea of the informal organization into an analytical relationship with the prior stress of systematic management theory on formal organization, they sought to reconcile the dualism of formal and informal, body and soul, structure and culture. The key to reconciliation was seeing the informal as a functioning entity within the whole framed by the formal organization. It was a solution called 'functionalism' in which the central concept was that of authority, not power. Moreover, the solution did not read backwards to grasp the political economy of the body as itself a project of power. Instead, the earlier history was seen simply as one in which a simple, formal, and mechanical view of the body needed to be supplemented by a stress on the soul of the individual, the authority of the leader, and the culture of the group. It was the prioritization of functional knowledge of the individual as the way to foster efficient practice through common ideas. Modern management ideas did, indeed, become uncommonly familiar to almost everyone as the *Zeitgeist* of the modern age. Although they were born inside the factory in the late nineteenth century, by the early twentieth century the ideal of efficiency had conquered society as well as the economy and work.

Reforming efficiency

Efficiency reforming economy

What we have been doing to this point is to investigate the ways in which, at a crucial point in its emergence, the idea of management was formed around knowledge of the individual that it produced, conceived in terms of a political economy of the body. On the eve of the First World War the discourse in which this political economy was transmitted became the first big management fad as a source of innumerable new truths about work and its organization. The truths were not uncontested. Opposition came largely from unsystematic managers, often internal contractors (Littler 1982) who were averse to their present power being eroded by the planning departments that Taylor favored. Union opposition grew, especially from the American Federation of Labor (AFL), who supported the attempts by the International Association of Machinists to have Taylor's practices banned.

The new system was adopted in military arsenals and in naval yards in the period leading up to America's involvement in the First World War in 1917 (Taylor died in 1915). In Du Pont's powder works, managers discovered the direct relationship between efficiency and safety. Interestingly, safety was not an issue that Taylor had considered. When two explosions occurred in Du Pont's powder works on the eve of its First World War expansions, they not only hastened the firm's shift from efficiency to safety but also raised the possibility of a link between increasing efficiency and diminishing safety.

The most notable arena of contest around Taylor's ideas occurred in the legislature. A special subcommittee of the US House of Representatives was established from 1911 to 1912 to inquire into the Taylor system, especially as it was implemented in the Watertown Arsenal (Aitken 1960). It was believed that industrial unrest was being created by the adoption of the system. One small result of the enquiry was that laws were passed banning the use of stopwatches by civil servants. Taylor was interviewed extensively about his system and, controversial as it was, used these interviews as a platform to promote his ideas.

Taylor was not a popular figure, even amongst the nascent community of management scholars. Many of those who saw themselves as having labored for decades in similar endeavors, without the attention that Taylor attracted, were somewhat disgruntled with his fame, while others, more nimble in using elements of Taylor's ideas and blending their own mix, made capital out of the fashion. Taylor's intellectual predecessors amongst the engineering fraternity opposed scientific management; they saw their own programs as suffering in the wake of its notoriety and as lacking the branding that Taylor had achieved. These were individuals such as Alexander Hamilton Church, Frank C. Hudson, Leon Alford, and Dexter Kimball who had been associated with proselytizing earlier approaches to systematic management (Shenhav 1999: 114–16).

Some sought to reform Taylor's ideas. An important reformer of orthodox strategies was Henry L. Gantt who developed welfare work policies (see Nelson and Campbell 1972). Other advocates of systematic management sought to put space between themselves and the controversies surrounding Taylor. Lillian Gilbreth, together with her husband Frank, sought to differentiate their program from Taylor's, cleaning up the image of motion studies by taking out the emphasis on time, seeking to redefine it as benign and pro-worker human factor engineering (Gilbreth and Gilbreth 1916), at least in their presentation of it as a discipline to workers; for employers the efficiency arguments remained paramount. The Gilbreths introduced the therblig (their name reversed) as the basic unit for motion studies as a micro-measure of motion.

Efficiency reforming management, organization and work globally

Taylor's ideas and those of his contemporaries such as the Gilbreths spread rapidly and globally; for instance, in 1910 Louis Renault visited F. W. Taylor and Ford in the United States and, on his return to France, his attempts to introduce some of Taylor's ideas in his factory led to a major strike. In the post First World War era the rationalization of work became a major movement in Europe, and spread in different ways in different countries (see Maier 1970). Taylorism in France came in two waves. The first wave involved the adoption of the principles of Taylor by Louis Renault in 1912, with organizers trained by Taylor himself (Peaucelle 2000); the second was generated by France's leading Taylorist Henri Le Chatelier, who translated Taylor's work and introduced scientific management throughout state plants. One person influenced by the import was the French economic theoretician Henri Fayol, a key figure in the turn-of-the-century Classical School of management theory, who published *Administration industrielle et générale* in 1916 (Fayol 1949), emphasizing organizational structure in management and concepts of administration. Fayol synthesized various tenets or principles of organization and management with Taylor's views on work methods, measurement and simplification to secure efficiencies. He stressed management training to a far greater extent than Taylor, for whom management, at best, only saw to the implementation of scientific time and motion. Fayol's work paralleled that of the French Taylorists until the 1920s when the two streams converged to create a new organization theory dedicated to improving organizational efficiency. The first generation of French Taylorist managers formulated their practice in a rhetoric that the heavily unionized and militant French workers could agree with. In a way, these Taylorist managers were storytellers able to translate their own rhetoric into French workers' culture. Even as late as the 1950s, in the postwar reconstruction, Taylorism was still being developed in France (Besson 2000).

Taylorism was translated to the newborn state of the Soviet Union, whose founders were strong believers in Taylor's scientific management. It is easy to understand that for Lenin and Stalin, Taylorism constituted a solution to their objectives of fast industrialization with a massive workforce drawn largely from the peasantry (Peaucelle 2000). Taylor's ideas were also exported to Japan, where psychologist Yoichi Ueno, who later became the first Japanese management consultant and was a founder and first president of the SANNO Institute of Management, introduced Taylorism in 1912. Criticisms developed as well. While Taylor, the Gilbreths, and Fayol, among countless others who were less celebrated, created specific technologies of power, they did become subject to important critiques of dehumanization as early as the 1930s by the French scholar, Georges Friedmann (1946). Franz Kafka, in his *Conversations*, was to say of Taylorism that

> Time, the noblest and most essential element in all creative work, is conscripted into the net of corrupt business interests. Thereby, not only creative work, but man himself, who is its essential part, is polluted and humiliated. A Taylorized life is a terrible curse which will give rise only to hunger and misery instead of the intended wealth and profit. (Janouch, 1971: 115)

However unpleasant was the Taylorization of work, the Taylorization of society went even further, shaping not only the time 'spent' in work but also the time that was allowed for recuperation from it.

Efficiency reforming society

The powerful stress on efficiency was instrumental in increasing the income of employees and their hours of leisure because it contributed to a shortening of the working day and an increased emphasis on rest pauses in that day. Increasingly, remuneration from work was being seen not only as income for present purchasing power and leisure but also as the basis for shielding the employee against the hazards of unemployment and retirement, and all the other eventualities of economic life, throughout a generation. New instruments of finance were being developed both to assist workers to insure their futures better and to plan their consumption now of income that they would earn later. Together with the rationalization of production there was a rationalization of credit that accompanied the rise of a widespread industrial system for the manufacture of goods, as Stuart Ewen (1976) has argued. Credit helped democratize consumption and extend its pleasures of seduction from the lifestyles of the rich and famous to those of the poor but honest. A war was waged on working-class habits of thrift, seeking to channel consumption into home and recreation, using advertising to nullify customary habits and create new ones, fuelled by hire purchase, with a little present income put aside for future social insurance (Nyl 1995).

The shift to shorter hours and higher wages created the conditions in which employees could spend their wages and leisure time on consumer goods, with their desires fuelled by constant advertising, creating dissatisfaction with existing modes of life, discontent with what they had, and a will to consume that which they did not yet have but could obtain now and pay for later. Asceticism in the sphere of production, ensured by the new disciplines addressing the political economy of the body, supported a new kind of calculating hedonism in consumption, embodied, as Turner (1984: 102) suggests, in a new personality type, that of the narcissistic person (also see Lasch 1991). By the 1920s seductive images, signs, and slogans depicting lifestyles that could guide people's consumption became widespread in the press and the radio. Department stores increasingly became tutelary sites. Lillian Gilbreth applied scientific management to the layout of department stores such as Macy's after her husband's death in 1924 (Graham 1998). In Michael Schudson's words, with the advent of the department stores, 'looking replaced doing as a key social action, [and] reading signs replaced following orders as a crucial modern skill' (1984: 156–7). Increasingly, the legitimation for the relations of domination at work was the pleasure of consumption it afforded at home.

It was Lillian Gilbreth who was responsible for extending the sway of the efficiency movement from the workplace to the home, as she adapted Taylor's ideas to kitchen planning, extending to the design of appliances and the architecture of the home. Lillian Gilbreth conducted experiments in the kitchen, developing a floor plan for kitchen spaces she called 'continuous'. Anyone who has ever been involved in having a kitchen designed will have learnt about this continuous space in terms of the domestic triangle of cook-top, sink and fridge.[1] Unnecessary motions and movements were to be eliminated through using flow process charts and micromotion transfer sheets to organize the domestic space as efficiently as the workspace in the factory. From an efficient workplace one could return to an efficient household, especially in its nerve center, the kitchen, perhaps traversing the space between in one of Mr Ford's automobiles. Efficient work made you free to consume what was increasingly advertised effectively.

Walter Dill Scott (1911) established the psychological bases for advertising, discussing human efficiency as a function of diverse factors including imitation, competition, loyalty, concentration, wages, pleasure, relaxation, etc. The latest gadgets and domestic devices were designed to be efficient, manufactured on efficient production lines, by efficient employees, using efficient machines, marketed through efficient advertisements on radio, billboards, magazines and newspapers, purchased through efficient hire purchase, and projected into the imagination through the efficient dream machine of Hollywood. Seductive images were beamed into the national (and then the global) subconscious from the depths of the imagination of the most talented writers, directors, and set designers, to be indelibly associated with desire, beauty and fulfillment. Imagine, desire, and realize all this and one could be truly modern. As Langdon Winner (1995) wrote:

> These images projected novel possibilities for living in modern society. They told a story in which people's orderly role in production was to be rewarded with an equally orderly role in consumption. Of course these efforts did not completely determine people's lives. But the experience of societies such as those of contemporary Europe where consumerism does not yet dominate understandings of self, family and society helps us appreciate the artificiality of these strategies of social control. The advertisements and *tableaux vivants* always depicted the future as something whole and inevitable. People were to be propelled forward by larger forces into a world that is rational, dynamic, prosperous, and harmonious.

Much of the contemporary efficiency movement achieved its aims by disciplining not only the employee but also, in the post Second World War era, the customer (Ritzer 1993). First it was supermarkets; self-service rapidly spread to other areas, such as gas stations and banking, leading to an externalization of the costs of labor to customers, encouraging urban sprawl and blight, through the Wal-Martization of everyday life. Undoubtedly these routines shave a few dollars off average costs but in doing so they create a brutal and joyless aesthetic of cost saving, encourage urban congestion and reduce potentially enjoyable experiences, such as shopping, to treks through huge warehouses with all the charm of an aircraft hangar. Efficiency has been so naturalized as to be almost invisible, its logic so entrenched that we have a hard time identifying its impact:

> Taylor's thinking ... so permeates the soil of modern life we no longer realize it's there. It has become, as Edward Eyre Hunt, an aide to future President Herbert Hoover, could grandly declaim in 1924, 'part of our moral inheritance' ... Taylor bequeathed a clockwork world of tasks timed to the hundredth of a minute, of standardized factories, machines, women and men. He helped instill in us the fierce, unholy obsession with time, order, productivity, and efficiency that marks our age ... Taylor left a distinctive mark on American life and the world ... he quickened the tempo of our lives, left us more nervous, speedy, irritable ... all concur that if we obsessively value time, jealously guard what we have of it, and contrive to use it 'efficiently,' we must look to Taylor for the reasons why. (Kanigel 1997: 7)

With the McDonaldization of service delivery and the Wal-Martization of consumption, as rationalized workers became rationalized consumers, the meta-routines of efficiency established in work percolated into the broader society. The ultimate promise of modern society was held to be individual, material satisfaction powered by restless motion and desire. The American Dream became an endless road movie running from one identikit mall to another (Winner 1995), in which a dream of efficiency dominated waking as well as working life and, in some, raised dystopian nightmares.[2]

Community against efficiency

Power, community and democracy: Mary Parker Follett

Not everyone contributing to the imagination of futures at work in management theorizing shared the same dreams. There were signs that what for some augured a dream of efficiency, for others foreshadowed a nightmare of isolated sociability, alienated being, and wasted humanity. Additionally, it became increasingly evident that it was an insufficient level of reform and innovation to be merely mechanically efficient in terms of the relation between the body and the immediate environment. Such reform, while necessary, could not be relied upon to create the desired results because the free will of the workers interceded. If rational calculations were to be as effective as possible, then a new kind of actor needed to be inscribed into practice, one who gave their consent willingly. Initially, these ideas of willing participation were imagined in terms of quite classic debates about democracy, although these terms of trade were rapidly forgotten, along with their author, Mary Parker Follett.

Mary Parker Follett conducted community studies and enquiries into local democracy in Massachusetts. Optimism about management was widespread in the early years of the twentieth century and was captured in the management texts of the day, most notably by Follett (1918; 1924). Born into a wealthy and privileged Boston family, Follett was passionately committed to democratic ideals. After graduating from the Women's College at Harvard, she became involved in social work in a diverse Boston neighborhood. Follett never lost her commitment to democracy and local group organization, which she honed in her community work in Boston. What she learned in making community centers work for people lacking in the obvious resources of a wealthier society was that, with experience in 'modes of living and acting which shall teach us how to grow the social consciousness' (1918: 363), many people were far more capable than they or others might have imagined. Follett sought to establish conditions in which management and workers cooperated together to achieve not only productivity but also social justice. She suggested that Taylor's ideas were incomplete. In particular, they had not been thought through for their democratic potential. Taylor's lone individuals, in a massive functional structure, under strict control, did not accord with American ideas of democracy. Something had to change in management thinking if this were to be the case.

Central to Follett's worldview was the concept of power. She saw power as legitimate and inevitable. But because power is so central it does not mean that it need be authoritarian. Follett was concerned to democratize power, distinguishing between 'power with' and 'power over' (or coactive power rather than coercive power). She argues that it is the former that needs developing and the latter that needs diminishing, in an effective strategy for challenging silence about how power relations were by talking about how they were not. Here, naming 'power' functions as a way of shaping power.

Follett believed that people in a democracy had to be able to exercise power at the grassroots level. Democratic diversity had great advantages, she said, over more authoritarian homogeneity. Organizations must be developed democratically as places where people learn to cooperate, especially managers and workers. We should welcome difference because it feeds and enriches society, while differences that are ignored feed on society and eventually corrupt it (Follett 1918). Given democratic opportunities, she thought that people could make the most of their situation, even if they seemed relatively impoverished in their access to resources. Her view of democracy was that it should be participatory, because the experience of being participative was empowering and educative.

Follett saw the central questions of organization in terms of power, legitimacy, and authority in a way that few of her contemporaries did. She produced a rationale for authority distinct from Taylor's 'scientific' approach, which identified management as a responsible discharge of necessary functions rather than the privilege of elites. Authority and responsibility should derive from function, not privilege. Both politics and business require an understanding of how to produce collaborative action between different people integrated in a common enterprise rather than creating their mutually assured destruction through the incivility and non-democracy of a despotic regime of formal organization borne on the body of the worker.

It seemed to Follett that Taylor's system of scientific management might have achieved efficiency but at the cost of eroding civility. Her model took as its norm the quintessential small-scale communities of American democracy. Mass production and large scale were made possible through efficiency in the division of labor, but this division had gone too far. It had removed the social bonds that constrained individuals and now pitted them ruthlessly and relentlessly against each other in a highly competitive individualism. What was required was a reinstitution of civility, society, and fellowship in and through work and its organization if the corrosive effects of possessive individualism on the moral character of the American employee were to be halted. People needed to think not just of themselves and the individual benefit to be gained through competition at work but how they fitted into an overall pattern of functions, responsibilities, and authoritative entitlements to command and to obey.

Follett had an appreciation and anticipation of what was required in fully bringing democracy to the USA of her time. In her own words, 'democracy rests on the well-grounded assumption that society is neither a collection of units nor an organism but a network of human relations ... We shall have democracy only when we learn to produce this will through group association – when young men [and women] are no longer lectured to on democracy, but when they are made into the stuff of democracy' (1918: 142, 7).

Her views of Taylor's influence were evident in her assertion that individuality is represented best in the capacity for union between people, rather than in their non-relation, which she defined as evil. In her view the potentialities of the individual remain potentialities until they are released by group life. Only through the group can men and women discover their true nature, and gain their true freedom. On this basis, she opposed the modern legal conception of the corporation as an individual fiction. She thought that corporations had the capability for 'real personality' only when their members were able to interknit themselves into genuine relations, as a human group. Out of this vital union comes creative power (1918: 7–8). Or, more poetically, 'We find the individual through the group, we use him always as the true individual – the undivided one – who, living link of living group, is yet never embedded in the meshes but is forever free for every new possibility of a forever unfolding life' (1918: 295).

Follett is a long way from Taylor and his view of the person as an individual unit whose body is to be disciplined in a scheme of engineering efficiency. She points, instead, to a belief in the importance of human relations as essentially communitarian. She emphasizes conflict resolution as well as the importance of learning from disputes, and the necessity of drawing leadership skills from the group through partnership and coordination rather than just relying on hierarchy, ultimate authority, or competition (which later becomes a major stream of tutelage in its own right: see Lewin 1950). In contemporary terms, she was for polyphony in organizations, for diversity, rather than strong cultures and homogeneous recruitment and training. By getting rid of conflict, she said, most managers mean getting rid of diversity so that their ideas are never challenged. She saw conflict as 'a normal process' which enabled 'socially valuable differences' to be registered 'for the enrichment of all concerned' (1995: 86). What was important was, first, not suppressing, eliminating or denying conflict, and second, how the conflict was dealt with. Three approaches were possible. First, there was what she called domination, where there was a victory of one side at the expense of the other. Second, there was compromise, where all parties relinquish a part of their original interests. Third, there was her favored option of integration, in which a new, and better, solution emerged from negotiation that preserved the original interests of both sides.

Follett's stress on unfolding democracy is a decisive shift from Taylor's enveloping autocracy of expertise being imposed on the body. It enlists a new subjectivity to shape the ranks of those persons being subjected. As Rose puts it:

> To rule citizens democratically means ruling them through their freedoms, their choices, and their solidarities rather than despite these. It means turning subjects, their motivations and interrelations, from potential sites of resistance to rule into allies of rule. It means replacing arbitrary authority with that permitting a rational justification ... to rule subjects democratically it has become necessary to know them intimately. (1996: 117)

Power positive and negative; power coercive and coactive

Follett's communitarian democracy has been seen not only as the opposite pole to Taylor's individualism but also as a program for 'management, owners, and labor working together in a theory of *coactive power*' (Boje and Rosile 2001: 90). The meaning of coactive power is normatively contrasted with that of coercive power in terms of a contrast between 'power with' and 'power over' (Follett 1924: 101). Her

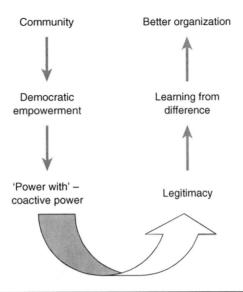

Figure 3.1 Follett's diagram of power

view was that 'Coercive power is the curse of the universe; coactive power, the enrichment and advancement of every human soul' (1924: xii). Given the nature of Foucault's (1977) argument that contemporary forms of power are engaged in a struggle for the soul, her use of language in this respect is quite revealing. She believed that coactive power could be achieved through cooperative governance in which workers were trained in the knowledge of the whole business and its markets, thereby making democratic governance through joint situation search processes workable. Employees need empowering, rather than disempowering, as in Taylorism.[3]

Follett's ideas can be represented diagrammatically as in Figure 3.1. Experience in the community is the seedbed of democracy, where ordinary people are able to discover that they have extraordinary abilities to get things done in concert with other people. In communities they learn about democratic empowerment and coactive power.

Through experience of positive power, people come to accept the legitimacy of power when it is coactively constituted. The legitimacy that they build through sharing in grassroots democracy means that they learn from difference. When organization can incorporate this sense of virtuous and positive power then it will become more robust, more capable, and more able to tap the creative energies and abilities of all its members.

Situating Follett

Follett represented a break with earlier – and subsequent – conceptions. Her work was obviously very different from Taylor's views. She also differed greatly from the approach to sociology that was institutionalized in the Sociological Department at Ford in 1914. One might think that there were continuities: the latter sounded the death knell of the conception of the person as merely a repository for external coercive powers directed by engineers at a subject conceived of only as a body. Ford's innovations signaled a shift in focus from the body of the worker to their moral life. However, it was a concern that differed significantly from Follett's approach.

First, the concern with morality at Ford was in large part simply a displaced concern with the body. As we discussed in Chapter 2, only moral bodies, those that lead sober, disciplined and wholesome lives, were worthy of the five-dollar day. Rather than have an extensive apparatus checking the body at work, Ford instituted the Sociological Department to monitor and survey whether or not the desired balance between maintaining the rhythm of toil and the restorative powers of recreation, mediated through sober and disciplined consumption and social reproduction, was being achieved.

Second, although the Sociological Department was of some significance, it was neither widespread nor long standing. Few other organizations had the resources to support something similar. And, from the 1920s onwards, they barely had the need. The knowledge required moved from the interior space of the organization to, on the one hand, the prohibitions of the state, and, on the other, the positive power emanating from the universities. There was an institutionalization of the disciplinary knowledge of the body, both the individual bodies of the workers and the collective body of the workforce.

One important source of institutionalization, the Harvard University Fatigue Laboratory, was to play a significant role in a double shift of knowledge: from the workplace to the universities and from the management of the body to the collective consciousness. It was through Harvard's sponsorship that the next lesson in the construction of a manipulative power at work was to be constructed. A shift was under way from a focus on the political economy of the body to a focus on the moral economy of the collective soul.

The Hawthorne experiments

The Fatigue Laboratory at Harvard

Western Electric served as the manufacturing arm of the Bell System for more than 100 years in the United States. It produced many of the breakthrough technologies developed by scientists at Bell Laboratories. Inside the Hawthorne works, more than 40,000 people designed, assembled and tested a wide variety of switchboards, cable and wire harnesses, relays, switching systems and other state-of-the-art telecommunications equipment. This was the plant chosen by General Electric for a series of experiments designed to help it sell more light bulbs to businesses. General Electric sought evidence that better lighting of the workplace improved worker productivity. GE funded the National Research Council (NRC) of the National Academy of Sciences to conduct a study at AT&T's Western Electric Hawthorne plant located in Cicero, Illinois. The research examined the relationship between light intensity and worker efficiency. The hypothesis was that greater illumination would yield higher productivity; in a derivation of ideas about scientific management they sought to find the one best level of illumination. Two work groups of female employees were selected as a control and an experimental group. By manipulating lighting in the experimental group and comparing worker productivity with that of the control group, the researchers thought that they would be able to validate and measure the impact of lighting. The study, however, failed to find any simple relationship, as both poor lighting and improved lighting seemed to increase productivity. Indeed, in the final stage, when the researchers pretended to increase lighting the worker group reported higher satisfaction.

George Pennock, Western Electric's superintendent of inspection, suggested that perhaps the reason for increased worker productivity was simply the interaction between the researchers and the female employees, which was perhaps the first time anyone in authority had shown any positive interest in them. He thought that maybe the workers responded favorably to this interest by increasing their output and reporting satisfaction, irrespective of the changes they were being subjected to. He decided to invite researchers from Harvard to conduct investigations.

In 1927, Harvard created the Fatigue Laboratory, under the direction of L. J. Henderson, a chemist and physiologist, at the Harvard Business School. Fatigue was high on the research agenda not only because of the intensification of work that Taylorism had inspired but also because, during the First World War, the problem of tired workers had become the basis for a new intellectual movement. The work of the US Public Health Service during the war, and closely related work by the Committee on Industrial Fatigue, which had been set up to increase productivity in the face of the long hours deemed necessary for war readiness, had put industrial tiredness on the national agenda (Derickson 1994). Henderson, although a physiologist, was to hasten the shift from a physiological focus on the body to one that was more psychological by including Elton Mayo in the work of the Fatigue Laboratory. Labor turmoil contributed to a postwar reconceptualization of fatigue as students of industrial relations increasingly emphasized the psychology of fatigue as the outcome of the maladjustment of individual laborers to industrial reality. Henderson would contribute to the development of systems theory, influencing management theorists such as Chester Barnard (1938), and he was a founder member of the influential Pareto Circle at Harvard (Heyl 2002), to which Talcott Parsons also belonged. One of the early research projects that the Harvard Laboratory conducted in 1927 took over the work of the Hawthorne research project, the most significant – if flawed – finding of which was that informal organization existed and it was this that motivated performance.

The body in the physical environment

There were four waves of subsequent research at the Hawthorne plant, each in a different location. The first was in the relay assembly room from 1927 to 1929. Hundreds of women worked in the relay assembly room where they assembled 40 different parts into the mechanical relays that were needed for telephone switching. The assembly consisted of putting together a coil, an armature, contact springs and insulators in a fixture and securing the parts by means of four machine screws to form each relay unit. Each assembly took approximately one minute to complete. Under normal conditions with a 48-hour work week, including Saturdays, the assemblers produced 2,400 relays a week each. Six women were selected whose prior production rates were known. They were removed from the large assembly hall to a special test room with standard assembly benches, tools and equipment. The researchers wanted to test the effects of changes in length and frequency of rest periods and hours worked. The test room was separated from the main assembly department by a 10-foot-tall wooden partition. Temperature, humidity and lighting conditions were controlled, and an observer in the room recorded events as they happened.

Five assemblers worked at the benches, while one woman procured and distributed parts. The production rate was monitored as each completed relay was placed on a chute, activating an electric counting gate as it passed down. The women had no supervisor, but they increasingly assumed responsibility for their own work and were allowed to share in decisions about changes in their work. The experiments consisted of 23 changes in the working environment. For instance, rest breaks were added and maintained at various lengths and periods of time. Shorter workdays and elimination of Saturday hours were also tried. Output increased no matter how physical conditions were varied. In fact, even when conditions were returned to what they had been before, productivity remained 25 percent above its original value. Absenteeism was only a third of that in the main assembly room. Output averaged 3,000 relays a week per assembler. Physical changes appeared to have no effect on output rate. The relationship between pay, incentives, rest, and working hours had little effect on productivity, even when the original, more demanding conditions were reimplemented.

From 1928 to 1930, another experimental group was established whose work involved mica splitting. For this group the workers' piece wages were held constant while work conditions were varied. The women were moved to a special test room where, unlike their cohorts, they received 10-minute rest breaks at 9:30 a.m. and 2:30 p.m. After a brief decline in performance following the move, the women's output increased by an average of 15 percent and remained at that level for the duration of the experiment. When they returned to their department, losing the rest periods, their output dropped back to the original rate. Since no other conditions had changed, the researchers attributed the increase in output to the beneficial effects of rest periods, not to the effect of the experiment itself.

A program of plant-wide interviews followed from 1928 to 1931. These recorded employee concerns and grievances, with 21,000 employees being interviewed. These data would support the research of the Harvard team for years and led them to conclude that work improved when supervisors began to pay attention to employees, that work takes place in a social context in which work and non-work considerations are important, and that norms and groups matter to workers. The final stage of the research took place on the bank wiring observation group from 1931 to 1932. In this study 14 male workers had incentive pay introduced and were observed but nothing happened. The work group had established work norms defining how much work they should perform in a day and stuck to it, regardless of pay. This strengthened the anthropological interpretation that informal groups operated in the work environment and that these groups, the informal organization, managed behavior in the formal organization. The organization had a collective soul – constituted as an informal organization – which would later be conceptualized as a culture.[4]

Social and human problems: Elton Mayo

Situating Mayo

While Roethlisberger and Dickson (1939) were to write up the Hawthorne research, they did not do so before Elton Mayo (1933) had leapt into print, causing some subsequent confusion about who actually conducted the studies. Mayo did not, but he used the research to mount a critique of scientific management's technologies of power. However, he was not so naive as to suggest a critique of power *per se*. He realized the necessity of technologies of power but sought more efficient and effective interventions.

The interpretations that Mayo (1933) made of the Hawthorne Studies were in large part already well rehearsed and accorded with views that he had formed in Brisbane in the aftermath of the First World War, in his work with 'shell-shocked' soldiers returning to sunny Queensland from the dark horrors of trench warfare in the European theater. It was Mayo's early and incomplete training as a doctor, and his collaboration with a Brisbane specialist, which provided the occasion for the formation of his ideas about the importance of psychological subjectivity. From the treatment of maladjustment on the part of veterans, it was a small step to the treatment of industrial malaises: 'Industrial unrest is not caused by mere dissatisfaction with wages and working conditions but by the fact that a conscious dissatisfaction serves to "light up" as it were the hidden fires of mental uncontrol' (Mayo 1922: 64; cited in Bourke 1982: 226). Elton Mayo prescribed several short rest breaks per shift, to relieve physiological strain and to disrupt the negative feelings that led to industrial unrest. These ideas were subsequently to develop much further, as a result of his research involvements during the Second World War.

Mayo's wartime studies of absenteeism and labor turnover led him to critique excessive individualism as a technology of power, and to propose an alternative approach. Unlike Follett, he did not come up with an explicit communitarian approach but he did develop a 'doctrine of human cooperation'.[5] Against excessive individuation Mayo (1975: 8) pits collaboration, his version of community. Individualism has served the nation well, he says, but only in one dimension, that of organizing for material efficiency. What it has not been able to do, even in wartime conditions, is 'ensure spontaneity of co-operation' or 'teamwork' (1975: 9), that is, social efficiency based in the skills of individuals to cooperate with others. The ability to display a capacity for receiving 'communication from others' and responding to the 'attitudes and ideas of others in such a fashion as to promote congenial participation in a common task' (1975: 12) has been lost because scientific management has destroyed it, creating anomie and shattering community, through 'the skill required of a machine-hand [having] drifted downwards; he has become more of a machine tender and less of a mechanic' (1975: 13). All the organizing energy has been focused on developing technical skills in a more and more divided manner while 'no equivalent effort to develop social or collaborative skill has yet appeared to compensate or balance the technical development' (1975: 13).

From the body to the soul; from coercive to manipulative power

Mayo's theoretical background guided the selection of issues he was familiar with and the marginalization of the issues that did not match the theory he chose to promote. Mayo's ideas had already been formed in Brisbane; in the US the Hawthorne Studies provided him with the opportunity to promote them to the world and to do so before the researchers formally associated with the project did so. It may be said that Mayo achieved first-mover advantage. He used it to argue that small groups had their own sources of positive power, derived from group morale. When Mayo (1933) looked at the findings from the Hawthorne Laboratory investigations he thought that the results showed that employees had a strong need for shared cooperation and communication. Merely by asking for their cooperation in the test, Mayo believed, the investigators had stimulated a new attitude among the employees. The assemblers considered themselves to be part of an important group whose help and advice were being sought by the company. He believed that if consultation between labor and management were instituted it would give workers a sense of belonging to a team. Here we can see the transformation produced in the modes of surveillance. A new strategy of government of the body/soul in the factory was to be based on the construction of a sentiment of freedom (and responsibility) without – apparently – any kind of surveillance:

> The improvement in production, they believe, is not very directly related to the rest pauses and other innovations. It reflects rather a freer and more pleasant working environment, a supervisor who is not regarded as a 'boss,' a 'higher morale.' In this situation the production of the group insensibly lifts, even though the girls are not aware that they are working faster. Many times over, the history sheets and other records show that in the opinion of the group all supervision has been removed. On occasion indeed they artlessly tell the observer, who is in fact of supervisory rank, very revealing tales of their experiences with previous 'bosses.' Their opinion is, of course, mistaken: in a sense they are getting closer supervision than ever before, the change is in the quality of the supervision. (Mayo 1975: 75)

These studies changed the landscape of management from Taylor's engineering approach to the political economy of the body to a social sciences approach that focused on the interior life, the mental states, the consciousness and unconsciousness – what Follett and Foucault termed the 'soul' – of the employees. Worker productivity would, henceforth, be interpreted predominantly in terms of patterns of culture, motivation, leadership, and human relations (Maslow 1978). The locus of power shifted from the engineering expert, designing the job, selecting and training the right worker, and rewarding performance, to the manager, responsible for leading, motivating, communicating, and counseling the individual employee as well as designing the social milieu in which work takes place.

Human relations

Mayo developed what became known as the Human Relations School. The emphasis of this approach was on informal work group relations, the importance of these for sustaining the formal system, and the necessity of the formal system meshing with the informal system. In the informal system special attention was to be paid to the satisfaction of individual human needs, focusing on what motivates different people, in order to try and maximize their motivation and satisfaction. Mayo thought the manager had to be a social clinician, fostering the social skills of those with whom she or he worked. Workers who argued with their managers and supervisors were expressing deep-seated neuroses lodged in their childhood history.

Therapeutic interviews were recommended as a management tool, to create better-adjusted workers, and training in counseling and personnel interviews was touted as an essential management skill. The advice was simple. Pay full attention to the interviewee and make it clear that this is the case; listen carefully to what they have to say; do not interrupt; don't contradict them; listen carefully for what is being said as well as any ellipses in terms of what is left unspoken; try and summarize carefully what has been said by the speaker as feedback for the interviewee; and treat what has been said in confidence (Trahair 2001).[6]

An ideal interview would be a form of confessional, working through positive power. The individual subjects who are interviewed will reveal themselves to themselves through these interviews; 'they will reflexively turn in upon themselves as an object of truth', as Haugaard (1997: 90) suggests, but the presentation of truth will be one which mere employees 'are not competent to interpret so the expert [the manager] is needed to weave a discourse of truth out of their deepest desires and most secret longings'.

The body having been re-engineered, it was now time to get to work on the soul, or at least that secular synonym for it, the unconscious. Trained dispositions are disciplined and responsible and will conduct the body through self-control. Mayo contributed to the new technologies of the self and counseling (Rose 1996; also see Baritz 1974). With Mayo, power moves from a focus on the body of the worker to the voice of the worker, to the signs of the unconscious that are interpretable through eliciting employee participation in therapeutic counseling. Now, it is evident that this is not a meeting of equals. These sessions are to be neither friendly chats nor a meeting of equals but a meeting of clinical expertise lodged in superior power, claiming the mantle of authority, with human weakness, frailty and illness.

Just as Taylor's focus on disciplining the body was tempered in practice by Ford's concern with the morality of his five-dollar-a-day workers, so the theoreticians of management shifted their focus from the body to the soul (consciousness and unconsciousness). The locus of the moral being was defined as one who not only is but also wants to be an obedient subject. The self became 'an object of reflection and analysis, and, above all, transformable in the service of ideals' (van Krieken 1990: 353). The ideals were only too clear, given that the meta-routine that had already been established was efficiency. What was under construction here was an attempt to establish patterns of spontaneous obedience as similar meta-routines that could be depended on utterly.

Mayo unequivocally unleashed a program for reforming the individual as an object of reflection, analysis, and transformation, and much of subsequent management was to extend this technology of power by normalizing it as simply the constitution of management. Rose (1989: 2) noted that the 'management of subjectivity' became 'a central task for the modern organization' and those who profess expertise about organizations.

The group

What was crucial about the Hawthorne Studies was that they reconstituted subjectivity not as a unique quality of the individual's psychology but as a phenomenon of the group and a resource for the organization.

> The group represented a field for thought, argument, and administration that was genuinely supraindividual and yet not of the order of the crowds or the mass. The group would exist as an intermediary between the individual and the population, it would inhabit the soulless world of the organization and give it subjective meaning for the employee, it would satisfy the social needs of the atomic and fragmented self isolated with the rise of the division of labor and the decline of community, it would explain ills and could be mobilized for good, it could bring about damage in its totalitarian form and contentment and efficiency in its democratic form. In the medium of the group a new relay was found where administration in the light of psychological expertise could come into alignment with the values of democracy. (Rose 1996: 136)

The attitudes of employees; their feelings of control over their working lives; the sense of cohesion within the work group; and their belief in the good dispositions of bosses and supervisors towards them created 'a range of new tasks' that 'emerged to be grasped by knowledge and managed in the factory' (1996: 138). Things that were not known had to be made knowable, to be given shape and form. Non-directive interviews were used to find a 'way into the emotional life of the factory, the emotional significance of particular events in the experience of the worker' (1996: 139). These could then be slotted into the emergent discourse of functionalism that Parsons and others at Harvard were developing: manifest and latent functions could be distinguished so that one could analyze problems scientifically, in terms of underlying causes rather than apparent explanations.

Human relations approached these matters through more psychobiological constructs, preparing the way for organizational behavior to emerge as a self-referential discourse, while functionalism goes on to define contingency theory as the triumph of organization studies. Organizationally, knowledge of existing patterns of relations could be incorporated into change programs to make them more efficacious; interviews could fulfill therapeutic functions by making latent issues manifest. Managers could then manage in full knowledge of those sentiments and values belonging to their employees and act upon them appropriately. Specialized functions, such as personnel management, emerge to deal with these issues, through counseling, easing adjustments to change, planning and collecting data. Other new disciplines such as organizational communications also emerge as instruments for realigning misaligned values within organizations. Definitions of the situation could be arrived at that were shared in management's terms rather than being opposed by workers' terms. A culture of commitment could be built. And its builders should be leaders. Groups needed leaders. Leadership prowess was evaluated on the basis of an ability to get others to do what it was that the leaders wanted them to. And when they did this they could be seen to be leaders who cheapened the costs of surveillance greatly (Bavelas and Lewin 1942). Such leaders learnt how to use the democratic potential of groups to manage so that they could relax their vigilance in consequence. Group dynamics, leadership, sensitivity could all become the object of training and the subject of a new disciplinary apparatus that could be forged, just like a science, in the laboratory (Cartwright and Zander 1953). The raw materials for its forging were provided by Chester Barnard.

Leadership and authority

Chester Barnard

Chester Barnard joined forces with Mayo when he cited him to the effect that 'authority depends upon a co-operative personal attitude of individuals on the one hand; and the system of communication in the organization on the other' (1938: 175). What managers should communicate are strong moral values, which it was management's duty to provide, said Barnard. Good management requires emotional work, and it is the task of the managerial elite to configure others as servants of responsible authority through guiding them emotionally, thought Barnard, and Mayo (1975) seemed to agree with this diagnosis.

For Barnard, authority relations were not a given but had to be worked at by managers. Authority only exists in so far as people are willing to accept it. The pervasiveness of authority can be expanded by gradually enlarging the 'zone of indifference' within which compliance with orders will be perceived in neutral terms without any questioning of authority by employees. Managers should seek to extend the borders of this zone through material incentives but more especially through providing others with status, prestige, and personal power.

Communications, especially in the informal organization (which Mayo had 'discovered' in his interpretation of the Hawthorne experiments), are absolutely central to decision making. Management's responsibility is to harness informal groupings and get them working for the organization, not against it. Everyone should know what the channels of communication are and should have access to formal channels of communication that should be as short and direct as possible. All of these new technologies of power should not replace the scientific management of work and organization design but should supplement it, be added to it as new forms of persuasion.

Where individuals worked with common values rather than common orders, they would work much more effectively. While Barnard had realized that it was more effective to work on the enrichment and advancement of consciousness as a technology of power rather than merely the body, Mayo also seemed to realize that the unconsciousness and the state that he referred to as 'reverie' – a kind of semi-consciousness – needed attention as well. It was the hidden fire that had been illuminated by Freud and his followers. Most people's actions were driven by the unconscious, and this was as true of people at work as at war. Agitators and radicals were victims of neurotic fantasies that could be traced, invariably, to infantile history. If individuals could be guided by therapy in work, they would be healed of their neuroses. Organizations should organize teams and use personnel interviews to aid members, as Mayo (1985) put it, to get 'rid of useless emotional complications', 'to associate more easily, more satisfactorily with other persons – fellow workers or supervisors – with whom he is in daily contact', and to develop in the worker a 'desire and capacity to work better with management'. The manager was to be a good shepherd, educating and leading his flock, through 'clinical' and 'counseling' skill.

One should note that Barnard did not always represent authority in such a pastoral mode. More often than not he was, as Wolin (1960: 411) suggests, a no-nonsense rationalist who, in common with later theorists such as Nobel economics laureate Herbert Simon (1957), saw authority in far more rational and power-full terms. When superior power in a hierarchy commands the other to do as they are told, whether they want to or not, that is power. Communication skills can soften power but they do not replace it. Behind the smooth words and clever communication campaigns it is evident that power relations are still being constituted, ready for managerial intervention and action, should the gentler, softer tools of persuasion prove less seductive than imagined.

The humanization of work

In the UK, Australia and much of Europe, especially in Scandinavia, these concerns fused into the humanization of work movement.[7] Morale and attitude surveys became significant instruments for calculating and ranking the importance of specific issues and measuring the effectiveness of measures taken to address them. The measures taken were usually drawn from the new disciplines of management communication, leadership studies and the explicit management of the person and collective body of employees – personnel – or, as it became in the 1980s, human resource management (HRM). Communication had a special role to play. HRM should align employee values with the objectives determined by management authority. It would do this by 'explaining the situation, clearing up misunderstandings, and allaying fears and anxieties' (Rose 1989: 72). The nature of managerial authority should not be left to chance. It should be shaped by the appropriate leadership style. As Rose put it, 'autocratic leadership produced aggression or apathy ... laissez-faire leadership produced chaos, democratic leadership produced not only feelings of loyalty and belonging but also the most work of the highest quality. Democratic leadership was ... good ethics ... good psychology and good business' (1996: 145). And, in a faint echo of utilitarianism, such leadership offered a science of the happiness of the greatest number:

> It appeared that one could utilize the dynamics of group life to rethink work in a way that fused the values of democracy, productivity, and contentment. There was no

antithesis between what was good for the worker and what was good for the enterprise. The worker's interest in work was more than merely that of maximizing wages and minimizing the severity of labor in terms of effort and hours. Through work, the worker obtained psychological and social benefits: fulfillment and a sense of belonging. And as a corollary, the productive worker was one who felt satisfied and involved in work. Hence the boss's interest in the laborer should not be restricted to the technical organization of the labor process, and the establishment of effective systems of command, authority and control. It had to encompass the happiness of the worker, the human relations of the enterprise ... This psychology of the worker as a social subject was explicitly fused to a radical project for transforming the conditions of labor and the authoritative relations of the workplace in the name of ethical principles, political beliefs, industrial efficiency, and mental health. (1996: 142–3).

The conduit from leaders to employees ran through the personnel department, where these new truths were lodged in the many innovative personnel management techniques that were developed.[8] The personnel officers (a term that seemed to have been incorporated seamlessly from military usage) documented values and sentiments, diagnosed malaises, and dispensed good counsel to 'create the internal harmony that was the condition of a happy and productive factory' (Rose 1989: 72).

The institutionalization of leadership

Phillip Selznick

In one of the most sophisticated accounts, Phillip Selznick's (1957) *Leadership in administration* explicitly divides the soul from the body. The organization is a corporate body, a tool or instrument rationally designed to direct human energies to a fixed goal, an expendable and limited apparatus. However, the body has a soul, something largely natural, living, and unplanned, a distinctive identity, something which Selznick identifies as an 'institution' (1957: 21). Organizational tools evolve into something infused with value and meaning, becoming soulful institutions. Or they will if they are managed properly and there is specificity about how to achieve such proper management.

Management is the job of the elites: 'Maintenance of social values depends on the autonomy of elites' (1957: 8). These autonomous elites must produce that commitment and identification, that great soulful boundless leap, which makes the bodies of the employees more than a mere tool. The elites must make the individual components of the tool identify with and feel committed to the elites and their purposes. They will do this both by stimulating soulful feelings and by controlling them 'to produce the desired balance of forces' (1957: 100). These soulful individuals sound closer to well-made Replicants than to real flesh and blood people (Scott 1982; Dick 1968). They will have the freedom of human agency but it is one that will always be exercised in such a way as 'to be consistent with the organization's objectives' because of the 'organization personality' (Simon 1957: 109) that the elites will have implanted in the Replicants – those simulacra of free men and women – who people the instrument. It makes the Tyrell Corporation seem less science fiction and more organization science. Management, in the form of its elites, seeks to normalize the psyche of subordinates such that obedient self-supervision becomes a reflexive instinct. (Appropriately, the Tyrell Corporation's emblem in the movie *Blade runner* is an all-seeing eye.)

There were other options, however, to the *Blade runner* strategy. One of these drew directly from Follett's early-century and neglected insights, and only came into definition towards the end of the century whose early possibilities she sketched. The trick was to bring the routines enacted in political economy into creative tension with the routines being constructed to create obedient subjects, and to draw from the soul thus constructed a creativity that both the political economy of the body and the moral economy of the soul denied.

The mind in the soulful machine

Incorporating knowing

Fortifying the meta-routine of efficiency required perfecting supporting routines; thus political economy shaded into moral economy as the 1930s developed. Slowly, it became evident that efficient routines could only be founded on the social and cultural rehabilitation of the worker as a whole person rather than merely their perfection as an instrument of political economy. The political economy project was doomed by one simple substantive fact. What people ordinarily know and do – sometimes in ways that a theory never captures – is essential to how organizations are able to do what they do. The one best way could never be entirely prescribed; and where it was attempted then, by definition, something close to a non-learning organization would be instituted. Even scientific managers could realize this in the main lesson of the Hawthorne Studies. It was a realization that became the impetus for Mayo's moral economy project.

The moral economy project was not really as radical as some of its prophets, such as Mayo, assumed. It built on what Taylor bequeathed. It didn't deconstruct the legacy. Contemporary theory builds on the legacy of both of these schools. In this approach, the ordinary knowledge of ordinary people is regarded as a neglected resource that managers must access, use and routinize. They will do this through the simple strategies of building social capital (brought into focus primarily through the work of Robert Putnam 1993; 1995) and through the use of those coactive power strategies that Mary Parker Follett had recommended for building such capital all those years ago. Once social capital has been identified, then new routines can be constructed. Social capital takes care of the coactivity while knowledge management will structure the new routines. It is tempting to see the former as a continuation of the concern with the moral economy and the latter as a simple extension of scientific management – to incorporate the mind as well as the body and soul of the employee. We explore this proposition in what follows.

Social capital

Social capital is a new idea with deep roots that go back to Mary Parker Follett. In theories that draw on the same wellspring of ideas that we find in Follett (whether it is realized or not), social capital is defined as 'the sum of actual and potential resources embedded within, available through, and derived from the network of relationships possessed by an individual or social unit' (Nahapiet and Ghoshal 1998: 243). Firms are 'understood as a social community specializing in the speed and efficiency in the creation and transfer of knowledge' (Kogut and Zander 1996: 503). Organizations, designed to bring people together for task completion, supervision and coordination, result in frequent and dense levels of social contacts, creating coactive power in Follett's terms. Social capital, as Follett realized, makes it possible for ends to be achieved that, in its absence, could otherwise only be achieved at additional cost.[9]

The social capital concept privileges the worker as a 'knowledge worker' with embrained rather than embodied knowledge (Blackler 1995). Such employees are potentially mobile and can go to another employer; thus, they must be kept loyal by avoidance of coercion (which, much as the use of tight contracts, destroys trust) and by use of soft power (see Fox 1974 on power and trust relations).

Trust and control can be viewed as structures of interrelated situated practices that influence the development of different forms of expert power in particular organizational contexts. In this view, trust and control relations are generative mechanisms that play a role in the production, reproduction and transformation of expert power. Trust is based on predictability of behavior, where some type of control or self-control mechanism influences such predictability. Trust and control are closely associated (Reed 2001; Maguire et al. 2001). Many organizations attempt to 'manage' trust as a means of control (Knights et al. 2001). Maguire et al. (2001) have suggested several ways in which this happens including actively manipulating the employee using rewards, acquiring information about the employee and thus rendering him/her more predictable and hence controllable, and actively manipulating the goodwill of the employee by increasing his/her identification with the organization.

The rhetoric of 'trust' often sits uncomfortably in the context of all the routines constituting a 'low-trust' workplace of design of technologies and of work by standardized procedures. Contemporary labor process studies carried out or reviewed by Thompson and Ackroyd (1995; 1999) and Thompson and Warhurst (1998) suggest that we need to untangle the managerial rhetoric and intention from the realities of the situation.

Knowledge management

Knowledge management is another new idea with deep roots that go back to Frederick Taylor and scientific management. Two aspects of knowledge management are relevant here. First, there is the treatment of knowledge as a commodity, through the mechanization and objectification of knowledge creation, diffusion, and storage. Treated this way it increases management's sense of control. Second, there is soft domination of the knowledge worker by identification-based control. The highest degree of trust is when the person completely identifies with the organization, in which case his/her self-image is aligned with managerially determined objectives (Alvesson and Willmott 2002). What knowledge management seeks to do is to draw from the tacit knowledge of individuals and the social capital of the group to construct new and improved routines. The thrust of scientific management and the many subsequent clones spawned from its political economy, such as knowledge management, was that routines produce increased efficiency where the correspondence between relations of knowledge is closed, where the worker does exactly what the scientific manager prescribes. Taylor and his heirs sought to make workers functionaries of knowledge relations defined externally to the 'being there' of the workers. Yet, paradoxically, as the Hawthorne Studies first revealed, efficiency is determined by the extent to which individual knowledge and expertise are accessed and utilized (Grant 1996a: 380).

In the most current clone of scientific management – which is knowledge management – efficiency is based on *common knowledge* as a prerequisite to the communication of direction and routine. Translating specialist information depends on the sophistication and level of common knowledge. Second, the *frequency and variability of task performance* change the efficiency of knowledge integration (Nelson and Winter 1982). The efficiency of comprehending and responding appropriately among employees involved in tasks is a function of frequency of task performance. Third, *organizational structure* that reduces the extent and intensity of communication to achieve integration assists efficiency, and to this end the employee has to be integrated into the enterprise as an obedient rather than a resistant subject. Knowledge management grows out of the cross-pollination of scientific management and human relations theory to make obedient subjects creative.[10]

Knowledge management is an instrument producing new routines that result from acquiring and distilling knowledge of tacit experiences and action that is embedded in social and institutional practice (Spender and Kijne 1996; Brown and Duguid 1991). Individual public performances draw on private parts of the self – the soul in Follett's terms – in interactions (Nelson and Winter 1982). Thus, as recent theory has it, 'the primary role of the firm is in integrating specialist knowledge resident in individuals into goods and services' (Grant 1996b: 120). Knowledge management institutes what Garrick and Clegg (2000) have referred to as an 'organizational gothic' at the heart of organizational life, a capacity to suck the vitality from the individual body and soul in order to enhance the vitality of the corporate body for increased efficiency and reduced costs, through greater coactive power. The allusion to Dracula is intended; the practice seems as gothic as any Hammer horror movie.

Power/knowledge management

Individuals share uniquely held knowledge on the basis of what is held in common among them. Common knowledge refers to the 'common cognitive ground' among employees that facilitates knowledge transfer through promoting dialog and communication – what Nonaka and Takeuchi (1995: 14) term 'redundancy'. Redundancy creates an intentional overlap of information held by employees that facilitates transferring and integrating explicit and tacit knowledge. Knowledge about elements not directly related to immediate operational requirements that arises from images in tacit knowledge can be shared through redundant information about business activities, management responsibilities, the company, products and services (1995: 81–2). Competitive, individuated, relations of power make this knowledge difficult to surface. Coercive power leads to zero-sum games, win/lose scenarios, power/resistance, and resource dependency (see Chapter 5). It creates power effects more akin to rape than seduction, as Stokes and Clegg (2002) argue. The rape and seduction analogy suggests that seduction would seek to elicit expert knowing representing a rich and anchored context, whereas rape absconds with the partial acquisition of knowledge without context, and thus, lacking situated meaning, promotes only a wrenching of something unwillingly given. That is why the projects of knowledge management and social capital are seeking to become aligned. First, use coactive power to seduce knowledge that can become the basis for the new routines. Then, when the new routines are established they take on a coercive power of their own, as individuals can be held accountable to them. The major problem with the knowledge management project is that we all carry a great deal of redundancy around in our heads. If you don't know what you know until you need to know it, how can you know what you have stored away in the junk room, so to speak, as 'redundant knowledge'? When the time is ripe, relevant knowledge surges forth unbidden, but you cannot take an inventory of the 'redundant' when the time isn't ripe.[11] There has to be someone knowing something in some context before knowledge can be known, let alone abstracted. The study of knowledge management should really be a study of power/knowledge management because its processes are indivisible from those of power:

> At the core of management is the legitimation, extension, and normalization of dominant property rights, the practical disciplining of the everyday organizational life of members, and the framing of knowledge that can be ascribed a key role in extending, limiting, and otherwise shaping these rights. I call this the discourse of power/knowledge – a discourse that, in academic terms, functions as a surrogate for discussion of sovereignty. (Clegg 2003: 536)

All forms of organization are forms of organization of social relations. All social relations involve power relations. Power is evident in relations not only of ownership and control but also of structuration and design. These relations take many forms. They may be embodied as financial capital, intellectual capital, or social capital. Such relations are likely to be both differentially distributed and socially constructed as well as to exist in differential demand in differentiated markets. Power is also evident in the various forms of knowledge that constitute, structure, and shape these markets and organizations, what is referred to today as knowledge management. What is novel in knowledge management, in its variation on the repertoire of scientific management, is the orientation to the brain rather than the body, the fusion with the moral economy of social capital, and the combination of coactive with coercive power. It frames the new combinations of power/ knowledge that are so evident in soft power today, as we will explore further in Chapter 12.

Conclusion

While this chapter has been historically rooted in the period 1900 to 1945, focusing on scientific management through to the human relations era, it has connected this earlier period to some of the most recent work in organization theory on knowledge management and social capital, where most literature is situated between 1995 and 2005. With these themes we foreshadow the analysis of soft domination, which will recur in Chapter 12.

Knowledge of power was more or less implicit amongst these early theorists, with the exception of Follett. With her exception, theorists steered away from explicitly forging an analytical account of power and, partly in consequence, Follett's explicit address of power seemed to fade from sight as the century unfolded. In some respects, early management and organization theorists were situated too close to its practice to reflect overly on its theory. In these early texts, power, in so far as it was a topic, was to be found embedded, precisely, in the strategies for making sense of management that the pioneers forged and the managerial techniques they advocated.

Hitherto power had been embedded in practice that did not theorize it as such. None of what we have addressed thus far in terms of the political and moral economy of the body, and the emergence of a concern with the soul of the employee, constituting what we might term the 'standing conditions' legitimating existing regimes of power, was to enter greatly into subsequent accounts. Where it did so enter then it was as an assumption of 'authority', defined in terms of legitimate power, which could be safely bracketed as an unproblematic set of relations requiring no address. The marginalization of power was a trend strengthened further by the fillip that the Second World War gave to all matters related to personnel and organization design in the most advanced military of the day, that of the US forces.[12] In fact, power was being written into a corner where it was destined to become the antithesis, the other, to authority, as we shall see in Chapter 5. The ascendance of a concern with authority went hand in hand with a view that resistance was counterproductive and identified with organizational power; thus, power was expunged from authority.[13] Perhaps this is one reason why the discourse of knowledge management has grown, so uncritically, out of the ashes raked over in this chapter, with little or no address of power and hardly any connection to Follett. Knowledge management with the addition of social capital seems to amount to little more than her coactive power.

Follett's ideas lay fallow for most of the twentieth century. However, in the late-twentieth century knowledge management drew implicitly on Follet-like ideas of social capital, coactive cooperation, and creativity, to refashion and repackage contemporary thinking. Bringing her back into this picture tells us what's wrong with it: it lacks power. Rather than knowledge management, one should, we think, refer to power/knowledge management because there are quite complex and sophisticated power dynamics at work, although they are rarely addressed as such.

It is not that power was absent from what the theorists in this chapter did in their theorizing. It was explicitly there in Follett and in Selznick. In Mayo and Barnard it was more implicit as they developed accounts of people at work and their leadership that staked out conditions for governing the soul and producing obedient subjects. Although they were not explicit about this they focused on shaping power at work. Bodies had been disciplined; now new subjectivities were being constituted through new disciplines, frames, and practices that these early pioneers talked and wrote into being. But, simultaneously with their talking and writing these practices into being there was a surprising silence about the nature of what was being created as, explicitly, practices of power. In large part this was because the intellectual apparatus that would enable one to make an explicit interpretation in power terms had yet to be constructed. Thus, we should stress that interpreting these historic texts through the lens of power is not an understanding that coevolved with the understandings of those who wrote the texts. It is very much a consequence of later and more sophisticated accounts of power – as we shall subsequently see – than of any account that these authors might have had readily available to them. Formal acknowledgement of power, as a concept in its own right at the heart of organization practice, was something that waited in the wings where it had scuttled with the neglect of Follett's work for most of the century. The translation of Max Weber's work into English from the late 1940s onwards saw it reappear but not in quite the way that its progenitor seemed to have intended. In the time and the space between scientific management and human relations, between political and moral economy, after Weber but barely touched by his concerns, a concept of power was about to emerge in theory, hesitantly, but with distinct characteristics, as we shall see in the next two chapters.

Notes

1   Taylor's impact on domestic science, and space more generally, is covered in Bell and Kaye (2002) and Banta (1993), as well as Game and Pringle (1979).

2   During the inter-war era, desire shifted from finding creativity in production to displaying imagination in consumption. Consumption became the next frontier of freedom, after indigence, after work. In fact, in a routine world of work, consumption offers an escape and promises freedom. Thus, it may be said to fulfill some imaginative and utopian dreams. The possession of that which is desired will serve to transform the meaning of life. Of course, wherever there is utopia, dystopia lurks close at hand. This arises when desire impels purchases motivated by psychological and sociological factors (Holt 1995; O'Shea 2002), and becomes the motivation for pleasure which, when desire is not consummated in consumption, is accompanied by feelings of discomfort caused by the absence of fulfillment (Belk et al. 2003). Compulsive and impulsive consumption when shopping (Rook 1987) implies that immediate gratification can relieve those negative motivations often associated with permanent and momentary loss of control (Baumeister 2002) in other spheres of life. While certain categories of goods meet needs or wants, anything can become the object of desire and, then, only *that* can satisfy. Driven by the need for self-actualization, in the language of Maslow (1962), desire for consumer goods became the source of relief from dull, deadening and routine work, giving rise to the figure of the instrumental worker (Goldthorpe et al. 1969). Interestingly, some writers, such as Belk et al. (2003: 44), suggest that the outcome of all desire will always be perpetual disappointment.

3   But Taylorism still had a lot of steam left in it. For example, in the postwar era the total quality management (TQM) movement owed a great deal to the engineering auspices of Taylorism (Hetrick and Boje 1992). The *kaizen* system of 'continual improvement' was based upon

extensive work measurement to establish standards (see Merkle 1980), with its 'standardized work sheets' where 'transferable work components' are defined and assigned standard 'cycle times' for execution (see also Adler 1993:103–4). Some elements of Taylorism gave vent to quite unexpected outcomes, which contributed greatly towards a shift from the project of seeking to govern the body to one attempting to govern the soul – in order to create subjects whose morality was evident in their obedience to the authoritative principles of management.

4   Critics have been quick to point out flaws in the research, especially the relative lack of consideration given to the changing economic context (the onset of the Depression in 1929) and the role that incentives played in improving worker productivity (important early critical contributions were made by Landsberger 1958 and by Carey 1967; 2002; also see Gillespie 1993; O'Connor 1999). Other common criticisms are, for instance, that the supervisors were friendly rather than authoritarian which needs to be factored in; that the group composition was changed to get better results during the experiment; that the rest periods were a major innovation but were overlooked in the accounts proffered; that the women's productivity rose because they had a clearer idea of the relationship between their output and earnings in the smaller experimental group, and better and more immediate data to provide feedback.

5   Mayo did this in explicit opposition to what he termed the 'rabble hypothesis', whose lineage he traces back to Hobbes, but which for him was epitomized by the innovations of scientific management. We discuss Hobbes in Chapter 7.

6   Mayo's intent was clearly manipulative. Contemporary forms of workplace counseling are handled off site, away from work, and confidentially. Mayo's interest in counseling was not about helping employees but about helping managers better manage these employees through control and manipulation.

7   Abrahamsson (1980) focuses on the Swedish and broader Scandinavian developments while Child (1969) and Rose (1989) both focus on the British developments. As Rose (1996: 143ff) notes, J. A. C. Brown's (1954) Social psychology of industry, which enjoyed considerable sales success in its many editions, played a considerable role in the UK in circulating humanization of work ideas. The humanization of work movement was never as influential in the United States as it was in Europe, especially Scandinavia and the Netherlands.

8   A huge fillip was provided to these techniques by their systematic development and application during the Second World War, as officers in the armed forces increasingly drew on personnel techniques and applied psychology for selecting, training and counseling troops. One upshot was that the strategies that would be available to personnel officers after the conflict was over grew exponentially, to encompass more sophisticated knowledge of the workforce, the work, and the worker (Townley 1994: 13), based on the techniques of the new behavioral sciences. Townley (1994) writes extensively on how these further developments helped constitute practical techniques of power. Of course, these techniques were constructed not as techniques of power but as management techniques pure and simple. In other words, power did not enter into their self-conception, albeit that it was present in their constitution. By the 1950s authority relations on the American model were emblematic of modernity, especially as it appeared to have been US know-how and management that saved Europe, not only in the Second World War through the efficient mass mobilization of the Normandy landings, but also from the ruination that ensued as its aftermath with the Marshall Plan. To European intellectuals the only alternatives to chaos appeared to be decentered enterprise, governed by authority and management, or communism governed by centralized power, which outside of left-wing circles did not appear attractive. Not surprisingly perhaps, in the context of Cold War politics, where theorists addressed themselves to the nature of organizations in those states committed to enterprise, they saw power not in legitimate structures but in sources of countervailing resistance to the dominant motif of authority.

9   Social capital as it is conceptualized most often in organization theory has three dimensions: structural, cognitive and relational. The discussion of structural and relational concepts is drawn from network theory, favoring separation. Structural elements comprise the overall patterns of connection (Burt 1992). These are to be found in the presence or absence of network

ties, network configuration, and morphology, such as patterns of linkages. Density, connectivity and hierarchy characterize the linkages. Networks that are created for one purpose may be used for another (Nahapiet and Ghoshal 1998; Coleman 1988). The relational dimension of social capital captures references to assets created and leveraged through relationships. Among these are trust, trustworthiness, norms and sanctions, obligations and expectations, identity and identification. Relational embeddedness refers to the kind of personal relationships that people have, such as respect and friendship, which influence their behavior in fulfilling socially ascribed motives (Blum and McHugh 1971). The cognitive element refers to resources that provide shared representations, interpretation, and systems of meaning among parties (Nahapiet and Ghoshal 1998).

10 Not too creative though: it is a creativity that remains highly framed. Grant (1996b) identifies four mechanisms for accessing the creativity of, and simultaneously framing, specialized knowledge in organizations. The first three integrate knowledge while reducing the need and cost of communication and learning, while the fourth is dependent on interaction and crossover learning in the decision process. The first mechanism stresses rules and directives involving direct forms of coordination (impersonal coordination including plans, schedules, forecasts, rules, policies, procedures, social norms and etiquette) and indirect forms (education and training) (de Boer et al. 1999). Standardized information and communication systems are supposed to govern interaction and reduce the quantity of directions in communication necessitated by specialist knowledge and roles (Demsetz 1991; de Boer et al. 1999). Teece et al. (1997: 520) press Mayo's discovery of culture into service by arguing that culture is a *de facto* governance system mediating the behavior of individuals. Second, sequencing activities and inputs allow individual specialist activity to be coordinated continuously, reducing communication. Activity independence varies depending on the product and technologies involved such as sequential, overlapping or concurrent. Third, routines as simple sequences of an automatic nature will be differentiated by supporting complex patterns of interactions among individuals, permitting transfer, recombination or creation of specialized (tacit) knowledge (Dyer and Nobeoka 2000). Routines are highly interdependent, and changes in one routine, or in a higher-level system or architecture, result in new routines required to integrate and coordinate related routines (Teece et al. 1997). They occur between individuals in the absence of rules, directives or significant verbal communication and are expressed via a repertoire of responses (Grant 1996b: 115). Fourth, group problem solving and decision making support low communication and direct transfer of knowledge arising from the first three mechanisms. As task complexity increases, the need for interpersonal communication, interaction in decision making, and group input for non-standardized coordination also increases: meetings and open forums should be arranged in which consensus on unusual, complex and important tasks involving mutual adjustment can be achieved. Devices that decentralize knowledge integration serve to increase participation and thus increase the scope and flexibility of knowledge integration (de Boer et al. 1999: 387).

11 A friend, Tim Ray, after he had read this section on knowledge management (KM), wrote the following to us: 'KM seeks to empower people by being objective about subjectivity in order to exclude people and power … If KM were an old dog, you'd take it out and shoot it because it would be cruel to leave it in the pain of its own contradictions.'

12 It was not just in the military that such an impact was felt; there was a more general impact leading to the bureaucratization of employee relations more generally if we accept that the account that Boron, Dobbin and Jennings (1986) offer of large scale organizations in the steel industry in the North Eastern US applied generally across the country.

13 The approach to power that we develop in this book will lead us to rethink this view of resistance: as we shall see in the later chapters, resistance, being undefeatable, became incorporated, such that it is viewed today as productive. Our genealogy of power is thus, simultaneously, a genealogy of the idea of resistance – as well as obedience – that has been thought from the outset as the antithesis of resistance.

 **4** The Curious Case of
Max Weber

Chapter outline

In this chapter we will:

- Establish the importance of the work of Weber for any understanding of power in organizations.
- Show how this work was systematically distorted in its reception by virtue of the translation strategy followed by Parsons.
- Situate Weber in his proper context, which is that of German intellectual life at the turn of the nineteenth century, where figures such as Kant, Marx and Nietzsche were central.
- Elaborate Weber's theory of rationality and the will to power.
- Elaborate Weber's central concepts of domination and discipline.
- Relate Weber's ideas to those of his close friend, Simmel, and demonstrate how these are still eminently serviceable terms for discussion.

Introduction

Modern organization and management theory is very largely an American invention. The leading journals are primarily American; the leading theorists are mostly American; the organizations and practices from which their knowledge is generalized and on which it is normalized are usually American; the curriculum that most students of these journals will follow is mainly American in derivation; the textbooks that distill and simplify what management means for the masses who shuffle though their pages are invariably American, even when they are 'adaptations' for local markets. But it could easily have been otherwise.

When the Wharton School first developed a management curriculum it was to Prussia – to Germany – that they turned and deferred. And it was a Prussian, Max Weber, who first developed a systematic account of organizations in which power was both absolutely central and essentially pivotal. Yet, few people who were his contemporaries knew this. There is no evidence that many of those early-twentieth-century theorists constructing universal management and organization theory from American roots were familiar with Weber's work. Its impact was limited even in his native German, let alone in translation – most of which did not occur until after the Second World War. By that time it was too late: the institutional tracks were well rutted and Weber's concerns rattled noisily in them. Thankfully, in the interest of peace and quietude, Talcott Parsons was at hand. Through application of liberal doses of Parsons' good oil the realism of Weber's German prose was translated from domination to authority, which became the single most important conceptual cornerstone of postwar theorizing about power, as we shall see in the next chapter. By this we do not mean that this theorizing explicitly concentrated on authority, seeking to explain it; on the contrary, its importance resided in the fact that it seemingly required no explanation. The terms had become almost 'second nature' to the emerging discourse of organization theory (Bauman 1976). The assumption of authority and its identity with forms of hierarchy did not need to be explicated because it could be taken for granted. It simply was the way of the world, something natural, functional and prime.

Reading Weber

Translations from America

While Taylor was prescribing how work should be designed in America, or at least the Midvale Steel works and one or two other establishments, that continent received a visitor from Europe. Max Weber, recovering from a prolonged period of intellectual inactivity associated with deep depression, attended the World's Fair in St Louis in 1904 on the invitation of Hugo Münsterberg, a compatriot of Weber's and a follower of Taylor. We do not know what Weber saw there but it would not be surprising if there were not exhibits celebrating the achievements of systematic management, something which was not only a central interest for Münsterberg but also at the cutting edge of management innovation in 1904.

Max Weber was already a minor if not yet significant intellectual in Germany. He had recently completed his essays on the 'Protestant ethic' (Weber 1976)[1] and was soon to create most of what we now know as his writings on power and organizations in the first 20 or so years of the twentieth century, almost contemporaneously with F. W. Taylor's promulgation and defense of his program. In the period between the wars Weber's infinitely more sophisticated ideas were circulated only among a small number of scholars in Germany and barely established any sort of program at all, either in theory or in practice. These ideas received widespread reception in English only after the second of these wars, initially due to Talcott Parsons.

After a fairly conventional undergraduate education, Parsons studied at the London School of Economics and from there, at the end of 1925, he went to Heidelberg. It was in Heidelberg that he encountered the influence of Max Weber, who had lived and worked there from 1896 to 1918. Parsons first read Weber's work during this period and became a sympathetic interpreter and subsequent translator of Max Weber. Parsons was the son of an ascetic Protestant family (his father was a Congregational minister in Colorado Springs). Thus, we might surmise that Weber's essays on the Protestant ethic may have held especial interest for him, explaining why he chose these to translate into English.

Parsons became the leading 'functionalist' theorist of the 1950s, whose theory stressed the importance of consensus and a central value system for social order. Thus, not surprisingly perhaps, Weber's rugged realism, which was most evident in the centrality of *Herrschaft* or domination to his scheme of thought (see Roth, in Weber 1978: lxxxviii, noting in his introduction to *Economy and society* that the sociology of domination is the book's core), was invariably translated as if it had the qualifier of legitimacy attached to it, thus rendering it as authority, the core notion for functionalist theory. From Parsons' point of view, rendering domination as legitimate *per se* makes obvious sense, due to functionalism's general concern with stability and endurance. For Parsons, the other to authority/domination is less power/conflict than it is instability/disorder. So, from that perspective, it makes sense to equate (enduring) domination with authority. It effectively rendered power in such a way that it could be analyzed without considering conflict and confrontation between forces. While domination rests on a variable probability of obedience, power does not necessarily do this (it might involve compliance by force). Thus, domination is always to some extent legitimate while this is not necessarily true of power (it might involve violence). Hence, while some instances of power may be only episodic (where violence rules), domination has some extension; it is enduring and (more) permanent. In other words, while there might be instances of an illegitimate exercise of power, domination is implicitly both enduring and potentially legitimate. It might have made for good functionalism but it was bad translation.

In the German language, *Autorität* is rarely used to denominate a *process*; in fact, it is almost exclusively used as an *attribute* of a particular person or office. So, one does not usually 'exercise authority' (*Autorität ausüben*), as one would say in English, but one would only 'exercise power/domination' (*Macht/Herrschaft*). Hence, someone is more likely to have (possess) *Autorität* rather than to exercise (*ausüben*) it. Also, *Autorität* would be only loosely coupled to legitimacy (someone can have *Autorität* as a person, although the legitimacy of the office is in question and vice versa). So, *Autorität* is more a personal attribute that tends to accompany (if not necessarily so) the exercise of power/domination, at least in German. In English the matters are somewhat different: authority is not merely a positional attribute but can also be something that is observable in process when words and deeds deepen or cheapen the legitimacy of authority; it is not irrevocably attached to positions. While Weber's translation by Parsons emphasized a fair German interpretation it was also one which happened to correspond with the assumptions of functionalist theories. As Cohen et al. (1975a; 1975b) establish, following Gouldner's (1971) tracks, there is every need to 'de-Parsonize' Weber despite Parsons' (1975) objections to the contrary. Talcott Parsons and A. M. Henderson translated Weber's (1947) sociology of domination into a sociology of authority, thus establishing what became the dominant meta-routine in the repertoire of postwar organization and management theory.

Situating Weber

Weber is not a classical management theorist

After the English translations were available, the organization scholars who read Weber largely worked outside of contemporary German scholarship. Few, if any, knew precursors such as Nietzsche, Hegel and Marx or contemporaries such as Simmel. And, to add a further barrier to the reception of his ideas, while Weber foreshadowed a more critical scholarly approach to the analysis of organizations and economic action, in the period that had elapsed since Taylor's work was first received, a discourse on management had developed that regarded Taylor as a founding intellectual father, someone to build on, to respect, and with whom to engage rather than someone to criticize or question. When Weber's ideas were received they were normalized into the canon that this scholarship had already constituted. Weber became seen as a classical scholar of administration, someone whose concern with bureaucracy rounded out the concern with the shop floor exhibited by Taylor, and which meshed nicely with other contemporaries, such as the Frenchman Henri Fayol. The Max Weber known to most management and organization theory was therefore an exceedingly simplified caricature in which the nuance, depth, and cultural embeddedness of the original had been lost.

Weber's inscription as a part of the classical canon by management writers (Pugh 1971) added a touch of class to a rather pedestrian set of concerns. However, Weber was never a conscious part of the classical management canon in any contemporary's calculations, least of all his own. While Weber (1978) was familiar with the work of Taylor and other scientific management writers, they were not familiar with him. While Taylor proposed technologies to exert power, Weber explained them. It would be wholly incorrect to bundle Weber up as a scholar of the Classical School akin to F. W. Taylor (Pugh et al. 1971) or to situate his corpus within the narrative of formal management theories (Robbins and De Cenzo 2005). They have very little in common at all.

Weber both acknowledged the origins of modern bureaucracy in military auspices and demonstrated an awareness of Taylor's 'scientific management', but as formal theories of management were first initiated in the late nineteenth century, in a great wave of mobilization around the notion of engineering, they barely occupied the same conceptual universe as Weber. These pioneers of management argued that the applied science of engineering, if applied appropriately, would not only legitimate the manager as a new class of highly skilled employee but also justify the entire structures of control in which they were inserted. It would make these structures authoritative, for what could be a better basis for authority in the new world than the legitimacy of science (Shenhav 1999)?

Engineering rationality replaced older legitimation grounded in the Protestant ethic (Weber 1976) or ideas about the survival of the fittest, flourishing as social Darwinism from the nineteenth century (Therborn 1976). Scientific management was able to position itself as a rational and irrefutable bastion against the privileges that ownership allowed. Installing scientific management, it was claimed, would eradicate arbitrary and socially destructive domination, tame it, and make it authority. It would create a legitimate model of hierarchy and management conceived not just as the expression of a dilettante or capricious will. It was based, its protagonists said, on facts and technical analysis of the organizational situation. It was grounded in functional analysis of necessity rather than the arbitrary exercise of will by an overseer or a master. It would fit the person to the job, after the job had first been scientifically analyzed. Thus, people were to be slotted into their positions on the basis of their aptitudes and abilities, formed through whatever circumstances. Above all, the achievement of efficiency would ensure management authority and inscribe it in the ultimate value that flourished best in modernity.

Weber foresaw that ultimate values would be in inexorable decline as modernity developed, defined in terms of an increasing rationalization of the world through new institutions and a concomitant decline in beliefs in enchantment, magic and fatalism. In large part this would be because the 'calculability' contained in the disciplinary rationality of modern management techniques, such as double-entry bookkeeping, would progressively replace values. As techniques increasingly achieved what previously only great value commitments could ensure, then the necessity for these values would diminish. The future would be one in which we strive to work ceaselessly in jobs and organizations that neither serve ultimate values nor adequately fill the space left by the values they purported to replace. The outcome of this process of rationalization, Weber suggests, is the production of a new type of person, the specialist or technical expert, well represented by engineers in the twentieth century (Layton 1986). Such experts master reality by means of increasingly precise and abstract concepts. Statistics, for example, began in the nineteenth century as a form of expert codified knowledge of everyday life and death, which could inform public policy (Hacking 1991). The statistician became a paradigm of the new kind of expert, dealing with everyday things but in a way that was far removed from everyday understandings, a little like Frederick Taylor, perhaps, with his fascination for statistical data.

The understanding of the rationalization of power and domination that has been developed thus far can be used to analyze the history that early figures in management, such as Taylor, were constructing. Weber sometimes referred to the process whereby all forms of magical, mystical, traditional explanation are stripped away from the world as disenchantment. The world stripped bare by rational analysis is always open and amenable to the calculations of technical reason under the tutelage of the expert. It holds no mystery. New disciplines colonize it and Taylor evidently promulgated one such new discipline. However, he did not produce a new authority, something that was uncontested. In Nietszche's terms, he found that the will to power he proposed was widely opposed by resistance.

While Taylor was an unabashed utilitarian, the philosophical auspices of Max Weber were very different indeed. He was no Benthamite reformer intent on discovering the one best way to be efficient but a scholar schooled in the classical German traditions of Kant and Hegel. As such he provided the vocabulary and grammar for the analysis of power, one that, due to translation, became increasingly available from 1947 onwards. But knowledge had already been too systematized, literally. The system and rationality were the hallmarks of the new management thinking, one from which Weber's grammar of power and domination had been formally expunged in favor of authority by Parsons and Henderson's translation of Weber (1947). Being expunged, power would now largely be treated as marginal (Hardy and Clegg 1996).

Weber's major interest was in the development of the great world civilizations. In this sense, he took up the themes of G. W. F. Hegel's (1998) philosophy of history, especially the specific and peculiar role of rationalism in the development of Western culture. Weber was also concerned with the debate concerning science and history, between interpretive understanding and causal explanation. Weber felt that historical sociology should be concerned with both individuality and generality (Ritzer 1992: 114).

The philosopher who dominated German philosophical thought during Weber's life was Immanuel Kant, who lived from 1724 to 1804. Kant argued that the methods of the natural sciences as he understood them at that time provided indubitable knowledge about the external phenomenal world as we experience it through our senses. Kant argued that empirical analysis and moral judgment were two separate systems. Weber believed that while sociology must be concerned with empirical analysis of society and history, the method of sociology would have to be different from that of the natural sciences, because it dealt with the ideational, and thus moral, world. It meant examining social action within a context of social interaction, not just viewing people as objects driven by impersonal forces. For Weber, the person could not be reduced to the utilitarian calculating machine that Taylor conjured up.

Along with this emphasis on universal cultural history, Weber's detailed training as a legal and economic historian led him to reject the overly simplistic formulas of economic base and corresponding cultural superstructure that were so often used to account for cultural development in Marxist analysis. Weber, given his legal training, sought to generalize across cases and developed the method of ideal types to do this. Amongst his enquiries were a series of ruminations on organizations, on power, authority and domination. Unlike Taylor, Weber had an explicit concern with issues of power and domination, and a particular interest in their organization (Clegg 1975).

Weber's obscurity

Parsons was somewhat unusual in having read Weber when he did, shortly after Weber's death. The national and international reception of Weber's work during his lifetime was muted. What distinction he enjoyed came almost exclusively from his work on the Protestant ethic (1976) and the printed versions of the lectures on *Wissenschaft als Beruf* (1919a/1948) and *Politik als Beruf* (1919b/1948). After Weber's death from influenza in 1920, his widow, Marianne Weber, extended awareness of his work through her success in bringing *Gesammelte politische Schriften* (Weber 1921), *Gesammelte Aufsätze zur Wissenschaftslehre* (Weber 1922a), *Gesammelte Aufsätze zur Sozial- und Wirtschaftsgeschichte* (Weber 1924a) and *Gesammelte Aufsätze zur Soziologie und Sozialpolitik* (Weber 1924b) to fruition, but none of these succeeded in making Weber well known. Even Weber's (1922b) epic *Wirtschaft und Gesellschaft* was not widely distributed. As Kaesler (2004) observes, in a most instructive essay addressing the critical reception of Weber's *oeuvre*, fewer than 2,000 copies of this text were sold between its initial publication and its translation into English in 1947.

Weber was not well known outside of certain select circles of scholarship, such as Parsons' (1937) recognition of him as a founder of the theory of social action and Schutz's (1967) recognition of the centrality of his account of social action as an appropriate point of departure for a phenomenological sociology. In Germany he was perhaps better known as an economist rather than a sociologist concerned with social relations in antiquity and modernity (Swedberg 1998).

He was not much read by Anglophone management theorists until after the Second World War, when his works were widely translated into English (Weber 1930; 1946; 1947; 1949; 1954; 1962; 1965; 1970; 1974; 1976; 1978). However, in a measure of the limited distribution that still pertains, in 1981 Mohr Siebeck (a German editorial house in Tübingen) announced the publication of an edition of the full works of Weber in 34 volumes with approximately 21,000 pages. Such data give us an idea of the still limited knowledge of Weber's work in English at the time that his ideas were being introduced into the language.

In some respects, even if the founders of modern management theory had known something about Weber, it is doubtful that they would have been able to make much of him. For one thing, despite being lauded in some (mistaken) quarters as a founder of value-free science, he did not represent himself as anything other than an engaged scholar. The nature of his engagements with certain scholarly and liberal imperatives that were closely related to national values were pre-eminent (see Weber's 1946 two essays on 'vocation') and are barely explicable to postwar American concerns. His attitude to work, as a vocation, did not resonate with the values of Taylor's pragmatism, which saw work as little more than a set of efficient tasks sequentially stitched together.

Weber was rather less a classical management theorist and rather more a student of culture; indeed he practiced what today we might call 'cultural studies'. He concentrated on subjectivity, the relation of culture to the individual, and its historical genealogy. His concerns were light years away from the more pragmatic interests of Taylor and his followers. For instance, Weber did not use the term 'efficiency', preferring instead to write about technical rationality and the formally most rational mode of political domination. Today, efficiency is not only taken for granted as a pre-eminent value but is also bundled up with other cultural values such as the pursuit of 'innovation' or 'profit'.

Weber (1978) noted that Taylor's scientific management hastened the rationalization of the world. Taylor's innovation was to create a practice of domination in which the employee became oriented towards a new external disciplinary regime. Not only did they orient externally; they also learnt a rationalized self-discipline. Taylor's interventions represented a historical 'switching point', a moment when a new rationalized regime of work became possible. For Weber, rationalization meant the ordering of beliefs and action according to specific criteria. While Taylor's practice of rationalization dwelt on the corporeal dimension, with its political economy of the body, Weber's account of contemporary rationalization focused more on the imposition of bureaucratic routines on intellectual labor (Berdayes 2002: 37). However, these forms of rationalization, which stressed the relation of means and ends, were not the only ways of being rational.

Weber's theory

Rationality

Weber listed four forms of social action based upon the principle of rationalization. They are, first, *Zweckrationalität*, making decisions according to planned results. This is a form of decision making in which the social actor chooses both the means and the ends of action. In bureaucracy, one effect of this form of rationality is to concentrate control in the hands of managerial elites and legitimate this power on the basis of procedural rules, because they define the ends and police the means. Thus, as Berdayes suggests, 'even as it becomes more uniform and pervasive throughout an organization, power is depersonalized, so much so that managerial personnel themselves become subject to impersonal bureaucratic control' (2002: 38).

Second, there is *Wertrationalität*, where one makes decisions according to an absolute value or belief, such as a religious or other ideological commitment, where there is a 'self conscious formulation of the ultimate values governing the actor and the consistently planned orientation of its detailed course to these values' (Weber 1978: 21). In this form of decision making, the actor chooses only the means of his actions because the ends are predestined. Now, it might seem, at first glance, that from the perspective of *Zweckrationalität* action, value rationality will always appear irrational, if only because *Wertrationalität* orients action to a chosen value or end, without regard for consequences. However, for one whose sense of calling in their belief in *Zweckrationalität* is unassailable, the inimicality disappears.

Means–ends calculation as a form of life can become an ultimate value; think, for instance, of the reliance of business on sophisticated legal advice concerning the probabilities of adverse action being contingent on a chosen course of action. A faith in the reasoning that creates such probabilistic advice represents an ultimate value. It would be faith in an ultimate value of formal rationality, the pursuit of the most efficient and technically correct, calculable, impersonal, and substantively indifferent choice of means guiding any social action. Weber seems to come close to this with his idea that formal rationality was, in his time, increasingly becoming characterized by abstraction, impersonality and quantification, even to the extent of seeking to quantify that which seems essentially unquantifiable (Gronow 1988).

Third, there is emotive rationality, where decisions are made in terms of specific emotional states of the action, which is usually interpreted in terms of affectual action. Finally, there is traditional rationality, when people make decisions according to an orientation to a specific tradition, producing traditional action. The forms of rational behavior most common to modernity are *Zweckrationalität* and *Wertrationalität*, but Weber claimed that industrial civilization produces a totally new form of formal rationality, which George Ritzer (1993) defines in terms of the rational search by some people for the optimum means to a given end, where that search is shaped by rules, regulations, and larger social structures.

The will to power

The institutionalization of formal rationality depends on a will to power becoming material. Weber saw relations of power (for which he employed a number of different concepts) as the absolutely central aspect of all organized social life, and politics as the expression of resistance to the imposition of their will. Two central Weberian categories, in the original German, were *Macht* and *Herrschaft*.

The precise translation of these terms is contested. Initially, they entered into usage as 'power' and 'authority', respectively. While there is little controversy surrounding the translation of *Macht* as 'power' (as an active verb rather than a passive noun, although, it should be noted, that 'might' is seen by some scholars as a more appropriate translation), there is considerable dissent surrounding the translation of *Herrschaft* as 'authority' that was initiated by Parsons and Henderson in their edition of *The theory of social and economic organization* (Weber 1947).

Later translators do not follow this lead but instead translate *Herrschaft* either as 'rule' or as 'domination', depending on the context of translation. For one thing, it is necessary in order to recover some sense of the indebtedness that Weber had to German philosophical and literary figures, such as Nietzsche and Goethe (Kent 1983; on the Nietzsche connections see Fleischmann 1964; Eden 1983; Schroeder 1987; Sica 1988; Hennis 1988; for the most obvious connection to Goethe see the new edition of his *Elective affinities*, 2005).

Weber (1978) introduces *Macht* and *Herrschaft* as fundamental concepts of interpretive sociology, and he does so after a discussion of social relationships and prior to a discussion of social action. It is evident that both concepts are sociologically defined as relational concepts. To say that they are sociologically defined is to note only that they are framed within the context of a science 'concerning itself with interpretive understanding of social action in order to arrive at a causal explanation of its course and consequences' (1978: 4). A causal explanation that is adequate entails both understanding (*Verstehen*) and explanation (*Erklärung*). The former is an essentially interpretive activity, premised on the relation between a specific case and a general context of understanding within which it can be framed, as a type. The latter entails that 'there is a probability, which in the rare case can be numerically stated but is always in some sense calculable, that a given observable event (overt or subjective) will be followed or accompanied by another event' (1978: 11–12). It is such probabilities that define social relationships as an expectation of the continuity of a meaningful course of action (1978: 27).

Weber defined power in various but related ways in his writings, but his most concise definition is that power is 'the possibility of imposing one's will upon the behavior of other persons' (1954: 324), and, as he often added, especially where this will is resisted by those over whom it is exercised, regardless of the basis on which the probability of obedience rested (1978: 53). We may recognize a debt to Nietzsche's (1973) 'will to power' (Schroeder 1987) in the centrality of the notion of will to his conception of power.

Weber's domination and Parsons' authority

Weber introduced the term *Herrschaft* 'as the probability that a command with a given specific content will be obeyed by a given group of persons' (1978: 53). Where obedience occurs, we have an example of legitimate *Herrschaft*, which Parsons and Henderson appropriately translate as 'authority'. The concept of legitimate

Herrschaft refers to legitimate, non-coercive rule. Thus, authority is a relationship of legitimate rule, where the meaningfulness of the social relation rests on assumptions accepted without imposition by all parties to that relationship.

Relations of both power and legitimate rule must occur within specific spheres. In organizations this is the structure of dominancy, an order 'regarded by the actor as in some way obligatory or exemplary' governing the organization (1978: 31). In a later parlance, the structure of dominancy might be thought of as an obligatory passage point (Clegg 1989), something that is decisive in framing how a phenomenon unfolds.

> Without exception every sphere of social action is profoundly influenced by structures of dominancy. In a great number of cases the emergence of a rational association from amorphous social action has been due to domination and the way in which it has been exercised. Even where this is not the case, the structure of dominancy and its unfolding is decisive in determining the form of social action and its orientation towards a 'goal'. Indeed, domination has played the decisive role in the economically most important social structures of the past and present. Viz, the manor on the one hand, and the large scale capitalistic enterprise on the other. (Weber 1978: 941)

The formal structures of dominancy will be experienced as differing substantive types of rule, within which it is probable that there will be willing obedience. Any bureaucracy is an example of a structure of dominancy, although they might vary in their substantive particulars; should it be the case that values infuse its members, binding them with commitments to its rule, then the structure of dominancy may be transformed into a structure of authority, perhaps where the rule is infused with an ultimate value or is taken for granted and accepted as a legally rational basis for constraining action.

In modern organizations, Weber argues, formal rationality would be best institutionalized, and domination most complete, when rationality is accepted as legitimate in its own terms. Such a state of affairs would be what Weber defined as 'authority'. Thus, authority is legitimated domination, one leading to the other. They are not qualitatively different from each other. The differences between them are ones of degree, not of kind. In this regard power and authority are opposed to violence as a mode of dominance, and are themselves specific forms of dominance.

Simmel (1971), Weber's intellectual peer, argued that domination is dialectically related to freedom rather than violence, although coercion, especially when it is institutionalized, is important because of its form; it keeps people together. In its institutionalized form, such as the labor market, coercion (in this case to work rather than be idle) serves social ordering. For Weber, social relations of power often involve coercion when dominance is not legitimated and social action that seeks to intervene in social relations is enacted, whether proactively or reactively as resistance. To speak of authority, however, presumes that legitimacy is present.

In history, domination rarely is as one-dimensional as the Weberian ideal type deliberately represents it to provide an accentuated and heightened model of a real phenomenon to aid its recognition and analysis in empirical cases. For example, as Bendix (1977) notes following Weber (1954), fully consistent charismatic leadership is inimical to both rules and tradition, but disciples who wish not to see their discipleship lose meaning seek to routinize that charisma, usually through instilling either a system of lineage based on sanguinity or rule by rules. The charisma is reconstituted on another basis of rule.

Somewhat confusingly, although Weber defines four types of rationality he only defines three types of domination, and it is not entirely clear what the relation is between them. It is evident that *Zweckrationalität* corresponds pretty closely to rational-legal domination, and that traditional rationality corresponds to traditional domination; while his third type, charismatic domination, where obedience is given because of a belief in the extraordinary grace and powers of the person deferred to, seems close to the type of emotive rationality. The absence of a specific category for *Wertrationalität* might suggest that as a category it is almost indivisible from the others. For instance, one could make decisions according to an absolute value or belief, such as a religious or other ideological commitment that is traditional, or they could be based on a belief that the absolute value is manifest in a particular charismatic individual. Or, it might suggest that Weber thought that value-based authority would not be of significance in the modern world. Like all sociologists of his time, he underestimated nationalism and religious fundamentalism, which are paradigmatic instances of this type of authority (see Haugaard 2002b).

There is another possibility related to the missing value-based rationality: one could imagine the categories of *Wertrationalität* and *Zweckrationalität* becoming fused and intertwined, in a situation where rational-legal authority is so institutionalized that obedience to it becomes an absolute commitment or, as Weber (1947) termed it, a 'vocation'. On such occasions, as Weber stated, 'The fate of an epoch which has eaten of the tree of knowledge is that it must know that we cannot learn the meaning of the world from the results of its analysis, be it ever so perfect; it must rather be in a position to create this meaning itself' (1949: 57). Where *Wertrational* meaning surrounds, embeds and saturates the meaning of organization and its work as a call to duty, an obligation to some sense of a greater purpose than the nature of just doing the work itself, then this will surely be the case. Value-rational action, or *Wertrationalität*, is the 'self-conscious formulation of the ultimate values governing the actor and the consistently planned orientation of its detailed course to these values'. From the perspective of *Zweckrationalität*, value-rational action will always appear irrational, since *Wertrationalität* orients action to a chosen value or end, without regard for consequences.

Although Weber is commonly construed as a theorist of authority, the three types of what he refers to as *Herrschaft* are, in fact, types of domination. Authority is a social relation that stands at the outer limits of a more probable range of social relations of domination. These relations constitute the normalcy of organization – where there is a probability of resistance – which only shades into authority when, for reasons of tradition, charisma, *Zweckrationalität* or *Wertrationalität*, the subject owes an allegiance that enables them to legitimate their subjection to an external source of domination. It should be evident that authority derives its legitimacy from the ruled, not those ruling. Hence, organizational politics, premised on the necessity of acts of power by putative authorities to counter resistance to their imposition of their will, is something to be expected as normal. It will usually be the case that, despite charisma, tradition, discipline or vocation, situations ensue where there is resistance by some to the will of some other.

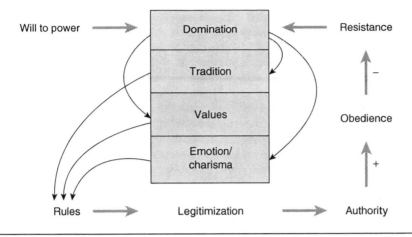

Figure 4.1   The Weberian view of resistance as something to overcome

As we see in Figure 4.1, at the center of Weber's conception is the notion of the individual having a will to power that seeks to overcome resistance through domination, whether though values, emotions, tradition or rules. However, if any of these are to endure then they must eventually be routinized through rule by rules, as a more stable and authoritative form of domination. Rule by rules offers the prospect of legitimization – the alchemy that turns domination into authority and, through obedience, minimizes resistance.

Domination and organization

Domination and organization are inescapably mutually implicated. Domination requires organization – concerted action by a body of people employed as staff – to execute commands; and, conversely, all organization requires domination in that the power of command over the staff must be vested in an individual or a group of individuals, in an organization of any scale. Hence arises the necessity of a division of labor.

What is most remarkable about any organization is the way that it shapes superordinate goals that others orient to; in this way, these others will do things that they would not otherwise do and thus will be subject to power. Their social action is constrained and enabled by the manifest will or command of the ruler, rulers, or rules. These are meant to influence the conduct of the rule; that is what they are designed for. Whether or not the rules achieve their purpose is not something to take for granted; the effective legitimacy of rule should never be assumed but is always an empirical matter. Should the rule(r)s positively influence the social action that occurs within the context of organizationally enabled action, it will only be so to the extent that those ruled make the content of the command – its will to power – the maxim of their conduct for its own sake. Of course, the rulers can tilt the probability in their favor by acculturating others to the habitual obedience of commands; they can constitute the others as subjects with a personal interest in seeing the existing domination continue because they derive benefits from it, which was the philosophy behind Taylor's advocacy of piece-rates; they can hold out the promise of the pleasures of future rule through participation in domination to the subaltern ranks by dividing some elements of the exercise of functions among them; and they always hold a power of dismissal should these incentives fail.

The power of command can exist irrespective of the sense of duty to obey; when that duty is present then the command may be felt as a legitimate obligation to an authority; with a sense of duty, power is transformed into authority, where the legitimacy of rule and rules is accepted. Where power is bereft of that sense of duty it shades into domination, defined as the non-legitimate imposition of will. It should be evident that the judgment of the legitimacy or otherwise of rule – whether it is authority – is a prerogative not of the rulers but of the putatively ruled. It is for this reason that power, as a social relation, will be inherently dynamic. While claims as to power's efficacy are made each time that an organizational action is enacted through command (whether habitual, written, spoken, ruled, or construed in any other way whatsoever) there is always the probability that the command will be met with resistance, either because it is not construed as being legitimate in the context in which it is interpreted by those subject to it or, which amounts to the same thing, to resist it fits better with another more highly valued course of action than obedience to rule.

Command may be interpreted quite flexibly. Organizations seek to replace the necessity of frequent interventions into the body politic through a discipline of power that institutionalizes the domination of formal rationality; that is, the probability that a command with a given specific content will be obeyed (Weber 1978: 53). Now it is important not to interpret 'command' too literally. A command is not simply something that is necessarily expressed vocally, as in 'I command you to cease that at once.' A command also encompasses the orders that are received in writing or through other forms of representation, as well as the generalized duties associated with a particular office. Let a historical example suffice to make the point.

King Henry II of England appointed his friend Thomas à Becket as the Archbishop of Canterbury, the head of the Catholic Church in England. However, Becket proved recalcitrant to his will with respect to ecclesiastical reform, leading to a long dispute between King and Archbishop. In October 1164 Henry had Becket condemned on trumped-up charges of contempt of court over a land dispute in Pagham, and ruled that the Archbishop should forfeit all his goods. Becket was summoned to attend a Council at Northampton, where, at morning mass, he pitted the rule of the Church against the rule of the Monarch, when he said 'Princes also sit and speak against me; but thy servant, Lord, is occupied in thy statutes', and entered the Council bearing his archiepiscopal cross of office. Becket maintained that the Council had no right to judge him, as a servant of God. Nonetheless, to escape its judgment he fled to exile in France.

The dispute dragged on for the next six years, despite frequent attempts at intermediation between the two powerful rulers, one of Church, the other of state. Finally, on May 24, 1170, the Archbishop of York crowned Henry II's son, Henry the Younger, as successor at Canterbury. Becket, of course, as the head of the Church, took this as a grave snub, and on July 22, 1170, the King and the

Archbishop agreed to a compromise that allowed Becket to come home from his French exile in Fréteval and recrown Henry the Younger in a second ceremony. However, the reconciliation was hardly consummated. Henry the Younger refused to meet Becket when he arrived at Windsor.

Becket's authority was now severely compromised. He attempted to reassert it through an act of power, excommunicating his old ecclesiastical enemies, including the Archbishop of York who had done the crowning. When this news was brought to him in his Christmas court at Bures in Normandy, Henry exploded and is said to have uttered the words, 'who will rid me of this troublesome priest?' The result, of course, was that Henry's knights took this as a royal command and killed Becket in Canterbury Cathedral.

A question, perhaps rhetorical, when uttered by a ruler, can be interpreted as a command because command encapsulates the claims to authority of an office. That obedience to it will always be probabilistic suggests that resistance to power – politics – is a normal part of the rationalization process, and thus of organizations. In this case, Henry was unable to exercise authority over Becket; Becket could counter all attempts on his part to do so by claiming to serve the 'honor of my God', as his ultimate value. Nor could he assert his domination over him as Becket claimed that his dominion was the rule of the Church not the rule of the state, and that the two were indubitably separate, with the Lords Spiritual owing a greater allegiance to their ultimate ruler, God, through the will to power manifested in His servant, the Archbishop, than to their temporal ruler.

The only card that Henry could have played in this complex political game was blocked. He could have won the Pope to his cause – in fact he even threatened to support the Holy Roman Emperor's anti-pope if Pope Alexander III did not decide in his favor – but the Pope was unlikely to settle a dispute on terms that, ultimately, weakened his authority and that of the God in whose name he ruled.

The discipline of organization

Although Weber's interests were broad and many, for the contemporary organization and management theorist the most important types of power discussed by Weber derive from a constellation of interests that develops on a formally free market and from established authority that allocates the right to command and the duty to obey (Weber 1954: 291). According to Weber the modern world increasingly strips social actors of their ability to freely choose the means and ends of their actions, particularly as it organizes through bureaucracy. In modernity institutions rationalize and organize affairs, cutting down on individual choices, replacing them with standardized procedures and rules. Rational calculation becomes a monstrous discipline. Everything and everyone seemingly had to be put through a calculus, irrespective of other values or pleasures. It was a necessary and unavoidable feature of organizing in the modern world.

Weber greatly admired the achievements of bureaucracy, as he saw them. In many respects these achievements were quite limited. Twentieth-century bureaucracy (that specifically modern form of organization that Weber saw) never achieved its full realization. We are confronting at the beginning of the twenty-first century its full realization in what has been named paradoxically 'post-bureaucracy', a more flexible and subtle form of organization that embodies bureaucracy in technological devices such as computers, cell phones, PDAs, etc. In other words, Weber saw an initial version of bureaucracy but not its full realization in modernity.

Weber was pessimistic about the long-term impact of bureaucracy. On the one hand, bureaucracies would free people from arbitrary rule by powerful patrimonial leaders, those who personally owned the instruments and offices of rule. They would do this because they were based on rational legality as the rule of law contained in the files that defined practice in the bureau. On the other hand, they would create an 'iron cage of bondage' (or more literally, as translated directly from the original German, a house of hardened steel). The frame was fashioned from the 'care for external goods' (1976: 181), by which Weber meant that if these goods were to come into one's grasp in a market economy then one could gain them only by mortgaging one's life to a career in a hierarchy of offices that interlocked and intermeshed, through whose intricacies one might seek to move, with the best hope for one's future being that one would shift from being a small cog in the machine to one that was slightly bigger, in a slow but steady progression.

The iron cage would be fabricated increasingly from the materialization of abstract nouns such as calculability, predictability, and control, to which one must bend one's will. Thus, power concerned less the direct imposition of another's will on one and more the ways in which the conditions of one's existence were increasingly inscribed in a rationalized frame which one's will had to accommodate as a part of its assent to normalcy. Weber's example is bureaucracy, characterized by rules and regulations, hierarchy of authority, careers, and specialization of roles. The bureaucracy operates in a predictable manner, seeks to quantify, and emphasizes control over people and products through standardized and formalized routines, such as those that Taylor advocated. Recast this way, Taylor had a very specific role to play, materializing the will to power.

If power were never resisted there would be no politics. For Weber, economic action based on the best technically possible practice of quantitative calculation or accounting would be the most formally rational display of the form of rationality. By contrast, substantive rationality would denote concepts of goal-oriented action that will vary according to context and hence be indivisible from the real substance of specific settings. The second chapter of Max Weber's (1978) *Economy and society* deals with the relationship between formal and substantive rationality (see the excellent account of the different conceptions of rationality in Kalberg 1980), where substantive rationality is the basis from which resistance springs as a menace to power, at least where it entails a project for humanity instead of a project for private individuals.

Where an individual has so internalized commitment to a rational institution, such as the civil service, or science, or academia, that the commitment shapes their dispositions in such a way that their will knows little or no resistance to its formal rationality, then this represents obedience to an institutionalized will to power. Power, at its most powerful, is a relation that institutes itself in the psyche of the individual. Simmel explored this when he examined how personality accommodates to the requirements of contemporary urban environments, emphasizing that punctuality, calculability and exactness become part of modern personalities to the exclusion of 'those irrational, instinctive, sovereign traits and impulses which aim at determining the mode of life from within' (1964: 413).

Increasing self-discipline, meshing with intensified bureaucratization, rationalization and individualization, marked modernity in the social world. External constraint (sovereign power, traditional power) increasingly is replaced by internalization of constraint (disciplinary power, rational domination), assisted by the new technologies of power that figures such as Taylor were developing. As Robert van Krieken puts it, 'being modern means being disciplined, by the state [and other organizational forms], by each other and by ourselves; that the soul, both one's own and that of others, became organized into the self, an object of reflection and analysis, and, above all, transformable in the service of ideals such as productivity, virtue and strength' (1990: 353). More recent writers such as Elias (1982) and Foucault (1977) are wholly in accord with Simmel (1971) and Weber (1978) in these respects.

The modern, rationalized person was increasingly disciplined in the discourse on power that Simmel and Weber jointly orchestrated. Simmel also saw domination as in part a function of the symbolic content of widely held ideas embedded in everyday practices of life and discourse. These are conceptualized as 'precepts', a term derived from the Latin *praeceptum*, meaning instruction, tutelage, injunction, or command. The relevance to Taylorism thus becomes evident as a specific program of instruction and tutelage in domination, in the making of certain precepts obligatory and exemplary, of framing a wholly rationalized way of organizational life. It prepares the social and cultural foundations of a domination already secured economically by relations of production, ownership and control. As Simmel puts it, one becomes 'habituated' to the 'compulsory character' of these precepts 'until the cruder and subtler means of compulsion are no longer necessary' – indeed, until one's 'nature' is so 'formed or reformed' by these precepts that one 'acts ... as if on impulse' (1971: 119). When this occurs:

> [T]he individual represents society to himself. The external confrontation, with its suppressions, liberations, changing accents, has become an interplay between his social impulses, in the stricter sense of the word; and both are included by the ego in the larger sense ... At a certain higher stage of morality, the motivation of action lies no longer in a real-human, even though super-individual power; at this stage, the spring of moral necessities flows beyond the contrast between individual and totality. For, as little as these necessities derive from society, as little do they derive from the singular reality of individual life. In the free conscience of the actor, in individual reason, they only have their bearer, the locus of their efficacy. Their power of obligation stems from these necessities themselves, from their inner, super-personal validity, from an objective identity which we must recognize whether or not we want to ... The content, however, which fills these forms is (not necessarily but often) the societal requirement. But this requirement no longer operates by means of its social impetus, as it were, but rather as if it had undergone a metempsychosis into a norm which must be satisfied for its own sake, not for my sake nor for yours. (1971: 11)

The individual in a situation of formal domination increasingly comes to be subordinated to 'objective principles' which they experience as a 'concrete object' whose necessity takes the form of a 'social requirement ... which must be satisfied for its own sake'. Foucault (1977) did not put it better or clearer.

Conclusion

Weber and Simmel provide a sophisticated set of terms, an analytical frame, and a family of concepts for addressing power in organizations. Chief amongst these concepts are power, domination and authority. These are necessary – but not sufficient – terms. The intention, in contrast with Taylor and other management practitioners, was to explain power rather than to further its operation.

Given its genesis one might have expected that postwar organization theorists would have latched on to the Weberian corpus, maybe added some Simmel, and gone out and addressed the types of organizational power that had conquered the twentieth century. Oddly, few chose to. Had they done so, then a dominant ortho-doxy would have emerged that made the practical accomplishment of both author-ity and obedience as meta-routines analytically problematic. Instead, what postwar theorists saw was conditioned by what they had learnt from the previous genera-tions of thinkers, in terms of the need to integrate, conceptually, the informal and the formal organization, and to concentrate on issues of efficiency. The legacy of Taylor's and Fayol's concern with organizational design and Mayo's and Barnard's concern with consciousness and culture was to be integrated. Parsons, that col-league at Harvard of the great biological theorist of the system, L. J. Henderson, had developed the precise terms with which they could be so integrated, in his transla-tion of systems theory into a theory of the social system, a conception that was shortly to become metonymic to the whole discourse of organization theory.

Parsons was a great social theorist. Strangely, while the notion of system rapidly achieved dominance, there was little resonance from two other of his great works of translation, both of which had a bearing on power. One was, of course, *The theory of social and economic organization* (Weber 1947), which we have considered in this chapter. The other was his translation of the concept of power into a lead-ing role as the positive force that animated the social system just as money moved the economic system, which we will investigate in Chapter 7. In the next chapter we shall track the development of what management theory and organization theory were to constitute as power in organizations. We shall see that, despite Weberian citations, it ended up being less a source of enlightenment than one of opacity.

Note

1   After some consideration, we decided not to cite the original publication date of Weber's work, for a number of reasons. As we will argue, matters of translation are important, so the editions rather than the original date of publication are the key datum. Moreover, given the long lags in the English translation of most of Weber's works from the time of their composition, the origi-nal date of English publication is hardly a good guide to the period of their composition, which in many cases involved various posthumous editors, starting with Marianne Weber, his widow, as the reader shall see shortly.

 5   The Rational System and
                        Its Irrational Other

Chapter outline

In this chapter we will:

- Establish how the concept of efficiency and the social system became established in organization theory.
- Elaborate Parsons' framing of organization theory in terms of a systems metaphor.
- Show how the concept of power was radically decoupled from that of efficiency and how power was marginalized as deviance, the other to authority, related to uncertainty.
- Elaborate the alternative vision for the analysis of organizations that was presented in Goffman's institutional theory.
- Argue that the concentration of systems views of power on a conception of it as something embedded at the subunit level led to a lack of questioning of the relation between power and hierarchy, and do such questioning.

Introduction

In the previous chapter we saw how Weber's ideas about power, which were embedded in a conception of domination, were translated as really having been about authority, a term already secured in organization theory through the earlier work of founding fathers such as Chester Barnard, and a term that seemed far less questioning and problematic than the notion of domination.

Thompson (1956a) contributed an important editorial to the inaugural volume of the *Administrative Science Quarterly*, which in many ways set the tracks for much subsequent development in calling for management knowledge to be built by identifying unambiguous, basic principles, which transcended specific contexts. For this exercise in decontextualization, systems theory was perfect, and Parsons (1956) was invited to contribute essays on organizations as systems to the first volume. Thus, at the birth of the journal which is seen in the US as one of the, if not the, leading outlets for scholarship and research on organizations, *Administrative Science Quarterly,* Parsons turned his functionalist conception of the social system to analysis of organizations. He defined 'primacy of orientation to the attainment of a specific goal' as the 'defining characteristic of an organization which distinguishes it from other types of social systems' (1956: 63). Now, what is interesting about this definition is that it assumes that goal orientation is authoritatively given rather than something that is empirically problematic. One of the reasons why Parsons (1956) may have held this view has to do with his peculiar interpretation of Weber.

Although Parsons' invitation to systems theory was taken up with alacrity, on the whole, his earlier invitations to Weber and his later, sophisticated, reading of power were not to be as widely entertained. When early contributions to the *Administrative Science Quarterly* discussed Weber it was in the context of his concerns with 'power, conflict, authority, and domination within organizations as well as the effect of broader social structures on organizational life ... core Weberian issues [which] became more peripheral to organizational theory in the 1970s and 1980s with the ascendancy of the organization – environment tradition' (Lounsbury and Carberry 2004: 4–5). While Weber was referred to as a theorist of bureaucracy in the 1950s and 1960s, even up to the 1970s, since that time 'current researchers rarely cite Weber, and if they do, it is more often than not a mere ceremonial nod ... Much contemporary organizational research completely ignores Weber, and his intermittent cameo appearances suggest that his work has dramatically diminished in status' (2004: 3, 5).

As focus switched to the organization and the environment in organization theory, its key meta-terms increasingly coalesced around the notion of efficiency. Efficiency had a long career, as we have seen. It was the point of application for the earliest programmatic practices of power; now its engineering roots were to be joined by the very latest terms in the engineer's conceptual toolbox, which was the notion of system. Who better to do this and to make power systematic other than Talcott Parsons?[1]

Systemizing the world

First, the word: Vilfredo Pareto and Talcott Parsons

It was the emergence of a common discourse of the organization as a social system that settled matters in favor of efficiency rather than a discussion of domination. The seminal figure in this conception was L. J. Henderson at Harvard, the central figure in the Pareto Circle, and the director of the Fatigue Laboratory, whose work at Hawthorne was an initial occasion for Mayo (1933) to address some human problems of industrial civilization.

Pareto was an Italian who held an economics chair at the University of Lausanne in Switzerland, and, at a time when the disciplinary boundaries had not firmed as much as they were to do subsequently, also contributed to sociology as the author of *The mind and society* (1935), the translation of his *Trattato di sociologia generale* (1916). The major conceptual innovation that he contributed was that social action could be neatly reduced to residues and derivations. People act on the basis of non-logical sentiments (residues) and invent justifications for them afterwards (derivations). It is the residues that comprise the real underlying problem, the particular cause of the squabbles that lead to the 'circulation of elites', and the appropriate subject matter for social science scholarship. Residues are rooted in the basic aspirations and drives of people and these are not necessarily coherent or logical.

Two types of residue are of particular importance: first, those associated with rule by guile, whose bearers are calculating, materialistic and innovating; second, those that rule by force and are more bureaucratic, idealistic and conservative. Societies tended to oscillate between rule by the two types, Pareto argues. There would be a tendency to equilibrium when the two types of residue were balanced in the governing elites. Because elites are circulatory, balance can be achieved but not guaranteed. On occasion, when the balance is too uneven, another set of contenders will replace the current elite. If there are too many guileful types in the governing elites, this means that the 'lions', the violent conservative types, will be in the lower echelons, itching to take and capable of taking power when the cunning 'foxes' finally make a mess of things by being too cunning and corrupt. If the governing elite is composed mostly of the violent conservative types, then it will fall into a bureaucratic, inefficient, and reactionary muddle, easy prey for calculating upwardly mobile guileful types, a theory that he illustrated with numerous classical, historical and contemporary illustrations.

His economic ideas, expressed in the *Manual of political economy* (1971), were no less influential. He regarded individual preferences as the fundament of economics, not utilities. A utility was simply a way of rendering the underlying fundamental preference order. One of his most important ideas, for students of power as well as of economics, was the idea of Pareto optimality. Society enjoys maximum ophelimity (a non-utilitarian term that Pareto coined to mean economic satisfaction) when making someone else worse off makes no one better off. It introduces a non-zero-sum conception of positive power, one that influenced Talcott Parsons (1964).

Pareto was at the heart of Parsons' great works that dominated mid-twentieth-century sociology. Pareto was instituted as one of the founders of sociology in *The structure of social action* (Parsons 1937) and Pareto dominated *The social system* (Parsons 1950), a project that had enormous influence on the unfolding of studies of organization and the placement of power within them. The acknowledgement of Pareto's centrality is one of the first things one reads in the latter book:

> The title, *The Social System*, goes back, more than to any other source, to the insistence of the late Professor L. J. Henderson on the extreme importance of the concept of system in scientific theory, and his clear realization that the attempt to delineate the social system as a system was the most important contribution of Pareto's great work. This book therefore is an attempt to carry out Pareto's intuition. (1950: vii)

Institutionalizing the organization as a social system

Parsons (1950) viewed organizations as systems in their own right, as did Roethlisberger and Dickson (1939: 551–68), who also developed a clear delimitation of the goals of the industrial system seen in terms of internal and external equilibrium (see also Barnard 1938). Indeed, in many ways Barnard saw these goals as sharp examples of social system characteristics rather than other, more amorphous, entities. Usually, he believed, the identification of organizational goals is relatively unproblematic. Moreover, they usually have well-defined hierarchies of relations of authority, often spelled out in organization charts. The services that goals perform are often stated as part of the organization's mission statement. Hence, in an open systems perspective, organizations seem to be a suitable object for analysis.

'Organizations' is not a common ordinary language category. The generic concept of organization is *ambiguous* because it refers to a *non-existent reality* that has been synthesized in an abstract concept.[2] It allows substitution for other terms, such as 'corporation', 'monopoly' or 'bureaucracy'. These words, because of their association with the power of money and state actions, or more precisely with the consequences that private accumulation and unchecked state intervention have for employment and citizens' welfare, became strongly questioned by some important sectors of society in the postwar era. Corporations were seen as having been responsible for the Depression, while state bureaucracies were seen to have been responsible in both Japan and Germany for the war. Neither the corporation nor the bureaucracy seemed especially liberal or neutral categories. The nascent discipline of organization studies had to be careful not to appear as a servant to power, or to employ terms that would undoubtedly compromise its declared objectivity and neutrality. Theoretical asepsis was an indispensable condition for combating any suspicions that could have brought into question the scientific nature of this knowledge, serving the interests of increased productivity and combating the human problem at the core of organized employment relations – that seemingly docile bodies may harbor intractably resistant wills – through disciplined routine for efficient operation of organizations.

By utilizing a sufficiently general and abstract concept, substantive differences that existed between establishments as varied in nature and social function as the business, school, university, prison, hospital, government agency, church or political party were eliminated (March and Simon 1958). It was a designation that permitted distinct realities to be made equivalent and comparable, having reduced these spaces to the behavior of certain structural variables in relation to their environment. Relying upon their inalterable *faith* in positive science, these approximations assumed that the discovery of such relationships, which were thought to be deterministic, would permit the experts to establish the most appropriate structural design for the organization to achieve a perfect match with its environment (Pugh and Hickson 1976). In short, through the terminological cunning represented by the term *organization*, and with the new language that would follow, the large corporation recuperated social legitimacy to the point of being situated as the exemplary experience for all other types of organizations to follow. Thus, the corporation's economic success, manifested in the accumulation of great fortunes, projected itself as a preferred laboratory for experts in organization; the universal principles of structural design and guidance that guarantee the rational operation of any formal organization were to be discovered in these spaces as readily as in a public sector bureaucracy.

The structural vision synthesized ambivalence towards modernity expressed through the progressive bureaucratization of the world and the growing dissemination of market-based rationality. The tensions between general regulation mechanisms and freedom of exchange prefigured the landscape of a world dominated by an institutional isomorphism in which organizations essentially *operate with freedom* but are always subject to the pressures of competition and the demands of their contingent media of mobilization: technologies, environments, size, and so on.

The modern world is a huge market into which, over the course of the last century, the institutions that preserve the unity of society and protect the public interest have been gradually incorporated. However, their original purposes have been gradually displaced, as they have been forced to operate under commercial rules that turn their functions and responsibilities into commodities and their establishments into bureaucratic corporations oriented towards efficiency, in order to develop competitive advantages that translate into economic success. Undoubtedly, this tendency towards incorporating all human activity into a commercial logic generates grave distortions that have led to the dismantling of the social contract upon which welfare capitalism had been built (Jacoby 1997).

The study of organizations and the examination of their structures and management are considered to be *non-problematic*, since the normality of instrumental rationality from which they are organized and operated, associated with the introjection of work routines and rules of conduct of individual existence, make it difficult to appreciate the phenomena on any other terms. Because of this, it is precipitously assumed that organizational problems are essentially technical and that experts should properly solve them, which implies recognition of the problems as inescapable ingredients of modern human existence. Due to the fact that we have become accustomed to living under their mandate, we all too easily forget that the modern operation of these rules and organizational and governmental instruments gives rise to profound practical consequences. It is a question of mechanisms that bring about certain effects; these give rise to particular forms of social distribution, to arrangements of individuals, groups and populations grouped and differentiated in order to determine their social position. In only observing the technical content of the organizational mechanisms, one loses sight of the social effects produced by their operation, setting aside the fundamental importance of the forms of regulation and governance from which conduct is directed. Because of this, the means become, indeed, *are* the ends, as the study of intentions and effects increasingly rests on an understanding of how things get done.

The implications are obvious. A non-reflective approach to organizational problems gives rise to incomplete interpretations of social problems, to the tacit acceptance of the everyday realities in which we find ourselves immersed, leading us to the acceptance that little can be done in the face of these problems, which are essentially generalizably organizational rather than qualitatively specific.

In synthesis, organization science, as a field of knowledge dedicated to the analysis of organizational forms and governmental actions and means, assumes that very specific attention is given to the systems and procedures that regulate action. However, this is always undertaken with the understanding that these systems and procedures are a product of highly contingent social relationships and processes from which society is established, organized, and transformed. An organization conceived as a social system is merely an amplification of abstractedness, a double-order magnitude of abstraction. What makes the abstraction possible? The key notion is the goal. All social systems have a central value system that integrates all the disparate abstract systems that comprise it into a holistic entity. The central value system provides shared orientations towards action. The shared central values of organizations are expressed in its goals. Values and goals originate from the cultural and institutional environment. Organization goals must always be legitimated by organization values, which, in turn, are required to be consistent with social values. The legitimacy of organization goals arises from the contribution that can be made to the functional requirements of the wider social system. Thus, these goals stand in an overarching relationship to subsystem goals, and, in turn, are subordinated to the overarching societal system goals with which they are integrated.

The integration of society's values into organization goals should mean that organization roles are harmoniously designed and structured in terms of the normative expectations that individuals bring to their membership of the organization. Being a member is seen as a more or less explicit acceptance on their part of equilibrium between their preferences and the opportunities available. The opportunities must offer sufficient inducement or they would not choose to express their preferences by becoming members. The assumption is that there is a balance between inducements and contributions, as both Barnard and Simon developed. One consequence of this assumption is to make any actual exchange necessarily, *a priori*, a fair exchange. The overall processes of socialization in the broader social system help make this possible. Individuals internalize societal norms through socialization and strive to gain both psychological and instrumental satisfaction in these terms; that is, they seek satisfaction through socially sanctioned means to achieve socially given ends, or in organizations, they accept the legitimacy of organizational means to achieve given organizational goals.

As the values and specific normative requirements accord, they regulate the system. They do so through dealing with four general problems, which have to be solved if survival of the organizational system is to ensue. These are the four functional problems that any system must address and resolve:

1 *Adaptation*: acquiring the necessary resources for day-to-day functioning and reproduction.
2 *Goal attainment*: how the system mobilizes resources once they have been obtained.
3 *Integration*: how subsystems are tied together and subordinated to overall goal attainment.
4 *Latent tension management*: how the system deals with latent tensions, disagreements or lack of shared values, which might arise from time to time.

For Parsons, change is either endogenous or exogenous. Endogenous change arises from disequilibrium between two sets of functional subsystems: those that stress efficiency, which include adaptation and goal attainment, and those that stress stability, which includes integration and latency. However, exogenous change is more likely, suggests Parsons, especially as there are changes in the central value system. When change occurs, the organization system will strive for a new equilibrium position (see Henderson et al. 1937). Much of this is apparently Paretian, although Desmarez (1986) disagrees, indicating that Pareto's conception is dynamic, looking at deep changes or ruptures of the system rather than adaptive adjustments.

Apparently Paretian it may be; improbable it undoubtedly is. Extra systemic changes do not always produce adaptive responses. Social systems have no necessary affinity for virtuous cycles of equilibrium; they can as easily disintegrate as integrate, in vicious cycles. Changes can sometimes occur in a revolutionary fashion; they can be sudden and profound. Internal conflicts and contradictions can sometimes generate change. Values and goals, as Parsons sees them, are reifications (Silverman 1970). Moreover, they are reifications that, in Weber's terms, imply a structure of dominancy.

Parsons' systems theory

The differentiation of organization from social theory had been under way for some time. In the wake of the call to systematicity that was inscribed in the first volume of the *Administrative Science Quarterly* by its editor J. D. Thompson (1956a) and by the doyen of social scientists, Talcott Parsons (1956), it was evident that organization theories' key concerns were to be constituted within the assumption of the individual as an element in an organization conceived as a system. The system approach in contingency theory appeared necessary because it referred to the organizational level, complementing the level of disciplinary relations inside groups which personnel and human relations theory, later human resources theory, had carved out. The shift in focus on power from personnel to systems was fully achieved only with the publication of J. D. Thompson's (1967) *Organizations in action*, but it had been well signposted.

Slowly, gradually, in the period between the wars, a twofold set of changes occurred that framed the way in which organization theory would approach power in the era after the Second World War. These were a displacement of central focus from personnel to systems, and a shift in concern from rationality to uncertainty. The models of organization and administration derived from scientific management and formal theories of administration and the ideas that were developed in human relations came together in the notion of an organization as a social system, open to changes introduced from its environment, in which the informal organization of Mayo and the formal organization of the Classical School were separate subsystems.[3] There is sometimes a distinction made between rational and natural systems, or between closed and open systems, but few theorists are concerned with a closed system model any more. The notion of the organization as a functional and open system is a paramount conception and leads to a particular view of power.

An explicit organization theory of power emerged in the postwar era. However, its practitioners seemed unable to recognize, authentically, what it was that they purported to be addressing. The claim to address power was made from within a systems framework. Within its terms, the most rational world would be one that accorded with the patterns of a closed system, in which uncertainty had been removed. Uncertainty basically signals freedom rather than closure; it signals the limits of the organization in controlling the actions of others. It was in seeking to define the limits to systematicity that control and power became key elements. That which was uncontrollable, unexpected, unanticipated, – in a word, uncertain – spoilt the systematic picture. And for the spoilers there was a name. And the name was power. Power was seen as the antithesis of authority, undermining attempts to increase efficiency.[4] A consequence of this shift was that, as far as power was concerned, the focus on rationality had to shift to uncertainty. Uncertainty became seen as one of a number of resources that conferred power. (As we shall see subsequently, lists of these resources were compiled and theories of the lists constructed. It was dull stuff but one supposes someone had to do it.)

The conception of open system organizations presumes that, in principle, a total rationality is possible; however, in practice, as Thompson (1967) theorized, although organizations strive to be rational, because they are open systems, they can rarely if ever achieve such rationality. Reed (1985: 21) characterized the tension between the cult of theoretical rationality and the struggle with irrational practices as an intellectual schizophrenia in organization studies. Organizations are always open to irrationalities even as they strive to be rational. When the failure of the system to rationalize all relations within it creates dependencies that are not mapped on to the formally rational structure of dominancy, or, in other words, when what is taken for granted as authority does not extend its remit to all niches, segments or strata of the organization in question, then there is power.

Power is the enemy of reason and rationality but also of the individual's freedom to act. Where there is irrationality in the organization then there we will find power, because power derives not from rationality, from reason, from rule, but from irrationality, unreason and an absence of rules. That is the scene seen from the systemic heights; from within the system's depths there is also the informal realm of the organization. In other words, power is a dysfunction when seen from a system point of view, while informality is the result when seen from a psychological point of view.

Where residual sources of uncertainty remained in otherwise rationalized systems then these were to be seen as unanticipated irrationalities of rationalizing systems. These residues had a name, a special status, and denoted a distinct space in the emergent pantheon of organization studies. The name was uncertainty; the status was indicated by an absence of rule, and a consequent inability to predict, control, and contain what those who inhabited this space might be able to do. All of this denoted an absence of functioning authority.

Disrupting systems and organizing identity

Goffman and organizing identity

Authority, with its assumptions of legitimacy, necessarily implies consent to the rule that is invoked. Erving Goffman makes this absolutely clear, writing in relation to the small things of everyday organizational life, which 'provide instruction' in the essence of the organization's power: 'For example, to move one's body in response to a polite request, let alone a command, is partly to grant the legitimacy of the other's line of action' (1961: 165). To accept the privileges that any organization offers is already to legitimate its claim to organize one and one's world, 'placing one in a position of having to show a little gratitude and cooperativeness (if only in taking what is being given)' and through this some acknowledgement of the right of the agents doing the organizing to do as *they* please and feel entitled to do. That what they feel pleased to do may be within the normative universe of the formal rationality guiding their action is merely incidental, as far as those who are *subject* are concerned. As Goffman (1961: 167) suggested, discrepancies between the authorities' and the subjects' views of what an organization can command, expect and receive are not unusual; and a great deal of organizational life consists of strategies that seek to close that gap on the part of organizations, and open it up as far as possible on the part of the people, the employees, within these organizations, both managers and employees more generally.

People's definitions of the situation rarely accord entirely with those scripted and expected of them by organizations. Real people rarely conform to expectations that they will act in the prescribed way. What the participant in an organization is expected to do, and what is actually done, *may* cohere, but, as Goffman observes, this 'is not the real concern' because 'expected activity in the organization implies a conception of the actor and ... an organization can therefore be viewed as a place for generating assumptions about identity' (1961: 169–70). That is, the organization has a prior claim to defining the identity of those individuals that comprise it. Organization theory in much of its discussion of power in organizations starts from the analytically strange position of accepting the formally legitimated assumptions that organizations make about identity rather than starting with the actors themselves, their definitions of the situation, which is to favor the analytical abstraction over that which is existentially and empirically real.

> In crossing the threshold of the establishment, the individual takes on the obligation to be alive to the situation, to be properly oriented and aligned in it. In participating in an activity in the establishment, he takes on the obligation to involve himself at the moment of the activity. Through this orientation and engagement of attention and effort, he visibly establishes his attitude to the establishment and to its implied conceptions of himself. To engage in a particular activity in the prescribed spirit is to accept being a particular kind of person who dwells in a particular kind of world ... to forgo prescribed activities, or to engage in them in unprescribed ways or for unprescribed purposes, is to withdraw from the official self and the world officially available to it. To prescribe activity is to prescribe a world; to dodge a prescription can be to dodge an identity. (1961: 170)

The point is that legitimacy is not something given; it is an effect of some actor's construction of the situation. Interestingly, the constructions that organization theory so often chooses to make are already those of the prescribers, not the prescribed (choices which are often claimed to be made in the interests of 'value-free' analysis). It seems strange to take one set of social constructions – those of the abstracted and corporate organization – as somehow more real than the definitions of the situation that the actors themselves construct. Of course, as we shall see subsequently, what is important is to analyze the discourse which makes either abstracted or embodied constructions possible (see Chapter 10).

Goffman was aware that 'every organization ... involves a discipline of being – an obligation to be of a given character and to dwell in a given world' (1961: 171), and that every individual can make 'adjustments' to absent their self from the prescribed being through use of either or both unauthorized means and ends to enact 'practices' that evade the organization's assumptions about what one should do and be. These escape attempts are what make one a human agent: purposive, someone with dignity and integrity rather than the cipher that so many organization roles seem to assume. In systems theory the display of such humanity is castigated as an illegitimate act of power, the illegitimate 'underlife of public institution' as Goffman (1961) termed it. In Goffman (1961) it is what makes for human being. What Goffman had to say was available to organization theorists, almost contemporaneously with the Parsonian framing of the world, a framing that irrevocably switched the tracks of analysis to functionalist system theory assumptions over and above agential concerns. But it largely went unnoticed.

In Parsons' functionalist social theory, given the centrality of a cultural institutional viewpoint, what are constructed as values and goals in organizations cannot be treated as empirically contingent on structures of dominancy or, indeed, as fundamentally problematic. If it were the case that values and goals were problematic or experienced as domination then the central value system would not be doing its theoretical work. If the central value system does its theoretical work properly then power would have little role to play in organizations because there would be no need to make members act in terms of the organizations' preferences, over and above their own preferences, because, by definition, these preferences would be aligned. Thus, by definition, power could only ever be enacted *against* the organizations' preferences. The reason for this is simple: organizations' preferences are always already authoritative; action that seeks to ensure they are enacted is thus, by definition, legitimate authority. Thus, power could only enter the picture if members sought to enact preferences other than those of the organizations; power, by definition, would always be illegitimate if it were not in the service of the organizations' goals. It was precisely this conclusion that was reached by Parsons (1964): that power, if it were to be legitimate, could only ever be deployed in the service of goal attainment. It was this insight that framed his discussion of positive power, which we shall consider in Chapter 7. Where this left any other instances of power, other than in pursuit of system goals in the organization, was quite clear: they could only be constituted outside its normative order, as illegitimate and deviant. Goffman's organizational underlife was thus transformed into an informal organization, one that was conceived to be both underground and illegitimate, in which power flourished.

Fixing the system

From the underlife of institutions to formal systems

If one accepted the systems theory view of authority, given its acceptance of established claims to legitimacy, then it was evident that it had no place for power which did not serve organizational goals. Other forms of power could only reside in unruly spaces where the remit of authority did not extend. These forms of power were something done *against* authority rather than *in* its name. Power would be found in the gaps and niches that rationalizing systems neglected or created. Rationalizing systems were equivalent to authority; what they colonized was legitimate and authorized, *a priori*, by definition, as it emanated from a rationalizing and sovereign center. What is not authority and is not authorized, what is residual and remains obdurate to the will of rationalizations, must be power. Power represents deviations from normalizing rationalization because it is embedded in those spaces that authority does not extend to. From an organizational point of view, power will invariably be related to resistance because it is outside of and other to authority.

Power was 'discovered' in systems theories of organizations from the 1950s onwards, although Mary Parker Follett (1924; also Follett 1918) had anticipated these concerns. We can date formal recognition of its discovery within modern organization theory quite explicitly as 1956:

> The usual definitions of power are properly applicable to the internal structures of formal organizations. One reason why research workers have seldom regarded actual power in such organizations may be that the classics of bureaucracy have stressed the rational aspects of organizations, with emphasis on authority to the neglect of unauthorized or illegitimate power. And it was not that long ago that informal organization was 'discovered' in bureaucracies. (Thompson 1956b: 290)

There are several aspects of this discovery of power that are worth remarking. First, it is utterly Parsonian and functionalist in its stress on authority. Second, it sets up a contrast between rational authority and irrational power. Power is what happens when rationality is not secure. Power is irrational and it is illegitimate. Hence, power is the other, or opposite, of authority. In fact, it is what occupies that space that authority has not colonized. Power is brute, uncivilized, and dirty, in contrast to authority, which is rational, legitimate and clean. In fact, the distinction between power and authority is making reference to that distinction between the formal and the informal organization that the open systems conception was supposed to resolve. Other researchers were to echo this distinction as they followed in Thompson's footsteps. Bennis et al. (1958: 144) made a distinction between 'formal' and 'informal' organization. In the formal organization there resides 'authority', a potential to influence based on position, while in the informal organization there exists power, 'the actual ability of influence based on a number of factors including, of course, organizational position'. Formal organization is the repository of authority; informal organization, outside of the formal, is the home of power.

Power is what occurs when authority is not enacted or respected. Power occurs when people who should not exercise their will, in the formal scheme of things, are in a position to do so. Note that these definitional binaries do something rather subtle. They strip power away from the formal structure of the organization entirely; its will is authority, and it is only where this will is resisted or opposed or sidestepped in some way that power exists. The formal organization is now conceived of no longer as a thing of power but merely as a thing of legitimate authority. However, within the psychological literature, Bennis (1978), amongst others, recognized the formal organization as the main cause obstructing people's psychological growth in organizations. In this context, authority may become irrational and power can be viewed as a positive resource of the organization, in a manner analogous to the uses that Follett had prefigured.

A number of empirical studies of power in organizations make these distinctions quite clear, with the first being the paper by Thompson (1956b) with which this stream of discussion commenced. As well as making some very general and dubious theoretical points, the paper in question also reported an empirical study. The subject organization was two United States Air Force (USAF) bomber wings. The work of the USAF personnel was characterized by highly developed technical requirements in the operational sphere, for both aircrew and ground crew. While the aircrew possessed greater formal authority than the ground crew, the latter were in a highly central position within the workflow of the USAF base, relevant to the more autonomous aircrew. Briefly, what Thompson (1956b) found surprised him; despite their lower status in the authority system he saw that the maintenance engineers who worked on the planes had bases of power available to them that they were able to exercise over the flight crew. These bases were, as is necessary in a systems theory, expressed in terms of general attributes of the system. These general attributes were the 'technical requirements of operations', being in a 'centralized' position within the organization, and being involved in strategic' communication' within it. In other words, the engineers controlled the major source of insecurity for the flight crews, the safety of the plane as a flying machine. In general theory terms this substantive instance was to be translated into control of uncertainty, a move in which the work of Crozier (1964) was vital, as we shall see shortly. The aircrew depended upon the ground crew for their survival and safety, which conferred a degree of power on the latter not derived from the formal design of the base relations. Thompson attributed the power of the ground crew to their technical competency *vis-à-vis* the flight security of the planes and the strategic position it accorded them because of the centrality of concerns for the aircrew's safety.

Other writers confirmed Thompson's (1956b) view that it was the technical design of tasks and their interdependencies that best explained the operational distribution of power, rather than the formal prescriptions of the organization design. Dubin (1957: 62), for example, noted how some tasks are more essential to the functional interdependence of a system than others, and the way in which some of these may be exclusive to a specific party. Mechanic (1962) built on this argument, extending it to all organizations, saying that such technical knowledge generally might be a base for organization power. In this way, researchers began to differentiate between formally prescribed power and 'actual' power, which was also regarded as illegitimate. Thompson puts it quite precisely when he says that researchers 'have seldom regarded actual power ... [but] have stressed the rational aspects of organization to the neglect of unauthorized or illegitimate power' (1956b: 290).

Crozier's (1964) study of maintenance workers in a French state-owned tobacco monopoly, whose job was to fix machine breakdowns referred to them by production workers, proved absolutely essential for the emerging functionalist consensus concerning power. The maintenance workers were marginal in the formal representation of the organization design compared to the production workers, who were at the technical core of the organization and central to the workflow-centered bureaucracy that characterized the organization.

In practice, however, the story was very different. The production workers were paid on a piece-rate system in a bureaucracy designed on scientific management principles. Most workers were effectively 'deskilled' in a bureaucracy which was a highly formal, highly prescribed organization, where there was little that was not planned and regulated, except for the propensity of the machines to break down, and thus diminish the bonus that the production workers could earn. Hence, to maintain their earnings the production workers needed the machines to function, which made them extraordinarily dependent on the maintenance workers. Without their expertise, breakdowns could not be rectified or bonus rates protected. Consequently, the maintenance workers had a high degree of power over the other workers in the bureaucracy because they controlled the remaining source of uncertainty. Management and the production workers were aware of this situation and had attempted to remedy it through preventive maintenance. But manuals disappeared and sabotage sometimes occurred. The maintenance workers were indefatigable in defense of their relative autonomy, privilege and power. Through a skilled capacity, the result of their technical knowledge, they could render the uncertain certain. The price of restoring normalcy was a degree of autonomy and relative power, enjoyed and defended by the maintenance workers, well in excess of that formally designed within a system whose limits they defined. Workers knew well how to exert their knowledge to control the speed of the line as well as how to stop it. Soldiering was a practice sustained by the control of knowledge that others – the supervisors – did not have. To control these practices, organizations constantly evolve new systems and procedures but they can never do so fully. There are always new spaces of knowledge controlled by a few. Even outsourcing places the organization in a delicate relation to the contracted outsourcer at contract renegotiation time.

Crozier's (1964) study was a landmark. He had taken an underexplicated concept – power – and had attached it to the central concept of the emergent theory of the firm, which was uncertainty. In a different way, March and Simon (1958) recognized the role of uncertainty (bounded rationality) in organizations and suggested effective structures to confront it. A central feature of organizations as they were conceptualized in the 'behavioral theory of the firm' (Cyert and March 1963) was that they attempted to behave as if they were systems. Yet, they did so in an uncertain environment. The ability to control that uncertainty thus represented a potential source of power. Crozier subsequently revisited the links between power and uncertainty as a critical resource (Crozier and Friedberg 1980). Members of an organization meet each other in spaces that offer relatively open opportunities for control of rules and resources. People do not adapt passively to the circumstances that they meet; they use these circumstances creatively to enhance the scope of their own discretion, through shaping and bending rules and colonizing resources. Power was still seen in terms of the control of uncertainty as it was played out in daily struggles over the rules of an uncertain game, largely in zero-sum terms.

After Crozier (1964) and Thompson (1967), the field developed rapidly. A theory emerged, called the 'strategic contingencies theory of intra-organizational power' (Hickson et al. 1971), which built on these ideas. It explicitly acknowledged its debt to Thompson's (1967: 13) 'newer tradition' that conceives of the organization as 'an open system, indeterminate and faced with uncertainty, but subject to criteria of rationality and hence needing certainty'. The approach combined Crozier's (1964) stress on 'uncertainty' with sociological functionalism and the behavioral theory of the firm in economics (Pennings et al. 1969), as well as Blau's (1964) social exchange theory, and operationalized a definition of power that used Dahl's (1957) and Kaplan's (1964) behaviorist approaches to its definition. We shall return to this aspect in the next section.

> The open system had a behavioral essence: Limitation of the autonomy of all its members or parts since all are subject to power from the others; for sub-units, unlike individuals, are not free to make a decision to participate, as March and Simon (1958) puts it, nor to decide whether or not to come together in political relationships. They must. They exist to do so. (Hickson et al. 1971: 217)

The subsystems of the open system organization are conceptualized as if they were autonomous actors, with goals and values that cohere. This is, of course, a theoretical abstraction. Their behavior is guided by the economic rationalism of the open-system/bounded-rationality construct, so they are inescapably free in a double voluntarism and determinism, because they are only free to do what they must. Thus, there is no alternative for the subsystem but to be freely subjected by its own natural rationality. Subunits of organizations conceived as systems may be conceived as having powers of action but the assumption that these powers are unified and homologous, that they override competing interests and subjectivities, strategies and meanings, is a theoretical *a priori*, not an empirically nuanced observation. To assume a subsystem is to make an assumption of unitary calculability inhering in it. It renders the conceptual abstraction of the organization as system as strangely flat and one-dimensional. Authority is condensed down into the subunits while the relations between them are conceptualized as inherently ones of power. But the power that is conceptualized is not relational but structural; if one can identify the subunit that handles most uncertainty for the system, with a few caveats one will have identified power, irrespective of what these unitary actors do. In fact, they can do anything, because what they do does not enter into the theory. The theory is purely structural.

The core idea is that these subunit subsystems reduce uncertainty for the overall organization. In doing this they exchange resources with each other and with the environment to which they are open. The institutional environment is the source of change in goals (Pennings et al. 1969: 420); thus, it is a key factor introducing uncertainty into the rational system. To the extent that organizations are more structurally dependent on certain subsystems to cope with the uncertainties generated from the environment, from the processing of those inputs that the subunits receive, and from their output, then these subunits, the theory predicts, will be most powerful. Power is thus related to control of uncertainty, as this is measured by responses to a formal survey, in which departmental managers, who were presented with a series of hypothetical scenarios for evaluation, responded in terms of Likert scales. In this way, the functionally specific subunits that used esoteric technical knowledge to control uncertainty and thus increase their power relative to the formally designed hierarchy were identified.

The four subunits, not surprisingly, seemed to correspond to Parsons' four functional imperatives. The subunits were interdependent, but some were more or less dependent, and produced more or less uncertainty for others. What connected them in the model was the major task element of the organization, 'coping with uncertainty'. The theory ascribed the balance of power between the subunits to imbalances in how these interdependent subunits coped with this uncertainty. Thus the system of subunits was opened up to environmental inputs, which represented a source of uncertainty. Subunits were characterized as more or less specialized and differentiated by the functional division of labor, and were related by an essential need to reduce uncertainty and achieve organizational goals 'to use differential power to function within the system rather than to destroy it' (Hickson et al. 1971: 217).

According to this model, power is defined in terms of 'strategic contingency'; in parallel and related work it was to be defined as 'strategic choice' (Child 1972). Strategically contingent subunits are the most powerful, because they are the least dependent on other subunits and can cope with the greatest systemic uncertainty, given that the subunit is central to the organization system and not easily substitutable. The theory assumes that the subunits are unitary and cohesive in nature whereas, in fact, they are more likely to be hierarchical, with a more or less problematic culture of consent or dissent. To be unitary, some internal mechanisms of power must exist to allow such a representation to flourish, silence conflicting voices, and overrule different conceptions of interests, attachments, strategies and meanings. The theory assumes that management definitions prevail but research suggests this is not always the case (Collinson 1994). Nor can we assume that management itself will necessarily be a unitary or cohesive category. For management to speak with one voice usually means that other voices have been marginalized or silenced.

For a long time the key journals found space for contingency contributions that provided very little insight into important aspects of power. Even with the manifestation of a strategic contingencies theory of power, existing patterns of legitimacy were not challenged because hierarchy was not addressed. If anything, in contemporary systems theory, the situation has deteriorated further. While, recently, open systems theory has been revivified by diverse developments in chaos and complexity theory, these newer approaches to systems, which stress how organizations cope with rapidly changing environments through complex evolutionary adaptations, tend to downplay the role of agency and thus power (Kaufmann 1993). Change is increasingly seen in terms of complex and somewhat random interactions between large numbers of elements in interaction in computer models (Sorenson 2005).

Power and the metaphysic of uncertainty

Maintaining bounds

A whole metaphysic of uncertainty was at work in these rediscoveries of power. What is uncertainty? In some general way it denotes a lack of assurance or conviction in what will transpire. Certainty, by contrast, represents a situation where one can predict with absolute surety what a future state of affairs will be. For instance, one may be certain that the sun will rise tomorrow morning. Certainty represents a situation in which outcomes are absolutely predictable. Certainty is the state of affairs that formal organization theories sought to be midwife to through their commitment to one best way of organizing. They sought to drive out soldiering, craft control, and production rates that were inexplicable and unpredictable. What was wanted was no possibility of untowardness. Inexplicability, strangeness, and surprise would be strangers to the formal organization just as much as they were to be strangers to the rational system. Within the dreams of rationality one should have a situation in which a rule existed for each and every thing that might ever occur, but of course, following March and Simon (1958), it was realized that rationality was not a dream but a world bounded by cognitive capabilities, human processing, and incomplete information.

The notion of bounded rationality is meant to capture the way in which organizational decisions are actually made; evidence is searched for, usually through channels of information that are known in advance. The evidence weighed is by no means exhaustive, but it is usually thorough in terms of the familiar ways of making sense that the organization and its decision makers use. Hence, rather than seeking optimization, in an economic model of the rational consumer under conditions of perfect competition, organizations typically seek to 'satisfice', a term that Simon created to capture the process of drawing on limited but familiar channels of information to arrive at the most satisfactory decision with regard to the evidence available.

The links to Pareto and his opposition to utilitarian theory should be clear. Satisficing is not too far removed from another made-up meaning, ophelimity. From this perspective, uncertainty would represent an inability to go on, doubt as to how to apply a rule, or what rule to apply. Thus, metaphysically, uncertainty represents a situation in which rules for remedying surprise have yet to be enacted, in which the bounds of action have not yet been staked. When one thinks of where the whole metaphysic began, with Thompson's and Crozier's maintenance workers, then this account seems substantially correct. What these employees did was to handle, by resolving, the uncertainties contingent on machine usage and maintenance. And, at least in Crozier's case, there was evidence to suggest that the uncertainty that others had *vis à vis* the machines was a state of bounded ignorance that the maintenance workers actively conspired to keep reproducing.

Bounded rationality is the recognition of a limited freedom to act, of the irrationality/emotionality of the actions of individuals and of the need to control as much as possible of these behaviors through the design of structures of control in organizations. It implies, in a first historical stage, the design of the disciplinary society and the bureaucratic organization, and in a second (current) stage, the design of the control society and the post-bureaucratic IT organization. The second stage has deep implications because it entails a paradoxical freedom of individuals to become obedient cyborgs. Everyone is free to move inside limits; the composition of the limits changes, but the centrality of restraint remains.

Who has what resources?

Similar to the strategic contingencies view of power, in terms of theoretical approach, is the resource dependency view (Pfeffer and Salancik 1974; Salancik and Pfeffer 1974; Pfeffer 1992). It derives from the social psychological literature that Emerson (1962) developed and which was implicit in Mechanic's (1962) study of the power of lower-level participants. Sources of power include not only uncertainty but also information, expertise, credibility, position, access and contacts with higher-echelon members and the control of money, rewards, sanctions, perceptiveness, social capital, etc. (e.g. Crozier 1964; French and Raven 1968; Pettigrew 1973; Benfari et al. 1986; Krackhardt 1990; Burt 1992). Such lists of resources are infinite, however, since different phenomena become resources in different contexts. They are also extremely *ad hoc* and tautological, as Kramer and Gavrielli suggest: 'we infer what social actors have power by observing what they are able to obtain. We explain what they actually obtain, in turn, by invoking the notion of power' (2005: 322). Without a total theory of contexts, which is impossible, one can never achieve closure on what the bases of power are. They might be anything, under the appropriate circumstances.

Possessing scarce resources is not enough in itself, however, to confer power. Actors have to be aware of their contextual pertinence and control and use them accordingly (Pettigrew 1973). This process of mobilizing power is known as politics (Pettigrew 1973; Hickson et al. 1986), a term whose negative connotations have helped to reinforce the managerial view that power used outside formal authoritative arrangements was illegitimate and dysfunctional. It was the dichotomous nature of power and authority that created the theoretical space for the contingency and dependency approaches. The concept of power was thus reserved primarily for exercises of discretion by organization members, which were not sanctioned by their position in the formal structure. Such exercises are premised on two assumptions: first, that there is an illegitimate or informal use of resources; second, that the legitimate system of authority may be taken for granted and its existence as such rendered analytically non-problematic.

All resource dependence theorists view a certain resource as key in organizations, but they differ in which resource is regarded as key. Pfeffer and Salancik (2002) argued that power could be both vertical and horizontal in organizations, and their focus, similarly to Hickson et al. (2002), was on subunit power. They hypothesized that power would be used in organizations to try and influence decisions about the allocation of resources. Subunits may be thought of as departments in the organization. To the extent that subunits contributed critical resources, including knowledge, that the organization needs, other subunits submitted to their demands and ceded power to them. The similarities to strategic contingencies theory are striking. Using archival data on university decision making in the University of Illinois, they confirmed their hypotheses, suggesting that power is a positive-sum game for those that have control of critical resources. Using the power these resources bestow means yet more resources can be obtained to leverage more power. Those that have resources attract more resources and thus more power.

Power was still played out in daily struggles over the rules of an uncertain game. There is no doubt that uncertainty, as well as the other contenders for strategic resource status, can be a source of power, but not in a context-independent way. What counts as a resource can be made to count only in specific contexts. For instance, box cutters, which are used for cutting paper and cardboard, are not usually thought of as a powerful resource, or at least they were not until September 11, 2001. Then, in the hands of determined terrorists, they were responsible for what has now passed into history as 9/11. So, if information, uncertainty or box cutters are to count as resources for power, they will do so only in specific contexts. For this reason control is always the key word.

To the extent that specific resources are related to power in a general way, without regard for context, they are not very helpful. Anything can be a resource in the right context but it is the context that is important. Thus, possessing scarce resources is not enough to deliver power over and above that formally authorized; one also needs to have an explicit knowledge of context (Hickson, et al. 1986; Pettigrew 1973; 2002) and of how to use resources accordingly.

Power, possession and causality

Systems theory used general attributes to explain phenomena, because the theory was supposed to function as a set of coherent and transcendental terms. Along with the key conception of power being an emergent property that appears at the limits of rationality, where there is uncertainty, some other key terms were imported from political science. These were that power was something people possessed where these possessions could be conceptualized as bases of power, or resources, which could be mobilized in causal episodes.

The definition of power that entered these open systems theories stressed that power is a causal relation predicated on possession of situationally valued resources. Many different entities can possess the resources that enable power. We have encountered organizations, subsystems and individuals, but had we delved into political science we would have found other entities such as groups, roles, offices, governments, nation-states or other human aggregates (Dahl 1957). Where these exercise power then any one of them, conceptualized abstractly as an A, has to be able to get some other party, conceptualized as a B, to do something that the B would not otherwise do. The basis for this causal exercise is important, as there will be a source, domain, or base to it, conceptualized in terms of resources that A possesses and can exploit *vis à vis* B. Power will be expressed through means or instruments of power, such as love, fear or money. It will be a probabilistic capability, not an absolute one: where an A's probability of securing consent is higher than a B's then one may say that A is more powerful in respect of that specific probability. Finally, it will be a conditional capability, having applicability that is limited in scope over B to some specific areas of B's behavior.

The political science definition of power was enormously influential in debates from the 1950s to the 1970s (see Clegg 1989), although its provenance stretched back to debates that occurred from 1924 to 1926 in the American Political Science Association (Caton 1976: 155, n. 1). Its importance for organization theories was in the promise that it held of a scientific definition of power as a properly causal concept. The subsequent Nobel laureate Herbert Simon saw this importance clearly:

When we say that A has power over B, we do not mean to imply that B has power over A ... [It is] a problem of giving operational meaning to the asymmetry of the relation between independent and dependent variables ... identical with the general problem of defining a causal relation between two variables. That is to say, for the assertion, 'A has power over B', we can substitute the assertion, 'A's behavior causes B's behavior'. If we can define the causal relation we can define ... power. (1957: 5)

Such a treatment of power as a causal relation is consistent with the epistemological source in logical positivism that seeks to explain facts only in terms of their objective relations. Simon (1957) was articulating a representative experience in terms of his conception of power, one shared by other theoreticians, including Dahl (1961: 41), March (1955: 437) and James (1964: 50). McFarland (1969) asserted that power and causality were fundamentally equivalent. That this was not a new assertion would be familiar to anyone that had studied Hobbes (see the discussion in Clegg 1989: 21–38). What was new was that the grammar in which causal relations were constructed had shifted from the mechanics of Hobbes' (1651) clockwork, or Hume's (1902) billiard balls, to a stripped-down behaviorism of stimuli and responses. It was to be through the responses of a B to the stimuli of an A that power should be registered, according to these political science accounts.

The organization theory accounts of power as a causal phenomenon that we have encountered thus far either look at what elapses in specific cases (such as Thompson 1956b and Crozier 1964) or adopt a conception of causal power that conceives of causal statements in terms of what Blais (1974) refers to as 'if ... then' statements, referring not to actual occurrences but to the independent variable's ability to affect a dependent variable, in probabilistic and theoretically coherent terms. It is in this sense that strategic contingencies theory conceptualizes power. Gibson captures this sense when he says that 'It is simply not the case in any but the most idiosyncratic use of the word "power" that to have the power to do something is the same as actually to cause it to happen. It is merely to be able to cause it to happen' (1971: 102). It is this formulation that translates a causal conception of power as a relation into a conception of power as something structural; it shifts it from a property of relations to a capacity of actors. These capacities are such that 'if something were to occur, such and such effects would happen' (1971: 105). Power becomes equivalent to it being possible to produce certain effects, theoretically, given certain environmental conditions, which is how strategic contingencies theory operates. It regards power as a conditional state.

Clayton's power: the kind of power you have when you're not really having power

Is power a visible and deployable asset?

What one can do and say with the causal conception of power, as something given by possession of resources, is very limited.[5] First, it appears to be not a social relation but a possession. One has power rather than being in a relationship of power. Second, if power is not to be a conditional state, in which case it ceases to be relational, then it must be seen to have happened for one to say that it has happened. The stimulus has to produce a response. Whereas Weber bequeaths a grammar of power, structured around relations of dominancy, these conceptions of power as equivalent to causality and premised on resources whittle away the relations of dominancy. Power becomes merely an effect observable in specific episodes of action. Each episode starts from rest, and rest doesn't have to be addressed. The organization theorists of the open system regard authority as corresponding to the conditions of rest. It need not be addressed; it does not require explanation because it is *a fact*. Politics can be denied as other than a deviant activity.

The result of the conceptual decisions – which are, of course, also political decisions – made by systems theorists as they elect to work within the discourse their concordance produces is a strangely schizophrenic representation of organizations. On the one side, deemed the right side, is the bold confident formal representation. On the left side, there is a shadow system, little talked about other than by a few theorists of 'power' and largely ignored by the rest. Here is the dark side of the dialectic that turns domination into authority. Authority produces and is produced by rules and, while rules produce obedience, they can just as easily, where opportunity presents itself, produce deviance, as we represent figuratively in Figure 5.1.

Opportunity is given by space for resistance – small patches of local indetermination – in which 'irrationalities' that do not accord with the formal system logic can flourish. Where these irrationalities can gain some leverage by exerting control over uncertainty, then small acts of power can be generated as local resistance to the dominant logic of organizational relations. Thus, down amongst the oilcans thrives a degree of relative autonomy that might surprise system designers.

Resistance is never of a piece; it only looks that way from the perspective of those authorities who find resistance to their rationalities simply irrational. In fact, as Ford et al. (2002) have argued, the quality of resistance varies greatly with the contexts in which it occurs. When there is resistance to the power relations inscribed in the authorities' views of the world, then what makes it possible are alternative

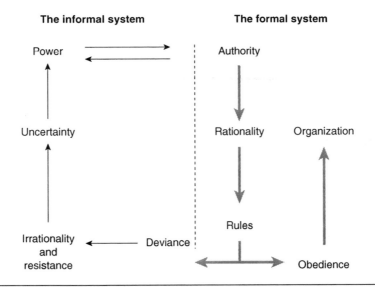

Figure 5.1 Systemic schizophrenia between the realm of authority–rationality–obedience and the realm of power–resistance–deviance

assemblages of conversations about the nature of that rationality that is taken for granted by authorities. Ford et al. (2002) identify three typical modes of resistance, depending on the nature of what they call the 'background conversations', which one might think of as subordinated and alternative rationalities to whatever is posited as the official and authoritative story in organizations. These are conservations that are complacent; resigned or cynical. Each differs in positing the mechanisms of resistance differently. Complacent resistance is premised on 'denial', 'procrastination', 'avoidance' and 'withdrawal' (Ford et al. 2002: 113). Resigned resistance is motivated by a belief inscribed in the modes of rationality that characterize everyday conversations that the authorities and their projects are not defeatable, even while they are unappealing; it is characterized by 'lack of attention', 'reduced morale', 'non-participation' and other forms of 'covert' withholding of commitment (Ford et al. 2002: 113). Cynical resistance entails more overt action such as 'sabotage', and can feed into analysis of actions in terms of their 'hidden agendas', generating hidden agendas of its own, leading to a norm of 'politicking' in the organization (Ford et al. 2002: 113).

We should stress that resistance is normal. Only an inability to see that the nature of social reality is socially constructed and thus appears differently to people who have different interests in its co-construction, negotiation and de-construction, would lead one to see resistance as in some way deviant. It only becomes seen as deviant if one starts from the premise that the authorities authorized constructions of the world are the only reality, and that they describe an ontologically given condition of existence rather than a politics of such construction, a position that no respectable social science, one would have thought, would want to adhere to, because such adherence throws away the possibility of analytic leverage as something that is unencumbered and unbeholden to extant interests vested in situations. Instead, it invests the analyst as the handmaiden of the authorities, a tool of the masters, and a stooge as far as alternative rationalities are concerned.

Does power imply conflict?

In the management literature the focus is almost exclusively on the use of power in situations of conflict that arise when actors try to preserve their vested interests against authority (e.g. Pettigrew 1973; 1985; MacMillan 1978; Pfeffer 1981; 1992; Gray and Ariss 1985; Schwenk 1989). One group (usually senior management) is forced to use power to overcome the opposition of another (perhaps intransigent unions or dissident employees) to maintain order and impose authority. It is a view reinforced by a common definition of politics in the management literature as the unsanctioned or illegitimate use of power to achieve unsanctioned or illegitimate ends (e.g. Mintzberg 1983; 1984; also see Mayes and Allen 1977; Gandz and Murray 1980; Enz 1988). The majority of management writers defined power in terms of conflict that ensued when illegitimate action challenged the bounds of rationality (e.g. Mayes and Allen 1977; MacMillan 1978; Gandz and Murray 1980; Narayaran and Fahey 1982; Mintzberg 1983; Gray and Ariss 1985; Pettigrew 1985; Enz 1988; Schwenk 1989; Pfeffer 1992).

Eisenhardt and Bourgeois (1988) supply one of the most exquisite examples of the illegitimacy of power. In commenting on an empirical case, they observed respondents saying that:

'There is a lot of disagreement. We air opinions and they're often heated. They're even abusive and insulting sometimes … We argue about most things.' Another VP said: 'There is a lot of debate. There is a lot of disagreement … Art [the president] doesn't want yes people.' *Despite this conflict, we saw little evidence of politics at Forefront. Rather, the executives seemed to operate using open argument* (1988: 751, our italics).

It is not only that authority is taken as unproblematic, so that it need not be addressed, but also that the conception of power that is developed tends to be limited to a specific conception of causality as a contiguous relation between discrete entities in the same space but in a time-lagged way.

There are other notions of causal power available from science. Notions of structural causality – such as a bridge collapsing because it is ill-designed – are rather different from process causality causing its collapse, for instance where its supports rust (Ball 1975: 218). However, it becomes very difficult to consider structural causality in the analysis of organizations where the structure is assumed, *a priori*, to be one of authority. What could be ill-designed in an authoritative set of relations, where the goodness of design is tied up with its legitimacy? Legitimacy attaches to the fact that it is, it exists, it is designed as such, which makes it legitimate, as an *a priori* that defines it, irrespective of any weaknesses that it might exhibit.

Such approaches clearly imply that the use of power would be dysfunctional. First, it doesn't flow from imperative command lodged in authority. Second, it is usually seen in terms of individual self-interest aimed at thwarting managerial initiatives that are intended to benefit the organization as a whole, which have the whole force of system legitimation behind them. When legitimacy is defined in terms of the 'organization', writers usually mean organizational elites, such as senior management or top management teams. Distilled to its essence, the conventional view of organizational politics refers to behavior that is 'informal, ostensibly parochial, typically divisive, and above all, in the technical sense, illegitimate, sanctioned neither by formal authority, accepted ideology, nor certified expertise (though it may exploit any one of those)' (Mintzberg 1983: 172). Thus, power became equated with illegitimate, dysfunctional, self-interested behavior. Managerial interests are equated with organizational needs and the possibility that managers, like any other group, might seek to serve their own vested interests is largely ignored (Watson 1982).

Some echoes of the functionalist view of conflict can be found, such as in the literature on beneficial conflict, which emphasizes power balance and open argument as the way to avoid a 'win/lose' mentality (Gudykunst 1998; Hocker and Wilmot 1991; Johnson and Johnson 1982; Jehn 1997; Jehn et al. 1999). Here, echoes of Parsons' positivity may be heard, dimly. Moderate levels of conflict enable organizations to adapt to changes, coordinate different constituents, and innovate (Ting-Toomey 1985). When conflicting views are encouraged, innovation evolves around the creation and resolution of conflict. Therefore, in this 'innovation mode', conflict is constructive because argumentation provides 'credits' which represent other group members' positive attitudes toward that person (Moscovici and Faucheux 1972). Positive means to become collaborative, to accept the rationales of authority and to help the organization solve the problems it confronts, considering that this authoritative view is the only legitimate one. Moderate levels of conflict also motivate argumentation in order to clarify differences between opposed positions and enable opposed parties to build cooperation (Folger et al. 1997). Moderate levels of conflict are characterized by experimental or flexible behavior and preparedness to switch strategy from, say, threats to jokes, thus preventing harmful escalation or 'sticking points' so that 'no single strategy takes over' (Conrad and Poole 1998: 334). There is also a distinction in the literature between task conflict and relationship conflict. Jehn (1997) found that groups that institutionalize the acceptance of disagreements about work processes or goals and that discourage conflict related to personality traits and interpersonal relationships have higher production output, lower error rates, and higher customer satisfaction. Yet, these positive accounts of power and conflict are exceptions rather than the norm.

Does power imply hierarchy?

People are strange. They can become addicted or phobic to almost anything. On the evidence of both organization theory and three lifetimes spent around many of the more significant organizations of at least four countries, we would have to conclude, with Fairtlough, that most people seem to be strangely addicted to hierarchy and phobic about any alternatives that might be posited to it:

Talk about organizations usually centers on who should be in charge. We're used to hierarchy and know how it works. It's a familiar and comfortable habit, the obvious fall-back, the default option. When it works, it feels precise and clear – we know Bloggs is the boss, he tells us what to do. When it doesn't work we blame Bloggs. We accept that hierarchy has its faults, but we think it's inevitable. We may try to ameliorate its bad effects, but we never question the basic idea. (2005: 7)[6]

We may note that this lack of questioning is both practical and theoretical. Practically, from our earliest experiences in school, organized by a 'principal' or 'headteacher', we spend all our formative years in a hierarchical organization. For those who attended really elite schools the sense of hierarchy was probably much more pronounced, which means that, given dominant models of social reproduc-tion whereby elite groups tend to reproduce themselves, the experience of most elites who actually run organizations is imprinted in terms of hierarchy. And if practical experience were not sufficient, as we have seen in the previous chapter and in this, in management and organization theory the normalcy of hierarchy has been a constituent aspect of almost all English-language thinking about power in organizations, which, revoking domination, placed authority at center stage and deviation from it as power, a resistant and insubordinate property of hierarchical systems.

One reason why the way of seeing things organizational as hierarchical has been so pervasive in the English-speaking world is the profound importance that the foremost commentator on civil strife gave to hierarchic notions of sovereignty as essential to organization designs desirous of minimizing disorder. Having lived through the English Civil War and having served the nation's monarch as secretary, Thomas Hobbes (1651) was inclined to regard the only alternatives to ordered hier-archy, profound authority, and peaceable subjects to be a life that was solitary, poor, nasty, brutish, and short. Hierarchy and authority were the joint guarantors of order, for without them only anarchy, disorder, and disorganization would flourish.

As discourse about power and organizations was institutionalized in the latter half of the twentieth century, the concern with authority and hierarchy was nor-malized. Power was conceived not as reproducing normal authority and hierarchy but as undermining it, never more famously than in Crozier's (1964) maintenance workers, lowly individuals in the pecking order, who were supposed to have organi-zational power because of their control over uncertainty! In retrospect this seems errant nonsense, and it is hard to believe that one ever could have taken seriously the implication that the oilcan keepers were more involved in relations of power than were top management teams or the leaders of organizations. Of course, if the discourse on leadership had filled in for the deficiencies of that on power then the situation might have been different, but it didn't, as Gordon (2002) argued; con-sequently, given that leadership appeared not to be concerned with power, perhaps it was not surprising to find power in the most unlikely places, down among the oilcans.

The functionalist theory of organizations preserves one aspect of the hidden history of power that started with Taylor in the nineteenth century. Taylor explic-itly sought to redesign the human body in its accommodation with the material and social environment that he created, in terms of one necessary way of being. Latter-day functionalists believe, just as strongly, that organization will be as it is because, when it is in fit with those contingencies that it has to deal with, it will have evolved to the one best way of dealing with them. And an unquestioned aspect of that being, in any normal organization, will be for hierarchy to divide tasks, set rules, and design structures. All of these divisions, rules and designs are necessary for organizations to exist; thus, it is extrapolated, hierarchy must be a necessity. Hierarchy is a necessary bulwark against disorder, against lower-order members exerting their agency and using power to mess up the rules, task divisions, and structural designs. Hierarchy is the necessary prerequisite for lower-order members to have sufficient fear and loathing of authority and its strict discipline, so that, similar to the poor subjects of the Panopticon, what members of organizations know about the conditions of their existence as members holds them submissively in thrall to the necessity of power's devices.

Fairtlough suggests that 'hierarchies tend to learn slowly, especially because a lot of effort goes into preserving the superior status of those at the top, inevitably an anti-learning activity' (2005: 18). The alternative to hierarchy is not chaos or anarchy. Only our powerful addiction to hierarchy, bred in habit, leads us to believe it to be so. And it is a 'powerful' addiction in a double sense: first, it is strong; and second, it is obfuscatory, because, where power is concerned, it creates blind spots, absences, and silences where critical reflection should be. In the absence of critical reflection alternatives are not thinkable; where there is critical reflection then alternatives become visible. Hierarchical rights, interpreted through a traditional conception, presume an established order of domination in which is vested a *repressive* right to exercise power over subjects.

Hierarchy has useful functions. It can be used to settle dispute unilaterally as disparate views are rejected in favor of hierarchically preferred options. But the risk is that it will produce stifling cultures of orthodoxy; structures which cannot easily learn from the diversity of their component strengths and voices; leaders who believe their own rhetoric rather than trust that wisdom might possibly reside in the views of those that they seek to rule, sell to, supply, and employ; and power which can only understand resistance to it in terms of illegitimate choices of illegitimate ways to express being an organization member. In shorthand, being a member, it is assumed, means being someone who accepts that the terms of trade for receipt of a wage or salary are that one keeps one's opinions to oneself where they conflict with those of authorities; that one's daily bread buys one's daily acquiescence to whatever authorities choose to do.

Hierarchy has many celebrated advantages, not least being familiarity, unity of powers, and a theory of sovereignty that few would criticize openly. After all, we all know that what bosses do is rule. And the whole legal framework of common law, derived from Masters and Servants Acts, assumes definite powers distributed differentially in terms of relations embedded in the hierarchy. Little wonder that hierarchy is so normalized, so hegemonic, so deeply embedded legally. Within the limits of legal frameworks, those in dominant relations of hierarchy can do drastically bad things to the immediate life chances of those of us who are not, such as making us redundant. That is why in analysis of any system of power relations one should never stop at the organization door, looking only at what goes on inside the organization. One also needs to consider the changing balance of forces in the industrial relations arena, as political parties of differing ideological persuasions use government to shift the balance of power between labor and capital over the legal definitions of what constitutes a contract of employment and its breaches. Often, the balance of power intra-organizationally changes dramatically as a result of changes registered in the political arena. Rights – to strike, to dismiss, to parental leave, to statutory entitlements – ebb and flow with shifts of the political current, as does resistance to their creation, preservation, extension or erosion. Moving in one direction they embolden employers; shifting to another they create anxiety when they offer succor to employees, at what seems to employers to be their expense.

Of course, the law is always an imperfect instrument. Confining resistance to power within its limits sometimes only serves to foster resistance to it, creating confrontation and conflict over its meaning and implementation where this had previously not existed. Recall that, even after 25 years of legal imprisonment of Nelson Mandela as an enemy of the state, this power did not preserve the state that imprisoned him, and its legality, against the resistance of a people and a movement committed to their own freedom and liberation. The law provides obligatory passage points through which, using its monopoly over the means of violence, the state can seek to channel freedoms and repressions, define rights and obligations, and corral consent as legitimate and exclude dissidence as illegitimate. But history is replete with laws being challenged and overthrown by subjects empowered with the moral necessity of their convictions. In the recent past one thinks of the repeal of the Poll Tax in the UK; the Orange Revolution in the Ukraine; the defeat of segregation in the USA by the Civil Rights struggle, and of apartheid in the Republic of South Africa. Legitimacy does not always equal right; courageous people can dislodge the most entrenched hierarchies, even when they are backed by might.

The paradigm of a sovereign master and commander is almost second nature. It provides an implicit and pervasive model of sovereignty for all strong, macho, business leaders. However, there are alternative definitions of sovereignty, significantly different from the paradigm of master and commander, as traced by Kalyvas (2005) in terms of a model of constitutive power: 'It erupted on the political scene with the invention of modern constitutionalism', in the form of 'an original constituting power', which founds and grounds 'a constitutional order while remaining irreducible to and heterogeneous from that order' (2005: 226). In the constitutive alternative, the emphasis is on the creation of a new order in which power is *productive*: 'The sovereign constituent subject is not a repressive force, but a productive agency' (2005: 227). Instead of 'stressing the discretionary power of a superior command emanating from the *top*, the notion of the constituent sovereign redirects our attention to the underlying sources of the instituted reality located at the *bottom*' (2005: 227). In short, modern notions of sovereignty acknowledge *demos* and *poly* – both *democracy* and *polyarchy* – as well as *hierarchy* and *bureaucracy*.[7]

Fairtlough suggests that we simply do not know how desirable hierarchy is in particular situations, 'because it never gets tested against anything other than anarchy or chaos' (2005: 9). What it should be tested against, Fairtlough suggests, are contemporary models of polyarchy, including heterarchy and responsible autonomy. Heterarchy means the separation of powers; it builds sovereignty into practice rather than the precedent of domination. It sets up, at best, internal systems for the exercise of voice, the calling to account, and the checking of power, and encourages coevolutionary learning because each party has to pay close attention to the cues and signals that the others are attending to; it cannot simply impose 'one best way' or 'my way or the highway' on members. It works from a team basis, enabling cooperation and fostering coevolution, learning and innovation, and is committed to pluralism. In diversity it sees strength rather than division. Contemporary forms of virtual communication make the provision of transparent information easier, immediate and cheap. Whereas in the past the slow transmission of information, its necessary archiving and storing in written files, the high costs of reproduction, and limited literacy may all have conspired to make hierarchy more effective, because control was premised on institutionalized routines; that is no longer the case today. The conditions exist in which organizations can empower their members to be more responsibly autonomous, where members can be autonomous but responsible subjects with clear modes of accountability.

Malone (2004) argues that the emergence of virtual immediacy and instantaneity is driving hitherto hierarchical organizations to become increasingly either more heterarchical or more responsibly autonomous or both. Decisions can be made by secret ballot in virtual labs, where arguments for and against actions can be made anonymously on a shared screen. Here the power of good argument will prevail rather than the power of hierarchy, which presumes enlightenment and wisdom reside in domination, a very dubious proposition (if one with a long historical pedigree emanating from the Age of Reason). Organizations can move from command-and-control to coordinate-and-cultivate models, suggests Malone. In this shift management ceases to direct and instead starts to facilitate organization processes for goal setting, standard setting and value articulation. One corollary is that the cultural ties that bind will flourish and grow stronger in a climate of genuine responsibility and respect rather than in an inauthentic parroting of what are presumed, on the rule of anticipated reaction, to be views that will accord with those who are in positions of dominance.

Social scientists have rarely felt it necessary to explain why it is that power should be hierarchical (Hardy and Clegg 1996). It is because of this that hierarchy is reinforced. We have seen in the previous chapter how this hegemony has deep intellectual roots in the development of an orthodox consensus around a functionalist interpretation of Weber's (1978) work. It is so strongly held that, as Hardy and Clegg (1996) explained, contemporary theory could only imagine that power was what 'bad guys' used to try and get their (illegitimate) way while good guys could just rely on the hegemony of authority and hierarchy as a 'second nature', a culture that was so acculturated that for most people who lived its everyday life nothing other than it could be imagined (Bauman 1976). Thus, power served the hegemony of hierarchy and this hegemony deepened its service by simultaneously obscuring those relations of power that it served, making them feasible, visible and accountable only as authority.

Both *heterarchy* and *responsible autonomy* are specifications of different forms of rule by many, *polyarchy*. It was Ogilvy (1977) who introduced the concept of heterarchy, meaning multiple rulers, a balance of power rather than a single rule, as in hierarchy. There are many examples of heterarchy that one can identify, such as partnerships in professional organizations including law or accounting firms, or alliance relationships between separate firms. Responsible autonomy is a concept that we first encountered in the work of Andrew Friedman (1977). Responsible autonomy means getting things done not through hierarchical control – which Friedman called direct control – but through the autonomy of a group or individual to decide how they will do what they will do, where what they will do means that they are accountable to some others; hence, the notion of *responsible* autonomy. Earlier, something very similar seemed to have been captured by David Hickson (1966) in terms of the contrasting specificity of role prescription in different organization theories. He identified a convergence around the centrality of the issue of the degree of role prescription but a sharp cleavage between those researchers who thought it desirable and efficient and those who did not. It was a cleavage that broke down, roughly, along the lines that higher prescription was favored by the formal theorists of administration and classical management theory, while lower prescription was favored by the more humanistic researchers.

Many organizational examples of low prescription with high responsible autonomy come to mind, and Fairtlough gives an instance that is especially dear to our hearts:

> Basic scientific research, in academe and in research institutes, is largely conducted by autonomous groups, which are led by principal investigators. These groups develop their reputations by publishing reports in peer-reviewed journals. Principal investigators apply for research grants from various funding bodies. Grants are given subject to the novelty and significance of the group. The principal investigator's freedom to choose research topics and to recruit people provides autonomy. The group's continued existence depends on it continuing to publish good science – this provides accountability. (2005: 30)

Another example is that of investment fund management, where, if a fund does well, the manager may be given more funds to invest and earn more accordingly from fees and commissions; here, autonomy is provided by the internal policies of the financial institution where accountability is evident in the way that the fund performs in a competitive market. Fairtlough (2005: 31–3) sees responsible autonomy as flourishing best where it is encapsulated within rules that are widely understood, transparent, legitimated and shared, and where action is open to critique, such as regular audit, or being held in some way accountable for the actions taken as a responsibly autonomous subject or unit. Many forms of audit are increasingly institutionalized to deal with conditions of power at a distance – holding people accountable at a distance – such as the growth of standards (Brunsson et al. 2000). The essence of responsible autonomy is that there is audit and disputed determination by some independent and third party held in good standing, and institutionalized as such.

In heterarchy, as Fairtlough explains it, through rotation of office, and reward schemes related to risk and innovation rather than position, tendencies to domination can be reduced. Heterarchy builds democratic skills and capabilities in what has the potential to be a virtuous circle; it encourages more sophisticated general skills for interpersonal processes, dialogical relations, teamwork, mutual respect and openness (see the 'alliance culture' reported in Pitsis et al. 2003). Admittedly, as Fairtlough (2005) suggests, heterarchies work best when the size of the organization is small, below about 150 people, he recommends. Heterarchy cannot be extended indefinitely as it is impossible to work in what are highly direct democracies once the number of participants rises beyond the circle of people who can know each other reasonably well. However, responsible autonomy within forms of heterarchic organization enables encapsulated boundedness to be created – with devices and agents for boundary spanning – thus extending functional capabilities. Of course, the establishment of efficient responsible autonomy means critique must be in place from the start; the rules and accountabilities need to be clear, and dispute resolution mechanisms must be in place.

Hierarchy is premised principally on 'power over' others while the polyarchic alternatives are principally premised on 'power to' get things done (see Chapter 7 for more on the 'power to' and 'power over' distinction). What distinguishes heterarchy from responsible autonomy is that in the former there is a constant and continuous interaction between entities and agents in deciding what and how to do something. In many instances, this means that for heterarchy to be successful it needs to develop an identity for instances of it that is separate from whatever organizational bodies comprise and host the constituent parts (Clegg et al. 2002). Responsible autonomy means that there can be a lot more distance between agencies. Both differ from hierarchy in not being subject to arbitrary power vested only in relations of domination. No pure versions of these types will be found in reality; they are abstracted 'ideal' types, in the Weberian sense. Most organizations will comprise different mixes of hierarchy, or direct control, heterarchy, and responsible autonomy. The benefits and costs of each will differ in different contexts.

Fairtlough (2005: 79) echoes a general view in seeing the development of knowledge-based organizations as major drivers of a shift away from hierarchy towards heterarchy and responsible autonomy. A knowledge economy's virtual communications replace the need for rules, precedents and files to record them, and greater knowledge means increased scrutiny, awareness and possibility of audit or whistle blowing. If Fairtlough's (2005) optimism, born of experience as well as wisdom, is half-right, many of the studies recorded in this chapter of the dynamics of illegitimate power will fade into irrelevance in future. Power will not die with these accounts but the contours of its representation will change markedly, as hegemonic silences fade away, and analysis of power is directed less by hierarchical norms and instead by norms more open to its recognition as a truly constitutive aspect of organizational relations. Neither heterarchy nor responsible autonomy, as distinct forms of polyarchy, are an alternative to power but they are alternative to hierarchy, and they do configure power relations quite differently, around polyphonic rather than hegemonic principles, less concerned with imperative coordination from a single and superior point of view and narration and more concerned with deconstructions and translations of alternative accounts (see Kornberger et al. 2005). But they still remain modes of power – with all that implies – as we shall see in Chapter 12, when we develop the conceptualization of power under polyarchy further.

Conclusion

It is not that organization theory has not produced much in the way of theories of power; as this chapter indicates there are many accounts available. However, perspectives in which power is seen as the illegitimate antithesis to authority, and in which hierarchy is hegemonic, characterize nearly all of these accounts. It is seen as something deviant to be explained rather than something that is somehow embedded in the normal functioning of organizations.

Our view is that organizational structures and systems are structurally sedimented phenomena that result in part from a history of victories and losses already embedded in the organization, and in part from the ways its roles and relations have been shaped historically. Organizations are not neutral or apolitical. We should think of an organization as a collective lifeworld in which traces of the past are vested, recur, shift, and take on new meanings. In Weber's terms, organizations already incorporate a 'structure of dominancy' in their functioning. Authority, structure, ideology, culture, and expertise are invariably saturated and imbued with power in their relations. Thus we may conclude that, with the significant exception of Follett, whom we encountered in Chapter 3, the relations of power vested in formal organization design have been taken for granted by mainstream organization and management researchers. Where they did stop to consider power, they did so largely through models that saw it as a form of deviancy, a deviation from a normal order of authority and obedience. Thus, the exercise of power has been seen as an illegitimate and unauthorized aberration within a given structure of dominancy (Perrow 1986a; 1986b). Such an approach constitutes power as that which escaped rationality.

Oddly, while Parsons developed a theory of power in the 1960s, most organization theories of power do not relate to it, although we will address it in Chapter 7 of this book. They do, however, follow his thinking in seeing authority as a rational, natural and normal system asset. Thus, it is not managers or the system that is the source of power relations in organizations; power relations only reveal themselves when the system breaks down in some way, when deviance occurs, when authority cannot ensure the achievement of commitment to system goals by all those who are incorporated within the organization. As we shall see in the following chapter, it is precisely the normalcy of organization power embedded in authority and hierarchy that enables many things to be done in its name that are morally reprehensible. And although in the next chapter we shall concentrate on a particular type of organization, the total institution, to exemplify this thesis, we shall be at pains to point out how many 'normal' features of 'normal organizations' have the same potential for reprehensibility. It is a price we pay for the organizations that functionalism and hegemony tell us we must have.

Notes

1   Parsons was the key symbolic figure, because of his celebrated status as a theoretician. However, in terms of his own intellectual formation we should also consider the influence of Henderson and his systemic biological view, the role Pareto's work played for Henderson (Henderson 1935), and the recreation of Pareto's view by the Harvard Circle, especially by Homans and Curtis (1934). Contributions by Merton (1952) and his group, especially Selznick (1957) and Gouldner (1954), were also relevant to understanding the subsequent institutionaliza-tion of organization theory, which became materialized in the publication of the *Administrative Science Quarterly* and the creation of departments and programs on the subject of organiza-tions (Ibarra-Colado 1999: 103, 106–12).

2   The philosopher Alasdair MacIntyre once wrote, rather wittily, on the ontological problems of talking up a general and ordinary language category into being as a scientific object: 'There was once a man who aspired to be the author of the general theory of holes. When asked, "What kind of hole – holes dug by children in the sand for amusement, holes dug by gardeners to plant lettuce seedlings, tank traps, holes made by roadmakers?", he would reply indignantly that he wished for a general theory that would explain all of these. He rejected *ab initio* the – as he saw it – pathetically common sense view that for the digging of different kinds of holes there are quite different explanations to be given: why then he would ask do we have the concept of a hole?' (1971: 260). He wrote about holes. If one substitutes the notion of a system, or indeed an organization, for that of a hole, one raises quite mischievous issues.

3   The consolidation of a system approach did not mean the death of the personnel approach, because it made very important psychological contributions in terms of behavioral research during the Second World War, notably in personality theory and in terms of operationaliza-tion, both of which were to have a delayed impact on organization theory through the Aston School in the 1960s (Clegg and Dunkerley 1980).

4   Efficiency had been built into organization theory from Taylor onwards; it 'swarmed', to use one of Foucault's terms, into a variety of organizational settings, such as the Ford Sociological Department, and thence into the Harvard Fatigue Laboratory. Mayo sought to further its application to the individual in the personnel counseling applied at the Western Electric Company. Loren Baritz (1974) developed a view of this experience, which showed its similarities with the psychiatric couch and the Catholic confessional box, while George Friedmann (1946) developed an early critical examination. The claim to scientific neutrality expanded 'the nature and array of personal infractions … open to control' (Berdayes 2002: 39). For instance, with Mayo the moral economy that had emerged with Ford shifted not just into a concern for the welfare of the body of workers, but into a specific concern with the individual 'soul' of the employee, to use the phrase that Follett found felicitous and which contemporary Foucauldians such as Rose (1989) were subsequently to utilize. The new disciplines isolated a field of 'deviance': in Ford's time, they did so quite literally. With Mayo, the deviance was becoming more metaphorical, and by the postwar era the deviance became fully metaphorical. Now power played the part of the deviant other in the systems theory that had become the orthodox ground for the possible construction of management knowledge.

5   To attach the term 'Clayton's' to anything as a possessive, in Australian slang, dates back to the late 1970s when an advertising campaign for a soft drink, Clayton's, tried to position it as the drink that real men had when they weren't having a drink. The marketing failed but the phrase stuck: anything Clayton's is a fake, a substitute, not the full quid.

6   Gerard Fairtlough, in thinking about alternatives to hierarchy, is not some ivory tower theorist, or hippie dreamer, we should add. In fact, he is one of the few current organization theorists to have run several multimillion dollar enterprises (including Shell Chemicals UK and Celltech, the most successful European bio-technology company) and, as he explains elsewhere, many of his ideas were worked out in the practice of running these companies (Fairtlough 1994).

7   Other writers also recognize that hierarchy is by no means the only form through which power relations may be condensed and concentrated – nor is it necessarily the best. Manuel Castells (1996a) argues that we are seeing the emergence and rise of the network society, and Phillip Bobbitt (2002) sees the nation-state being replaced by the market state, wherein numerous diverse private organizations take over governmental function, thus reducing the role of hierarchical government.

 **6** The Heart of Darkness

Introduction

The study of extremes is important for organization science. Extremes serve to demonstrate that irruptions to normalcy and taken-for-granted assumptions are not some deviation from normal but regular, albeit unpredictable, occurrences. They serve to establish that the assumptions of equilibrium that anchor systems theory are profoundly misleading. In cases where equilibrium is assumed, then the expectation is that there will be a typical standard deviation occurring around the norm. The point of looking at extreme cases is to see normal phenomena in a condensed and concentrated form, especially as these normal phenomena center on the person in the institution.

In this chapter we will focus on what is one of the most important and extreme instances of organizational power in the twentieth century, the Holocaust. The Holocaust was an extreme because its workflow was oriented to the organization of routinized, standardized, centralized, mass production of death as its overarching systematic goal. What made the systematic approach to death possible, however, were a whole series of organizational accommodations. The Holocaust was a total institution designed to mass produce death. The Canadian sociologist Erving

Goffman first advanced the idea of 'total institutions'; similar generic ideas are to be found in Michel Foucault's (1977) work, and Zygmunt Bauman (1989) provides more substantive accounts of the Holocaust.

Erving Goffman and Michel Foucault

Situating Goffman

If Weber's relative neglect is one curious absence in the annals of organization theory, then it is not the only one. The litany of unsung heroes must also include Erving Goffman, especially his work on total institutions,[1] not least because he anticipated, in so many ways, themes that were later to attract dedicated followers of Foucauldian fashion. Goffman's approach to organization power owed nothing to the rationalism of systems theory and seemingly little to earlier writers, such as Weber.[2] It was substantial, significant, and stylish, yet has hardly been accorded its due in the field. There is an initial question that this chapter will address. Why does Goffman not figure as a prominent precursor of institutional theory?

In *Asylums* (1961) Goffman decided to study those social acts which rational society had placed in special contexts, outside of its definition of reason, in those psychiatric hospitals known in his day as 'asylums'. Goffman's research question was to ask what habits were socially constructed through symbolic interactions in such organizational contexts. Thus, his work was resolutely organizational in its focus on the effects of organizations on individuals and the framing that the organization structure and processes provided. Goffman saw his research question in terms of how such institutions served as a 'forcing house for changing persons, as a natural experiment on what can be done to the self' (1961: 12).

It is the extreme possibilities for transformation of the self that recommend total institutions as research settings. Practices come into sharper focus in a world of extremes. The self becomes so much more pliable and plastic in these institutions: the inmate is separated from others not classed as being essentially similar by virtue of their institutionalization; their sense of the self is subject to abasement, degradation, humiliation, and an insistent stripping away of who and what they are by withdrawal of the physical and social supports that normally sustain them. Goffman documents the self's resistance to its erosion, its insistence on retaining some authentic sense of who one was and struggles still to be. Inmates practice secondary adjustments, such as developing close relations with other inmates, with pet rodents, insects or imaginary others, that do not directly challenge the staff of the total institution but that, by representing forbidden satisfactions, affirm that the inmates are still their own person, still embodying personhood as unique spontaneous agency. The self demonstrates 'expressed distance', 'holding off from fully embracing all the self-implications of its affiliation, allowing some ... disaffection to be seen, even while fulfilling ... major obligations', and 'defaulting not from prescribed activity, but from prescribed being' (1961: 188). Goffman elaborates the many 'make-dos', those small acts of adaptation, adjustment and improvisation that are prevalent in total institutions such as Central Hospital, and the ways that inmates of the institution capture special assignments for themselves or access to special places or patrons that extend autonomy – even life – a little.

Goffman argues that the self emerges from the way it defines itself against obdurate otherness and others. Goffman documents the tenacity of the self to be what it is and resist being prescribed as that it should be. No matter what were the sins, the crimes, the craziness that opened the doors of the institution, to strip the self from the person without allowing some expressed distance is intensely inhumane. That this inhumanity usually takes its course under a public rhetoric of care and concern for the selves at its fulcrum is the greatest betrayal of their selfhood. Like Bob Dylan (1964), another great observer of the scenes of everyday life, we may say that Goffman alerts us to the chimes of freedom flashing in the most unlikely places and for the most unlikely people:

> Through the wild cathedral evening the rain unraveled tales
> For the disrobed faceless forms of no position
> Tolling for the tongues with no place to bring their thoughts
> All down in taken-for-granted situations
> Tolling for the deaf an' blind, tolling for the mute
> Tolling for the mistreated, mateless mother, the mistitled prostitute
> For the misdemeanor'd outlaw, chased an' cheated by pursuit
> An' we gazed upon the chimes of freedom flashing.

Goffman drew on symbolic interactionism at a time when structural functionalism was the dominant paradigm in sociology. Perhaps this is why he is so slighted, so little cited: maybe he just didn't become sedimented in the collective consciousness of the field as it became defined. Yet, Goffman drew from the same anthropological tradition as some of the pioneers of the human relations movement (for example Lloyd Warner, but also Elton Mayo and later W. F. Whyte) in introducing what were nonconventional ethnographic research methods. His misfortune was to do so at about the same time that the case study, the ethnographic method, and the importance of the root social science disciplines of anthropology and sociology were being marginalized by the professionalization of organization theory as a disciplinary space in its own right, institutionalized within business schools. The historical moment and the academic space in which Goffman worked are important elements in understanding the silence about his work and the lack of attention given to it until now. In the early 1960s organization theory was cementing its own project of domination; the systems framework was being locked in place and, as Wittgenstein once remarked apropos another set of issues, of that which it could not or would not speak, thereof there was to be silence. Goffman's analysis of total institutions largely ceased to feature.

That functionalist theory, not knowing what to do with Goffman, should dismiss him, is hardly surprising. The approach to institutional theory that he developed simply was too multifaceted to fit in the world busy being built in the 1960s, and his work seemed to miss the boat when second-generation institutional theory was launched in the 1980s.[3] What is surprising is that in the 1970s, when some 'critical' theorists were struggling to shake off the stultifying analytics of labor process 'theory' and found the succor they sought in *Discipline and punish* (Foucault 1977), with its emphasis on power, surveillance, and resistance, Goffman was still largely ignored. Perhaps Goffman, who showed no interest in Marxism or structural themes, was insufficiently chic; for instance, he was condemned as quietist in his political allegiances by the leading American social theorist of the post-Parsonian generation, the mantle that Alvin Gouldner (1971) assumed when he moved on from organization sociology to social theory and from the United States to Europe. At best Goffman could be accommodated to the radical canon as a humanist (Burrell and Morgan 1979). By the late 1970s radical humanism had lost its charm; it was a time when French structuralism seemed so much more radical in its denial of the 'problematic of the subject' (Althusser 1971).

Situating Foucault

In 1960s France the main points of reference for leftist intellectuals had been Marxism and the actually existing social conditions in society. After 1968, and Althusser's subsequent fall from analytic and everyday grace, and as poststructuralism gathered pace, these points of reference seemed to converge on the figure of his former École Normale Supérieure student, Michel Foucault, an authentically left but non-Marxist intellectual.

The ascendancy of interest in Foucault mirrored the decline of interest in Althusser, and a number of the early discussions of Foucault were by some people who had previously been Althusserian Marxists (Barry Hindess (1996) is a good example of someone who trod this path). In Foucault, as was evident by Poulantzas' (1978) response to him in *State, power, socialism*, there was to be found an account of power that did not rely on familiar notions of the state as its fulcrum. At a time when new politics were emerging around personal issues such as sexuality and gender relations, Foucault seemed a better guide than those who would reduce social relations to a *pas de deux* articulated between the economic base and the ideological superstructure.

The English-language reader who knows little of intellectual politics and the history of ideas might think that Foucault must be celebrated in France as an authentically Gallic organization theorist. Nothing could be further from the truth. He is virtually unknown and unused by the French organization and management theory community. In fact, he is probably no more read there than he is in its United States equivalent, even though he may be better known. Oddly, Foucault's fame in organization theory is almost entirely due to his discussion in British and Australian English-language accounts. Foucault has become a celebrity *French* intellectual for Anglophone readers, much as, in earlier years, Sartre and Althusser.

In more than one respect there is some continuity between Goffman and Foucault. Goffman (1956; 1961) did not make it easy for those who wish to pigeon-hole; he preferred to work through the empirical materials rather than through abstracted analytic models, as did Foucault. It is time to retrieve Goffman for the canon of organization theory – as well as to incorporate Foucault – but in each case it is imperative that it be done critically. While each grasped a great deal they also made startling errors of omission, especially Foucault.

Total institutions

Goffman coined the term 'total institutions', to refer to a class of concentrated power. In many ways he anticipated the themes that were later to become popular in Foucault's (1977) work – the power of incarceration, rules and surveillance – although instead of focusing on *design* he studied *action*, which undoubtedly gave greater acuity to his analyses: in Goffman we are dealing with what people actually do, not what the designers of their institutions would have them do. In this respect Foucault is as erroneous as Parsons, dwelling in the space of normative expectations rather than enacted social actions.

Institutions are total when they surround the person at every turn and cannot be escaped; they produce and reproduce the normalcy of life inside the institution, however abnormal it might seem from outside (Deleuze 1992). Thus, total institutions are organizations that contain the totality of the lives of those who are their members. As such, people within them are cut off from any wider society for a relatively long time, leading an enclosed and formally administered existence. In such contexts, the organization has more or less monopoly control of its members' everyday life. Sometimes, total institutions comprise practices and operating mechanisms which inscribe domination on a particular bio-political target, such as those classed as insane, criminal, Jewish, indigenous, fallen women, schoolchildren in elite boarding schools, orphans, sailors, etc. Goffman's argument is that total institutions demonstrate in heightened and condensed form the underlying organizational processes that can be found, albeit in much less extreme cases, in more normal organizations. He chose extremes because the everyday mechanisms of authority and power were much more evident there than in the world of the corporate 'organization man' (Whyte 1960).

If Goffman (1961) anticipated some aspects that Foucault (1977) was later to stress, the latter still missed a great deal. Total institutions are not just premised on surveillance, on the gaze, as Foucault suggests. While Foucault stresses that 'the techniques of surveillance, the "physics" of power, the hold over the body, operate according to the laws of optics and mechanics, according to a whole play of spaces, lines, screens, beams, degrees, and without recourse, in principle, at least, to excess, force or violence' and that it 'is a power that seems all the less "corporeal" in that it is subtly "physical"' (1977: 177), he misses the characteristic aspect of the most significant total institutions of the twentieth century. Their means have been overwhelmingly violent, based upon confinement against the will of those subject to it, and abuse of the dignity and bodies of those confined. Foucault suggests that in the total institution there

> is no need for arms, physical violence, material constraints. Just a gaze. An inspecting gaze, a gaze which each individual under its weight will end by interiorising to the point that he is his own overseer, each individual thus exercising this surveillance over, and against himself. (1980: 155)

One must protest that this makes power far too ideational. With David Ackles (1969) we might ask 'Do your absent bodies hear your souls' lament?' The soul may become the prison of the body, but the body can become, literally, the inmate of the institution, and once therein, free to be inscribed in the worst possible ways – as we shall see. Thus, although using a concept of *total institution* associated with Goffman (1961), and ideas of *surveillance* often associated with Foucault (1977), we shall take these concepts into a *far more corporeal modernity* than the latter entertained as a part of the modern condition. For Foucault, the corporeality of power belongs to pre-modern times, not the modern age.[4] As has been suggested by Hacking (2004), there is a need to bridge between discourse in the abstract and face-to-face behavior, between Foucault and Goffman.

Total institutions are often parts of a broader apparatus, such as a prison or detention center, as a part of a criminal justice or immigration system. Total institutions do not just include organizations that make people inmates against their will, however, or in which people can become institutionalized to an accommodation. They can also include organizations founded on membership contracted on voluntary inclusion: for instance, a professional army, a boarding school, a residential college, or a religious retreat, such as a monastery or nunnery. Several types of organization can be a total institution:

- Places to put people that the state deems incapable of care for the self (these people, who vary historically and comparatively, have included the 'feeble', the 'lunatic', the 'disabled', the 'indigent' and the 'old').
- Restrictive organizations that institutionalize people who pose a threat to others, such as people with communicable diseases of contagion who are legislatively contained in sanitaria for the duration of their disease.
- Punitive organizations, such as prisons, gulags, concentration camps, reform schools, prisoner-of-war camps, or detention centers for asylum seekers.
- Organizations dedicated to a specific work task, such as boarding schools, military barracks, and vessels at sea, or remote company towns.
- Retreats from the world, such as monasteries, abbeys, convents, or growth and learning centers.

What these very different types of organizations have in common that make them total institutions are the following. Each member's daily life is carried out in the immediate presence of a large number of others. The members are very visible; there is no place to hide from the surveillance of others. The members tend to be strictly regimented by formal rational planning of time. (Think of school bells for lesson endings and beginnings, factory whistles, timetables, schedules, and so on.) People are not free to choose how they spend their time; instead, it is strictly prescribed for them. Members lose a degree of autonomy because of an all-encompassing demand for conformity to the authoritative interpretation of rules.

If we accept Goffman's analysis, it becomes evident that the essential core of organization is power. Organizations exert power over their members by making them do things that they would not otherwise do and take on identities that they would not otherwise have assumed. And, if people obey orders voluntarily then the power is sanctified as authority. Authority is experienced in the normalcy and legitimacy of power, as what it is one will do and should do, in terms of legitimate, often superordinate, expectations. Under certain conditions these expectations can frame surprising outcomes.

Authority at work

Ordinary people can do extraordinary things when authority tells them to, as an experiment by Milgram (1971) demonstrated. Milgram's research question was simply to ask to what extent ordinary individuals, people who are not authoritarian personalities but display all the signs of normalcy, follow the commands of figures perceived to be in authority. His answer demonstrated that the kind of situation in which people are embedded determines, in part, how they will act. He designed an experiment in which white-coated scientists instructed ordinary people (the subjects) to do cruel and unusual things to other people (the participants) as part of an experiment in a laboratory. In a nutshell, the subjects were instructed to administer increasing levels of electric shocks to the participants as part of a behavioral learning program. They did so under a range of circumstances. When participants gave incorrect answers to test questions, they were to be administered a shock, with each one to be higher than the one before. (No shock was actually administered; the participants, unbeknownst to the subjects, were actually actors.) When the subjects were face to face with the participants and told to administer the electric shock directly to their hands, using force if necessary, only 30 percent did so. When the subjects could still see the participants but used a control lever that administered the shock instead of having to force the hands of the participants onto the plates administering the shock, 40 percent did so. When the subjects could no longer see the participants but could only hear their distress as the current apparently surged, 62.5 percent were able to apply the current. Moving the others out of earshot marginally improved the rate to 65 percent. The more distance – both physical and psychological – there was between the controllers and the controlled, the easier it seemed to be to do seemingly inhumane and cruel things. The closer the relation between the controller and the supervisor, and the more removed the subject, the easier it became to continue. Obedience to authority flows more easily when the subjects of action are at a distance. When these subjects can be transformed into objects in the controller's mind, when they are dehumanized or reduced to just another example of a specific case, obedience flows even more easily.

Another factor facilitating the application of current was the incremental threshold. Once someone had committed to the action, each increase in the threshold was just a small step, just another slight increase in pain to be endured. It is not as if they started out to kill another person or cause them irretrievable injury. They just did what they were instructed to do – only they did a little bit more of it each time. Where such action should stop, once started, is not at all clear. And after someone has committed to the action, especially if others are complicit, there arise what Milgram (1971) termed 'situational obligations'. In organizations with complex divisions of labor, sequential action invariably makes us complicit with many others, in many interactions.

Milgram (1971) made one crucial change to the experiments to test out a further hypothesis: that plurality produces space for reflection and pause for consideration. In the experiments reported thus far, there was only one expert giving instructions. Milgram introduced another expert and instructed them to disagree with each other about the command being given. The disagreement between authorities paralyzed the capacity for obedience of the research subjects: out of 20 subjects in this experiment, one refused to go further before the staged disagreement; 18 broke off after it; and the remaining subject opted out just one stage further on. *Polyphony* – the presence of competing and conflicting voices – increases the probability that people will think for themselves rather than just do what they are told. Thus, strong organizational cultures that suppress value difference are more likely to produce unreflective and sometimes inappropriate organizational action than more democratic and pluralistic settings.

Discussion of Milgram leads us back to total institutions. It is in these, precisely, that we would least expect to find polyphony and difference. As Bauman suggests, '*the readiness to act against one's own better judgment and against the voice of one's conscience is not just the function of authoritative command, but the result of exposure to a single-minded, unequivocal and monopolistic source of authority*' (1989: 165) Total institutions – as organizations that presume to exercise strong cultural control over their members, to the extent that they diminish pluralism – squeeze the space in which civility, reflection, and responsibility can thrive. Bauman urges that 'The voice of individual moral conscience is best heard in the tumult of political and social discord' (1989: 166).

Even in times and circumstances that are considered normal, you might find powerful total institutions at work, which the following case demonstrates. Again, the absence of polyphony is one of the preconditions for the establishment of total institutions. Haney et al. (1973) designed an experiment that resonates with government practices that are accepted as normal and routine in many societies. The researchers divided a group of male American college students into two types of people, those defined as guards and as inmates. They created a mock prison in a laboratory basement, using as subjects 21 healthy male undergraduate volunteers. Each person was to receive $15 a day for two weeks. Nine were randomly selected to be 'prisoners', with the remainder designated as 'guards' who were to supervise the prisoners in a rotating three-shift system. Each wore the symbolic garb of the role. Prisoners were given unflattering uniform clothing and tight caps to simulate shaven heads. Guards were put in a militaristic-type uniform and given LA cop sunglasses. Names were suppressed with norms of impersonality, and complex rules and penalties for their infraction were promulgated. Then the experiment began.

The experiment had to be aborted after less than a week. An escalatory chain of events occurred; the construed authority of the guards was enforced by the submissiveness of the prisoners, tempting the guards to show further and increasingly illegitimate displays of the power that their authority allowed them to exercise, leading to further humiliation of the prisoners (Bauman 1989: 167). Bear in mind that the subjects were all normal, well-adjusted people before the experiment began but that after one week they were playing their roles with such conviction that the experiment had to be abandoned because of the real possibility of harm to the 'prisoners'. No sense of solidarity developed between the two groups, and almost all of their conversation centered on the roles assumed in the experiment.[5] Of course, these were just little experiments, play-acting one might note, wryly, so let's look at a real-life experiment in which the stakes were somewhat higher and the drama existentially real. We shall begin with an account provided by the eminent sociologist Zygmunt Bauman.[6]

Zygmunt Bauman: another curious absence

It is not only that Weber and Goffman have been written out of the history of organization theory. Others were never written in. Zygmunt Bauman is one of the world's most eminent intellectuals, notable for many outstanding contributions to social science, especially *Modernity and the Holocaust* (1989). It is a work of great organizational significance, although this fact seems to have escaped the majority of writers and authorities in the field, for it is rarely cited in the standard journals or subject outlines.

Bauman's argument is that bureaucratic rationality was one of the essential factors that made the Holocaust possible. The usual explanation of the Holocaust is that it was a reversion to barbarism. On the contrary, says Bauman. The mechanics of the Holocaust were made possible by precisely those features of society that made it 'civilized', chief amongst which was rational bureaucracy. Rational bureaucracy was used to try and resolve what was referred to as the 'Jewish Question', one which flowed from the premise that Jews were a contagious plague, a pestilence, the other on whom hatred could be focused. The answer was to be found in a 'Final Solution' organized around extermination, the Holocaust.

If a central aspect of the Holocaust concerned its organizational possibility, wouldn't one think that this might be a central theme of contemporary organization studies? Wouldn't organization studies want to focus on this case as an exemplification of how what was good in organization could produce what was evil in human action? Might it not want to comb through the records of the Holocaust to identify the trail that the Gestapo left behind or conduct oral histories of the few of its victims to survive? Or should it simply seek absolution for its silence? The sound of silence and the need for absolution are overwhelming: we know only of one such oral organizational historical account (through the work of Chris Grey 2005) that explicitly engages with the Holocaust, by Madsen and Willert (1996), who examine the structure of daily life in a Nazi work camp. They do this through conversations with the Danish social psychologist, Gunnar Hjeholt, who was arrested by the Germans in 1944 and spent nine months in the Porta Westfalica concentration camp before being liberated. Much as Bauman, he concludes that the most frightening thing about the camps as a system was the fact that they were, organizationally, not at all unique. Once inside the logic of their system, certain actions became routine. They were much like other systems with which we are all familiar. Many victims (or their relatives) of Gestapo terror are still fighting for compensation, so such systematic organizational oral histories have important legal as well as ethical significance. In the face of missing formal evidence about Gestapo crimes, gaining such compensation has proved a rather hopeless cause for many of the victims or their representatives. Until very recently, most slave laborers who worked for German companies during the Second World War fought in vain for compensation. Only about a year ago, 60 years after the events, was a fund eventually set up to compensate the victims. Needless to say many of the latter have meanwhile died.

Apart from Madsen and Willert (1996), the only work of significance that does address the Holocaust, which is not entirely without discussion in the organizations literature (see Clegg 2002; Grey 2005: 25), is Bauman's, although much of the discussion misses the mark. For instance, du Gay (2000b) argues that Bauman's representation of bureaucracy is one-sided, since he only refers to the potentially amoral character of bureaucratic procedures and not to the bureaucratic ethos of justice. According to du Gay, racist and party-political convictions, normative and moral sentiments, rather than the application of rules, drove the Nazis. Armbrüster and Gebert (2002) argue that the SS was more a social movement than a rational bureaucracy, animated by spontaneous improvisation rather than rule-driven behavior. The Nazis overthrew the legitimate rule of legal-administrative bureaucracies through politicizing the institutional organs of the state by forced appointments of party members to leading institutional positions (see du Gay 2000b: 48–51; 1999). When ends become detached from means, as Grey (2005: 25) says, substantive ethics are dangerously weakened.

Irrespective of the arguments about bureaucracy, there is no doubt that the Nazis were experts in moving from the gaze, through the selective use of members' categorization devices, to the construction of a career, in the sociological sense of that term, often terminal, in a total institution. (The wonderful autobiography of Janina Bauman, *Winter in the afternoon: the recollections of the life of a young girl in the Warsaw Ghetto*, 1986, is a narrative account, by one who resisted and lived to tell the tale, of how the controls of that total institution tightened.) [7] The juridical eye of the state increasingly promulgated special laws and decrees. These fixed the gaze with the use of devices such as the star that all Jews were obliged to wear prominently on their clothing, or the labeling of businesses as Jewish with prominent signage. After the gaze came confinement, initially through being rounded up and herded into ghettos, where began the career inside the total institution proper. For many millions it was to end, after transportation jammed in cattle-trucks on the rail systems of Europe, in some unknown place in Eastern Europe that the world ought never to forget. The final total institutional experience might last no longer than it took to strip and have a communal shower. For many, the final destination of the gas chambers was the end of what had been a long and slow career in total institutional settings of increasing intensity, while for a few the struggles to survive continued in the work camps associated with the whole business. And business it was, as we shall see.

Total institutions as instruments of genocide in total war

The roots of evil

Anti-Semitism was not a novel experience in German life. Weber, for instance, encountered it in his support of the academic careers of friends such as Simmel.

Higgins (2004: 89) suggests that the Prussian elite had constructed the German project of modernity exclusively in terms of an ethnic nationalism. It was a nationalism that demanded its own strangers, outsiders, and enemies to be viable, a role which Jews had been playing for centuries. They were shortly to be cast the starring role in the horror that fascism was to orchestrate. And orchestrate is an apt verb. The Nazi state was a despotism that relied on stage management, propaganda, and spectacle as its major organizational devices for creating unity, coherence, and support to eliminate not only Jewish people but also polyphony more generally.

The Third Reich was a state developed on the basis of power and myth. Power came from National Socialist command of the state apparatuses after 1933. German history provided the myth it orchestrated. The myth was that of the German *Volk* and its supremacy, which provided 'values and meaning and ideas and plans and stratagems and alternative forms of social organization ... an oversimplified representation of a more complex reality' (Bailey 1977: 7). It created a mythical cosmos that deified the human and demonized the barely human, those others whose not-being defined being German (see Zeraffa 1976: 77 on 'myth'). The signifier of the myth, the ascendant Reich, presented itself as belonging to a history of the German people. In this way its meaning was already complete and projected into the future; it postulated a past, a memory, and a comparative ordering of facts, ideas and decisions, a destiny denied, most notably by the 1919 Treaty of Versailles, but insistent (Barthes 1984). When this destiny assumed a form that captured the state, it rapidly adopted caricature, pastiche, and elaborate stage managed symbols that did 'away with all dialectics, with any going back beyond what is immediately visible ... a world which is without contradictions because it is without depth, a world wide open ... wallowing in the evident' (from *Mythologies*).[8]

The consequences of authoritarian populism and aborted modernization meeting the naturalized myth of the *Volk* were alarming. The defeat of the First World War aborted German nationalism. Nationalism had been achieved and imposed from above by elites, positioning the German nation as a people of manifest destiny, which the First World War stopped in its tracks. When it was revived by Hitler the Nazis changed the nationalist project from one that was defined by elites to one that was to be defined in more popular ways. It became a popular project in a context where, after the collapse of the Weimar Republic, there were few state or civil society resources and few national or civic sources of moral values, education, or authority outside of the National Socialist Party. Moreover, there was little in the way of 'constitutionalism, the rule of law, democracy, civil society, the institutions to negotiate cultural and racial diversity ... There was nothing to prevent the normalization of discrimination and oppression' (Higgins 2004: 90). The project of normalization fused several rationalities, not just the rationality of modernity as Bauman (1989) sees it, but also elements that in themselves were hardly remarkable, as they could be found in comparable polities elsewhere. The Swedish social democrats of the inter-war period, for instance, were as keen on eugenic projects and no less statist. However, what the Nazis had in addition was a much stronger degree of racism and a very clear sense of the other through which to define their German self, using the category of the Jew. Moreover, at the level of micro-politics, the Nazis sought to implement their myths – based on blood, race and territory – in all the spheres of everyday life, such as the family, the youth group, and the neighborhood, through capillaries of power such as the Hitler Youth (see Rose 1999: 25–6).

The Final Solution

It was sometime between the June 1941 offensive against the Soviet Union and January 1942 that the decision was made to exterminate the Jews of Europe (see Mosse 1978), although something of the idea was already evident in speeches by Hitler in 1919 and in *Mein Kampf* (1924). It was not a sudden decision. The pressure against the Jews built up steam after the Nazis came to power on January 30, 1933. Judicial harassment intensified in the period leading up to war with 'bans on employment, on practicing professions, on owning a car or a phone, on going to the theater, on marrying or having sexual relations with gentiles' (Higgins 2004: 86). At the same time, various options were sought to deal with the Jewish Question, including forced resettlement, with Madagascar being suggested as a destination. Once extermination was adopted as an end the top management team concentrated on the project, with the rule of anticipated reaction mobilizing management sentiment. As Higgins notes, in the disorderly and crony-ridden world of Nazi politics, much as in any organization where to succeed means impressing the boss, senior Nazis who were 'rivals tried to outshine each other in Hitler's eyes through their bold initiatives in carrying out what they often had to second-guess as his intentions. Massacring the Jews in one's jurisdiction offered a sure-fire way to impress the boss. Once one crony hit on it the rest followed suit' (2004: 87).

It is not clear who decided that extermination was the appropriate solution, or when they decided. It was certainly the case that it was formally communicated to the top management team of the Nazi project who met on January 20, 1942, in Wannsee, to plan the extermination of Europe's Jews. Adolf Eichmann, one of Hitler's deputies and the Head of the Department for Jewish Affairs, was chosen to organize the Holocaust. He led the Reich's effort for the Final Solution, efficiently organizing the roundup and transportation of millions of Jews to their deaths at infamous camps such as Auschwitz.[9] Two-thirds of all victims were liquidated in just 18 months, from June 22, 1941 to December 31, 1942, according to the Third Reich's chief statistician, Richard Koherr (Higgins 2004: 98).

Six million bodies disappeared from the face of the earth as a result of the Holocaust, including one and half million children. The ultimate goal would have seen the extermination of 11 million Jews; the war's end saw about 50 percent of the target achieved, given that the 6 million also included other categories constituted as deviant, such as the feeble, homosexuals, communists, gypsies and so on. By any calculus the efficient dispatch of millions of state-stigmatized people to their deaths by the German state during the Second World War was an enormous organizational achievement.[10] Indeed, Rose suggests that the actual power of Nazism 'was its capacity to render itself technical, to connect itself up with all manner of technologies capable of implementing its nightmarish dreams into everyday existence' (1999: 26) There were quite specific rationalities – techniques, one might say – behind the technologies. We shall now turn to these.

Identity and power

The project of fascism *entailed an ongoing construction of an organizational politics of identity and non-identity.*[11] Identities were established through the use of various stigmatizing 'membership categorization devices' (Sudnow 1972; Sacks 1992).[12] There was no need for any subtlety in interpreting the Nazis' use of membership categorization devices. Terms such as 'Jews', 'gypsies', 'homosexuals', and 'the feeble', which the Nazis used, needed no inferential reasoning. They were not 'natural' categories but were produced by a vast organizational apparatus to appear naturalized. A fundamental organizational condition of the Holocaust was the identification of individuals as members of specific categories, and the marking of their membership categorization with devices. In the case of Jews, these were the distinctive markers that all those who were defined as Jews were obliged to wear; in Germany the yellow star, in the Warsaw ghetto a white band with a blue star.[13] Businesses were also marked: during the boycott upon Jewish stores that the Nazis declared on April 1, 1933, yellow Stars of David were painted on windows. These markers of identity singled out those who were destined for special categorization and total institutionalization, entailing *concentration of clearly inscribed identities in specific spaces*, initially in ghettos such as that in Warsaw, and latterly their spatial segregation in camps.[14] Confined, segregated, and marked, they were much easier to control. The *orderly and efficient marshalling of bodies* was required. These bodies were transported across Europe in cattle-trucks and efficiently scheduled as inputs into the death camps. If the trains had not run on time, the points not been set up correctly, the machinery of death would have been interrupted. One historian, Goldhagen (1996), argues that the order and efficiency depended on hundreds and thousands of small acts of organized goal orientation by civilian German citizens and collaborators in the occupied territories.[15]

Expert knowledge

When the trains arrived at the camp, doctors made a 'selection' using *expert knowledge* to decide which of the new arrivals were fit to be worked to death. Life for the slave laborers was often unbearable and many would die of overwork, starvation and disease. Less than 10 percent were chosen to be slave laborers; most were dispatched straight to the 'showers', after first disrobing. Those who were selected for the gas chambers *had all markers of identity removed*, by being stripped and shorn, and having personal items such as jewelry taken. Such denial and degradation of identity is typical of total institutional practice, even if extermination is not.

Efficient power means that systematic attention has to be paid to its means. By 1944, when the Jews from Hungary were deported to Auschwitz, the death factory was unable to absorb the mass numbers. It was estimated that in the spring of 1944, 46,000 Jews were killed in one day. Such efficiency requires a dedicated organizational apparatus. Crude organizational technologies assisted in this huge project. The Hollerith machine was used 'to track the Jewish populations and accumulate information regarding the "success" of the Genocide' (Leventhal 1995). The machine was 'a primitive calculating engine and precursor of the modern computer developed by the statistician and census taker, Herman Hollerith', and manufactured by the IBM subsidiary Deutsche Hollerith Maschinen Gesellschaft (DEHOMAG) (Leventhal 1995).

The destruction of those collected and defined in their identity as Jews and other stigmatized categories would not have been possible without application of *an intrinsically instrumental and value-free science*. It is, of course, this kind of science that lies behind the conception of the organization as an open system. It is this abstraction that enables one to conjure up an organization science in which the specificities and particularities of concrete practices can be reduced to the mechanism of variation, selection and retention, the resolution of equivocality in an open system fed by inputs, organized around a central workflow that defines the throughput, producing outputs. The inputs were live bodies; the transformation process one of chemically induced death; the outputs corpses with the value stripped out of them. *An efficient total institution premised on the efficient transformation of its raw material inputs required a factory system for its flows of power, with efficiencies of scale in processing inputs and creating outputs*, that could, literally, reduce something to nothing (Ritzer 2004), people to ashes, dust and detritus. In so doing it not only created efficiencies but also destroyed futures by dividing societies, families, friends, communities, workers, creating a vacuum where the foundational identity of generations yet unborn should have made its mark, inducing guilt and shame about surviving for those that remained.

Achieving efficiencies

Bauman referred to Feingold's (1983: 399–400) argument to establish that Auschwitz was an extension of the value rationality of the modern factory system:

> Rather than producing goods, the raw material was human beings and the end-product was death, so many units per day marked carefully on the manager's production charts. The chimneys, the very symbol of the modern factory system, poured forth acrid smoke produced by burning human flesh. The brilliantly organized railroad grid of modern Europe carried a new kind of raw material to the factories. It did so in the same manner as with other cargo. In the gas chambers the victims inhaled noxious gas generated by prussic acid pellets, which were produced by the advanced chemical industry of Germany. Engineers designed the crematoria; managers designed the system of bureaucracy that worked with a zest and efficiency more backward nations would envy. Even the overall plan itself was a reflection of the modern scientific sprit gone awry. (1989: 8)

In the early stages, bullets delivered death, but these were needed for the front line. Anyway, they were slow and inefficient; it would have taken hundreds of years to shoot every Jew in Europe. Initially, there were many concentration camps, in which death was an incidental cost of confinement in horrific conditions, while originally there were only four death camps (Chelmno, Belzec, Sobibór and Treblinka, which were all in rural Poland). These resembled a cottage industry of killing compared to the two conglomerates (combining slave labor with extermination) that the Nazis established, Majdanek and Auschwitz, of which Auschwitz was the larger and more developed. In pursuit of their key performance indicator, the extermination of the

Jews, the Nazis organized for economies of scale. Estimates are that 1,500,000 people, most of whom were Jews, died at Auschwitz. Others who died at Auschwitz included Soviet prisoners of war, gypsies or Roma, Poles, Jehovah's Witnesses, homosexuals, and political opponents of the Nazi regime.

Auschwitz was designed so that two transports per day, each with 6,000 Jews, could be 'processed'. These 12,000 Jews would have their heads shaved and their clothing collected and stored, and would be gassed and cremated, all within a 24-hour period. Within 24 hours, all traces of their bodily existence were obliterated from the face of the earth, apart from their hair, skin, gold fillings, prosthetics, dentures and anything else that could be recycled, because, short of a budget for the killing machine, a user-pays philosophy prevailed as the victims funded their own deaths through their corpses being made a source of value. The SS ran profitable industries dealing in what it recycled from the dead and produced through slave labor. It also got kickbacks from Krupp, Volkswagen and IG Farben, amongst others, for the labor it supplied (Leventhal 1995; see also Borkin 1978; Hayes 1991). And there were willing accomplices in power networks elsewhere. Vincent (1997) demonstrates how the Nazis were able to use the secrecy associated with Swiss banking to bank the assets realized (also see Bower 1997; Levin 1999). These were not isolated crimes by a few evil people but required considerable networks of expertise and involvement (Raab 2003). In this way, the Holocaust can be seen as a bureaucratic regime of power with many capillaries and considerable expertise in its service.

On the whole, the process that was adopted was a simple system of *mass destruction*, of flows, throughputs, and outputs. It wasn't designed like this from the outset. The Auschwitz complex included three main camps and 39 smaller camps, 40 miles southwest of Krakow. As Higgins (2004: 133) tells it, Auschwitz grew from a barracks left over from the old Austro-Hungarian Empire, which was initially equipped with a small gas chamber and crematorium. Innovation was concentrated on Auschwitz II, a satellite camp adjacent to the village of Birkenau. Most of the 1.5 million were killed at Auschwitz–Birkenau, the second of the main camps. It was here that the railway ran right into the camp, beneath the sign reading 'Work makes us free' (*Arbeit macht frei*). Initially, it too was run on pre-industrial lines. There was a 30 meter run from the undressing sheds to the gas chambers and the corpses were bundled into pits and burnt after dispatch. However, in March 1943 a modernized, integrated high-capacity infrastructure was established as a greenfield development, with four separate plants, each with its own crematorium and gas chamber. Here is how Higgins describes the setup in his *Journey into darkness:*

> The new underground undressing room, disguised as a disinfecting station, measured 30 by eight meters in each of the larger two factories. Deceit was essential to the factory's orderly throughput ... Few Germans were to be seen, as the SS believed in the progressive virtues of self-management (*Selbstverwaltung*). From the undressing room the Sonderkommando [trusted inmates] ushered the naked victims into the adjacent gas chamber disguised as a shower room. It had the same dimensions as the undressing room and a two and a half meter high ceiling. Usually around 2,500 people were packed in at a time. Cramming them in like this quickly brought the temperature in the chamber up to body heat, the optimum temperature to evaporate the Zyklon B pellets into gas ...

Only German personnel could throw in the gas pellets. Death came painfully, on average after 10 minutes, given an adequate gas supply. The gas chambers were equipped with peep holes so the Germans could check on the process. Sometimes they amused themselves by putting in too little gas which prolonged the death agonies of the victims. Not a single person came out of a gassing alive.

Around thirty minutes after the introduction of the gas the Sonderkommando opened the doors of the gas chamber opposite the entrance and began the backbreaking task of lugging the corpses to the electrical lift. Their SS supervisors forced them to work at a furious tempo. The 'dentist' removed gold teeth, and the women's hair was cut off and collected. Mucus, urine, excreta, and menstrual blood covered the corpses, making them slippery and hard to handle. Each lift took between ten and twelve piled-up corpses to the ground floor, where they had to be dragged to the hatches of the 15 crematorium ovens.

The new crematoria represented another technological breakthrough in that they centralized combustion: three ovens shared the same energy source. They used minimal amounts of precious coke and mainly ran on human fat. A prominent German manufacturer of crematoria plant, Topf and Söhne, successfully tendered for the project, and custom-designed and built the new crematoria. (Like IG Farben, their business flourishes to this day in Germany.) The ovens operated at temperatures between 800 and 1,200 °C. The high operating temperatures meant Topf and Söhne's engineers had to make twelve service calls during the facility's working life. Within 40–45 minutes the ovens reduced the corpses to ash and bone fragments, which found their way into the nearby Vistula River, Even in this respect, the German designers stuck to good industrial tradition, dumping the tailings in the nearest waterway. (2004: 134)

The actual chemical agent of death, Zyklon B, was initially used as an insecticide (for delousing clothing) in the First World War but was subsequently developed as an agent for human extermination during the Second by the German chemical multinational IG Farben. Many experiments and refinements were involved, with great scientific rationality being devoted to the topic of extermination by chemists and their co-workers over several years, to establish the appropriate level of concentration, temperature, and time of application to suit the new purpose (Dworkf and van Peltz 1996). The gas was a cheap means of destruction: that was its attraction for the economic rationalists running the camps. Other economic efficiencies of the day involved practicing sustainable recycling for profits, minimizing service intervals to contain running costs, and externalizing the costs of side products, such as tailings. The management was exemplary in its technical and economic efficiency. As a business it used the best practice principles of its day.

An open system

The death camps were a simple open system in which the inputs were living bodies that were subject to an initial selection, variation and retention. Those selected were gassed and burnt, although at times of peak throughput, those who could not be accommodated in the gas chambers and crematoria were shot and burned in mass pits in the grounds of Birkenau. Variation was simple as those able-bodied enough were retained and worked until death. The outputs were the elimination of the great uncertainty that stalked Nazi Europe, seen as the possibility of contagion of Aryan purity by Jewish bodies. The equivocality was resolved by the death of the contagious bodies.

How was such a system possible? First, it was highly authorized: *the highest authority sanctioned this organizational action.* That a strong leader tells followers to do things, management scholars might think, could be a good reason actually to do them, because they are the leader and their will is usually fulfilled. A strong leader is assumed to have good reasons, so the person follows in good faith. In addition, the leader commands a mighty organizational apparatus, which, in this case, had a monopoly over the means of violence. Eichmann's commitment to Hitler as a strong authority figure shaped his behavior. The SS themselves were an authoritative elite; most 'of the leaders of the *Einsatzgruppen*, the mass-shooting squads who murdered up to a third of all the Holocaust victims, held PhDs or Doctors of Laws. They were the principal bearers of German civilization, not low-lifers, misfits or retards' (Higgins 2004: 98). Many careers were advanced in academia, science, philosophy, economics, genetics, geography, education, social work, and history in the service of the Holocaust. And their authority and actions were minutely documented in memoranda, data, statistics, and reports.

Second, it was highly routinized. Routines eliminate the need or the space for reflection. *When actions that enact the organizational action in question are routinized, the acts in question become easier to enact.* Routine is important because it facilitates action without reflection (and responsibility), as an automatic response to a stimulus. Individuals become merely a cog in the big machinery that turns them around. One sees only a small part of the whole organizational machinery when accomplishing a task; one cannot see where and how the task fits into the big picture, nor can one see its consequences as an outcome of the task or organization. This may seem an absurd point – for are not all modern organizations premised on routines and routinization? The point is not that this, on its own, makes horror possible, but that in the appropriate context it can do so when other conditions are present. Routinization, we might say, is a necessary but not a sufficient condition. For instance, Reserve Police Battalion 101, comprising 500 middle-aged reservists who were active in Poland, was engaged in the task of shooting defenseless civilians. They 'ended up murdering 38,000 individuals and consigning another 44,200 to the maw of the Treblinka death camp. 500 ordinary men with a combined body count of 83,000 civilians … as it carried out more massacres, the majority of the men fell into a matter-of-fact routine, whilst a minority began to enjoy their work, embellishing it with gratuitous humiliation of and cruelty towards their victims' (Higgins 2004: 100).

Third, in exercising total institutional power *it is much easier to act with extreme prejudice towards those who are the victims of the action, or the subjects of power, when they are dehumanized.* When ideological definitions and indoctrination convince organizational members that the victims are less than human, it creates distance between organizational members and the people who are affected by the action, and the human costs can be borne with greater equanimity as a necessary cost of a greater good – progress, the state, the party or whatever it takes to still the conscience. Representing victims as numbers rather than people also makes it easier to forget the ethical consequences of actions. A generalized condition of organizational modernity is that only what can be counted counts (Power 1997; Brunsson et al. 2000). In Spielberg's (1993) film, it is when Oscar Schindler spots a little girl in a bright red coat amidst the black and white and drab colors of those being rounded up, when her individual humanity shines out to him in all its bright luminosity, that he ceases to be a bystander (Higgins 2004: 94–5). He sees an individual amidst the mass, something that organizational modernity discourages.

When actions are performed at a distance on people defined as administrative categories, the people are effectively dehumanized (Kelman 1973). The more dehumanized they are, the easier becomes the application of pure technique to their cases. Dehumanization involves the production of others whose most characteristic feature is their otherness, their being different in essence from those who constitute them as such, as outside a space in which there exists a shared moral scope. The novelist Ian McEwan notes that the 'trick, as always, the key to human success and domination, is to *be selective in your mercies*. For all the discerning talk, it's the close at hand, the visible that exerts the overpowering force' (2005: 127, our emphasis). Those whom one sees as essentially similar to oneself, as sharing in a common being and meaning, are that much harder to destroy. What you don't see or can't recognize as someone who is just like you needn't bother you. What you can keep at arm's length outside your intimate fold of humanity is easier to defile. There is a poem that indicates this well:

> They came for the communists, and I did not speak up because I wasn't a communist;
> They came for the socialists, and I did not speak up because I was not a socialist;
> They came for the union leaders, and I did not speak up because I wasn't a union leader;
> They came for the Jews, and I didn't speak up because I wasn't a Jew.
> Then they came for me, and there was no one left to speak up for me.
> (Martin Niemöller 1892–1984)[16]

When the subjective can be reduced to the objective, when the qualitative can be represented quantitatively as a bottom-line calculation, it is so much easier to make rational decisions (cut costs, trim fat, speed throughput, increase efficiency, defeat the competition) without concern for the human, environmental, or social effects of these decisions. Again, it goes back to the value-free basis of management science. If one is cutting costs to become more efficient it is much easier, morally, to represent these costs abstractly rather than to have to deal with them personally (Moore 1989/2003).

Note that in this framework of total institutional power there has, as yet, been no mention of resistance. Where there was such resistance it often occurred in individual rather than collective terms through acts of self-annihilation by ultimate gestures of existential choice that refused total power its routinized predictability. Organizationally, it is extremely difficult to outflank a total institution from within its strategies of totalization. Control of the organizational apparatus, routinization of power in many small acts, extensive division and dehumanization, and responsible, regulated violence are hard to overcome when one is incorporated in the total institution, especially without recourse to any countervailing institutional powers, such as a system of rank and command. It is, perhaps, for this reason that the

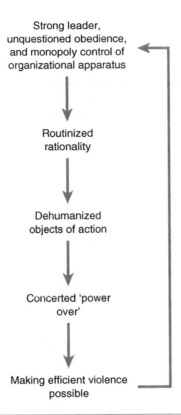

Figure 6.1   Total institutional power

literature of total institutions so often celebrates the small acts of individual resistance that do occur, because there is so little chance of organized resistance as access to organizational means is so limited.[17]

Analytically, the diagram of power that maps how such a total institution functions may be thought of in the terms of Figure 6.1.

Resisting the Final Solution

On average, two-thirds of the Jews in German-controlled territory during the Second World War did not survive (Seibel 2002), but there was significant territorial variance. That it is an essential sense of a shared humanity that enables survival from horrors that wait unleashing may also be seen in the Danish case, which offers a strong counterfactual. The Danish resistance movement, assisted by many ordinary citizens, coordinated the flight of some 7,200 Jews to safety in nearby neutral Sweden, suggesting that it was indeed many small acts of omission and commission that were important in enacting the Holocaust. On September 11, 1943, the man in charge of the German occupation in Denmark told his head of shipping operations, Georg Ferdinand Duckwitz, of plans to round up all of the approximately 8,000 Jews in Denmark and transport them to the Theresienstadt concentration camp. A week later Duckwitz was given more details. Ships would arrive on September 29 and a coordinated lightning raid would occur on the night of October 1. On September 25, Duckwitz flew to Sweden and met with the Swedish prime minister to ask him to help save Danish Jewry. The prime minister sent a telegram to Berlin offering to accept all of the Danish Jews if Germany would agree to let them go. Duckwitz returned to Denmark and waited for news. When none came, he assumed the Germans had ignored the Swedish request. On September 28 he looked up his friend, Hans Hedtoft (who became prime minister after the war) and told him of the plan. Hedtoft and three of his friends set out to warn as many as possible. One of the first he spoke to was the head of the Jewish community in Copenhagen, who in disbelief first accused him of lying (German officials had convincingly denied earlier rumors of the raid). When Copenhagen Jews came to prayers on Wednesday morning September 29, they were told there would be no services that morning or on Rosh Hashanah, which was to begin that evening. Instead they were to spread the word of the raid and go into hiding. Christian Danes told their Jewish friends and neighbors. Some even looked through the phone book for Jewish sounding names to call and warn.

When the Nazis carried out their raids on the night of October 1, they found fewer than 300 of the 8,000 Jews. Eventually they rounded up only 475 Jews who were sent to Theresienstadt. The others had gone into hiding. Within the month of October, fishermen had been recruited to transport them to Sweden (which had broadcast its willingness to provide sanctuary after Niels Bohr had convinced it to act publicly); money had been raised to pay fishermen for the risks they took; Jews were moved from their hiding places to new hiding places near the ports and beaches used to transport them; Danish police were recruited to keep others, including the Germans, away; and the Jews were ferried to Sweden. One tally was that 5,919 Jews, 1,301 half-Jews, and 686 Christians married to Jews (a total of 7,906) were successfully transported to safety. A tally of Jewish Holocaust victims in Denmark said only 30 had died while *en route* to Sweden, another 30 committed suicide, and only 51 of the 475 sent to Theresienstadt did not survive. (The Danes maintained constant contact with Nazi officials about the fate of the Jews shipped to Theresienstadt.) The toll among the Danish Jewish population was slightly more than 1 percent, which was a remarkable record. Thanks to this extraordinary mass rescue effort, at war's end Denmark had one of the highest Jewish survival rates for any European country.[18] In some other European countries, such as Lithuania and Latvia, non-survival was over 90 percent. In these countries, it was hardly a question of the local populations overlooking the Holocaust; rather they actively furthered it. There are reports of German troops being shocked by the cruelty shown by the local population to the Jews who lived there.

No other country came close to the Danish percentage of survivors. Here, the active engagement of the people as a whole in resisting the Final Solution made an enormous difference, one that could have occurred elsewhere but did not. Thus, we may draw a further implication, that *power needs to delegate authorities to dispatch its projects,* without which it can be deflected, even in total institutional situations.[19]

Organization overcoming humanity

The most effective way of overcoming humanity is to treat those categories of person with which one will deal harshly as in some respects not fully, wholly or essentially human in the way that normal, well-formed people like us can be taken to be. Make them the other. Such sleights in casting identity enable one to maintain distance. There are many ways of *maintaining distance.* One technique, of course, is through physical separation and isolation. The constant trains and fumes from the furnaces perhaps occasionally perturbed ordinary Polish citizens going about their everyday life, yet nonetheless they remained separate from the camps, which were a spatially confined zone. Technique enables distantiation. When we master a technique, even when it comprises methods of brutal interrogation, intimidation or torture, the skill in the technique has its own charm, aesthetics, and beauty, such that technicians can take sheer delight in using it, irrespective of its moral effects:

> Technical responsibility differs from moral responsibility in that it forgets that the action is a means to something other than itself ... *the result is the irrelevance of moral standards for the technical success of the bureaucratic operation.* (Bauman 1989: 101, italics in original)

Divisions of labor in complex chains of power enable elites to maintain distance from power's effects. Where these effects can be represented in terms of intermediary forms of data (kill rates, efficiency statistics, and so on) it also helps. Whatever may be our small labor input, it moves minute cogs in a bureaucratic machine necessarily intermeshed with so many others that we are just one small element in the overall scheme of things. We don't even have to try to understand the totality. And if perchance we do understand, then, as we shall meet in the second dimension of power in the next chapter, we realize that we can't do anything to change the situation, thus producing immobility and reinforcing conformism. The system of which we are a part is responsible, not us.

When *technique is paramount,* action becomes purely a question of technical power in terms of the use of means to achieve given ends. For instance, as a master of logistics, Eichmann was enormously proud of his achievements in the complex scheduling of trains, camps, and death. He was, as he said, a good bureaucrat. There are two profound effects of an organizational power that makes people technically accountable and responsible for results expressed in a purely quantitative form: it makes the person doing the task utterly transparent – either the targets are achieved or they are not – and it relieves one of moral indeterminacy. If one is authorized to do something and given targets to achieve by superordinates guiding strategies and plans, obedience surely is appropriate, and authority should be served.[20]

Obedience to power is encouraged where organization work is *a ceaseless round of activity with little room for reflection,* where activity is mostly just a small link in a great chain of doing. Most organizational members are in the middle of organizational chains whose links are not always clear. People are not always aware of the consequences of what they do and do not do. Most of the time, they are just doing what they are told (shred those files, write those checks, dispatch those troops, and maintain those train schedules). In the death camps, *those who were the subjects of power were made complicit in its exercise.* Orderlies, handlers of dead bodies, strippers of skin, hair, gold, jewelry, and dentures, were nominated from amongst those who had yet to meet their fate. Participation in the horror preserved them for the time being.

Barbarism and modern organization

Seeing excesses of instrumental rationality or even Western enlightenment as consequentially culminating in mass murder does not explain all genocide. Consider the slaughter of Armenians conducted by the Turks in the early twentieth century, for example, or that committed in Rwanda more recently, where 1.5 million people were murdered, not in total institutions, but in the midst of their villages, by a brutalized mob, often using just machetes or bare hands. The uniqueness of the Holocaust is that it was organized and industrialized mass murder, not pure hate, hysteria, or collective ethnic vengeance and 'cleansing'. Its organizational basis is what makes it unique. However, the Holocaust is not a necessary outcome of the sufficient conditions. Bauman's location of evil within a particular mode of organizing is, perhaps, too narrow. The same mode of organizing (e.g. bureaucracy) can assist the perpetrators as well as the victims; also, for some scholars, barbarism is at least as much a matter of personality – that is, a result of internal not external distancing – as of organizational form, at least according to Adorno et al.'s (1968) account of the 'authoritarian personality'. The mode of organizing (that is, the means) would here reside in favor of individuals' intentions, biography, and personality, or at least the conditions that enabled a specific personality type to flourish and be rewarded. Adorno's account would imply a more socio-psychological perspective. It would stress the specificity, the uniqueness, the abnormality of those who perpetrated the Holocaust; however, as scholars such as Bauman and Higgins make clear, it is its very mundane, organizationally routine qualities, the normalcy of its technical rationality, which is most compelling about the Holocaust. The organizational apparatus defined the identities not just of its victims but also of its perpetrators, just as Goffman (1961) would lead us to think.

The Holocaust, rightly, is claimed as occupying a special case in the annals of twentieth-century history. While organizational form, in conjunction with an overemphasis on instrumental rationality, helps distance human suffering, it is not a sufficient condition for terror, nor is it even necessary in certain circumstances. Excesses of instrumental rationality (organizing) and disregard for substantial rationality (human rights) can lead to barbarism. But the opposite also holds. Disorganization and chaos, or a lack of instrumental rationality and overconcern with substantive rationality, such as are furnished by racism and fundamentalism, can provoke similarly disastrous consequences, as Rwanda demonstrates.

The Holocaust is *the* crime of the last century, largely because it was not some gruesome means to some other end but was an end in itself. Six million people were annihilated; national histories were irrevocably marked, and generations were sundered. Nothing else that follows in this chapter will, or could, possibly compare with the atrocities recorded there. Nonetheless, although the atrocity of the Holocaust was unique, its organizational form as a total institution was not. While industrially organized genocide may not have recurred since the Nazis' death camps, despite the many atrocities that have occurred globally in the intervening 60 years, the total institutional form did not die out with the Nazis, as we shall see in what follows.

Marking identity in peaceable total institutions

Total institutions for marking life rather than creating death

The focus switches now to less harrowing but no less total institutions. First, we shall consider the case of the Irish Magdalene Laundries, in which young girls were held captive in a kind of forced labor serving as a moral penance. Second, we shall look at the Australian case of the Stolen Generation, where children of Aboriginal descent were forcibly removed from their parents. Third, we shall consider the case of a totalitarian society that sought to be a total institution by building around itself a wall that none could penetrate, as was the case of the GDR. The wall collapsed under the creative powers of the citizens it held captive, when democracy overcame bureaucracy and politics overcame economics, at least in part, marking an exchange to a different system of freedoms and repressions. Finally, we shall update the picture with a look at the case of the inmates of the Coalition prison in Iraq, Abu Ghraib, made infamous through the photographs of humiliated prisoners taken by a number of US armed forces personnel.

Bureaucracy may be neither a necessary nor a sufficient condition for organizing total institutions but it is, nonetheless, a pervasive aspect. The sources of fear that lead societies to enclose people in total institutions vary historically and comparatively. Everywhere, criminals are confined. We are concerned, however, with more specific fears leading to total institutionalization. In theocratic Eire, even up to 1996, fear was inspired by young women's sexuality, and became institutionalized in the system of the Magdalene asylums, run by the Sisters of Mercy on behalf of the Catholic Church. It was a highly gendered example of what Foucault referred to as the 'gaze'.

Gendering the gaze

Foucault's accounts of surveillance and the notion of the gaze are gender blind. While Foucault was analytically acute he did not focus on the different ways in which men and women experience being the object and the subject of a gaze. The total institution needs to be engendered, as the case of the laundries demonstrates. The gaze as experienced by men and by women is different as a consequence of a politics of sexuality in which, conventionally, men gaze and desire, and women are gazed at and desired. There is no sense in Foucault that that which is being gazed upon, or over which surveillance is being exercised, is as an embodied being, with sexuality. It is pathological to feel that one is permanently under gaze in normal life but of course that would be an experience that many women would be familiar with. Think about women walking past construction sites. Not only are the attractive women whistled at, but also others who fail to make the cut are commented upon and graded.[21] While Foucault missed the element of gender in relation to surveillance it is noteworthy that Goffman did not. One of his later works was a veritable handbook of gendered gazing, titled *Gender advertisements* (Goffman 1976).

In *Gender advertisements*, Erving Goffman sought to explore the other aspect of communication that he inherited from Mead (1938), gesture, as Richard Hoggart's (Goffman 1976: vii) foreword makes abundantly clear. Goffman analyzes how gender displays affirm what are taken to be basic social arrangements (keeping women in their place) and at the same time frame and fix gendered identity. Goffman makes it absolutely clear that he is concerned with power in relation to gesture and signification:

> [I]n our society whenever a male has dealings with a female or subordinate male (especially a younger one), some mitigation of potential distance, coercion, and hostility is quite likely to be induced by application of the parent–child complex. Which implies that, ritually speaking, females are equivalent to subordinate males and both are equivalent to children. Observe that however distasteful and humiliating lessers may find these gentle prerogatives to be, they must give second thought to openly expressing displeasure, for whosoever extends benign concern is free to quickly change his tack and show the other side of his power … The expression of subordination and domination through this swarm of situated means is more than a mere tracing or symbolic of ritualistic affirmation of the social hierarchy; these expressions considerably constitute the hierarchy; they are the shadow and the substance. (1976: 5, 6)

The text of Goffman's *Gender advertisements* consists of a series of black and white photographs[22] (of advertisements, art works, etc.) with laconic comments by Goffman that make his analytic points. Originally the book was a visual presentation: the photographs were shown as colored slides and the comments functioned as a verbal commentary on the visual text, which was a presentational format that worked much better than the eventually published form.[23]

Washing away sin in the Magdalene Laundries

The Magdalene Laundries case presents an instance where the specificity of gendered power relations is only too apparent. The gaze that some young women of Eire were subjected to was not one that touched their boyfriends, their brothers, their priests and those others who may have contributed to their 'fallen' state. The Magdalene system was named for Mary Magdalene, Christ's follower in the New Testament who, for many years, was considered by the Church to have been a reformed prostitute. The Church subverted Mary Magdalene's treatment by Christ in its regard for girls who conceived out of wedlock, or committed other sins of the flesh. Christ's explicit code on the woman taken in adultery was to let he who is without sin throw the first stone, the exact opposite of the code that came to be adopted in his and her name.

The organization of the Magdalene Laundries inverted the Christian code. While one could argue that Christ displayed a feminist sensibility in his treatment of Mary Magdalene, those intuitions enacted in her and his name were resolutely anti-feminine. Magdalene institutions began in the late 1700s but became most prevalent in the mid nineteenth century, when secular asylums designed to reform prostitutes and return them to society with usable skills were taken over by the Catholic Church across Ireland. They slowly changed into homes for unwed mothers and then prisons for any girl or young woman deemed by society to be acting sexually promiscuously.

The Magdalene Laundries received young girls sent there by families or orphanages. Their stay was not voluntary, nor was it normal paid labor. They were there because they were 'sinful'. The sins varied from being unmarried mothers to being too ugly, too simple minded, too clever, or a victim of rape who talked about it; or, if an orphaned teenage girl, they could be incarcerated as a precautionary move if they were thought to be too attractive. And for their sins they worked 364 days a year unpaid, some were half-starved, beaten, humiliated, and raped, and their children were forcibly removed from them. Their sentence was indefinite and their confinement palpable. At the Magdalene institution in Cork, there were 20-foot-high brick walls, topped with shards of broken glass mortared into the concrete (CBS 1999).

Over the course of the existence of the laundries it is documented that over 30,000 women worked in them (Humphries 1998). The work was hard, relentless, raw and physical, involving washing, scrubbing, and ironing. It started at five in the morning with mass, followed by breakfast; then the women worked, with institutional breaks for meals, until they went to bed at about seven o'clock at night. The choice of work – washing and laundering – was deliberate. By scrubbing, they were supposed to wash away their sins along with the stains on the laundry that they dealt with, as it came in from the nunneries, monasteries, schools, orphanages and local businesses.

The way out of the laundries was to be claimed by a relative who was willing to take responsibility. The chances of being claimed were slim, because of the stigma attached to being in the laundries. If they were released they usually could not locate their families or their illegitimate children. Thousands of women lived and died there, as virtual slaves, in an environment controlled and dominated by celibate women, servants of God and Brides of Christ who acted as remorseless reminders of the wages of sin and the consequences of a fall from grace.

The laundries were extremely profitable and required a larger and larger number of workers. These workers were supplied by Catholic priests in ever increasing numbers. Thus, the system developed in a society and a time when authority was not questioned, women were second-class citizens and women's sexuality was a perceived threat to social stability. It was an era ruled by double standards and the importance of keeping up appearances. As Kay Lorraine (2003) writes, there were also laundries elsewhere, in Britain, mostly Protestant, the last of which closed in the 1970s, and in virtually every Catholic city across Europe and North America, especially Quebec, as well as in Australia.[24] The last Magdalene asylum in Ireland closed in 1996 (see Mullan 2004). New Magdalene asylums are opening in Asia and Africa, where oppression and double standards for women are still the norm, run by some of the same orders that previously operated the Magdalene asylums elsewhere.

The system came into question as a result of the sale of Church property in Ireland:

> In the 1970s, a former convent laundry property held by the Sisters of Charity in Dublin was sold to the Republic government for public use. 133 unmarked graves were discovered on the property, containing the bodies of abandoned Magdalene girls. Family members who had never been notified of the deaths claimed some of the bodies. Many others remained unidentified. Finally, in 1991, the remaining bodies were buried in historic Glasnevin cemetery in Dublin, marked with a single memorial. (Lorraine, 2003; also see www.netreach.net/~steed/magdalen.html)

The asylums were total institutions in every sense (Lorraine 2003). Many of the girls were very young when they were admitted and were often given a different name, as part of the process of breaking them down psychologically and stripping them of their individual identity, making them easier to control. After 10, 15, 20 years in the laundries under constant psychological abuse, many women could no longer remember their original names or the names of their family members. What makes it more terrible is that some of the young women who were committed there were themselves victims of sexual abuse in total institutions, such as Catholic orphanages, or in the Church, such as rape at the hands of a priest. Still, in the view of many of the Sisters of Mercy, through suffering and hard work in the laundries, for the greater glory of God, fallen women might find salvation. *Be convinced that the regime of the total institution is the best for all concerned, both those in and those outwith, such that its purpose is wrapped in the rhetoric of being in the 'real' interests of both the other and the society at large.*

The Stolen Generation

Australia is today a vibrant multicultural society, one that is highly inclusive of most of those who are its citizens.[25] Its original peoples were deemed to exist formally in the 1960s when they were first included in national statistics and electoral rolls, having failed to be written out of history by death or breeding.[26] The original peoples of Australia were hunter-gatherers who traveled there from Asia at least 60,000 years ago. They have not, on the whole, fared as well from the migratory and nation-building process as have the settlers who made their homes there over the past 220 years or so. In fact, their life chances, to use a sociological term, often approximate those of people who live in far less affluent societies, especially in terms of morbidity rates, live birth rates and other health-related statistics. Light was cast on some of the systematic disciplinary mechanisms that contributed to the destruction of Indigenous cultural capital through an enquiry that commenced in 1995. The National Inquiry into the Separation of Aboriginal and Torres Strait Islander Children from Their Families was established in May 1995 in response to efforts made by key Indigenous agencies and communities, and resulted in a report to the Human Rights and Equal Opportunity Commission (HREOC). The report was titled *Bringing them home* (HREOC 1997), from which much of what follows is taken verbatim.

The practice of forced removal of Indigenous people and their placement in total institutions was established early in the colonial history of Australia. Violent battles over rights to land, food and water sources characterized race relations in the nineteenth century. Indigenous children were kidnapped and exploited for their labor or otherwise forcibly removed from their families for two main motives. One was that they provided cheap labor (Reynolds 1990: 169), as there was no requirement to pay them beyond providing food and clothing. The second was to 'inculcate European values and work habits in children, who would then be employed in service to the colonial settlers' (Mason 1993: 31).

During the nineteenth century the predominant policy regime was one of social Darwinism, where the survival of the fittest was interpreted as justification enough for the superiority of the settler society and the inferiority of the hunter-gatherers that had lived off the land for at least 60,000 years.[27] It was widely believed that Indigenous people, being unfit to survive in the modern world, would either die out or be so blended in as to be indistinguishable. To this end, government and missionary protectorates set up reserves to which Indigenous people were to be confined. Management of the reserves was delegated to government appointed managers or missionaries in receipt of government subsidies. Enforcement of the protectionist legislation at the local level was the responsibility of 'protectors' who were usually police officers. Near total control was exercised. Entry and exit from reserves was regulated, as was everyday life, the right to marry, and employment. Children were housed in dormitories and contact with their families was strictly limited to encourage conversion of the children to Christianity.

The number of children of mixed descent was increasing as a result of sexual contacts. Owing to changing definitions of what constituted Aboriginality, those with 'European blood' were not allowed to live on the reserves. Government officials thought that by forcibly removing such children from their families and sending them away from their communities to work for settlers, this mixed descent population would, over time, 'merge' with the settler population. As Brisbane's *Telegraph* newspaper reported in May 1937:

> Mr. Neville [the Chief Protector of WA] holds the view that within one hundred years the pure black will be extinct. But the half-caste problem was increasing every year. Therefore their idea was to keep the pure blacks segregated and absorb the half-castes into the white population. Sixty years ago, he said, there were over 60,000 full-blooded natives in Western Australia. Today there are only 20,000. In time there would be none. Perhaps it would take one hundred years, perhaps longer, but the race was dying. The pure blooded Aboriginal was not a quick breeder. On the other hand the half-caste was. In Western Australia there were half-caste families of twenty and upwards. That showed the magnitude of the problem. (Buti 1995: 35)

Many of the familiar techniques of total institutions were used. Great 'care was taken to ensure that [Aboriginal children] never saw their parents or families again. They were often given new names, and the greater distances involved in rural areas made it easier to prevent parents and children on separate missions from tracing each other' (van Krieken 1992: 108). Female children were singled out for 'special treatment'

(Kelly 1992):[28] 'Indigenous girls were targeted for removal and sent to work as domestics. Apart from satisfying a demand for cheap servants, work increasingly eschewed by non-Indigenous females, it was thought that the long hours and exhausting work would curb the sexual promiscuity attributed to them.'[29] It was not just the long hours and exhausting work; there was also little in the way of medical provision or treatment when calorific shortfall had its inevitable consequences.

> A common feature of the settlements, missions and institutions for Indigenous families and children was that they received minimal funding ... The lack of funding for settlements, missions and institutions meant that people forced to move to these places were constantly hungry, denied basic facilities and medical treatment and as a result were likely to die prematurely. [30]

In 1937, official government policies adopted a policy of 'absorption' and 'assimilation' by white society of children of mixed descent. Assimilation was a highly intensive process necessitating constant surveillance of people's lives, judged according to non-Indigenous standards. The results of these judgments were that, from the 1940s onwards, under the general child welfare law, Indigenous children were often forcibly removed from their natural families if they were found to be 'neglected', 'destitute' or 'uncontrollable'. As *Bringing them home* argues, interpretations of those terms assumed a non-Indigenous model of child-rearing and regarded poverty as synonymous with neglect.

The role of knowledge is evident and central in these policies, providing the arguments that animated power and moved authorities into action. The result was a continued process, utilizing the neglect procedures that removed just as many Aboriginal children from their families as before. During the 1950s and 1960s even greater numbers of Indigenous children were removed from their families to advance the cause of assimilation. Not only were they removed for alleged neglect; they were removed to attend school in distant places, to receive medical treatment, and to be adopted out at birth. As institutions could no longer cope with the increasing numbers, and welfare practice discouraged the use of institutions, Indigenous children were placed with non-Indigenous foster families where their identity was denied or disparaged. 'A baby placed with white parents would obviously be more quickly assimilated than one placed with black parents. So ran the official thinking, but more importantly, so also ran the feelings of the majority of honest and conscientious white citizens' (Edwards and Read 1989: xx).

Not only did the placement of black babies with white families lead to a subsequent loss of identity, and then, in those cases where the children did not pass as 'white', confused and absent identity, it also had significant intergenerational effects. These were experienced in terms of the displacement and dispersal of individuals and family members. Contacts were lost; family and kin relations broken; clan relations disrupted; and the rights of access to and ownership of traditional lands forfeited. The loss of land was a significant loss, because under the terms of Native Title legislation, establishing land rights is based on continuous possession of the land. But the loss is more than merely a matter of legal entitlement; it is also a deep spiritual loss, a loss of meaning at the center of life as much as an economic loss of access to the land that provides for life, the reproduction of habitual ways of life, and the preservation of traditions and the identity of a culture. As the father of a professor at the University of Technology, Sydney, explained:

> We bond with the universe and the land and everything that exists on the land. Everything is bonded to everything.
>
> Ownership for the white people is something on a piece of paper. We have a different system. You can no more sell our land than sell the sky.
>
> Our affinity with the land is like the bonding between a parent and a child. You have responsibilities and obligations to look after and care for a child. You can speak for a child. But you don't own a child. (Behrendt 2003: 33)

Such views of the world had great difficulty surviving baptism in the religious and work ethics provided by the various total institutions to which Indigenous people were consigned. Traditional rights of access to the land, to places of religious and other cultural significance, were broken; in fact, the expropriation of the people, their alienation from the land, and the entitlement of the land passing to those white settlers who squatted on it or otherwise asserted title over it, meant the end of Aboriginal sovereignty, defined in Aboriginal terms:

> Sovereignty can be demonstrated as Aboriginal people controlling all aspects of their lives and destiny. Sovereignty is independent action, it is Aborigines doing things as Aboriginal people, controlling those aspects of our existence which are Aboriginal. *These include our culture, our economy, our social lives and our indigenous political institutions.* Wrapped up in all this is health, housing, education, legal matters and land rights, and many other things … [when] Aboriginal people are able to exercise absolute control over these essential areas without penalty being imposed by non-Aboriginal society, then our Aboriginal sovereignty will be recognized … (Behrendt 2003: 100; cited from National Aboriginal Island Health Organization, q0985, written comment, NAIHO Conference, www.kooriweb.org/foley/news/story8.html)

White society might not have intended harm although it caused great damage, injustice and wrong, which has never been formally acknowledged at a governmental level as a responsibility that should be assumed for past actions. As Ibarra-Colado (2004: 25) writes, the failures of modernity were not simply the price to be paid in order to achieve the universal goal of progress. The price of conquest and subjugation was a necessary way of establishing the practical and moral superiority of the difference represented by the colonizers over the colonized. The state and the religious institutions that enacted policy acted out of what their custodians thought was for the best in the world, and this consisted of desocializing Indigenous people through resocializing them in total institutions. Of course, this meant destroying their sovereignty but this had never been recognized anyway. The ideas of confinement in total institutions designed to resocialize continued to shape policies into the 1970s, until the election of a government committed to Aboriginal self-determination shifted the policy practice.

What is noteworthy is that while the policies of institutional incarceration were being followed for Indigenous children, the influential ideas of John Bowlby (1951) were being adopted in the care of non-Indigenous children, stressing the centrality of the mother and child relationship. Although total institutionalization was often the outcome of policy, the policy itself was conceived and represented as being in the best interests of the children, despite this evident counterfactual knowledge.[31]

The German Democratic Republic: a total society?

Next, we shall consider what happens when total institutions seek to impose total control on a society. While such control is difficult to achieve organizationally it is almost impossible societally, where subtle forms of control have to be involved in the fabrication of total – not just organizational – identities by the imposition of styles of life deeply linked with the management of desires by consumption, mass media, success as spectacle, etc. We have one example of such an attempt at generalizing a total institution to a total society in the country that used to be known as the German Democratic Republic (GDR). The GDR was more often referred to as East Germany to signify the socialist bloc state that was set up in the eastern part of Germany after the Second World War. At the core of this state was the secret police organization known as the Stasi. The control of society as a whole is based on the design and control of spaces and mobility (Deleuze 1992), on how openness and closedness is defined, rather than on a disciplinary society and the total institution regime. Is a society possible that is the extreme expression of a total institution, that is, one in which, while individuals are imprisoned, they can move freely inside the limits established in this new configuration of spaces? Until we have more knowledge of North Korea than we do at present, the GDR represents the best-documented case study available.

East Germany was the front line in the Cold War between Soviet communism and Western capitalism. It was taken by the Soviet Red Army, advancing on Berlin from the east in the closing stages of the Second World War, and assigned to the Soviet sphere of influence at the Yalta Peace Conference of February 1945. It was a frontier society whose boundary was defined to its west by the Berlin Wall, erected on August 13, 1961, *to maintain order at its border by locking the people in* and denying the freedom to move out, and shooting or imprisoning people if they were caught trying to escape. Across the Wall was West Berlin, symptomatic of a land of market opportunities largely denied in the East.

While the GDR, by some accounts of its ex-citizens, wasn't too bad a place – it didn't assassinate too many people – the whole society was premised on being a gulag. One could not easily get in and get out of the GDR, unless the regime chose to sell one into exile and profit from one's export to the West, which was a trade not engaged in to the same extent by any of the other Eastern bloc countries. Of course, people applying often had to face severe repercussion and persecution (sometimes even jail) and sometimes these repercussions were even extended to their relatives. But that did not stop (tens of) thousands from applying and from eventually emigrating to the West and earning the GDR hard currency by doing so. Thus, the GDR was never a closed or total society although it was difficult to escape from, physically. The GDR authorities sought to stop people from inside getting out, which they did by trying to block every avenue of escape, never entirely successfully.

There were also many other interior *escape attempts* (Cohen and Taylor 1976) such as TVs tuned to the Western channels, the Red Flag not flying on the appropriate occasions, the jokes against the regime, and the refusal to seize the opportunities it afforded its subjects. Everyday knowledge of the world outside the Wall was beamed across the border from West German TV stations. However, such information was the most dangerous commodity because it gave knowledge of alternatives to the official story provided for the people of East Germany, represented by a set of beliefs that were insistently parroted, such that they became an ideology held by the elites as an act of faith. These escape attempts were even more dangerous because they involved not just bodies getting away but minds that roamed free outside the limits imposed by the official ideology. Dangerous escape attempts needed to be nipped in the bud; a security organization, the Stasi, was established to defeat resistance. At least every seventieth person ended up as a Stasi operative, according to official data published by the German government (Bundeszentrale für Politische Bildung) and confirmed by associations of Stasi victims. However, when the number of people who were enrolled as informants – neighborhood and workplace spies – is included, then, according to Funder's (2002) data, as many as one in three people were involved. What they did was to produce a simulacrum of total control. Masses of information was collected and filed, much of it as useless as the files that J. Edgar Hoover had the FBI keep at the same time in the US but, in the same way, having the potential for leverage, inducement and influence in a paranoid society:

> The Stasi was the internal army by which the government kept control. Its job was to know everything about everyone, using any means it chose. It knew who your visitors were, it knew whom you telephoned, and it knew if your wife slept around. It was a bureaucracy metastasized through East German society: overt or covert, there was someone reporting to the Stasi on their fellows and friends in every school, every factory, every apartment block, every pub. Obsessed with detail, the Stasi entirely failed to predict the end of Communism, and with it the end of the country. In its forty years [it] generated the equivalent of all records in German history since the Middle Ages. Laid out upright and end-to-end the files the Stasi kept on their countrymen and women would form a line 180 kilometers long …
>
> Information ran in a closed circuit between the government and its press outlets. As the government controlled the newspapers, magazines and television, training as a journalist was effectively training as a government spokesperson. Access to books was restricted. Censorship was a constant pressure on writers, and a given for readers, who learned to read between the lines. The only mass medium the government couldn't control was the signal from western television stations, but it tried: until the early 1970s the Stasi used to monitor the angle of the people's antennae hanging out of their apartments, punishing them if they were turned to the west. (2002: 4, 17)

The main role of the Stasi was to protect the German Democratic Republic from its citizens through producing a huge surfeit of information on them for its controllers. In fact, the state defined the republic as the Communist Party; effectively, the Stasi was there to protect the party from the people. Thus, a state that was in principle the supreme power, because it owned and controlled the means of production in the society, was unable to exercise the power it held theoretically because it was not a state based on legitimacy. Its control was constantly weakened by the necessity to exercise power almost continuously, in so many small ways, that it had nothing behind it and could not build power as a free, creative and empowering positivity. Nothing much that was positive could survive in a civil society suffused in negativity, articulated by a sovereign power able to do whatever it thought necessary to maintain its members in fear. It arrested, imprisoned, and interrogated anyone it chose. It inspected all mail in secret rooms above post offices (copying letters and stealing any valuables), and intercepted, daily, tens of thousands of phone calls. It bugged hotel rooms and spied on diplomats. It ran its own universities, hospitals, elite sports centers, and terrorist training programs (2002: 59). The GDR was a totalitarian society, anything but the ideal speech community that another German, Habermas (1971), was theorizing across the border. The Stasi was a perverse, brutal, and criminal instrument of oppression.

While the Wall was one of the most disgusting buildings in German history it pales into insignificance in the face of the inhumanity that characterized the gas chambers of Auschwitz; moreover, the intimidation spread by the Stasi did not match that of the Gestapo's terror. To Jews, gypsies, or mentally ill people in Nazi Germany assimilation, consent or submission was not an option to evade extermination; in the GDR, being a good socialist could ensure a measure of freedom in a society that sought for a total control that was never entirely achievable. As Arendt (1970) observed, effective terror is enhanced by extensive social atomization. The best way to maintain and intensify such terror is through a network of informers. They are a perfect Panopticon: as one never knows who is in the pay of the police, potentially every person one comes into contact with might be – so one must always be on guard.

Dense networks of bureaucrats characterized the GDR's state-approved and state-dominated civil society organizations, which thrived on the premise that membership has its privileges, especially for the authorities. *The guardians of order in the GDR enjoyed extraordinary privileges,* denied the ordinary citizenry, for their pains in its service. It was a society built on an obsession with order. It was also a house of cards, built on the denial of the citizens' Nazi history. Fighting this history was its initial justification; however, the justification rapidly shifted to fighting the West as decadent capitalism. In turn, this was translated into fighting any of its citizens who showed a fascination for the freedoms that the West offered, who refused the state's dictatorship over their needs, or who failed to be seduced by the lure of the official ideology. The house of cards only survived because it was the front line for the Soviet bloc, and the Red Army could intervene at any time it chose to restore its version of order, as it had in Hungary in 1956 and Czechoslovakia in 1968. However, when *glasnost* and *perestroika* came into Soviet fashion with Gorbachev after 1985, the GDR was done for as the Red Army could no longer be relied on. The Soviet Union was changing and the GDR was failing to change with it.

Glasnost spread to the GDR, initially to Leipzig, where in 1989 the Nikolaikirche became a focal point for protest against the regime. In August the Hungarians cut the barbed wire at their border and the people poured across. They demanded access across the wall to the West as well, and the border guards allowed it but were instructed to survey the identity papers of those returning so that they could be dealt with later. Coming back into the GDR, people started to destroy their identity papers *en masse* in revolt against the regime. The demonstrations got larger and larger and the regime became less able to control them. They stopped trying and fled to their offices. The government decided to relax border controls and the rest was history, with people dancing on the wall and then tearing it down, followed by the reintegration of Germany, after the only successful revolution in German history. Nonetheless, while it lasted good bureaucrats protected the GDR and left plenty of evidence of that fact. The Stasi's overconcern with formalization left kilometers of data, which name both victims and perpetrators, and which document the crimes committed – something that has, since the demise of the GDR, eventually served the cause of the victims in their claim for legal action and compensation.[32]

The Stasi sought to exercise a dictatorship over needs on behalf of the ruling elite of the party in the GDR, but failed. The most forceful critique of East European state socialism (Fehér et al.'s 1983 *Dictatorship over needs*) was that the state in communist societies dominated civil society in the name of civil society's freedom. Such societies denied civil society any autonomy from the party-dominated state in the formation of opinions and needs. In the absence of markets, the state could exercise dictatorship over the needs of the people, such that consumers could not obtain freely what they wanted, unless they capitulated and joined the party's privileged ranks. In many ways it was this control over needs as much as the control of surveillance that characterized power relations in the GDR. Control of individuals by control of their needs is the first step in control, before surveillance with cooptation/repression, before fabrication of identities or self-surveillance as the (never full) realization of control.[33]

An illegal and immoral war, betrayed by images that reveal our racism

That was the byline of an article that appeared in the respected UK newspaper *The Independent*, by Robert Fisk, on May 7, 2004.[34] The reference was to the infamous photographs of Abu Ghraib. Apparently, the goal of the US forces in photographing sexual humiliation was to blackmail Iraqi victims into becoming informants against the insurgency, McFate (2005) argues. It has been asserted that what occurred at Abu Ghraib was the result of a few 'bad apples', but there is ample evidence to suggest a more deliberate strategy in accord with Fisk's concerns. For instance, in Abu Ghraib, the 'War on Terror' was used to legitimate and sanction extreme measures, in which the individuality of inmates was removed with their clothing and with the degradation of their dignity through brutality, in a regime in which gratuitous violence became routinized. The greater good of the War on Terror could be used to justify lesser evils, as if avoiding a bigger harm with a lesser one were not totally irrational (and immoral) and destructive of whatever moral ground its project might be based on.

Theoretically, the case of Abu Ghraib is a clear example of a total institution. It is spatially circumscribed and heavily guarded; people are confined against their will without legal redress; they are subject to bizarre and unusual practices over which they have no control and which are designed to dehumanize and render them powerless. They are institutionalized in terms of being stripped of markers of identity, quite literally stripped in some cases. The organization of Abu Ghraib is precisely the kind of organization that one would expect leading practitioners of organization studies to be engaged with, although there is little evidence that this is the case.

Greenberg and Dratel (2005) have collected and published *The torture papers: the road to Abu Ghraib*, in which they establish that there was a systematic attempt by the US government to prepare the way for torture techniques and coercive interrogation practices, forbidden under international law, with the express intent of evading legal punishment in the aftermath of any discovery of these practices and policies. A systematic decision was made to alter the rules governing the use of methods of coercion and torture that lay outside of accepted legal norms. Not only did the lawyers and policy makers knowingly overstep legal doctrine, but they also did so against the advice of the Secretary of State and the Legal Advisor to the Secretary of State. Thus, the decision to use the opportunities afforded by Abu Ghraib as a total institution to exceed the rights accorded under law was deliberate. The torture of prisoners became standard practice, as the internationally accepted tenets of the Geneva Convention were bypassed and ignored. What made it possible to do this were the opportunities for total institutional control and isolation afforded by the prison. What should be evident is that Abu Ghraib represents a gross offense to the standards of a civil society normally espoused by people who deem themselves the upholders of liberal values that emerge from the post-Enlightenment stress on the importance of individual human rights. It should be clear that we are not equating the abuses of Abu Ghraib with the atrocities of Auschwitz but are drawing an organizational analogy. It is the total institutional qualities of the two settings, the death camp and the interrogation camp, which make their respective atrocities possible. In both cases some of the same organizational processes render extreme obedience to power not only thinkable but also doable.

Not only is Abu Ghraib an example of a total institution that stands at the heart of darkness of US imperial power, it is also a chilling example of what can happen when those civil rights that Weber saw as essential to rational-legal bureaucracy are trounced. Of course, we understand the context in which the institution is inscribed, but what strength do moral claims to a superior form of life have when they are so contradicted by everyday practice?

Twenty techniques of total institutional power

Many of the techniques that were evident in total institutions can be used to make everyday acts of extreme power easier to think and to do. What these extreme cases do is throw everyday power practices into sharp relief. Any one of the techniques in Table 6.1, abstracted from the cases reviewed here, is a significant and subtle power practice; combined they are a formidable weapon against ethical rectitude in everyday life.

Table 6.1   Twenty ways of constructing total institutional power relations

Techniques of power	*Cases from which they are abstracted*
1 Construct an organizational politics premised on identity/non-identity	The Holocaust – around identities such as 'Ayran' and 'Jew' but we see this technique present in other cases as well: 'fallen women' and 'nice girls' in the Magdalene Laundries; 'defenders' and 'enemies' of the state in the GDR; 'half-breed' and 'full-blood' in the Stolen Generation
2 Concentrate and marshal bodies on the basis of clearly inscribed identities in a specific space	The Holocaust – where the death camps played a key role; but also prisons, the Laundries, and even whole societies in the case of the GDR can be made a specific and concentrated space
3 Delegate authorities to enact centrally conceived power projects	The Danish resistance to the Holocaust serves as a counterfactual highlighting the importance of such delegation. Where delegates don't behave as emissaries but act as authorities able to exercise discretion, then central plans can be sabotaged
4 Use expert knowledge to render power efficiently	The role of the medics in the death camps; the importance of the white-coated experts administering the Milgram experiments; the role of the 'protectors' and expert committees in the removal of the Stolen Generation
5 Strip members of markers of individual identity	Uniforms, head shaving and tattooed numbers in the camps; nakedness in Abu Ghraib and the infamous 'bag over the head' of the photographed victim with the electric leads connected to him; uniforms in the Magdalene Laundries; forced removal from families and clans of the Stolen Generation
6 Pay systematic attention to means while accepting ends	This applies to every case
7 Apply intrinsically instrumental and value-free science	Characterized by the Holocaust and the Stolen Generation most obviously. In the Magdalene Laundries, medical opinions were sometimes sought; in the GDR, deviants were sometimes classified as psychiatric cases and locked in another kind of total institution. The evidence is still not clear about Abu Ghraib: was this systematic torture science at work or not?
8 Construct a factory flow of power – with efficiencies of scale in processing inputs and creating outputs	The Holocaust and the Magdalene Laundries are most clearly characterized by this mode of organization

(Continued)

Table 6.1 (Continued)

Techniques of power	Cases from which they are abstracted
9 Have the highest authority sanction the organizational action in question	In each case this applied; the state in the Holocaust and the GDR; the Church in the Magdalene Laundries; the state and the Church in the Stolen Generation; the US president in the case of Abu Ghraib
10 Routinize the actions that enact organizational power	Most obviously in the Holocaust; least obviously in the Stolen Generation, where the power was exercised intermittently and unpredictably from outside the routines of everyday life. In the Holocaust and the Laundries the very nature of organizational routine was the means of enacting power
11 Dehumanize those subject to power	In the Holocaust, the Laundries, Abu Ghraib, and the Australian outback, all those subject to power were regarded as less than fully a part of the civilized community of humanity
12 Be selective in your mercies	The Stolen Generation exemplifies this best; at the same time that children were being stolen from their mothers, concerned experts such as Bowlby were widely read on the importance of mother–child bonding and relations. Ample evidence exists to suggest that those responsible for administering the Final Solution, from rounding up victims to their extermination, enjoyed happy family lives while not working
13 Maintain a distance between the designated exercisers and subjects of power: divisions of labor in complex chains of power enable elites to maintain distance from power's effects	This is most evident in Abu Ghraib. The Church has tried, unsuccessfully, to use this plea. It was the basis, in part, of Eichmann's defense
14 Make technique paramount in the dispatch of power	The Holocaust
15 Obedience to power is encouraged where organization work is a ceaseless round of activity with little room for reflection	The Holocaust; the Laundries

Table 6.1   (Continued)

Techniques of power	Cases from which they are abstracted
16 Make those who are the subjects of power complicit in its exercise	This characterized the Holocaust, and the organization of the camps, but in the cases reviewed it reached its peak in the GDR
17 Be convinced that the regime of the total institution is the best for all concerned, both those in and those outwith; wrap its purpose in the rhetoric of being in the 'real' interests of both the other and the society at large	Racial purification and ethnic cleansing marked both the Holocaust and the Stolen Generation. In the GDR the party had a historic destiny to fulfill in securing the real interest of its citizens in achieving socialism
18 Minimize the possibilities of escape attempts, by spying on everyone and making everyone aware that they may be being spied on and informed about	The role of the Stasi; the role of the police and the Aboriginal protector in the case of the Stolen Generation. In the death camps, inmates did not survive long enough for this technique to be important
19 Lock members inside, keep outsiders outside, and systematically misrepresent the reality of the situation	The Berlin Wall round the GDR; the prison compound; the razor-glass topped walls around the Magdalene Laundries
20 Reward the institution's keepers with perks and benefits and keep them secret from other members	Especially the GDR

Although total institutions make it easier to practice rigid adherence to a legal instrumental rationality which makes it possible for actors to do things which they wouldn't do if they were not bracketing their value rationality, it is still the case that, in everyday life, such bracketing can all too easily occur. Think of the tax official who bankrupts someone; the insurance official who figures out how not to pay an insurance claim to a loyal customer based upon some technicality; the official who insists that an old lady puts down her pet because its a 'health hazard' and against regulations; the health inspector who closes down small family run restaurants; and the safety official who closes down a playground. But when rigid adherence to a legal instrumental rationality is fused with a total organizational apparatus we have a fearsome instrument.

In total institutions, whether we like it or not, we see the techniques of everyday organizational power in sharp relief and focus. For their techniques are assuredly organizational techniques, not techniques of caprice, will or individual voluntarism. Moreover, their techniques are deliberate acts of domination. By this we refer not to the violence but to the ordering, the social organization of ethical horror, in such a way that it is domesticated, tamed, made normal. If such horrors and monstrosities can be tamed, how much easier is it to enact the many lesser calumnies and sins of everyday power in ordinary organizational life?

Total institutions are a significant type of organizational rationality for eliminating equivocality, with practical lessons in variation, selection and retention. What is surprising, as we remarked at the outset of this discussion, is that so little attention has been paid by organization science to total institutions in general (Burrell's 1997 'retro-organization theory' is an exception, as is the discussion in Burrell 1994. For a contrary view, one should see Weiss 2000; also see Adams and Balfour 2001; Hinings and Mauws 2004). Why do organization theorists give so little attention to the realities discussed in this chapter? Is it because their knowledge is an instrument of power? Are these scholars parts of a movement that designs and operates its systems and maintains its silences in return for some perks, such as tenure in well-salaried positions in business schools? The position of such scholars is always ambiguous; of necessity they exist somewhere between power and the 'subjects' of that power, the authors of this volume being no exception to the general rule. Still, it is a matter of choice as to whether one focuses one's gaze on those operating the machinery of power, on the machinery itself, or on those it damages. Overwhelmingly, the organization theorists' gaze has seemed more fascinated by designing a better machine in the interests of those it serves rather than those it damages.

The sounds of silence

Sometimes that which is left unsaid is more important than that which is carefully articulated. The silences of power speak from the words they don't pronounce as much as those they do. Texts speak to us by the words they tell but also by the words they keep quiet. In *A theory of literary production* Pierre Macherey (1978) argued for the significance of what is not said and of what is placed in the margins, noting that what needs to be explained is not the apparent unity of meaning but the presence of an opposition between elements, disparities which point to a conflict of meaning.[35] This conflict is not the sign of an imperfection; it reveals the inscription of an *otherness* in the work through which it maintains a relationship with that which it is not, that which happens at its margins. Thus, it is the silences and gaps in a discourse that are significant to an understanding of its ideological milieu.

These indicate the unconscious of the discourse, in so far as it possesses one, an unconscious in which the play of history beyond its edges may be seen. We have identified several such edges here.

Our purpose is not merely historical. The astute reader might recognize that, between the lines, reside more general and contemporary points being made about the nature of power and total institutions, as well as about the nature of contemporary organization theory. By the tally of this chapter it is a theory of surprising reticence; indeed, it is more than surprising; it is strange. In a science devoted to understanding how organizations do what they do, the organizational crimes of the century remain largely a black hole, a vast empty space, a void of intellectual nothing, an absent presence in a science dedicated, in the words of its leading journal, 'to transcending the bounds of particular disciplines to speak to a broad audience'. Transcendent it may aspire to be, but this science hardly seems able to speak to central manifestations of power. What we have in its place is the radical absence of such address in, precisely, a surfeit of irrational rationality, with an empty and missing center.

What was lost in translation does not reflect an absence in life, however, as this chapter has sought to make absolutely clear. Despite the fact that domination went missing with action inside systems theory, in not one of the cases reviewed should what was inscribed in its place ever be graced with the name of authority. Legitimacy there was not, at least not from the point of view of the wretched inmates of the institutions constructed. But there was power aplenty. And it is important to differentiate between the violence that was embedded in these total institutions and the power that they expressed.

Power is not violence, but power makes violence easier to impose, both morally and practically, as Arendt (1970), who was very careful to distinguish between power and violence, makes clear. Violence, she argued, is an instrument that should never be confused with power. Power is the ability of a social entity to act in concert, enabling its components to function together. For Arendt, acts of violence are the antithesis of power as they 'can always destroy power' – in the sense of a collective concertative 'power to' – but, as she says, while 'out of the barrel of a gun grows the most instant and effective obedience ... [w]hat can never grow out of it is power'(1970: 57). Where action is exerted by violence then it is a one-sided act that entails domination and subordination. While violence was the means deployed, it was not this violence that signified power but the capacities realized in establishing stable social relations of domination that incorporated so many bodies within the vortex of that violence, and which made that violence possible.

In every case, what violence does is to violate the state of being that Arendt (1993: 167) terms 'freedom', that which enables human beings to transcend necessity and to act creatively and imaginatively. By attacking the bodies of those subject to power, by extermination, torture, seizure, confinement, these manifestations of power seek to obliterate resistance through total domination. An essential step is classification of bodies as sharing an essential similarity as Jews, enemy combatants, citizens, sinful girls, etc. Uniqueness and individual identity are denied; just the big essential category is used to order confinement. When individuality is so denied, then the possibilities of individuals acting in concert, in power, to resist, are minimized. It is no accident that it was the tearing up of their identity papers that mobilized the final resistance against the Stasi in a creative act of resistance to a power that had always insisted on its rights of inspection, a power which reaffirmed the individual human freedom of each putative subject. Yet, even individual acts of resistance can deny power. One thinks of Gramsci (1971), writing his prison note-books in tiny script on toilet paper and other filched resources; Primo Levi, work-ing in the IG Farben slave labor camp, surviving in part because, as a chemist, he knew that he could safely eat cotton wool and drink paraffin. After his liberation, he was to liken resistance to just surviving, much as a frog in winter:

> Consider whether this is a man,
> Who labors in the mud
> Who knows no peace
> Who fights for a crust of bread
> Who dies at a yes or a no.
> Consider whether this is a woman,
> Without hair or name
> With no more strength to remember
> Eyes empty and womb cold
> As a frog in winter.
> (Levi 1992, 'Shemá')

Domination in total institutions in the twentieth century worked on both the body and the soul. Its subjects may have been produced by power, but that power depended on relations of domination that stripped subjects of their life-enhancing pluralities, their identities as more and other than that which they were classified as being. While power might create a certain kind of visibility, in total institutions its relations seek to deny resistance through a form of invisibility. Classifications, degradations, and stripping of identity work to make the subject invisible as a person already thought of in terms of being an already-dominated category, whose ability to act is thus diminished.

Relations of domination should not be mistaken for particular acts of violence. Relations of domination are stable sets of social relations capable of confining bodies – and sometimes souls – in ways that deny individuality, identity and dif-ference, filling their existence with a totality that denies their freedom. That vio-lence thus becomes so much easier to enact is an effect of totality rather than power *per se*. Power, which depends on mobilization, real political energy, and creativity, is antithetical to violence. Violence is an instrument not so much of power as of domination. When the organizational relations sustaining intense domination – total institutionalization – break down, then violence becomes far less probable, as the case of the GDR shows most clearly. Once the people no longer were held in the web of fear and paranoia constructed by the government, once they destroyed the identity bestowed on them with a sense of freedom, then the situation changed abruptly. As Arendt argues, it is where 'commands are no longer obeyed' that 'the means of violence' cease to be of use:

[T]he question of this obedience is not decided by the command–obedience relation but by opinion and, of course, by the number of those who share it. Everything depends on the power behind the violence. The sudden dramatic breakdown of power that ushers in revolutions reveals in a flash how civil obedience – to laws, to rulers, to institutions – is but the outward manifestation of support and consent. (Arendt 1969; retrieved on March 4, 2005, from http://www.nybooks.com/articles/11395)

The superior organization of power has less to do with the subordination or domination of people and more to do with the ability of power to transpose the means of subordination into legitimate currency, into authority. As the list of 20 attributes in Table 6.1 demonstrates, power has many pressure points; it is the multiplicity of these, their interactive effects, their dulling of the thresholds that are crossed, that are significant in the ways in which total institutional power is accomplished. Mark these points well, for they are often present long before violence or horror manifests itself explicitly; they ease power over the thresholds from authority into sheer domination. What is most sobering is that such domination is not necessarily done in the name of evil, violence or terror: sometimes it comes clothed in moral authority, religious piety, or ideological legitimacy. Why, it even comes disguised as normal organization, authority or leadership.

Conclusion

As a result of this chapter, we can conclude that power is not only a social relation, one that has to be seen as embedded in specific social relations of domination, but also a relation between human beings who are, in theory, free to act by being in the world and projecting this being onto the world, which entails acting in concert with others if they are to be effective. *Destroy the possibility of concerted action and the capacity to resist diminishes and domination fills the near horizon.* It would be more reassuring if the number of cases cited in this chapter were just the extreme and documented extent of total institutional cases. It would be reassuring but it would be wrong. Sadly, this chapter could easily be expanded to whole volumes, as the cases of what are sometimes referred to as man's inhumanity towards man are legion, as they are expressed through organized mechanisms rather than singular acts of violence and terror. We could, for instance, have looked at the origins of concentration camps in the Boer War, or their most current use as detention centers as part of the Australian government's solution to the 'problem' of asylum seekers; we could have looked at the ways in which in the contemporary US, prisons function as one of the major forms of social organization to which one in three young urban black men graduate after schooling and in which an increasing number of people, largely black men, spend their entire lives in a total institutional career; we might have looked at the movement of North American indigenous peoples to reservations rather than the Stolen Generation in Australia; instead of the GDR we might have looked at the apartheid regime in South Africa; rather than choose the Catholic institutions of the Magdalene Laundries we might have looked at the institutions designed for the moral education and security of young women in many Islamic societies; or if we really wanted to plumb the depths of despair, we could have considered the fate of young East European women forced into prostitution and held imprisoned and coerced in total institutional submission to the worst forms of sexual exploitation.[36] It should be evident that there any number of substantive cases of total institutions waiting research, both contemporaneously and historically.

Recalling Follett's work from Chapter 3, all the instances of power discussed in this chapter are cases of 'power over' people. There is also the possibility of a far more benign 'power to' being organized into existence. And, had we chosen to do so, we could probably have provided cases of power being organized more benignly in total institutions, such as elite boarding schools. Here, confined circumstances enable an extraordinary concentration of positive social capital to be developed that will amplify the range of relations that the young men and women who are confined will take with them from the school into their subsequent life. Total institutions can be enormously facilitative as well as destructive; they can create power as well as destroy lives. They are, in certain countries, absolutely central to the reproduction of elites. Thus, the total institution is never always a bad thing; it depends on the circumstances and the type of power that is enacted. Where it is 'power to', rather than 'power over', as the next chapter will demonstrate, there may be more grounds for optimism and less occasion for moral outrage. But, in the face of the many outrageous things that have been done, organizationally, through total institutions, it is vitally important that we realize that the price of human dignity and freedom is eternal vigilance against undoubted capacities for domination. Organization studies needs to recognize these priorities as a premise of those proposals it makes for organizational design; otherwise it will never play an enlightenment role as a part of the solution to the betterment of the human condition, but will merely be another utilitarian brick in the wall.

Notes

1   When the terms "Erving Goffman" and "institutional theory" were entered into Google, with the inverted commas, 45 hits were generated, none of which were recognizable publications contributing to institutional organization theory. It is not that Goffman is not used; he is cited extensively by organization behaviorists and students of framing and impression management. However, his contribution as an institutional theorist is largely overlooked.

2   Goffman's analyses are centered on a problem area seemingly removed from organization analysis, namely the everyday habits of ordinary people. Yet, he draws on the same symbolic interactionist roots that organization theorists such as March and Simon did: George Herbert Mead's (1934) *Mind, self and society*. What March and Simon (1958) took from Mead (1934) was a stress on habit and routine as key elements of pragmatism; what attracted Goffman (1956) was the analysis of experience from a perspective which saw communication as essential to the social order. Language communicates through significant symbols involving two types of conversation: that of 'language' and that of 'gestures'. The analysis of language produces discourse analysis (see Chapter 10). A significant symbol is a gesture that signifies an appropriate response to others to whom the gesture is directed (Mead 1938: 47). Gesture short-circuits rational consciousness, defined in terms of reflection and prior anticipation of action enacted. In the conversation of gestures, communication takes place without awareness on the

part of the individual of the response that their gesture elicits in others. The individual is unaware of the reactions of others to these gestures, unable to envisage their gestures from the standpoint of others. The individual participant in the conversation of gestures communicates unconsciously. For Mead (1938), participation in the social act of communication is the means through which thought, as potential significant symbolic behavior, is realized. In Mead's terms, the individualized focus of the communication process is signified in symbolic interaction: it is here that the mind becomes evident. There is, then, no mind or thought without language, and language, (the content of mind) can only be the development and product of social interaction (1938: 191–2). Thus, mind is emergent in the dynamic, ongoing social process that constitutes human experience (1938: 7). The mind is social: the human individual is a member of embedded social contexts whose acts must be viewed in these contexts. Society is not a collection of pre-existing atomic individuals but a processual whole within which individuals define themselves through participation in social acts.

3   Although in cognate areas, such as the sociology of the professions, he remained a respected figure (Freidson 1986), and his work on 'impression management' was taken up by organization behaviorists such as Rosenfeld et al. (1995).

4   Especially in his work on gender Goffman (1976) was far more attuned to the embodiment of power, as we shall see. Few other writers on organizations stress the embodiment of power; the anthropologist James Scott (1990) is an exception but one hardly regarded as a contributing author to the organization and management theory canon, despite his analyses of total institutions.

5   The experiments are written up and enacted in a slide show on a fascinating website at http://www.prisonexp.org/ that Phillip Zimbardo has established. The site also contains many links to accounts by Zimbardo, and others, that draw connections between the research and the experience of Iraqi prisoner abuse.

6   It is conventional to issue product advisories when there is some expectation that the material in question might offend more delicate sensibilities. In keeping with this tradition it is incumbent on us to issue a warning. For those more used to abstractions such as systems theory or resource dependency, the remainder of this chapter might be challenging. We make no apology because for too long the analysis of power has been silent about the organizational capabilities that lie at its heart of darkness.

7   Janina Bauman's account is brilliant and should be read, but one should also look at the following website: http://www. war-experience.org/history/anniversary/wghetto0443/pagetwo. htm. In a later publication, Janina Bauman (2002) reflects, methodologically, on the writing of her life histories. We use the plural, advisedly, as there is a successor book, *A Dream of Belonging* (Bauman 1988), which recounts her postwar experiences.

8   Accessed on March 29, 2005, from http://carbon.cudenver.edu/~mryder/itc_data/barthes/myth_today.html.

9   After the Second World War, Eichmann escaped capture and lived in Germany for five years before moving to Argentina, where he lived under an alias for another 10 years. Israeli agents finally captured him in 1960, and he was subsequently tried in Israel for crimes against humanity. Eichmann's defense was that he was a bureaucrat who just followed orders. (An account of his trial was written by Hannah Arendt 1994, who coined the memorable phrase 'the banality of evil' to register interpretation of the events reported there.) Although Eichmann was subsequently found guilty and executed, his defense was important because it posed the question of the extent to which a person who is obedient to organizationally legitimate authority can be held accountable as an individual for his or her actions. It is a point that has a contemporary salience. In relation to recent corporate scandals in the US and elsewhere the guilty managers often say that they were simply following orders.

10 Of course, as we shall discuss subsequently, it was by no means unique. If the growth of Western modernity is a story of organization, it is also a story of death and destruction wreaked by these same organizational capabilities. The conquest that followed the 'discovery' of the Americas or the Antipodes, for instance, was another enterprise requiring enormous

organizational achievements of shipbuilding, navigation, occupation, extraction and exploration. Of course, in the case of the Americas it was military and religious bureaucracy that played the main role. This historical event, considered by scholars such as Dussel (1995) as the beginning of modernity, needs to be re-evaluated in organizational terms. What was unique about the Holocaust was that it was much more spatially and temporally concentrated and confined, and the other that it constituted dwelt in the midst of the categories of reason, not outside, not as something constituted as savage, wild and alien. The European other was, in fact, at the heart of some of its most celebrated cultural achievements.

11   Marking prose in italics is something that will be reiterated throughout the chapter. These italicized elements will later be used to create Table 6.1, towards the chapter's end.

12   Sacks (1992: 338) showed how analysis of membership categorization devices could be used as a tool of political analysis of organizations with an example from the former Soviet Union. The USSR used to publish the names of 'profiteers'. People could see that these were Jewish names. The Soviet state could thereby continue to deny that it was anti-Semitic (since it did not call these people Jews), while deflecting grievances aimed at its own economic inadequacies. It used members' categorization devices – ordinary language ways of making sense in common currency – from which all could infer the meaning clearly enough.

13   There is a good discussion of the introduction of the yellow star by the Nazis at http://history 1900s.about.com/library/holocaust/aa031298.htm. Interestingly, as the site says, the Nazis merely intensified, magnified, and institutionalized an age-old method of persecution with this labeling, which goes to the heart of the thesis that this chapter is developing: that the practices of total institutions are not something substantively different to normal organization practices. In 807 Abbasid caliph Haroun al-Raschid ordered all Jews to wear a yellow belt and a tall, cone-like hat. But it was in 1215 that the Fourth Lateran Council, presided over by Pope Innocent III, made its infamous decree, Canon 68, which declared that 'Jews and Saracens [Muslims] of both sexes in every Christian province and at all times shall be marked off in the eyes of the public from other peoples through the character of their dress.' This council represented all of Christendom and thus this decree was to be enforced throughout all of the Christian countries. While the star is usually represented as being yellow, it was not always. It varied with local practice. In the Warsaw ghetto it was blue, as Janina Bauman explains: see http://www.war-experience.org/history/anniversary/wghetto0443/pagetwo.htm. The practice of using a badge to single out and identify Jews was instituted in the fifteenth century in Germany and Austria. The practice was not new. Indeed, like much else associated with the Holocaust, there were traditions associated with it.

14   Again, the existence of camps was not new. The British first used concentration camps in the nineteenth-century Boer War against the Afrikaners in Southern Africa; prior to this time, camps were a common device for holding those captured and about to be sold into slavery in other parts of Africa.

15   There are not only all these *small acts of commission*, agency and responsibility to consider. There are also the *small acts of omission* by the allies. The news about Auschwitz did get out: the Vatican and the western allies were informed by one of the four escapees from Auschwitz, Rudolf Vrba. One consequence was that the USAF bombed the synthetic fuel and rubber plant that formed a part of the complex; as Higgins (2004) suggests, it was a target enjoying strategic significance.

16   Retrieved on February 13, 2005 from http://www.rockingham.k12.va.us/EMS/Holocaust/ Holocaust.html.

17   These small acts of resistance are the stuff of great fictional contributions to organizations studies; one thinks, for instance, of Milos Forman's (1975) film of *One flew over the cuckoo's nest,* adapted from a novel by Ken Kesey (1973), as well as of Alexander Solzhenitsyn's *One day in the life of Ivan Denisovich* (1963) and *The gulag archipelago* (1995). These novels offer a greater understanding of the nature of extreme power than is to be found anywhere in the canons of organization theory and, on the assumption with which we started the chapter – that the extreme condenses and concentrates the normal – they represent some of

the strongest examples to be found anywhere of the analysis of power and resistance in organizations. Especially with the focus on the individual incarcerated and their struggle to preserve autonomy, limits of freedom and dignity against overwhelming odds, they represent a central contribution to any analysis of power and organizations.

18 The details of the Danish case were retrieved on February 13, 2005 from http://www.goleta-publishing.com/jstamps/1001-2.htm.

19 The question of Denmark's relation to the Germans and the Jews during the Second World War is very much a current issue in Denmark. In 2005 a central debate in the Danish media and historical circles focused on the Danish Coalition cabinet's actions during the war, especially on whether a 'public apology' should be made to the Jews for Danish cooperation with the German authorities. The discussion received fresh impetus when the prime minister of Denmark, the liberal Anders Fogh Rasmussen, demanded in a meeting with the president of Russia, Putin, that he should make a 'public apology' for the Soviet suppression of the Baltic countries during the Cold War. Putin denied the request but it raised the issue of whether Denmark should make a 'public apology' to the Jews, given that recent research is critical about the way co-operation with the occupying Germans was carried out from the Danish side and how many large Danish companies were involved. At the center of the debate are decisions made by Erik Julius Christian Scavenius (1877–1962), who was the Danish foreign minister 1913–20 and 1940–2, and prime minister 1942–3. After August 29, 1943, Erik Scavenius lost all of his real powers when the German authorities dissolved the Danish government following the refusal of that government to crack down on unrest to the satisfaction of the German plenipotentiary. Scavenius was thus prime minister for some of the Second World War as head of a Coalition cabinet, and before that he had been the foreign minister, the most important liaison between the Danish government and the German authorities. He was a diplomat, not an elected politician, and had an elitist approach to government. He was very afraid that emotional public opinion would destabilize his attempts to build a compromise between Danish sovereignty and the realities of German occupation. Scavenius felt strongly that he was Denmark's most ardent defender. After the war there was much recrimination about his stance, particularly from members of the Resistance who felt that he had hindered its cause and threatened Denmark's national honor. He felt that these people were vain, seeking to build their own reputations or political careers through emotionalism. Debate continues over Scavenius' legacy. For example, on the 60th anniversary of the August 29 dissolution of government, Prime Minister Rasmussen chastised Scavenius for his stance, saying that it was naive and morally unacceptable. However, many historians contend that it was only through Scavenius' policies that the Danes – amongst whom the Jewish population were regarded – escaped the worst hardships of the war and the atrocities of the Holocaust.

20 A great source on the bureaucratic form of the Holocaust is Claude Lanzmann's (1985) brilliant film *Shoah* based on interviews with people who participated in its unfolding. Lanzmann spent 11 years tracking people down, cajoling them to talk, asking them questions they didn't want to face. *Shoah* shows the mundaneity of terror. For instance, German Railways carefully invoiced the Reich for transportation of people to the concentration camps. A Treblinkan landowner who sold the land for the camp shows disdain for and disinterest in what was done with it, refusing the evidence that had been before his eyes, in the smell of the air he breathed in his nostrils, and in the anguished sounds he could hear in his ears.

21 The author of this passage worked on several construction sites at one time in his life; hence, the sources for these observations derive from participant observation.

22 The photographs are all of people, mostly women, who are all apparently white. It would be interesting to speculate what the analysis might have produced had it also contained photographs in which were depicted relations of color as well as relations of gender – but it did not, so one cannot.

23 The author of the chapter, Stewart Clegg, was present at such a presentation made by Erving Goffman at a conference organized by the journal *Theory and Society*, whose editor at that time was Alvin Gouldner, Professor of Sociology at the University of Amsterdam.

24 In Australia the institution was associated with the slogan 'Bad girls do the best sheets'.

25 For those who are not its citizens but who seek to be by washing up in its waters as asylum seekers, it maintains concentration-camp-like total institutions: see Clegg et al. (2005: 180–1) for a related discussion.

26 There is no doubt that building the nation destroyed a great deal of Indigenous people's culture, the actual extent of which has been the subject of aggressive 'history wars' – see Macintyre and Clarke (2003) – sparked by an initial provocation from Windschuttle (2002), which was, in turn, his response to the interpretation of the history of black/white contact in Australia in recent times. It is significant that such a debate has taken place, irrespective of what one might think of Windschuttle's abstracted empiricism: he will only give credence to data recording the deaths of black Australians that were compiled in official statistics and formal reports. One could hardly contemplate a similar debate occurring in organization and management theory over total institutions, for the simple reason that there is so little with which to engage debate. The indifference is staggering.

27 Eurocentrism assumes the other simply to be defective natural material, usable but finally expendable, giving rise to this linear history inevitably built upon the sacrifice of its victims. The future, if we wish to improve, requires us to recognize these acts in order to promote a different way of thinking that restores justice and eliminates the usually unrecognized barbarism of the conqueror, as Ibarra-Colado (2004: 25n) puts it. Of course, he was writing of the fate of the indigenes of what is now Mexico – but it is an inscription that could equally mark the graves of those millions of unknown indigenous casualties of colonization elsewhere in the world, were such monuments deemed productive. They are not: such national symbolism seems only to begin with the birth of the nation-state and its immolation in the blood of battle. Unknown soldiers may be marked but not unknown peoples. Essentially, unknown soldiers are always celebrated as 'people like us', the settlers rather than the dispossessed, even in the finest examples of the genre of such celebration: see http://www.anzacs. net/Unknown% 20Soldier.htm.

28 For more details of the special treatment that was meted out the reader may refer to the work of Paul Kelly (1992), an acute Australian ethnographer whose major medium is the short story in song.

29 Retrieved July 22, 2005 from http://www.austlii.edu.au/au/special/rsjproject/rsjlibrary/hreoc/ stolen/stolen08.html.

30 Retrieved July 22, 2005 from http://www.austlii.edu.au/au/special/rsjproject/rsjlibrary/hreoc/ stolen/stolen08.html.

31 There is a general point to be learnt from this sorry history of contact across cultures: '[I]f we recognize the world as a mosaic of differences, the modern as well as the non-modern must critically confront each other regarding the history of modernity. Each one must review the role that they have played, the responsibilities that they assumed and the effects that their presence and their relationships generated, having changed themselves in the presence of the other, but also changed the other with their presence. Only in this way can one respond to the challenges of the present day: How to restore the value of the conquered peoples' originating identities, while at the same time preserving the modern ideals of liberty and equality; how to preserve a sense of community side-by-side with the modern principle of individual autonomy, achieving their reconciliation?' (Ibarra-Colado 2004: 26).

32 Elsewhere the authorities were faster at covering their tracks. In Romania, files were burnt immediately after the Ceauşescus were executed in the streets of Bucharest. Here, according to Trondheim academic Delia Wirth, who grew up in Romania but now lives in Norway, the situation was worse than in the GDR. There was no physical wall – but there was no need because the country was so deep inside the Soviet imperium. However, there was, as she says, a wall in the mind, censoring everything one said and did because of the widespread system of informers. If these informers did not report one to the authorities they were as likely to bribe and extort money or scarce resources, such as meat (the monthly quota was 500 grams of meat per person), in order to buy their continued silence.

33 One might doubt whether the Stasi was actually very effective in controlling the population. Most of the 85,000 Stasi employees were bureaucrats who went home at 5 p.m. So, the active control of the Stasi was far from being total, notwithstanding that such control was exerted over the very many informants, numbering every third person according to Funder. (These figures are disputed by some of the ex-GDR citizens we have talked to and we have no way of knowing the exact proportion.) Control took place in a space that was physically inescapable, other than at great risk or expense. Many of the kilometers of data (surveillance reports, interview protocols, etc.) that were produced are virtually untouched to date and still rest in the archives. Hence, it is difficult to see how – in the face of its sheer inability to deal with its own stock of information – the Stasi could have effectively controlled an entire population. Yet, that was hardly the point. Much as the Panopticon could not guarantee that everyone was under surveillance all the time, it hardly mattered if the individual subject experienced the reality of surveillance in his or her psyche. It was to buttress the sense of being under control by surveillance that the state produced sustained propaganda about the moral legitimacy of its practices and recruited informants to spy on others, often family members, while maintaining border controls which, if breached, meant at best imprisonment and at worst death for the surveyed subjects. These attempts at total control took place in a context that not only policed its subjects attentively but also afforded extraordinary privileges for its elites.

34 Retrieved from http://www.robert-fisk.com/articles400.htm#FullStory on May 22, 2005.

35 A similar point is also made by Ernesto Laclau in a 1981 paper called 'Politics as the construction of the unthinkable', which is, unfortunately, unpublished in English but which has been translated from the French by David Silverman and discussed in his book *Interpreting qualitative data* (1993: 78).

36 For an analysis of the extent of this trade one can look at Victor Malarek's (2003) *The Natashas: the new global sex trade,* according to which there are hundreds of thousands of women from Russia, Ukraine, Moldova and Romania, amongst other countries, who have been sold into slavery as prostitutes since the 'liberalization' of Eastern Europe, for as little as $500 or as much as $10,000, depending, of course, on their use value. The place that they ended up most frequently, he says, is Bosnia, where they service the UN peacekeeping troops, but there are estimated to be half a million in Germany alone. Many of the girls come from orphanages, as young as 16, and many have been kidnapped off the streets. A distressing excerpt from the book, detailing how the betrayal of trust and naivety operates, can be found on the website of Penguin Canada, at http://www.penguin.ca/nf/Book/BookDisplay/0,,0_0670043125,00.html?sym=EXC. The book offers a detailed account of how the trade is organized, the houses in which the girls are locked and policed, and the appalling methods used to defeat their spirit and will as they are 'broken in' to the trade that their pimps make them ply.

7 Power To and Power Over

Chapter outline

In this chapter we will:

- Distinguish between 'power to' and 'power over'.
- Examine the debate between conflict and consensus theorists in the light of the analysis of power; elaborate Parsons' conception of power as a positive circulatory medium; and critique some of its assumptions through the work of Habermas and Giddens.
- Examine the work of Luhmann, which is increasingly influential on European organization theorists, and of the social theorist Mann on elaborations of power as a 'positive' phenomenon.
- Critique the one-, two- and three-dimensional views of power, as abstracted by Lukes from the works of Dahl, Bachrach and Baratz, and Gramsci, respectively, and their empirical extension by Gaventa and theoretical extension by Hardy.
- Consider the important work of Laclau and Mouffe and its critical development by Žižek.
- Establish that power is better analyzed relationally rather than dimensionally, as Allen argues.

Introduction

There are at least two major theoretical auspices for the social theory we shall consider in this chapter. One is to follow through the idea that power is facilitative, that it is 'power to', a view that made one of its earliest appearances with the work of Mary Parker Follett, whom we reviewed in Chapter 3. This conception was at the core of Parsons' positive theory of power, which will be reviewed forthwith, and has been especially influential in Kanter's (1977) 'positive' account of the power of the *Men and women of the corporation*. The other conception of power is more familiar; it stresses that power operates largely as 'power over', which is to see power less as a capability that is facilitative than one that is prohibitive.[1]

Of course, it is rare that instances of power will fit unambiguously with just one or the other of these two categorical ways of thinking about power, in part because the conception of power that one has is dependent on the point of view taken. One person's 'power to' may involve asserting 'power over' many other people; the capabilities of an organization to have the power to do something will invariably mean that its delegated agents have to assert power over others and have it asserted over them.

The relevant point is that the effects of power as productive or negative are strictly contingent, so for some people the effect may be positive while for others it will be negative. Power itself isn't 'over' or 'to' in a transcendent way; it is 'over' or 'to' depending on the specific situation and the contingent position of the agents involved in the relation. You have the power to access certain areas on the corporate website that are closed to the public while your employer has power over your life chances: offend or upset the employer and you can be retrenched, or if the employer fails to develop successful strategies, you may both be retrenched – their capital and your labor. Power will always exist in a complex contingent tension between a capacity to extend the freedom of some to achieve something or other and an ability to restrict the freedoms of others in doing something or other.

The facilitative *power to* conception builds from the work of Talcott Parsons, who represented power as a property of the political system, analogous to money in the economy. It is a view of power that sees it in overwhelmingly positive terms. Power conceived this way is creative, it accomplishes acts, and it changes the nature of things and relations. The *power over* conception builds on a primitive notion of power first articulated clearly in models of classical mechanics. The facilitative conception starts from a complex conception of power playing a specific role as a positive system property in social systems, while the mechanical view starts with a more reductionist conception of power being exercised either when people and things are made to do something that they would not otherwise do or when their preferences, dispositions or natures to do something are arrested or stopped in some way.

Power, conflict and consensus

Conflict theory, the major rival to functionalism, centered on power (Bartos and Wehr 2002), especially as developed by Ralf Dahrendorf (1959). Dahrendorf had incorporated important aspects of Weber's (1978) work into a basic schema derived from Marx (1976). From Weber, Dahrendorf derived the concept of authority lodged in imperatively coordinated association as the fundament of organizational life, in which there are institutionalized superordinate and subordinate positions. The distribution of authority created the basis for competition that plays itself out in specific conflicts. Conflict was seen as the basis of organizational life. The resolution of one conflict would become the foundation for the next. Social change was seen as ubiquitous, rather than unusual, and conflict was normally one of its major mechanisms. Order emerges because some members of society are able to constrain others. Their acts of containment are episodes of power, usually accompanied by conflict. Thus, in conflict theory power plays the role of a key mechanism. It creates conflict and conflict hastens change.

Because the stress in functionalism had been on social order and consensus rather than on contradiction and conflict, it had been widely believed that it lacked a theory of power – until Parsons (1964) provided it with one. Parsons had been

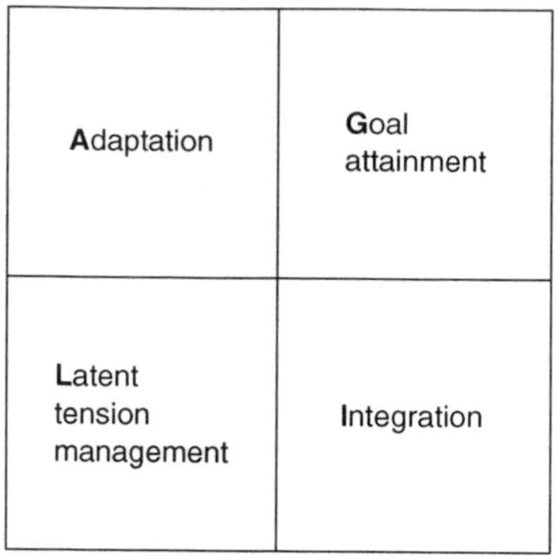

Adaptation	Goal attainment
Latent tension management	Integration

Figure 7.1   Parsons' basic AGIL model of everything

the leading sociologist in the US, and much of the rest of the world, since the 1930s, when, relatively late in his career in the 1960s, he turned his attention explicitly to the concept of power. That Parsons (1964) developed a theory of power was significant for functionalist analysis. Parsons defined the central problem of social theory as being able to answer how social order is possible and why society exists, rather than there being a bleak and violent war of all against all in a life that is solitary, poor, nasty, brutish, and short. In other words, how was it that what Hobbes (1651) had conceptualized as a state of nature did not prevail?

The conflict theorists' answer was that order occurred because dominant elites imposed it on their terms through imperative coordinated association in and through organizations. Parsons sought to show how order was possible on the basis of uncoerced action. He conceived of all forms of social action being organized in terms of four subsystems (Figure 7.1): two of these were specialized on political and economic rationalization, with the attendant risks of change and conflict, but there were also distinct spheres of integrative and normative processes whose task was to deal with those conflicts that arise.

These four processes were referred to as the conceptual and analytical universe of subsystems of adaptive, goal-oriented, integrative and normative processes. The latter two subsystems provided a plurality of moral orders which countervail economic and organizational adaptation. Think of religious ethics holding up scientific research on human gene technology, for instance. There is always a gap between the expectations raised by some moral categories and the possibilities created by economic and political rationalities. Power is the medium whereby this gap is narrowed, in either direction, such that, despite moral and other differences, effective goal orientation is facilitated and efficient organization produced, using sanctions if necessary. These sanctions should be authoritative: for instance, shooting abortionists dead might be a sanction of the extreme right-to-life community, but it is not authoritative. What would be authoritative would be to use the law courts to challenge existing rulings and thus change the legislative framework

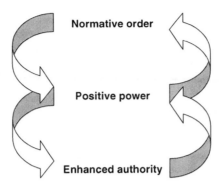

Figure 7.2   Talcott Parsons' positive power

within which abortion is practiced. Challenging and changing existing rulings would indicate the sanctioned exercise of power. Thus, power is facilitative in Parsons' schema: it helps create binding obligations. And, if these are not obeyed, then authoritative sanctions can be enacted.

'Power to' conceived as a functionalist relation

Power as a circulatory medium

Power is similar to money, says Parsons (1964): both are circulatory media. Just as money functions as a generalized mechanism or means for securing satisfaction of desires within the economy – without money you may want things but you cannot buy them because you lack 'effective demand' – so does power in political systems. Both power and money are anchored in popular confidence in their currency; it is this which provides them with their legitimacy. Given this perception of legitimacy, power can be deployed in the expectation that others will respect it and follow its injunctions, because those over whom its remit runs will regard its obligations as binding. Symbolic legitimacy is the orderly background within which Parsons' view of power is embedded. Indeed, he theorizes power as the medium of order for social systems, including organizations. We may diagram Parsons' account of power as in Figure 7.2.

Power is defined as a generalized capacity to influence the allocation of resources for attaining collective goals. Members share institutionalized obligations by virtue of being members and, within the context of membership, certain sanctions are legitimized through those obligations and institutionalized roles involved in the power system. Power is the legitimate mechanism regulating commitments. Authority, on the other hand, comprises the general rules that govern the making of specific binding decisions.

Parsons' view of power diverges from Weber's formulation of power within a context of domination. Instead, individuals are conceived as moral agents acting within a normative context; they are effectively socialized to be so. Where they are not, then socialization must be amiss. Thus, actors routinely use power not as a form of resistance to domination but as a way of ensuring the reproduction of authority, as a positive force, as a capacity to produce an effect. 'Power is exercised within the context of norms,' as Clegg (1989: 132) suggests. Thus, when power is exercised organizationally it is always within the context of binding obligations shared by the power wielder and the power subject, and the sanctions that are threatened for non-compliance are always normatively constrained. One may not agree to consent but one does so in the knowledge of what one can expect the authorities to do in consequence. Deviance and resistance to power, because they call forth the appropriate sanctions, actually strengthen the organizational order rather than weaken it, something captured in US criminal justice parlance when it is said that 'you've done the crime, so you serve your time'.

Barnes (1988: 26) refers to Parsons' views as normative determinism: it is easy to see why. The assumption is that norms are invariably operative and shared; when they are not then a failure of socialization mechanisms is held responsible. However, this is too strong a line: many forms of social action can flow from authentically held norms that do not happen to be shared by others who hold equally passionately to the authenticity of their norms. Much of organizational life is like this.

The solutions to current problems that are provided by one specialist form of knowledge may differ markedly from those offered by another: each may be held authentically but they may not share much in the way of normative assumptions. As skilled social actors navigating their way in complex organizations, such as hospitals, people may share a common commitment to the wellbeing of the patient. However, this is at such a general level of normative framing that it is less consequential as a practical relevancy than the contestation concerning appropriate courses of treatment that arise from time to time. Concerned, conscientious providers from different systems and perspectives can interact with the same client in situations of crisis but have marked differences of opinion concerning what constitutes the best care that the client should receive. In such cases, a framework of clinical governance has to deal with the conflicts that ensue.

Sometimes the public realm within which individual actions are enacted lacks the normative clarity and coherence that Parsons assumes.[2] Consequently, the discursive availability of norms often functions to fuel competing calculations of interest by different agents, who make estimates of the probability of sanctioning for the actions that they propose. Whatever normative order ensues is not so much the cause of the power actions that are taken as the result of these actions. Or, as Clegg put it, 'normative order is the emergent effect of their calculations and differential access to, utilization of and effectiveness in sanctioning resources, just as much as is normative disorder' (1989: 133). We cannot assume *a priori* that the structures of what Weber termed dominancy will be legitimate and thus function as authority: it is a matter of empirical determination.

The limitations of power/money analogies

Habermas (1987b) has drawn attention to some important differences between the analogies of power and money in Parsons. Money is a free-floating resource: a promissory note can buy anything anywhere that its value and legitimacy are recognized. By contrast, the power that one might have as a result of being a professor in a particular university is much more limited. It may relate to an ability to compel students to submit to assessment and examination and not much else; it certainly would be insufficient to be the basis of a generalized power out with specific contexts of classrooms and committees. In a word, power requires and is specific to a particular organizational context.

Given a certain structure of relations, enacted through hierarchies, committees and routines, certain limited powers may be available but they are hardly transferable to other contexts. Bob Dylan (1965) may have said that 'money doesn't talk, it swears', but it does so in a way that almost anybody can translate, in market transactions. The authority that enables an organizational incumbent to do as they wish, within certain limited contexts, is much more circumscribed, normatively. It requires legitimation. If the organization collapses then power lodged in it collapses. A currency collapse is hardly analogous: it represents a catastrophic generalized system breakdown where there is an overall loss of confidence in the currency but, for as long as the central bank can cover what is drawn on it, it retains a diminished legitimacy. In 1992 when the British pound fell out of the European Monetary System the currency lost 25 percent of its value. In the circumstances of a specific organization collapse, legitimacy in the overall system of organizations may remain intact, while in any specific organizational case in question it does not.

Authority and power are closely related in Parsons. Habermas is good on this: he sees that the relation between the two concepts entails a systematic lack of reciprocal balance between them because 'a person taking orders is structurally disadvantaged in relation to a person with the power to give them' (1987b: 271). In trying to make the subject do what is wanted, the ultimate sanction against noncompliance is the threat of withdrawing the continuing condition of organization membership. The right of withdrawal is clearly not reciprocal. The power subject in a hierarchical relation lacks the authority to impose this as a sanction: some obligations are more binding than others, and some actors, those who are hierarchically superordinate, are in a stronger position to impose them. They determine the conditions under which legitimacy is defined and authority dispensed. They can define what is seen to be authority, because it is legitimate, just as they can define what is not taken to be legitimate. Those who are not in the top management team, and are thus not hierarchically superordinate, cannot enter into the process of goal formation, unless invited to do so, and thus can never offset their organizational structural disadvantage. The currency of their ideas will never be spent because, unlike economic actors, they are not free to spend.

The point of these comments should be clear: power may be positive and may serve collective goals, but only if one is incorporated within its remit. If one is other to power, if one is the object of its exercise by those who are its subjects, then its authority to do what it wants with one's life chances might seem rather less than legitimate. And this is what usually happens: few organizations operate on polyphonic or collectivist principles. Discursive participation in consensual goal formation is not a normal condition for most subordinate organization members. I don't need to agree with you to spend my money on something you sell; however, if I sell my labor to you, then there has to be some subjugation of my preferences, dispositions and attitudes to those that are organizationally defined as legitimate. By accepting the offer of employment one makes the assumption that this is a fair exchange – that one *wants* to be in *this* specific position of subordination. It all depends on the alternatives; short of many, most will accept almost anything, no matter how repugnant it may be. 'To be invariably told, infrequently consulted, and be expected not to participate in the formation of collective goals' is hardly a secure basis for obtaining commitment to these goals' (Clegg 1989: 135). Parsons focuses on 'power with' but unfortunately does so to the extent that he neglects that what often seems to one party to be 'power with' may seem to some other party to be much more a case of 'power over', where, given that the superordinate has power over one, it is not surprising that one should string along with the power that is being shared.

Parsons' power – a theory half-right

'Power to' works creatively, it is facilitative; should such power fail then the power to enforce sanctions authoritatively will be exercised as power over deviants. The latter is the unusual and intermittent aspect of power: power does not normally work through coercive exercise to secure its objectives, but only does this when the order that is ordinarily secured breaks down. Parsons argued that the creation of power normally 'presupposed consensus on system goals' (Haugaard 2003: 90), thus providing a framework within which facilitative power operated. Power only needed to be coercive when order broke down, periodically, and members needed to be disciplined – in order to reassert the central value system of the normative order.

Power flows through the social order as a circulatory medium that positively reinforces authority through creative facilitative episodes as well as being invoked negatively when deviance is punished. Power, much as money, is a circulatory and symbolic medium. The modern market economy requires some widespread shared confidence in the currency for orderly transactions to occur. Think what happens when there is a run on the currency and it is rapidly devalued: assets are frozen, banks close and confidence crashes. Similarly, power resources have to be viewed as a source of confidence by the society at large, much as are monetary resources: thus, as they circulate in an orderly way they build confidence by reassuring members of the appropriateness of the consensus that exists about their appropriate use. Hence, power resources have what one of Parsons' successors, Niklas Luhmann (1986), was later to call an autopoietic – or self-referential – quality (see Hernes and Bakken 2003).

Parsons did get it half-right. He perceived that power was not the exception which is somehow outside the system. He understood that for power to be effective it had to be a constituting and systemic property. Viewing it as a circulatory medium he prefigures the postmodern perception of power. Furthermore, he was not totally mistaken in linking it to legitimacy and authority. His crucial error was in the assumption that authority and legitimacy derive 'naturally' from system goals, rather than that the consent behind legitimacy and authority will always be constructed through complex means which have nothing to do with the realization of system goals and are very far from a Habermasian ideal speech situation. Legitimacy grounds truth somewhat more than truth grounds legitimacy, as we shall see in Chapter 8, when we consider the work of Flyvbjerg (1998).

Giddens' conflict critique of Parsons' functionalism

Parsons' theory was sophisticated – but at odds with the experiences of liberal democracies in the 1960s characterized by civil rights demonstrations, race riots, student demonstrations, and the 'Paris Events of 1968' which marred General de Gaulle's last year as president of France. All of these events questioned existing authority rather than obeying it. None of them seemed to suggest that the moral order was one that was widely shared. It was hard to see the youthful student protestors or the militant blacks just as people for whom the socialization project had failed.

For Giddens, a young scholar making his initial impact in the heated times of the 1960s, authority was the Achilles' heel of Parsons' system. All around him, in the universities in which he and colleagues taught, the cities in which they lived, the evidence that society seemed conflict-ridden and fractured along significant cleavages of age and race, let alone class and gender, was everywhere visible. Parsons may have been reflective of the assumptions of Eisenhower's USA in the 1950s, but by the 1960s and the presidencies of LBJ and Nixon, the Civil Rights movement, the dog-days of the war in Vietnam, and the stirrings of feminism, social order seemed more problematic – especially on campus in university organizations.

Giddens observed that Parsons' power is 'directly derivative of authority: authority is the institutionalized legitimation which underlies power' (1968: 260). Such a conception hardly seemed adequate to describe a situation where, seemingly everywhere in the world's big cities, one could hear 'the sound of marching, charging feet', as the Rolling Stones sang at the time (Jagger and Richards 1968). At base the criticism is that Parsons neglects 'power over' in favor of 'power to'. In consequence, Parsons is seen to play down hierarchy and division, which give rise to different interests, and thus overstates the degree of authority in the social system. Not only was social order seemingly more challenged than theory predicted, but there did not seem to be much positive power about:

> What slips away from sight almost completely in the Parsonian analysis is the very fact that power, even as Parsons defines it, is always exercised over someone! By treating power as necessarily (by definition) legitimate and thus *starting* from the assumption of consensus of some kind between power-holders and those subordinate to them, Parsons virtually ignores, quite consciously and deliberately, the necessarily hierarchical character of power, and the divisions of interest which are frequently consequent upon it. However much it is true that power can rest upon 'agreement' to code authority which can be used for collective aims, it is also true that interests of power-holders and those subject to that power often clash. (Giddens 1968: 24)

Later, Giddens (1984) was to change his ideas quite markedly (see Clegg 1992 for an overview of Giddens) by making a distinction that was premised on Parsons' systems view: the distinction between allocative and authoritative resources. The former are material resources in the normal sense of the term in the power literature: things that people have access to or can deploy. Authoritative resources are premised on normative order and are clearly closely related to Weber's sense of legitimacy as Parsons had translated it. Both types of resources, as Allen says, 'refer to sets of capabilities' (2003: 45). These resources are 'the media through which power is exercised' writes Giddens (1979: 91), something drawn on in the course of social interaction. Resources can be held in store, he suggests, and as resource capabilities expand, then so does potential power. Storage is achieved through symbolic and representational devices, which in contemporary times extend to phenomena such as IT systems, and the reach of other media. Actual power is demonstrated by the leverage that can be exerted across space and time. The greater the space and the longer the time over which power extends, presumably, then the more will be the power. Thus, Giddens sees the ability to mobilize and deploy resources across space and time as an indication of the pervasiveness of a power that is 'distanciated'. To the extent that what occurs in one space is affected by social relations in another space that reach into the first space, then this corresponds to what Giddens (1984) thinks of as distanciated power. It represents, for example, the power of a higher court to settle appeals from a lower court; the power of the Royal and Ancient St Andrews club to settle matters of dispute arising from interpretation of the rules of play of the game of golf; or the power of a video referee to determine a matter of ambiguous interpretation of play on a rugby league field. It also extends to situations such as President Gaddafi, of Libya, in anticipation of the likely consequences of maintaining a nuclear arms policy in the face of the US Bush presidency's policy of preemptive strikes, deciding to declare his nuclear capabilities and to desist from their further development. In this case, an anticipated reaction concerning the US military resources demonstrates the perceived power of US policies and capabilities.

On this criterion, argues Giddens (1990), we are at the cusp of a decline in the powers of states relative to organizations operating globally in increasingly globalized markets. Organizational action at a distance is increasingly made possible through the storage of resources in phenomena such as databases that can both enable and constrain social actions, rather than through military extension and hardware:

> [D]istanciated forms of power may be considered to manifest their abilities through a series of often routinized and repetitive practices 'stretched' over space. Administrative power, in transnational institutions for example, can be seen to work through an ability to regulate the timing and spacing of social activities ... power generated in one part of a distanciated network is transmitted intact across it ... [through] ... conduits ... [which] ... seem to undergo little in the way of displacement or transformation. (Allen 2003: 46–7).

Elsewhere, Giddens makes power a necessary component of the human condition, in a move reminiscent of Arendt: 'an agent ceases to be such if he or she loses the capability to "make a difference", that is to exercise some sort of power' (1984: 14). Hence power seems to be both the transmission of agential capabilities across space and time and the ability of all agents to make a difference: if the former constrains the opportunities for the latter for anyone, they cease to be fully human. Of course, making a difference can always be constituted in positive dialectics as the denial of the will of another by the exertion of one's will – even to snuff out one's life as a way of denying the other the opportunity to take it. It is this fundamental and irreducible active human agency that denies power the mechanics assumed by the organization theorists and political scientists who follow Hobbes' causal models. The knowledgeability, skill, reflexivity and recursivity of the human sciences, embedded in language, ensure a radical separation of them from the natural sciences.

Human rationality is always context dependent because, as Wittgenstein (1972) demonstrated unequivocally, no rule could ever account for its own interpretation: thus, context cannot be reduced to rules. All science occurs in the context of what realist philosophers of science refer to as 'standing conditions'. These standing conditions provide for the prevalence of the sense that the science makes of the world of object relations, against naturally occurring conditions. Standing conditions are definite sets of contextual experimental conditions, such as ensuring a sterile laboratory environment, maintaining a vacuum, or holding a stable temperature. Without these conditions, maintained by the experimentalist, the predicted relations that the research setting seeks to display would not occur. Thus, a context for stable object relations has to be artfully contrived so that the context has no effect other than that sought experimentally. A science of objects needs to appear to be context-free; otherwise, it cannot provide a general theory.

Put simply, iron filings should always display the same dispositional behavior when introduced to the poles of a magnet, irrespective of whether the experiment occurs in Japan or the United States or of who is the experimentalist. These variables simply are not important to the 'sense' that the filings make of their patterning around the magnetic poles. Which is to say, as phenomena from the object realm rather than the subject realm, they can make no sense whatsoever. Nor is it relevant to the sense that the experimentalist makes. They do not index the particulars of their own identity in making this sense.

Had we been thinking about how managers might respond to the twin poles of a strategic threat, rather than iron filings responding to a magnet, the situation would be very different. The patterns that emerge are not the result of laws that inexorably create a certain pattern. There is far more indeterminateness. Patterns are established by rules that are applied locally *in situ* by the actors themselves. These rules are not external – even though they may exist as such, as material traces, in manuals or procedures. They are, instead, the result of a complex mastery of skills that enable the actors to cope with new situations according to some categories for making sense that involve the application of members' implicit rules. That is what constitutes skill. But, once such skills are well learnt they become reflexively automatic. That is, they cannot be analyzed simply in terms of those rules that might be thought to constitute them. Such rules become themselves the unspoken and tacit ground of any action, action that is capable of improvising in unpredictable ways around and between any senses that the rules might make. Rules cannot account for their own interpretation *in situ* by actors. It is such interpretations that provide the social science sense of context. Studies that take these interpretations as their frame of reference are only ever as ontologically secure as these intersubjective interpretations are stable.

Giddens says that power is inescapable because all social contexts involve relations of power in which actors who exercise power draw on structures. Structure is 'the practical accomplishment of the reproduced conduct of situated actions with definite intentions and interests' (Giddens 1976: 127). How does one know what these intentions and interests are? Well, one way would be to ask the people to whom these putative interests and intentions belong of what they consist. These people may not provide the answers that the theorist requires in order to demonstrate that they are, indeed, shaped by structure. Perhaps if they had read Giddens they would have the appropriate answers, but reading Giddens is only slightly less painful than reading that other grand theorist, Parsons, and neither have the excuse of being translated from the German, as does Luhmann. All three strangle prose, make their meaning opaque, and construct systems that rely upon one accepting the overall systemic worldview. It is the kind of prose that gives sociology a bad name – which makes it seem like some kind of Esperanto that one must learn to speak. Nonetheless, in Giddens' theory, it seems clear that structures make resources available to actors with which they can then constitute rules. These rules create relations of autonomy and dependence, which actors, drawing on resources, reproduce as relations of domination (Giddens 1981: 28–9). Structures are rules and resources; systems are reproduced and regular practices. Actors draw on structures to produce systems:

> Power is an integral element of all social life as are meaning and norms; this is the significance of the claim that structure can be analysed as rules and resources, resources being drawn upon in the constitution of power relations. All social interaction involves the use of power, as a necessary implication of the logical connection between human action and transformative capacity. Power within social systems can be analysed as relations of autonomy and dependence between actors in which these actors draw upon and reproduce structural properties of domination (Giddens 1981: 28–29). These structures do not just produce domination, as a negative, restraining experience – they also make possible the creation of power through social order because the reproduction of structure presupposes structural constraint ... whereby actors who threaten systemic stability by new and innovative structuration practices are met by the non-collaboration of others in the reproduction of these new structures. (Haugaard 2003: 94)

It sounds a lot like Parsons' Weber defunctionalized – where *Herrschaft* is once again rendered as domination rather than authority and is conjoined with a theory of resource dependency. Power is stored in resources that can be stockpiled and drawn on. The more strategic resources are held, the greater autonomy and the less dependence. Power relations deploy resources which can be depleted as they are used or which, though their use, can increase in value. As Haugaard (2003: 93) suggests, creating power through the reproduction of social order presupposes consensus and the regular predictability of others' actions. But, of course, as the post 9/11 world knows, sometimes very surprising things happen.

Niklas Luhmann's system building, revising Parsons' analogies

Giddens was not the only contemporary European theorist to find ideas from Parsons useful; at least two other theorists beat a path to Parsons' intellectual door. The first of these we shall consider was a German, Niklas Luhmann, another grand theorist with a desire to create a total system of thought. He does so successfully – but with a high degree of opacity. To pierce the opaque veil of Luhmann's thought through erudite knowledge is, for some scholars, a life's work. We have less time available but shall seek to be as pointed as we can by concentrating on his view of power. Luhmann begins his analysis of power with a fairly conventional point of view: 'power involves causing outcomes despite possible resistance, or, in other words, is causality in unfavorable circumstances'. But he immediately urges that the important questions are to be found not in the specification of these causal relations but in what makes them possible. Hence, attention switches to the macro-social system and the functions of power formation at this level. Much as Parsons, his analysis commences with an analogy: power is a *communication*, rather than a *circulatory*, medium. Thus, it is closer to language and meaning than capital and money.

Social theory has two elements according to Luhmann (1979: 109): on the one hand, a theory of social differentiation into strata and into functional subsystems; on the other hand, a theory of social and cultural evolution leading to increasing sophistication. The bearer of this differentiation and evolution is writing and the possibilities for extended communication that it prepares. These are carried by communication media, defined as 'a code of generalized symbols which guides the transmission of symbols' (1979: 111). For people to interact successfully in an infinite world of possibilities they must choose to relate through activities which will be mutually beneficial. Mechanisms need to exist that induce others to accept the basis for selections made. Communications media are formulated whenever the manner of one partner's selection serves simultaneously as the motivating structure for the other. It serves to bind both partners. Think of a sexual relationship: physical attractiveness, empathy and good sex may be the initial media of communication, but they can spin out into contracts of marriage, children, and mortgages – the whole package. However, there is always an irreducible element of uncertainty, according to Luhmann. Once again, think of a sexual relationship: is she cheating, does he love me, can I trust her? The power holder always has at their discretion more than one alternative. At the same time, they act to remove uncertainty from their partners. The one subject to the power also has other alternatives. Power is greater when it can shape action in the face of attractive alternatives. Unlike power, coercion removes all choices from the subject. Power requires agency and requires choice. Coercion indicates a weakness of power, not strength; in many cases it is what one has recourse to when there is a lack of power.

Power functions as an alternative medium of communication to trust through which dominant and subordinate groups can coordinate and control their social interaction. Trust is easier to use but harder to rely on; I may be able to deploy power but might not need to because I have a relation with you that creates a binding obligation. Where obligations already bind the other then power over them

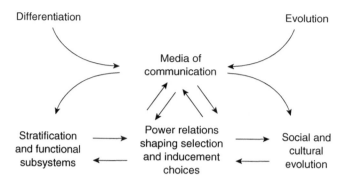

Figure 7.3   Luhmann's Power

need not be exercised. Trust is of more value, as Bachmann (2001) and Lane and Bachmann (1998) argue. Reed (2001) proposes that it is the combination of limited and rule-bound trust relations with focused and sanction-based power relations that institutionalizes binding social arrangements where uncertainty and risk are high. Trust and power provide alternative functional mechanisms for coordinating social interaction by reducing complexity and uncertainty. By providing generalized media of communication and coordination that reduce complexity, power mechanisms facilitate more effective system management of uncertainty, consequent upon increasing structural differentiation, which undercuts the intimate face-to-face basis on which trust is established.

The parallels with Parsons are evident, although Luhmann explicitly rejects Parsons' use of norms as underlying actions. Norms may evolve, according to Luhmann, but they do not form *a priori's* to social life. As Luhmann put it: '[Norms] come into demand and are developed to the extent that generalizations that must be retained counterfactually become necessary' (1995: 326). We provide a diagram of Luhmann's power in Figure 7.3.

Power is inextricably connected with the ability to impose sanctions, not necessarily those that are prohibitory. Luhmann proposes that positive sanctions can be an instrument of power to the extent that they change the preferences of another actor such that they perceive losing the reward as a threat. In his later work, self-referential or autopoietic systems are central; these systems come to exist when (1) they reproduce themselves, by (2) following an internal logic driven by a system-specific binary code.

Humberto Maturana and Francisco Varela (1980), Chilean cognitive scientists, developed the theory of 'autopoiesis'. An autopoietic system is organized to respond to the world while preserving its integrity. The system has a memory that organizes the parts even while those parts may be adding up to produce the functioning whole. The opposite of an autopoietic system, which is found in living organisms, is one which is allopoietic and found in machines, such as an assembly line, where each of the assembled parts has a different mechanism to the one in which it eventually serves. An autopoietic system builds up certain expectations about its environment which it then sees confirmed or not, in a binary way. There is a single binary code steering 'understanding' from within the system. In this sense the system is closed because it can only make sense of external stimuli in relation to its own internal operations, lodged in memory. On the other hand, the system is open and not deterministic, since the feedback from the environment, deciphered in the binary way of the code, influences its reproduction. The system is not deterministic but is contingent over time, meaning that choices made lay the basis for later choices. Earlier choices are not determinate of later ones, but they help form contingencies.

Thus, power becomes restricted in Luhmann's later work to the political system rather than being a generalized medium of communication. Also, the individual subject who came clearly into focus in his work on power now disappears: in their place are social systems as systems of communication. By defining power and politics narrowly as system attributes, Luhmann places power outside agency. It is not clear how such a theory, ultimately, can be of much use, given the Weberian exposition of power as a social action, enacted by agents, within an essentially interpretive frame: it reduces authority to a property of systems as an *a priori* rather than as something contingent on how human action reproduces structures of dominancy. The subject disappears from focus in favor of the system of communication. The system is still contingent: it continually emerges through distinctions that are drawn with other systems – which is how it keeps reproducing.

Within Luhmann's 'social semantics', *power* is that 'language' that is prevalent within the political system and that cannot easily be 'translated' into the language of another subsystem (e.g. money). *Hierarchy*, on the other hand, appears as one possible *steering medium* of complex social systems, one that is suboptimal to what Luhmann calls 'contextual steering'. For Luhmann, *order* is possible without reference to hierarchy: it can emerge spontaneously in much the same way as it does as an emergent property of the market in neoclassical theories of economic liberalism. While power is a special 'language', hierarchy is a special 'principle' to generate social order – and not a very effective one either (contemporary systems, according to Luhmann, are not stratified but are functional and thus polycentric in nature). Luhmann's conceptualization strips power of the centrality that it plays in many other social theories. Luhmann is more interested in understanding how a hierarchical system, for example, becomes established. After all, power is no longer the prime medium for securing social order but only one among several media, and it is not the most effective medium either (to that extent, Luhmann seems to echo Parsons) In fact, the more power becomes 'visible', the less effective it is. Contemporary social systems can no longer be steered by power alone. So, the gradual 'erosion' of power does not pose a problem to social order because other media have taken over. For Luhmann, power is compartmentalized within the political system and, as system complexity and sophistication increase, it is becoming devalued.

Michael Mann's historical functionalism

Parsons displayed little historical sensitivity, preferring to construct vast synthetic schemes that were similar to Russian dolls: open one box and you will find it replicated inside, all the way from the state to the psyche.[3] They were all boxes in Parsons' schema and any historical or substantive material could be squeezed into them. Not so for one of Parsons' English admirers, Michael Mann, who had made a name for himself as a student of conflict theory. Mann used an essentially Parsonian schema to construct his magnum opus *The sources of social power*, of which two volumes are available at the time of writing, and a third is planned.

While Mann (1986) is another grand theorist, as we have identified he is one for whom the grandness of theory is best measured by its historical sweep. The ambition is enormous: when the third volume is completed it will offer a history of power from the beginning to the present day of human history. We cannot review all of what Mann has to contribute; thus we shall focus on the analytics rather than the substantive histories. As most of what Mann writes concerns very detailed exegesis of the historical accounts, a kind of meta-sociology of meta-history, we have decided, strategically, to try and pull out the central elements of his theory without recourse to the considerable detail. Of course, this does a grave injustice to the forcefulness of his endeavors, for which we apologize in advance – but we do this in the context of an audience for whom his historical erudition and reach are, on the whole, of somewhat less importance than one might wish. While the theory of organizations has a great deal to learn from the detailed accounts of history that Mann provides, this is not the place in which to reinforce them. Thus, we seek to provide a somewhat stripped-down and historically bereft account of the underlying analytics.

Mann argues that power, historically, is managed through interlacing networks that mobilize around four types of resources, entwining with each other in the process, creating significant unintended consequences that make history. These correspond to the Parsonian four functional prerequisites model. In Mann (1986) they are defined as economic, ideological, political and military resources. The four types of resources typically correspond to two types of power. A distinction is made between authoritative and diffused power. *Authoritative* power is found most typically in military and political organizations. It is characterized by 'willed commands' and 'conscious obedience by subordinates' (Mann 1993: 6). Ideological and economic power organizations are typically characterized by *diffused* power. Here power works less by direct command and more by 'relatively spontaneous, unconscious, and decentred' means (1993: 6). Market exchanges in capitalism are provided as an example where there is 'considerable constraint' but the constraints are not experienced in the form of 'imperative commands' (Weber 1978) but are often seemingly natural. They have become what Bauman (1976) terms 'second nature', acculturated to such an extent that the sway they exercise is experienced as so institutionally embedded and pervasive that it is inescapable; it has become one of Durkheim's (2002) 'social facts'.

Authoritative power is spatially bounded. In military organization, for instance, authoritative power is intensive, tightly controlled, highly concentrated, coercive and mobilizable only in very specific places. While military power may readily call forth obedience from those who are enrolled within its ranks, as Allen remarks, when 'stretched over large expanses of territory or enacted at great distance, however, coercion is limited in what it is able to achieve' (2003: 49). At the time of writing the US and Coalition troops are still occupying Iraq, and each day the news brings a new tally of suicide bombers destroying lives in occupied zones. The spatial bounds of military power in this situation are indeed tightly constrained. Even the 'Green Zone', the heart of Baghdad, has been subject to attack. Ranged against the authoritative resources of the military are the far more diffuse ideological powers of the Islamists and Ba'athists and of Sunni and Shiite Muslims (themselves opposed). Their resources are far less, in terms of hardware, than those of the military, but their ideological resources are clearly far more extensive in spatial reach and scope, as well as being capable of causing extensive damage. The basis of ideological power is persuasion, moral commitment to abstract ideals and shared ideas, and a willingness to participate in common rituals and social practices.

Staying with the Iraq example, we may observe that the early planning of the campaign against Saddam Hussein envisaged the destruction of a totalitarian regime by superior military power, which, once the regime was toppled, would be replaced by extended diffuse power. This is what has happened – but the diffuse power of a market economy has yet to find much purchase in the mayhem caused by ideological power. Of course, what typically happens when a state is destroyed is anarchy rather than a spontaneous emergence of a market economy. In the void created, diverse powers will struggle for control, using the types of power and resources that they have at hand. The power of the 'insurgency', whether exercised in the name of the Ba'ath Party, Sunni nationalism, or a radical and fundamentalist Islamism, is clearly great. It is able to summon people to commit suicide in the hope of destroying a few more enemies – and thus the resolve, will and institutions of the occupying powers – with daily regularity. The reach of these extensive powers is far greater than that of the military occupation; it extends to the diasporic communities of radicalized Muslims in the cities of Western Europe, such as Leeds, Hamburg, and Paris.

In Iraq we appear to have a situation of struggle between different forms of organization specialized in distinct modes of power. The military are unable to deploy diffused powers, while the insurgency has few authoritative powers and, as the Iraq Assembly comes into being, may well have even fewer – if the body is capable of building legitimacy. Nonetheless, through organizational outflanking by the use of non-conventional warfare, for which the Coalition forces are ill-prepared, such as motor vehicles turned into media for suicide bombing, the insurgents are seeking to create systemic change by denying the occupying troops and their collaborators any legitimacy by systematically attacking them. Lacking access to organized authoritative resources, they have recourse to ideologically charged resources.

We may represent Mann's contribution in the simplified diagram of power, shown in Figure 7.4. Where organizations that have access to all four types of resources are thus able to exercise both authoritative and diffused power then highly effective institutions of power have been created, best represented in the organization of the modern constitutional democratic state with extensive powers of revenue raising through taxation and possessed of a professional military and other coercive organizations. The positive 'power to' achieve things, however, seems to have a primary relationship with the negative 'power over' to command and prohibit, to create order out of disorder. There are good organizational reasons why this should be so. The positive power to achieve things depends first on having established a stable

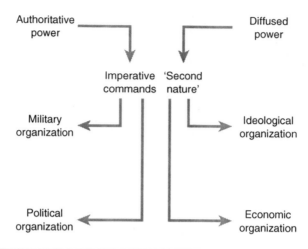

Figure 7.4   Mann's diagram of power

structure of dominancy, in Weber's (1978) words. Power over people and things has to first be stabilized. Once 'power over' has been established then a collective power to achieve things collaboratively can be countenanced – at least by those who dominate the structures of dominancy. It is important to remember this: authority may be one of the power resources of dominant elites but the elites remain dominant, in positions of dominancy and structures of dominancy, even where they are regarded as authoritative. Authority does not neuter the capacity to exercise power; it merely clothes it in legitimate self-righteousness.

There are cases of 'power to' which can exist independently of structures of dominancy, and Hannah Arendt (1970) is the theorist who has done most to advance thinking about these. For her, power corresponds to the human ability to act in concert. It is embedded in groups who enable each other to act in certain ways to achieve certain goals, much as the classic definition of the organization from its origins in Follett, Barnard and Mayo would suggest. The stretch and reach of such groups can be extensive in these days of virtual communities of practice. With minimal resources, and using the Internet, the public space can be extended globally – a good example being the social movement banned in China but known the whole world over as Falun Gong. Collective acts of mobilization through virtual space are capable of generating moral and political energies.[4] Networks of virtual power are capable of creating global issues out of local and highly place-specific conflicts, such as the judicial execution of the Nigerian Ogoni poet and environmental activist Ken Saro-Wiwa, and his nine co-defendants, on the orders of the then Nigerian dictator General Abacha.[5]

In summary, although there are similarities between Parsons, Luhmann and Mann, in that they sought to develop the positive aspects of power from essentially functionalist social theory, there are also significant differences, as highlighted in

Table 7.1   Comparing functionalists

	Parsons	*Luhmann*	*Mann*
Metaphor	Power circulates	Power communicates	Power networks
Key analogy	Money in the economy	Trust	Resources that correspond to Parsons' fourfold model constructed as the economy, ideology, polity and military
Style	Dense theorizing	Even denser theorizing	Meta-history
Key problem	Order	Communication	War

Table 7.1. Parsons is very much the inspiration for this group of theorists. Luhmann takes his basic ideas and produces an entire system of thought out of it. Mann uses Parsons to construct his model – but interestingly, while he addresses power, he does not do so using the model of power that Parsons developed. Instead he uses the basic categories of the AGIL model and conceives of them as institutional resources. Of the three theorists, Mann is the most substantively significant; Parsons the most original; and Luhmann the most complex.

'Power over', in one dimension, conceived as a mechanical relation

Parsons saw himself as explicitly addressing Hobbes' problem of order – how society is possible – while the others did not choose to do so through the approach to power that he pioneered. They accepted the Hobbesian question but not the Hobbesian tools.[6] Hobbes' tools were fashioned from the dominant intellectual resources of his day – the emergent ideas of classical mechanics and a conception of the mechanical world as composed of wheels, springs, and counterbalances in a causally harmonious clockwork. At the center of this conception was a basic idea that power was equivalent to a cause: it held things balanced, in restraint, it produced order and made things happen.[7]

Thomas Hobbes was the first really great English-language theorist of power and he constituted a modern understanding of the concept that has been remarkably pervasive in debates down to the present day. It is a minimalist definition of power: that power is equivalent to cause (Hobbes 1651). Power and cause are identical terms, he maintains. If an individual can make something happen, something spring into motion where previously it was at rest and there was no action, then that individual has power (see Hindess 1996). It is a mechanistic conception of power, premised very much on Galileo's physics of inertia, where changes in state are a result of forces acting on each other. Certain corollaries flow from this primitive, or initial, conception of power. Things have to be visibly related for us to say that they are causally connected. Hobbes thought of clockwork as the appropriate analogy: small flywheels might drive other wheels to effect motion, with a complex system of weights and springs connecting and holding everything in tension.

Indeed, the idea that power and causality are identical has been remarkably durable: the atomistic, mechanistic and causal representation of the world of power became a decisive image. It was picked up by later theorists of political philosophy such as John Locke (1976) and David Hume (1902), who traded the movement of clockwork for the slightly more fluid movement of balls responding to the force of the cue, either directly or intermediately, on the billiard table. With Hume the underlying idea of causality was clarified: if one phenomenon was to be the cause of some other phenomenon they must be entirely discrete or separate from one another in space and time but must share a contingent or contiguous relationship. Effects must be logically, conceptually and substantively separate from presumed causes. In social phenomena the universe of causal relations will occur between separate, distinct and discrete subjects: the subject is identified by their possession of a unique body, occupying a unique space. Different subjects have different interests and will shape their preferences accordingly; thus, their actions are not merely mechanical but also purposive. These notions of power as a causal relation do not seem amiss when modern conceptions of political power, constructed in the twentieth century, are considered.

Galileo's ideas have continually been pressed into service: bodies will remain at rest unless outside forces act on them; the distance that they traverse is an operational measure of the force exerted; power is thus equivalent to the force exercised. Even Foucault (1988a: 50), the man who pronounced the death of sovereign power, respects the micro-physics of power. Foucault recreated a conception of power that returned analysis to the core of Hobbes' concerns: the body politic considered not simply as a metaphor but also as a materiality that was not only physical and biological but also anthroposocial (see Ibarra-Colado 2001b: 300). Isaac (1987: 27) suggests that the mechanical causal view of power has almost become second nature for contemporary theorists, who tend to think of causality purely in terms of contiguous phenomena acting on one another in the same time–space continua. Causality retains its mechanical push and shove imagery, rather than attending to genetic or structural conceptions of causality.

When the American political scientist Robert Dahl (1957) defined the concept of power, cause was as central to his conception as it had been to classical forebears of the Scottish Enlightenment, such as Hume. Power, he says, occurs as a relation between actors, where the category of actor may refer to individuals or to collective entities. Underlying these relations is differential access to resources that finds expression through different instruments of power, whose efficacy is limited to specific arenas (1957: 207). Within these arenas there will be a variable range of key issues over which power is exercised. Empirically, argues Dahl (1961), the fact of different issues confronting people with different preferences will tend to bear out the fact that the distribution of power (at least in political communities) will be pluralistic.

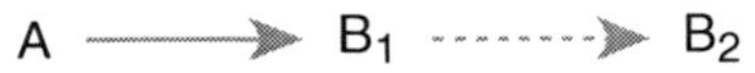

$$A \longrightarrow B_1 \dashrightarrow B_2$$

Figure 7.5   Causal power

Such consistency of definition around the bare essentials might suggest to the casual reader that there is great consistency and certainty surrounding the nature of the phenomenon under discussion; power indubitably is a matter of proximate things related by clashing causal forces. To the less casual reader it should suggest no such certainty; instead what we may deduce is that a set of representational terms has become well entrenched as devices for thinking about power. They have become so because they tap into powerful discourse, the rhetoric of classical mechanics, extended from the world to which it initially referred – a world of object relations – to a world of subject relations. The diagram appropriate to this conception of power is very simple, as we see in Figure 7.5. Power occurs when A gets B to move from rest by doing something that they wouldn't otherwise do, i.e. moving from position B1 to position B2.

Once the social reality of a world of subjects rather than the object world of billiard balls and cues is approached then it becomes evident that what is of far more importance than the impact of cue on ball is the strategy and gamesmanship behind the cue: the understanding of the rules, the state of play, and the skill of the contestants at the table. We might say that while the billiard cue presents only one face to the ball, it is the face that the skillful player presents in taking his or her cue from the evolving state of play that is crucial to the outcome of any competition.

'Power over': two faces and three dimensions

In an influential critique that was published in 1970, two American political scientists, Morton Bachrach and Peter Baratz (1970), argued that power has two faces. One face concerns the outcomes of decisive battles between different actors over specific issues. It corresponds to the diagram of power in Figure 7.4 . The other face is subtler, however. It concerns the 'mobilization of bias' (Schattschneider 1960: 71) that can result in 'non-decision-making'. Some things never make the political agenda; they are either implicitly or explicitly ruled out of bounds, hence they are not raised. To adapt Haugaard's (2003: 94) terms, the existing elites do not collaborate in the reproduction of these new issues as phenomena to be taken seriously rather than ignored, disdained or dismissed. Only those issues that conform to the dominant myths, rituals and institutions of politics will be admitted. Hence, important issues that challenge these dominant ideas will not be heard. Their exclusion from consideration signals a neglected face of power. If analysis is restricted merely to those issues which elites sanction, we miss the power shaping and restricting agendas; we miss the way in which, anticipating the likely reaction to what are perceived to be contentious issues, these issues are never raised (Friedrich 1937). The major marker of the influence of Bachrach and Baratz's (1962; 1963; 1970) work (discussed at length in Clegg 1989) was that the imagery

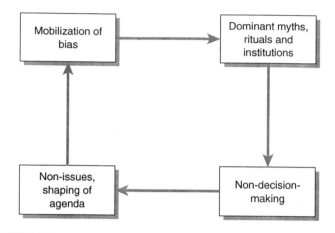

Figure 7.6   The second face – or dimension – of power

of two faces of power was shortly extended by the British political theorist Steven Lukes (1974; 2005) to include an account of three dimensions of power – where the second dimension accorded with their second face. The diagram of two-dimensional power is represented in Figure 7.6.

Lukes' (1974) book *Power: a radical view* was a major landmark in the conceptualization of power. It sought to bring what had hitherto been a largely liberal and individualist tradition of theorizing about power as a causal relation into a fruitful dialog with broader traditions of thought. He shows that each dimension of power rests on a different set of moral assumptions: the one-dimensional view of power is premised on liberal assumptions; the two-dimensional view of power is premised on a reformist view; while it is the moral assumptions of radicalism that underlie the three-dimensional way of seeing power.

The *one-dimensional view of power* pivots around an account of the different preferences that actors might hold and how these will be settled empirically. It concentrates on observable behavior and concrete decisions that are expressed in overt conflict concerning specific issues, revealed in political participation. The focus was on community power – who was powerful in local communities and what issues were the key ones over which power was exercised. (Clegg's 1989 *Frameworks of power* discusses the community power debate.) It is power as Dahl (1957) saw it. The *two-dimensional view* adds some features to the primary view. It does not focus just on observable behavior but seeks to make an interpretive understanding of the intentions that are seen to lie behind social actions. These come into play, especially, when choices are made concerning what agenda items are ruled in or ruled out; when it is determined that, strategically, for whatever reasons, some areas remain a zone of non-decision rather than decision. What is important is how some issues realize their potential to mature while some others do not; how some become manifest while others remain latent. Given that an issue may remain latent then conflict is not merely overt; it may also be covert, as resentment simmers about something that has yet to surface publicly. One may address these two-dimensional phenomena not so much through discrete political participation as through express policy preferences embodied in subpolitical grievances.

From Lukes' point of view, the two-dimensional position is an improvement on the one-dimensional – but it could be improved further. Hence, he provides what he calls *a three-dimensional view* – a radical view to be contrasted with liberal and reformist views (Figure 7.7). While the previous views both define their field of analysis in terms of policy preferences, with the second dimension relating them to subpolitical grievances, the radical view relates policy preferences to real interests. Real interests are defined as something objective, as distinct from the interests that people think they have and express themselves as having through their preferences. He summarizes the distinctions that he is making in the following terms:

> Extremely crudely, one might say that the liberal takes men as they are and applies want-regarding principles to them, relating their interests to what they actually want or prefer, to their policy preference as manifested by their political participation. The reformist, seeing and deploring that not all men's wants are given equal weight by the political system, also relates their interests to what they want or prefer, but allows that this may be revealed in more indirect and sub-political ways – in the form of deflected, submerged or concealed wants and preferences. The radical, however, maintains that men's wants may themselves be a product of a system which works against their interests, and in such cases, relates the latter to what they would want and prefer, were they able to make the choice. (1974: 34)

Implicitly, Lukes is suggesting that power distorts communication and that by imagining it away, by thinking of a utopia undistorted by power, one could be in a situation to reflect on the nature of one's real interests. Otherwise, whatever preferences people might express can always be charged with being subject to systematic distortion and thus a result of 'false consciousness': that is, if they do not accord with the preferences that one would expect, analytically, on the basis of one's moral preferences or their theoretical articulation, one can always see them as something other than real interests. By definition, real interests are what the analyst would have them be. They cannot be judged by the subject who does not express them, because such subjects are systematically deluded about their interests – a condition which he refers to as being subject to hegemony, a term that he borrows from the work of Antonio Gramsci (1971).

The term 'hegemony' derived from debates that occurred in Western Marxism in the 1920s: the fundamental issue, according to the theorists of the Soviet Union, was why the Western working classes had not joined together in revolution against the ruling class, as had the workers and peasants of Russia. The reason, according to Gramsci, is that potential revolutionary consciousness has not been able to emerge because of the intellectual leadership enjoyed by the ruling class. Where this intellectual leadership is established, the concepts with which people ordinarily analyze their situation are those of the rulers rather than the ruled. For Gramsci (1971) hegemony is the normal form of control, and it is rare for ruling groups to have recourse to explicit force or violence to assert their will; in fact, that they have to do so shows that they lack real power – because it means that they have not successfully established hegemony. Hegemony occurs when the ruled consent to their rule and imagine the reality of their everyday existence in terms of concepts that cannot do other than reproduce their consent and subordination. Usually, these concepts are provided by organizations in civil society rather than the state: it is to the church, schools, unions, media that one should look to find the loci of hegemony. Here organic intellectuals attached to the dominant class reproduce its worldviews, concepts and categories for popular consumption.

One consequence of Gramsci's view is that power rarely needs to be exercised where hegemony reigns. Hegemony legitimates existing distributions and structures of power. It is only when there is some crisis in the normal reproduction of these powers, when the illusions of hegemony are exposed, that those in positions of power seek to exercise it in order to reassert control. Hence, the exercise of power, rather than being a talisman of forcefulness, becomes a tacit admission of weakness. Real power, power that is secure, power that rules successfully, does so through hegemony. Thus, there is a contradiction in Gramsci. On the one hand Gramsci views hegemony as *real* power, but on the other, when he actually mentions power, it is equivalent to coercion which, just as in Arendt, is actually the absence of power.

Under hegemonic conditions the favored groups that dominate have their interests routinely attended to by all the everyday aspects of existence that are taken for granted in the ways things normally work. As Westergaard and Ressler argue, we should look for power as something present in uneventful routine rather more than 'in conscious and active exercise of will' (1975: 144). These uneventful routines attain naturalness and are reproduced as if they were natural in such a way that they are rarely if ever challenged. To do so would be, in a word, unthinkable – unthinkable under normal conditions, that is. Lukes (1974; 2005) suggests that under extraordinary conditions, when routines break down, people may be able to pierce the veil of their everyday 'consciousness' and grasp their real interests. Or rather, they may grasp their interests in terms of another discourse made available to them, or which they have only glimpsed dimly previously. Lukes (1974) is not explicit about the nature of such alternative discourses. In Western society they have usually been identified with various oppositional movements that define their meaning against whatever they determine is the ruling orthodoxy, such as socialism against capitalism, feminism against patriarchy, animal liberation against meat eaters, and so on. Typically, reality is reduced to a great cleavage around some category of difference that is regarded as absolutely fundamental, morally, such that it is seen as the essential basis defining existence.

Notice that with the third dimension of power the concept has shifted into a radical interiority: it is tied up with what people find themselves able to articulate and say, what their consciousness, defined in terms of normal discourses and language, enables them to think and feel. In other words, what we have is a kind of negative account: rather than shaping consciousness positively, through discourse, radical theorists such as Lukes (1974) see power as prohibitory, negative and restrictive. If it were really more radical it would have to be about what people are *able to articulate and say* and what language *enables them to think and feel*. However, in the second edition of his book, Lukes cites Przeworski approvingly to argue a slightly different tack: that hegemony '*does not consist of individual states of mind but of*

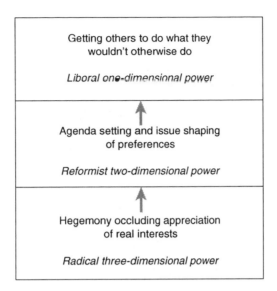

Figure 7.7   The three dimensions of power according to Lukes

behavioral characteristics of organizations', noting that when wage-earners 'act as if they could improve their material conditions within the confines of capitalism' they are consenting to capitalism (2005: 9, citing Przeworski 1985: 145–6). It is a long bow. If there is only one game in town, one has to play it. Lukes (2005: 10–11) also relates his position to that of Tilly and, in so doing, shows that his fundamental views of 'real interests' have not changed in the intervening 30 years since he first wrote *Power: a radical view*. In Tilly's words, with which Lukes concurs, 'subordinates remain unaware of their true interests' because of 'mystification, repression, or the sheer unavailability of alternative ideological frames' (1991: 594).

Benton (1981) has argued that what Lukes creates with his thesis of hegemony as 'control of consciousness' against the real interests (or true interests) of people is a 'paradox of emancipation'. If people are systematically deluded about their interests they cannot emancipate themselves. If their individuality and autonomy are to be respected then no one else can emancipate them; only they can emancipate themselves from mental slavery but, lacking the tools to do so, they never will unless some external agency interferes. But, if it does so, then it will be acting in their interests as that external agency constitutes them – not as the people whose interests they are would define them. Perhaps governments whose armies invade and occupy countries in the name of essentialisms such as markets and democracy would do well to consider the paradox of emancipation?

Lukes (1977) was to argue that subjects have a relative autonomy in being free to choose, notwithstanding that the choices they make will be made under conditions probably not of their own choosing. Their relative freedom will be indicated by the possibility of rational discussion occurring about the plausible relation of means and ends. However, as Barbalet argues, this is a long way from real interests – perhaps because if 'to be subject to power is to have one's real interests contravened, and if real interests can be identified only outside of a subordination to power, then it is impossible ever to determine whether one is subjected to power, except when it ceases to matter' (1987: 8).

The debates around the third dimension of power are a replay of early debates in Marxism drawn from Marx and Engels' (1998[1847]) *The German ideology*. There the idea of people having a false consciousness arose in relation to the proposition that the ideas of the ruling class are in every epoch the ruling ideas: thus ordinary people will not know their own minds other than through the dominant ruling ideas, which will make them see things falsely and occlude their understanding of their real interests. Lukes' views of power seem to be influenced by the work of Sir Isaiah Berlin on freedom, when, as Berlin puts it, people 'would not resist me if they were rational and as wise as I and understood their interests as I do' (2003: 205). The analyst is placed in the position of determining what the subject would choose if that subject were really free to choose (2003: 205). Similarly, the idea of a third dimension of power seems not too far away from Berlin's defense of negative liberty:

> To threaten a man with persecution unless he submits to a life in which he exercises no choices of his goals; to block before him every door but one, no matter how noble the prospect upon which it opens, or how benevolent the motives of those who arrange this, is to sin against the truth that he is a man, a being with a life of his own to live. (2003: 199–200)

The idea of free choice seems illusory. For instance, when one joins an organization and accept its conditions of existence as those in which hierarchical power over one will be exercised, how different is one as someone 'free to choose' than the subject that Berlin sketches above? Moreover, in such a situation, where the only freedom is either to show loyalty or to exit – the opportunities for voice being limited – isn't holding on to the idea that one is really free a form of false consciousness (Hirschman 1970)? That is to say, wouldn't holding an idea of freedom in such a setting be a situation of systematic delusion?

To suggest that someone is in a state of false consciousness presupposes that there must be a correct or true consciousness as its counterpart, which is theoretically problematic (Haugaard 2003: 101), in exactly the terms that one might think from Berlin's (2003) positive account of liberty. Of course, in some situations it might seem quite unproblematic to say that one is more rational and wise and understands the other's real interests better than the other. Where such ideas are applied to deliberate systems of manipulation of knowledge, as, for instance, where cigarette manufacturers mislead their customers about the health risks associated with their products, then it might be appropriate to speak of a 'false' consciousness. Cigarette manufacturers or other 'economical with the truth' product liability statements are hardly the focus of false consciousness theory, however. Instead, false consciousness theories of ideology, hegemony and so on have been applied to issues of much wider scope, which are less specifically intentionally created and are lacking in clear-cut criteria of truth and falsity. In the strong case, such views of power assume a transcendent position which enables the theorist to determine what the real interests of other people are – even when the interpretations that theorists make rule against the sovereignty of individuals interpreting their own will. According to the theory, people cannot do this because they will always do so through the inauthentic and dominated categories of thought. Only the analyst, equipped with a transcendent theory, can pierce through to their real interests, as three-dimensional theories propose: however, with Miller (1987) and Rose (1999) one must question the morality of any critical apparatus that corrects the human subjectivity of others in a 'calculus of domination and liberation' (1999: 95). Not only does it miss the ways in which power is constitutive rather than distortive, it also opens up the possibility of some rather dubious moral practices. The theoretical consequences of a radical three-dimensional position might seem insignificant. Theoretically, some Marxist or feminist scholars might ruggedly insist that the people about whom they theorize simply do not really know their own interests. 'So what?' the democrat might say, 'Just ignore them.' The practical consequences can be considerably more serious, however. Think of the practical consequences of a theoretical position that suggests that parents do not know their children's real interests but that the employees of the state, with their superior theoretical consciousness, do. Then think about the 'Stolen Generation'. Or, think about a theoretical position that sees young people at risk because of their biological or sexual maturation. Then think of the Magdalene Laundries. As another option, think about a theoretical system which brands anyone who wishes to leave the society and reject the values that it has created an enemy of the state – and then think of the consequences of the Berlin Wall for the GDR. It existed not to keep deviants out but to keep them in – presumably because the theory created so many of them. Alternatively, think about some eugenics theories that declare that different 'races' populate the world and that some of these races are impure, along with other 'scientifically' constructed categories such as the feeble, gypsies, homosexuals, and Slavs. Then think of the 'Final Solution'. Theoretical positions that presume to know the real interests of others, despite the views that the others articulate, are deeply dangerous.

In order to avoid these theoretical pitfalls, while still attempting to retain the essence of three-dimensional power, Haugaard suggests that 'undermining power relations' may be 'a matter of facilitating individuals in converting their practical consciousness knowledge into discursive consciousness knowledge' (2003: 102). This is not a question of some enlightened theorist presenting subject actors with some external truth. Social life presupposes a large tacit knowledge of everyday life and in routine social interaction this knowledge remains practical consciousness. The moment of insight is when what they *already know* – in terms of their lived experience and their practical consciousness of it – informs them that what is articulated discursively for them as an adequate and true account of this experience is, in fact, false. It doesn't ring true. When this occurs, people are facilitated in critically confronting their everyday social practices as part of a system of relations of domination which are reproduced, with their complicity, through everyday interaction. Practical consciousness is a tacit knowledge which enables us to be competent and capable actors in our everyday lives, while discursive consciousness comprises knowledge which we can put into words. These two forms of knowledge are not entirely separate. The relative separateness of the two types of social knowledge is an important element in the maintenance of systemic stability. If practical consciousness has never been critically evaluated, never formed part of discursive consciousness, then it will be reproduced virtually as a reflex. Marx and Engels argued that most people, lacking the critical education to see through the fancy words of political economy that hold them captive, can nonetheless grasp enough of them to know that their everyday life contradicts these words; and, once they are provided with an alternative way of interpreting their reality, these intuitions become the departure for social critique.

As Haugaard (2003) argues the case, the radical feminist and the Marxist do not dispense true consciousness. However, they may make actors aware of aspects of their practical consciousness, knowledge that they have never previously confronted in a discursive fashion. In consequence, they can see things differently. Thus, social critique entails converting practical consciousness into discursive consciousness. Once knowledge of structural reproduction becomes discursive, the actor may reject it or they might simply shrug and accept that this is how things are and there is little they can do to make them otherwise. In this event, it may become apparent that certain structural practices contribute to relations of domination and/or are inconsistent with other discursively held beliefs. What is useful about this approach to the matter of consciousness is that it accommodates arguments about the definition of the situation (Thomas 1923; McHugh 1968). On balance, as the adage has it, if people define situations as real they are real in their consequences, and while interlocutors may try and argue different definitions with different consequences, they rarely have any suitable fulcrum outside of the consciousness of the people whose definitions they are. Theorizing Lukes' third dimension of power in terms of a form of consciousness raising through the conversion of practical consciousness knowledge into discursive consciousness knowledge is theoretically consistent and avoids the chief pitfalls of Lukes' analysis – that it requires the theorist to adopt a transcendent position.

In his study, Gaventa (1980) suggests another aspect to three-dimensional power that also does not hinge on the theoretically problematic dichotomy between true and false consciousness. Given the definition of the situation prevailing, there can be no guarantee that what is learnt will not reproduce domination and hegemony as easily as question it. In Gaventa's (1980: 136–64) analysis of disempowered miners in the Appalachian coalfields, it tended to be the case that those communities which were the most dominated were the most passive about their dominance, and the least likely to strike and agitate. The miners had learnt the practical conditions of existence only too well; the contradiction between what they experienced and what they might be brought to think simply did not arise as a realistic definition of their situation. They were effectively governed by a complex confluence of two- and three-dimensional power. Gaventa (1980) argues that the third dimension of hegemonic power comes into play under specific conditions:

- When subordinated groups keep losing whatever struggles they mount, it is easy for them to become dispirited and to stop struggling.
- Where people are unable to express themselves positively through concertative power relations, then they have no opportunity for building skills in and knowledge of power.
- Where people are subject to many competing interpellations that chronically disorganize their consciousness, so that they cannot decide what to believe, then they will be more likely subject to hegemony.

All of these correspond to 'organizational outflanking' (Mann 1986), where subordinated groups lack collective organizational capacities in relation to, and relative to, the capacities that their dominators exercise. Definitions of the situation accept rather than question it.

Four dimensions?

What characterizes the three-dimensional view of power is that these dimensions, as Lukes (1974) conceived them, are dimensions of the same essentially contested concept – the underlying notion of power as A getting B to do something that they would not otherwise do. Lukes did not seek to synthesize disparate conceptions of power that did not inhere in their essential contestation but sought to advance the case that the three dimensions described different layers of the same concept. There have been attempts to extend the three dimensions further.

According to Hardy and Leiba-O'Sullivan (1998), a fourth dimension of power exists that goes beyond Lukes' third dimension. They call this the postmodernist dimension of power and claim to find this fourth dimension in Foucault. Foucault, they suggest, conceptualizes power as a network of relations and discourses, which capture advantaged and disadvantaged alike. The intentions which actors have concerning outcomes do not necessarily produce the desired outcomes; instead, it seems to be implied that it is the discourse which produces effects. According to this view, as they argue it, all actors are subjected to a prevailing web of power relations, a network which resides in every perception, judgment and act, and from which the prospects of escape are limited for both dominant and subordinate groups.

Looked at through the model of a dimensional analysis, in their terms, power may be exercised through the mobilization of scarce, critical resources as the first dimension; through the control of decision-making processes as the second dimension; and, at a deeper third-dimensional level, through managing the meanings that shape others' lives. Deeper still, they suggest, is the fourth dimension, where power is embedded in the very fabric of the system; here power is conceptualized as constraining how we see, what we see, and how we think, in ways that limit our capacity for resistance. They see power as being embedded in the system, which defines how and what we see, and how we think (1998: 460). According to this view, postmodernism handles power as a network of relations and discourses. The subject is socially produced by the system of power that surrounds it, and power is no longer a manipulative, deterministic resource under the control of autonomous, sovereign actors because all actors are subjected to 'disciplinary power' (1998: 458–60).

Hardy and Leiba-O'Sullivan's (1998) superstructuralism hardly does justice to the complexity and sophistication of Foucault's thought, any more than it does to the reality of power. It seems to offer little more than a further version of the third dimension as a total hegemon. In this view, Foucault is seen to suggest that the subject is socially produced by the system of power which surrounds it and is a socially constituted, socially recognized, category of analysis, one with multiple and fragmented identities rather than the one suppressed identity of a real interest that is unexercised, unknown and unrealized. Thus, from this perspective the subject is not a 'given' but is produced by power and knowledge. However, the register of dimensions is still in a position of analytic dominance here. What we have, by definition, is a further development of the 'radical' third dimension, a dimension in which the discourse of real interests is already inscribed. Against this stress on interests, essential to the discourse of dimensions, were we to read Foucault more broadly than as a theorist of surveillance we would appreciate that identity as it is constituted, construed, and performed in organizations will be multiple and contradictory; it will be not so much lodged in some remote analytic concept of interests, real or not, but much more the stuff of idle chatter, speculation, gossip, personal desires, the judgments and (dis)affections of significant and imaginary others, as well as formal organizational imperatives and accountabilities. In short, when we are at work and working, analytic notions of interest have little more purchase than do generalized theories of discourse.

In this 'four-dimensional' view, the diagram of power in Figure 7.8 suggests that the three dimensions are surrounded by a fourth dimension shaping subjects' subjectivities. The gray shade represents the pervasive systemic power, constituting the subjectivity of the actors in each of the other dimensions. It is, as suggested, superstructuralism of the highest order. Seeing Foucault in relation to an interest-based view of power is analytically inchoate. The notion of real interests that are not realized is entirely alien to his analysis. To argue that identity and interests are related within the framework of a dimensional view, and that the identity shaping mechanisms are a fourth dimension, can only mean that this fourth dimension somehow shapes the identities of the other dimensions. To see the ways that people act, what they think are significant issues and decisions and what are not, how their sense of their interests is shaped, against some privileged conception of what these interests really should be, is to conceive of the person as a cipher, as a cultural dope, a thing not free to choose, and the analyst as an oracle.

Following Lukes (1986: 4–5), we can argue that variations of different power views are too many and what unites these variations is too thin and formal to provide a generally satisfying definition that we could apply to all cases. Recall that for Lukes it was not *all* conceptions of power that were essentially contested but a particularly influential causal conception – which Clegg (1989) tracks back to Hobbes (1651). Foucault does not draw from the essentially Hobbesian conception of causal power that shapes Lukes' account. As has been argued elsewhere (Clegg 1989), Foucault's classical auspices owe much more to Machiavelli than to Hobbes. There is no elective affinity between this conception of power and that purloined from Foucault

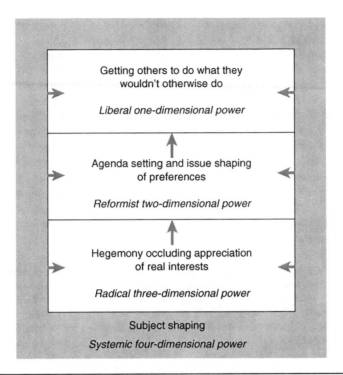

Figure 7.8   The four dimensions of power

and 'synthesized' into the fourth dimension. Ideas have distinct provenances and to simply blend clashing principles of composition, in an *ad hoc* manner, especially where there are contradictory political, ontological, epistemological and moral presuppositions, may result in a mixture that is somewhat indiscriminate. It should be noted that other approaches have adopted a similar synthetic mode – notably Hardy (1996), Fulop and Linstead (1999) and Digesser (1992).[8]

Power and subjectivities

Clearly subjectivity is important in the discussion of power, but unfortunately neither Lukes' discussion nor its extension in Hardy's work quite grasps what is important in subjectivity. The basic point of reference for any contemporary discussion of subjectivity has to be Laclau and Mouffe's (1985) *Hegemony and socialist strategy*. It was this work that introduced the basic poststructuralist ideas into discussion of power. Briefly, these are that there are no privileged grounds of theoretical truth from which the theorists can write or speak; knowledge is contested and reality is something known only through knowledge of it. Hence, as Žižek says, 'there is no transcendental Signified; so-called reality is a discursive construct;

every given identity, including that of a subject, is an effect of contingent differential relations' (2005a: 271).

The argument of *Hegemony and socialist strategy* effectively puts an end to discussion of real interests because it deconstructs the notion of the subject as something that is a substantial entity, already there and fully formed, except for realization of its real interests which the structure of reality occludes. Instead, interests are never given – any more than is the nature of the subject. Subjects are an effect of the play of contingent discursive possibilities, the signification of which is not fixed in advance because all of its possible terms are relational. It is the play of differences that is important. It is how we see ourselves in the discursive possibilities that determines how we, as subjects, constitute ourselves as 'the' subject with specific sets of interests that relate to other subjects with other interests. However, going beyond this poststructuralism, Žižek sees the 'real achievement' of Laclau and Mouffe's work to be more than merely its poststructuralism (whose general approach has been discussed in greater detail in Clegg 1989):

> The real achievement of *Hegemony* is crystallized in the concept of 'social antagonism': far from reducing all reality to a kind of language-game, the socio-symbolic field is conceived as structured around a certain traumatic impossibility, around a certain fissure that cannot be symbolized. In short, Laclau and Mouffe have, so to speak, reinvented the Lacanian notion of the Real as impossible, they have made it useful as a tool for social and ideological analysis. (2005a: 271, 273)

Being constituted as an ideological subject by responding to those interpellations that constitute our subject positions, we are, Žižek suggests, by definition deluded. We see ourselves in terms of antagonisms – for instance, as man not woman, as religious not an infidel – which have an *a priori* impossible relationship. Each of the terms stands in an impossible relation to the other. Each of them prevents the other from achieving its identity with itself. As soon as one defines oneself in terms of a religious identity – for instance that one is a Muslim and not an infidel – then one is engaged with a social reality that these terms construct, always the other to those many infidels whom one encounters, and whose being there and being that is a constant affront to the identity that is assumed. Or think of it in class terms. The proletarian demands the capitalist; it needs the capitalist as its other, if only as an illusion, as something to struggle against in rhetoric and through other forms of engagement. The capitalist serves as an illusory figure for the proletarian just as does the infidel for the Muslim or the Christian – where each is the other to the infidel. The real existence of those others who are not bearers of the same subject positions as oneself does not challenge one's identity, however; in fact, it constitutes it.

> However, to grasp the notion of antagonism, in its most radical dimension, we should invert the relationship between the two terms: it is not the external enemy who is preventing me from identity with myself but every identity is already in itself blocked, marked by an impossibility, and the external enemy is simply the small piece, the rest of reality upon which we 'project' or 'externalize' this intrinsic, immanent impossibility … This is also the real ground for Freud's insistence that the *Verdrängung* cannot be

reduced to an internalization of the *Unterdrückung* [the external repression]: there is a certain fundamental, radical, constitutive, self-inflicted impediment, a hindrance of the drive; and the role of the fascinating figure of external Authority, of its repressive force, is to make us blind to this self-impediment of the drive. (2005a: 274)

Indeed, the authority figures that block us in organizations function in precisely these ways. We need them for our identity; overcome them and we are forced to confront the painful emptiness of our own failings rather than project them on to others whose responsibility they can be assumed to be rather than a responsibility that we will not assume. What we imagine that the other deprives us of having or being does not exist as something that the other possesses – the Hegelian moment of 'the loss of the loss' or the 'negation of the negation', 'that moment of pure antagonism where it is brought to the point of self-reference' (2005a: 274, 275). It is the negativity of the other, as an externalization of one's own self-hindering, to which we ascribe in terms of the interpellations constituting our sense of who we are. The other functions as a form of positivity for the subject position claimed, as a symptom: the believer needs the infidel to measure the worth of his belief, the other always functioning as a reflexive determination of its other term. As Žižek puts it, 'the subject is correlative to its own limit, to the element which cannot be subjectivized, it is the name of the void which cannot be filled out with subjectivization: the subject is the point of failure of subjectivization' (2005a: 276). The subject is always a work in process whose interests are produced as something seemingly real only in the name of certain antagonisms that are always already there to mask the empty space of the subject: the sinner and salvation; the worker and oppression; the capitalist and exploitation, for instance. We should be happy in the indetermination of subjectivity rather than clutch at the straws of 'real interests', for they are only ever a fantasy of the categories we conjure and conceive.

To have or have not: power as a relation in space, not a thing

Digging deep into power

The dimensional view of power resolutely dissects power into layers. Analytically, the imagery is of the theorist digging deeper into the topic, but the topic is rather static. Nothing much flows. Power is all about stopping things happening in this radical view of power. Lukes' account of power moved steadily towards a view of power as something oriented to preventing people, 'to whatever degree, from having grievances by shaping their preferences, cognitions, and interests' such that they 'can see or imagine no alternative' (1974: 24). It moved power into the control of consciousness, not bodies in space, as we saw in the previous chapter's concerns with total institutions.

In many ways these dimensional views of power match the structural view of organizations in their timelessness and motionlessness. Just as, in organization theory generally, such static synchrony has come under attack from writers such as Weick (1969), with their emphasis on organizing rather than on organization, on process and verbs rather than nouns and structures, so we need to move towards a more relational view of power and of organiz/ation/ing as the complex recursive articulation of order–disorder, in which structure regulates the relations (and their settings) that produce–reproduce–transform such structures.

One might note, in addition, that these analyses are confined to inner space, consciousness, rather than to outer space, the material world. If we think about the analyses of power that we have presented, space was obviously important for the early political economies of the body, as well as for the sense of confinement found in total institutions. Yet, by the time that the debates have switched to dimensions, space fails to make an appearance. Inner space – in terms of consciousness – is traversed but not the space between people, the situation of bodies in relation to each other, at a distance, embedded in space (see Deleuze 1992).

When organization theorists started to think about power from the 1950s onwards they often took over the definitions and causal assumptions from their colleagues in political science: indeed in some cases, such as J. G. March (1955), the scholars who were contributing to both debates were equally at home in either. But there was little connection between these analyses of causal power and the analyses of total institutions by theorists such as Goffman (1961). The former confined themselves to space as defined proximately in small slices of time; the latter explored how confinement shaped power over time in small slices of space. The former confined themselves to situations that could be defined as 'normal', while the latter were confined to the 'abnormal'. Indeed, it may well be in the perception of the abnormality of total institutions that their neglect by those concerned with the normal can be located.

There were methodological issues as well. The mechanical-causal views of power were quite strict: they placed restrictions on the possibility of action at a distance that flowed from the initial specification of power in mechanical-causal terms. For something to have caused something else to have happened the two putatively connected events or phenomena had to be coterminous in space and connected, and the effect had to time-lag the cause. Analyzing power empirically in relatively small political communities was ideally suited to these restrictions. Had power been analyzed in total institutions, using the mechanical-causal models, then it would hardly have had much more to say other than to identify order givers and order takers. That power might somehow have been constituted in the relational and constitutive fabric of the organization was not something that a purely episodic and causal-based view of power could grasp easily.

Grasping power relationally and spatially

Confinement clearly aids power over people. Total institutions are all strongly bounded by physical barriers marking out space: the Berlin Wall; the asylum wall; the walls bounding the reserves and the Magdalene Laundries; the barbed wire of the death camps. It is confinement within space that made total institutionalization possible. As John Allen recently suggested, the connection of space and power is familiar:

> Most political disputes over land and territory, in Europe and beyond, where borders have been torn up and redrawn by coercive states or countries subjected to the dominant force of neighbouring governments or ethnic groupings, have geography at their core. Closer to home, the gated communities which sprung up in major cities to enable the affluent to live beyond high walls and electronic fences are an integral mix of geographic and economic constraint. (2003: 1)

In the terms used in the previous chapter, these are all further examples of total institutions. But, of course, dramatic as these examples are as peculiar condensations of power, they are hardly typical of the way that power traverses space.

Not all space is experienced as confinement, as Deleuze (1992) identifies. Power 'is a relational effect of social interaction,' suggests Allen (2003: 2). It may traverse space but usually less through the confinement of space and more through 'mediated relationships or through the establishment of a simultaneous presence' (2003: 2). Allen opposes any unduly centered notion of power as well as any overly ubiquitous concept. Power should not be seen as concentrated in particular organizations, institutions or the resources they have available to them, he suggests. The 'odd tall fence, high wall and exclusionary boundary marker' are easier to recognize than 'the many and varied modalities of power' constituted differently in space and time (2003: 4).

Organizationally, power and resources are often confused, perhaps most famously by Crozier and Friedberg (1980), or possession or access to resources is somehow said to proffer power to their possessors, as we have seen in Chapter 5. With Allen we believe this to be a fundamentally mistaken view:

> Resources may be misused, incompetently applied, mobilized for all the wrong reasons, and, perhaps worst of all, simply wasted by a misguided yet otherwise well-meaning bunch of individuals. Those in charge may make a string of bad decisions, or those nominally in control may pool all available resources, yet to no avail. What can go wrong may well go wrong, and if it does not it may succeed only partially or hardly at all. In short, power as an outcome should not be 'read off' from a resource base, regardless of its size or scope. Power is in this sense no more to be found 'in' the apparatus of rule than sound is to be found 'in' the wood of musical instruments. (2003: 5)

Power is above all a relational effect, not a property that can be held by someone or something. Thus, metaphors of its seizure – as if power were a tiller waiting to be grasped so that the crew might set a different course – or of its destruction – as if power could be blown up – are profoundly unhelpful because they lack a basis in primarily embodied metaphors of power (Lakoff and Johnson 1980). We experience power not as a thing but as a relation. And we are quite capable of understanding the relation and accepting it nonetheless because, for practical reasons, most of our social knowledge has to be based in those relations in which we are involved, and this tends to reproduce these relations. We cannot easily deny those relations we experience every day, if only for the ontological reason that most actors would become chronically insecure if they were, to any great extent, to confront critically the knowledge that they hold in their practical consciousness. The relational quality of power is a potentially great source of systemic stability.

When the Stasi could no longer translate the authority of their office into fearful subordination by the people, they could no longer exercise the power that they had done previously. If the heir to the throne of a country cannot even organize his own wedding as he would like, despite all the organization of flunkies, courtiers and advisors; and if, when he occasionally deigns to visit one of his mother's dominions, he is largely ignored by his 'loyal subjects'; then it is not clear that the authority claimed due to tradition translates into much power outside of the immediate spatial circumstances of the specific locale in which he knows that this authority will be recognized. Being an heir to a throne enables one to access resources but not necessarily to translate this access into the power to achieve specific outcomes – such as not being treated with indifference when one steps outside the boundaries within which authority can be orchestrated. While primogeniture may provide access to valuable resources of power, what one is able to do with its instruments of rule is not given by their access.

Instruments allow us to use them to exert our will; whether that will is repaid by sweet music or merely discord is a separate matter. To exercise power over an instrument to unlock its capabilities to produce great music requires considerable skill, discipline and practice. It is not enough to have a Stradivarius; one must be able to unleash what a Stradivarius is capable of being and doing. Often, this will require the concerted actions of many others – the orchestration of power – where it is less the power over some entity held by its possession that matters so much as the concertative power that surrounds and embeds this potential power over resources (see Bourdieu 1977: 72 on orchestration).

Orchestration implies a great deal. First, it implies a sign system that those who are being orchestrated can read and understand in common. Second, the sign system should be infinitely translatable from any one place to another. It should be capable of travel. Third, its instantiation requires a high degree of concertation across space and time. Orchestras are often found in theaters, and the theater metaphor is one that has been stretched far from its original usage; one talks, for instance, of a theater of war, where opposing forces seek to orchestrate their sway over a physical space defined as territory. With this metaphorical switch we shift from the orchestration of effective governance with a limited and spatially confined theater – the orchestra pit – to one that is far more diffuse but still territorially defined. We can make the territoriality aspect clearer with an example used earlier. Iraq, one of the venues for the 'War on Terror', is a definite physical space even if it is one in which the remit of sovereignty is highly contested and authoritative power is extremely limited by the pervasive use of violence on all sides.[9] Power does not exist apart from its constitution; it is, as Allen puts it, 'coextensive with its field of operation. Power is practiced before it is possessed and it is this that gives rise to the roundaboutness of power, not some facile notion that it is a shadowy force lurking in the murky recesses' (2003: 9). In the next chapter we shall consider the views of Foucault, which are the most significant statement of a constitutive analysis of power.

Conclusion

In this chapter we have considered two major but rather separate approaches to power in social theory. On the one hand, we have looked at views that see power as facilitative, as creative, as something that may be positive. On the other hand we have looked at views of power that emanate from a primitive conception of power as a causal mechanism that makes things happen, often against the will of those to whom it is applied. These debates, although rather separate, have been at the core of social theory concerns with power in the last quarter century or so. One tendency of these debates has been to focus power either on resources external to actors or on states of minds internal to actors. In the first case, the risk is that power becomes seen as equivalent to the possession of a thing rather than something whose effects are always played out in specific relations. And, because things tend to be fixed in space and time, there is a further tendency to concentrate on power in confined arenas in which resources might be deployed. In the second case, the concentration on matters of consciousness has led to a rather futile debate about what people's real interests are, how they might know these, and how analysts might know them better. The effrontery to ordinary life is astonishing: for most of us, our interests, we suspect, are beyond the supposedly historic role that grand theories have written for them, are unstable and contingent, and are changing all the time, depending on the relation and on the circumstances. The debate about real interests is futile because it pits the individual's definition of the situation against analytic privilege, and unless one wants to accept the paradox of emancipation – that others can be coerced into democracy – then the only reasonable thing to do is to accept the consciousness that the other claims rather than to tell them it is false. To tell someone that their consciousness of their self is false, and that the consciousness that some other person has of their consciousness is less false and truer, is as arrogant a theoretical position as one can embrace. It presumes the absolute authority of a point of view external to the consciousness of the other. The arbitration of what interests are real requires the analyst to occupy some transcendent and omnipotent position from which judgments may be made. It is almost as if, without some fixed point of reference, theory cannot determine power relations. As Castoriadis (1988) has said about such determinism, it is a lazy methodology *par excellence*. Whether these fixed points of reference are rooted in Marxism, feminism or some other intellectual system, the fixity of the points seems to be an effect of first sharing the beliefs that the theoretical positions articulate. It is almost as if one has to have some fixed, external and transcendent point of view from which error may be determined. However, there is always the possibility of error attaching to the putatively transcendent position – because nothing grounds it other than the security of its own convictions.

In the work of Haugaard and Gaventa we see an attempt to retain the radical edge of three-dimensional power while, simultaneously, avoiding the dichotomy of 'true' and 'false' consciousness. In the case of the former, the dichotomy is replaced by the contrast between practical and discursive consciousness. In the work of Gaventa, we see a carefully documented account of how the constant exposure to organizational outflanking results in a transformation of the consciousness of the dominated into agents who are incapable of organized resistance. In the work of Allen, we also see how domination is not actor specific, as in the Lukesian tradition, but is externalized into the spatial locales in which social interaction takes place. However, while these perspectives take us away from the actor-specific and truth-oriented rut of the three-dimensional power debate, the workings of power are not exhausted by these conceptualizations. In the next chapter we will seek to explore how power may be seen as constitutive of organizational reality and of agency.

Notes

1   The distinction between having power over someone and the power to do something is one which is embedded in ordinary language usage. The latter approximates far more closely to the verb usage of *to power*, as one might refer to an engine powering a car, while the former lends itself to saying that someone *has power*, where power is a noun – as if it were a thing that could be possessed. In French the distinction between *puissance* and *pouvoir* reflects the distinction between the two ways of thinking about power. The English word 'power', in fact, stems from the French word *pouvoir*, meaning 'to be able'. In English, power is thus often thought of as the exercise of an ability that, without such exercise, would lay fallow, as it were, awaiting enactment. It is this sense of being a capacity unexercised that is rendered by the French word *puissance* (Emmet 1953). *Puissance* is closer to the notion of power as 'power to'; in English the concept of power, while retaining more of the sense of its French root in *pouvoir* as an ability exercised, also has to stand in for *puissance*, the capacity concept. We will find that these ordinary language auspices echo through the debates addressed in this chapter.

2   In some universities, such as the University of Sydney, an inability to reconcile political and philosophical differences has led to there being two departments of economics (Economics and Political Economy) and two departments of philosophy (Philosophy and General Philosophy), an expedient adopted precisely because of the failure of the rival camps to achieve normative coherence.

3   Our colleague, Eduardo Ibarra-Colado, suggested to us another metaphor, one that implies personal discomfort, which is that using Parsons' model is akin to stripping the layers of an onion.

4   On Falun Gong see the following news sites: http://www.time.com/time/asia/features/ falun_gong/; http://edition.cnn.com/SPECIALS/2002/falungong/).

5   See http://www.thirdworldtraveler.com/Environment/ShellNigeria_environ.html. For more on the ways in which the interests of powerful transnational corporations such as Shell can be damaged by virtual mobilization, the reader can consult http://www.africaaction.org/docs97/ shel9705.2.htm and read about the alleged 'Crimes of Shell'.

6   These Hobbesian tools were, as the Canadian political philosopher C. B. Macpherson identified, those of possessive individualism. Possessive individualism is a doctrine that Macpherson (1962) traces back to Hobbes' (1651) idea that social order results from a social contract between individuals and an overarching authority. It involved theorizing the subjects of the contract as if they were highly competitive self-possessed atoms. The nature of their competition always threatens social order; thus, they defer to a supreme authority that can mobilize sufficient power in protection of the overall social order that it makes sense to bestow legitimate authority on this symbol. For Macpherson, a particular model of society gives birth to the expression of this doctrine, and that is the emergence of a possessive market society. In such a society, the hallmark of modernity, there is no 'authoritative allocation of work or rewards' (such as through caste or some other status ascription) but 'a market in labor as well as in products'. The essence is that labor is fully a commodity, 'i.e. that a man's energy and skill are his own, yet are regarded not as integral parts of his personality, but as possessions, the use

and disposal of which he is free to hand over to others for a price ... market relations so shape or permeate all social relations that it may properly be called a market society, not merely a market economy' (1962: 148).

7   It was this aspect of the Hobbesian problematic that Parsons, as a member of the Pareto Circle, was to find useful. Other theorists were more impressed with the causal mechanics rather than the ensuing order. There is an excellent analysis of the sociological significance of the Pareto Circle by Barbara Heyl (2002).

8   This is not to say that one cannot use ideas from a context, such as Foucault's writings, and apply them in a framework that is not of their making (see Clegg 1989 for such use). However, care needs to be taken in constructing the terms with which accommodation will be made, especially with a thinker whose ideas concerning power went through a number of distinct phases, which is the case with Foucault (see Chapter 8).

9   These words were written on May 9, 2005, three months after the Iraq democratic elections were held.

8 The Foucault Effect

Chapter outline

In this chapter we will:

- Analyze the impact of Foucault's work and consider some extensions of Foucault's ideas by other scholars, looking in particular at actor network theory (ANT).
- Elaborate the work of Flyvbjerg and Clegg.
- Consider some of the major critics of Foucault's approach.
- Look at some empirical methods for extending Foucault's ideas further – notably the method of life-path analysis that is used in social geography.

Introduction

Where some commentators saw only scientific management we see a political economy of the body; where others welcomed the humanization of work we saw a moral economy of the soul; where still others ignored the horrors of total institutions, for whatever reasons, we see less a statistical aberration from the norm and more a condensation and concentration of the norms of powers. It is in the little things of socially constructed normalcy that we see power in organizations being slowly constructed. The slow, the small, the normal – this is where we find power. As Nietzsche suggests, 'All the problems of politics, of social organizations, and of education have been falsified through and through, because one learned to despise "little" things, which means the basic concerns of life itself' (1967: 256). Asking small questions often leads to bigger answers than one might have anticipated (Flyvbjerg 2001: 133).

Flyvbjerg (2001) focuses on particular events, narratives, and storytelling as an analytic approach to understanding power, which he calls, after Aristotle, *phronetic* approaches. Phronetic research focuses on many aspects: know-how (skill, art and competence), context and judgment, 'the particular', dialog, incorporated knowledge and the narrative aspect. It is 'the narrative or storytelling aspect' that is more and more widespread. The phronetic and narrative approaches have been seen to be especially appropriate for analysis of power (2001: Chapter 10).

The narrative approach can be related to Geertz's 'thick descriptions' (1973: 6), when he writes that those facts 'that we call our data are really our own constructions of other people's constructions and what they and their compatriots are up to', something which 'is obscured because most of what we need to comprehend a particular event, ritual, custom, idea, or whatever is insinuated as background information before the thing is directly examined ... ethnography is thick descriptions' (1973: 9). As we have seen in Chapter 6, if we set the particular case, the extreme, to one side, because it is not 'normal', then 'it leaves us helpless in the face of the very difference we need to explore' (Geertz 1995: 40). It may simplify but it hardly clarifies.

Foucault's power

Reading Foucault

Something termed 'the Foucault effect' (Burchell et al. 1991) has been noted, not always favorably. It is perhaps not surprising, given the undoubted influence of Foucault's work on power, that such a powerful effect should have been noted. A vast critical industry is now addressed to Foucault's *oeuvre*.[1] Foucault has become an icon and a fashion (Ibarra-Colado 2001a) in organization studies,[2] despite the fact that the author in question declared himself against the role of the 'author', while nonetheless being quite willing to exploit his own success.

Foucault's work on power is scattered, although *The Foucault reader* edited by Paul Rabinow (1984) provides a good introduction; Kendall and Wickham (1999) provide a good guide to his approach. However, the best guide to his account of power is undoubtedly provided by Mark Haugaard (1997; 2002a), who, following convention, divides Foucault's work into three distinct preoccupations: with archeology; with genealogy; and with the care of the self. Rather than being three distinct approaches these represent different emphases that are more or less predominant at different stages in Foucault's work. While in his late discussion of governmentality he seeks to bring these different accounts into a patterned relation with each other, nonetheless there are distinct emphases. The archeological approach seeks to demonstrate the arbitrary nature of that which confronts us as the assumed nature of everyday life; in Bauman's (1976) words, the present ways of seeing the world seem to us to be almost a second nature, as overwhelmingly there, as something natural. The discourses with which, in their assemblage and grammar, we render the world as something knowable and as true provide us with the means to make the facticity of the world. It is not that the world we experience in some way denies a human essence – because it represses us through unreal interests (Lukes 1974) – or can be remade in a more ideal or utopian form in which discourse will be less distorted.[3] It is the world that was made historically and, in its own terms, rings true.

Using Foucault

We live our lives as organizational subjects bound by a whole world of normalcy: hierarchy; rigid rationalities; domination experienced as authority; and everyday work as a complex of mechanisms in which we strive to amass the resources, pull the levers and thus exercise power. Yet we do not constantly question the normal, nor do we acknowledge its power over us. However, we can see, as we have done in the earlier chapters of this book, that many foundations of organizations and management, and organization and management thinking, not only are bizarre and strange by contemporary views (the political economy of the body; the 'Sociological Department'; efficiency in the abattoir) but have helped to translate (Parsons' work on Weber and on social systems theory), selectively discard (Follett's work) and prepare the foundations for today's normal science (the naturalness of the rational system; the unnaturalness of power).

In the past, we would insist, the main function of 'normal' organization and management theory was the design of mechanisms to exercise power, coupled with a simultaneous way of constituting them, discursively, that negated their reality as power; instead it constituted them as social problems, industrial problems, human problems, and so on, in ever more technically specialized forms and concepts. For instance, having never thought about the relation between the body and power, conventional organization and management theory can see only efficiency at work in Taylor rather than a political economy oriented to the body; later it cannot see a political economy of the soul at work in human relations, or a political economy of the unconscious in the later literature of excellence and the more sophisticated proposals of organizational culture; and, as we saw earlier in Chapter 6, it can find no place for the Holocaust or other total institutions. We need to grasp the history of the present to redefine the tools with which we understand it: that management and organizations began as (knowledge of) a political economy of the body makes these total institutions seem less exceptionable and more comprehensible.

Power as techniques of social relations

Foucault teaches us that, rather than being a resource that can be held or exercised – a capacity inanimate but potential – power is inseparable from its effects. We have already encountered this view of power at the outset of the book: it underlay the viewpoint from which Chapters 2 and 3 of the book were written. The focus for analysis is the play of techniques, the mundane practices that shape everyday life, structuring particular forms of conduct and more especially structuring the ways in which people choose to fashion their own sense of self, their dispositions and those devices with which, through which, by which, they are shaped and framed.

> [A] thoroughly heterogeneous ensemble consisting of discourses, institutions, architectural forms, regulatory decisions, laws, administrative measures, scientific statements, philosophical, moral and philanthropic propositions – in short, the said as much as the unsaid. Such are the elements of the apparatus [*dispositif*]. The apparatus itself is the system of relations that can be established between these elements. Secondly, what I am trying to identify in this apparatus is precisely the nature of the connection that can exist between these heterogeneous elements. Thus, a particular discourse can figure at one time as the programme of an institution, and at another it can function as a means of justifying or masking a practice which itself remains silent, or as a secondary re-interpretation

of this practice, opening out for it a new field of rationality. In short, between these elements, whether discursive or non-discursive, there is a sort of interplay of shifts of position and modifications of function which can also vary very widely. Thirdly, I understand by the term 'apparatus' a sort of – shall we say – formation which has as its major function at a given historical moment that of responding to an *urgent need*. The apparatus thus has a dominant strategic function. (Foucault 1977: 194–5, italics in original; also see Deleuze 1989: 157–8)

These are techniques of power in so far as they induce appropriate forms of conduct in those others whom they target. Hence, power is only visible in its effects. However, these effects are not at all mechanistically related to some initiating prime mover. Instead, technologies of the self work initially by inducing people to regulate their own behavior and actions in accord with idealized representations that are institutionalized in specific contexts: the worker who strives for excellence; the manager who strives to be enterprising; or the service worker who aims to leave every client delighted. This is only one of the three ways that relations of power unfold. In the first unfolding the subject is constituted as a particular body/soul in relation to others – an enterprising worker, for instance; second, the subject is constituted in relation to those social bodies or populations defined in relation to authoritative categorizations – the official employee of the month, for instance; in the third unfolding the subject constitutes knowledge of itself, in relation to itself and in relation to others – the employee as coach and mentor (Ibarra-Colado 2001b: 20–7, 29). These are rarely pure forms but a complex mixture of articulations that, together, form specific local regimes of governmentality – how power is constituted locally in specific organization settings.

Power produces truth

Power produces its own truths – which is why, occasionally, epochal and seismic shifts occur, some more perceptible than others, in what is taken to be true: as power shifts, so do those truths held to be self-evident.[4] The power of systems theory as the normal science of management and organization theory produces deviance from authority – as power. Its rules of discourse produce power as a deviant effect of the system. And, as we shall see in the next chapter, there were equally orthodox but opposed ways of rendering the truth of power not as systemic deviance but as the imposition and control of a capitalist labor process that de-skilled craft workers. Both accounts, incidentally, refer to the same historical events of the growth of Taylorism, while seeing in these events quite different grounds for different histories of the present. They posit different truths.

Our interest is not in adjudicating between different truths; such an activity seems utterly pointless given that we reject the transcendent position. We are more interested in the conditions of their existence, their possibility. The key element for the production of contemporary discourse is the understanding of current practices. When practices change, then there is an opportunity to re-produce (produce again and in a different way) their knowledges. The knowledge that we are interested in is that of power in organizations. Increasingly, as Greenwood and Hinings

(2002) have argued, such knowledge, to the extent that it is produced at all today, is increasingly produced from the business schools. These institutions are the main locale for the production of what we take to be correct and true knowledge of power in organizations. Of course, just as in any other sphere of endeavor, the field of knowledge production is stratified. The business schools most enmeshed in the global circuits of power – the elite US business schools and their global clones, which can recruit the 'best students' and maintain the most 'elite' 'strategic conversations' – tend to have the inside track in defining the possibilities of what is taken to be true. Their intellectual capital is most highly prized: its investments and the returns on these investments, built up over many years, are the bluechip knowledge stocks. Few with investments to protect would wish to liquidate them, so the temptation is always to demonstrate that the old canon can address the new problem.[5] For instance, when scholars argue that only a functionalist view of power is valid (Donaldson 1985) we do not see someone wishing to demonstrate just that the propositions he uses are the outcome of verifiable procedures. Rather, we see someone attempting to invest his or her particular discourse with the effects of that power which attaches to the talisman of 'science'. Like a dog, they are marking their terrain – but with the totemic power of exclusionary canons of knowledge rather than the more usual substances. What they mark out is a terrain that is divided between that which is conjecturally true and that which is not.

The study of organizations is a seemingly minor and inconsequential territory in the social science universe – at least looked at in terms of prestige ratings of knowledge (Pfeffer 1993). Yet, the offices marked 'organizations' in the corridors of business school knowledge have 'an importance that almost passes unnoticed, to the extent that their primary function is found more in the production of practical consequences than in the institutionalization of great theoretical discourses or the defense of a certain regime of truth' (Ibarra-Colado 2005: 15).[6] If one practical consequence of their knowledge is that those who pass through the portals of the business schools leave with little understanding of how power works, what its manifestations are, and how its relations may be analyzed, other than in the simplest mechanical terms, then relative ignorance serves some functions. It serves to maintain an idea of modern organizations as if they were merely technical apparatuses, with some causal attributes, in which individuals occasionally exert leverage, when they are proximate to the right resources and dependencies.

By contrast, the account that we are presenting is not premised on power as a mechanical fulcrum: it does not rely on a model of possession or access to resources with which to leverage others. In short, we are moving towards an immanent view of power, one in which, as Allen says, 'Power does not show itself because it is implicated in all that we are and all that we inhabit' (2003: 65). The immanent idea of power is not dependent on an analytical claim to omnipotence, to a pure form of knowledge that stands apart from and outside of power, and which legislates on what power is and is not. We wish to dissolve any sense of there being a privileged and transcendent position from which the truth of power is visible. Such positions can only ever be constituted within specific discursive practices. Within some institutionalized forms of these, some representations will achieve dominance: for instance, power may be registered as an overwhelmingly mechanical and causal relation between people who possess differential access to differential resources. What one might say is that, discursively, some representations of the world, which of necessity have a historical specificity (ways of seeing the world are always diachronically shifting and contested language games), become fixed in usage, are normalized, become the common currency of thought and conceptualization. Specific discursive practices become institutionalized and thus have common currency among other discursive practices, even as they are resisted.

Discourses are always in permanent dispute; there is no meta-discourse of/for everyday life. The tactical polyvalence of discourses indicates the unstable, contingent articulation between knowledge and power in discourses, marking possible displacements and reutilizations (Ibarra-Colado 2001b: 20); they denote the possibilities of appropriation of some discourses (the discourses of the opposition, for example), changing their meaning. Some discourses may become temporally and temporarily ontologized – that is, taken for granted as a necessary aspect of (thinking about) being. (For instance, in the relatively recent past it was a fact widely assumed that women did not make good managers; if they were married, it was assumed that they would be having babies and that it was their husband's job to support them, and thus they were obliged by law to exit from the workplace. Women's being was ontologized as secondary to men; as producers of babies, and as not managers.) Hence, part of the task of analysis is to provide an understanding of how the ways of thinking and conceptualizing the world that have become normalized are possible. What are the grounds of what passes for reason in any given epoch? And what concordance and dissonance does this buried history prepare?

Discipline and punish

Power does not become an explicit concern in Foucault's work until the genealogical phase of its development with *Discipline and punish* (1977), in which he introduces his view of power as productive, as creative, as much closer to the 'power to' conception than to that of 'power over'. Here the concern is less with power as something that is distributed, so that some have it, or have more or less of it than others, and more with how the techniques and practices of power are normalized into ways of being in and thinking of the world that we share discursively, and which structure conduct in the world – including resistance to these techniques and practices. Such resistance merely serves to demonstrate the necessity for the further application or refinement of those techniques and practices so that, in future, resistance will be overcome. Power feeds on its failures to achieve the ends that those who wield it desire. In fact, failure is its most essential ingredient as it continually demonstrates to the elites of power the necessity of the power they invariably wield imperfectly.

The phase of Foucault's work indicated by the publication of *Discipline and punish* centered on the 'explicit recognition that meanings are central to the constitution of social life as a complex set of petty and ignoble power relations' (Haugaard 1997: 43). So it is not just that our sense of the world in which we live is embedded in our institutionalized conventions for making sense of it; these also form the warp and weft of everyday power relations. We cannot understand our present without knowing its history; a history of the present is the first step to rethinking the pasts we might imagine, to see 'how that-which-is has not always been' (Foucault 1988b: 37). Thus, from this perspective, power is always at work. It is both inescapable and also something active, something done, something exercised. 'Power is the consequence of petty confrontations between actors fighting within or over a regime of truth production' as Haugaard (1997: 69) suggests. It is produced through the strategies and tactics of local conflicts 'carried out by actors with specific strategies and objectives', rather than being the effect of some capacities to access resources, or real interests, or ideologies that obscure these. Power is always embedded in those forms of rationality with which actors will be held accountable.

The objects of knowledge are the consequence of power; it is the inscription and normalization of power relations in the field of knowledge that call truths into being, which produce its realities, its 'domains of objects and rituals of truth' (Foucault 1977: 194). Thus, in closely related times but in radically disjunctive conjectures of knowledge, justice can be served both by imposing its design on the body and by seeking to discipline the soul (Foucault 1977). It is not an either/or relation: that the political economy of the body gave way to a moral economy of the soul in terms of regimes of punishment does not mean that the body disappears from the discourse or the practices of power (although Foucault tends to neglect the body with his enthusiasm for the power of the gaze, as we argued in Chapter 6).

We are dealing with social facts (Durkheim 1983: 67) rather than an evolutionary sequence in regard to the relation between body and soul: that the body was neglected in preference for the soul does not obviate the continuance of the technologies visited on the soul. Specific ways of acting, thinking and feeling constitute the body and soul as objects of reflection and as sites of power: there is no hierarchy of powers at work. In our embodied selves we are at one with the body and the soul, the conscious and the unconscious, and any other legacies of that Cartesian dualism that has marked our knowledges (Lakoff and Johnson 1999; also see Clegg et al. 2004 on Cartesianism and its effects).

Different social facts are sustained by different practices. The facticity of the factory, the total institution, the Panopticon and other organized sites of power is maintained by techniques of power that organize the spaces within which social relations are constituted. Allen refers to these as the zoning, partitioning, enclosing, and serialization of activities, in which matters of spacing and timing are institutionalized – as we have seen graphically in the case of the total institutions:

> The arrangements of space, the particular assemblages of space which make up institutional complexes, are understood as integral to the ways in which particular forms of conduct are secured. In this line of argument, different spatial arrangements reflect the possible ways of acting inscribed in different schemas and serve to regulate, as well as enable, movement through them. (2003: 70)

But it is not just a matter of spatial arrangements; as in Bentham's Panopticon, these are designed to generate a certain sort of subjectivity. There are those who know indubitably that they are under power, who have power and surveillance exercised over them, and there are those who stand in hybrid relations to power – partly constituted by it and partly enacting its constitutions. And there are those who move effortlessly through the elite portals of power: they switch smoothly from boardroom to executive suite, from the cabinet office to the corporate headquarters, traversing spaces that are just as designed as the Panopticon – but designed to pro duce *legitimate* asymmetries of authority, asymmetries that the hybrids will want to *desire*, by which they will seek to be *seduced* (Rosen et al. 1990). Still others may be *forced* to accept such relations through *coercion*, while others may be *deceived* as to the intent that resides in these relations and are thus *manipulated*. Different actors may generate power effects through these different modalities.

Essentialism?

Ordinarily, if power is going to do something then some agency or other has to do it. Of course, this can lead to a problem – thinking of power as a thing that one may have or not have, or may have but hold in reserve (reserve powers) – a problem that, hopefully, this chapter will not dispose the reader to accept. The tendency to reify power, to make it an active agent in its own right, betrays a certain lack of reflexivity in the way in which the Foucault effect has played out. He criticizes the totalizing power of past ways of thinking, saying that we need to break free from discourses of sovereignty that see power centered on certain essential ways of society being structured. Yet, the alacrity with which his view of power as premised on the gaze of surveillance has been taken up, especially in organization studies, seems to be itself creating a new essentialism (Sewell 1998).

A part of the new essentialism is to confine power purely to organizational settings that comply with some elements of a total institution, in which a notion of the Panopticon functions as a metaphor, capable of extension to the electronic Panopticon, and so on. Certainly, people walk the streets and the halls of public spaces throughout the world and are subject to cameras that follow their every move – but with little effect except in so far as people are called into account retrospectively. Most of the time there is no one constantly monitoring the results of the watchful electronic eyes. It is usually only when it is established that some crime or misdemeanor has occurred that the tapes are checked. If it is not established fairly quickly, the evidence has often disappeared, as the tapes are routinely wiped and reused if nothing has come to notice. The mere fact of there being panoptical possibilities does not mean quite as much control as many of the more enthusiastic followers of Foucault would suggest. Panoptical possibilities are not necessarily wholly inclusive. In Australia, Aboriginal people were not included in the census until the 1960s – meaning that in some essentially modern respects they did not exist. This was also the case for indigenous people in Mexico; they were denied as part of the Mexican reality for about 500 years, until the Zapatista insurgency of the early 1990s obliged the modern state to check its memory, when the Internet and insurrection met in a widely publicized actor network.[7]

Governmentality

Foucault used the notion of 'governmentality' to connect the idea of 'government' with that of 'mentality', as a neologism based on a semantic merger. He was pointing to a fusion of new *technologies* of government with a new political *rationality*. 'Governmentality' refers both to the new institutions of governance in bureaucracies and to their effects. These effects are to make problematic whole areas of government that used to be accomplished through the public sector, seamlessly regulated by bureaucratic rules; now they are moved into calculations surrounding markets. Foucault defines government as a specific combination of governing techniques and rationalities, typical of the modern, neoliberal period. Bureaucracies, rather than regulating conduct, now enable individuals in civil society to act freely through markets to get things done, in normatively institutionalized ways governed increasingly by standards, charters, and other codes, and enable public administrators to recreate themselves as entrepreneurial actors, chasing after and trailing 'excellence' in the private sector (Peters and Waterman 1982). When we talk about 'mentality' we can distinguish different sets of knowledge that are dominant in different moments. For example, the Keynesian welfare state was an expression of the dominant mentality from the 1930s to the 1960s, while neoliberalism begins to dominate from the 1970s onward (see Foucault 2003b). As the designs of government change, so do the mentalities of those who administer and are subject to them. If the Weberian bureaucrat valued ethos, character and vocation, the contemporary neoliberal bureaucrat is expected to be enterprising.

Foucault introduced the term 'governmentality' in a series of lectures that he gave at the Collège de France on the 'Birth of Biopolitics' in 1979 (Marks 2000: 128). These lectures engaged with the changing face of liberalism as a political project in the Reagan and Thatcher administrations. For Foucault, governmentality meant both strategies of organizational governance in a broad sense, and self-governance by those who are made subjects of organizational governance. The concept of governmentality sought to capture new liberal approaches to political management. The focus was on 'the totality of practices, by which one can constitute, define, organize, instrumentalize the strategies which individuals in their liberty can have in regard to each other' (Foucault 1988b: 20). As du Gay suggests, governmentality 'create[s] a distance between the decisions of formal political institutions and other social actors, conceive[s] of these actors as subjects of responsibility, autonomy and choice, and seek[s] to act upon them through shaping and utilizing their freedom' (2000a: 168). What is novel about liberal forms of governance is that the personal projects and ambitions of individual actors become enmeshed with, and form alliances with, those of organization authorities and dominant organizations.

A number of scholars have written about the later aspects of Foucault (see especially Szakolczai 1998: 258; Clegg 2000; Clegg et al. 2002; Ibarra-Colado 2001b: 34–7). However, with the exception of du Gay (2000b), Jackson and Carter (1998), and van Krieken (1996), they do not explicitly address organizational issues (e.g. Hunter 1993; Miller 1992; Burchell et al. 1991). As the governmental concept is quite close to some aspects of organization theory, this is surprising. In particular, the practice of governmentality *aspires* to create a common sensemaking frame (Peters and Waterman 1982; Weick 1995; Colville et al. 1999) or, in terms of political theory, a common 'practical consciousness' (Haugaard 2000). In Jackson and Carter's (1998) terms, governmentality means that 'people should, voluntarily and willingly, delegate their moral autonomy and moral responsibility to obedience to the rules, to being governed in their conduct by a "moral" force ... which is external to the "self"'. As they go on to note, the requirement for obedience 'usually is rationalized and justified in terms of a greater collective interest' (1998: 51). Or, as Townley suggests, 'before a domain can be governed or managed it must first be rendered knowable in a particular way' (1998: 193).

Some organization theorists have interpreted knowability very much in terms of earlier Foucauldian conceptions of surveillance. However, knowability can often be quite selective rather than generalized, as surveillance theories suggest. Knowability, as a shared property of organizing, a practical collective consciousness of those doing the organizing, reaches

> [d]eep into the lives of a disparate population to the extent that people more or less internalize its effects ... in the absence of any sanctions, we opt to restrain our behaviour because we may freely choose what is appropriate and what is inappropriate behaviour ... the freedom that people have to get things done or to make themselves up in certain ways [is] a necessary part of what it means to govern. A degree of freedom is implicit in the art of governing, in the liberal sense that the promotion of freedom, rather than its denial, is the most efficient way of achieving governmental ambitions. (Allen 2003: 80–1)

Governmental power operates largely through facilitative rather than prohibitory mechanisms, using forms of institutionalized regulation to achieve their effects, through 'the continuous and relatively stable presence of a series of ideals, expectations, received "truths", standards and frameworks which provoke individuals to govern their lives in quite particular ways' (2003: 82). As Allen goes on to say:

> Subjects are constituted by the spacing and timing of their own activities as much as they are by those of others who seek to influence their behaviour; their conduct is shaped as much by what they absorb and imagine the 'truth' of their circumstances to be as it is by the physical layout, distribution and organization of their settings. (2003: 83)

The mechanisms of power are not only the spatial mechanisms that Allen (2003), as a geographer, is sensitive to; they would also include the communication media defined as 'a code of generalized symbols which guides the transmission of symbols' to which Luhmann (1979: 111) attended. Indeed, it is largely through these generalized media of communication that power achieves its reach: hence, the centrality of the bureau to the old models of bureaucracies; the pervasiveness of information systems in newer forms of organization; and the increasing governance of organizations, everywhere, by codified standards (Brunsson et al. 2000). The case of standards makes it clear that the modalities of power that can operate are many and varied and should not be reduced to any essential category, such as domination (see Rose 1991). Standards can dominate us; but they can also produce many other experiences, some delightful, some expensive, some safe, and so on. Nonetheless, power effects are embedded in the text of the standard. There is a difference between the form of the files or the information system and the content of that which they convey. It is both the reach of the form and the regulatory potential of the content that matter. These produce causal powers that can be enacted by actors with variable and indeterminate effects, often theorized in the form of actor networks.

Actor network theory

Actor network theory (ANT) is a misnomer, for it offers not so much a theory as a method. Analytically, it owes a great deal to the tradition of ethnomethodology that was initiated by Garfinkel (1967), in as much as it starts from the premise that ordinary actors in everyday situations must already be skilled and accomplished methodologists if they are able to manage the complexity that everyday life presents. Similarly to ethnomethodology, ANT is concerned to research how the actors do what they actually do. It does this by studying the mechanics of power as the actors develop them as they construct and maintain actor networks. An actor network not only includes human actors but can also include non-human actors. Hence, the networks of everyday life are invariably heterogeneous: they include machines, such as automobiles, mobile phones, and PDAs, software such as Plaxo and LinkedIn, as well as other people. ANT is concerned to trace the transformation of these heterogeneous networks, how they are constituted, how they emerge and come into being, how they are maintained, how they compete with other networks, and how they are extended over space and time.

ANT understands an organization as a network of entities that do things; the network is constituted by the entities that connect themselves in the network. Both actor and network constitute, define and redefine each other. Thus, an actor network is not necessarily enclosed within the organization, nor do the people or positions in an organization chart necessarily describe it. Both organizations and actors may be thought of as being indistinguishable from the networks in which they are constituted, where they seek to enroll, mobilize and translate each other to what they constitute as their interests. Of course, from a power perspective, we are all engaged in these activities all the time, so power necessarily resides in the dynamic social relations constituted in the network. ANT thinks of these relations in terms of performances, rather as Goffman does, where actors enact what they take to be what they want to be taken to be, with all the room for error, ambiguity and confusion that such performance entails. To try and achieve their objectives, actors in networks have to try and problematize issues, arouse others' interest, enroll their energies, and mobilize the capabilities enrolled; they seduce, induce, translate, and otherwise persuade others of the rightness, correctness, and appropriateness of the courses of action that they persuade these others are being undertaken, such that these others accept the projects and allow themselves to be enrolled in them. Of course, these others are probably doing the same things in terms of their projects, so it should be expected that, despite blandishments, resistance will often occur.

One of the ways in which politics ensues in the networks is by seeking to create interest relations where the different projects of different actors become mutually implicated, such that a shared interest emerges as an outcome of the dynamic processes that occur in the constitution of the network. The notion of interest carries no ontological baggage associated with discourses of 'real' interests and 'false consciousness'. It merely describes what the actors constitute.

Within an actor network, the multiple and conflicting interests of various actors become translated and inscribed, embodied and embedded, in material artifacts, such as texts, programs, skills, dispositions, machines – all those phenomena on which the achievement of our agency depends (Callon 1991: 143). Where stable patterns are established between such phenomena and the processes of translating and inscribing multiple others, we may say that an actor network has been established (Callon 1991). At this stage the network begins to take on durable qualities. The dynamic of network formation is that the entities comprising it require the network to be able to perform as those entities (Holmstrom and Stalder 2001).

Inscription is perhaps the most important way in which an actor network is 'translated'. Inscriptions may take place through documentation, reportage, modeling, programming, formal discussion, argumentation, strategic planning, hierarchy, relationship formations – almost any way of persuading others. All these can serve as the means whereby meanings are inscribed in a network and, as such, represent the truths of that network (Holmstrom and Stalder 2001). Through inscription, actors embed agendas into artifacts that then play a role in the network. Networks are small zones of stability amidst the overwhelming complexity and confusion of everyday life; indeed, Callon (1986) suggests that a network relies for its stability and its continued existence on maintaining a degree of order in the ways in which it keeps at bay the complexity that always threatens to overwhelm it.

Allen (2003) notes that different modalities may be engaged in the construction of complex actor networks: they may be networks of domination; they may achieve legitimacy and be accorded authority; they may eschew the necessity for authority and seek to operate wholly through coercion, being induced to do something, perhaps through fear of the alternatives or expectation of the rewards. They might seek to manipulate or seduce the other: when manipulated, the others are misled; when seduced, they are intrigued, sensually involved, and emotionally ready to be compromised. There is thus great freedom in contemporary forms of power: our present is a complex reality with a large and varied set of materials and technologies to constitute individuals, a relational palette with plenty of options for composition. While all these may be examples of power, they are examples of different modalities.

A central idea concerns the spatially constitutive nature of the particular ways in which different modalities of power take effect (Allen 2003: 94–102). The two major dimensions of spatiality are reach and intensity. Power may be either more or less instrumentally hierarchical or collaboratively associational, but is only ever as effective as its effects – not the resources that it can deploy. That there is paint on the palette means little until it is creatively deployed on the canvas – in this case the canvases we co-construct and co-destruct as lives and times that are lived, shared and denied. Reach and intensity may be achieved either by power constituting a field of social relations through traversing space in some way or, alternatively, by the instrumentality of power dissolving space through technologies of governmentality, such as those of surveillance, virtuality and so on. It is important, however, to remember that the modalities of power that can operate on the self are many and varied (including at least authority, inducement, seduction, coercion, and manipulation) and thus should not be reduced to any essential category, such as domination. These modalities may all crosscut, of course, and those involved may not always be clear which they are actually being enrolled in or are offering:

> Acts of authority and seduction may well play across one another ... acts of authority may mutate into outright coercion should recognition be withdrawn; or such acts may overlap with the effects of institutional domination as options are narrowed down and fixed to eliminate political choice. Seduction as a peculiarly indeterminate mode of power may even be eclipsed by a more determinate form. (2003: 121)

Power is not a force that intrudes on a stable situation from the outside so much as a way of talking about the structuring of social action in normal ways (Falzon 1998; Heiskala 2001). The general idea is that rather than power being something exercised between two or more conflicting combatants or adversaries divided over some issue, one to the other, it is 'more a question of ongoing and active structuring of the possible field of action of the others – a process that is always open to resistance, transformation and renegotiation' as Peltonen and Tikkanen (2005: 275) put it. Together with Munro (1999), they have contributed explicit ANT accounts of power to the literature that draw directly on the works of Foucault.

Circuits of power

The Aalborg case

Foucault says: 'power produces knowledge . . . power and knowledge directly imply one another . . . there is no power relation without the creative constitution of a field of knowledge, nor any knowledge that does not presuppose and constitute at the same time power relations' (1977: 27–8). In such a view, rationalities and powers are fused. Rationalities are always situational. And because they are always contextually situational they are always implicated with power. No context stands outside power. If that were the case, then power would exist nowhere, outside of understanding, outside of possibility, outside of sense. Different power actors operate in and through different rationalities, which have different rules for producing sense and, at the more formal outer limits, for producing truth. In fact, sense and truth cannot be separated from the ensemble of rules that constitute them – and their obverse – as such.

To adopt a discursive analysis of rationality is to see what people say as the means whereby rationality and power become interwoven. People may be in a position to say anything, given the infinity of discourse, but they rarely surprise the well-grounded analyst with their discursive moves. Language games are not predictable but they are explicable. We can understand and constitute the senses that are being made as well as the conditions of existence and underlying tacit assumptions that make such sense possible. And in this way we can begin to understand the different forms of agency that find expression in organizational contexts, where the players make sense of rules that they actively construct and deconstruct in the context of their action.

Clegg (1989) has used the idea of circuits of power to represent the ways in which power may flow through different modalities. Relatively simple is transitive power, where one agency seeks to get another to do what they would not otherwise do. Power in this sense usually involves fairly straightforward episodic power, oriented towards securing outcomes. The two defining elements of episodic power circuits are agencies and events of interest to these agencies. Agencies are constituted within social relations; in these social relations they are analogous to practical experimentalists who seek to configure these relations in such a way that they present stable standing conditions for them to assert their agency in securing preferred outcomes. Hence, relations constitute agents that these and other agents seek to configure and reconfigure; agencies seek to assert agency, and do so through configuring relations in such a way that their agency can be transmitted through various generalized media of communication, in order to secure preferential outcomes. All this is quite straightforward and familiar from one-dimensional accounts of power.

Episodes are always interrelated in complex and evolving ways. No 'win' or 'loss' is ever complete in itself, nor is the meaning of victory or defeat definitely fixed as such at the time of its registration, recognition or reception; such matters of judgment are always contingent on the temporalities of the here-and-now, on the reconstitutions of the there-and-then, on the reflective and prospective glances of everyday life (Schutz 1967). If power relations are the stabilization of warfare in peaceful times then any battle is only ever a part of an overall campaign. What is important, from the point of view of the infinity of power episodes stretching into a future that has no limits, are the feedback loops from distinct episodic outcomes and the impact that they have on overall social and system integration. The important question is whether episodic outcomes tend rather more to reproduce or to transform the existing architectonics – the architecture, geometry and design – of power relations. How they might do so is accommodated in the model: through the circuit of social integration, episodic outcomes serve to either more or less transform or reproduce the rules fixing extant relations of meaning and membership in organizational fields; as these are reproduced or transformed they fix or refix those obligatory passage points – the channels, conduits, circuitry of extant power relations. In this way dispositional matters of identity will be more or less transformed or reproduced, effecting the stability of the extant social relations that had sought to stabilize their powers in the previous episodes of power. As identities are transformed, then so will be the social relations in which they are manifested and engaged (see Figure 8.1).

System integration also needs to be considered. Changes in the rules fixing relations of meaning and membership can facilitate or restrict innovations in the techniques of disciplinary and productive power, which, in turn, will more or less empower or disempower extant social relations that seek to stabilize the episodic field, recreating existing obligatory passage points or creating new ones, as the case might be. (The model is discussed in detail in Chapter 8 of Clegg 1989; in Chapter 9 of the same text it is applied to matters of state formation.)

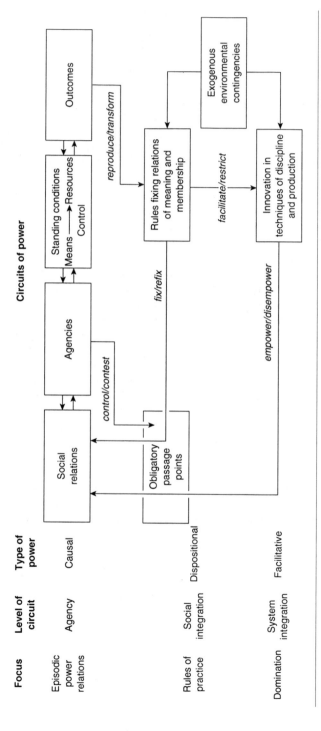

Figure 8.1   Representing circuits of power

As an empirical instance, one can consider the detailed case study of planning in Aalborg conducted by Bent Flyvbjerg (1998), which is easily interpretable in terms of the circuits model, even though it does not use it explicitly. Clegg (1989) and Flyvbjerg (1998) are both influenced by Foucault, albeit that both use the resources that he provides creatively. Clegg's recognition is that there is no fundamental power that should be seen as constitutive of nearly anything and everything: that is, power should not be seen as ubiquitous and that it flows through different circuits of social relations, with different effects, is useful in representing the Aalborg case.

High-level city officials initiated the Aalborg Project in October 1977, as a plan intended to limit the use of cars in the city center. Soon after its initiation, several agencies, trade unions, police, local and national consultants, the business community, private corporations, the media, and interested citizens became involved in order to decide on issues such as redirecting traffic by creating a rational local and national bus traffic system. A task force was established to formulate a three-year plan. The first conflict arose between architects and the bus company over the location and size of a bus terminal. Originally just a minor disagreement, the discussion turned into embittered conflict and division among the main players. There was a public hearing and the production of a counterplan by the Aalborg Chamber of Industry and Commerce, and a revised plan was approved in 1980.

Small business people with retail outlets in the planning precinct grew increasingly dissatisfied with the original urban renewal plan. Without a constant stream of cars coming into the city center they feared they would lose business. They succeeded in halving the original plan to construct the bus terminal. The Environmental Protection Agency then began to question the environmental hazards and impact of the proposed bus terminal, while another source of local conflict concerned a subplan designed to try and maintain the authentic charms of the old shopping streets. The City Council forbade all non-retail businesses (banks, insurance companies, and offices) from occupying ground floor premises, to try and preserve the street's character. However, non-retail business leaders were also present in the local Chamber of Industry and Commerce, and they agitated against this plan. In its first four years the Aalborg plan underwent six rounds of reconstruction and modification. Although the overall plan was never actually rejected, specific projects became more and more minute, as well as more problematic in content and scope, generating further subordinate and specific episodes of power between local factions: cyclists and planners; planners and small business people; motorists and public transport; and so on.

Unexpected and unanticipated environmental contingencies had an impact on the project, such as the Mayor and several high-level local officials being jailed on bribery charges, thus challenging the overall legitimacy of the urban renewal plan. By this time the original plan had undergone its eleventh revision. The Chamber of Industry and Commerce reversed its original stand and began arguing that redirecting traffic would hurt businesses by causing falling revenues. However, the City Council survey rejected this fear by revealing that retail profits were increasing. Meanwhile, new Social Democratic politicians came on the scene, deciding to bolster the urban renewal project by emphasizing positive aspects of the original plan adopted a decade earlier, which led the Aalborg Project into a total impasse.

The outcomes were not what any faction wanted: instead of reducing car traffic, it increased by 8 percent; instead of creating an integrated system of bicycle paths, unconnected stretches were built; instead of reducing traffic accidents, the number of fatalities and injuries among cyclists increased 40 percent; instead of reducing noise, the levels substantially exceeded Danish and international norms; and air pollution increased.

Flyvbjerg's (1998) main theme is that power shapes rationality. At various stages the various political actors sought to steer the project through their preferences; they sought to structure what the circuits of power model terms 'obligatory passage points'. Different claims were made for participation in different committees; differential participation produced different outcomes at different times, favoring different preferences. Small battles were fought over who, and what, could be introduced in which arenas and meetings. In this way the relations of meaning and membership in the various locales were contested, reproduced or transformed. As these changed then the obligatory passage points shifted; as these shifted the relations of power that had prevailed shifted also – most dramatically when the Mayor and officials were indicted and imprisoned. Thus, small wins in specific episodes of power had the capacity to shift the configuration of the overall circuitry through which power relations flowed. The actors engaged in the plans were constantly seeking to fix and refix specific schemes, and although the play of power was very fluid, the underlying social integration of the small business people with each other, the Chamber of Industry and Commerce, and the editorial views of the local newspaper, seemed to mean that the small business people were the prevailing winners in the many struggles. The attempts to respecify the system integration of the traffic plan in Aalborg consistently foundered on the reef of social integration. How Aalborg was planned, designed and looked, as well as how it was not planned, was not designed and did not look, was an effect of power relations.

Flyvbjerg (1998) alerts us to one very important fact of power relations and rationalities: that when power and knowledge are entwined then the greater the power the less the need for rationality, in the sense of rational means–ends justifications. The relation between rationality and power was an uneven relation: power clearly dominated rationality. That is, those who presently configured power sought to continue doing so and were quite ready to define the reality of the project in any way that seemed to them to further their preferences, using whatever strategies and tactics were available to them. In this sense, what was defined as rationality and reality was an effect of power, as it defined and created 'concrete physical, economic, ecological, and social realities' (1998: 227). What was advanced and argued as rationality depended wholly on power relations; the more disadvantaged in these the agents were, the more they were liable to have recourse to conceptions of rationality that downplayed power, and sought to position themselves through factual, objective, reasoned knowledge. The most powerful rationalities took the form of rationalizations rather than authoritatively grounded accounts. Often these were public performances of rationality which other agents who were witness to the rationalizations felt compelled not to reveal because they lacked the powers to do so; they anticipated and feared the reaction that their actions would in all probability produce, should they move, for dangers lurked in open conflict and identification of differences.

The greater the facility with which agencies could have recourse to power relations, the less concerned they were with reason, and the less they were held accountable to it. Access to more power produced less reason. In other words, the more that they were able to seduce, manipulate, dominate, induce, rationalize, and so on, the less likely that they would be amenable to the authority of reasoned argument. The Enlightenment project of a rational public sphere is a strategy of the weak and is opposed by the strong, according to Flyvbjerg's analysis. Power relations were, on the whole, more marked by the gentle arts of power – persuasion, inducements, seduction, etc. – than by antagonistic strategies. The antagonisms were the most visible and publicly reported aspects of power – but they were hardly the most typical. They rarely are: the necessity to throw one's weight around usually signals a position of relative weakness rather than strength, such that if one needs to use force one is demonstrating that one is weak. Establishing agreements between agents creates the power of ongoing action, a much stronger relation of power than specific episodes enacted in response to conditions of crisis.

In Aalborg, what was most typical was the constant attention to the small things of power relations that continually reproduced the status quo; rather than attempts at transformation, it was largely reproduction that prevailed. The most skilled strategists of power were those for whom reproduction was the preferred strategy; in the case of Aalborg this was the small business community, whose institutionalized voice was much more actively represented to governmental rationality than that of the various citizen groups – the cyclists, the greens and so on. In turn, these relations were embedded in deeply held local loyalties and relations defined by the forms of symbolic and cultural capital that Bourdieu analyses. When, in openly antagonistic settings, these relations came up against contra-points of view that were well researched and represented in rational terms, power-to-power relations dominated over those defined in terms of knowledge or rationality against power.

Mostly, power relations were both stable and inequitable. Where power relations could be maintained as stable and characterized by consensus and negotiations, rationality could gain a greater toehold; the more power relations became antagonistic, the easier it was to deploy less rational arguments and strategies. Thus, rationality must remain within the existing circuits of power if it is to influence them. To challenge them is to play a losing hand.

Circuits of power in practice

The theorization of circuits of power has been used in a number of studies,[8] but the one that we shall discuss here is a recent study of 'Circuits of power in practice: strategic ambiguity as delegation of authority' by Sally Davenport and Shirley Leitch (2005). It is a study of positive power enacted through the facilitative circuit, which is the reason that we have chosen to discuss this particular application. It pulls together an analysis of power with an analysis of strategic ambiguity to empower stakeholders. Strategic ambiguity (Eisenberg 1984) involves deliberate use of ambiguity to create a 'space' in which multiple interpretations and responses by stakeholders are enabled and possible (Davenport and Leitch 2005). The case study analyzes the attempt by the Foundation for Research, Science and Technology, a public sector research-funding body in New Zealand, to transform the national science system. Given that unclear goals, restive and sometimes resistant stakeholders, and a process of creative engagement between the organization and its stakeholders marked the attempt, the use of strategic ambiguity was highly appropriate.

In 1999 New Zealand research funding changed from being a very explicit rules-based funding model in which power relations were highly episodic, with strong non-collaborative competition between grant getters. What changed the situation was the fashion for a 'knowledge economy' that had blown across the Pacific and into New Zealand. In the new knowledge economy the idea was to create facilitative knowledge sharing and building capacities rather than encourage zero-sum games between researchers in a very small country (less than 4 million people). Policy statements were issued; things were going to change – things *had* to change. What was changing was that the Foundation was moving from funding research to investing in innovation. Where previously there had been disciplinarily defined fiefdoms there was now to be one investment operation in an innovation strategy accompanied by 'disinvestment' in existing areas of research that failed to show promise for future wealth creation.

The focus of the research is on the second circuit of power, the positive facilitative circuit, which comes into play when the existing rules of practice characterizing a power arena are changed or destabilized in some way, either by authorities or others internal to the circuits of power, or by some exogenous contingency that has an impact on these circuits. When the existing rules of practice fixing relations of meaning and membership change, then relations of power in the circuit may be either empowering or disempowering of members, stakeholders and others. Here the focus is on stakeholders who are particularly susceptible to what Clegg defines as the central paradox of power: 'the power of an agency is increased in principle by that agency delegating authority; the delegation of authority can only proceed by rules; rules necessarily entail discretion and discretion potentially empowers delegates' (1989: 201). The use of strategic ambiguity is one way of achieving 'high discretionary strategic agency' through enabling creativity in sensemaking about what changing meanings mean. Strategic ambiguity introduces purposeful discretion into the space between organization and delegates. Contested sensemaking shifts the circuits of power in unanticipated but partially creative ways. For anyone familiar with university research circles the immediate results were predictable: confusion, resentment and resistance. However, researchers who were involved in research institutes that already had a private sector funding orientation saw it quite differently – much more positively. The Foundation sought to engage research providers and end users of research in a creative dialog – one into which the institutes jumped with alacrity while the universities were far more hesitant about what the changed conditions meant. Previously they never had to negotiate; they just submitted research applications and were either funded or not, according to the recommendations of expert panels – in a very small national system. Now the priorities were being set by the Foundation in terms of investment criteria that were opaque to the community of researchers until they entered into negotiation with the Foundation. The researchers speculated that perhaps, as the rules became more fixed, as meanings settled down and settled in with the new system of funding, the system of relations might shift back into a more episodic mode of circuitry. In which case, one might expect periodic bouts of reformed purpose and renewed use of new sources of strategic ambiguity.

Engaging Foucault's critics

Preamble

Perhaps the single most important outcome of the trajectory that runs through Follett to Foucault on the axis of positive power is to shift attention away from an over-concentration on power as a negative and zero-sum phenomenon. At the outset of this book we discussed how analysis of power in terms of outcomes was not such a good idea. What is an outcome shifts with the here-and-now from which it is viewed. It also shifts in its meaning depending on who is doing the viewing, and the relevancies they hold. These relevancies themselves are an effect of existing power circuits. It is for this reason that the circuits of power framework is so useful: it enables us to concentrate on process rather than become too bogged down in questions such as 'Who won?'

Traditions die hard. Thinking of power in terms of both causal mechanisms and essential interests has become a veritable tradition in power analysis. We shall now address some of the major criticisms that have been made of Foucault's reconstitution of some of these key and associated terms. It is a difficult task because of the extent and dispersion of Foucault's formulations of power as well as Foucault's recognition of the futility of searching for the 'correct' interpretation or the 'real' meaning of his (or any author's) words. We will deliberately confine our analysis to a focus on power; this is not to say that we are unaware of the broader criticisms that have been made of his overall body of work from philosophy, social and literary theory, and so on.

There have been many critiques – if only because the impact of Foucault's work across diverse fields of knowledge has been considerable. In addition, he became something of a celebrity intellectual, in common with any number of other Parisian intellectuals before him, and the fame of his scholarship, as well as, occasionally, the notoriety attached to his private life, attracted attention much as a brilliant stadium light attracts moths (Eribon 1991; Miller 1993). He burned brightly, although his luminescence was extinguished in 1984, when he died of AIDS. Still, even more than 20 years later, his work remains influential and, as we shall see in later chapters, has had a considerable impact on 'critical' and 'discourse' scholarship on power. Here, however, we concentrate on some of his critics.

Criticism from essentialism

An early set of criticisms of Foucault arose in the context of feminist theory, a position committed to the idea that there are some essential structures of patriarchal dominancy at work in gender relations (for example, Fraser 1981; 1989; Cooper 1994; Deveaux 1994; Harstock 1990; Sawaki 1991; and especially Hekman 1996 which collects much of the critical commentary). From this perspective there was little doubt that men and women had real opposed interests, and that men's inter-ests, represented in the patriarchy, dominated those of women. Such a view of dom-ination did not sit easily with what was seen as Foucault's overly generalized account of power. If power does not concern questions of sovereignty, and if sovereignty needs to be overthrown as a prime mover for power analysis, if power comes from everywhere, if power is neither an institution nor a structure but 'the name that one attributes to a complex strategical situation in a particular society' (Foucault 1984: 93), then power seems so diffuse that it cannot be pinned down, dissected and used in analysis of specific structures of domination, such as those of patriarchy.

Domination is inescapably a part of what it means to be human; through the normal forms of domination we learn to assert our powers as historically consti-tuted subjects having the capacity to act upon the limits of our freedom, 'through practical, technical and procedural inventions ... embodied in ways of thinking, speaking and judging that emerged at a particular time and place and are destined to disappear' (Rose 1999: 95). What truths maintain domination will vary from era to era and this will be a result of the dominant power practices defining that era, producing its objects, its rituals, and its truths. In this way are power and domina-tion related, such that, for instance, the power of feminist critique produces the conditions both of its liberation and of that domination which it will liberate. Structures of dominancy are not power, they are the outcome of historical strug-gles for power. In this sense, power does not stake out and hold some essentialist ground, position or viewpoint, but is distinctly empirical and strategic. Power priv-ileges no essential struggles in society; what different interests ensue will be largely contingent upon, precisely, these struggles.

It is through struggles and resistance that the legitimacy of domination as authority is enacted. Authority is never given *per se*; it has no transcendent ethos but is merely representative of the state of play of power relations. That they are as they have become speaks of no necessary unfolding of the rights of man – or woman; it merely indicates those normalcies which have become taken for granted as necessary nodal points of contemporary existence, necessities that key texts or movements can question, sometimes even transform (de Beauvoir 1953; Friedan 1965; Greer 1970).

The point is not that there will not be struggles – of course there will, and many of them may be articulated by their protagonists in terms of some essential con-ceptions that privilege particular cleavages around notions such as gender, class or, for that matter, any number of alternative constructions of identity – but that para-doxically, unlike many feminists seem to promulgate, these struggles should not be seen as necessarily eternal or somehow in the nature of things. They are not *the* truth at the expense of other truths (e.g. Harstock 1987); rather, they are the effects of whatever relevancies are at work, are capable of mobilizing support and of being translated into actions of various kinds. In this way, an essentialism that might seem quite surprising to some other essentialisms – such as the renaissance of the religious right might seem to old-school socialists and feminists – will irrupt not because it articulates some fundamental sovereign principle but because its supporters mobilize around it as if it did. Thus, one can remain agnostic about the various essentialisms that enthusiasts of whatever persuasion might proffer, while not denying the analysis of their effects.

Inspired by Foucault, there have been several developments of non-essentialist feminism. Judith Butler (1990) uses the distinction between 'power to' and 'power over' to demonstrate how each conception hinges on a different conception of the human subject. The theorists who stress 'power over' assume that subjectivity is already there in a pre-given form, while the theorists who stress 'power to' see it as producing subjectivity. The former corresponds to notions of patriarchal power subjecting gendered relations to its pattern, while the latter indexes a notion of subjection as subject making embedded in discourse (Probyn 2005: 518). These discourses institutionally produce – legally, nationally, culturally – what is contested as normalcy.

Criticism of negativity

Ironically, one critique of Foucault picked up precisely on his implicit agnosticism. Deleuze (1988) criticized Foucault's ideas because, despite Foucault's protestations to the contrary, he argues that power is mainly negative for Foucault, in his institutional analyses. Although Foucault's later work argues that power is positive, his analyses mostly show power as a restrictive and oppressing force – hence the linkage with total institutions. Only when he talks about power and pleasure (in his last two volumes of *The history of sexuality*) does Foucault's notion of power become more productive. However, it is not productive enough for Deleuze who argues that power is always linked to desire – or to the very strong instinct or drive that underlies desire. So power is linked to very strong emotions like passion or desire, and it is for this reason that it is positive. Thus, one seeks a certain kind of liberation or experience as a result of what we might term an essentialist desire, but, to realize or achieve this, one must exert power.

For Deleuze, Foucault talked about a more passive pleasure that might come with power: he was insufficiently positive. This is a very different spin on positive power to those we have encountered thus far: as Foucault acknowledged in his preface to Deleuze and Guattari's (1983) *Anti-Oedipus*, it is 'the connection of desire to reality' which is important; because we desire something we exert power positively to try and bring it within our grasp. In this sense, quite contrary to Deleuze's critique, Foucault views power as always being positive in that it brings about a change in state; he acknowledges, however, that the outcome of this change may not be something that is welcome (Haugaard 1997). Nonetheless, it is clear that the project is not one of total control or domination; power does not always get its way. Consequently, we may agree with Foucault that power is never

a phenomenon of mass and homogeneous domination – the domination of one individual over others, of one group over others, or of one class over others; keep it clearly in mind that unless we are looking at it from a great height and from a very great distance, power is not something that is divided between those who have it and hold it exclusively, and those who do not have it and are subject to it. Power must, I think, be analyzed as something that circulates, or rather as something that functions only when it is part of a chain. It is never localized here or there, it is never in the hands of some, and it is never appropriated in the way that wealth or a commodity can be appropriated. Power functions. Power is exercised through networks, and individuals do not simply circulate in those networks; they are in a position to both submit to and exercise this power. They are never the inert or consenting targets of power; they are always its relays. In other words, power passes through individuals. It is not applied to them ... The individual is in fact a power effect, and at the same time, and to the extent that he is a power effect, the individual is a relay: power passes through the individuals it has constituted. (2003a: 29–30)

Thus, the effects of power cannot be simply read off as domination, despite some critics' point of view (Allen 2003).

Criticism of Eurocentrism

Another common criticism of Foucault is that he presents a Eurocentric view of power, and one that is oriented far too much to the centrality and importance of texts and discourses in explicating this history. In fact, his view of the world is even more restricted: it is essentially Francophone and actually misses opportunities to engage with other scholars working, at various times, on similar themes, such as the English E. P. Thompson (1967) and the German Max Weber (1978) on aspects of discipline, or the Canadian Erving Goffman (1961) on *Asylums*.

Certain scholars have engaged with Foucault's works from a broad perspective and, in doing so, have shown ways in which the focus on discourse may not be as limited as might be imagined. Typically, Foucault's analyses demonstrate that the growth of a phenomenon such as Western rationalism, in the Age of Reason, had a dark, dialectically related side – in this case the emergence of madness as the other of reason (Foucault 1965). As the Age of Reason cast its spell over a benighted and bewitched Europe, so it also was extended globally through the European colonization of the world, albeit that, as we have seen in Chapter 6, it did not necessarily incorporate that which it found there as indigenous. On the one hand, reason promised emancipation from enchanted and traditional beliefs at home; at the same time it offered nothing much more than domination globally, as it imposed a developmental discourse on the rest of the world judged inferior by the criteria of Euroreason.

The very discourses that established the Enlightenment in the West, through reasoned knowledge, using a language of emancipation, created new discursive systems of power, of which notions of development were one. In the postwar era, huge swathes of the world in Africa, Asia and Latin America were consigned to the category of underdevelopment. A whole discourse of development and underdevelopment was created, employing what Escobar (1984/5; 1992; 1995) refers to as a new political economy of truth, replacing earlier orientalist themes (Said 1979). Discursively, a vast institutional network of agencies was talked into being using the terms of the new discourse: that development meant achieving the state of existence of those societies that were already wealthy, which created an apparatus linking knowledge about the Third World with specific powers to intervene in the knowledge objects thus created (Escobar 1992: 23).

Linkage was achieved discursively through three strategies: first, the definition of the situation of some countries as less developed or underdeveloped, seen as a problem to be treated by specific kinds of interventions from outside, from the West; second, the recasting of these problems into appropriate technical problems (of economics) to be resolved through the application of scientific expertise; third, the institutionalization of development through the formation of a network of new sites of power, defined in terms of specialist expertise and knowledge, which then bind people to certain behaviors and rationalities. In this way, Escobar argues, a spatial field of power and knowledge emanates from the West and percolates out, pulling actors into the orbit of its rhetoric of 'development'. The rhetoric is powerful; it resonates with Enlightenment ideals as well as the aspirations of poor people in those countries at which the discourse is aimed. The exchanges were not all one way, however, and we should not be blind to this because, as has been argued elsewhere, many syncretic forms of the colonizers being colonized in reverse have created much of the vitality of the contemporary world through media such as music, gastronomy, and religion (Clegg 1996).

Escobar provides applications of Foucault that demonstrate that discursivity has material effects. Yet, how these effects are created, theoretically, is troubling. Power becomes equivalent to its discourse; the discourse seems to take on a reified power apart from any of the agencies that might be articulating or resisting the discourse. Power becomes a verb that does things – a troubling state of affairs for English usage wherein power is ordinarily a noun and is only a transitive verb in specific instances, such as when one notes that a car is powered by a four-liter alloy engine.

Criticism of a singular focus

While Foucault's later work on governmentality brings power outside of confinement and into more nuanced arenas, as Hannah notes, Foucault 'never precisely spelled out the ways in which the panoptic logic of visibility had to change to operate effectively in an environment where its subjects did not suffer continuous confinement' (1997: 344). From this perspective, Foucault maintained too singular a focus on surveillance.

A closely related critique comes from Bourdieu which says that the emphasis in Foucault is too much on a 'simplifying vision of social constraint as discipline, i.e. as a constraint exercised upon the body from the outside' (Wacquant 1993: 35). The emphasis remains on 'external disciplines and constraints' rather than the processes of 'inculcation of cognitive schemata of perception, appreciation and action'. Thus, the criticism is that while Foucault may be quite good at describing the disciplines of power as an external imposition on the body, he is far less sophisticated in his discussion of the 'subtler forms of domination which come to operate through belief and the pre-reflexive agreement of the body and mind with the world – whose paradigmatic manifestation is masculine domination'. Here, Bourdieu is actually quite close to Lukes (1974; 2005), when he asks: 'Indeed, is it not the supreme exercise of power to get another or others to have the desires you want them to have – that is to secure their compliance by controlling their thoughts and desires?' (1974: 23). In fact, this criticism suggests that Bourdieu was, perhaps, not as familiar with the Foucauldian *oeuvre* as one might expect of one Parisian and Collège de France intellectual of another. It is evident from the earlier discussions that Foucault does attend to these matters – and in a way which is less rhetorical and more empirical than Lukes (1974).

Bourdieu approaches power differently: it is practical social action that links what is past to what is yet to happen, for which he reserves the term 'habitus'.

> Habitus is a tacit knowledge of how to 'go on' as a competent social agent. It is a form of disposition derived from life experience. In this sense, habitus is both an internalization of reality and, at the moment of practice, an externalization of self as constituted through past experience. Through the use of habitus in social practice, history, as past experience, becomes projected into the future. When actors interpret their past they impose particular order upon it, which, in turn, determines their ordering the future. Hence the ability to reproduce the orderdness of social life as a whole, is a reflection of the ordering which actors perceive to exist in the past. (Haugaard 2002a: 225)

Bourdieu was alert to the symbolic manifestations of power relations, looking at the way in which the dominant symbolic order of any arena, such as a society or an organization, generates a system of highly visible distinctions and discriminations which stratify those populations subject to them. The dominant symbols and meanings stratify status in orders of distinction, based upon many small and subtle markers of identity: tastes, deportment, education, residence, sports, life interests, and so on, all represent a surplus of meaning denoting membership in particular strata of society. The symbolic order is never stable or fixed but is an effect of previous and current power relations and competitions in which actors seek to position those symbols of distinction that define them, or which they aspire to, as the desirable forms of seduction.

> Because status represents past experience, status has a tendency to be self-reproducing and self-reinforcing. It is self-reproducing in the moment that the dominated class use their past experience to shape future expectations, in this case, habitus, as embodied history, repeats itself as an endless, self-fulfilling prophecy. Individuals find themselves in a particular place in society; as a result they undergo certain experiences, they then internalize a habitus concerning the order of things, and, consequently, structure their future behaviour in a manner which reproduces their social position. Instances of this include the expectation by working class children that education is 'not really for them'. They order their actions relative to this predisposition and the more they do so, the more accurate they find their habitus to be – they underachieve within the educational system.
>
> The alternative to the self-fulfilling prophecy is to try and move up the social ladder. This has the unintended consequence of reinforcing relations of domination. What constitutes status is valued because people desire it. Consequently, the act of raising expectations towards social mobility is, ironically, to validate the system of hierarchy. Furthermore, the attempt at advancement usually culminates in failure because the newly acquired habitus, the new manners and meanings, do not form part of the actor's deeply internalized habitus, the habitus of childhood, which is what renders actions easy

and natural to perform. The recently acquired condition of the habitus of social advancement is betrayed in the actions of such individuals. Their actions are characterized as 'affected', 'unnatural', or 'pedantic' in contrast to the 'natural ease' and 'effortless elegance' of those who carry out the very same actions with reference to a habitus which is truly 'theirs'. (Haugaard 2002a: 226)

Bourdieu, like Foucault, was something of an outsider: a working-class child, from Algeria, who drew mainly on one source of capital to get ahead in the world of academia – his intellectual knowledge – in dealing with elites. Many of his colleagues with their middle-class and aristocratic backgrounds had other forms of capital that worked for them – social and cultural – which gave them access to forums, arenas and other possibilities, much more readily. Bourdieu also lived in one of the most status-conscious cities in the world, Paris, and no doubt had an acute eye for the slights, the stings, the cruel put-downs of distinction and its claimants, protectors and assailants (Bourdieu 1984). What is maintained as *distinction* is social or symbolic capital that exercises a form of symbolic violence wrought by the state, educational institutions and appeals to the natural order of things (Bourdieu 2002). All these establish, stabilize and reproduce distinction, making of specific cultures a form of capital with which people seek to impress some and simultaneously suppress others. Education, particularly in universities, is vital to this process as it is the field in which struggles over the truth claims of knowledge are played out (see Harker et al. 1990).

   While maintaining distinction might as easily involve seduction as manipulation, inducements as much as coercion, in Bourdieu it is invariably reduced to domination, which, once institutionalized as a legitimated set of orderings, acquires the gloss of authority. These symbols serve solely to legitimate domination; they provide the velvet glove that cloaks the iron fist because 'no power can be exercised in its brutality in an arbitrary manner ... it must dissimulate itself, cloak itself, justify itself for being what it is – it must make itself be recognized as legitimate by fostering the misrecognition of the arbitrary that founds it' (Wacquant 1993: 25). Through the impositions of symbolic violence tied up in cultural capital the dominated come to misrecognize their reality and begin to see it in the terms – and they are plural and fragmentary – of the elites, a game that they can never win.

   Thus, from the perspective of this critique, the Foucault effect requires qualification: most of us do not live in total institutional organizations. Nonetheless, knowledge of the parameters of these is invaluable in helping us assert our freedoms as citizens in a civil society employed by and interacting with organizations, subject to imperfect surveillance, negotiating distinctions, and having a variable awareness and regard for the governmental regimes that do exist. Power is complex, heterogeneous and multifaceted. In fact, towards the end of his life, Foucault demonstrated an awareness of the rather one-dimensional focus that he had developed:

When I was studying asylums, prisons, and so on, I insisted, I think, too much on the techniques of domination. What we call discipline is something really important in these kinds of institutions but it is only one aspect of the art of governing people ... Power consists in complex relations: these relations involve a set of rational techniques, and the efficiency of those techniques is due to a subtle integration of coercion-technologies and self-technologies. (1997: 182)

With this in mind, Bourdieu's critique of Foucault's lack of sophistication in regard to the inculcation of cognitive schemata is justified. However, Foucault's treatment of the constitution of knowledge, and the effects of this knowledge on the self and how one might overcome these, must be acknowledged, particularly in his later address of the 'care of the self'.

Critique of power as structuralist

In his earliest discussion of Foucault's work Steven Lukes (1977: 8, 139) categorizes him as a structuralist: a theorist who regards individual wills as of less significance than structural factors within systems. Against this, Lukes takes the side of human agency. For him one cannot discuss power without also discussing responsibility. If one exercises power one could have chosen differently; one could have chosen not to have done so. Attributing power is equivalent to attributing responsibility: that one exercises power over another demonstrates a deliberate choice rather than a structural necessity. However, as Hoy notes, 'The claim that a structural system restricts what an agent *can* do does not entail the claim that such a system determines what an agent *will* do' (1986: 128). In other words, structural patterning can coexist with individual choices and responsibility. Where does this leave Foucault?

In contrast to Lukes' views, Foucault eschews any problematic of the subject as much as he does one of structure. Neither subjects nor structures are seen as determining and determined. It is not a matter of levels or dimensions of analysis, in a geological metaphor; instead, because of the discursive shaping of power, power exists in terms of 'intentionality without a subject, such that power relations are intentional and can be described without being attributed to particular subjects as their conscious intentions' (Hoy 1986: 128).

Power operates through a network of relations, micro-politics and capillaries of power, as discourses shape the structure of society and those common attributions of motive and meaning with which claims to intentionality can be made, through patterning truth relations in knowledge (Blum and McHugh 1971). Foucault's power/knowledge nexus illustrates the importance of historical ways of constituting knowledge claims, which will differ markedly from episteme to episteme. If Foucault were the structuralist that Lukes would have him, then power should be something that the structures distribute, so that who possesses it depends on where they slot into the structures. Yet, he argues strongly against any conception of power as a possession. Power is not something that dominant classes have and those subordinated lack. Power is not the property of the state and it is not implicit in specific resources. Power is a strategy, and those who are dominated are as complicit in its strategic web of relations as those who are dominant. Power is not something that is situated in some sovereign center from which it radiates. By contrast, its capillaries permeate many small, local spaces.

Foucault is structuralist in one respect: he is interested less in who has power and more in the possibilities of how anyone is able to exercise power; how the fields or arenas in which power is exercised are structured in such a way that power could be exercised. In this respect he is much closer to Clegg's (1989) reformulation of the underlying issues of the exercise of episodic power than he is to Lukes' (1974) formulation. In fact, he even uses a metaphor to discuss how he sees power that Clegg (1975) had used earlier. In Foucault (1982), when he answers the question 'How is power exercised?', he draws an analogy with the game of chess. That one piece may exercise power over another is, in Foucault's (1982) terms, 'an effect of the overall arrangement of the pieces at the time as well as of the strategy leading up to and including the capture' (Hoy 1986: 135). Or, in Clegg's (1975) terms, the moves that are possible are embedded in the rules of the game – but in reality power is less like a game of chess with fixed rules and more akin to a game where some of the players can make up and interpret the rules as they go along (as seen to great effect in Flyvbjerg's 1998 analysis). Hence power/knowledge – precisely because the knowledge of the rules is not a stable and externally given datum but is an effect of the power being played out.

When power is everything it is nothing ...

Lukes (2005), in the second edition of his celebrated book on power, makes a further criticism of Foucault's account of power as being so general and diffuse in its effects that it is indeterminate and empty, almost akin to socialization as a catch-all category. He is not alone: Lynch (1998) makes a similar critique. Because Foucault's power lacks any other, anything that is outside and opposed to it, such as freedom or autonomy, some state of being opposed to being subordinated or dominated, it is seen to be utterly nihilistic – a position that is often met with the critique 'How can it be true that there is no truth?' In large part this charge of nihilism arises because of Foucault's opposition to any Whiggish history, as a story of progress, of increasing emancipation (of knowledge; from power). However, the charge misses Foucault's point entirely.

It is not that Foucault does not acknowledge truth; rather, he does not acknowledge a *single* truth. That is, he does not privilege any one version of truth over another; rather, he recognizes that different social systems or cultural regimes will have versions of truth that reflect the regime's historical constitution of knowledge. Haugaard (1997) adds weight to Foucault's observation by adding that there is no culture on earth that believes their version of truth is not true. Foucault gives truth a plurality; rather than there being a single truth out there waiting to be discovered there are multiple truths, each of which has a cultural significance (Foucault 1984; 1997). In this sense, he is not a nihilist; as Haugaard (1997) points out, it is not that Foucault does not have values, it is just that he does not trust them. For Foucault it is the privileging of one's values or version of truths that prevent one from recognizing those of others from which one might learn, a position that is central to his 'care of the self' writings.

Foucault sees power as having a specific relation with freedom which 'is both the condition and the effect of power. It is a condition because power is only exercised on free beings, and it is an effect since the exercise of power will invariably meet with resistance, which is the manifestation of freedom' (Hoy 1986: 139). At this point he comes quite close to Lukes' (1974) position on the relation of power and responsibility; hence, where there is no freedom, no responsibility, just pure coercion, for instance, then there can be no power. Power is closely and deeply related to ethics, because the exercise of freedom is related to the election of a particular mode of existence as a life project – and, as we shall shortly see, as a life-path.

Where there is power, then the appropriate question to ask is: how is this power possible? How are power relations arranged? Not taking a transcendent position, Foucault would not expect power arrangements everywhere to partake of some essential quality, such as class struggle or resource dependency. They will be contingent on the effects of local struggles in specific fields and arenas of power. Again, in this respect he joins Lukes' (1974) way of thinking – that power is an essentially contested concept – but he adds the rider that it is not just in political theory but in everyday practice that the contestation occurs.

Power that is not practical, not morally responsible, and not usefully evaluative

Lukes (2005: 65–9) takes the point that power is a significant term in everyday practice in his second edition of *Power: a radical view*, and in so doing adds to the general critique of Foucault. In everyday practice power will be contested for three reasons, he suggests (following Morriss 2002). First, for practical reasons: we need to know who can exert power on us and whom we can exert power on. Second, there are moral reasons: denial of the power to have done something is tantamount to a denial of responsibility; one cannot be held responsible for things over which one has no control, in other words. Third, we use power in everyday life for evaluative purposes: where people are rendered powerless to better their conditions because of the actions of others – whether specifically intended and targeted or not – through the structural arrangements they design (such as a shifting balance of citizenship versus consumer rights in a society, tilting state provision of things like education and health care increasingly into the laps of consumers rather than holding them to be rights of citizens), then power is palpable. Things could be otherwise; different choices could be made; different designs would have different consequences. Foucault evades these three uses of power, according to Lukes (2005: 90), because his account of power as something that both represses and produces is 'wildly overstated and exaggerated'.

The problem, according to Lukes, is that Foucault is too much in thrall to 'Nietzschean rhetoric, within which power excluded both freedom and truth'(2005: 91). Because truth is contingent on regimes of power, one cannot make judgments about the relative merits of forms of life; because power is inescapable, one has neither practical inclination nor moral responsibility to liberate oneself – or others – from particular instances of it. Moreover, he produces far too strong an account of power in works such as *Discipline and punish* (1977) because he confuses design with efficacy: after all, the Panopticon may have been a fiendish design but it was not that widely used, and, Lukes (2005: 93) suggests, hardly achieved the 'one-sided, monolithic image of unidirectional control' that pervades both his work and that of his disciples. Indeed, for Lukes (2005: 97) his views seem much like old-fashioned sociological functionalism with their accounts of the centrality of the socialization process. Power in Foucault becomes so general that it is virtually indistinguishable from socialization. Only late in his life was he able to make more fine-grained distinctions that enabled discrimination to be made about the different types of power and its asymmetries – and when he did so he trod familiar paths that had already been well prepared, for instance in Weber's (1978) account of domination.

A science of design rather than practice

Foucault focuses on big schemes, whether they be great men's grand designs such as Jeremy Bentham's Panopticon, or overarching discourses that are said to determine a society's 'regime of truth'. As we saw in Chapter 5, when compared with Goffman, in Foucault there is little focus on the inmates of the institution and more concern with the designs that incarcerate them. The anthropologist James Scott (1990) also focuses far more on the inmates of the institutions and his conclusions point to a world of power and resistance that Goffman would have immediately recognized. He studied the 'hidden transcripts' of power – the subliminal utterances of power that never cross powerful thresholds but circulate among the servants, in the taverns, the carnivals, the marginal areas of the lower orders in social life. It is here that news, stories, and dissent circulate freely through rumor, humor and bawdy, mocking behavior, reflecting upon the pompous and pretentious official stories – the polite fictions – maintained by those in power as 'public transcripts'. In public the lower orders, knowing where their interests reside, pay deference to the official stories, enact their scripts with style and aplomb; but when out of sight and out of mind they creatively, joyously, viciously, and with the flair of the carnival, mock and subvert the dominant order and authorities. In literary theory, one may think of Bakhtin's (1984) emphasis on carnival, or in organization analysis Rhodes' (2001) celebration of *The Simpsons* as the most effective critical analysis of organizations available, Willis's (1974) *Learning to labour*, or Linstead's (1985) wonderfully anarchic work on humor.[9] All of these texts share with Scott the importance of retrieving the underbelly of formally organized life; of piercing through the official stories and capturing not only the deep bows but also the silent farts, double entendres, and profane moments that puncture and deflate local rituals, identities and powers.

In such accounts the actors who are subordinated to power may well be exposed to various panoptical devices but they are always able to subvert them, subtly resist them, push, prod and probe for the weak spots in power, or show up its absurdity. Moments of resistance such as these will rarely if ever overcome the system, but these small bursts of pleasure do serve to make domination more bearable and less injurious through skilled performances, albeit that they breed from, trade off, and depend on that domination they mock (Roy 1958; Burawoy 1979). Sometimes they might act as a safety valve that supports the existing relations of power; at other, rare times, when the probe reveals a rotten body politic, a hollow façade, or an empty windbag, they might suggest real modes of resistance and real alternatives.

In these accounts, the lower orders treat the grown-up world of power, its celebrity and façade, with all the respect of a *Sun* editor on the trail of another Tory sex scandal or a royal balls-up – which is to say, with no respect at all. These popular forms of contemporary carnival have long served the function of allowing prurient interest in those upholders of the moral order caught in breach of it, permitting them to be ritually humiliated and the moral order to be mocked for the licentiousness, wickedness, and perversity it conceals. Simultaneously, the prurient interest, whether taking positions such as 'there but for fortune', 'lucky bastard', or 'it serves them right', reinscribes the moral order – the function of deviance displayed. The order violated, publicly revealed and then mocked, is an order accommodated and re-established, according to these accounts. By partaking in the pleasure of seeing the rich and famous misbehave, we affirm that the moral order is re-established (misbehavior leads to punishment, so best behave), while its essential inequalities are revealed through peccadillo and spectacle as a form of moral entertainment and thus enjoyed vicariously.

An approach that researches hidden transcripts has great applicability to organization researchers who seek to capture from beneath the surface and behind the scenes the authentic experiences of reactions to power, rather than its stylized representation as a design. That Foucault was more concerned with the design than the practice of power thus becomes another criticism.

Repositioning Foucault

Life-paths

How might we use Foucault? We shall suggest some applications developed from human geography, namely the idea of life-paths as developed by Hannah (1997) from the work of Hägerstrand (1970), to show how Foucauldian ideas might operate outside the confines of institutions – and in more open organizations. The life-path is a way of representing and understanding how people ordinarily move through time and space (a method that has been elaborated by Pred (1977), but which we need only address in its fundamentals in this context). The reason why the life-path methodology is important is that it enables us to take some of Foucault's ideas about total institutions and apply them to more mundane situations.

Some life-paths are almost entirely confined and visible: the prisoner in a high-security jail with closed-circuit TV surveillance of the cell, for instance. Such a person may move only through a very limited and very visible set of spaces – from cell to dining hall to exercise yard and back. Most life-paths are not like this: they have many moments of invisibility and a lack of confinement, as we move and mingle with others from one arena of action to another. We may be confined, in the classroom, the office, the factory floor, for intervals in these trajectories, and we may be more or less visible during some of them; but in other areas, at home, in the cinema, on the subway, we are largely invisible as a *specific* object of any surveillance or inspectorial gaze, even though in a generalized sense we may be captured in the lens of multiple electronic Panopticons – albeit that they are not explicitly focused on one, as would be the case in a prison. The electronic eyes are both more plural in number and aimed at much more generalized bodies, and we are aware of their existence in creating a normative environment – but it becomes a matter of choice as to whether we allow them to target us specifically. Our deviance defines their acuity; in total institutions their acuity defines our deviance. The everyday life that is confined differs dramatically from that which can, apparently, wander free. The extent of wandering free, however, is often more of an illusion than a reality. Bear in mind Bourdieu: we are always subject to and subjects of discriminatory judgments made in terms of fine distinctions in the various fields through which we roam.

Outside of total institutions we are able to interpret the normative environment in such a way that we have a degree of freedom to orient our actions as more or less in accord with whatever knowledge we have of the situational constraints, such as speed limits, office hours, the use of the office phone, appropriate deportment, bearing, and language, and so on. In other words, we can get away with things – and the more that we are not being subject to surveillance the more that we can get away with, should we choose. Nonetheless, no one is entirely free to be whomsoever he or she chooses to be – from the discourses of choice available – because we do share some features with the confined. We are not fixed permanently by confinement in space – but we are often confined at prescribed times of the day and subject to more or less systematic surveillance either in real time (CCTV; computer monitoring; keypad entry and exit, etc.) or in audit time, retrospectively (tax returns; standards; legal notices, etc.). Moreover, we are confined through the many data traces we leave in the world: our permanent address; tax file number; passport; driving license; credit cards; bank accounts, etc. These devices, which Rose (1999) and Power (1997) argue are the modern liberal technologies of regulation, make us partially visible, not always in real time but sufficiently so that our life-paths, or critical incidents in them, can be made accountable. Not only that, but we are aware, constantly, of the threat of observation by the authorities – the tax audit, the speed trap, and so on – as well as being found out for not passing adequately as a member of those communities of practice in which we claim membership (see Garfinkel's (1967) discussion of Agnes's strategies for passing as a female).

As Hannah (1997: 352) says, 'despite only imperfect success', there are authorities to whose power we are, in principle, held accountable. They govern our idea of ourselves: we are people who take risks with speed limits or always observe the letter of the law; we are likely to park where and when we should not or only where and when we should; and so on. 'For the average "free" citizen the life-path of information traces is full of gaps, but retains its unity through the matchability of names, permanent addresses, social security numbers, etc.' (1997: 352). Moreover, there are those internal governors of the soul: the sense of self that we seek others to have of our self through the presentations that we make of it (Goffman 1956). The responsibility for the judgments we make lies entirely with us: as Foucault (1988b) put it in his later work, we have 'a care for the self' – we are responsible subjects – but we are responsible not only to our sense of our self but also to governmental norms that will have variable salience for us, depending not only on who we think we are but also on where and when we think we are. To be able to conduct one's self implies some degree of consciousness and reflexive capacity.

We face not total institutional powers but a variety of normalizing, imperfectly coordinated, partial regimens of authority and power of sanction. These will be vertically and horizontally fragmented organizationally. Vertical fragmentation means that the three moments of normalization (receipt of information traces, judgment, and enforcement of normality) may all take place in uncoordinated and distinct arenas with only imperfect communication between them. Horizontal fragmentation occurs when the individual leaves traces across different organizational arenas, in which these organizations, for reasons of law, technology, or ignorance, are unable to exchange and match information regarding different activities. Omniscience recedes dramatically in possibility as the walls of the total institutions are breached and the citizen moves in everyday life; nonetheless, some citizens have greater freedom of unsupervised movement than others, in various organizational arenas, and are subject to more or less coordinated authorities. Additionally, we 'have some leeway to protest, appeal, and complain about the exercise of normalizing authority. We may demand a certain degree of balance between our visibility and that of the vigilant authorities' (Hannah 1997: 353). Of course, crises such as 9/11 may lead the authorities to step up their attempts at coordination and we may become less inscrutable in more places in consequence.

A life-path is a metaphor (Lakoff and Johnson 1999). It suggests a journey. Now, that journey may be temporally extended or restricted: we might consider a path through a day at work, a week at work, months at work. For many people it would hardly matter, for their discretion is so limited that repetition of the same routines is the order of the day: think of one of those jobs designed by F. W. Taylor that we encountered in Chapter 2. For others, however, there may be little repetition of routines even though the life-path remains tightly constrained physically: the life-path of the writer of this text would fit this pattern.

The writer's day might strike many as a dull life, but it is one he enjoys, nonetheless. Every day the journey to and from various keyboards is clearly delineated – but the nature of the work that is pounded out through the fingers and the neural connections to the brain is very different. Already today the writer has planned a research paper in a meeting with colleagues; written some of this text; answered the phone and addressed and read e-mails; and scoped a commercial development of a research center – all in the space of two hours.

Clearly the life-path is insufficient in itself as a mapping device, because while life-paths through organizations may be represented and analyzed they also require the addition of Elliot Jaques' (1967) ideas on the time-span of discretion. The time-span of discretion points up responsibilities; the life-paths show the limits to those freedoms enjoyed organizationally. Indeed, as Ibarra-Colado (2001b: 361) shows, for academics especially, these limits are particularly evident: the CV and periodic reports on performativity (how many papers published in which journals) make the university a particularly clear case of the state steering a neoliberal course from a distance. Although academic work is often creative, always producing new results, we are also prisoners of our own careers, institutions, routines, schedules, etc. We are inscribed as academics, as 'subjects' of the structures that modulate our careers and trajectories. If we want to be successful we need to represent properly our role as researchers and scholars, appropriately interpreting and following the rules to win a privileged position. In this sense we are, as routinized workers, prisoners of our own existence, always institutionally modulated. And, in the end, maybe we are happy and content with our own conditions of life – like a contented cow chewing on its cud as it surveys the rich pastures around it, ripe for grazing and it fresh for milking.

We can compare the life-paths of individuals through organizations. We can analyze the visibility and accountability of organization members in terms of different regimens of authority, as well as in terms of the different members' time-span of discretion (Jaques 1967). As a general rule we may hypothesize that:

- the greater the individual members' time-span of discretion
- the less the surveillance of their organizational life-path
- the less that the subjects correspond to the 'usual suspects' thrown up by bio-power analysis
- the less subject they will be to disciplinary power.

Organizationally, the majority of those who are outside total institutions live under the conditions of an imperfect panopticism and regimes of governmentality that are never perfectly socialized; deviance is always possible, and is likely to occur from time to time. Of course, deviance is hardly a governmental surprise: specific segments of the population can be targeted for renewed governmental focus through the mechanism of bio-power, as the authorities learn to anticipate their deviance statistically on a probabilistic basis. One can predict accurately on past probabilities that drivers under 25 years of age are more prone to break the speed limits and be involved in accidents, or that supporters of a particular football team are more likely to be 'soccer hooligans' than those who support some other teams.

Through using life-path analysis in conjunction with an account of the responsibilities of members' time-spans of discretion we can make comparisons between the power relations to which different categories of organizational member are subject. While power is exercised in specific episodes (for instance, of domination, authority, seduction, coercion and manipulation), it has some presence as a capacity that retains potential effectiveness even when it is not being used, something which life-path analysis can illuminate. Organizations, we may say, are theaters for the constitution of power and all its attendant dramas, as so many life-paths traverse them.

To say that power is constitutive does not mean that it should be seen as constitutive of nearly anything and everything, as being ubiquitous. Power can be woven through different media: through domination, authority, seduction, manipulation, and coercion, for instance. Moreover, rather like the character from the evocative song of ceaseless travel that Bob Dylan (1974) conjured, the effects of power are always 'tangled' up in the rhythms and routines of everyday life. And everyday life is always lived in specific places: the East Coast; out West; New Orleans; outside of Delacroix; a topless place; or Montague Street. They are a part of a topological landscape through which we move here-and-now, there-and-then, in the present, the recollected and imagined pasts as well as those futures we aspire to. And as we move we seek to conjure up the powers we wish to exercise and vanish those we wish to avoid, seeking to stabilize interaction rituals associated with specific places; these can place people in terms of markers of their identity, they can be displaced, they can be contained in specific places or may spill over into other places, they can be recognized, mocked, disdained, subverted or copied. In short, we seek to stabilize our causal powers; the fact that others will also be doing this, and doing so on life-paths and projects opposed to those we pursue, is a sufficient reason to always keep a certain indeterminacy, a certain contingency, even randomness, in play. Hence the possibilities of transformation can never be eliminated, because of all the intentional agents who intermingle, act at a distance and often produce only unintended effects as well as those non-intentional agents, such as viruses, natural disasters, and technologies that lay waste to life-paths and projects (Clegg 1989: Chapter 9).

Causal powers

Depending on the different life-paths structured for one organizationally, or which one achieves, these capacities constitute what Harré and Madden (1975) term 'causal powers': abilities inherent to the relations of power prescribed in the life-path, dependent on the structure of relations between people and with things that this path entails.

The notion of 'causal powers' emerges first from natural science premised on a realist ontology, in which causality is regarded as being inherent to the structure of relations between phenomena. Under certain standing conditions (stable structuring of relations and environment), circumstances which enable causal powers to be realized will prevail – for as long as the enabling standing conditions are maintained. In other circumstances, standing conditions may restrict the causal powers of some people and things. Hence, the tendencies of any given phenomenon within specific relations to exert its implicit causal powers will be contingent upon the standing conditions prevailing. In this respect all power agents are analogous to practical experimentalists. They seek to ensure the reproduction of those stable conditions that enable them to create causal regularities. But if we are all doing this – if we are all practical experimentalists – then it becomes evident that we have a situation of radical and unstable contingency. We seek to do power unto others as they seek to do power unto us; and organizations, similarly to families, with their close physical intimacy and proximity, provide the perfect theater with appropriate cues, settings and props for such causal powers to be rehearsed, practiced, reproduced, and transformed.

We are all practical experimentalists. Think of some everyday examples: we seek to *seduce* the other with sweet talk, cool flowers and intimate candlelit dinners because we know that these props often produce the desired results. Perhaps, after desire has been sated, and it is some years later, the other may be contractually locked into an exploitative and loveless relationship in which *domination* occurs through the exercise of powers that have narrowed down choice to the strict binary of 'Should I stay or should I go?' Often, the fear of the unknown is greater than the desire to escape domination. In yet other circumstances, we continue to turn up at the classroom each day because we accept the legitimacy of the instruction that we know we will receive there; accepting its *authority*, we admit our self-interest in learning and being taught just as much as the teacher does in having students who want to learn. Of course, this is not always the case: sometimes the student is there because the law, in the case of a young person, says that they must be there, or maybe they are forced to attend to receive a mandatory attendance grade necessary for earning a course credit. Without the *coercion* of either the truancy laws and inspectorial system or the grade point system we would not choose to attend: we are coerced by these to accept the choice on offer. Of course, staying with the student example, we may also be *manipulated* into attending: the teacher has let it be known that the examination will closely parallel the lessons and that to miss a lesson is to risk failing the exam because we will not acquire the necessary know-how.

Conclusion

We may speak of the ways in which different regimes of power relations create different elites: elites of blood, land and estates in feudal relations; elites of capital, industry and production in modern relations; elites of symbolic analysts, celebrities, magicians of money, and wheelers with deals in postmodern relations. In each case these elites (who by no means will be separate but will be intermingled, tangled up with each other in their pleasures, seductions, and schemes) are an effect of the prevailing discourses, the meanings and phenomena that circulate through them. Of course the elites are individuals – but without the organizational circuits of power that sustain them they would be as nothing. A king with a crown is but a pretender when there are no courtiers, no sycophants, no deference, no taxes, no palaces, no crowds, and no functions to sustain the man in his myth. Elites are sustained by those myths about power that circulate widely – which, in turn, are embedded in the many small wins sustained in the battles and the warfare of everyday life, in the boardrooms, the media, the courts, all the institutions that organizations traverse. Politics in everyday life is, as Foucault acknowledged, institutionalized warfare, with all the attendant ritual, ceremony and drama to which Goffman (1956; 1961) was so alert. (In many ways, Goffman was sufficiently alert as to have anticipated much of what Foucault had to say as well as some of what he, perhaps, should have said.)

Power is contingent in Foucault. Maintaining contingent standing conditions of social relations that enable one to assert one's powers is analogous to domination; where others desire these standing conditions to be maintained as the environment that they choose to be in, we have seduction; where we freely and readily accept that there is mutual benefit and self-interest in existing relations of domination, we have authority; where we are deceived into thinking that there is mutual benefit and self-interest in existing relations of domination, we have manipulation; and where we are forced to accept the existing standing conditions, then we have coercion. We may say that these are all different ways in which the relations of causal powers may be structured. Causal powers may be manifested to the extent that not only certain structural conditions of social relations prevail but also there are no impediments pertaining to the realization of those powers. Hence, in each of these circumstances of domination, seduction, authority, manipulation and coercion, causal powers may be exercised in terms of the inherent dispositions structured into the social relations that pertain.

Thus, contrary to much of the Foucault effect, power may be seen as equivalent to specific social relations making accessible the use of various resources mobilized to produce a succession of mediating effects. These effects occur across space and time and can often be crosscutting. Hierarchical or collaborative associational power is only ever as effective as its effects – not the resources that it can deploy. One cannot read off from actual resources and draw necessary conclusions about probable effects. Power constitutes a field of social relations by traversing and dissolving space through technologies of governmentality, such as those of being under surveillance, being accountable to the files, or being regarded as an enterprising subject, and so on. It is important, however, to remember that the modalities of power that can operate on the self are many and varied (including at least authority, seduction, coercion, and manipulation) and thus should not be reduced to any essential category, such as domination.

Notes

1   See http://www.untimelypast.org/bibfou.html#byFou, which offers a good guide to original texts by Foucault as well as critiques of them.

2   Unfortunately, the reception of Foucault's work has been such that only one or two of his better-known formulations have been used, with organization studies researchers failing to pay attention to his overall project (Ibarra-Colado 1999: 133–7; Starkey and McKinlay 1998: 236). Some researchers began to use Foucault's power/knowledge matrix to reinterpret the role of accounting techniques and psychological disciplines (e.g. Hoskin and Macve 1988; Rose 1989; van Krieken 1990). Other contributors sought to redefine disciplinary analysis in the organizations field (Burrell 1988; Calás and Smircich 1999; Clegg 1989; 1994; Knights and Vurdubakis 1994).

3   Flyvbjerg (1998) discusses the later Habermas/Foucault debate, as does Mumby (1992); also see Habermas (1986; 1987a). M. Kelly (1994) reproduces the actual debate.

4   Foucault (1980) distinguishes repressive and positive power: the distinction is much the same as that which we found in Follett and Parsons, or that which we also found in the work of Mayo, where we can see the transformation of modes of surveillance. The Human Relations School designed a new strategy of government of the body/soul in the factory based on the construction of a sentiment of freedom (and responsibility) without, apparently, any kind of surveillance. As Mayo reported the observations at Hawthorne, the history sheets and records showed that in the opinion of the group all supervision had been removed, when, as Mayo (1933: 75) insisted, they were getting closer supervision than ever before, but of a different type and quality. Foucault's notion that one of the characteristics of positive power is a link to the production of truth is something that we can certainly see at work in Mayo's (1933) classic construction of the 'truth' of Hawthorne.

5   It is a different story for those seeking the best return: they may well be tempted into more speculative areas of the knowledge market.

6   They may produce some more general positive power through work done according to the norms of scientificity that the peer review practices of the journals inscribe in their more productive and public practitioners – who are of course, as in any field, a minority – and which eventually becomes published. But only a minority of scholars achieve widespread citation and discussion. Most languish in citation black holes. More often than not, complex ideas are interpreted in the more easily digestible form found in so many introductory textbooks or popular journals.

7   See http://www.eco.utexas.edu/faculty/Cleaver/zapsincyber.html).

8   See, amongst others, the following: Cerny (1994); Hallsworth and Taylor (1996); Hallsworth et al. (1997); Coopey et al. (1997); Orssatto and Clegg (1999); Orssatto et al. (2002); Lycett and Paul (1999); Lagendijk and Cornford (2000); Taylor and Hallsworth (2000); Lucio (2000);

Tantoush et al. (2001); Prasad and Eylon (2001); May (2001); Bathelt and Taylor (2002); Bathelt (2002); Clegg et al. (2002); Clegg and Ray (2003); Leiser and Backhouse (2003); Rodrigues and Child (2003); Johnston (2004); Muir (2004); Latimer (2004); Marshall and Rollinson (2004); Vaara et al. (2005).

9 Once, when asked to share his analysis of humor with the viewers of the website www.ck management.net, Steve Linstead was unable to do so because he started giggling. The camera had to stop and the take start again. The reason, he explained, was that all of his primary sources were scatological or contained what the advisories politely refer to as 'sexually explicit language' and, as such, were hardly fit to be presented 'on air'.

 **9**   Critical Theories of
Organizational Power

Introduction

The development of management studies as a field concerned almost single-mindedly with the improvement of management practice and an ever-increasing quest for improved efficiency created a sense of disquiet among some management scholars. In the 1980s, this feeling began to gel into an area of study founded on the belief that something fundamental was being overlooked in the rush to build 'better' (i.e. more efficient) organizations and to educate 'better' managers to manage them.

The scholars associated with this area of study began to attack the basic foundations of management as a field including the unquestioned belief in the value of efficiency and the use of 'value-free' quantitative methods for the investigation of management issues. Their interests led them to consider at some length the inherent contradictions in organizations (in particular, in corporations), and the resulting work forms a central plank in the array of approaches to the study of issues surrounding organizations and power. It is this area, generally referred to as critical management studies (CMS), which will occupy us in this chapter.

The development of CMS has been driven largely by a desire among some management scholars to provide an alternative perspective to mainstream work in management. As such, it is defined more by what it is not than what it is. The area is therefore fragmented and crisscrossed with tension and debate drawing on different traditions from sociology and philosophy and focusing on different substantive topics. At the same time, a cohesive field of CMS is increasingly discernible:

> Eclectic by design, CMS has combined various schools of post-Marxism, post-structuralism and also contemporary feminist theory to provide something of a discernible approach to analysing management; one that attempts systematically to interrogate its philosophical assumptions, and the imperatives and techniques associated with its practice. In particular, such critical analyses of work organizations and their management have raised broad questions concerning the management of subjectivity and the scope of organizational power relations to shape social identity and the lived experience of organizational life. (Hancock and Tyler 2004: 621)

The underlying concern with power and management knowledge makes CMS one of the few areas of management to have dealt systematically and deeply with the topic of power. While this work cannot be said to be central to the organization and management theory canon (in as much as there is such a thing), it has developed into a significant and accepted body of work. At the same time, it is also clear that the work of CMS scholars has had little impact outside the confines of its own academic journals and conferences. On the whole, this work is not found in the curriculum of major business schools, nor has it gained much traction in changing corporations or the management practices upon which they depend – its avowed goal. Even less can it be said to have affected the mainstream research conducted by most academics, particularly in the elite American business schools.

Interestingly, this new area of CMS has become an established area of study in management despite its openly political aspirations. CMS not only sees the pretensions to objectivity of more orthodox theory as a dubious fig-leaf for interests that are closely aligned with existing power elites, but also sees the necessity of producing a value-driven theory of management which is open about its values. As Alvesson and Willmott argue:

> instead of assuming the neutrality of management theory and the impartiality of management practice, [CMS] challenges the myth of objectivity and argues for a very different, critical conception of management in which research is self-consciously motivated by an effort to discredit, and ideally eliminate, forms of management and organization that have institutionalized the opposition between the purposefulness of individuals and the seeming givenness and narrow instrumentality of work-process relationships. (1992a: 4)

Despite its critical nature and avowed political goals, CMS has become an accepted part of management studies to the point that it is now an official part of the Academy of Management Meetings and has been the subject of articles and special issues in prestigious management journals such as the *Administrative Science Quarterly*. The role and position of CMS in management studies more broadly is therefore an interesting conundrum in and of itself: to what degree can CMS participate in the structures of power and privilege that characterize management research and education while still maintaining the necessary distance and legitimacy for real critique? Our interest in the future possibilities for further development of views of power in organizations makes this question a particularly pertinent one which we will return to later in the chapter.

In this chapter we will proceed in four steps. We will begin by situating CMS in the broader field of management and discuss some of the institutional characteristics of management studies as they relate to the development of this stream of work. We will then discuss what we have called the European tradition of CMS, focusing first on the theoretical foundation of this stream of research, Critical Theory,[1] and then discussing the direction and contribution of the work in this stream. Third, we will discuss the more eclectic North American stream of research, providing a broad outline of the common themes in this literature as well as considering several key contributions. Finally, we will end the chapter with a discussion of how CMS can contribute to further investigations into organizational power.

Irony in the academy

CMS and the emergence of 'critters'

So where did CMS come from? While this may seem like something of an odd question, it is an important one in terms of understanding the potential of the philosophical framework that CMS represents. Charles Perrow, for example, has described CMS as 'an oxymoron', alluding to the internal tension, if not outright meaninglessness, of the term (Zald 2002: 365). If, as some critics have suggested, it is simply a political move by those disaffected with mainstream approaches to management studies, then it may well have little to offer as a coherent stream of literature (although this says nothing about its potential as a political movement) and is really of little interest to us here. If, on the other hand, we can discern a theoretical perspective shared across at least a subset of approaches, then there may be a case for more optimism in the future of CMS. Even more, if we can identify a coherent approach to power in organizations, then this becomes of great interest to us here.

CMS has become increasingly visible in the United States as a result of events at the Academy of Management Meetings over the last five or six years. While these events have resulted in the formation of a discernible public identity for American critical management scholars (including the rather unfortunate innovation of the label 'critter' which some have adopted), they have also created something of a crisis of purpose among CMS scholars more broadly. In particular, the development of a CMS interest group,[2] and the way it developed, have had implications for the nature of CMS as it had already been developing in Europe and Australasia.

CMS divided by a common language

It is useful, perhaps, to begin with a brief discussion of the differences between management studies as it has developed in North America and as it has developed in the rest of the world, particularly Europe, the UK, and Australia. While business schools have been a part of the American university system for over 100 years, they are relatively new phenomena in other parts of the world. In the UK, for example, the first business schools were only founded in the 1960s, and only two were founded in that decade (Fournier and Grey 2000), one of which, London Business School, was designed to be in many respects more American in its orientation than British. The same might be said of schools established elsewhere on the same model, such as the Australian Graduate School of Management in Sydney. These particular schools carefully screened and recruited their staff for prior business school experience and orientation.

In contrast to the elite schools, however, many of the academics who joined other schools moved from cognate social science departments in universities as business schools were founded and staffed through the 1960s, 1970s and 1980s. Many of these newcomers were escapees from areas in decline, such as sociology. They brought with them a broad social theory perspective that imbued UK business schools with an eclectic theoretical and methodological perspective. By contrast, scholars had existed for many generations in the elite American business schools, in which they had developed their own very clear managerial perspective, and partly as a result of this, their points of contact with social science more broadly were highly attenuated. One consequence was that the methodological and theoretical perspectives common to these schools were much narrower and much more ingrained, with less infusion of vitality from broader debates in the social sciences.

One index of the major difference between the corporate disposition of British universities and US universities in the 1960s was that in Britain they still had residual elements of fourth-estate radicalism. For instance, the close ties of the new Warwick Business School, founded in 1967, with the Rootes automobile company, were the subject of a trenchant critique by one of the employees of Warwick's History Department, E. P. Thompson (1970). A critique of corporate complicity and corruption of knowledge by too close a relation to big business must have struck many US readers, even then, as quaint. Today almost everyone would find it so, inured as we are to developing close links of this kind. Thompson's critique indicated that the encompassing university environment for business schools in the UK (and Australasia, one might add) was characterized by very different political and social dynamics from their American counterparts. [3]

The difference in attitudes between the UK and the US was reflected in different approaches to scholarship and research. In the UK the strong labor movement and the corresponding attention paid by management scholars to areas like labor process theory and industrial relations added a concern with the dynamics of power in the workplace rooted in a framework that recognized the opposed and conflicting interests of management and workers. During the 1980s the assumptions of this framework, which viewed plural and conflicting interests as the normal situation in the workplace, with these interests split between capital and labor, bosses and workers, management and the unions, came under challenge from a changing political environment.

In the UK, the rapid changes in the political environment concordant with the rise of Thatcherism, and what was perceived as its more American neoliberal approach to economic and social policy, created an impetus for a whole discourse of analysis and critique of what was seen as a rising managerialism in government and politics, one which sought to obliterate these entrenched traditional sources of difference. For those British academics in industrial relations, industrial sociology and organization theory that were politically opposed to Thatcherism, areas such as labor process theory provided an opportunity to align their theory with their political interests. An annual labor process congress was held from the early 1980s onwards, at which many of these ideas were developed. In addition, there existed a long tradition of critical approaches in other subjects, such as accounting, all of which made a general CMS more legitimate (Tinker 1985; Cooper and Hopper 1988; Hopwood and Miller 1994).

While there were earlier roots, such as the production of an edited collection on *Critical issues in organizations* (Clegg and Dunkerley 1977) and a textbook *Organization, class and control* (Clegg and Dunkerley 1980)[4] that developed a critical perspective, the arrival on the European scene of something actually called CMS was shaped and aided both by the climate that developed after the emergence of Thatcherism and by some shifts in theoretical emphasis that accompanied it. Internal tensions arose among people committed to labor process theory, as factions developed in what had been a broad-based critical approach. Some adherents, who were more focused on the classical texts of Marxism and its more recent development in Braverman (1974), were aghast at the incorporation of fashionable French theory from evident non-Marxist scholars such as Foucault (Thompson 1990; 1993; Thompson and Ackroyd 1995). From this split came the genesis of CMS as a platform and legitimate interest area (Fournier and Grey 2000: 9). Thus, in the UK CMS was a platform for developing theoretical issues alien to more orthodox labor process and industrial relations theories. In particular, there was a concern with issues of subjectivity and identity, conceived in much broader terms than those of class identity and class politics, to which Knights and Willmott (1987) and Willmott (1997) provide good guides.

The first major work drawing together writings under the banner of CMS was Alvesson and Willmott (1992a) who made an explicit link between a growing area of management studies which they called CMS and the work of the Frankfurt School and associated thinkers, often referred to as Critical Theory:

> [T]his collection contributes to a rapidly expanding body of knowledge that questions the wisdom of taking the neutrality or virtue of management as self-evident or unproblematical. From the standpoint of Critical Theory ... management is too potent in its effects upon the lives of employees, consumers and citizens to be guided by a narrow, instrumental form of rationality. (1992a: 1)

In Europe, then, the link between a particular set of concerns and theoretical approaches and CMS was clearly made and, while there was much 'fraying at the edges', this connection to the concerns and approaches of Critical Theory more broadly formed an important anchor for CMS. While the concern may be with critiquing management theory and practice and the relations of power that characterize it, the theoretical roots are clearly visible.

In North America, in contrast, the term 'CMS' took a very different turn with the founding of the Critical Management Interest Group at the Academy of

Management. Their founding statement provides some insight into the very different understanding of the meaning of CMS. It reads, in part, as follows (http://aom. pace.edu/cms/):

> Our workshop is open to a broad range of critical views. We aim to foster critiques coming from labor, feminist, anti-racist, ecological, and other perspectives. We are open to critiques formulated from a broad range of theoretical standpoints. In particular, our use of the term 'critical' is not meant to signal a specific commitment to any particular school of thought such as Frankfurt School critical theory. Rather we include proponents of all the various theoretical traditions that can help us understand the oppressive character of the current management and business system. To use some of the labels ready at hand, these traditions include, but are not restricted to: marxist, post-marxist, post-modernist, feminist, ecological, irreductionist, critical-realist, post-colonial.

The idea of CMS suggested here is therefore a much broader one than that proposed by Alvesson and Willmott (1992a). It is not a moment of critique founded in a particular theoretical tradition but something much broader, bound together by a political interest rather than either an empirical topic or a theoretical tradition. And, furthermore, the tension between them is clear. The sort of CMS envisaged by the founders of the Critical Management Studies Interest Division is a broad category of work that is joined together by the simple act of critique. Their inclusiveness is in stark contrast to the theoretical program of CMS in Europe and also to the ethos of management studies more broadly. The result is more of a political movement to foment change in management studies (and perhaps management practice) broadly and less a coherent theoretical platform for analysis. American CMS, one might say, tends to be more fragmented, less theoretical and more activist in its orientation.

   Why is all of this important? It is important for the simple fact that 'CMS is a composite beset by internal strains and tensions, not a unified movement' (Grey and Willmott 2002: 411) and our discussion needs to reflect this. The tension between political program and field of study is integral to understanding CMS and its tensions. Our challenge in the remainder of the chapter will be to straddle this divide somewhat and try to glean some coherent picture of CMS as a discipline. Our starting point will be the Critical Theory of the Frankfurt School in the next section, because if CMS has a theoretical distinctiveness then it is from this work that it will be built, as was envisaged by Alvesson and Willmott (1992a). At the same time, we will stray somewhat from their narrow view without being tempted to simply adopt the 'any critique is CMS' approach which is more prevalent in the US. The result is somewhat fragmented but provides a useful view of management and organizations that offers a functional platform for examining power in organizations.

CMS's theoretical auspices

Critical Theory

In this section we will briefly discuss Critical Theory in sociology and outline its history and broad characteristics. Critical Theory is a cohesive body of work that has been highly influential across the social sciences and more broadly in the new left and other left-leaning social movements. We will begin by situating Critical Theory historically and theoretically. We then discuss the influence of Critical Theory on one branch of CMS – the branch we will refer to as the European School of CMS, which draws explicitly on Critical Theory as a foundation for the examination of management and the modern organization. While a relatively small body of literature, the well-developed theoretical foundation of Critical Theory provides analytical power and impact that makes this an extremely important literature for those interested in power in organizations.

Critical Theory refers to both a group of scholars, or 'school of thought', and a form of 'self-conscious critique that is aimed at change and emancipation through enlightenment and does not cling dogmatically to its own doctrinal assumptions' (Carr 2000: 208). The body of work produced by this school of thought is interesting as much for its societal effects as it is for its influence on sociology and related disciplines. As Held explains:

> The writings of what one may loosely refer to as a 'school' of Western Marxism – critical theory – caught the imagination of students and intellectuals in the 1960s and early 1970s. In Germany thousands of copies of the 'school's' work were sold, frequently in cheap pirate editions. Members of the New Left in other European countries as well as in North America were often inspired by the same sources. In other parts of the world, for example in Allende's Chile, the influence of these texts could also be detected. In the streets of Santiago, Marcuse's name often took a place alongside Marx and Mao in the political slogans of the day. (1980: 13)

The writings of this group of scholars, often referred to as the Frankfurt School, became an important influence in the development of various radical protest movements in the 1960s and 1970s, especially, as Held suggests, through the ideas of Herbert Marcuse (1964; see Ali 2005b). The alternative interpretation of Marxist theory provided by the Frankfurt School, and their focus on issues and problems of common concern such as mass culture, the family, and sexuality, and their search for a transcendental subject able to spearhead change, resonated with the concerns of many of the people involved in the radical protest movements that characterized this period around the world.

The Frankfurt School was established in 1923. Its proper name was the Institute for Social Research and it was formally associated with the University of Frankfurt. However, an endowment from Felix Weil, the son of a wealthy grain merchant, provided a significant amount of autonomy. The first director of the new Institute was Carl Grunberg. Grunberg was unique in being the first professed Marxist to hold a chair at a German university. He was also unique among chaired professors of his time in his concern for what he saw as a tendency for German universities to focus on teaching at the expense of research and to produce academics who were only capable of supporting the status quo upon which their privilege and power depended. He also believed that Marxism provided the theoretical infrastructure to challenge this situation. It was a combination that led him to focus the attention of the Institute on a program of critical research, bringing together a range of scholars who shared his interest in theorizing about social life and development. He also founded a journal, *Grunbergs Archiv*, which was the first major European journal of labor and socialist history. The journal published articles on a broad range of topics focusing on the history of capitalist and socialist economies and the workers' movements by economists, sociologists, historians and philosophers.

Marxism provided the basis of the Institute's program for the empirical investigation of the social world from the outset. But Grunberg's view was very different from the mainstream view among Marxists at the time. He believed very strongly in a version of Marxism that was highly situational and limited in focus, a sharp contrast to the monistic materialism of many Marxists of the time who believed in transhistorical laws that explained the relation of the social and the economic in simple, universal truths.

While setting the stage for Critical Theory, his view, however progressive, was largely rejected by the central figures of the Frankfurt School. In particular, his belief (commonly held by Marxists at the time) that the social was simply a product of the economic was rejected along with his optimism about the general improvement of social institutions over time. What was retained, however, was a commitment to empirical research and a belief in the importance of history. The critical moment of Marxism combined with these latter beliefs in methodology (see Morrow 1994 for an extended discussion) provided an initial foothold for the development of Critical Theory, as it became known.

The turning point for the Frankfurt School occurred when Grunberg retired in 1929 and Horkheimer took over as the director of the Institute. Horkheimer quickly gathered together a diverse group including Erich Fromm, Theodore Adorno, and Herbert Marcuse. Horkheimer continued Grunberg's concern for theoretical analysis and empirical investigation (not to mention his belief in the 'dictatorship of the director') but moved the focus of the Institute towards a much more radically historical and theoretical mode. He also believed strongly in the need for a reintegration of the disparate disciplines of the social sciences, as the state of fragmentation he saw was so advanced that no discipline could say they had any real ability to explore the historical reality that existed in a particular place and time.

The Institute was closed by the Nazi regime in 1933 for 'tendencies hostile to the state' (Jay 1996: 29). Many members of the Institute were Jewish, which was problematic in those times; in addition, their obvious interest in Marxism and their rather suspect international connections marked them out as enemies of the fascist state. Fortunately, Horkheimer had arranged to transfer much of the Institute's financial endowment out of Germany. The Institute first moved to Geneva and then, in 1935, to Columbia University in New York City. It may seem somewhat ironic for a openly left of center group to move to what is arguably the heartland of capitalism. At the same time, this forced emigration resulted in changes in the tone and focus of the work of the Institute and provided exposure of their work to the English-speaking academic world (particularly through their English-language journal *Studies in Philosophy and Social Science*). Arguably, this period was at least partially responsible for the later popularity of their work among English-speaking scholars.

Critical Theory as a term was introduced by Horkheimer in an early essay in 1937 (Horkheimer 1993), but its meaning was initially far from clear and has evolved substantially over time. At its most basic, Critical Theory 'is most succinctly defined as an empirical philosophy of social institutions' (Steffy and Grimes 1986: 325). It combines a conceptualization of the nature of social investigation with a belief in empirical investigation carried out within a Marxist framework:

> Critical theory aims to produce a particular form of knowledge that seeks to realize an emancipatory interest, specifically through a critique of consciousness and ideology. It separates itself from both functionalist/objective and interpretive practical sciences through a critical epistemology that rejects the self-evident nature of reality and acknowledges the various ways in which reality is distorted. (Carr 2000: 209)

Morrow (1994) has identified three phases in the development of Critical Theory. The first was characterized by a kind of interdisciplinary materialism that sought to analyze factors that might contribute to the development of a revolutionary working class. The term 'materialism' referred explicitly to Marx's historical materialism but, as we mentioned above, rejected the reductionist view of the link between the economic and social that characterized orthodox Marxism. Instead, it was argued that a new version of materialism was required with a more nuanced and complex idea of culture, a more developed social psychological investigation of class, and a much more reflexive view of method. And, at all times, there was to be ongoing empirical investigation to explore the applicability of the resulting ideas. At a more practical level, the focus was on understanding when the German working class would mobilize and overthrow the Nazi dictatorship that was then in power.

In the second phase, the work took a decidedly more pessimistic turn. With the failure of the German workers to organize and overthrow Hitler, and the distressing turn of the Soviet revolution to Stalinism, Critical Theorists began to lose their faith in Marx's theory of revolution. The general mood of Critical Theory turned unmistakably gloomy and became a view of modernity 'where every increment of Western progress, every step on the ladder of (instrumental) reason was adjudged to be simultaneously its obverse, a regressive retreat into myth and repression' (Howe 2001: 179). While retaining the belief in the destructive effects of capitalist forms of production, they began to focus on the stabilizing dynamics of capitalism. Instead of a focus on what would lead to the revolution, they tried to understand the dynamics that were preventing it. In particular, they looked to the rise of the welfare state and the development of the mass media, or the cultural industries as they referred to them, and their role in distracting the working class from their 'real' interests.

Underlying this work were two important concepts: reification and dialecticism. 'Reification' refers to the tendency in social science and philosophy to remove ideas from their historical context and to believe they are independent of that context. It is a recognition that the 'researcher both is part of what they are researching, and is caught in a historical context in which ideologies shape the thinking' (Carr 2000: 209). Horkheimer drew on Lukacs' concept of 'reification' to describe this tendency and the rejection of reification became a distinguishing feature of Critical Theory and an important center point of its debate with mainstream social science and philosophy.

The term 'dialectical' is one that has been the source of much misconception in social science as it is too often understood as some sort of a compromise of opposites. Instead, Critical Theorists meant something much more subtle. In developing this notion they drew on Hegel's notion of dialectics involving the recognition that the particular and the universal were interdependent. In this dynamic relationship of interdependence, contradictions emerge which in turn promote the generation of a new totality. The dialectic, as such, was conceived as involving three 'moments': thesis, antithesis and synthesis. The new synthesis was not some sort of middle ground but rather a new position that encompassed the old in their totality.

While the founding members of the Frankfurt School embraced the Hegelian foundation of dialectics, they rejected Hegel's claims to absolute truth, preferring a historical-contextual interpretation. Truth was always mediated, and part of that mediation was the historical period in which the truth claim was constituted. Many truth claims that were accepted as a constitutive part of normalcy derived from ideologies distributed through the cultural industries, while another part was to be found in the material reality of those needs, desires, and wants which, in their formation, bear the inscription of a specific history.

Based on this much more powerful notion of dialectic, the Frankfurt School rejected the simple class interest analysis that came with a traditional Marxist orientation and placed its emphasis on understanding cultural phenomena as mediated through the social totality. Counter to the orthodox Marxist view, the economic system could not be extracted and analyzed other than in its broader societal context. The focus of Critical Theory was to explore the aspects of the system that made the most dominating aspects of the social order appear normal and natural. The lack of knowledge of the real history of the social system in place at a particular time was not an academic matter but a political one with which Critical Theory worked to engage.

Finally, in the third phase identified by Morrow (1994), under the leadership of Jürgen Habermas[5] the foundations of Critical Theory were radically rethought. In its previous phase, Critical Theory had taken a very pessimistic turn. Against this deep pessimism, Habermas argued that while enlightenment and myth will always be entwined, the fundamental differences between them should not be lost, nor should our ability to discern one from the other be underestimated. While Habermas and his followers agreed that modernity is certainly characterized by pathologies and distortions of various kinds, it contains progressive elements too. For Habermas, one of the primary tasks of social science became to distinguish what was socially rational from what was not, and bring this distinction to bear on contemporary life. The term 'modernity' is not just the description of a historical condition. It is an unfinished project that could lead to a more rational society. To distinguish what might count as rational, the social sciences must seek to become 'reconstructive sciences' whose focus is on the emancipation of all members of society. The goal of Critical Theory for Habermas, like his predecessors in the Frankfurt School, was not to reflect reality, but to engage with it and create change.

Critical Theory and European CMS

Borrowings and linkages

Critical Theory was an obvious theoretical resource for the nascent CMS to draw on, but surprisingly there was very little explicit borrowing or homage for some time. Burrell and Morgan (1979) did introduce Critical Theory explicitly to the canon of organization analysis but, on the whole, the Frankfurt School remained underappreciated. Fifteen years later, Burrell (1994) extended an invitation to Habermas's thought for organizational scholars, but few took up the invitation. However, some key ideas from the Frankfurt lexicon have more recently entered into the vocabulary and analysis of one stream of CMS, in terms of a concern with emancipation, a belief in dialecticism, and a desire to avoid reification of theory. This leads to a very different view of organization studies than that which characterizes the mainstream of organization theory:

> Critical theory assumes that organization science is a social practice and, as such, must give account of itself. This means that research should include a critical discussion of the subjective, or theoretical, character of the observer and observed, as in the case of hermeneutics. Critical theory further expands its epistemic critique to include: (a) a discussion of the limitations of alternative forms of inquiry; (b) an analysis of the relationship between the community of organizational researchers and organizational practitioners and members; and (c) an acknowledgement of the practical aim of any particular mode of research. In sum, critical theory assumes that theories, systems of knowledge, and facts are embedded in and reflect relativistic world views. (Steffey and Grimes 1986: 325)

The stream of research in organization studies that draws on the tradition of Critical Theory is therefore fundamentally different from more traditional forms of inquiry. It is different in its view of method, in its understanding of the relation of researcher to researched, and in the sorts of empirical issues which are viewed as appropriate topics of enquiry. Additionally, different journals emerged to promote it, such as *Organization*, which were avowedly critical, while other more conventional publications, such as the *Handbook of organization studies* (Clegg et al. 1996), opened conduits for some critical perspectives to enter the mainstream. We shall consider a number of themes that are associated with critical perspectives.

Emancipation theme

In their early article, Alvesson and Willmott focus on the idea of emancipation, which they define as 'the process through which individuals and groups become freed from repressive social and ideological conditions, in particular, those that place socially unnecessary restrictions upon the development and articulation of human consciousness' (1992b: 432). They make it clear that by this they do not mean the various uses of emancipation that fall under the term 'quality of work life'. While giving them a sympathetic nod, they reject approaches to emancipation that legitimate moves in this direction through some link to improved organizational performance (here we see echoes of the logic behind Ford's programs to improve the lifestyle of his employees that we discussed in Chapter 3). For Alvesson and Willmott (1992b), emancipation cannot be bestowed by management, but is the result of a struggle for self-determination and a protracted and often painful process of self-reflection and change.

The paper then goes on to engage with postmodern and poststructural critiques of the notion of emancipation and of the modernist project more generally. In working through the conflicting philosophical perspectives of various positions, Alvesson and Willmott provide an excellent overview of some of the fundamental differences that characterize the more eclectic version of CMS that we will discuss in the next section. They also do an excellent job of defending the foundational assumptions of a Critical Theory approach by scaling down and contextualizing them:

> In a space between Critical Theorists' commitment to critical reason and radical change, the scepticism of poststructuralists about metanarratives and efforts to separate power and knowledge, and humanistic ideas for reducing the gap between human needs and corporate objectives, we locate an agenda for microemancipation. This agenda favors incremental change but, because it has open boundaries to more utopian ideas, it does not take as given the contemporary social relations, corporate ends, and the constraints associated with a particular macro-order. (1992b: 461)

The influence of Critical Theory in this work is clear. The concern with engagement, the recognition of a conflict of interests, and a focus on emancipation all stem directly from the work of the Frankfurt School. At the same time this is CMS, as the perspectives drawn from Critical Theory are used to examine uniquely situated questions of emancipation in the modern corporation.

Alienation theme

While Alvesson and Willmott (1992b) focused on emancipation, Jermier (1985) focuses on another central idea in Critical Theory, the concept of alienation. In his early writings, Marx introduced the concept of alienation as the necessary result of the private appropriation of labor value under capitalist modes of production. But in early capitalism, the shared awareness of the class-based oppression experienced by workers prevented their separation from their true selves. Workers were therefore objectively alienated but subjectively remained aware of their condition.

But later conceptualizations of alienation had to deal with the reality of the loss of awareness of workers. To the objective alienation that results from the capitalist system was added the subjective alienation of workers who do not appreciate their real interests. Two different approaches were developed to explain this situation. Lukacs (1968) argued that the system becomes mystified and workers, while experiencing the oppression of the system, are unable to understand it. For Critical Theorists of the Frankfurt School, the blame lies in the intensity of consumption made possible by the material success of capitalism and the effects of the cultural industries together resulting in a mirage of wellbeing, recalling Lukes's (1974) radical view.

Jermier (1985) represents these two very different conceptualizations of alienation in two different short stories. In both of the stories we follow Mike Armstrong through a day at work. However, the two stories present very different versions of Mike's life as a skilled operator in a phosphate plant in a large American city. In the first version, Jermier draws on Critical Theory and has Mike surrounded by a consumerist wonderland of big screen TVs, designer furniture, and new cars. His view of his work is one of a satiated consumer and he is unable to see his own alienation and to recognize the class-based identity that he shares with his fellow workers. He is the archetype of the worker going through his workday unaware of his own oppression and of the appropriation of his labor through the capitalist system. He has lost touch with his true self and is deeply alienated. Even more, the system in which he finds himself has been reified to the extent that no other system seems preferable, or ever, perhaps, possible:

> The major institutions in society (schools, churches, the family, advertising and enter-
> tainment, etc.) act in harmony to present a version of the work in society which denies
> oppressive realities. Cultural domination is completed when consumption is manipu-
> lated so thoroughly that consumers feel compelled to frenetically buy and use the cul-
> ture industry's latest products, even though they see through them. Workers are
> anesthetized by the persuasive rationalizations readily accessible in mythical structures
> and by manipulated, diversionary consumption, such that the injuries of class are
> neither perceived nor felt. (1985: 75)

In the second, darker version, Jermier draws on the dialectical Marxist version of alienation and we meet a very different Mike. Gone are the trappings of happy materialism and instead we meet a worker caught in the daily grind of an unhappy work life in a dehumanizing job. He tries to fight back but feels hopeless and frus-trated in the face of the power and seemingly unassailable arguments of his fore-man. He longs for something else but cannot imagine what that alternative might be. He is deeply alienated and experiences that alienation but sees no alternative:

> Dialectical Marxists characterize the ordinary worker as subjectively alienated (falsely
> conscious), but engaged in responsible, meaningful protest and new forms of class rad-
> icalism. Thus, workers are capable of understanding the actual operation of the system
> and there is an awareness of deprivation and disadvantage, even though this awareness
> rarely fosters revolutionary motives. Individual workers are not psychologically domi-
> nated by property-based power dynamics to the point of mystification or resignation.
> (1985: 78)

Jermier's work provides an interesting contribution for several reasons. First, he adds a challenging view of work, and particularly the subjective experience of work, to the rather limited and undertheorized discussions of self-actualization and quality of work life that are common in the management literature. His dis-cussion of alienation challenges researchers to look at the broader context of work, rather than just the narrow conditions of work, in thinking through the subjective experience of work. Second, his choice of fiction as a methodology provides a very different approach to the presentation of empirical work in management (see Phillips (1995) for a more developed discussion of fiction in management research). Third, he draws on critical management to deepen the discussion of a central theme in the management literature.

Manufacturing consent theme

One significant US-based writer who has made a contribution to CMS is Michael Burawoy, a British trained anthropologist who moved from researching labor in copper mines in Africa to labor in a plant in Chicago, which turned out to be the same plant in which Donald Roy (1958) had done his pioneering ethnographic work. Burawoy's theoretical inspiration is drawn from the work of the Italian theorist Antonio Gramsci (1971) and his theory of hegemony, which we have encountered in Chapter 7. Gramsci sought to account for the collapse of the Western working-class movements during the post First World War years. The reason, he concluded, could not be found within either the state or the capitalist economy; rather, the key lay in the institutional fabric of civil society, which in the West succeeded in eliciting the 'spontaneous consent of the masses' to the status quo (1971: 12). Burawoy took from Gramsci the importance of 'managing consent' for maintaining orderly legitimated power relations in organizations. In essence, the research question was why the Western working classes had not revolted as Marxist theory would have expected them do, under the burden of exploitation and the economic contradictions of late capitalism. The answer, said Burawoy, was that in their everyday working lives managers and workers manufactured consent to the dominant relations of production. Of course, the question only makes sense if one assumes that the hypotheses of Marxist theory are correct: that is, if one assumes that what needs to be explained is something that should have happened but did not. The question then becomes why it did not happen.

It was not a unique question: earlier versions of it had been asked by a number of industrial sociologists, but their answers were a little different from Burawoy's. For instance, the emphasis on cultural or normative domination is to be found in the classic text of William Whyte, *The organization man* (1960), which warned that corporations no longer sought merely the worker's labor (the main concern of industrial and organizational analysis at that point). Following Follett, whom we met in Chapter 3, he argued that they now wanted the worker's soul in terms of the willingness of the employee to identify with the company. British researchers had developed the theory of embourgeoisement, which saw the Western working classes as adopting middle-class values of acquisitiveness and individualism in place of an older class-based culture (Abercrombie et al. 1980; Goldthorpe et al. 1969).

Burawoy introduced a new spin on these accounts by hooking up these 'dominant ideology' accounts to Braverman's (1974) labor process analysis. He sought to identify the labor control systems that elicited workers' consent. Burawoy (1979; 1985) discerned several species of hegemonic factory regimes, each of which invites workers to align their interests with those of their employers; closely related, Richard Edwards (1979) saw corporations maintaining control over white-collar workers and increasingly manual employees through the spread of 'bureaucratic controls' encouraging workers to identify with the organization to a greater extent than any union or class affiliation (Joyce 1980; Vallas 1991). In particular, Burawoy stressed the importance of small everyday things in the life of the factory, the rituals and games, that made work tolerable and allowed the employees to distantiate themselves from the mind-numbing ordinariness of work. Thus, rather than see the explanation for their attitudes to work as arising from the orientations they brought to work, as did the Cambridge researchers of the embourgeoisement thesis (Goldthorpe et al. 1969), Burawoy, following Roy (1958), saw them arising from the nature of social relations in work.

The hegemonic thesis has been developed further by a number of people. For example, Guillermo Grenier (1988) conducted fieldwork at Johnson and Johnson's medical instruments plant in Albuquerque, New Mexico. He saw that initiatives such as quality circles, by imbuing work relations with the trappings rather than the substance of participation, chilled out dissent and implicated workers in enforcing managerial norms as a part of their everyday work. Barker (1993) provides an ethnographic account of ISE, a small electronics assembly plant spun off from a large corporation which adopted self-managed teams to ensure its competitive success. Workers were encouraged to embrace team principles and willingly assumed responsibility for mutual discipline and control. Kunda (1992) provides an ethnographic account of a computer engineering organization that systematically developed a system of 'normative control', which it used to gain the professional employees' consent. In all these studies, the manufacture of consent is seen to be an important aspect of what is done as a normal part of everyday work as it is shaped by various managerial devices, such as teams, quality circles and so on. Thus, the focus on power is dedicated to explaining the relative quiescence of employees and the ways in which their goals become closely aligned with those of management.

Dialectical change theme

In our final example of the application of Critical Theory concepts in management, we will consider Carr's (2000) discussion of a dialectical approach to the study of organizational change. Carr begins with an introduction to Critical Theory and focuses on the idea of dialectics as developed by the Frankfurt School. As we discussed above, the concept of the dialectic in Critical Theory refers to the notion of interconnected oneness of thesis and antithesis in both thought and social institutions. Carr (2000: 214) argues that the concept has been used in 'a somewhat loose and "undisciplined" manner' in management and that much of its analytical power has been lost. He calls for a radical rethinking of dialectic and for a return to the much deeper notion of this fundamental dynamic.

The ramifications of a return to a more developed notion of dialectic are significant. Carr goes on to argue that many organizational processes are better understood as dialectical where managers are an integral part of a process and not simply influencing processes in organizations:

> The manager/administrator should not simply become aware of dialectical relationships between structures and actors but become more critical in the appraisal of the options in carrying through their tasks. Instead of being preoccupied with control (and largely preserving the status quo), a dialectically aware manager/administrator would recognise, and work through, the tensions and strains that inevitably arise from contradictions, oppositions and negations. Dialectical sensitivity leads the manager/administrator to recognise that they are not only part of the transforming 'process' but themselves are also being acted upon. (2000: 14)

Carr's work again links important issues in management research and practice to the concerns and theoretical frameworks of Critical Theory. The resulting perspective provides interesting and unexpected insight into, in this case, organizational change and its relation of managerial action. As in the previous two examples, this example highlights the practical nature of Critical Theory and how its focus on engaging with the empirical world fits well with the pragmatic view of much of management theory.

CMS as critique rather than Critical Theory

Situating CMS today

In this section, we will examine some exemplars from the broad stream of litera-ture that has collected under the banner of CMS but which does not grow out of the tradition of Critical Theory and the Frankfurt School. This eclectic mix of per-spectives shares almost nothing beyond some sense of an underlying conflict:

> Goodies and baddies; imperialists and freedom fighters; evil lords and young heroes; forces for 'good' rising up against their oppressive rulers! Such imagery has not only been central in myths, science fiction and fairy tales but has implicitly underpinned critical social research. Critical research across the social sciences has been strewn with presuppositions of essential conflicts between women and men, between capital and labour, between colonized and colonizer, between managers and subordinates, between blacks and whites, and so on. (Grice and Humphreys 1997: 412)

The underlying conflict perspective means that many of the works gathered under this banner deal explicitly with issues of power in and around organizations and therefore are of interest to us here. However, at the same time, this is an area of research that is deeply divided. Work in this tradition includes contributions from diverse theoretical orientations that are often in deep conflict in terms of their underlying philosophical assumptions. In fact, it is arguable that this area is not an area at all but simply a trendy label or brand (Thompson 2005).

At the same time, some writers have provided arguments to the contrary and have argued that a discernible field is forming. In a very interesting article on the topic, Fournier and Grey begin with the observation that the '1990s have seen the emergence of a new conjunction of the terms "critical" and "management", and even the birth of a new sub-discipline dubbed "critical management studies"' (2000: 8). They then go on to argue for three defining characteristics of CMS: an anti-performative stance; a commitment to some form of denaturalization; and a reflexive approach to methodology.

By 'anti-performative' Fournier and Grey mean an approach to knowledge that does not privilege efficiency as the measure of value or usefulness. It seeks to estab-lish a foothold for management scholars such that the worth of their contributions does not have to be firmly grounded in their contribution to national productivity, in the way in which, in the UK, the new performativity sweeping through univer-sity research cultures demands. Fournier and Gray (2000: 8) base their discussion on Lyotard's (1984) notion of a performative intent – 'the intent to develop and cel-ebrate knowledge that contributes to the production of the maximum output for the minimum input' (2000: 17) – but reverse it to describe CMS. Obviously, most of organization and management studies are based on a performative intent, making this characteristic a clear boundary.

The idea of denaturalization refers to work that intentionally challenges the taken-for-grantedness of current versions of capitalism and organizations. While much of organization and management research assumes the naturalness of current arrangements and works to understand their nature, work in this vein seeks to unveil the systems of power that hold the current arrangements in place and to show that other arrangements are possible and even, maybe, preferable. One criticism of mainstream management research is that it legitimates and reifies current arrangements; CMS works towards the opposite ends.

Fournier and Grey (2000) argue that CMS differs from its more traditional counterparts due to it being more reflexive (see Alvesson and Kärreman (2000) for a more complete discussion of reflexivity). They suggest that in mainstream management research 'some (often rather weak) version of positivism is simply assumed, there is no explicit reflection on epistemology and ontology, and discussion of methodology becomes limited to issues of method and statistical technique' (2000: 19). Critical management research, on the other hand, is much more reflexive and consciously examines its philosophical foundations, its theoretical assumptions, and its methods.

Combined, these three characteristics give us a rough frame for recognizing this more eclectic version of CMS. The degree to which the work that falls within this boundary is a nascent field or simply a collection of oppositional points of view remains to be seen. Nonetheless, CMS provides a range of work that is of direct interest to us here. We will now consider two very different examples of work from this growing literature, which serve to develop the foundations for an alternative view of power. First, we will consider queer theory, which is a set of ideas based around the premise that identities – and particularly the aspects of identity related to gender and sexuality – do not fall into clear and distinct categories. Challenging such deeply held aspects of the social world becomes a point for contesting all categories and even theorizing as an activity. Second, we will discuss postcolonial theory, a perspective that focuses on the dynamics of colonialism and how the experience of a colonial relationship shapes the subsequent nation.

CMS and queer theory

In this section, we will focus on the potential of queer theory (e.g. Butler 1990; Sedgwick 1994) as a foundation for work in CMS. Fundamental to queer theory is a broad challenge to categories, boundaries and limits. While its history lies in rethinking categories of gender and sexuality, and in the broad literature on feminist theory, poststructuralism and postmodernism, its theoretical interest is now much broader:

> So queer, then, in the very broad terms in which I have reviewed it here, is an approach which seems to be centrally concerned to politicize the terms upon which knowing is almost always conceptualized. Its key move is to question the existence of the boundary,

not simply to demonize that which lies on one side and to celebrate that which lies on the other. Queer eschews simple finger pointing, it avoids resting on the simplicities that separate the innocent from the guilty, the victim from the oppressor, or real experience from mere abstraction. (Parker 2002: 156)

Queer theory, then, involves thinking through the contingency and social constructedness of the categories that we commonly take for granted. While this sounds much like strains of postmodernism and poststructuralism, the distinctive contribution of queer theory is to focus attention on what this means for basic categories of identity and what happens when you take this view to its logical conclusion. Queer theory suggests that we can negotiate the boundaries that characterize historically and culturally situated social life. We can 'think about the *how* of these boundaries – not merely the fact that they exist, but also how they are created, regulated, contested' (Namaste 1996: 199, emphasis in original).

Parker's (2002) work applies queer theory to management. He begins by identifying three problems he sees with management theory, problems he believes queer theory can help illuminate. First, he finds the notion of 'management' in the sense of a category of work to be problematic. From a 'disparate collection of occupational nouns – owner, supervisor, administrator, overman, foreman, clerk – a term has emerged that appears to represent anyone engaged in the co-ordination of people and things' (2002: 146). Second, he finds the idea of 'management' in terms of a practice equally unsatisfactory, particularly as it has become widely used to refer to the management of everything from supply chains to relationships, and to be used in a way where managing something is good while not managing it is bad. Finally, the idea of management as a field of research separated from the practices of management is also a problem from Parker's perspective. He wants to problematize the taken-for-granted relationship of theory to practice.

Butler's (1990) notion of doing drag has been used by Parker to see managers doing management as 'performing'. They are accomplishing a particular identity in a complex social space:

Doing 'manager' is playing a role. Management means wearing the costume. It calls upon the bodily comportment, the props and scripts and gestures that signify 'manager'. The problem, or one of 'my' problems, is that the role has become hardened into a series of predictable scripts, an unreflective rehearsal of what the type 'manager' does. But treating management as 'drag' – not just dramaturgy – suggests both its provisionality and a possible playful form of resistance. (Parker 2002: 160)

Parker argues that management as a practice, and the taken-for-granted categories through which we understand it, need to be 'queered'. By this he means that we need to challenge the categories and limits that are bound up in the notion of management as it is applied in all realms of life. We need to draw on the ideas and practices developed in queer theory to work through the settled and stable meanings that have grown up around management and reclaim the provisionalness and playfulness that underlie it. As he suggests, '[a]gainst managing, in the sense of control, this is a continual, permanent, neverending movement of asking "who are 'we'?"'(2002: 161).

Finally, in terms of management as a field of study, Parker argues that queer theory also helps us to rethink the relationship of management theory and management practice. But what does it mean to queer the academy? It means, first, to recognize the highly heterosexist and male-dominated nature of management as a field. Its sexual politics and its power relations are highly concordant. But beyond that, it means something much more profound about the nature of knowledge. Queer, argues Parker, 'insists on a reflexivity about knowledge, about the places and spaces whereby certain forms of knowing are legitimated, about the subjects and objects of enquiry and the manners that pertain to its production and distribution' (2002: 162). In other words, the entire basis of management as an academic enterprise, the idea of an academy separated from practice, allowing it to be disinterested and value-free, and the practices of academic knowledge production, all need to be queered, a prospect which the Academy of Management, somewhat surprisingly, seems not yet to have embraced wholeheartedly.

CMS and postcolonial theory

Another area of increasing interest in CMS draws on the literature on postcolonial theory (Bhabha 1994; Said 1979; Appiah 1991; Barker et al. 1994; Williams and Chrisman 1993; Young 2001) to examine various issues in management and organization theory. While this literature remains small, there have been notable recent contributions (Banerjee and Linstead 2001; Jaya 2001; Prasad 2003; Vaara et al. 2005). It is to this literature that we will turn our attention in this section.

The roots of postcolonialism lie in colonialism. Colonialism, which saw the routinization of the plunder, enslavement and extraction of precious metals and minerals characteristic of the earlier period of imperialism, was the experience of imposed foreign political and administrative rule, through which most of the world's people were inducted into the global economy. Europe dominated much of the world in the 1800s and early 1900s (Loomba 1998), with Central America, the Philippines and parts of Oceania effectively US colonies. Postcolonialism is, by extension, a theoretical standpoint which is critical of colonialism and in particular of its subsequent effects on the colonized nation and its people. The related term 'neocolonialism' implies continued economic and cultural dependency by postcolonial nations and highlights the ongoing influence of former colonizers and other Western nations upon former colonies (Nafziger 1988). There is, therefore, an important nuance in the usage of the terms 'postcolonial' and 'neocolonial', as countries may be postcolonial in that they are politically independent, while at the same time neocolonial due to prevailing cultural and/or economic dependency upon existing imperial powers (Loomba 1998; Young 2001). The postcolonial era can be positioned within global processes of hegemonic influence, whereby historical transformations give rise to evolving states of more subtle subjugation and reconfigurations of power.[6]

The inherent temporality of the postcolonial condition is also problematic as the colonization of nations and their subsequent political independence are both historically and geographically situated. Indeed, although postcolonialism is often applied to nations in Africa and Asia, the same sort of approach may also be applied to

Western nations such as the United States, Australia and Canada as former British colonies, yet which also have exerted their own 'colonization' of indigenous peoples (e.g. see Banerjee 2000; 2003; Banerjee and Linstead 2001; Neu 2003). There is, however, as Whitlock observes, 'active hostility to the inclusion of Australian, Canadian, South African and New Zealand colonial settlements in the framework of the post-colonial' (2000: 41). This causes theoretical thinking about European settlers to remain underdeveloped and unfashionable in postcolonial criticism. Such texts are seen as politically contested, whereby representing or giving a voice to them invokes the uncomfortable reminder of giving credence to ancestral forces of colonial oppression and dispossession. At the same time, we see no reason that postcolonial analyses should be restricted to only the less economically advanced former colonies. While macro-level theories of phenomena usefully delineate those global structural forces at play, there is a need to investigate 'postcoloniality as a variegated historical situation that is embedded in specific locations' (Prasad 2003: 28).

In addition to a theoretical interest in the effects of colonialism, postcolonialism also contains an oppositional or interventionist movement against oppressive economic, political and social forces. Said effectively articulates the tension between theoretical discussion and political engagement when he reflects that:

> We belong to the period both of colonialism and of resistance to it; yet we also belong to a period of surpassing theoretical elaboration, of the universalising techniques of deconstruction, structuralism, and Lukacsian and Althusserian Marxism. My home-made resolution of the antithesis between involvement and theory has been a broad perspective from which one could view both culture and imperialism and from which the large historical dialectic between one and the other might be observed. (1993: 234)

The work of Edward Said is especially important in postcolonialism because it is one of the first major statements of what the Enlightenment looked like from outside of its project, from the perspective of those others that it constituted as beyond reason, as wild and barbarous rather than calm and enlightened. It represents a re-return of the noble savage, bearing learning rather than arms, but using this learning to disarm the certainties, orthodoxies and knowledges of the West. Said was a humanist critic of the great tradition of the Western Enlightenment, speaking from the vantage point of being other and in some ways outside that which it constituted, while, paradoxically, doing so through the mastery of all of its tools. He argued that in understanding the Enlightenment we have to see how the bringers of liberty, equality and fraternity in the West were avid purveyors of subjugation, domination and enslavement elsewhere in the world.

Central to postcolonial theory is an interest in the impact of postcolonialism on local cultures and identities. But it is not solely focused on the local. Bhabha (1994), for example, discussed the politics and spaces of dislocation that affect both the colonizer and the colonized. Within this critique, both identities are based upon a type of psychoanalytical ambivalence or 'hybridity'. The postmodernistic mixing of 'self' and 'other' is located at the heart of postcolonial culture. This perspective is of relevance here as there is a complex and dynamic overlap between externally generated, constraining structural forces and local indigenous experiences.

One area in which a significant amount of work has been done is in connecting postcolonial ideas to discussions of globalization (e.g. Banerjee and Linstead 2001; Gopal et al. 2003). The central thrust of this work is that one must not critique processes such as globalization merely in terms of their purported advantages and disadvantages. Rather, it is necessary to understand the historical elements that have shaped and molded these processes. Therefore globalization, as an inherently Western discourse of capitalism and industrial progress, involves tensions between the global and the local. The embracing of this notion and the associated processes that have infiltrated managerialist discourse and practice, such as multiculturalism, merely extends and facilitates the promotion and adoption of the dominant occidental ideology (Banerjee and Linstead 2001). Thus the arguments for what would appear to be altruistic and well-intentioned systems of inclusion merely camouflage neocolonial processes of organizational and managerialist assimilation. This may be particularly witnessed in the multinational corporation that adopts methods of human resource best practice in an attempt to 'manage diversity'.

One of the most interesting applications of these ideas is in rethinking the role of multinational corporations in postcolonialism. Parallels can be drawn between the power of the multinational corporation and the hegemonic power of Western nations manifested in their ability to assert control over other nations. It can be argued that a subtle component of hegemonic power is when acquiescence is achieved through the socialization of local leaders and elites. Therefore, 'hegemonic control emerges when local elites buy into the hegemon's vision of international order and accept it as their own – that is, when they internalise the norms and value orientations espoused by the hegemon and accept its normative claims' (Ikenberry and Kupchan 1990: 285). This process occurs due to the desire for modernity and improved economic development. The Western model of modernity is thereby embraced, despite obvious differing historical legacies and operational variations in resources and indigenous culture.

For instance, Vaara et al. (2005) examine the way in which postcolonial relationships are recreated through language, whereby enforcing the specific language policies of the colonizer in multinational corporations tends to create organizational hierarchies along the colonizer–colonized axis. Local distinctiveness is legitimate where this is not in conflict or inconsistent with the homogenizing principles of (rational) business decision making. This is where the role of the indigenous manager is particularly beneficial for the corporate entity as they legitimize globalizing forces through glocalization strategy as a representation of, and intermediary for, local management methods and interests. In closing, it is worth noting that postcolonialism poses a conundrum when thinking about CMS as a field. Given the attention paid to other alternative sociological perspectives such as postmodernism and poststructuralism, postcolonial theory has received little attention (Prasad 2003: 28–9), perhaps because CMS is itself largely a project of white academics in UK and other First World universities, with little interest in or knowledge of non-Western societies. The ideas potentially open up exploration of a range of issues of central concern for organization and management theory. We therefore believe that postcolonialism is an area of particular opportunity for further work in CMS.

Conclusion

Our goal in this chapter was to provide a broad introduction to CMS and to link it to power in organizations.[7] The explicit focus on power in CMS makes it one of the central traditions from which to understand the dynamics of power in and around organizations. The attempt to move beyond a focus on efficiency and the assumption of 'value-free' methods of enquiry allows scholars in this tradition to consider questions of conflict of interest, power, and the distribution of privilege in a way that eludes mainstream researchers. CMS provides a unique perspective from which to consider many of the pressing questions that society is asking regarding corporate governance, the environment, globalization, and other central questions that are created by the increasing dominance of the corporation and the market (e.g. Hancock and Tyler 2004).

At the same time, providing a comprehensive introduction to CMS is a challenge given the highly fragmented nature of critical approaches to the study of organizations. We have distinguished two broad streams that are separated theoretically and geographically (although there are, of course, many overlaps).[8] On the one hand, we have the more theoretically cohesive stream of CMS that has developed largely in Europe, which draws on themes of the Frankfurt School, such as emancipation and political practice, but transferred to a management context. The stream, though small, is increasing in institutional importance in UK management schools, making a clear and lasting contribution to more mainstream approaches to management research, that connect with some theoretical currents reviewed in the previous chapter. Indeed, this institutionalization may well blur its distinct boundedness as an alternative discourse; although, equally, it may drive some members to more quixotic flights of fancy remote from the mainstream (Jones and O'Doherty 2005).

The second stream of literature is larger but lacks the institutional embeddedness of European CMS. The North American stream of literature is bound together by an underlying view of the world as riven by conflict and struggle but by very little else. But despite the many different perspectives that have been adopted to study the various conflicts that have been identified (e.g. man versus woman, humankind versus the environment, management versus labor, etc.), researchers in this tradition increasingly share a common identity and an increasingly dense professional network including participation in prestigious conferences and the founding of dedicated journals. However, somewhat surprisingly, in an age when criticism of modern management and organizations has become a lucrative industry, in the films of Michael Moore (1989) and the books of Naomi Klein (2001), George Monbiot (2000), and John Pilger (1999), none of the CMS contributions has had much public exposure or wider discussion. Given that the objective of changing management practices would require some currents of popular support, the lack of a broader audience and the failure to develop one may well be the fatal distraction that leads to a gentle decline of the area into academic obscurity.

At the same time, both streams of literature share an avowed interest in creating social change. While they may not agree on the problem or the solution, there is a complete consensus that the status quo needs to be changed. But this raises an important question. Why has Critical Theory had so little impact in terms of the mainstream management literature and, even more, in terms of management practice? One part of the answer may lie in the conceptual frameworks used in critical management. As Agger suggests, the theoretical sources upon which critical management scholars draw result in work that has less impact 'because they are incredibly, extravagantly convoluted – to the point of disastrous absurdity one would think' (1991: 106). In other words, the inaccessibility of the theoretical perspectives in CMS, combined with the incommensurability of CMS and more traditional streams of research results, have led to an almost complete disconnection between CMS and mainstream management research.

When considering the relation of CMS to management practices, the underlying conflict perspective has had a rather unfortunate effect: the managers whom the critical management researchers would like to affect are generally seen as the problem. One consequence has been that critical management theory has little to say to managers and management practice beyond making value judgments about the legitimacy of management and management actions – which most managers would find challenging. At the same time, there is no clear audience in whose interest CMS speaks, leaving critical management scholars without an audience in the world of practice.

But this is not the only reason why CMS has had so little effect. There is also the real problem of internal contradiction and incommensurable theoretical approaches that dog any real accretion of knowledge. When it drew on Marxist roots, CMS shared a position on the nature of knowledge as ideology as well as on the central and general importance of critique, but this stream of research had little or no impact on theory or practice. Most managers and management students do not see the value in a critique that seems to leave them no room for improvement, other than the embrace of ideas discredited by their association with failed states and political movements. It may also be thought, given the discrediting of Marxism and misconstrual of postmodernism, that CMS is sufficiently incoherent, that little possibility of academic influence or political engagement exists, such that there is only a limited possibility to make much contribution in this context. However, the potential of CMS to contribute to broader discussions in organization and management theory is significant. Many of the problems – such as the realization that gender relations are power relations – with which critical management scholars grapple are of tremendous societal and organizational significance. At the same time, critical management as a field must develop better ways to connect to mainstream conversations and to make their work accessible and practical.

In terms of power and organizations there are huge opportunities to take understandings of power in organizations forward through this work. The underlying conflict perspective provides a fascinating counterbalance to the conflict-free world of mainstream management theory. Rather than a world where conflict is a sign of failure by managers to control and coopt, the world becomes a place characterized by irresolvable conflict that can only be recognized and managed. The interests of management become just one interest to be studied and the dynamics of power and politics that characterize organizational life inside and outside the organization take center stage. While CMS has so far failed to find much traction in the world of management theory and practice, there is every reason to believe that there is real potential for this to change in the near future.

Notes

1   We will follow the common convention of capitalizing the term to make it clear that it refers to the Frankfurt School tradition of German scholarship.

2   The Academy of Management is the largest conference in management, attended by approximately 5,000 academics each year. Although it is *de jure* the American Academy of Management it is increasingly *de facto* a global academy; thus, there are increasing numbers of international members. (There is an International Federation of Scholarly Associations of Management that meets in a different place every four years but not many Americans go to it.) The Academy is divided into a number of divisions based around member interests such as innovation, organization and management theory, and international management. In order to found a new division, a group of interested members begin by founding an interest group and proceeding to sign up members. If they are able to sign up enough members, then the interest group can seek to become a full fledged division. Interestingly, CMS has the largest proportion of non-Americans amongst its members, and thus it would seem empirically safe to say that it is the most globally representative and aligned in its interests.

3   As late as 1990, in an ancient university in an old European nation, one of the present authors heard one of several professors of history proclaim, in the context of a general critique of the social sciences after a management department had been established in the institution, that 'after management', 'Whatever would be next? Plumbing? Hairdressing?' It seemed to go down quite well with the crustier fellows of the university body in which it was spoken, which is to say almost everyone: they knew the thin end of a wedge when they saw one. Later, perhaps, they would come to recognize a gift horse, but the author in question cannot be sure as he did not stick around to find out. Their subsequent prolific growth of professors would seem to suggest some source of cash flow, although they may have found a 'magic pudding'.

4   Most of which was actually written in Australia but with a keen interest for UK events.

5   See McCarthy (1989) for an excellent overview of Habermas's work.

6   There has been an extended debate concerning the use of the prefix 'post' in postcolonialism, with the 'post' in postcolonial being debated almost as much as the 'post' in postmodern (Appiah1 1991). This is due to its association with something that has passed, such that some may surmise that colonialism is designated in the past rather than being regarded as an omnipresent force within the auspices of neocolonialism. We argue that it is useful to explore theoretical assertions of the postcolonial, which can be used to refer to the period following colonialism in both an ideological and a temporal sense and, when viewed solely as a descriptive label, has been used by some scholars since 1990 in preference to the term *Third World* (e.g. Goldthorpe 1996). This temporal feature is useful in as much as it highlights the importance of an appreciation of the historical moments which mark processes of decolonization.

7   The chapter should be read closely with Chapters 8 and 10, in which some related matters are discussed in more detail, as well as in conjunction with Chapter 13, where some of the issues of postcolonialism are taken up with more specificity.

8   The restrictions of space in a book which adopts a broad focus, such as this one does, entail economies that one regrets. The coverage of Europe has been highly selective, focusing principally on the UK contributions. We are aware of many significant contributions made by Scandinavian colleagues, such as Barbara Czarniawska and Guje Sevon's excellent (2003) collection *The Northern Lights: organization theory in Scandinavia*, as well as colleagues from elsewhere. For the same reasons we did not retread the ground covered by scholars such as Wilson (2003), Linstead et al. (2004), and Thompson and McHugh (2002), and the many labor process volumes such as Jermier et al. (1995). Neither have we focused overmuch on the distinct antipodean contributions to the genre, in part because these have been addressed elsewhere (Clegg et al. 2000).

 **10** Discursive Theories of
Organizational Power

Chapter outline

In this chapter we will:

- Introduce discourse analysis as an important approach to the study of power in organizations.
- Explain how the linguistic turn in philosophy led to the development of linguistically oriented approaches to the study of social phenomena.
- Discuss the development of discourse analysis as a method and a methodology.
- Present critical discourse analysis (CDA) as the foundation of a discursive analytic for the study of organizational power.
- Explore how organizational scholars have drawn on discourse analysis broadly, and CDA specifically, to develop organizational discourse as an area of study.
- Analyze the role that research on deconstruction and translation can play in informing analysis of negative and positive power, respectively.

Introduction

The linguistic turn in philosophy, and its subsequent reverberations throughout social science, produced a new way to view and study the social world. According to its proponents, language should be seen no longer as a passive reflector of reality that is at its best when seen least, but rather as the key to understanding social phenomena. Following this linguistic turn, language is seen as playing an active and indispensable role in the constitution of the social world and the idea of reality as a social construction appears on the scene. Alvesson and Kärreman succinctly put it that from this perspective 'societies, social institutions, identities, and even cultures may be viewed as discursively constructed ensembles of texts' (2000: 136). Language becomes the core concern of social research, and linguistic methods of research its primary tools, as the social world is understood as fundamentally linguistic.

Body, soul, mind ... and language

In earlier chapters we have seen the gradual expansion of the subject of power from the person conceived as a body, with a soul, to one with a mind. In discourse analyses we see the mind reconceptualized in terms of a speaking, writing, spoken and written subject that discourses through public language. The breakthrough conceptualization was most evidently that of Wittgenstein's *Philosophical investigations*, with its notion of meaning being embedded in 'language games'. Over several decades this view moved across the social sciences leading to new methods of systemically examining the social, including social semiotics (e.g. Hodge and Kress 1988), critical hermeneutics (e.g. Phillips and Brown 1993), narrative analysis (e.g. Czarniawska 1998), conversation analysis (e.g. Psathas 1995), ethnomethodology (e.g. Garfinkel 1967; Gephart 1978), and discourse analysis (e.g. Fairclough 1992; Phillips and Hardy 2002). All of these approaches share an interest in meaningful social action and its role in the construction of social reality; they differ in their level of analysis, the object of study upon which they focus, and their varied approaches to power. Combined, they extend the boundaries of social studies in a number of important directions to include a broad appreciation of the role of language in the production of social phenomena.

While this repositioning of language as the centerpoint of the study of the social world drove the development of this family of new approaches, the result was anything but a cohesive stream of research. Instead, what resulted was more like water spreading across a broad delta, with many small and intertwined rivulets that touched here and there only to separate again as researchers explored the many and complex ramifications of the linguistic turn. Our focus here will be primarily on one of the broader streams of this work, discourse analysis. We will, however, occasionally stray into other related approaches as we explore this complex topic.

Our specific focus on discourse analysis as an appropriate topic for a chapter in this volume grows out of the fact that other interpretive approaches have often failed to grapple directly with questions of power. Many of the methodologies that have arisen from the linguistic turn take for granted the power dynamics that frame the social world that they are seeking to explain, and work to explain the nature and constitution of social action and structure without any real interest in the dynamics of power that underlie their social construction. While this work has, in many cases, been highly insightful, it has little to say about the questions of power and organizations that concern us in this volume and we will not deal with them here. Furthermore, looking forward, we believe discourse analysis is the area with the clearest potential for further development in studying organizations, making it all the more appropriate as a focus of interest here.

While the development of a discursive approach took some time to appear in the quiet cul-de-sac of organization studies, it has slowly taken hold as a significant approach to understanding organizational phenomena. It is not without its detractors, as we will see, but it is an area of increasing significance which has culminated in the publication of a handbook on the topic of organizational discourse whose editors argue that organizational discourse is now an established approach to organization studies: 'Discourse analytic approaches therefore allow the researcher to identify and analyze the key organizational discourses by which ideas are formulated and articulated and to show how, via a variety of discursive interactions and practices, they go on to shape and influence the attitudes and behaviour of an organization's members' (Grant et al. 2004: 25). In other words, the editors argue for the delineation of a field of study focusing specifically on the discursive foundations of organizational phenomena. One of our tasks here, then, is to examine this proposition and see if, in fact, organizational discourse has become as established as the existence of this handbook suggests.

Accepting the existence of organizational discourse as an established area of study does little to solve the obvious problem of theoretical fragmentation. Within discourse analysis there remain broad divergences in approach and foundational assumptions that make much of the work incommensurable (see Putnam and Fairhust (2001) and Kaiser and Muller (2003) for two accounts of this diversity). Our challenge here, then, will be to draw together these disparate strands and show the common threads that bind together what is often seen as a bewildering array of work only connected by the term 'discourse analysis'!

In this chapter, we will examine the contours of discourse analysis as an approach to the study of power in organizations. As we mentioned, our task is complicated by the diversity of approaches and the more or less obvious ways in which power appears in this growing body of work. We will begin by examining the roots of discourse analysis in the work of linguistic philosophers such as Wittgenstein and Winch. Building on this foundation, we will then move on to trace the history of discourse analysis, focusing on the work of Foucault and Fairclough and their explicit interest in power. We will then focus more closely on the development of organizational discursive analysis driven by an explicit interest in the dynamics of power in organizations; in other words, we will present a discourse analytic for the study of power in organizations drawing on the growing literature in the area.

Wittgenstein and the linguistic turn

The roots of the linguistic turn lie in a stream of work in philosophy concerned with the nature of meaning and experience. The linguistic turn describes a particular philosophical understanding that proposes 'a particular relation of language to social/historical embedded "seeings" of the world and every person's situated existence' (Deetz 2003: 421). One important group of philosophers that contributed to the linguistic turn includes German phenomenologists such as Heidegger (1977), Husserl (1962) and Gadamer (1989). Their work explored the question of what it means for something to exist as well as the nature of our phenomenological experience of reality.

In addition, linguistic philosophers such as Wittgenstein (1967), as well as Winch's influential (1958) commentary on Wittgenstein, contributed to the ongoing development of this approach through their specific focus on the nature of language and meaning. Their work highlighted the central role of language in the construction of social reality by attacking correspondence theories of language that argued for a one-to-one relationship between language and the world. They argued that language was not a mirror of reality but something much more important. The result of all of their work, put simply, was a well-developed perspective that argues that language and, more broadly, meaningful action are much more than a simple reflection of reality; they are, in fact, *constitutive* of social reality.

The new view of the relation between the constituting practices of social groups and the reality that they constitute has several important ramifications. First, the relation between reality, as it is constituted, and the process of its constitution, is not fixed. Different practices will result in the constitution of different realities as reality lends itself to many, but not all, constitutions. Reality as it is constituted depends on the sedimentation of practices and language that has developed up to that point. Second, the nature of the social reality that is constituted is situated historically and socially. It is the result of historical events and the acts of various actors. As such, it will change over time and from social group to social group. Third, the nature of social reality as it is constituted assumes a matter-of-fact or taken-for-granted nature. The sedimentation of practices that leads to a particular constitution of reality loses the uncertainty and conflict that characterized their development and what remains takes on the character of simple truth. The way things are now is understood to be the way they always were, minus certain errors, which have now been cleared up. Naturalness is necessary for social life to proceed (Schutz 1967), but it effectively hides the processes of social construction that underlie everyday social reality.

The effect of this view can be seen across the social sciences. For example, one of the most influential books in twentieth-century sociology – Berger and Luckmann's (1967) *The social construction of reality* – emerges directly from this perspective. Berger and Luckmann outline the process by which social reality comes to be constituted through ongoing processes of interaction among societal members. Similarly, in anthropology, Geertz builds directly on this view to produce a semiotic view of culture where humankind is seen as 'an animal suspended in webs of significance that he himself has spun' (1973: 5). The constructivist view reaches something of a peak in the work of Gergen, who argues not only for a very strong form of constructionism, but for one that 'invite[s] us into new spaces of under-standing from which a more promising world can emerge' (1999: vi). The linguistic turn leads not only to a politically sensitive view of the construction of the social but also to one that is actively engaged in changing the nature of social reality.

From a researcher's point of view, the recognition of the constructive role of language problematizes the very nature of research as the objectivity, neutrality and independence of the researcher are called into question, as the nature of what passes for truth and knowledge is scrutinized, and as the question of how things work is replaced by questions about what things *mean* (Winch 1958). Today, the social sciences are no longer only about counting, a relatively recent and histori-cally aberrant view of their project in which defining and measuring variables and the relationships between them were seen as paramount; they also concern what, historically, they were always concerned with, namely interpreting what social rela-tionships signify, to which a long history of qualitative research bears witness. With the linguistic turn, however, the demands of interpretive research are multiplied. As researchers we are no longer simply interested in what the social world means to the subjects who populate it; we are interested in how and why the social world comes to have the meanings that it does.

The role of power, from this perspective, is twofold. First, the powerful are able to intervene in this ongoing process in an attempt to change understandings and, if successful, to change the very nature of social reality. This aspect of power and discourse is closely linked to ideas of ideology and Gramsci's (1971) notion of hegemony, as discussed in Chapter 7. The degree to which the construction of hegemony is possible, however, remains an empirical question, as the powerful are equally affected by the naturalized discourses into which they are born. Second, the discourse and practices that constitute social reality are also implicated in the distribution of power. To the extent that meanings become fixed or reified in certain forms, which then articulate particular practices, agents and relations, this fixity is power. Power is the apparent order of taken-for-granted categories of existence, as they are fixed and represented in a myriad of discursive forms and practices (Clegg 1989: 183).

Different discourses constitute different realities that privilege different actors as they pursue their interests such that 'the distribution of power among actors, the forms of power on which actors can draw, and the types of actor that may exercise power in a given situation are constituted by discourse' (Hardy and Phillips 2004: 299). While this aspect of social construction involves analysis of changing interests and complex interactions of different aspects of social reality, which result in difficult to analyze dynamics regarding who is helped and who is hindered in what situations, it is absolutely necessary (Clegg 1989).

Unraveling the complex dynamic between discourse and power is therefore one of the central challenges of discourse analysis. The mutually constitutive relation between power and discourse is exactly the relation we will explore in the remainder of this chapter. The secret to understanding this relationship is, of course, to understand the role of time. While discourse shapes power relations at a moment in time, over time the actions of differentially powerful agents accrete and modify discourses. This dialectical relationship is crucial to understanding not just power and discourse but structure and discourse more generally. It is this complex theoretical frame that we will explore in the next section, where we analyze the ways in which the development of discourse analysis in organization studies was foreshadowed by the development of an interest in the constructive effects of discourse in sociology. Understanding organizational discourse therefore begins with an understanding of discourse analysis in sociology more broadly. While there are many different approaches to discourse analysis in sociology, due to our interest in power we will focus on the most central works that include an explicit interest in the topic. Our focus will therefore be limited to three related streams of research. These link language games to power; draw on Foucaldian discourse analysis; and develop critical discourse analysis.

The sociological roots of organizational discourse

Language games and power

Wittgenstein's analysis of language games in his scattered texts, notably the *Philosophical investigations* (1972[1953]), was thin. Central and key concepts for thinking about language were introduced, including the notions of 'form of life' and 'language game', but were analytically underdeveloped. That this should be the case was hardly surprising given that many of the texts come from notes that his students took in his lectures, and were only constituted as books subsequent to his death in 1951. It was part of what made them so useful; that they were underdeveloped provided ample room for subsequent theorists to be creative (see, for instance, Pitkin 1972).

From the point of view of organization studies and the analysis of power, the most significant use of these key concepts remains the early work of Clegg (1975). Clegg, taking his cue from ethnomethodology but not using its conversation analysis approach, realized that the world of organizations is rich in discourse; whatever else managers may do, a large part of their work consists of the interpretation of key texts and the articulation and rationalization of different accounts of these. The research he conducted took as its empirical material audio tape recordings of naturally occurring conversations that were largely, but not entirely, framed by project meetings held on a construction site. In addition some of the data took the form of recordings of more consciously contrived interrogative interviews that he conducted.

Power came into the analysis in a way that blended Wittgenstein (1972[1953]) with Garfinkel (1967). One of the key concepts of the latter was the notion of 'indexicality', a term that originated from linguistics, where an indexical term would be defined as one that could only be understood in context. Classically indexical terms would be 'it' and 'this'. For instance, in the following sentence one cannot know what either mean without an appropriate context being supplied: 'It is this, then.' It could be an interrogative or a factual statement referring to the relation of two terms, but without a context being provided then the meaning of the terms is utterly inscrutable. One could as easily imagine the sentence to be one spoken by an explorer, a lover, or a politician, or, indeed, almost any identity.

What relates indexicality to power is context. In the context of construction sites the contract and its associated documents are the central framework shaping managerial discourse. The contract in question in Clegg's (1975) research was of the kind that is referred to in the construction industry as a hard money contract, where the construction being undertaken was bid for on the basis of the specifications in the contract, for a definite price, and where the most competitive tender won the contract. What this does is to set up a constitutive framework in which the *meaning* of the contract plays an essential role. Despite recommendations in the procedural handbooks of the industry, the contracts are never unindexical: they cannot be read simply as a precise and unequivocal set of instructions for building a building. There are at least two reasons for this, argued Clegg (1975). Both are questions of context – one immanently material to the conditions in which the specific contract is enacted and the other transcendentally constitutive of all contracts.

The immanent reasons are simple. Contractual specifications, typically, are large and complex bodies of documentation. Not only are there the documents on which the work is bid but there is also an associated 'bill of works' comprising detailed consultants' reports and associated documents. In an ideal world these would exist in an absolute and seamless correspondence of all detail from one document to another such that no document ever contradicted another or was in conflict with it. Given the vast amount of paper – comprising detailed specifications, reports, and projections – associated with relatively complex construction projects, that there actually is such correspondence is a large assumption to make. Many hands, at many times, with many distinct skills, produce the papers. More often than not there will be points of ambiguity or even disagreement between them. The precise meaning of them is not stipulated in the documents themselves. In Wittgenstein's terms (1972[1953]) there is no meta-rule that provides the rules for how the meaning embedded in the documents should be interpreted. It is this that provides the immanent grounds for indexicality and substantial opportunity for extensive language games to be conducted between project managers and other significant actors on construction sites, such as consultant engineers, architects, and other managers and employees, in which the precise meaning of what is often imprecise documentation is translated into contested action.

A distinction between the 'surface' and the 'deep' structure is central to Wittgenstein's thought. The classic case of the difference between surface and deep structure is one that Wittgenstein uses on several occasions and it involves the relation between any given instances of speech and the idea of grammar. Speech is on the surface; it is what one hears or reads in a written form. Underlying it, however, are the rules of grammar. Unless speech is making no sense, because it is almost random in its utterances, the sense that is made must be one that occurs because there is a shared sense of grammar informing both speaker and hearer. Sharing does not necessarily mean agreement. One may understand only too well what the other is saying while disagreeing strongly with it. But the matter of agreement or disagreement is predicated on the fact that the rules that underlie the speech as sensible speech are shared. These rules comprise the deep structure of speech. They are such that any competent speaker/hearer/reader recognizes that they are in play and is thus able to make sense, but that does not mean that any such person could provide an adequate account of them. Formulating the rules is inordinately complex and something that only a skilled linguist is able to do properly. To do it laboriously as one spoke or made sense would be absolutely inimical to sensemaking. It is this insight that underlies the whole of structural linguistics.

Wittgenstein thought of the deep structure in terms of grammar. Clegg argued that the texts that he recovered through audiotaping from the construction site had a social grammar underlying them, one that was embedded in their 'form of life', another Wittgensteinian concept. On some occasions of use the concept seems to mean no more than a mode of life; on other occasions the meaning is more inscrutable, possibly even genetically constitutive. It is with this concept that we begin to understand why the action should be contested, by reference to a transcendental framework.

Quite what Wittgenstein meant by form of life is not entirely clear. Clegg regarded the form of life as transcendentally constitutive and with this move brought together the surface structure and the deep structure. On the surface was what people said; underlying this was a deep structure of rules in the use of which people were more or less skilled game players, using a social grammar as a generative device for making sense of what it was that was being said and what it was that could – and should – be said. Skill is the crucial issue in this regard, and the skills were basically a mastery of rhetoric, of being able to make something out of the opportunities presented by the contractual documents. Deeper still was a transcendental frame, the form of life, that made what was constituted by the grammar, the deep structure, sensible and rational, by stipulating the need for the organization to be as profitable an enterprise as it could be.

The action played out in specific arenas. Project meetings were the main arena. These meetings were held to discuss issues. Sometimes they had fairly formal agendas, other times they were impromptu. Many of these were taped over a three-month period of intensive fieldwork. The issues invariably related some actions, or absence of actions, to the contractual documents contained in the bill of works. Thus, much of what was said in these meetings was said in relation to some putative but contested state of affairs in terms of the alignment of that state of affairs with the state that should have pertained in terms of the contractual specifications. The gap between these states was the matter at issue. Hence, the discourses involved attributions of responsibility for variance. What got to be said was spoken from different positions of material interest in the contract. For the head contractor the main issue was to find indexical particulars in the contract that could be exploited in order to win some contribution to the profitability of the site through processing variation orders for which additional payments could be demanded. The architect and client team sought to see that what they thought they had designed and were paying for was actually constructed for the price contracted. That is the point of a hard money contract: it is supposed to provide for a 'what you contracted for is what you get at the price agreed' outcome – at least in theory. In practice industry people know that skilled and shrewd project managers will find ways of creating significant and costly variance.

It can be seen that the rules underlying the surface production of text were quite clear; the project manager and his team sought systematically to exploit any indexicality in the contract in order to maximize profitability, while the architect and the client team sought to resist this at every turn. In turn, that these were the rules of the game only made sense in terms of a form of life of capitalism, in which the creation of profit was the fundamental aim.

To make it more concrete, the matter under discussion in a project meeting might be something apparently simple such as the meaning of clay. But while the meaning of clay may appear simple it soon becomes apparent that, from a perspective that sees the talk as exhibiting a surface structure, a deep structure, and a form of life, in fact the meaning is, precisely, a matter of power. The actually recorded material – what people said in situated action – provides the surface structure of the text. The contested matter was the depth of clay that should have been excavated to prepare the site for foundation pillars that were to be constructed out of poured concrete. The issue was simple. The consultant engineer's drawings instructed excavation to a minimum of 600 mm into 'sandy, stony clay'. They did not specify the depth at which such clay could be found. Accompanying the drawings were a series of reports from drilled test bore holes done as a site survey of the ground that had to be built on. These recommended excavation to a depth of two meters into clay. The project manager argued that there were different qualities of clay across the site, running at variable depths. There was 'puddle clay' and 'sandy, stony clay'. He defined 'normal clay' as 'sandy, stony clay'. The resulting depth of the excavations done became the subject of an acrimonious letter from the client's architect to the construction company. The points at issue resulted from investigation of

Table 10.1   Power, rule and domination: three dimensions of power

Concept	Level of analysis	Structural level	Ethnographic questions	Primacy of analytic focus	Focus
Power	Situated actions as empirical texts	Surface structure	Who wins?	Episodic action	Immanent relations
Rules	Constitutive rules	Deep structure	What are the rules?	Enacted mediation	Rhetorical skills
Domination	The aim of the game	Form of life	Why are these the rules?	Structurational framing	Transcendent taken-for-grantedness

the claimed excavation levels, which, as the letter put it, revealed little or no consistency. The counterclaim from the project manager was that the normal clay substrata varied in level across the site: hence the need for additional – and unauthorized – excavation. It was a complicated dispute, reported verbatim in Clegg (1975: Appendices 2 and 4) and commented on extensively in the text.

The analytical importance of the case is that it demonstrates that in everyday organizational life language games can be inherently political. First, the contestation that occurs – the discourse of the site meetings – is not random. Second, contestation is patterned by the skillful use of the underlying rules for constituting issues – searching for indexicality in the meaning of the documents – by the participants in the arena. These comprise a mode of rationality – a way of acting that is, within the situated action contest, rational. Third, this patterning only makes sense where the ultimate aim is the maximization of profit. We can represent the analysis as in Table 10.1.

There are many other analyses of language games in *Power, rule and domination* (Clegg 1975) that apply the same model (which is later developed in Clegg 1979). The importance of the analysis is in showing how discourse can be looked at in terms of power relations that are focused neither merely on the hierarchical structuring of the organization nor on discourse as merely a set of floating signifiers. Signification is an essentially political – and profitable – business, as the text demonstrates. And fixing signification is a key element of power relations.

Foucault and the archeology of knowledge

As we discussed in Chapter 8, the work of Michel Foucault has had an important influence on thinking about power. In perhaps no area has he had more influence than in the development of discourse analysis. In a series of books that include *History of sexuality* (1990), *Discipline and punish* (1977), and *Archeology of knowledge* (1972), Foucault developed a complex and nuanced view of discourse. His ideas focused attention on the importance of discourse in the production of truth, the integral role of power in this process, and the role of discourse in social change (Fairclough 1992).

At the foundation of Foucault's work is an insistence on the complete abandonment of correspondence theories of truth and on the necessity of moving discourse to the center of social analysis. The problem facing social investigation was not one of comprehending the truth behind the vagaries of the available texts but rather one of understanding how what was thought to be true at a moment and among a particular social group came to be thought of as true. The task facing anyone wanting to understand the dynamics of history and social change was one of understanding how things came to be true at a particular time and what other possibilities existed; why what was said was said and what was not said was not said, and the effects that this had on the nature of truth, the patterns of power and privilege, and the complex social structures that were thereby produced. It became an exercise in the archeology of knowledge as the nature of truth was followed back and the manner of its constitution revealed.

In order to understand Foucault's approach it is useful to begin with the concept of discourse. Foucault defines discourses, or discursive formations, as bodies of knowledge that 'systematically form the object of which they speak' (1977: 49). At a fundamental level, discourse produces the social world to which it refers. Discourses retain a wide range of 'socio-historically contingent linguistic, cultural, technical and organizational resources which actively constitute fields of knowledge and the practices they instantiate' (Reed 1998: 195). In other words, discourses do not simply describe the social world; they constitute it by bringing certain phenomena into being through the way in which they categorize and make sense of an otherwise meaningless reality (Parker 1992).

> Each discourse is defined by a set of rules or principles – the rules of formation – that lead to the appearance of particular objects through the categories and identities that make up recognizable social worlds. Discourse lays down the 'conditions of possibility' that determine what can be said, by whom, and when.
>
> [Discourse] governs the way that a topic can be meaningfully talked about and reasoned about. It also influences how ideas are put into practice and used to regulate the conduct of others. Just as a discourse 'rules in' certain ways of talking about a topic, defining an acceptable and intelligible way to talk, write or conduct oneself, so also, by definition, it 'rules out', limits and restricts other ways of talking, of conducting ourselves in relation to the topic or constructing knowledge about it. (Hall 2001: 72)

Discourse 'disciplines' subjects in that actors are known – and know themselves – only within the confines of a particular discursive context and the possibility that that provides (Mumby 2001). Discourse thus influences individuals' experiences and subjectivity, and their ability to think, speak and act, resulting in material effects in the form of practices and interactions, such that 'language defines the possibilities of meaningful existence at the same time as it limits them' (Clegg 1989: 151).

For Foucault, discourse – or at least the knowledge that it instantiates – is inseparable from power. Power is embedded in knowledge and any knowledge system constitutes a system of power, as succinctly summarized in Foucault's conception of 'power/knowledge'. Knowledge, in the form of broad discourses, constitutes the building blocks of social systems in a profound and inescapable way. As Clegg explains, 'the concern is with strategies of discursive power, where strategy appears as an effect of distinctive practices of power/knowledge gaining an ascendant position in the representation of normal subjectivity: forms of surveillance or psychiatry, for instance, which constitute the normal in respect to a penology or a medical knowledge from whose "gaze" and rulings no one can subsequently escape, whether prison or medical officer, or one carcerally or medically confined' (1989: 152). In constructing the available identities, ideas and social objects, the context of power is formed: 'it is in discourse that power and knowledge are joined together' (Foucault 1990: 100).

The discursive conception of power 'is not something that is acquired, seized, or shared, something that one holds on to or allows to slip away; power is exercised from innumerable points, in the interplay of nonegalitarian relations' (1990: 94). In other words, power is not something connected to agents but rather represents a complex web of relations determined by the systems of knowledge constituted in discourse.

> Power is everywhere; not because it embraces everything, but because it comes from everywhere. And 'Power,' insofar as it is permanent, repetitious, inert and self-reproducing, is simply the over-all effect that emerges from all of these mobilities, the concatenation that rests on each of them and seeks in turn to arrest their movements. One needs to be nominalistic, no doubt: power is not an institution, and not a structure; neither is it a certain strength we are endowed with; it is the name that one attributes to a complex strategical situation in a particular society. (1981: 93)

According to this view, power is embedded in a network of discourse that captures advantaged and disadvantaged alike in its web (Deetz 1992). Power is not a resource of a particular agent but a characteristic of discourse. Each situation has its own politics of truth, as the mechanisms that distinguish truth and falsehood and define knowledge vary according to the prevailing discourses (Foucault 1980). In every system of truth there is power and there can be no truth without systems of power to support it.

Foucault also rethought the relation between power and resistance. Just as power and knowledge are inextricably linked, so too are power and resistance. Resistance is never 'in a position of exteriority in relation to power' (Foucault 1990: 95). Therefore, where there is power there will also be resistance and, just as power is a broad and agentless web, resistance forms through a myriad of points distributed across webs of power/knowledge in an irregular, localized fashion. There is no centerpoint for resistance but, at every point where power is constituted through discourse, there is also resistance.

Foucault's perspective emphasizes the fact that an actor is powerful only within a particular discursive context as it is discourse that creates the categories of power within which actors act. It is thus the discursive context, rather than the subjectivity of any individual actor, that influences the nature of political strategy. The political strategies that exist at a point in time depend fundamentally on the structures of power/knowledge with which the actor is embedded. In fact, for Foucault, the notion of agents acting purposefully in some way not determined by the discourse is antithetical. Discourse not only constructs the nature of social reality at a particular point in time, but carries within it the blueprint for the future.

> To the extent that meanings become fixed or reified in certain forms, which then articulate particular practices, agents and relations, this fixity is power. Power is the apparent order of taken-for-granted categories of existence, as they are fixed and represented in a myriad of discursive forms and practices. (Clegg 1989: 183)

No statement occurs accidentally; no statement is unconnected to discourse. The task for the discourse analyst is to ask 'how is it that one particular statement appeared rather than another?' (Foucault 1972: 30). The structures of discursive formations form a cage within which only certain actions are possible and from which the direction of social and discursive change is determined. The nature of the discursive formation in place at any point in time is the source of power (and resistance), the social objects and identities, and the possibilities for speaking and acting, that exist at any point in time. Not only is the nature of the current relations of power determined by discourse, but so too is the future.

Foucault's work has received a significant amount of attention and has had a wide-ranging influence on social science, as we saw in Chapter 8. At the same time, his work has been roundly criticized on at least two generic counts, in addition to the specific substantive criticisms already discussed in Chapter 8. First, his work (and even more the work of those influenced by him) has been criticized for being unnecessarily cryptic and verging on a 'cult of obscurantism' (Clegg 1989: 152). Although part of the explanation of this tendency lies in the fact that his work has been translated from French, it is clear from even a cursory look at any of his books that there is a grain of truth in this criticism. It is an aspect of his work that has had the dual effect of making it of great interest to a particular group of scholars for whom the obscurity was a source of delight while also ensuring, unfortunately, that his work had little impact on mainstream work within organization studies. There clearly remains a significant opportunity for exploring further the relevance of Foucault's work for organization studies.

More importantly, Foucault's work involves a relatively fatalistic view of power (Burman and Parker 1993), which has been criticized for its failure to recognize that power/knowledge discourses are an expression of strategies of control by identifiable actors within a wider historical and institutional context. Critical discourse analysts, in particular, while sharing Foucault's unique theoretical perspective, argue that his work lacks a sufficient sense of agency. This approach makes it difficult to investigate the role of dominant groups in producing systems of advantage and disadvantage in society, let alone to introduce emancipatory interests. The concern with domination and emancipation is particularly clear in critical discourse analysis, to which we will now turn.

Critical discourse analysis

The work of Norman Fairclough (Fairclough 1992; Fairclough and Wodak 1997; Fairclough 2003; 2005) has been deeply influential in the development of a discursive approach to the study of organizations that he has termed critical discourse analysis (CDA). His work combines, in equal measures, a concern with the relation of discourse as social practice and social phenomena such as identity, social relations, and systems of belief and a concern with the relation of discourse as social practice and power. In doing so, he works to develop a perspective that connects close textual analysis with the social context in which the text occurs.

Fairclough's work builds on a broad range of approaches that he argues attend to the linguistic nature of discourse but fail to deal with the social aspects, or provide an adequate attention to the social aspects of discourse, but gloss its textual aspects. Researchers such as Sinclair and Coulthard (1975), Labov and Fanshel (1977) and Potter and Wetherell (1987) are given as examples of the first group. Their work focuses squarely on language but fails, from Fairclough's point of view, to make the connection back to the social world. Their approaches provide important insight into the nature of linguistic practice, but fail to link that back significantly to the social world in which they occur. They are therefore of great interest in understanding the nature of meaningful interaction, but of much less interest in understanding how the social world is produced through this meaningful interaction. A singular focus on the micro-dynamics of language leaves them unable to make a significant contribution to more macro-level social theory.

The primary example of the second tradition, according to Fairclough, is Foucault, to whom he devotes significant attention in his earlier work. In his discussions of Foucault, he explores Foucault's assertions regarding the connection between discourse and social reality (and in particular power). He sees Foucault as having much to say about the connection between broad sweeps of discourse and ideas such as social structure and the dynamics of social systems, but he also perceives a weakness in Foucault's work in that it is unable to make the connection back to instances of language production. While Foucault provides extensive and interesting examples, he is unable to provide a framework for the systematic examination of bodies of texts. His work stays at a very high level of abstraction and, while fascinating, is both impossible to replicate and very difficult to evaluate in terms of methodological rigor.

Fairclough's own approach combines aspects of these two camps to develop what he calls 'a synthesis of socially and linguistically oriented views of discourse, moving towards … a "social theory of discourse"' (1992: 5). At the heart of Fairclough's framework is a highly theorized approach to discourse that allows him to connect more linguistically focused approaches to the broader social context that concerned Foucault.

Fairclough's idea of discourse is based on conceptualizing 'language use as a form of social practice' (1992: 63). Two important ramifications follow. First, it means that discourse, as a form of social action, is constrained in important ways by social structure. What a certain actor can say at a particular time and place is limited by the social structures that exist at that moment. Social structure constrains discourse as a form of social action in just the same way as it constrains any other form of action. As Fairclough describes it, 'discourse is shaped and constrained by social structure in the widest sense and at all levels, by class and other relations at a societal level, by relations specific to particular institutions such as law or education, by systems of classification, by various norms and conventions of both a discursive and non-discursive nature, and so forth' (1992: 64).

At the same time, discourse as social practice is constitutive of the structures that constrain it. Social reality is, fundamentally, dependent on discourse as social action. It is through discourse as social practice that social structure is constituted. Discourse contributes to all of the levels of social structure that act back to constrain it as we described above. In other words, there is a complex and mutually constitutive relation between discourse and social structure.

It is also critical to keep in mind that discourse lies in the curious position of simultaneously stabilizing social relations and also functioning as a source of social change. It is through discourse that much of social structure is reproduced through discursive practices that reaffirm and re-enact social structure. But discourse can just as easily provide an arena for the struggles that lead to social change. Through discourse the social world is held in place and, equally, it is through discourse that it changes. Highlighting this complicated relation between discourse as a practice and the social structures that enable it provides the key to this form of discourse analysis and the point of entry for considerations of the role of discourse in the dynamics of power. Think of the way that George W. Bush used the rhetoric of old cowboy movies to articulate his opposition to Osama bin Laden and those who were alleged to support him: 'Either you're for us or you're against us.' It is a version of what has been referred to as the American Monomyth, in which the plot structure is always built around a superhero and a harmonious society threatened by evil forces (see Carlsen (2005: 47); also Jewett and Lawrence (1988)). It is through such positioning, which attempts to use identities familiar from hundreds of movies celebrating rugged individualism and straight shooting (preferably prior to asking questions and thus with a bias for action), that nodal points can be fixed discursively so that the parameters of power's circuitry are stabilized through flows privileged by elite positioning.

A particular understanding of the connection between text, discourse, and context grows out of this view of discourse and social structure and lies at the heart of Fairclough's approach. His diagrammatic representation of his framework is shown in Figure 10.1. His explanation of the dynamics of his model is as follows:

> It is an attempt to bring together three analytical traditions, each of which is indispensable for discourse analysis. These are the tradition of close textual and linguistic analysis within linguistics, the macrosociological tradition of analysing social practice in relation to social structures, and the interpretivist or microsociological tradition of seeing social practice as something which people actively produce and make sense of on the basis of shared commonsense procedures. (1992: 72)

In other words, the deceptively simple framework shown in Figure 10.1 provides a comprehensive attempt to combine an interest in textual production with an interest in social structures through the addition of the concept of a discourse as both a collection of texts and the social practices through which they were produced, distributed, and interpreted. The relation of discourse and social structure is dialectical and mutually constituting. At the same time discourse is both an object and a practice.

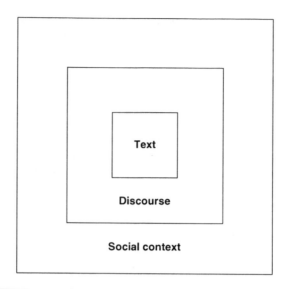

Figure 10.1   Fairclough's three-dimensional conception of discourse

Building on this relationship between text, discourse, and social context, critical discourse analysts commonly argue for the constitution of three categories of social phenomena, as subjects, concepts, and objects. Subject positions are locations in social space from which certain delimited actors can produce certain kinds of texts in certain ways. Different subject positions are associated with different rights to produce new texts (Laclau and Mouffe 1985; Parker 1992). Some individuals, by virtue of their position in the discourse, will warrant a louder voice than others, while others may warrant no voice at all (Potter and Wetherell 1987). Subjects who have the right to produce texts, to engage in discursive practice, are therefore able to engage in the process of shaping concepts, objects, and subject positions (Hardy et al. 2000). For example, the discourse of psychiatry includes the subject position of the psychiatrist who has the right to produce texts, such as medical diagnoses, that determine the sanity of individuals. Collectively, psychiatrists produce texts, such as books, academic papers, radio and TV shows, that shape our understanding of concepts such as the unconscious. The psychiatric discourse also includes the subject position of mental patient, a position with radically fewer rights to engage in the discursive practices that can change or maintain the discourse. In other words, inhabiting certain subject positions affords actors a degree of agency in producing texts that may affect discourse. However, the kinds of texts that can be produced are often highly constrained. Texts that break 'rules' prescribed and made meaningful by prevailing discourses may result in actors losing the legitimate right to take up the subject position.

Discourse also produces sets of concepts – categories, relationships, and theories – through which we understand the world and relate to one another. Concepts make up what Harré (1995) refers to as the expressive sphere: the ideas that constitute our cultural background. From a discourse analysis point of view, concepts are all of the constructions that arise out of structured sets of texts and that exist solely in the realm of ideas. They are more or less contested, and are culturally and historically situated; they are the fundamental ideas that underlie our understandings and relations with one another.

Concepts are historically contingent constructions that arise out of a discourse consisting of the texts produced, disseminated, and interpreted by a set of actors in a social situation. Concepts depend on the ongoing construction of texts for meaning and they may therefore change dramatically over time and from social group to social group. Since the meaning of a concept is dependent on discourse, and since individual understandings of the world depend on these concepts, participation in the discourse is political as discursive acts that succeed in transforming concepts change the world as it is understood. Discursive acts that are intended to redefine concepts are attempts to fashion preferable social relations and depend for their success on the resources available to the actor producing the text.

Finally, when concepts are brought into play to make sense of social relations or physical objects, then the discourse has constituted an object. Objects and concepts are obviously closely related. The primary difference lies in the fact that concepts exist only in the expressive sphere; they exist in the realm of ideas. Objects, on the other hand, are part of the practical order; they are real in the sense of existing in the material world. The concept of a 'river' exists in our minds as competent speakers of English. A particular river, say the River Thames that flows through London, is an object; it is made sensible to us by the concept 'river' and we can write about it using that same concept. But the river itself has a certain existence outside of the discourse that reveals it; it has an ontological reality beyond the discourse. It would continue to exist in a physical sense apart from our experience of it. Our deaths would not entail its disappearance as a material object, although it would necessitate its disappearance as 'river' as there would be no one left to attach that particular concept to it.

The role of discourse in constituting social objects is even more fundamental. The Thames flows without any awareness of the concept of a river. The Thames has no idea it is a river. In social objects, such as organizations, organizational members and others apply the concept of an organization to sets of material practices in a way that not only reveals the social nature of these practices and makes them meaningful (as in the Thames), but is fundamental to their performance. Changing the concept 'river', or convincing us that the Thames is actually a stream, may make us see it differently, but it does not change the nature of the Thames as a thing-in-itself. Changing the concept of an organization held by organizational members fundamentally changes the way the organization is socially accomplished. The thing-in-itself changes as the practical applications of what it is and what it can do change.

Organizations and other social interactions depend on the discursive construction of the underlying concepts and the discursive application of the concepts by members to make sense of their experience. By successfully modifying the discourse that underlies important concepts, and/or important objects, the actual accomplishments of social relationships can be changed. The act of creating and disseminating texts, of engaging in discursive practices, is therefore a highly political act and underlies the most fundamental struggle for power and control in organizations and in society more broadly. Underlying social reality is an intense struggle to determine the nature of constructs and to determine which construct applies in which case. The result is, not surprisingly, an ambiguous and contested set of discursive structures full of contradiction and subject to continuous negotiations as to their meaning and application.

The resulting framework 'provides a means of multi-functional analysis, attending to the interplay between knowledge, social relations and social identity, and a means of historical analysis, allowing the analyst to trace the articulation of texts over time and the constitution of orders of discourse' (Thomas 2003: 782). Even more importantly from our perspective, critical discourse analysis provides an approach to connecting the concern for language and discourse characteristic of the linguistic turn with a concern for power, domination, and ideology. It seeks to

> explore often opaque relationships of causality and determination between (a) discursive practices, events and texts, and (b) wider social and cultural structures, relations and processes; to investigate how such practices, events and texts arise out of and are ideologically shaped by relations of power and struggles over power; and to explore how the opacity of these relationships between discourse and society is itself a factor securing power and hegemony. (Fairclough 1993: 135)

Unsurprisingly, critical discourse analysis and related variants of discourse analysis play a major role in the discursive studies of organization. It is this development to which we will now turn.

Discourse analysis comes to organization studies

Situating discourse analysis

Discourse analysis was prefigured to a great extent by the concerns of ethnomethodology (see especially Zimmerman 1971) but these were barely institutionalized within the canon of organization theory. One significant British author did some early work using a discursive approach (for instance, Silverman 1974, which provides a good review of approaches to that point) but it seemed to be largely overlooked. The late Deidre Boden (1994; Boden and Zimmerman 1991) developed the ethnomethodological direction in her work and that which she edited, some of which we shall discuss below. Subsequently, discourse analysis has proven a useful and increasingly popular theoretical framework for understanding the social production of organizational and inter-organizational phenomena (e.g. Alvesson and Kärreman 2000; Grant et al. 1998; 2004; Hardy and Phillips 1999; Morgan and Sturdy 2000; Mumby and Clair 1997; Phillips and Hardy 1997; 2002). In fact, as Mumby (2004: 237) suggests, it has become a 'veritable cottage industry' with its own specialized conference, special issues in journals, several edited books, and a handbook. It explores how the socially produced ideas and objects that comprise organizations, institutions, and the social world more generally are created and maintained through the relationships among discourse, text and action. Accordingly, it involves not just 'practices of data collection and analysis, but also a set of metatheoretical and theoretical assumptions and a body of research claims and studies' (Wood and Kroger 2000: x) that not only emphasize the importance of linguistic processes, but also understand language as fundamental to the construction of organizational reality (Chia 2000; Gergen 1999; Phillips and Hardy 2002).

Organizational discourse as a field of study

In this section, we will introduce the notion of organizational discourse as a specific area of study and then examine two of the more important areas of investigation that have been initiated using a discourse analytic methodology. Our intention here is not to provide a comprehensive overview of discourse analysis broadly defined (see Mumby and Clair (1997) for a broader view), but to focus on areas of inquiry that fit the narrower view of discourse analysis described above and that have the potential to include a critical consideration of the dynamics of power.

The effect of the linguistic turn in the study of organization has been substantial. The broad range of methods that have been developed to explore the role of language in social interaction in social science more broadly has been reflected, if sometimes with a substantial delay, in organization studies. For example, as we have discussed one of the earliest contributions was by Clegg (1975) who went into the empirical world of a construction site armed with a tape recorder and came back with an analysis of management in practice constituted in power terms. Although he began from ethnomethodological auspices it is clear that he ended up in what would today be called discourse analysis. Gephart (1978) used an ethnomethodological approach to study one of the most political of all organizational events, an organizational succession. The work of Frost (1980) is representative of a stream of work that coalesced around a set of conferences held in Vancouver, BC in the 1970s and 1980s and which was concerned with a range of issues from an interpretive perspective. Clegg (1989), in *Frameworks of power*, considers the contribution of several linguistically oriented approaches, including the work of Foucault, and connects them explicitly to power in organizations. Phillips and Brown (1993) investigated the management of corporate identity using a critical hermeneutic approach.

In one of the most influential works in this tradition, Boden (1994), in her fascinating book on talk in organizations, introduced the notion of 'lamination' as a way of understanding the way in which everyday talk produces macro-structures like organizations. As Oswick and Richards describe it, 'the term "lamination" implies that "parts" (local conversations) (or what Boden also called "minor moves") are brought together, or layered upon each other, to form an unproblematic and relatively coherent "whole" (an organization)' (2004: 108). In describing the everyday micro-interactions that produce organizations through lamination, Boden provided a detailed and nuanced argument for the importance of everyday 'talk' in the production of organizations.

At the same time, it is only somewhat more recently that this broad stream of work has coalesced into something self-consciously referred to as organizational discourse analysis. Organizational discourse analysis, much like Boden's work on lamination, focuses on how discursive production leads to the construction of organizations and all the bits and pieces that make them up. As Boden argues, 'It is through the telephone calls, meetings, planning sessions, sales talks, and corridor conversations that people inform, amuse, update, gossip, review, reassess, reason, instruct, revise, argue, debate, contest, and actually *constitute* the moments, myths and, through time, the very *structuring* of organization' (1994: 8). Where it differs, of course, is in the primary position given to discourse as social practice. Grant and Hardy argue that

> The term 'discourse' has been defined as sets of statements that bring social objects into being (Parker, 1992). In using the term 'organizational discourse', we refer to the structured collections of texts embodied in the practices of talking and writing ... that bring organizationally related objects into being as those texts are produced, disseminated, and consumed ... Consequently, texts can be considered to be a manifestation of discourse and the distinctive unit ... on which the researcher focuses. (2004: 6)

Organizational discourse analysis, then, is the systematic study of the discourses and discursive practices that constitute organizations. It posits the organization as being discursively constituted, and scholars working from this perspective investigate organizational phenomena through the examination of discourse. Discourse is not, of course, directly accessible, but can only be researched through the study of the texts that constitute it. Therefore organizational discourse analysis is about systematically studying sets of texts that are implicated in the production of organizational phenomena. The point is well made by Mumby and Clair when they argue

> that organizations exist only in so far as their members create them through discourse. This is not to claim that organizations are 'nothing but' discourse, but rather that discourse is the principal means by which organization members create a coherent social reality that frames their sense of who they are. (1997: 181)

Organizations are largely produced and made sense of through discourse as a social practice. Furthermore, as we argued above, discourse is both a source of stability and a source of change. The actual role played by discourse in any actual situation is therefore an empirical question. At its extreme, this perspective leads to a view of organizations as a text. From this strong social constructivist position, the organization has no existence, no reality, outside of the discourses that constitute it. The organization is an unstable and constantly shifting achievement held in place by the constant discursive efforts of its members and other outside actors. Westwood and Linstead summarize this position succinctly:

> Organization has no autonomous, stable or structural status outside of the text that constitutes it. The text of organization itself consists of a shifting network of signifiers in dynamic relations of difference. Text does not have an entitive status either; it is a

process, a process in which meanings are emergent, deferred and dispersed ... The notion of structure is illusionary, representing only an ideological practice that pretends to stand in the place of the flux of shifting and seamless textual relationships ... Organization is a structure, but only when structure is recognized to be an effect of language, a tropological achievement. (2001: 4–5)

It is worth pointing out that this extreme position has received significant criticism for what is perceived as its nihilism and its collapse of epistemology into ontology (Fairclough 2005). Opponents have pointed to what they see as the internal contradictions of this strong form of social construction as well as the loss of an appreciation of the ontological reality of organizations and the value of the tension between structure and process. Proponents, on the other hand, argue that understanding discourse as a source both of stability and of pressures for change has the same effect, leaving two distinct camps and no resolution in sight. From our perspective, both camps have real potential in the quest more readily to understand power in organizations.

Setting aside this issue for the moment, one branch of organizational discourse analysis that is of particular interest here is the stream of research that has adopted a critical discourse perspective in the investigation of organizational phenomena (e.g. Orly and Gloclaw 2005; Hardy et al. 2000; Hardy and Phillips 1999; Thomas 2003; Vaara et al. 2004). These researchers have examined a range of organizational phenomena using a critical discourse perspective to highlight the dynamics of power in which the discursive activity is implicated. Given our interest in organizational power, this stream of research is particularly relevant and provides some initial examples of how effective this approach can be in exploring the linguistic nature of organizations combined with an explication of the dynamics of power. At the same time, this stream of research remains underdeveloped. Work from this perspective remains a rarity in a field that is itself marginal. For this perspective to begin to make the sort of contribution that it has the potential to make, much more research needs to be done.

To sum up, organizational discourse is a rapidly growing area of organizational studies with the potential to provide additional insight into our understanding of organizational phenomena. Interestingly, discourse analytic approaches are applicable to any traditional area of study but require a change in focus and method. At the same time, there are deep divisions in organizational discourse reflected particularly in the ongoing argument over the relation between ontology and epistemology in discourse studies. In any case, from the perspective of power in organizations there is great promise in the early application of critical discourse analysis to the study of power in organizations. While this method is being applied to a whole range of different substantive topics, it brings a welcome concern for power and politics to their investigation.

Themes in organizational discourse

In these final subsections, we will discuss some important themes that have been examined from the perspective of organizational discourse. While there are many others that have received attention, these topics have been particularly central to the developing literature and are important topics in their own right. They are also all areas where the research to date has dealt explicitly with power. They therefore act as important examples of the potential contribution of organizational discourse to our understanding of power in organizations.

Gender themes

The connection between gender and discourse broadly defined has been discussed for at least 100 years.[1] However, it wasn't until the 1970s that, stimulated by the new wave of the women's movement, gender and discourse emerged as a recognized field of inquiry (e.g. Cameron 1990; 1992; Kramarae et al. 1983; Roman et al. 1994; Spender 1980; Thorne et al. 1983). Since that time, 'the study of gender and discourse has achieved not only recognition as a full fledged field of inquiry, but one that is growing by leaps and bounds' (West et al. 1997). In the process, gender has become one of the central concerns of discourse analysis and a very significant literature on the topic has developed.

It is, therefore, not surprising that it was not long until the topic of gender and discourse emerged in organization studies. In her comprehensive review of gender, discourse, and organization, Ashcraft (2004) has identified four ways in which the relationship between these domains has been explored.[2] First, this connection has been explored in the literature by treating discourse as an outcome or a reflection of gender identity. By gender identity, Ashcraft refers to 'a socialized or relatively fixed identity or cultural membership, which is organized around biological sex and which fosters fairly predictable communication habits' (2004: 276). The earliest literature in this area focused on variation related to biological sex differences but this gave way to literature more focused on gender and which began to see the differences as the result of processes of socialization. Much of this latter literature focuses on feminine styles of communication and the ramifications of the differences in interaction between men and women (e.g. Tannen 1990; 1994). At an organizational level, this analysis led to a concern with the barriers that these differences create for women (e.g. Wilkins and Andersen 1991) and a parallel concern with women as leaders (e.g. Bass and Avolio 1994). However, this approach has also been the subject of much critique given the substantial variations in speech patterns across genders as well as between them. Furthermore, this perspective fails to really deal with the role of the organization in the complex relation between gender, discourse, and organization.

The second approach conceptualizes discourse as the performance of gender identities. From this perspective, discourse is constitutive of gender identities, but also can act to undermine them. Scholars working from this perspective adopt a performance metaphor (Goffman 1976) and understand actors as performing gender roles in the production of their everyday lives (Weedon 1987). The influence of this conceptual shift – from discourse as reflective of identity to discourse as constitutive of identity – can be seen in the stream of work that considers gender in everyday life as a provisional accomplishment (e.g. Alvesson and Billing 1992;

Butler 1990; Kondo 1990; West and Zimmerman 1987). In an organizational setting, this research focuses on how gender is accomplished within the constraints of the organizational stage. That is, it is concerned with how organizational members 'craft' (Kondo 1990) gendered selves through discursive practices in organizations.

From the third perspective, the discursive constitution of the organization takes center stage. This perspective adopts the radical position that organizations themselves can be gendered. The discursive constitution of organizations results in particular constellations of power and gender relations, constellations that disadvantage women (e.g. Acker and Van Houten 1974; Kanter 1977; Mills and Tancred-Sheriff 1992). From this perspective, the challenge for discourse analysts is to analyze the gendered nature of organizations and to attempt to develop alternative organizational forms that are not characterized by the oppressive aspects of current organizational forms.

Finally, the last approach to discourse, gender, and organizations focuses on broad, societal-level discourses and the role of these discourses in organizational life. These researchers see societal-level discourses as framing the constitution of both organization and gender. From this perspective, then, what is interesting is how organizations and gender are understood, communicated, and constituted at a societal level. Researchers have, to date, focused primarily on popular culture (e.g. Ashcraft and Flores 2003) and on organizational studies itself (e.g. Mills and Tancred-Sheriff 1992) with intriguing, if somewhat limited, results. It is clear that discourse analysis has much more to contribute as this literature develops.

Combined, the literature on discourse, organization, and gender constitutes one of the most developed areas within organizational discourse. While there is still significant work to be done in developing this stream of research, it is clear that discourse analysis provides important insight into the politics of gender that would not be available using more traditional methods. Seeing gender as constituted in discourse allows the politics of gender to be explored and critiqued in a powerful and convincing way.

Identity themes

A second empirical topic where discourse analysis has played a key role is in ongoing discussions of identity. Somewhat surprisingly there is little apparent reference to Goffman's (1961; 1963) path breaking work in this field. Recent examples of the application of discourse analysis to questions of identity range from studies in social identity (e.g. Phillips and Hardy 1997) to studies in occupational identity (e.g. Watson and Bargiela-Chiappina 1998), corporate identity (e.g. Salzer-Mörling 1998), and individual identity (e.g. Holmer-Nadeson 1996).

Identity has become a key concept in organization studies and one where there has been significant change over the last two decades. The effect of the linguistic turn has been felt very strongly as the traditional view of identity as a stable, essential characteristic has been replaced by a conceptualization of identity as fragmented, fluid and ambiguous as well as situated in time and space (e.g. Baak and Prasch 1997). Identity is no longer something that we are born with, or at least forms early in life, but rather a situated accomplishment that depends on time, place and circumstances.

The topic of identity is of central interest to researchers in organization studies due to the dual role of the concept of identity in the study of organizations. On the one hand, identities are linked to organizations in that organizations are one important location for their construction (Antaki and Widdicombe 1998). Individual identities are deeply affected by the work organizations of which the individual is a part (or by the fact that the individual is not part of any work organization and so is 'unemployed'). On the other hand, organizations also have collective identities, the shared beliefs that members have about the enduring and distinctive attributes of their organizations (Albert and Whetten 1985).

At both levels, the connection between identity and organization is a discursive one. At an individual level, individual identity is a product of discourse. It is in discourse that individual identity is constituted. At an organizational level, the discursive approach, 'by situating collective identity in the language in use among members, shifts attention from the intentions and attitudes of individuals to their observable linguistic practices and the effects of those practices on social relationships and action' (Ainsworth and Hardy 2004: 155).

As an example, consider Phillips and Hardy's (1997) study of refugee determination in the UK. Refugee determination is often presented as a quasi-legal process during which the available evidence is examined to 'reveal' whether an individual is a refugee or not. From a discourse analytic perspective, however, Phillips and Hardy (1997) argue that things look very different. Rather than being the focus of a highly rational process that separated 'real' and 'fraudulent' refugees, the identity of a refugee was contested, unstable, and discursively constructed. Furthermore, they found that actors in the refugee system had a stake in these different identities and acted discursively to support them. For example, the government juxtaposed 'political refugees' against the 'economic migrants' that had to be unmasked by their determination procedures. The white-led NGOs that spoke on behalf of refugees defined refugees as needy 'clients' to whom they, as professionals, could dispense services. The refugee-based organizations constructed refugees as fully functioning and equal 'members' of society who were willing and able to organize themselves.

By using discourse analysis to 'unpack' these competing refugee identities, Phillips and Hardy (1997) were able to provide insight into a number of aspects of the refugee determination system. First, in discursively evoking and drawing on particular refugee identities, *organizational* identities were also constructed. The government's role was to protect the public and stop the arrival of illegal refugees. One NGO viewed its mission as dispensing services to needy clients, while another saw itself as providing services but also representing a refugee constituency. A refugee organization saw itself as fighting against these other organizations to empower its members. These identities shaped organizational practice. So, for example, the service provider found it very difficult to engage in meaningful consultation with its 'clients' since its procedures for dealing with refugees were predicated on them being a passive recipient, not equal partners. The second NGO, on the other hand, introduced a series of mechanisms to give voice to its constituency, which were then used by refugees to influence and shape the organization and its policies. The refugee organization simply refused to cooperate with the NGOs, much to their frustration and amazement. The former was small and impoverished, and the larger and better-resourced NGOs could not understand why it did not take advantage of the opportunity to cooperate with them. However, an organizational identity that sees refugees not as silent clients, but as a vocal and capable constituency that is being marginalized, leads to an organization that is not going to collaborate with established agencies, regardless of how their interests might appear to overlap.

Second, in highlighting the discursive struggle around identities, Phillips and Hardy (1997) were also able to provide a better understanding of power. Traditional views of power – as derived from resource dependencies or formal authority – would suggest that the government was the dominant stakeholder and the refugee organization was virtually powerless. However, a discursive view reveals that power can be exercised by creating meaning for social objects and that certain identities are able to have an influence, even organizations that lack traditional power. So, the refugee-based organization, through its construction of an identity as the only legitimate voice for refugees as well as its confrontational relations with NGOs that tried to usurp its role, was able to secure a legitimate voice. It had a profound influence in pushing more established NGOs to change their practices and increase refugee participation. An organization almost devoid of traditional power resources had a significant impact on other organizations through its use of discursive power.

A discursive view of identity therefore provides a very different view of the dynamics of power and identity than a more traditional view. It also provides a useful frame for understanding the connection between individual and organizational identity and the complex processes of mutual constitution that exist between the two. It further provides important insight into the dynamics of power that surround the constitution of identity. Interested actors work hard to ensure that their interests are represented in the outcome of the discursive struggle, carried out through discursive practice as we discussed above.[3]

Deconstruction and translation themes

Following Foucault's (1980) idea of the truth effect, language does not naively mirror or innocently represent the world but actively creates and powerfully shapes it. Hardy et al. (2000) question this view by recognizing that discourse can have important positive effects and consequences in organizational contexts. They demonstrate that talk is far from 'ethereal', less an abstract entity and more a discourse mobilized by agents in order to act as a 'strategic resource' for the realm of management practice.

Discourse enacts and actively creates organizational reality (Hatch 1997: 368). According to Foucault (1972), language and power are bound together through the order of discourse. New discourses that have the power to enact new realities always imply a deferring of power relations (in terms of 'Who speaks?', 'What is an argument?', 'What creates truth effects?'). Often these do find expression through relatively dominant forms, as Clegg (1975) argued was the case in the construction site we encountered earlier. Where the analyst finds such closure then an appropriate theoretical stance to take to the discourse may be that of deconstruction.

Deconstruction focuses on procedures that subvert taken-for-granted realities and ways of world making (Derrida 1986; Chia 1996). Deconstruction is a form of intervention through maximum intensification of a transformation in progress (Derrida 1992: 8). It questions the taken for granted in order to demonstrate that it has an institutionalized history (Kallinikos and Cooper 1996: 5). Deconstruction makes us aware that the stories through which managers organize their own and others' thinking, which make organization thinkable, are a sum of human relations rhetorically intensified, transferred, and embellished, which, after long usage, appear to be fixed, canonical, and binding. They are metaphors whose metaphoricality we have forgotten to remember. Deconstruction questions 'truths' split off from the conditions and context of their production. It tries 'to identify internal contradictions in systems, to exploit the conflicts and absences present in the interplay between representations, using nominally stated arguments of those with voice ... to create openings for those without' (Jacques 1999: 216). In questioning the limits it allows the possibility of enacting different discourses that open up strange and ambivalent spaces not yet defined by the present 'texture of organizing' (Cooper and Fox 1990). Willmott suggests that deconstruction is a 'subversion of closure rather than providing an authoritative means of resolving ethical dilemmas' (1997: 211).

Narratives and stories constitute organizations; they guide the lives within them, and speak to those identities they constitute. Organization constantly talks itself into existence and we make sense of its experience through narratives and stories (Weick 1995; Boden 1994). These discourses shape organization through their 'truth effects' at the deepest levels (Foucault 1972). Practically, deconstruction is a means that allows one to question these truth effects and to analyze the language games that shape reality, opening up space for different concepts and perceptions. Deconstruction shows how the world is accomplished linguistically and its status quo maintained discursively. Even more important, it provides the space for things being different. As organizations are powerfully constituted and constantly enacted through languages, deconstruction is thus the precondition of change as it melts all necessities and shows that they were established at a very particular moment in history.

Deconstruction is something done by analysts, although it can be done by practitioners as well. In practice, at least, in complex organizations where the dynamics are more positive than negative, the opposite of the construction site that Clegg (1975) wrote about, the key practitioner skill will be that of translation. Translation is a term that has had a long and peripheral relationship with the social sciences as a topic of enquiry, as well as a practice of knowledge dissemination. While translation, as an analytic practice, was a central focus of Benjamin's (1982) contributions to the Frankfurt School in the 1930s, it lapsed into marginality, at least until the development of actor network theory. In the seminal paper titled 'Some elements of a sociology of translation: domestication of the scallops and the fisherman of St Brieuc Bay', Callon (1986) tells the story of a group of three researchers who worked in St Brieuc, a small fishing community near Brest in France, to repopulate the dwindling resources of scallops. The paper identifies three key agents of concern in determining the success or failure of the study. These included the researchers themselves, the fishermen, and the scallops. The focus is on the translation and non-translation of the needs of each of these into the terms of the others. Law (1996: 300) explains the complex interrelationship, described as translation, which occurs between the subject and the object, the non-living and the living.

Subjects endlessly turn themselves into objects, perhaps by creating rules and procedures which, for instance, assume the form of the standing orders or conventions that are performed at meetings, while at the same time objects are similarly turning themselves constantly back into subjects so that – in this case – they may judge whether or not the rules have been properly followed. Such syntax is a mode of accounting that is told and performed in documents such as agendas and minutes. And it is something that demands the performance of a constant weaving to and fro between subjectivity and objectivity. The former is not distant, strategic, and occasional. Rather, together with its interventions, it is continuous, reflexive, iterative, unfolding and tactical, distributed across time in ways that cannot be predicted or told in any detail at a single time or place.

Given that organizations are constituted through different language games – including the language game legitimated by top management as only one of them – no single language can be identified that could cope with the complexities emerging from them all. Drawing on philosophical (Benjamin 1982; Deleuze 1994) and sociological (Latour 1983) sources, we suggest using the concept of translation as an adequate means of understanding and conceptualizing management. Translation is concerned not with one language but with the differences between languages; it concerns not the elaboration of one single language but a moving from one to the other; it is not about speaking in one's own tongue but about understanding the other.

Translation, at root, is a process, a becoming rather than a being (Chia 1996). Translation will always be a temporary, imperfect and somehow improvised process. It cannot smooth over differences but tries to work with them, creating a resonance between languages, and can be understood as a form of mediation between different and contradicting languages and the realities they constitute. Following the current interest of organization theory in the space between (Cooper 1990; Bradbury and Lichtenstein 2000), the gaps, the interstices (Gherardi 1999), and the therein-unfolding in-tensions (Cooper and Law 1995), the process of translation focuses on the 'what is *between*' as 'where the real action is' (1995: 245). Translation explores 'the space between' different sensemaking; it explores the actual space where organizing occurs (Cooper 1990: 168). Translation becomes the process of linking, netting, connecting different language games through the use of stories and metaphors that display one as having rhetorical skill.

As actor network theory has demonstrated (Law and Hassard 1999), translation is a powerful process, especially where it involves enrolling others as relays in strategic agency. It is, of course, a fallacy of translation ever to think that others might be the passive beings that the notion of strategic relays suggests. Once others have been delegated to become relays then they are acknowledged as autonomous and have opportunities for the exercise of their autonomy in the pursuit of whatever action has been authorized. Here, the term 'authorized' bears a dual sense, referring both to the textual originator and to the legitimacy that is construed as the context within which any action will unfold. Delegates are empowered to speak and act as legates or envoys of those who represent authority. And in this role it is a rare delegate who is effective by sticking solely to the script and eschewing opportunities for improvisation and creativity. And it is in often-necessary improvisation that the most creative, the most powerful, and the most authentic moments will occur. Thus, translation is far more than a pure repetition of the same in the words of the other. Rather, translation always combines difference and repetition at one and the same time (Deleuze 1994). According to Benjamin, the 'essential quality' of translation 'is not statement or the imparting of information. Yet any form of translation which intends to perform a transmitting function cannot transmit anything but information – hence something inessential' (1982: 69).

Translation does not imply speaking on behalf of other people. Speaking for others implies defining common ground and identifying a common perspective. Such a strategy obviously implies exercising power since differences can get lost when someone claims to represent an issue better than the people who are directly affected by it. Translation works on a different level. It does not identify or unify, but takes the differences between languages and tries to deal with them in a constructive way. It does not speak for someone else, but repeats what someone said in a different language.

The translator does not become the author, but stays in the background. Translation is still a powerful process, of course, but rather than claiming to represent a standpoint for others, the translator has to explore different ways of linking languages between different people. Whereas speaking for someone else implies knowing their position and expressing it accurately, translation is much more of a hesitant and improvisational process. There can never be anything like a perfect translation; it is always a 'provisional way of coming to terms with the foreignness of languages' (1982: 75). The language of translation never fits perfectly; rather, it moves, folding and unfolding, enveloping and developing, and, with every single move, there (dis)appears a new but as yet hidden reality. Far from transporting a clear-cut message from one point to another, translation creates a bridge between differing language games that shape organizational reality, deferring to both of them.

It is through translation between different language games that positive power operates. Rather than just seeking the 'form of life' of an organization or a singular mode of rationality, contemporary discourse analysts can seek out the skilled uses of translation by managers who are oriented to the creative and positive use of power, at least, those managers influenced by teaching that adopts some of the strategies of positive power. Where there is less in the way of translation occurring, where there are blockages to the expression of positive power, then the analysis can focus on deconstruction.

Conclusion

Despite a growing body of literature, organizational discourse remains, at best, a nascent field in organization studies. While there has been much work done, there is still little agreement on the theoretical and methodological foundations of the field. At the same time, it is an area that has great potential for exploring power in

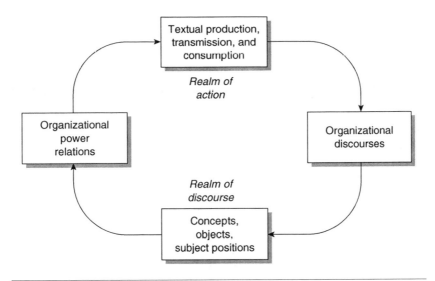

Figure 10.2 The mutually constitutive relation between discourse and power (adapted from Hardy and Phillips 2004)

organizations. A discourse analytic approach combines an explanation for the mechanisms through which reality is constituted with an explicit sensitivity to power (at least if we adopt a more critical perspective). The developing discourse analytic in organization studies therefore remains one of the most interesting developments in terms of understanding power in organizations, although much work remains to be done both in terms of developing the methodology and in terms of extending the empirical topics on which it has been applied.

Our view of the relation between discourse and power in organizations is shown in Figure 10.2. In the figure, the complex interaction between discourses and systems of power is shown in the mutually constitutive links between power relations and discourse. But these relations are not direct. The distribution of power fundamentally shapes the way texts are produced and disseminated; who can produce what texts in what way is conditioned by patterns of resources, legitimacy and the like. The nature of the texts produced both maintains and changes the discourse, leading to either stability or change. The collection of texts determines the system of concepts, objects, and subject positions that are constituted by discourse at a particular moment. The system of concepts, objects, and subject positions constitutes the relations of power that characterize the organization – and we have come full circle. This complex mutually constitutive relationship lies at the heart of the discourse analytic of power we have been exploring in this chapter.

The critical power of discourse analysis lies in the tensions between discourse and the linguistic and textual elements of which it is composed, and between discourse and the social world it constitutes. It is this combination that allows the connection to be made between micro-practices in organizations and the intra- and inter-organizational discourses that constitute the building blocks of organizations. While this is the real strength of discourse analysis it is also the source of the greatest challenge. Discourse analytic studies in the main focus either on the nature of the texts that make up the discourse, with only a limited discussion of the relation between the discourse and the social world it helps to constitute, or on the relation between the discourse and the social world while only dealing with the texts that make up the discourse in a cursory way. There is, therefore, a tremendous opportunity to expand and develop discourse analysis as a method by moving towards a more balanced approach to connecting social context to micro-practices through discourse analysis. Creating more balance between the three elements of discourse analysis will provide much more analytic power but also demands significant innovation in methods of data collection, analysis and theoretical discussion.

Organizational discourse analysis faces an additional challenge. It has, as we mentioned above, been increasingly criticized for its tendency to adopt 'extreme forms of social constructivism' that limit 'the value of one prominent tendency within current research on organizational discourse for organizational studies' (Fairclough 2005: 915). Reed (2004: 413) has described this tendency as the 'anti-realist, subjectivist, relativist, and ideationalist' tendency in discourse analysis. The postmodern tendency in discourse analysis grows largely out of the Foucauldian roots of many of the ideas that make it up. Fairclough (2005), in his recent critique, suggests that discourse analysis is losing theoretical traction due to its loss of a dualistic epistemology focusing on the relations between agency and structure. In other words, by seeing organizations as only discourse, it is missing the opportunity to deal with agency due to an overemphasis on structure. Discourse theory's brief history offers an opportunity for it to turn to sociological formulations that predate the current enthusiasm for discourse analysis and which do display a more sophisticated grasp of the relation of agency and structure.

Reed (2004) and Fairclough (2005) recommend the continued development of a critical realist approach to discourse analysis (see also Chouliaraki and Fairclough (1999)). A critical realist approach to discourse analysis begins with the premise that there is a difference between the world as it exists and our knowledge of it, which it maintains as a critical distinction. From this perspective the social world comes prestructured. Furthermore:

> This prestructuring process, and the material conditions and social structures that it reproduces, cannot be collapsed into language or discourse. If they are so collapsed or conflated, then the 'generative power' inherent in social structures cannot be accessed or explained because it remains imprisoned within its 'discursive moment' – within the linguistic and textual forms through which it is communicated and represented. (Reed 2004: 415)

In other words, critics are calling for recognition of how transcendent elements of structure act in and through agency to structure political performance, as we shall investigate in the next chapter. The result of neglecting structural factors is a loss of analytic power. Discourse analysis, from this perspective, needs to resist the temptation to conflate ontology and epistemology in order to retain its explanatory power.

How this particular discussion will work itself out remains to be seen. What is clear is that discourse analysis provides an important methodology for investigating the dynamics of power and politics that are intrinsic to organizations. As we said in Chapter 1, power is to organizations as oxygen is to breathing, and the study of power needs to become just as intrinsic to the study of organizations. Discourse analysis, and particularly critical discourse analysis, provides one important opportunity for further thinking and research on power in organizations.

Whereas organization theory may have been said to begin with the virtually mute body – think of Taylor's Schmidt, the dumb Pennsylvanian Dutchman – it rapidly moved to the soul and the mind. In discourse analysis it takes the mind out of the body and into discourse. The mind materializes in language. Organizations teem with texts, discourses, and language. The everyday discourse and rhetoric of organizational life comes to the fore as the real stuff of analysis. It is in these that power will be found, in the ways of categorizing, constituting and conducting everyday sense. With discourse analysis, organization theory finally catches up with the fact that organizational management – and resistance – are largely done discursively. There is no need to construct elaborate research instruments because there is all the complexity that one could desire in the mundane things of everyday organizational life.

Notes

1　For an excellent overview of the development of the more general discussion of discourse and gender, see West et al. (1997).
2　For a broad review of the gender and organization literature see Calás and Smircich (1996).
3　We will also address issues of identity in more detail when we consider the futures of power in Chapter 13.

 **11** Power and
Organizational Forms

Chapter outline

In this chapter we will:

- Situate the concept of power in the current and former debates about
  bureaucracy and the dynamics of bureaucracies.
- Explain the political dimensions of organizational forms, by introducing
  democracy and oligarchy as two major power regimes, and by presenting
  a model of analyzing political performance.
- Suggest the current social construction of specific hybrid political forms,
  encompassing contestation and coercive forms of power.

Introduction

The purpose of this chapter is to examine the direct relevance of organizational
power to the stability of political regimes of organizations, which we propose to
define as the *political performance* of organizations. The idea is to suggest that
theories of organization power can help us understand the dynamics of organizational forms and, what is more, that organizational dynamics are fundamentally
political. In the second part of the chapter we illuminate how organizational power
operates to generate hybrid political structures that we encompass in the *polyarchic*
model. We posit polyarchy as the most enduring contemporary political form.

Organizational form and power: the political
performance of organizations

Situating bureaucracy

Weber (1947) made the case for rational-legal bureaucracy as a bulwark against
the blandishments of patrimonial power and privilege. The argument is familiar.
Classical liberal bureaucracy, conceived on a rational-legal basis, stood for an *ethos*

of service to the public, through conformance to certain means, rather than the arbitrary treatment of people according to caste, status or resources. Rational-legal bureaucracy presumed democratic ideals, rule without regard for persons, and was intended as an abstract ideal as well as the basis for empirical description. Bureaucracy was a construct for Weber that served to represent in an accentuated form the qualities that any contemporary German liberal nationalist would admire as well as to condense the qualities appropriate to the construction of rational legality and bureaucracy.

In the last 20 years, a newer construct of *market liberal bureaucracy* has emerged with an alternative *ethos of efficiency* at its core.[1] With the creation of the new public sector management, modern conceptions of efficiency have emerged as the dominant characteristic for judging bureaucracy (Clarke and Newman 1997). Today the entrepreneurial type of public official, focused on value for money, is required by senior policy people (du Gay 2000a: 114). Added value has been sought through the implementation of internal management processes 'dominated by the twin rubrics of business planning and the building of corporate commitment to a specific organizational "mission" and purpose, linked to survival in a competitive environment' (Clarke and Newman 1997: 147).

In its application to practice, the original liberal bureaucratic construct has been criticized as failing to produce members emotionally committed to the pursuit of economic efficiency, which emerges as the central value of the new public sector management critique (see du Gay 2000b). Efficiency, which, as we saw in the early chapters, was originally derived from classical mechanics, has influenced much of the meaning surrounding contemporary management discourse on bureaucracy. As some have maintained, whilst an organization may be economical in its use of resources, it will not necessarily be efficient if it is focused solely on cost reduction (see Ransom and Stewart 1994). Efficiency, in this context, stands as a signifier against waste, such that, in the popular and reformist imagination, war against waste is associated with an assault on old-style (Weberian) bureaucracy (cf. Osborne and Gaebler 1992).

It is well known that Weber (1978) had no truck (Albrow 1997) with the ethos of efficiency that has been predominant in writings on bureaucracy in recent times. The central values embedded within the character of being a classically rational-legal bureaucrat, and all that this meant in terms of vocation (Weber 1947), have come under attack. Such ideals included a lack of self-interest; commitment to principles embodied in rules; allegiance to authority positions instead of individuals; and above all, a sense of personal responsibility in service provision, the stress on *being* a *public servant*. Weber's (1947) admiration for the culture of a professional administrative vocation is now seen as featherbedding and in need of replacement with a cost-cutting or entrepreneurial mentality.

The reception of efficiency has been one-sided. One dimension of public sector management – value for money – has been elevated above all other considerations in the 'war on waste' (du Gay 2000b). The rhetoric involves defining efficiency as the accomplishment of predetermined goals according to market-informed opportunities. Thus, efficiency has been constructed in such a way as to slice off the public value-dimension, so preventing discussion of goals by making discussion of the older type of efficiency out of bounds. What is now commonly defined as efficient involves neither questioning of public ends nor suggesting links to purposeful means (du Gay 2000b). Public servants understand the change in attitude. In the new climate, bureaucrats fear their jobs being contracted out to more 'efficient' markets (Rees and Rodley 1995). Advocates of bureaucratic reform conjure up a new ethic of accountability founded upon narrowly defined short-term commercial objectives. Decision making according to market-driven pressures will introduce the discipline of markets (Osborne and Gaebler 1992; see Stokes and Clegg 2002). Outputs should be defined and measured, and performance-based orientations developed towards them. Short-term goals are linked to accountability 'since these are the ones against which outputs and performance are measured' (Clarke and Newman 1997: 147). Finally, public employees will be inculcated with a culture oriented toward customer service, mediated by the managerial vision framing their goals.

Weber understood the function of technical virtuosity as a first line of defense in rational-legal bureaucracy against imprudent power, unbridled purpose, and visionary zeal. An intricate sense of due process could limit executive excess, as some critics of naive reform have noted (Stokes and Clegg 2002). When one examines what gets adopted from ideas such as efficiency, one sees a complex interplay at work. The process of identity switching often deforms when translating superordinate desires, such as visions, into subordinate practice (see various arguments of, for example, Latour 1987; 1996; Law 1999; Callon 1998; Law and Hassard 1999; Newton 1996). Bureaucrats might be required to invest new relations of meaning into old values and identities in ways that surprise would-be reformers, and old meanings can be attached to new things that are envisioned as efficiency (see, for example, Newton 1996; Cálas and Smirchich 1999; Mol 1999; Callon 1991; 1998; 1999).

Weber envisaged bureaucracy as supporting a growing pervasiveness of rational calculation as a central value in all spheres of life, and he was well aware that the ends that public administration serves are determined elsewhere by politicians. Nonetheless, Weber regarded the *means* for their accomplishment as a technical virtuosity which political vision should not interfere with. The contemporary emphasis in organizations is on new values and visions to drive meaning throughout organizational culture (see Bryman 1992). Ardent bureaucratic reformers, such as Peters (1992), Osborne and Gaebler (1992) and Kanter (1990), urge leaders of bureaucracies to develop new relations of meaning and purpose, framed by the vision conceived by their chief executive(s), or their consultants. Where Weber saw an increasing rationalization of the world, with the separation of bureaucratic means from whatever political ends drove their purpose, modern writers instead point to an increasing enchantment.

Chief executives and consultants have come to be defined as the enchanting visionaries of a secular age. Visionaries were not always so divorced from religious connotations. We should, perhaps, not forget the religious, pre-modern derivation of vision and visionaries. In feudal times – against which the economic conditions of a rational-legal conception emerged – one was as likely to be condemned as lauded for having visions (Roper 1994). Visions were generally dramatic and unsettling challenges to the keepers of knowledge, the priesthood. While they might excite the populace they were as likely to enflame them and hence were best avoided in favor of the reiteration of organizational orthodoxy. Visions are no longer enchanted religious convictions, or, rather, they retain their enchantment only in as much as they have made themselves in the image of people for whom the market is their icon (Schreurs 2000).

Modern managerial capitalism has solved the unsettling effects of visions by making them the preserve of the powerful rather than the powerless, of CEOs rather than peasant girls such as Joan of Arc. The vision becomes a tool of prescribed action rather than emancipatory change. The less bureaucratically powerful are urged to attend to futures imagined for them by the more powerful, rather than the vision being an articulation of an aesthetic made pure by its supposed distance from power, as enlightened knowledge. In the public sector the effects of visionaries upon employees' work are reasonably well known. Since the set of policy initiatives that analysts loosely termed 'Thatcherism' (Gamble 1988) emerged in the early 1980s, the preferred route for changing the public sector entailed replacing the dedicated career bureaucrat at their apex with political appointees who would ensure that technical virtuosity did not undermine their attachment to political visions.[2] Such appointments appear to require the adoption of a *new* subjectivity by public servants; they will be the key mechanism whereby classical liberal bureaucracy transforms into contemporary market efficient bureaucracy.

Creating efficient contemporary liberal market bureaucracies involves a change of sensemaking about purpose. While new sensemaking may throw old ways of public administration into bold relief, rarely will it produce the superordinately desired new rules for making different sense of organizational realities. Interpretation will always occur in the context of the previous knowledge of those whose responsibility it is to make sense of rules or business practices. Old ways of doing things stick and settle down, deeply sedimented, in both consciousness and organization, irretrievably there, prowling about like a ghost, as Weber (1976) might have said. New orientations to action can rarely be bought and adopted wholesale, once they come to market, and the old discarded. In this respect, the multiplicity of overlapping and incomplete language games, comprising ambiguous, shifting, and frequently undercodified rules, appears a normal part of bureaucracy (Zimmerman 1971).

The emphasis on the legitimacy of bureaucratically authoritative meaning as emanating from superordinate vision within the rhetoric of the new public sector management may well be mistaken. It is neither the conviction nor the vision of powerful zealots, any more than it is individual receptivity to new rhetoric, or the content of the rhetoric, that conditions the acceptance of such rhetoric. Legitimacy belongs not to privilege alone to ascribe; it also has a contingent relationship to the meaning projected on to executive action by those subject to it.[3] Increasingly, of late, classic bureaucracy has been delegitimated and alternatives to it have been widely discussed, especially the emergence of a new, post-bureaucratic or postmodern type of organization with different conceptions of power (Clegg 1990).

Essentially, the arguments about new organization forms boil down to a proposition that new power relations are emerging, based less on formal rules and dependent more on neoliberal forms of governmentality, with flatter hierarchies and proliferating projects and networks, in which employment relations become based less on career and more on contingent contracts. It may be 'post' but it is still political, as we have argued elsewhere (Clegg and Courpasson 2004; Clegg et al. 2002) and as we shall elaborate in the next section.

The politics of bureaucracy

All the debates and controversies about the demise of bureaucracy have not changed the fact that bureaucracy is *the* point of departure in thinking about organizational forms, and remains the central icon of organization studies. Bureaucracy is without any doubt 'the primary institutional characteristic of highly complex and differentiated societies' (Landau 1972: 167). Bureaucracy 'epitomizes the modern era' according to Blau and Meyer (1971: 10), because the meaning of bureaucracy is basically political. Bureaucracy is a political design as well as – indeed, even before – an organizational design. Bureaucracy aims to enhance the political performance of specific power structures.

As Weber noted in his speech to German army officers near the close of the First World War, the distant drum to whose beat they were likely to march in the future would be less probably shaped by socialism or capitalism than by bureaucracy. In this statement one can see the idea that bureaucracy is a purposeful social construction rather than a natural force coming from uncertain origins. Additionally, the deep political nature of the idea of administration is evident; it subsumes ideologies in this view. Bureaucracy has deep implications in terms of the management of power. The bureaucratic division of labor means that 'individual workers and employees can be exchanged and replaced at any time' (Dreyfuss 1938: 75). Bureaucracy is rather more a system of endogenous governance than a 'mere' organizational configuration stemming from exogenous contingencies and constraints. In other words, bureaucracy is a political shell functioning as a shield behind which the alternatives to bureaucracy dissimulate their inherent weaknesses.

Weber's seminal insight was that, in an organizational context, the rationalization process that produces bureaucratization results in a diminution of individual power. People are rendered into machine-like obedient objects, trapped in the 'iron cage', as we have seen in Chapter 2, such that from the outset, a political economy of the body and then the soul was oriented to achieving this outcome. Bureaucracy represents the institutionalization of the political efficiency of centralized authority legitimized by the power of knowledge, neutralizing, thanks to the proliferation and dissemination of experts into the social body, any possibility and any vague impulses of contestation. As Waters puts it, bureaucracy is a power structure that is in principle 'capable of being aggregated in an "upward" direction' (1993: 56). It is an 'upward-oriented' kind of political structure because it enhances the development of a professionalization of experts, as knowledge producers and knowledge holders, so to speak. To quote Weber,

> Bureaucratic domination means fundamentally domination through knowledge. This consists on the one hand in technical knowledge ... but in addition to this ... the holders of power ... have the tendency to increase their power still further by the knowledge growing out of experience in the service. (1978: 225)

Bureaucracy is an institutionalized power system where, according to functionalist logic, power flows as a circulatory medium in an inherently relational system. In Parsons' (1963) words, bureaucracy is a 'relational system within which certain categories of commitments and obligations, ascriptive or voluntarily assumed – e.g. by contract – are treated as binding, i.e. under normatively defined conditions their fulfillment may be insisted upon by the appropriate role-reciprocal agencies … in case of actual or threatened resistance to "compliance" … they will be "enforced" by the threat or actual imposition of situational negative sanctions' (in Scott 1994: 23). Power in bureaucracies is, therefore, a set of enforceable rules that prevents individuals from contesting and resisting binding obligations, such behaviors being likely to diminish the general political performance of the organization. As we saw in Chapter 5, this conception of power stands in opposition to that of authority; indeed, it is only when the remit of authority fails or is resisted that power comes into view, always as the action of the 'other' opposed to management.

Following Weber (and putting aside most of his critics), he acknowledged the possibility of a paradoxical domination (and thereby of a paradoxical power structure) when rational techniques and procedures became embodied in organizational forms (McNeil 1978). To put it differently, the meaning of bureaucracy lies in the forms that organizational leaders are able to design to control employees, implying that political asymmetries exist that will structure social action. Bureaucracy is concerned much more with 'efficiency of control' (Benello 1969: 268) than with economic efficiency. Or, more precisely, economic performance stems from the political efficiency of organizational control.

Power is *the* core issue. Corporate elites design structures and procedures aiming 'to gain information about labor, commodity, and capital markets, and then take strategic advantage of them' (McNeil 1978: 70). These administrative structures alone do not obviously explain the enormous political differentials existing within bureaucracies. Moreover, managerial leaders occasionally, from time to time, need the intervention of the state. We see this most clearly when, 'by not explicitly prohibiting exploitation in the making of contracts, the state was tacitly granting to private corporations extensive proprietary rights through contract law' (1978: 71). Still, it was the modes of calculation used by bureaucratic elites which were the major mechanisms shaping the use of power rather than some instrumentality of the state.

Weber's view of the exercise of power by corporate elites depends profoundly on the conception of leaders' and subordinates' respective rationalities, and the role these rationalities play in shaping efforts to transform the environment (Giddens 1977). Administrative rationalities are crucial to understanding how elites transform 'potential power' into the actual exercise of power from within structures of dominancy regarded as legitimate authority, the essential meaning of bureaucracy as an administrative apparatus. The dynamics of available organizational forms affect important underlying aspects of organizations: the rationalities at hand, the power structures, the exercise of power, and the legitimacy of power holders. In short, they affect the entire *political regime* of organizations.

Organizational forms generate enormous power for corporate elites because it is through these that they inscribe and express their *authority*. The important question, therefore, is how elites shape and design the dynamics for controlling expressions of their power, politically, as well as understanding those reactions that resist it. Indeed, Weber stressed that the only way for individuals to gain freedom against the overwhelming power of bureaucracy was through permanent political struggle. And yet, as McNeil puts it, 'rational-legal bureaucratic control is Hydra-headed' (1978: 76) and not easy to dismantle.

The stratification of struggles between a manifold of actors (business leaders, consumers, organizational sectors, cities, etc.) gives to bureaucracy the paradoxical aspect of a contestable regime requesting democratic forms of deliberation to come up with credible ways of ending debates and 'calling truces'. Democratic control has, therefore, to be relentlessly reasserted and strengthened, even if, contrary to what most critics have argued, bureaucratic control does not, *per se*, rule out democratic control (Albrow 1970). Specific organizational forms provide alternative solutions and rationalities to legitimate the concrete use of power. Once again, what certain critics of bureaucracy have neglected (Blau 1957) is the constant linkage that Weber makes between power and technical rationality, where power is the very means of developing and maintaining organizational performance. For modern organization theory, bureaucracy appears to be the demonstration that organizational forms should be conceived as the linkage between political and economic efficiency. Of course, the notion of bureaucracy being constructed in close relation to that of efficiency – rather than technical rationality – is not one that Weber would have been familiar with.

The meaning of (organizational) democracy and oligarchy

In the past, there has been little systematic reflection on democracy and organizations, other than in Follett and the organizational democracy movement, particularly in the Netherlands and Scandinavia, in the 1960s and 1970s, as we saw in Chapter 3. However, there are much older and well-established notions of democracy, which are highly controversial when applied to the organizational world.

Two major lines of thought serve as a basis for developing our understanding of the relationships between democracy and power. They help us to conceive of organizations as enabling, rather than tutelary, political systems. First, there is the work of Tocqueville, who presents a sophisticated theory of democracy through which we may see bureaucracies as associative rather than fragmenting and atomizing organizational systems (Goldberg 2001). Second, following Michels' insights, a theory of democracy can help us understand how democratic forms of power either break down (Linz and Stepan 1978) or shift and turn, fatally, into oligarchic forms of power.

Understanding Tocqueville today entails, as he himself put it, that one should 'adapt old values and ideas to new circumstances' (Goldberg 2001: 292). Tocqueville's theory of democracy can enlighten us on the influence that new organizational forms might have on equality and the concentration of power.[4] Democracy for Tocqueville (2000: 3–7) is not restricted to popular government but is assimilated to a process of increasing social equality. Democracy is a way to cope with the ever-growing threats of modern times and the atomizing effects of modernization. It is a political and cultural cornerstone of institutions capable of sustaining political equality, despite the fragmenting and 'disempowering' effects of modernity. A question arising from Tocqueville's work is whether 'organizations [can] be a credible alternative institutional setting replacing aristocratic institutions and values'. And in his terms, we need also to ask how 'communities can be protected from tyranny and license' (2000: 9). Thus organizational democracies are foundational settings in which every individual could be likely to

> achieve freedom and fulfillment by being an active participant in a dynamic, self-governing community characterized by tight solidarity and fundamental – though usually not absolute – equality. This solidarity does not proceed primarily from personal ties, particularly ties of personal dependence, but from common participation in an active community which forms a moral whole. (Weintraub 1979: 6, quoted in Goldberg 2001: 293)

Equality is generated through the same types of processes as authority. It is a slow and often contested social construction involving power struggles. It is the result not of a discursive construct, but of political debates and contestation. For Tocqueville, this is the very essence of democracy, as a set of institutions whose engineering facilitates the emergence of intermediary forms of power, enabling conscious democratic decisions and developing an individual and collective sense of responsibility. Democracy entails a whole set of moral values whose activation helps organizations to avoid both social isolation and the excessive domination of bureaucratic and centralized power. From a political point of view, Tocqueville usefully differentiates centralized government from centralized administration. The former refers to the concentration of power used to direct the general interests of the whole community, and is deemed necessary to the prosperity of any kind of collective. The latter refers to the concentration of power used to direct certain peculiar local interests, which, according to Tocqueville, is a threat to democracy.

To a certain extent, a neo-Tocquevillean theory of power would put forward the idea that reforms and redesigns of organizational forms should be carried out mostly by intermediary and associative groups. The treatment of equality within organizations, from a neo-Tocquevillean perspective, requires an understanding of power structures, as efforts to control inequality supposedly hinder the development of 'new aristocracies' (Goldberg 2001: 305). In other words, the first meaning of democracy in the context of organizations is how to avoid different corporate oligarchies taking over either from rule-governed forms of expertise, or from custom-governed forms of aristocracy, and developing more or less legitimacy in the process? The problem for democracy is oligarchy, in other words, as Michels (1915) recognized.

Oligarchy is located at the core of power; it is the means of monopolizing and perpetuating resources of power through perfectly legal and rational processes. Michels' basic reasoning was that organization precludes democracy, because '[I]mmanent oligarchical tendencies [exist] in every kind of human organization which strives for the attainment of definite ends ... [and that] ... the majority of human beings, in a condition of eternal tutelage, are predestined ... to submit to the dominion of a small minority' (1915: 11, 32). According to Michels, political leadership is 'incompatible with the most essential postulate of democracy' (1915: 390). Organizations necessitate oligarchy as a set of arrangements 'neither absolutely democratic nor absolutely autocratic' (May 1965: 419). Simply, any kind of association becomes more or less rapidly 'divided into a minority of directors and a majority of directed' (Michels 1915: 32).

Power struggles are evident as the core process of internal oligarchization, and thus create a paradox of democracy. According to Michels, organization necessitates delegation and dispersion of authority; thus, 'in the case of an association where one or just a few members have exercised all authority, the effect of organization will be counter-autocratic' (May 1965: 421). Even organizations that are democratic in conception, in the goals they promote as inclusive reasons for membership, will fail to be democratic in the procedures and rules they design and use; they may be democratic in the plurality of interests they objectively and institutionally represent, rather than in the causes they actually promote through their strategies (see May 1965). Consequently, even if organizational forms end up transforming democratic regimes into oligarchic regimes, this influence will be exercised concretely through power struggles. It is simply the underlying arguments and criteria, deciding who governs, which are likely to evolve.

Michels thinks that democracy, rather than being viewed as a 'simple equality', is more a regime which 'gives to each [citizen] the possibility of ascending to the top of the social scale ... annulling ... all privileges of birth ... the struggle for pre-eminence should be decided in accordance with individual capacity' (1915: 189). A meaning common to knowledge-based bureaucracy is therefore established. Oligarchy derives from the political process of the 'professionalization of leadership' more or less directly, because the interests of the experts in leadership are expressed in a struggle between leaders, who, in striving to compete to solidify their own personal positions, clash with those of the 'masses'. The political struggle is the very definition of democracy, according to Wilde, as it is defined by 'those rules that allow (though they do not necessarily bring about) genuine competition for authoritative political roles' (1978: 29).

To sum up, whatever the origin of the analysis, the fictitious political continuum between, say, bureaucratic forms embedded in oligarchic regimes, and post-bureaucratic forms (Heckscher 1994) embedded in democratic regimes, inevitably displays the existence of central political antagonisms which cannot be concealed. The relationship between the dynamics of organizational forms along this continuum and the dynamics of organizational power is at the heart of the construction of the political performance of organizations.

Political performance

The schema in Figure 11.1 summarizes the idea of political performance. As we proposed previously, the political performance of organizations lies primarily in the patterns of authority encompassed in the political relationship of subordination and in the political relationship between rival leaders. To be brief, political performance is produced by the interactions between four characteristics of political systems. These comprise the model of leadership (the basis of the distance between the elite and the governed), the model of inclusiveness (the degree of required and

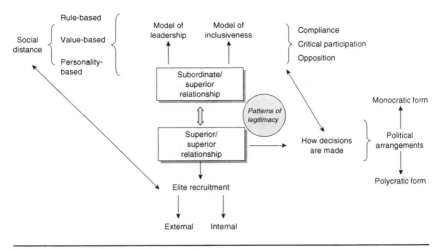

Figure 11.1 The production of political performance

tolerated participation), the decision-making model (from open dialog to monocratic forms of imposition), and the model of elite production (endogenously organized through career-functional types of backgrounds or exogenously generated through educational-familial-social kinds of backgrounds).

The figure suggests the existence of diverse types of political performance. For instance, an organization producing its elite through internal mechanisms of career, making decisions through deliberative settings, privileging personality-based types of leadership and critical participation, would generate a specific type of political performance, a sort of intermingling between social resistance, avoidance, and the power of charisma. An organization recruiting its elites externally, making decisions from the center, valuing a leadership based on rules and a compliance-based model of inclusiveness, would resemble a bureaucratic type of political performance, i.e. a mix of structural and procedural stability and of externally generated forms of values and authenticity. [5]

Usually, two categories of assumption help define the agenda when studying political performance. The first assumption is that the stability of governments is related to the way organizational forms are constructed (e.g. participative forms, decision-making processes and procedures, pathways to the top of an organization). Implicitly, this means that forms of governmentality are a mechanism 'that work[s] efficiently in any setting if properly engineered in accordance with rules distinctive to themselves' (Eckstein 1969: 275). A second assumption is that political performance depends primarily not on the internal structures of powers, but on external ingredients, such as geography, education, social stratification, and so on. Both approaches have been largely recognized as insufficient in the attempt to elaborate a model for understanding the stability of organizational/political regimes (Eckstein 1969; Linz 1978). It is in the patterns of internal structures and relations of power that the stability and dynamics of (democratic and oligarchic) forms of organization can be better grasped. Political performance is analyzed in Eckstein's (1969: 287) model according to the following items:[6]

- *durability*, i.e. the persistence of a certain government without major change over time
- *legitimacy*, i.e. the ability of a certain government 'to command positive commitments in a society'
- *strife avoidance*, i.e. the ability of a certain government to avoid or minimize social violence directed at the structure of rule
- *output efficiency*, i.e. the ability of a certain government 'to arrive at directives pertinent to demands in a polity, especially intense and widespread ones'
- *permeation*, i.e. the ability of the power holders to distribute resources and carry out reforms pertinent for the various segments of the social body
- *authenticity*, which means that all these aspects should be accomplished without deviating from some sorts of implicit meanings (what it means to be a democratic leader, for instance), the political formulas, to follow (Mosca 1939).

Accordingly, all these dimensions relate to three political characteristics of organizational forms. Organizational forms are designed to generate certain kinds of rules, of subordinate–superior relationships, and certain patterns of elite production. In other words, organizational forms might be the major ingredient of a system of governance. From the perspective of the power holders, the political purpose of any government is to perpetuate itself. It does not do so when a dominant leader is ousted for whatever reason and organizational lives are affected, when the organization necessarily lives a drama symbolized by the transfer of power, such as in the context of changes in political regimes at the level of nations or a change of top management team or CEO (Linz 1978: 3).

Where the very essence of the legitimacy of leaders is contested and, as is often the case, ends up in the unveiling of scandals or actual proof of incompetence, the lack of political performance is interpreted as a pivotal event and shatters the entire organizational edifice. In the upshot, it is the corporate elite as a 'ruling class' which is affected, and which, therefore, strives to recover both the trust of destabilized subordinates, and the dignity of an aristocracy. Unobtrusively, corporate elites use the power of their inter-organizational networks (Davis et al. 2003) and slightly reorient the rules of their most powerful resource, the system of elite recruitment (Putnam 1976).[7]

We turn now to the analysis of the dynamics of contemporary political structures of organizations. We remind the reader that the purpose of the dynamic we are going to emphasize, namely the polyarchic dynamic, is to stabilize, if not increase, the political performance of organizations as defined above.

Organizations as regimes

In the political realm of organizations, the social fabric of power structures is the pillar for the perpetuation of patterns of domination. Through the notion of political performance, the contemporary action of power holders is describable as a permanent striving for new forms of legitimacy and new forms of internal governance, which avoid or minimize the effects of possible contestations and oppositions. When we connect power to the social fabric of organizational forms we think of organizations as *regimes*. To describe an organization in terms of a regime is not to denote it as a place in which a particular model, a particular form, could serve as a perfect instantiation and implementation of a political structure (either of a democratic or of an oligarchic structure) but to see it as a space and occasion in which concrete modes of rule will be in struggle with each other. Organizations are politically pluralist settings, where the activity of leaders is to order symbolically and structurally a set of social relations between 'adversaries' (Mouffe 2000), between legitimate enemies, in an effort to organize human coexistence and contain relations of subordination in a context of inequality between people.

In a way, theories of organization power all converge on the understanding of how specific institutions (such as organizations) struggle to make things that are morally, ethically, and humanely unacceptable appear acceptable and necessary for the common good. The theory of organizations is an object lesson in how politics can overwhelm value-based rationalities by incorporating values in the business of politics. Theoretical efforts in the service of this ideal can be sketched as a permanent striving to find alternative political forms to those of the iconic bureaucracy, oscillating between patterns of permanent contestation and deliberation, and the production of durable consensus.

The payoff of most typologies of political forms proposed over recent decades is to stress the hybrid character of organizational power structures, which we analyze as polyarchic systems, stemming both from the polycratic Weberian forms and from the analysis of the approximations of 'pure' democratic regimes (Dahl 1971). In other words, political struggles about the production of a minimally acceptable power structure tend systematically to generate hybrids, more than to impose a given structure on the least powerful of the adversaries. From a theoretical perspective, power analysis stretches out from the understanding of consensus production to that of relentless contestation. Politics concerns the acceptance by a majority (or a powerful minority) of the conditions under which tolerance of contestation occurs.

From consensus to contestation: the nature and culture of power

In a sense, the project of Western political and organizational theorists of power since the 1940s has been to conceptualize the constitution of forms of power which are compatible with values that are as close as possible to democratic kinds of values. It is, perhaps, for this reason that the work on total institutions that we reviewed in Chapter 6 seems to have had such short shrift. It stresses totalitarian rather than democratic impulses. It is also why authority occurs much more than power in the indices of management textbooks. In this democratic project, organizations are seen as solutions to the establishment of particular institutions likely to limit and eventually contest domination.

We shall see in the next chapter that an underlying question that obsessed sociological theorists from Gouldner, Merton, and Selznick to Crozier, and more recently, in a different manner, to Bourdieu or Giddens, is to understand why the power of elites is barely contested in most Western societies – to understand how organizations have been constituted as means of limiting resistance and contestation rather than the power of the ruling few. The answer to this question refers to the existence of forms of distribution and structuration of power that obliterate, at least for a while, the necessity to deliberate about proper patterns of legitimacy. How do forms of power shift the focus of politics from *discourses* on power to *experiences* of power, and how do they produce outputs for most segments of a polity that offset the absence of true participation and resistance?

The types we are going to outline now (see Table 11.1) are related to these diverse aspects of politics, namely how leaders provide people with reasons to work, act and decide in the workplace, as well as with instruments, procedures, rules and values to help people accept and internalize the unfathomable limits of their individual power. As Giddens would put it, these forms are thought to facilitate the co-production of patterns of legitimacy by people and their leaders, the structures of power being the intermediate connection between both 'parties'.

In most approaches the difficulty in conceiving credible and convincing alternatives to bureaucracy stems from an inability to analyze hybrids in political terms. By this we mean hybrids are mostly conceived as more or less harmonious combinations between presumably opposite organizational characteristics, or as peculiar organizational devices devoted to a unique set of managerial preoccupations (such as organizational control in Greenwood et al. (1990), or transversal cooperation, and quasi-firms). We can find a similar tendency at more paradigmatic levels of reflection, which present new hybrid forms as a third alternative to market and hierarchy models (see for instance Adler (2001) on the community form). These attempts, however fruitful they are, do not address which antagonistic processes an organization must undertake to construct a hybrid; and, most important, never address *why* and *for whom* new hybrid forms might emerge. Moreover, these approaches to hybrids neglect that political forms mostly evolve through the 'production of authoritarian knowledge' via multilevel social mechanisms entailing contestations (Lazega 2000: 17). Political forms invariably do not respect the paradox of emancipation, that one can only free oneself and cannot be freed by others acting on one's behalf. New hybrid organizational forms may be designed with an increase of the freedom of others in mind but there can be no guarantees that the new freedom will not be another tyranny.

The central concern of the study of organizations, according to Greenwood and Hinings, is 'how organizations affect the pattern of privilege and disadvantage in society ... [and] how privilege and disadvantage are distributed within organizations'(2002: 411). In other words, how do elites produce power and perpetuate themselves? Or, how do subordinates demand this perpetuation because they interpret it as politically performative?

The study of organizations is often characterized as a politically neutral vision. It is one that accords with ideas of a value-free science. Organizations are conceived as places where political change occurs either for rational-calculative reasons or because the consensual-governed philosophy is so pervasive that nobody would even think to question its superficiality (Mouffe 2000). The poles that organizational debates on power operate between are, on the one hand, institutional models of power (Selznick 1957) and more flexible models such as that of the circulation of control (Ocasio 1994; Ocasio and Kim 1999); and, on the other hand, the resource-dependency approach (Pfeffer and Salancik 1978), in which light is shed on the actual apolitical character of these models, fitfully addressing (or shrewdly dodging) the question of the prominent struggles that arise when leaders are fired or when elites are put into question. These accounts present organizations as moved by relatively smooth events, concealing antagonisms and violence, partly because they would be mostly exogenous and generated by isomorphic processes (Fligstein 1985; DiMaggio and Powell 1977).

Political hybrids are contested social productions. In a sort of post-Michels analysis, we argue that the political instability of organizations goes hand in hand with the very prevalence of solid and durable oligarchies in organizations. The instability is apparent (companies merge, leaders circulate, plants close, people are dismissed, consultants consult, and disciplinary practices form and reform) but the institutional basements of organizations are steadily resilient. Thus, democracy needs oligarchs to be credible and oligarchy needs democratic principles to be accepted by the governed. We defend the idea that this apparent paradox is a promising way of analyzing the emergence of political hybrids in the organizational world. Political hybrids stem mainly from the deficiency of business leaders to address the cardinal political issue that a true democracy should cater for, that of inequality. We do not think the efficiency argument is well targeted to account for the transformations of bureaucracies, contrary to the relentless assertions of the recent managerial and new public administration literature (Osborne and Gaebler 1992; Peters 1987; Kanter 1990; O'Toole 1997). The growing move toward hybrids is mostly related to the search for proper forms with which to govern inequality. Organizations have a chance to become more democratic if business leaders understand or, more plausibly, accept that the establishment of hybrid regimes is at the heart of their political agenda, because that agenda concerns the distribution of power and privileges within organizational boundaries.[8]

To go further, we argue that a hybrid is not a smooth organizational combination of contradictory principles but a new creation, a singular model capable of politically challenging the very nature of bureaucracies (Ashcraft 2001). To move in this direction we need to think about hybrids from a political point of view, as controversial social constructions that imply the political nature of organizations and of authority; organizations are political because they entail hostile relationships and often violent antagonisms between their diverse constituencies. Organizations find ways of legitimating these disagreements, governing them and restricting the violence of the internal struggles aroused. That is why the contemporary question posed by hybrids is that of complex intermediary forms between oligarchic and democratic systems of government.

Table 11.1 naturally does not exhaust the numerous hybrids existing in the literature, but it highlights the most representative political configurations that have been proposed for managing the dynamic nature of authority by constructing intermediate

Table 11.1 A continuum of political forms

Oligarchy → Democracy

	Rational-based bureaucracy (Weber 1978)	Democratic hierarchy (Ackoff 1994)	Professional bureaucracy (Litwak 1961)	Collegiality (Waters 1989; Lazega 2000)	Post-bureaucracy (Heckscher 1994)	Collectivist democracy (Rothschild-Whitt 1979)
Nature of authority	Vested in individuals or through office, based on expertise	Circular power / No ultimate authority	Horizontal patterns of authority combined with strong administration	Vested in professional groups based on expertise	Personal qualities / Influence in networks	Collectivity as a whole / Expertise as an organizational resource
Type of hierarchy	Verticality	Verticality and power of intermediate committees	Dual hierarchy	Professional and knowledge based	Horizontality / Flexibility of hierarchy	No hierarchy
Decision-making process	Formal rules governed	Boards governed	Localizing discretion	Peers governed	Problem solving governed	Case governed
Core values	Law and seniority	Collaborative relationships	Mechanisms of segregation	Knowledge	Dialog	Equality
Nature of social control	Centralized rules and standardization of procedures	Autonomy of the subordinates	Physical distance between professionals and business departments	Commitment to professional norms	Commitment to collective purposes	Morality / Holistic work roles

Table 11.2 Three alternative political forms and their relationship with the nature and culture of power

	Bureaucracy	*Collegiality*	*Collectivist democracy*
Nature of power	Power distribution according to status stratification	Power distribution according to the 'stratification among equals' principle, based on professional achievements	Power distribution according to the principle of equality
Culture of power	Allegiance to the body of procedural and administrative knowledge	Allegiance to the body of accredited knowledge and to the representatives/ defenders of this body	Allegiance to the collective as an impersonal whole

models between 'pure' oligarchy and 'pure' democracy. The problem is that these models seem to be composed of mutually exclusive components. They are conceived not as real hybrids, i.e. new original forms, but as relatively coherent sets of criteria and principles put together to create a combination of contradictory factors.

The core features enabling a comparative analysis of these 'political regimes' are the degree of centralization of power (nature of power) and the values pertaining to the type of power distribution (culture of power). Following the classical definition of Montesquieu (1989), a political regime (form) is indeed the result of the congruence between a nature of authority (degree of political centralization) and the feeling of the governed. From this perspective, two political forms can be put forward when considering the social production of alternatives to bureaucracy. We present in Table 11.2 a possible 'confrontation' of these forms with bureaucracy, according to the above-mentioned criteria of the *nature* and *culture* of power.

The central question of politics in terms of our argument should be to ask for what end(s) is power exercised. Or, following Emmet (1958), we must address, fundamentally, how holders of power act politically by analyzing how their intentions are possible rather than how their decisions are made. These intentions do not necessarily reside, primarily, in the purpose of setting up and perpetuating a certain type of structure of dominancy, or in establishing the dominion of a small circle of the 'chosen few'. These are the features of a certain political regime we have called oligarchy. Nor are these intentions inaccessible or merely reportable inner mental states; they are accounted for in terms of the available vocabularies of motive for understanding the nature of political action. Thus, they are both recursive and reflexive of the analyses being promoted here.

The purpose of politics in the perspective we highlight in this chapter is to design congruence between a certain naturalization of socially constructed reality and a certain culture of power. In other words, it is to arrange things so that a certain form of power distribution can be viewed by a majority of members as naturally germane to a certain set of allegiance-generating values. No government can be legitimately designed and sustained without this political congruence. The social construction of political congruence gives obvious birth to contestation inside organizations. And this concerns democracy, where democracy is related to organizational forms and, reciprocally, the question of organizational forms is also that of the degree of inclusiveness allowed (the 'right to participate in public contestation' according to Dahl 1971: 4): that is, the degree of contestation which is likely to remain contestation and not turn into mere opposition, that is to say, the limits of permissible opposition. Organizational politics thus concerns separating the idea (and the consecutive types of behaviors) of participation from the idea of opposition. We will next suggest that this is at the center of the emergent polyarchy, which we present as the political regime in organizations that contemporary business leaders strive for.

Contemporary politics: polyarchy

There are specific contemporary conditions that might account for the current dynamics of political change in organizations leading to the social fabric of a polyarchic model of power. First, there is the knowledge-intensive economy, which has been extensively documented and investigated (Adler 2001; Blackler 1995; Alvesson 1995), and which we examined in Chapter 3, which tends to stimulate the (re)development of *collegial* forms of organization. Particularly, the development of project-based organizations (which are the organizational corollary of knowledge-intensive economies) facilitates the production of *new corporate internal subelites* and possibly a new generation of managerial suboligarchs: project managers, business unit leaders, key account managers, and so on. Collegial organizations are defined by Waters as 'those in which there is dominant orientation to a consensus achieved between the members of a body of experts who are theoretically equals in their level of expertise but who are specialized by area of expertise' (1989: 956). Consequently, political forms should more and more take into account the interests and power of internal subgroups generated by the needs of the organization, which comprise jobs occupied by an emerging new generation of executives (Cappelli and Hamori 2004).

Second, however mundane it might appear now, organizations are undoubtedly characterized by the pervasiveness of a culture of threat. The threat-intensive discourse of leaders is not a new phenomenon as it has always been part of the leadership and institutional communication apparatus. But it is nowadays used in a downright political way, aiming to justify and eventually legitimize unacceptable or hardly understandable managerial decisions, such as collective dismissals in periods of high profitability. A contemporary interesting fact is the absence of 'firestorms of protest', the absence of actual official resistance when illegitimate decisions are made. While 'victims' may have to explain why they would oppose these decisions, business leaders don't have to argue for them because of the supposed 'rules of the game'. The contemporary culture of threat seamlessly enhances the power of uncertainty in the workplace. There is a political paradox lying behind these dynamics, comprising

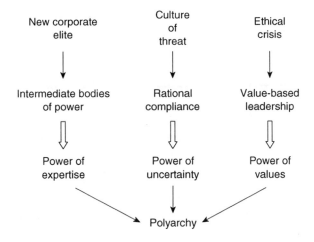

Figure 11.2   Some conditions of the generation of polyarchic structures of power

the fact that admitting powerlessness in the face of 'external threats' provides business elites with an easy way to refurbish a slightly severed legitimacy.

Third, evidently (and maybe even more mundane), the post-Enron period might be a highly favorable moment for any kind of critical opposition to contest the eternal evidence of contemporary elite power. One could therefore say that there is an urgent need for corporate elites to rejuvenate and restructure the political regimes of organizations, before any threat of being overthrown or overtly contested arises from the depths of organizations. Figure 11.2 sketches the mechanisms of the generation of polyarchy as the contemporary structure of power capable of bringing back the political performance of organizations onto an even keel. In a nutshell, the idea is that the three conditions outlined in the figure produce forms of power that might be difficult to combine in order to construct a congruent system of governance; in other words, a performing political regime. Weber stipulated clearly that one can never concretely observe a pure form of power and legitimacy in organizations and that the only possible model in action is a model of political hybridity. It remains the case that it is hard to design the political form enabling the hybrid to be constructed without too much social turmoil.

Hybridization resides between expertise, uncertainty, and values as political and cultural pillars of a political form. The hybridizing process entails in itself a democratic kind of social construction. For instance, combining compliant behaviors with the power of intermediate political bodies supposes a construction tolerating contestation and participation, which is what polyarchic forms might produce. In Dahl's perspective, a polyarchy is a political regime that has been 'substantially popularized and liberalized, that is, [it is] highly inclusive and extensively open to public contestation' (1971: 8). It is an imperfect approximation of democracy, which is likely to arise when the mutual security of governors and governed is preserved. Put differently, in polyarchic regimes, the chances of contestation are greater when they do not hamper the power of elites to act according to the values and principles on the basis of which they hold power. Contestation is therefore possible when it does not create rivalries in the polity. Polyarchy is therefore generated, thanks to a sort of political truce: oligarchs keep taking care of the political-strategic agenda and make 'crucial' decisions, while subordinates contribute (under the tutelage of local sub-oligarchs) the social construction of the local 'rules of the game', those which influence their personal fate.

As a result, polyarchy constitutes a political structure offering space to a great diversity of actors, while not disrupting oligarchic structures. The political 'polyarchic' model, therefore, defines organizations as sets of plural internal local oligarchies, under the tutelary power of a central clique of business experts. It does not allow business leaders to get rid of the issue of inequality but it does allow them to govern the consequences of asymmetries by forcing diverse kinds of actors to be involved in political struggles about *who gets power* within the firm, *to do what*, and *for whom*. It is utterly derived from the Weberian polycratic model of organizations: as Waters put it, 'polycratic organizations are those in which power is divided among the members on a theoretically egalitarian basis but which is in principle capable of being aggregated in an "upward" direction' (1993: 56).

Polyarchy is an ambivalent power structure enabling both the official recognition of a plurality of members and political actors, the right to disagree with the leaders, and the simultaneous concentration of political power. The regulation between contestation and political concentration is operated through the action of intermediate bodies (the corporate subelites) whose duty is to foster participation and to 'buffer' the potential consecutive development of oppositional behaviors. That perspective is in line with a theory of political pluralism, according to which, 'in a large complex society, the body of the citizenry is unable to affect the policies of the state' (Lipset et al. 1956: 15). That is why a polyarchic structure of power necessitates the fragmentation of the political body: 'democracy is most likely to become institutionalized in organizations whose members form organized or structured subgroups which, while maintaining a basic loyalty to the larger organization, constitute relatively independent and autonomous centers of power within the organization' (1956: 15). In a polyarchic structure, oligarchs strive to build a democratic plurality of actors while reinforcing unobtrusively the power of the inner circle. To sum up, a polyarchic structure of power is characterized by:

- soft and partly decentralized structures of governance with strict and relatively insuperable social and symbolic boundaries around oligarchic circles
- detailed social fragmentation through the multiplication of subgroups and the development of individualization, with strong intermediate bodies often articulated around internal professions and subelites.

We suggest placing the polyarchic model into discrete categories to help situate it with respect to the other political structures we have outlined in Table 11.2. These categories are dependent both on the level of fragmentation of the organizational body (political plurality) and on the level of admissible contestation (deliberative culture. The discussion is summarized in Figure 11.3.

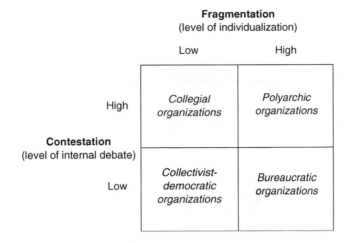

Figure 11.3 Variables Defining Polyarchy

Conclusion

In this chapter we have examined, from different angles, an old assumption of organizational theories of power: that power is about the constant and antagonistic search for equilibrium between possible contestation and uncritical allegiance. Weber was clear on that point: power is about the social fabric of obedience-generating technologies. In this chapter we have addressed one of these technologies, namely organizational forms, and its relationships with power structures. We have suggested illuminating the emergence of new organizational forms by unveiling how political dynamics and struggles in the workplace might generate legitimate political hybrids. In doing that, we have followed the traces of diverse schools of thought to help scholars think about organizational forms in a fresh way, albeit from a tradition that is, nevertheless, quite well established.

What are the strains that inform our theorization? First, traces of a Selznickian institutionalism: organizational forms are related to the meaning of the bridges existing between bureaucracy and democracy. Politics, for that matter, is about the production of specific values that could seamlessly or more violently be infused in the organizational body and in the polity. Second, there are traces of a pluralist tradition, nicely represented by Dahl, which sees organizational forms as the result of struggles and debates among a diversity of actors, all concerned with the same stakes and producing imperfect compromises.[9] The political forms in which they live and act are the temporary shapes given to these compromises. Third, there are traces of a Tocquevillean analysis of democracies: from that view, politics concerns the engineering of forms which render inequality approximately acceptable or inevitable, and which prevent inequality from hampering the performance of the whole organization. Politics is about the astute production of intermediate bodies and territorialized subgroups exercising power without contesting incumbent oligarchs.

The attempt to combine these traditions shifts the focus of organization power from the analysis of struggles themselves to that of the social creation of political performance. Political performance encompasses elements far beyond the production of outputs for people. It is the entire organizational edifice that is likely to be affected and involved in the construction of political performance. To put it differently, the success of an organization originates from its capacity to build a political system facilitating the congruence between a certain nature and a certain culture of power within the organization. Nothing is possible without a minimal congruence of that type.

By assuming political performance is of the utmost importance for organization leaders we do not mean that, once it is attained, no disequilibration is possible. That would suggest that a government or an organization that was performing well would never change. High political performance solidifies organizations, but does not prevent them from experiencing the influence of external factors that foster the emergence of internal opponents. For instance, as we will examine in the following chapter, it is highly likely that a change in the modes of elite production and, singularly, in the patterns and criteria of elite recruitment will affect the performance of organizational governments, however efficient they might be presently. The interdependence between different political ingredients, such as models of leadership and models of inclusiveness, creates unexpected knock-on effects on the structure of power.

Notes

1   The emergence of this debate demonstrates the salience and foresight of the diagnosis raised half a century ago by Gouldner (1955) under the rubric of 'metaphysical pathos': bureaucracy, as a political form, shrinks the scope of the organizational world in a one-dimensional view that is doomed to failure.

2   One may think of the character of Sir Humphrey in the BBC TV comedies 'Yes, Minister' and 'Yes, Prime Minister' as an example of this technical virtuosity.

3   English and Welsh readers may recall the poll tax as a case in point, in the early 1990s.

4   This aspect will also be addressed in the following chapter from another angle, that of the opposition between elitist and pluralist theories of power (see Chapter 12).

5   Once again, it is a different matter to evaluate the political performance *per se*. Here we only suggest that power structures and the organizational forms in which they are embodied generate different *natures* of political performance.

6   It should be specified at this stage that political performance is not to be confused with the view of a 'good' government, which depends on other types of criteria, such as moral judgments.

7   For instance, it is interesting to observe that the very rules shaping the road to the top of organizational hierarchies have undoubtedly changed over the past 20 years, as Cappelli and Hamori (2005) argue. Even though we will come back to this issue in Chapter 12, it is worth noticing now that the influence of educational backgrounds is dwindling, while pluralism of careers and of profiles seems to go hand in hand with the endogenous design of pluralist forms of organization and of political structures.

8   Political here also in the sense that it is the kind of decisions and processes which might affect deeply the future of the organization. This relates to the well-established Tocquevillean distinction between administrative and political agendas.

9   We will develop this theme in greater detail in Chapter 12.

12 Corporate Power Elites

Chapter outline

In this chapter we will:

- Analyze power as the cornerstone of elite production and perpetuation, in other words as the basis of corporate governance mechanisms.
- Shed light on the contemporary dynamics of the social and political foundations of corporate elites, by suggesting that they are an ambivalent phenomenon located somewhere between parochialism and globalization.

Introduction

The issue of power structures addressed in the previous chapter is closely related to the question of *Who governs?* (Dahl 1961). It is an important question and one just as deserving of an answer today as when first formulated by Dahl. In this chapter we address it by analyzing the dynamics of power in terms of elite production and perpetuation. First, we consider the debate between elitist and pluralist theories of elite power. The debate might seem endless but it requires contemporary examination in the light of recent corporate scandals that have, perhaps, reshaped the contours of elite groups and elite structures of legitimacy. Second, we consider current transformations in elite production, changes which lead us to consider the respective merits of organizational and inter-organizational accounts of elite production. Third, we examine how these changes might affect the very concept of power, by arguing that the contemporary concept of leadership is highly related to specific views of power.

Elite production: the meaning of pluralism and elitism

Situating elites

In his 1976 landmark *The comparative study of political elites*, Putnam writes wittily: 'Insofar as political decisions matter, political decision makers do, too.' He reminds us that behind the diverse façades of governance systems, which might appear to be quite transparent and accountable, 'power was always confined to a ruling few'. Indeed, addressing the issue of elite production and elite action in the context of organizations implies addressing a twofold debate. First, there is a debate concerning the appropriate level of analysis of elites. A controversy exists between an analysis in terms of inter-organizational networks (Mizruchi 1996) and an analysis in terms of endogenous generation of elites. We argue that elite power has to be analyzed in terms of 'the acceptance of irreversible commitments' which constitute what Selznick termed the 'character of the organization' (1957: 39–40). It is by analyzing formal policy commitments that one can distinguish between decisions pertaining to 'routine and critical experiences' (1957: 56). In this perspective, the question of elites is the question of leadership, that is the choice of 'key values and [of the creation of] a social structure that embodies them' (1957: 60). Leadership concerns the transformation of a neutral body of individuals into a 'committed polity' (1957: 90).

Second, there exists a debate about the degree of fragmentation and unification of the elite body, one that follows on from Michels' thought. Elite power is deeply related to the capacity of elites to create and maintain equilibrium between political and cultural cohesion as well as manage diverse practices and decision-making processes. As Miliband puts it, 'elite pluralism does not … prevent the separate elites in capitalist society from constituting a dominant economic class, possessed of a high degree of cohesion and solidarity, with common interests and common purposes which far transcend their specific differences and disagreements' (1969: 47).

Understanding elites means realizing that leadership concerns the professionalization of power holders; therefore, we acknowledge the fact that specific types of knowledge provide the circles of corporate power with resources to maintain their domination over the corporate body. We also acknowledge that constituting an elite body implies constantly engineering the beliefs of subordinates in the ability of a small circle of people to administer political affairs and reaffirming their legitimacy to take decisions that have large and potentially irreversible consequences.

Belief in the efficiency and legitimacy of rulers not only derives from discourses, as we suggested in previous chapters, but is mostly the consequence of actions generating relatively shared rationalities about what is the common good and who are the enemies of this common good. And these ideas never form in a vacuum. Constituting an organizational elite body is never an isolated act. One has to consider also that incumbent elites are permanently controlled 'by other elites exerting pressure, or by the public … or by institutional codes – that although there may be upper classes, there is no ruling class; although there may be men of power, there is no power elite' (Mills 1957: 16–17).

Understanding elites comes down to specifying rigorously the respective influence of elitist and pluralist views of power. In other terms, we present elites in this book as the missing link between studies of power and studies of democracy. Power concerns democracy and democracy implies power, as we have argued in the previous chapters. But there is a missing link between power and democracy in theories of organization power (well illustrated in March and Olsen's otherwise remarkable (1995) *Democratic governance*). The link is missing not only because of institutional disciplinary barriers between political science, organizational sociology and management studies but also because of the lack of an institutional perspective on elites. From this perspective, elites are responsible for the organization of political (strategic) action through organizing 'the interdependent obligations of political identities' (1995: 6); at the same time deep conflicts can occur when elites engage in political action, because they have to shape this action in such a way that their performance will be relatively acceptable to diverse political bodies.

In this chapter we focus on the 'professionals of power' as the cornerstone of the analysis of systems of governance. With C. Wright Mills we share the point of view that 'undue attention to the middle levels of power obscures the structure of power as a whole, especially the top and the bottom' (1957: 245). The purpose of theories of organization power should be to investigate power at the policy level instead of dissimulating its inherent weaknesses in the relentless analysis of power as 'petty politics and tactics and games'. Power is not just about little games over uncertainty and other irrationalities of systems theory, where some actors, who seem to lack any structural place, get others to do what they wouldn't otherwise do. Power should not be reduced to such games. It is the pillar of the social fabric of governing structures and regimes.

The meaning of pluralism

Dahl defines 'the fundamental axiom in the theory and practice of American pluralism' as the fact that '[i]nstead of a single center of sovereign power there must be multiple centers of power, none of which is or can be wholly sovereign' (1967: 24). Newton (1969) notes, aptly, that from such a perspective any political system 'which is not ruled by a power elite and which has different centers of power is guaranteed the title pluralist' (in Scott 1994: vol. III, 16). Some critics of pluralism question the possible tautology lying behind the term; after all, as Schils (1956: 154), among others, has pointed out, any complex society is to some degree (and in that view, everything is a matter of degree) pluralist, because it cannot be governed from a political center. But the meaning of pluralism is closer to that of democracy. In the pluralist perspective, pluralism is a political system enabling democratic decision-making processes, where the power to decide is shared between different bodies. More precisely, the behind-the-scenes pluralist thesis is that the existence and action of elites in a political system do not hamper democratic forms being developed. Elites are inevitable, but they can (must?) be plural. Here the statement of Rose is particularly germane: 'Pluralism is a theory of the power structure in which power is conceived of as dispersed and different elites are dominant in different issue areas' (1967: 282). A polity made up of what Dahl (1961: 190) called 'petty sovereignties' will avoid being confronted with any kind of competition. Competition might threaten democracy, as self-contained subelites do not necessarily act in the interests of the wider community.

The Schumpeterian vision of pluralism as a political system organizing and entailing competition between pluralities of elites is close to the core meaning of pluralist approaches to elite power. According to Schattschneider, 'democracy is a political system in which people have a choice among the alternatives created by competing political organizations and leaders' (1960: 141). Nevertheless, a plurality of competing elites is a necessary but not sufficient condition of democracy. What is more important is the institutionalization of a true system of responsiveness and accountability. Thus, as we suggested in Chapter 11, the examination of the relationships between elites and non-elites is the cornerstone of pluralist studies. To quote Dahl:

> Political power is pluralistic in the sense that there exist many different sets of leaders, each set has somewhat different objectives from the others, each has access to its own political resources, each is relatively independent of the others. There does not exist a single set of all powerful leaders who are wholly agreed on their major goals. Ordinarily, the making of government policies requires a coalition of different sets of leaders who have divergent goals. In this situation, it is probably easier for leaders to be effective in a negative way, by blocking other leaders, than in a positive way, by achieving their own goals. (1967: 188–9)

The problem with such an approach is the neglect of asymmetries between subgroups. In other words, it is indisputable that some groups and individuals are actually denied access to decision-making circles. As a result, power is not truly disseminated among subgroups, and remains a relationally unequally distributed resource. Here we get back to the idea of polyarchy as a system where 'each group has enough potential influence to mitigate harsh justice to its members though not necessarily enough influence to attain a full measure of justice' (Dahl 1961: 89). Newton points out that a major flaw of the pluralist approach is to consider that inequalities are not cumulative, i.e. that a political weakness in a certain area will be offset by a resource in another area (for instance, someone lacking money will have more time or more energy to devote to politics), contrary to Dahl's view that 'money and influence have a certain interdependence. The poor man is not likely to gain high influence; but if he does, somehow along the way he is no longer a poor man' (1961: 245). As Michels demonstrated a long time ago, this is likely to produce and perpetuate a small number of the 'chosen few' who pull most of the political strings, if not a single power elite.

The meaning of elitism

Elite theory is a well-established school of thought. It argues that a relatively small group of individuals initiate and monitor political and administrative decisions shaping the life of people and the destiny of collective bodies (Perrucci and Pilisuk 1970). Its central tenet is therefore that 'societies are divided into the few who hold power or rule, and the many who are ruled' (Etzioni-Halevy 1993: 19). Elitism derives from classical elite theorists such as Pareto, Mosca or Michels. Pareto distinguishes two types of elite: the governing elite, taking part directly or indirectly in government; and the non-governing elite, encompassing all the people endowed with excellence in their own area of knowledge, or *the experts*. Pareto writes, 'I use the word elite ... in its etymological sense, meaning the strongest, the most energetic, and most capable – for good as well as evil' (1935: 36).

For Mosca (1939), two classes of people appear in any society: a ruling class and a ruled class. To him, the political domination of an organized minority over an unorganized majority is inevitable. He distinguishes two elite structures, comprising the feudal structure, where the same members of the ruling class exercise all governmental functions (economic, judicial, administrative, military), and the bureaucratic structure, where a greater specialization in the ruling class separates the elite into different segments, especially in terms of the division between the administrative-bureaucratic and the military elites. According to Wright Mills, elite power constitutes three interdependent groups of the political, the military, and the corporate elite, whose perpetual uneasy coalition shapes the contours of an uncertain structure, a 'concerted power elite', sharing a commonality of interests, an ability to impose political unity, because, eventually 'elites ... agree on the "rules of the game"' (Etzioni-Halevy 1987: 4).

In most elitist studies, there is the assumption that the elite is 'internally homogeneous, unified and self-conscious' (Putnam 1976: 4). James Meisel (1962: 4) reminds us that no elite can be durable without group consciousness, coherence and conspiracy (common intentions). That these ideas are seen to be so necessary is largely related to Michels' tradition, according to which the division of labor necessary to any organization implies, *per se*, that a few people acquire the skills of leadership, the others being accustomed and socialized to being governed. However, the segmentation of the elite body into two restricted strata shrinks any view of a more open society, especially one that is more democratic. Once again, subsequent accounts of elites show a tendency to widen the scope and the endogenous variety of elite bodies, without renouncing the seminal elitist perspective outlined previously. For instance, the three-class theory of Mosca suggests the existence of an intermediate stratum of leaders 'who transmit information and opinion between the top elite and the citizenry, help to implement the elite's decisions, and provide new recruits for the upper stratum' (1939: 404–10). Thus, the possibility of a political stratification of elites is opened. Figure 12.1 illustrates this view, by displaying both the coexistence of diverse elite strata and the permanence of a hierarchy between elites. It also suggests the possible existence of a continuum between elites and the masses.

The relationship between elite composition and social structure shows a disproportionate recruitment among the diverse segments of society. Putnam puts forward two different models accounting for this relationship:

- an independence model, where the correlation between political status and economic status is negligible
- an agglutination model (Lasswell 1965: 9), where the powerful are also the healthy, wealthy, and well-educated people.

Mosca argued that 'Ruling minorities are usually so constituted that the individuals who make them up are distinguished from the masses of the governed by qualities that give them a certain material, intellectual, or even moral superiority; or else they are the heirs of individuals who possessed such qualities. In other words, members of a ruling minority regularly have some attribute, real or apparent, which is highly esteemed and very influential in the society in which they live' (1939: 53). Elitism, therefore, according to the elitist perspective, is also a way of

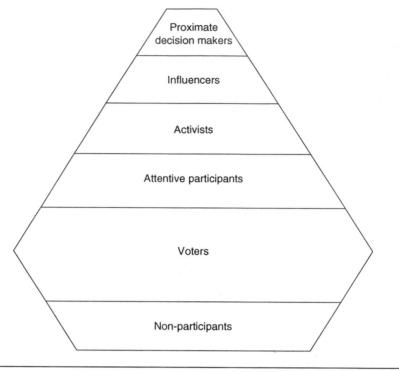

Figure 12.1   A political stratification model (from Putnam 1976: 11)

perpetuating a certain structure of dominancy and the patterns of legitimacy that accompany it. The meaning of elitism is related to the social acceptance by a majority of individuals that the act of governing necessarily implies a small number of individuals; that policies (and not necessarily politics) are a private business; and that participation might only be required at certain moments, under certain conditions, and following certain principles.

Elitism is not only a matter of social reproduction. It is also a cultural matter, deeply embedded in the political rationalities and identities of organizational members. As we proposed in the early chapters of this book, the constitution of management developed through the engineering of rules and instruments of calculation into a major achievement that was cultural. Having established management as a political affair, and elite managers as leaders who are the equals of statesmen as they make 'the transition from administrative management to institutional leadership' (Selznick 1957: 4), then a project that began with humble anatomical politics ends up having governance of the body politic through markets. To the political elites is left the role of regulation, in which people conceived as liberal individuals constitute themselves as entities who may or may not be politically self-regarding subjects (to the extent that they have a choice as to whether they vote or not); to the markets, and its elites, there is the delight of savoring the ascendancy of new forms of governmentality that make people economically self-regarding subjects, whether they vote for it or want it, or not. The notion of leadership is at the center of a struggle of legitimacy and signification between an administrative perspective on managing organizations and a socio-political perspective on governing institutions (Selznick 1992), in which governmentality plays the most recent role.

It is indisputable that the people who control the largest multinational corporations have enormous power and influence; indeed, as much as is the case for high-rank government officials, the fate and culture of entire nations and of millions of individuals reside in their judgments and actions. That is why it is of utmost importance to shed light on the patterns of corporate elite generation, as it is a way to understand better under which criteria, and what conditions, power structures are affected by the people designing and controlling them. Our assumption here is that while the models of analysis of elite production are well established and still pertinent for investigating the patterns and dynamics of elite production, the very criteria and concrete forms of contemporary pathways to the top are transforming, and are likely to affect on a long-term basis the power structures of organizations and, more widely, of the whole business world.

Dynamics of elite production

Historical snapshot

There are undoubtedly common features in Western societies concerning elite recruitment and grooming. In traditional European societies, the fundamental ingredient of elite production was heredity. The accumulation of both upper-class origins and wealth mainly brought by land in agrarian societies was the rule. The existence of alternative channels of recruitment derived either from peculiar favors accorded by a prince or a lord, or from military exploits and purchase of public offices. Alternative upward paths were partly founded on meritocratic criteria, enabling bright lowborn individuals to gain access to inner circles of power.[1] In the industrial revolution, as recruitment and promotion through patronage progressively gave way to elite recruitment via competitive exams and promotion by merit, meritocracy gradually supplemented privilege, but it never replaced it entirely.

With respect to elite education, it is noteworthy that for a long time there was no special dedicated educational system. Most heirs had private tutors or received the classical education given to upper-class sons by clergy. But the rise of new industries, such as chemicals, and the aftermath of the managerial revolution, which were analyzed by Burnham (1941) and Chandler (1962), gave way to a new salaried top executive class who gradually overthrew the heirs of the founding families. The professionalization of leadership underlined by Michels induced an increasingly specialized training and the education patterns of elites went through major transformations from the late nineteenth century onwards. Brezis and Crouzet (2002) remind us that the progressive democratization of higher education (re)created a new separation of the educational system into an elite system and a non-elite system.[2] Cassis (1997: 133) shows, for instance, that during the twentieth century the tendency is for a growing influence of higher education in the production of elites;

in 1907 respectively 35, 72 and 57 percent of English, French and German business leaders graduated from a university or an elite school, while in 1989 these proportions climbed to 64, 95 and 88 percent.

The channels of elite production have been affected by the successive social and industrial revolutions of the last two centuries. But the major consequence might be the resilience and unobtrusive reinforcement of elite separation from the masses, through the replacement of heredity and familial ties by selective dedicated educational systems and institutions. We shall return to these aspects later in an examination of the contemporary dynamics of elite production patterns.

Models of elite production

There is an extended literature on patterns and modes of elite production (Putnam 1976). From the idea of 'sponsored and contested' mobility (Turner 1960) to the analysis of interlocking directorates (Mizruchi 1996), from the analysis of the relationships between business and politics (Mizruchi 1992) to more recent analysis of the role of social networks in the 'small world' of business leaders (Davis et al. 2003), it is highly difficult to put forward unequivocal findings, given that this has been a very productive stream of research. Yet it is possible, following both Useem (1984) and Pettigrew (1992), to underline three major modes of elite production. These are the inter-organizational production of corporate elite cohesion; the condensation of upper-class principles; and the paths of corporate ascent. In a few words, Useem (1984: 103–5) suggests typifying five stages of movement into the inner circles:

1 company ascent, where movement into senior management ranks of a more or less large company operates under the scrutiny of top executives
2 outside directorships, when lateral movements operate to place representative individuals on the boards of several other companies
3 top management, when an individual gets access to the post of CEO or managing director
4 association leadership, such as participation in the management of a leading association in business
5 government consultation, such as becoming a 'business ambassador'.

Naturally, these features are germane to the highest rank of corporate elite production. They stress nevertheless the fact that in most cases pathways to the top are dependent on an ability to combine internal responsibilities and functions with external visible duties. The channels of recruitment, the routes through which most aspirants for corporate leadership reach the top, are marked by several mechanisms and criteria (Putnam 1976: 46–7):

• the existence of gates and gatekeepers (how and by whom are the chosen few chosen?)
• credentials (what criteria must would-be leaders meet, what are the most highly praised academic awards?)
• turnover and succession policies (how, and how often, do incumbent leaders leave office?).

Interestingly, Putnam adds a fourth criterion, the 'so what question'. In other words, from a political perspective, what is of utmost importance is to understand better the extent to which recruitment patterns affect the character of the elite and its politics. For example, as the methods shift from the permeability of the production channels, from hereditary systems offering one single path to the top, to lateral entries, from a selection by seniority (where, to quote Huntington 1973: 35, 'power goes not to the oldest son of the king, but the oldest child of the institution'), to a selection by efforts and performance, the meaning of being a leader is fundamentally affected. Take the difference between contested and sponsored mobility (Turner 1960: 856). Contested mobility is a system in which elite status 'is the prize in an open contest and is taken by the aspirants' own efforts. While the "contest" is governed by some rules of fair play, the contestants have wide latitude in the strategies they may employ' (1960: 856). In that case, established elites will not monopolize successful upward mobility. Under sponsored mobility, 'elite recruits are chosen by the established elite or their agents, as elite status is *given* on the basis of some criteria of supposed merit and cannot be *taken* by any amount of effort or strategy … Ultimately the members grant or deny upward mobility on the basis of whether they judge the candidate to have those qualities they wish to see in fellow members' (1960: 856). In the latter system, elite production turns into elite reproduction, as it is the foundation of the political agenda. Contested elite generation pertains to a pure democratic form of selection. Aspirants to leadership must think of themselves as competing because they form considerable identification with incumbent elites through the process of selection, which is actually a process of indoctrination and education. Sponsored policies of elite generation rest on the necessity to educate the masses so as to make them regard themselves as 'relatively incompetent to manage society' (1960: 859), cultivating the belief in the superior competence of the elite group.

Useem (1984) underlines compellingly that the three elite generative mechanisms act simultaneously but according to different degrees:

- In the upper-class principle, where the corporate elite is seen as a 'business aristocracy', a social network relying on specific kinship and private-familial connections, and academic pedigree is intermingled with social prominence.
- In the class-wide principle, where the corporate elite is produced through transcorporate networks such as acquaintanceship circles, webs of ownership, and interlocking directorates, Useem argues that the efforts of leaders to promote the broad needs of big business as a community instead of defending the interests of a single corporation are bolstered.
- In the corporate principle, the corporate elite is defined by organizational mechanisms of career and selection management and by the position of the organization in its environment, especially the economy.

The social and political foundations of these three principles are evidently different, even opposed. Each puts the emphasis on a specific political purpose. Upper-class mechanisms enhance the perpetuation of a restricted segment of the population based on the maintenance of a social and cultural distance with the governed, a distance which is the condition of legitimacy of the elite group; the objective is, therefore, to generate a belief in the persistence of disconnected and impermeable social worlds vested with different sources of political power and legitimacy.

Class-wide mechanisms and, singularly, interlocking directorates, are interpreted differently, according to the perspective chosen. From a resource-dependency perspective, they are means of facilitating economic interconnections, of exchanging rare resources such as highly skilled people. Interlocks are designed to reduce the uncertainties created by the relationships developed between firms (Pettigrew 1992: 166). From a 'class-based' perspective (Zeitlin 1974; Useem 1984), elite power stems directly from interlocks, because they generate and help the perpetuation of cohesive ties based on the class-wide interests of the corporate elite. But as Pettigrew argues, studies of interlocks say relatively little concerning how networks make use of such power. How and why 'the powerful' are 'bolstered by linkages outside the firm and checked by non elites inside the firm' (Pettigrew 1992: 179) remains a mystery if we do not include in the analysis the power of organizations to shape, at least partly, their own structures of authority through selection mechanisms of career management.

Useem sees 'the new powers of the transcorporate networks' as being the indirect product of 'the declining power of individual companies' (1984: 150). Nonetheless, studying elite power requires one to accept coexistence between class-wide logics and corporate logics in the social fabric of elite formation and reformation. The power of corporate elites is evidently based on their capacity to 'transcend the parochial interests of single companies and sectors, and to offer a more integrated vision of the broader, longer-term needs of business' (1984: 59). But such elites must also take into simultaneous account aspects of their internal political performance, as sketched in Chapter 11. Elites that are always hitting the airport tarmac and not taking care of business at home create vulnerability to a coup. In other words, elite production patterns affect the way management professionals are considered inside organizations. In charge of elite–mass linkages and/or in charge of the 'business as usual' parochial preoccupations, these are the people who are practically 'running the business'.

The political purpose of elite production is to decide to what extent the elite should be socially and culturally homogeneous (Mills 1957: 19) or should incorporate new blood and bodies, which raises, once again, the issue of pluralism and fragmentation of elites. Elite production patterns directly affect the degree of homogeneity of elites and therefore the degree of fragmentation of the elite body. We have already addressed the question of oligarchy because unified elites are potentially oligarchic. Dahl states that 'the actual political effectiveness of a group is a function of its potential for control and its potential for unity' (1958: 465). The more unified and cohesive the elite, the more capable they are of formulating moral reasons as to why they, and the other members of the dominant elite, should believe in their strength. We take the view that elite ideologies function more for the cohesion of the elite than they do for the subordination of the masses. If the masses believe them, well, that is an advantage, but it is not necessary: there are far too many mundane ways in which domination can be arranged for it to hinge on matters of ideology alone. For Mosca, people need 'political formulas', which are

Table 12.1 Some functions of the principles of elite production

Functions/Principles	Class based	Network based	Company based
Typical mechanism of production	Boarding schools 'Ivy League' kinds of educational system	Interlocks	Fast tracks Internal education programs
Typical leadership profile	Heirs	Political managers	Corporate professionals
Values bolstered	Business leaders as aristocracy and tradition defenders	Business leaders as political representatives	Business leaders as parochial defenders
Political purpose	Social perpetuation and elite unity	Cohesive ties and business as a whole power structure	Endogenous stratification monitored from the top

not 'mere quackeries aptly invented to trick the masses into obedience ... they answer a real need in men's social nature; and this need, so universally felt, of governing and knowing that one is governed not on the basis of mere material or intellectual force, but on the basis of moral principles, has beyond any doubt a practical and real importance' (1939: 71). Mills argues that elite power derives directly from a combination of factors, comprising psychological similarity, where elite members are of the same social type so that social intermingling occurs between different elite groupings, and coordination, as elites come to see that their diverse interests 'could be realized more easily if they worked together, in informal as well as in formal ways' (1957: 20).

We have summed up these different insights in Table 12.1. If anything, this table suggests that, as Davis and Mizruchi put it, in corporate governance 'the economic and the social are inextricably linked. Board members are typically recruited from among friends and acquaintances of current directors. Conversely, relations that begin as economic ties often become overlaid with the social relations, and the resulting social structures shape corporate decision making' (1999: 215).

When analyzing corporate elite power, one cannot eschew mentioning the central role played by commercial banks, especially in the US (Davis and Mizruchi 1999). Quoting Jackson in 1832 (cited in Roe 1994: 58), Davis and Mizruchi recall his words to the effect that 'it is easy to conceive that great evils to our country and its institutions might flow from such a concentration of power in the hands of a few men irresponsible to the people' (1999: 216). Nearly a hundred years later we find Wilson agreeing with him in 1911 that 'the great monopoly in this country is the money monopoly' (Brandeis 1914: 1). Board interlocks can thus be analyzed as means of domination by investment banks. The chain of interlocks is not a paranoiac phantasmagoria; the intermingling of banks and commercial enterprises is a reality. Kotz (1978) argues that banks control most of the largest US corporations through their trust departments. If we go back to the issue of elite homogeneity, it is interesting to note, with Davis and Mizruchi, that in the US, of the 648 largest US corporations in 1982, directors of 43 percent served either on the Chase Manhattan board or on other boards with Chase directors (1999: 218). One can draw the conclusion that, 'by anchoring the interlock network, bank boards provided a mechanism for political and governance cohesion among the corporate elite, albeit unintentionally' (1999: 220). Even if the social organization of corporate elites is more scattered and disorganized (Lash and Urry 1987) and more decentralized as economies move from a banking-based to a capital-market form of financial inter-mediation, the view of interlocks as institutionalizing a practice of power which produces cohesive and sometimes coercive kinds of inter-organizational ties remains valid (Perrucci and Pilisuk 1970). Palmer and Barber note that such a corporate elite *is* an actor and attains power not only because of their organiza-tional and institutional relations, but also because of their position in a 'multi-dimensional social class structure' (2001: 88). It is a view of power based on the assumptions that the 'corporate elite pursue acquisitions to increase their wealth and social status', which entails a classical Marxian analysis of the role of ownership in relations of production (see Marx 1976). Additionally, it assumes that social, familial and educational background (Domhoff 1967) as well as positions in net-works (Mizruchi 1996) are of considerable significance in relations of power. The established elite, in whatever way it criticizes and contests challenges, will resist new claimants through its participation in interlocking networks (Useem 1984). Maintaining or attaining power in these networks is achieved through extended social ties and, through these, control of business norms, which can be used to question, marginalize and otherwise seek to repel those 'challengers' who dare violate them (as when hostile bids are qualified as 'rapes').

Contemporary dynamics of elite production

As many commentators have noted, the corporate upheavals of the 1980s and 1990s have modified the power structure of most big corporations. In a nutshell, the idea is that the massive movements of mergers, acquisitions, re-engineering, downsizing and corporate governance dynamics may have affected the distribution of power between the organizational 'center' and the 'organizational body' (sub-sidiaries, senior executives, employees) through an ambivalent tendency of political recentralization and administrative (operational) decentralization. The differenti-ation of agendas between the top circles of corporate power and the manifold number of subunits and subgroups that are more or less vested with a delegation of powers has increased. The best gauge of this is the ratio of top to bottom salaries in an organization. The 1980s and since have seen the chasm grow much wider in many European and US businesses (and in the US it is notably wider than in Europe; in Japan the ratio is far smaller) such that the wedge between the 'governors' and the 'governed' is larger than ever.

What remains fascinating is the extent to which channels of elite produc-tion have been affected by those wedges and chasms whose materiality defines contemporary organizations. To grasp better the nature of corporate elite power in today's corporations, one still needs to evaluate the degree of resilience of well-established patterns of elite production. Here we follow the hypothesis that, if the channels of elite production have proved to be highly resilient, the criteria of recruitment and the consecutive leadership profiles may have started to transform.

The resilience of elite production patterns

In their study of the connective topography of the director and corporate board networks connecting the largest US corporations through interlocks, Davis et al. (2003: 307) raise the issue of the changes of the global network structure as a response to the political, economic and social transformations of the past 20 years. They found that the corporate elite still remains a 'small world'. In other words, the distance between directors is small and the strength of its ties is a very resilient property of elite networks over the last two decades. It is a finding that tends to confirm one of the major insights of Mills' study of elite power, according to which the mutually acquainted power elite is produced by a structural tendency toward concentration of institutions, not as the result of a rational and purposeful conspiracy, but because of the social fabric of common worldviews and standards of action for corporate executives.

At first glance, the connectedness of the corporate elite may be seen as shaky. In reality, Davis et al. (2003) demonstrate that the 'small world phenomenon' is still acting as a powerful mechanism of self-perpetuating power structures. Watts (1999: 4) defines the small world phenomenon as the materialization of the sensation of running into a complete stranger while progressively discovering that they know somebody unexpected in common. Short chains can connect many people, as Milgram (1967) puts it. From this perspective, an elite network might keep and sustain very resilient power only through short links, without recourse to institutions facilitating, or any particular ingenuity in, cohesion. Indeed, 'in spite of the rampant turnover among boards and directors, and nearly complete turnover in ties, distances among the corporate elite remained virtually constant' (Davis et al. 2003: 321).

The resilience of elite corporate production and the consecutive self-perpetuation of corporate power structures derive from the fabric and resilience of a community of power. It is the social foundation and organization of this community that provide the essential ingredients of its legitimacy. As Arendt noted, the most powerful form of power resides in the organizational sophistication of the few ruling groups, more than in the use of coercion or force. The resilience of elite composition in an ever changing and turbulent business world can be understood through the distance maintained between elites and the institutions they govern. Useem suggests implicitly that the social permanence of corporate elite groups flows from the fact that the organization of the class is largely independent of the organization of the polity constituted by organizations. In other words, social networks produce and reinforce the relative remoteness of elite members from the bodies they shape and govern through their common decisions. A possible contemporary definition of oligarchy production thus emerges from these debates. Michels analyzed the strong interconnections between organizations *per se,* and oligarchy as a by-product of organization. We could argue that, nowadays, because of the unknowability and rapidity with which the future encounters the present and the impermanence of contemporary organizational settings in consequence, oligarchy is produced by its *social disconnection from organization,* while reinforcing the inter-organizational social foundations of the elite class.

There is a further question: whether there is or there is not an intentional political design. Davis et al. (2003) suggest it is not necessary that there should be such a design, as the social construction of shared values and interests proves to be the 'obligatory' consequence of networks that frequently interact face to face. Intimate interactants may share common values as easily as a contagion might pass readily between the members. The network approach adds fuel to the elitist perspective, where elites are viewed as a set of interlocking centers of power, in which a few power holders master crucial decisions. The autonomy of elite organization does not, however, suppress any idea of pluralism, but it is a monitored pluralism, one where elite members themselves determine the distribution of power, and where the crucial organizational foundation is the purposeful fragmentation of elite strata. Eventually, strategic business decisions might largely be influenced by social ingredients, such as the sharing of values and the sort of 'neocorporatist' interests that emerge from a whole bunch of strongly interconnected individuals. Mimetic and normative isomorphism is of considerable value in explaining the emergence of surprisingly similar views amongst elites. At one level, it is almost a matter of good manners. One would not want to break ranks publicly, unless some element of either deep crisis or extraordinary opportunity presented itself. Interlocks not only provide a cohesive basis for the elite community; they also facilitate some decisions because bounded decision makers are provided with thick intelligence about what other competitors have done. Corporate governance is partly shaped by criss-cross observations at a distance; thus, power structures and consecutive political forms are likely to be increasingly similar, creating a dynamic circle of political resilience.

We can find comparable insights in many other studies. For instance, the studies by Brezis and Crouzet (2002), Temin (1999) or Baverez (1998) suggest the remarkable resilience of the origins of business elites both in France and in the US, countries characterized by very different institutional influences and values. Baverez researched the origins of the leaders of the companies whose shares are quoted on the Paris Stock Exchange (known in France as the CAC 40 firms, a sort of French Dow Jones). He shows the amazing stability of the origins and social foundations of the French corporate elite over the last two decades: from 1981 to 1997 the proportion of leaders that made their path to the top via a business career went from 20 to 25 percent; the proportion of members of founders/owners' families decreased from 43 to 20 percent; while civil servants represented 55 percent of the corporate elite in 1997 compared with 37 percent in 1981. The proportion of civil servants demonstrates, if needed, the resilience of the peculiar French structure of corporate power, marked by the ascendancy of a 'state nobility' (Bourdieu 1996) over the corporate world.

The interpenetration of state and civic power elites could be related, in part, to the emergence of the 'political manager' depicted by Useem (1984). The broadening of the managerial scope to encompass societal and political issues might indeed reinforce the tendency to educate and produce politically oriented leaders whose personal connections to the state might prove particularly efficient and necessary. In the US there is a remarkable ambivalence in elite culture, deriving from what Tocqueville suggested was the paradox of democracy, where the fantastic power of local institutions and the parallel power of the state and of the central constitution exist alongside the power of masters in a country marked by the unbelievable persistence of slavery and by a striking culture of initiative and freedom.

Notions of social mobility are central to US culture. Recall the highly popular biographies of figureheads of social mobility such as Andrew Carnegie or John Rockefeller, books whose main message to each single person in the country was that one could become part of the uppermost and wealthiest elite through hard work, ingenuity and innovation. Sorokin (1925), in his study of millionaires in the US, found that society was becoming less and less meritocratic and that the pathways to the top were increasingly imposing impediments to individuals without the basic upper-class capitals of wealth, access, culture, connections and kin. In a shrewd compromise, Joslyn and Taussig (1932) pointed out that elite production mostly rested on the fact that upper-class people were more able and competent than the sons (rarely the occasional daughter) of the lower social strata. They had received both a great deal more training and everyday practice in elite management and disposition.

The debate still rages between those who argue that exogenous social backgrounds are the most influential ingredients of elite generation, and those who counter that corporate careers can largely account for access to the top business ranks.[3] From the persistence of this debate, we draw the notion that the elite landscape is not that simple and, particularly, that the road to the top of the biggest corporations might have significantly evolved over the last two decades. Let us examine this latter hypothesis before concluding with a consideration of the political and theoretical implications of ruling elites for the study of power in organizations.

The transformation of elite paths and profiles

For decades scholars have posed questions concerning the attributes of individuals who make space for themselves at the top of elite circles. Recently, Cappelli and Hamori (2004; 2005) generated interesting results about the changes affecting the routes to senior executive positions in US business organizations between 1980 and 2001.[4] They collected information about demographical attributes, educational background, and career histories. Their analysis reveals significant differences in the attributes and experiences of top managers over the past two decades. In short, by the early 1980s, the principles and channels of recruitment of top executives were mostly similar to those in use from the 1940s or the 1950s. During these periods, the US economic elite came overwhelmingly from elite sons who attended elite colleges, strengthening the picture of the American elite as composed largely of white Protestant males (Temin 1999). In other words, elitism was fundamentally related to the restriction of recruitment channels, and to the self-perpetuation of narrow oligarchic circles of power (Bourdieu 1996).

Even narrow oligarchies can become more pluralist. Cappelli and Hamori's (2005) results support the hypothesis of a general progressive transition, between 1980 and the early twenty-first century, from a 'classical' elitist perspective towards a more pluralistic and, so to speak, a more fragmented picture of the corporate elite in the US. In short, compared to 1980, top executives in 2001 are younger, more likely to be women, and more likely to be educated in public institutions. To the authors of this study, these changes are more attributable to transformations in the organizational mechanisms of career management and control than to changes in the underlying populations in the two periods (2005: 31). Several dynamics are at the heart of the rejuvenation of elite production systems between the two periods:[5]

- Executive career paths are slightly different, which suggests that the skills and abilities tested are different as well. For example, selected individuals who get to the highest and supreme positions typically hold fewer jobs today; thus, having had tenure in one single company is much less important and the path to the top is significantly faster than was the case.
- Outside hiring is much more frequent among top executives. More than half of top executives now come from outside, despite the existence of strong and well-established internal career policies based on internal labor markets.
- A very significant gender dynamic is also unveiled. Female elites are much younger than their male counterparts (47 vs 52), are less likely to have been life-time employees (32 percent vs 47 percent for men), will have held their previous jobs for a shorter period of time (3.4 years vs 4 years for men), and will have got to the top faster (21 vs 25 years) (2005: 33).

How far these results can be predictive of an enduring trend is difficult to specify.[6] But overall, we might risk several hypotheses pertaining to underlying power dynamics shaping the subsequent form of the corporate elite:

1   The current globalization of the business world might be combining with the 'small world' phenomenon to force organizations to gain tighter control over their elite. In other words, the persistence of interpersonal forms of relationships in use in inter-organizational networks of different types necessitates companies to off-set consecutive 'externally produced' influences by endogenously shaping patterns of authority. Corporate leaders would then be groomed both within the corporate leadership nurseries and within the scattered external circles of power.
2   Globalization might be encouraging the creation of a 'profession' of corporate leader. The growing influence of MBAs, for instance, as the key for entry to the managers' job market and the decline in organizational tenure might signal the current construction of a 'profile' of top executives, based on common education and common types of inter-organizational experiences. A global job market of professional corporate leaders might therefore be emerging, largely monitored from the manifold elite networks surrounding organizations.
3   By and large, these hypothetical trends underline the effects of the fundamental interdependence of organizational power structures and of global economic structures of governance. It is not evident that organizations today are as capable

of producing internal power elites as once was the case. The diffusion of new types of behaviors regarding mobility and identity affects the composition of elite membership, as they strive to acknowledge and incorporate the growing influence of external actors and networks. A new oligarchy is emerging unobtrusively – one that is produced less in the shadows of class differentiation and Ivy League colleges than by application of the official standards of educational systems and in the rejuvenated shadows of pluralist interlocks. A pluralist *and* homogeneous corporate elite power seems to be emergent, at least in the US.

Corporate elite dynamics and the concept of power

Mechanisms of elite formation

Scholars grappling with the conceptual dynamics of the notion of power need to investigate the contemporary dynamics of elite production and its relationship with the meaning of elitism and pluralism in organizations (and more broadly in Western societies, with all their institutional specificities). Given that holders of key positions in power relations are today generated by different mechanisms than two or three (or more) decades ago, we might infer that this evolution sheds a different light on the basic concept of power. We think two major dimensions of the underlying idea of power are directly affected by the idea that we developed above of a relatively homogeneous pluralist corporate elite, one that is confusedly intermingling global and parochial dimensions in the 'profession' of leader.

The first dimension is legitimacy. Suchman (1995) suggests legitimacy is a generalized phenomenon involving the role of a social audience; according to Suchman, legitimacy is a 'generalized perception or assumption that the actions of an entity are desirable, proper, or appropriate within some socially constructed system of norms, values, beliefs, and definitions' (1995: 574). Legitimacy is socially constructed, as the long-lasting Weberian tradition puts it, because it mirrors the congruence between the behaviors of an entity and the beliefs of those it targets. With respect to this simple definition of legitimacy, our argument is that the evolution of the production patterns of corporate elites tends to generate *institutional* forms of legitimization. In other words, organizations are deeply affected by their interpenetration with external factors (such as elite networks, the role of external educational systems and credentials, and the role of social criteria such as gender). The reciprocal effects of external and internal mechanisms are particularly apparent in elite production, and it is clearly difficult to disentangle what pertains to organizational and what to external institutional dynamics. Elite production and, therefore, power structures are produced by the collective simultaneous structuration of networks and of a substantive set of shared professional obligations (potentially constituting a profession). Thus, power structures appear to be the result of the institutionalization of the reciprocal influences of individual experiences and life histories (paths to circles of power), and of established cultural frameworks shaping an approximately acceptable definition of what it means to be and not be part of elite groups. Singular intimacies are merging together with cultural standards and assumptions in the fabric of power structures.

The concept of power useful for explanation of corporate elite dynamics can make use of more refined managerial and resource-dependency explanations (a resource to manipulate in the course of life), as long as these are refined through contact with theories of an institutional and 'three-dimensional' type, to connect with Lukes' (1974) thoughts (something that their progenitors seem unable to do). A taken-for-granted belief system prevails but it suffers anomie as uncertain discourses come from people and issues of uncertain origins. The best case example is that of gender. The gender critique is now recognized by elite men and defensive strategies are in place to deal with it on the part of the corporate and other elites who strive now for legitimacy in this new arena of contest. It is for this reason that what has come to be known as the Summers Affair at Harvard was so shocking for the liberal intelligentsia. There was a sense that the battles about equity and gender had been won discursively, even if the practices that might reflect those discourses were slower developing than might fondly be hoped for. The rumination, in public, by Harvard Dean Larry Summers that there might be genetic variations between men and women in quantitative capacity thus unleashed a storm of controversy because it was seen and widely interpreted as an attempt to put the feminist genie back in the masculinist bottle. If Harvard deans can justify a lack of equity on genetic grounds then the other corporate elites could breathe more easily about their own failure to have addressed this issue adequately, if the issue was due to recede in importance. Of course, the fact that Summers (a neoclassical economist) knows little about genetics or sociology hardly equips him to contribute much of scientific worth on the matter, but that is not the issue. Just as it appeared that a fundamental legitimacy in discourse about the nature of gender had been established, his contribution short-circuited it. The obligatory passage points were uncoupling.[7]

Contemporary dynamics of legitimization rest upon a curious mixture of pragmatism (the instrumental part of political performance: see Chapter 11) and of morality (do they do the right things?), as Suchman (1995: 578–80) proposes. The Summers case thus created new opportunities for legitimization as Harvard hosed things down through the classic bureaucratic strategies of setting up subcommittees enquiring into the participation rates of females in select disciplines.

A further dimension of corporate elite dynamics relates to the current hybridization of different forms of subordination in the employment relationship. By and large, Simmel (1950) is valuable in the attempt to describe the circular nature of the dynamics involving elite production and forms of power for at least two major reasons. First, there is his idea of domination as a form of interaction, in which the desire of domination is more 'the mere consciousness of this possibility' than 'exploitation of the other' (1950: 181). The peculiar pluralism of the emerging corporate elite relates to the complex mixture between three kinds of subordination that Simmel perspicaciously delineated as follows.

Subordination under an individual

Subordination under an individual implies two different natures of power relationships. First, superordination means only 'that the will of the group has found a unitary expression or body' (Simmel 1950: 190). In that case, elites are in charge of the close unit, but it is the very identity of the elite that serves as the basis of the unity. Political asymmetry between the ruler and the ruled is the pillar of the efficiency and strength of the subsequent political form. Second, in case of opposition to the leader, the principle of superordination is not modified. 'Discord, in fact, perhaps even more stringently than harmony, forces the group to "pull itself together". In general, common enmity is one of the most powerful means for motivating a number of individuals or groups to cling together' (1950: 193). Simmel suggests merely that the ruler is always an adversary. Leading an entity means using the dual relation of people to the principle of subordination. Men cannot exist without leadership, without being led, an idea we find also in Tocqueville, because they 'seek the higher power which relieves them from responsibility' (1950: 193) and, simultaneously, they need to oppose the leading power in order to feel that they do more than merely exist but are free. Simmel reminds us that obedience and opposition are two sides of one consistent human attitude. In that perspective, power is a means of creating a common arena for the fight between rulers and the ruled, those who are for and those who are against the ruler, a struggle at the basis of the vitality of organizations and societies. Connecting elite production patterns with the concept of power implies analyzing the political consequences of enduring restrictions in the access to power circles, while the number of capable individuals who could claim to be potentially part of the elite body is growing. One of the most likely consequences is a naturally growing segmentation of elites, and the stratification of elites inside organizations, well illustrated by the pervasiveness of professionalization tendencies.

Subordination under a plurality

Essentially, subordination under a plurality creates a difference through its presumed objectivity, such that the collective behavior of the subjects is rid of 'certain feelings, leanings and impulses' (Simmel 1950: 225). The power of the ruler resides principally in the fact that this type of subordination enables 'every single individual who participates in a given decision [to] hide himself behind the fact, precisely, that it was a decision by the whole group' (1950: 226). We have already discussed this matter in relation to total institutions in Chapter 6. With respect to elites, Simmel thinks, this perspective suggests a solution for the misuse of power. Power holders are more collective than personally accountable individuals. As a result, increasing the power of certain elites might help to prevent misuses and abuses of power (1950: 227).[8] To go further, Simmel argues that subordination under a heterogeneous plurality has different implications to subordination under homogeneous elite rule. Being subjected to opposed superiors, as the child standing between conflicting parents, or employees being 'servants of two masters' (1950: 230), is the fate of modern individuals who are more and more dependent on a manifold of external 'power holders', while keeping a certain amount of freedom by not being entirely subject to any of them. In that respect, power derives from the interwoven mechanisms of differentiation operated, on one side, by the rulers among their subordinates and, on the other side, by the ruled among their different superiors. Power is at the crossroads of these two segmenting and stratifying practices. In a way, the ruled contribute to establishing and confirming a certain caste at the top from the moment a majority of the polity chooses certain power circles to gain relational positions of power; in exchange, the elite contributes by giving certain segments of the polity the capacity to make choices of that type, what Tocqueville called 'intermediate powers'. Hence the circular[9] nature of elitism and power contribute, paradoxically, to the reinforcement of elite structures. Power relations are the general consequence of the stability of certain elite groups, compared to the short-lived duration of other groups.

Subordination under a principle

Such subordination occurs especially under an objective law or set of rules, and means being accountable to the most 'uninfluenceable powers' (Simmel 1950: 250). Compared with personal forms of power relationships, the substance of the rule and of the emanating orders determines the legitimacy of power holders. Put differently, this type of subordination refers to the power of objectivity, i.e. the power of obligation stemming from the objective idealized validity of uninterrupted sources of rules generated by elite experts. The question of the corporate elite arises in a different manner. The confrontation of elite and non-elite is somewhat filtered by a flow of intermediate powers which become norm giving. Objectivity is defined by Simmel, that close colleague of Weber (1978), as 'the unquestionably valid law which is enthroned in an ideal realm above society and the individual' (1950: 256). But more importantly, subordination under objectivity supposes that the elite itself is subordinated to overwhelming principle; elites can give orders to non-elites and shape specific power regimes only in the name of the unit constituted by the objective principle, where 'the very commander subordinates himself to the law which he has made' (1950: 262).

The permanent mingling of objective and ultra-personal forms of power is one of the major ingredients of the social resilience of corporate elites. What we mean is that the remoteness of elite circles from the grassroots levels of organizations is a condition enabling the objectification of elite circles, who are represented as faraway uncontrollable worlds, as somewhat like the Greek gods of antiquity, enjoying a wealth, celebrity and life that few can ape and nearly all might envy. Their doings are fabled and the stuff of contemporary legend in MBA classrooms all over the world. At the same time, the individual qualities of leaders prove to be a sort of compensation of subjective arbitrariness. The power of leaders derives both from exemplar values and behaviors supposedly controllable and assessable by the polity, and from remote systems and networks hardly controllable by the latter. A shrewd mix of distant uncertainty and of permanently connected behaviors and decisions ensues. At its most potent it assumes characteristics of celebrity circuits of power, so that a star system ensues. The business of Hollywood and the Hollywood of business become ever more intermingled.

Conclusion

Corporate elites seem to operate a simultaneous movement towards seeking legitimization by refocusing on organizationally more parochial issues and stakes, while striving for the permanence of social structures of power outside the organization. Are these opposite tendencies or part of the same movement of political structures of organizations? Growing pluralism inside firms undoubtedly goes hand in hand with a strengthened political fragmentation between top elites and the rest of the organizational body.

These political ambivalences are well known and mostly derive from an established understanding of political dynamics. As Simmel said, 'all leaders are also led; in innumerable cases, the master is the slave of his slaves' (1950: 185). Light is shed on an interesting characteristic of leadership. Being a leader supposes that one follows those led to retain authority (1950: 185). Modern parliamentary leaders, increasingly reliant on focus groups and polling to tell them where their leadership should go, are only too aware of this. Power is the essence of a complex interaction hidden beneath 'the semblance of the pure superiority of the one element and a purely passive being-led of the other' (1950: 186). The social and political distance between corporate elite power and the powerlessness of contemporary workers conceal the circular nature of power relationships. The pure one-sidedness of subordination is not only nuanced by ethical fashionable requests. Contemporary leadership does not derive from the purchase of individual wills; it seems to be less class generated and more a fragile social construction based on astute political engineering.

Notes

1 Brezis and Crouzet (2002) cite for instance the case of Cardinal Mazarin, a lowborn Italian who became prime minister of France, or William Pitt the Younger who became prime minister of England at the age of 24.

2 Well illustrated by the French Grandes Écoles system.

3 See in particular the exchange between Sanford Jacoby (1999) and Peter Cappelli (1999) in *California Management Review*.

4 Note that their sample is constituted by the largest and arguably the most stable organizations in the world, namely those of the Fortune 100.

5 The authors of this study carefully remind the reader that there is still 'some stability' in the careers of top executives, and that the results should be interpreted as tendencies, rather than as definitive shifts.

6 The trends would have to be seen in terms of institutional specificity, anyway. They are not global but institutionally variable. For instance, many of the readers of this book will relate to large, divisionalized US corporations, because this is the US norm. But it is the US norm, not the norm everywhere. For instance, if we were to look at the next major economy in the world system, after the US, it would be Japan, and we would find quite a different corporate landscape with quite different corporate elites. In the US system of corporate capitalism it is self-evident that shareholders are sovereign and that the kingpins within the corporations are those finance managers who pursue their interests. Some commentators see a new type of 'stakeholder capitalism' emergent in Japan, in which several interests are vested and represented, and the main

stakeholders are employees, banks, and shareholders. The power of shareholders substantially increased during the 1990s because share prices declined considerably and shareholder dissatisfaction increased accordingly. When growth was the norm, shareholders were far more complacent. The number of foreign shareholders has increased by 10 percent over the last decade of economic recession. Overseas investors, whose primary interest is in shareholder value, are much more sensitive to share prices. Thus, many companies have come to place more emphasis on ROE (return on equity) and EVA (economic value added, net profit after interest and appropriate return to equity). Sony uses EVA as one of the measures of performance and it found that EVA was related to the share price. The EVA is estimated for three years to avoid too much commitment to short-term measures. Matsushita Electric has started to use ROE as a measure of one of its corporate goals. More specialized career tracks are emerging, in which considerable technological knowledge and core competencies are seen as necessary prerequisites rather than the generalist skills of the past. By the 1980s only 40 to 45 percent of Japanese firms had adopted a multidivisional form, at a time that it was widespread in the US. Japanese companies preferred a functional structure (Kono and Clegg 2001), and those that had adopted a multidivisional form were less divisionalized, less diversified and more centralized than comparable US corporations. And, rather than finance being the kingpin it is more likely that it would be human resource management that is the key obligatory passage point for strategic management (Jacoby 2005: 20–5). In part, suggests Jacoby, this is because of the importance of engineers in Japanese firms (as in German ones) whose 'productivist orientation made Japanese engineer-managers wary of finance departments, and it led them into alliances with HR departments, who provided the systems necessary to train workers to produce high quality products' (2005: 25). Additionally, of course, not following a hire-and-fire strategy as a way of coping with the business cycle meant that employees had to be managed properly: thus human resource functions rate as more highly influential than do finance or other functions in Japan. Indeed, in Jacoby's (2005: 26) terms, it is the human resource functionaries who are the elites of Japanese corporate organizations. They orchestrate and adjudicate the managerial tournaments that allow the cream to rise, late in their career, to the top. In addition, they keep the unions sweet in a system that has evolved into an institutionalized enterprise unionism. Not surprisingly then that, unlike their US counterparts, human resource managers are second only to marketing in gaining board-level appointments. The role of directors is to manage stakeholders, which, as well as shareholders, will also include banks, customers, and suppliers.

7   See http://www.abc.net.au/worldtoday/content/2005/s—84885.htm, accessed on May 20, 2005.
8   This refers to what Simmel called the stupidity of collectivities.
9   We do not say 'circulating' nature, as the process we describe here tends rather to perpetuate certain power circles instead of generating political circulations.

13 The Futures of Power?

Introduction

In this chapter we both look back and look forward. Looking back, we review the model of analysis that we have used to produce this book. It is one that is essentially historical and, in this respect, perhaps unfamiliar to many students of organizations. History has been out of fashion in the field for a long time, as well as regarded with disdain more generally. For instance, given the currency of recent views suggesting the end of history, we also review the debates around this topic. Basically, we find the thesis that the end of history has arrived in a world securely ordered on liberal economic principles to be overstated. The present state of the world is usually glossed as one of globalization, and so we consider how, in a global world, space is shrinking and time is being eclipsed, and consider the implications of these tendencies for power and resistance. A global world has been seen as one in which increasingly hybrid identities, lodged in the consumerist conditions of a postmodern society, will flourish. However, the organizational security of such a society is threatened not so much by the hybridity and insecurity of identities as by two distinct threats. Ulrich Beck (2002) names one of these as the 'risk society', where society is at risk from the unanticipated consequences of human action on the natural environment in ways that do not respect the boundaries of either societies or organizations. The second of these is what we term the 'state of insecurity', marked by the resurgence of some old identities in a modern form, namely the emergence of Islamist threats to civic order, leading to a heightened sense of surveillance and security in organizations.

Looking forward, if these are some of the external threats to social order that organizations have to buffer and absorb, what are some of the more immanent tendencies with which the futures of power will be decided? Power is likely to be increasingly institutionalized in the organizational world, we suggest, seeing the futures of power in organizations as revolving around two major issues. First, the balance between individual freedoms and initiative and the increasing concentration of elite power poses a major issue for the futures of power. Second, given the remarkable concentration of power in elites, how will they manage it? There are moral and ethical dimensions to consider in the futures of power. We have questioned the necessity of hierarchy and proffered a preference for heterarchy. How far can organizations be truly democratic and what is the peculiar interconnection between democracy, power and morality? Power without morality is despotism, while morality without power is sterile. Is this our future? How far do incumbent leaders have an interest in bringing morality back into business discourses and practices, and what risk do they take in doing so of facilitating the emergence of new collective actors? The underlying question is that of the dynamics of corporate elites as a genuinely efficient social movement. They are incorporating new issues, new agendas and new personnel simultaneously. A classic question of power has always been who rules, or who dominates. New agendas generate new players: one fascinating issue will be to analyze how far current social agendas for organizational leaders (corporate social responsibility and sustainability issues, in particular) will challenge the actual decision-making processes and power distribution, by including new experts in the political process of decision making, and by enhancing the rise of unexpected challengers whose interests are not presently considered in the political structure. A fruitful way of thinking about these issues is in terms of regime politics: hostile takeovers within commercial organizations often produce a 'violent' end of top management team careers associated with particular organizations. Contemporary violence is no longer essentially political but is shifting to the realm of interpersonal and hierarchical relations, especially as they are contingent on stock-market raids and coups.

The contemporary organizational world is increasingly precarious. Additionally, the individual member of organizations, find themselves exposed to pressures from new competitors, global players where once there were only domestic contenders, franchised chains or branded entities where once there were just other owner-operator competitors. Job insecurity feeds on new threats as overseas outsourcing increasingly comes into play. Cost pressures are experienced by organizations that once were protected by patronage, tariffs, quotas and political mobilization, as economic liberalism sweeps away these barriers to free trade and lower consumer and input prices. The problem is how to respond to constant and ceaseless change. The uncertainties are not merely externally induced: the traditional hierarchies of authority no longer command the respect and deference that they once did. One reason is the irruption of new agendas and issues that the old hierarchies barely grasp or manage, such as the ecology, ethics, and even, to some extent, a return-to-simple-life discourse and values. Managers are often caught in the middle, under assault from the new discourses but beholden to the old. One can imagine that they will strive to develop alternative means for achieving their goals and imposing their views by using parallel networks of influence, or gatekeepers' positions. Additionally, they are increasingly constituted within circuits of soft authoritarianism (Courpasson 2006), no longer as able to draw on unquestioned prerogative, but subject to greater forms of contestation, political opportunity and threat. One of these, which is the recurrence in a modern form of the nineteenth-century fear of the crowd, is the emergence of the mass spectacular, which may be the only means capable of mobilizing sufficient energy and social vibrations to foster collective social dynamics in the future. These occasional and unpredictable irruptions may be the future opposition that power has to deal with rather than the patterned oppositions of capital and class that marked the recent past. The future, as one of increasingly 'soft' power in organizations, looks blurred and unsure, pivoting around an implicit social pact between governors and governed. It is often supposed that mutual allegiance and obligations will hold relations together, even though the common good can never be captured in a mode of domination, in a vision imposed on others, in a claim based on any pretext of managerial fiat or ownership. Finally, we find that there is still great mileage to be made by asking the questions and using the analyses of a number of classical scholars of power, namely Weber, Durkheim and Simmel. And, amongst these scholars, we would also include Foucault, for he raises questions that are by no means as modish and superficial as some detractors suggest. The classical theorists, we suggest, are closer to Foucault than one might imagine.

Models of analysis

Bauman (in Bauman and Tester 2001: 40) suggests that neither experience nor knowledge of it comes divided into tightly sealed compartments. Although he was not writing about organization and management theory, we think his remarks, which seem to echo those of Alfred North Whitehead (1925) on the 'fallacy of misplaced concreteness', are applicable to this field of enquiry. In a spirit of skepticism, rather than defer to the quite recent foundations that organization science has built, our strategy in this book has been to take these foundations apart, attacking them with the intellectual intent of deconstruction and reconstruction. Thus, despite the appearance of our book in a series that provides foundations for organization science, as the attentive reader may well have inferred by this point, we have our doubts about organization science as a self-evident category; we propose a different conception of science to that which is often espoused; and we question the foundations that many of its practitioners claim.

In societies that have been settled and inhabited for long periods of time it is often the case that foundations of quite recent construction are built over those that had previously existed. Sometimes such construction is simply convenience; other times it is a way of politically intervening in the past and physically obliterating it. So it is with knowledge. Analysis, we believe, should not leave its history behind with ne'er a backwards glance, such that the present dulls, numbs, or overwhelms historical memory (Bauman, in Bauman and Tester 2001: 21). Sadly, that is the case with most organization theory, which usually is focused on either ideographic particulars or cross-sectional synchronicities but rarely on the historicity of its own becoming. In other words, an interrogation of what makes its foundations possible is not usually a feature of its practice. Lacking reflexivity, much organization theory dwells in the immediacy of its own presence to such an extent that it neglects those great disciplinary traditions from which it once drew sustenance. Once politics and sociology were a source of nourishment but now organization theory increasingly feeds on itself, cannibalizing its stock of knowledge. The traditions of older intellectualism have been cast off, like a security blanket that the child grown into lusty adolescence deigns to cling to, in a sign of maturity. Not that we think regard for the past is a form of infantilism; on the contrary.

More often than not, in its modern constructions, contemporary organization analysis seeks institutional isomorphism with a model of theory conceived as a scientific practice represented in terms of systematic manipulation of variables, because that is what it is thought that mature and proper sciences – and scientists – do. There are good classical auspices for this view of science, which, once again, have their roots in utilitarian philosophy and its view that only that which can be controlled and manipulated is of value in scientific work. It was early in the methodology of modern social science that the philosopher John Stuart Mill, whom we met at the outset of this book, referred to the method of concomitant covariation as one of the principal methods of all science. Using this method one manipulates the parameters of an experiment in such a way that one systematically varies theoretical controls until causal efficacy is established. Different parameters are held constant, such as temperature or time of exposure to some variable, while others are systematically varied. Once the desired causality is achieved one seeks to replicate that experiment systematically, in order to ensure the constancy of results, given the standing conditions. It is this strategy of systematic covariation that is the fundamental axiom of laboratory-based sciences, such as physics, chemistry and molecular biology.

There are no laboratories in nature. By definition, the laboratory is an artfully contrived environment. When we look at naturalistic phenomena – naturally occurring phenomena – that vary through time and space, the research questions that we seek to address are such that one cannot control experimental parameters. For instance, with the global warming hypothesis, one cannot isolate a low-lying Pacific atoll, such as Kiribati, and systematically increase the ecological heat surrounding it, perhaps by systematically thinning its immediate ozone layer. And, even if one could, there is the not so small ethical question of what happens to the nature so fried, including the Kiribatians, globally warmed and inundated on the atoll. The ecology, like the subject of other historical sciences such as the evolution of species, linguistics, or the galaxy, is not something that can be artfully constructed into a temporally and spatially bounded sphere of covariation.

> Historical sciences are concerned with narrative chains of proximate and ultimate causes. In most of physics and chemistry the concepts of 'ultimate cause,' 'purpose' and 'function' are meaningless, yet they are essential to understanding living systems in general, and human activities in particular ... In chemistry and physics the acid test of one's understanding of a system is whether one can successfully predict its future behavior ... In historical sciences, one can provide *a posteriori* explanations (eg, why an asteroid impact on Earth 66 million years ago may have driven dinosaurs but not many other species to extinction), but *a priori* predictions are more difficult (we would be uncertain which species would be driven to extinction if we did not have the actual past events to guide us). (Diamond, 1998: 422)

In historical science – and it should be clear that organization theory is such a science in the conception that has been advanced in this book – there are an enormous number of variables, great complexity, unique actors, and no possibility of artful laboratory closure. Thus, the organization scientist has to adopt different strategies to that of covariation.

We suggest the following research strategies. First, respect the natural scene. That is, take seriously the lived experience and understanding of the action scenes that the participants make. Don't just go in on a smash and grab raid with a questionnaire that might make sense to the researcher but not necessarily to the researched. Research is not just reportage: theorize the data, don't just describe it. Be theoretically informed even when being descriptive. Hear the stories: people organize their lives through narratives and research should adopt a narrative structure. Be reflexive: always remember that you are the author of the fragments that these others author. There is unlikely ever to be a definitive account. The narrative is more likely to be an *Alexandria Quartet* (Durrell 1968) than a definitive history.

There is one great advantage when researching socially constructed phenomena: provided we are able to translate the language in use, we are able to interpret the understandings that its subjects have of themselves and the phenomena that they found salient. Ultimately, we can seek to understand interpretively the stories that people construct to explain reality for them. (While this is easier if we are able to be co-present and ask directly, historical traces can also yield great returns.) Essentially, the human condition is a narrative condition open to understanding; it is a work in progress paused to create spaces for interrogation, enquiry, and conversation, although there have been suggestions that these have ceased to be as important as we face 'the end of history'.

The end of history

Some readers may recall, or have read about, those heady days when history allegedly ended, as the Berlin Wall collapsed.[1] When the wall came down it seemed to many observers as if, with the end of communism – at least in Europe – the only threat to existing democratic political power was vanquished. Liberal, plural democracy, the open society and open organizations seemed to stretch as a vista into a future full of promise offering peace in our time, with all its assumed dividends, and the triumph neither of the will nor of the state but of decent, ordinary democracy. Surely the chance to build a better world of organizations was imminent? To review this question in terms of debates about power we first need to backtrack a little to the world before the wall came tumbling down. Then we can begin to consider the current state of affairs.

To imagine the end of history is to imagine a world without surprise, contingency and drama, a world wholly of order. Social order is an emergent drama enacted through the clash of imaginations, encoded through circuits of relational power, and experienced as different orders of domination. It involves prosaic as well as implausible projects, dreams as well as nightmares, ambitions as well as anxieties. Ordering uses whatever devices, actors and technologies come to hand for its constructing. And it always occurs in contested spaces. There is never a single social imaginary, despite what conservatives, radicals, or functionalist theorists might think. Always there will be imaginings, striving to come into being and seeking to deny the strivings of other projects. Such is life.

We will briefly review the recent history of power, its social imaginary, recapitulating the relations between its changing theory and the context of political practice. Not surprisingly, in the 1970s many key debates overwhelmingly concerned power and the state, in part because in a number of European countries during this era, notably France, Spain and Italy, it looked as if the communist parties might gain electoral office.[2] Hence, the debates about power at that time were conceived in terms of the extent to which the state was an organizational instrument capable of being run by alternative elites in different ways (Poulantzas 1973; Miliband 1969).

By the 1980s it was clear that the chance that these communist parties might have to gain office was past. The neoliberal agenda was resurgent, with the pace being set in the UK and the US and other Anglo dominions such as Australia and New Zealand; while, on the left, the debates had shifted to consider how it was possible to construct coalitions and alliances between disparate and fragmented interests from green parties, from feminism, and from social democrat parties in opposition to these neoliberal projects. As rates of unionization declined and the old heartlands of the male blue-collar working class, such as mining and steel making, were decimated by the switch to a post-industrial services economy in most Western countries, the notion of class position securing clear-cut identities weakened greatly, in both theory and practice. The debates shifted to encompass the insecurity, multiplicity and indeterminacy of conceptions of identity in a postmodern world (Laclau and Mouffe 1985).[3] The proliferation of a plurality of identities introduces many more points of rupture into contemporary politics. The fundamental role previously assumed by relations of production in defining identity as that of either the ruling or the working class cannot be sustained in the face of new, shifting, unstable identities. These new identities are not so much articulated through traditional forms of political representation (parties and unions), but colonized and channeled through consumption, lifestyles and branding (consumer generations such as Gen X and Y, Boomers, as well as the new tribalisms of identity, such as dance, trance, Goths, etc.).

Increasingly, against the hybridity of identity, the business organizations that market and brand those identities with which people badge their bodies, possessions and lives were becoming increasingly global. Capital became ever more organized on a transnational basis. Branch offices dispersed yet coordinated production and marketing capacities, and spread all over the world, exploiting global migratory patterns, profiting from globalized labor markets and consumption (Hardt and Negri 2000). The world's space seemed to be shrinking, not only because of globalization, in at least three ways. First, time is *eclipsed* through virtual media. Second, whereas once there was a limited and secure set of identities planted in firm hierarchies in the social space, these are now *expanding*, proliferating, and complicating the nature of the social space such that it becomes simultaneously shrunk by overcrowding and much more difficult to navigate because of increasingly confusing signs. Third, social spaces that once were only colonized on the colonizer's terms are now *counter-colonized* in ways that threaten the security of these spaces. The buffering spaces of the social have shrunk.

Shrinking space: eclipsing time

Extending business globally

What made contemporary globalization possible, in part, was the virtual capillaries of instantaneous communication and trade embedded in the Internet. By the 1990s much of the focus of organization theories had shifted to the emancipatory possibilities of new virtual technologies potentially rendering hierarchy and bureaucracy redundant (see Clarke and Clegg 1998). Optimistically, as we suggested in Chapter 5, there is good reason to think that, however slowly, imperative coordination may be giving way to responsible autonomy and heterarchy; new forms of polyarchy as suggested in Chapter 12. There are now technologies available that can handle more distributed authority relations, through the use of digital and virtual communication. The Internet allows for far less centralized modes of organization – and, indeed, in the present state of anxiety in society about terrorist attacks, we are likely to see many organizations adopting more distributed and network structures, with responsible autonomy in each of their nodal points, if only to be sure that the organization can survive a cataclysmic event such as 9/11. It is evident that organizations that have distributed systems and networked leadership will better survive catastrophe. After all, that is precisely what the Internet was designed to do.[4]

While the optimistic scenarios envisage a world in which small and local business, offering unique products, will be globally connected by the Internet, there are more pessimistic aspects of globalization to contend with that are likely to have an impact on organizational power relations. Pessimistically, the times in which we live have grown more troubled in many respects and the necessity of imperative coordination is seemingly ever more pressing. As a result of digital capabilities, Western postmodern society not only surrounds those who live within its borders; its global media project images of it to the rest of the world, intensifying the powers of the market enormously.

Resisting globally?

In the past the major challenge to market power was the state (Clegg et al. 1983) or the organized labor movement. After the failure of Eurocommunism in the 1970s, and the *rapprochement* of social democracy with the neoliberal agenda from the 1980s, challenge from the state declined. The decline in left politics was paralleled in the industrial sphere as well. Today, the *international* organization of capital confronts *national* labor movements. When one considers the new global conditions of production it is evident that trade unions face a new reality.

Organized labor has had to match the learning trajectory of that capital in whose employ it is globally arraigned. The literature addressing the use of IT in business and administration, and its consequences for social and industrial organization (e.g. Sprague and McNurlin 1986; 1997), provides an archive of the learning process involved in these changes as organizations better manage the supply and value change in an increasingly complex business environment.

Significant global campaigns have emerged from within the trade union movement and from the critics of globalization to confront the new global realities (Hogan and Green 2002). However, trade unions remain, for the present, largely nationally institutionalized, and they do not afford much of a threat to existing organization of the relations of production, especially as their recruitment and penetration of the post-industrial services economy is far lower than was the case in the era of industrial labor and society. Also, they are increasingly irrelevant because their leadership is largely male and the domain of their traditional membership is female. Thus, the biggest issues that unions face today on the membership front are low female and ethnic minority participation rates such that the people doing the representing rarely share either gender or ethnicity with those they represent.

Inter-union coordination in response to the globalization of value chains was taken forward by the UK Liverpool docks dispute, which took place between 1995 and 1998. Extensive mobilization of support from within and beyond the labor movement was achieved through the use of the web in concert with more traditional forms of mobilization (Carter et al. 2003). Following the defeat of the union, the skills developed in the struggle have been carried forward to archive the dispute and to develop a sustainable skills base within the community.[5] Within 48 hours of the settlement of the UK dispute an identical dispute broke out in Australia, a locus of support for the Liverpool workers and, at that time, a regulated labor environment (Clegg 1999).[6] Of critical significance was the role of the federal Australian government in planning the dispute, involving overseas training of serving members of the Australian armed services.[7]

Clearly learning and counter-coordination are taking place globally on all sides – unions, employers and governments – and new forms of power and resistance can be expected (Little and Clegg 2005). The emerging global system is far from complete and far from determined, but it is having a profound impact on social and working life in the regions included within and excluded from it. Of course, the speed of change in markets, competition and technology means that there is a socio-institutional lag, something that occurs when any new techno-economic paradigm emerges (Perez 1983). It is information and communication technologies that are driving the distributed processes of globalization and providing new forms of cultural and political indexicality, as well as new forms of counter-coordination for excluded constituencies (Little and Clegg 2005).

Anticipating resistance? Simulation and identity in the electronic Panopticon

US federal legislation, which predates 9/11, requires GPS transmitters to be fitted to all US cell phones.[8] Organizations, not just in government, are increasingly making use of available surveillance technologies to seek enhanced supervision and control. The electronic Panopticon is going global in an increasingly insecure world, offering opportunities not only for hypersurveillance but also for a new kind of organizational simulation that is hyperreal, a world where we can '*simulate* a space of control, project an indefinite number of courses of action, train for each possibility, and react immediately with preprogrammed responses to the "actual" course of events (which is already over and through a simulacrum)' (Bogard 1996: 76). Organizations increasingly need neither to *handle* power via a political economy of bodies, nor to embed it in a moral economy of the soul through extensive *surveillance*. Instead, they project information in a mode that has been described as 'the purest form of anticipation' (1996: 76).

Almost all large scale organizations of any sophistication are increasingly premised on work whose doing is simultaneously subject to hypersurveillance of its being done, characteristic of both managerial work and work more generally. The traces of data that all information-laden actions leave automatically as they are enacted become the objects for analysis, for the speeding up of processes, for eradicating porosity through which some effort, time or work might seep, for eradicating the gap between the action and its accounts, the work and its record, the deed and the sign. The loop between being, doing and becoming tightens irrevocably on the terms of those elites that can channel and funnel information, closing down the unaccountable moments in the programmed loop between employees and technologies reporting data that managers have to act on.

Ideally, managers become adjuncts of expert systems, which will instil operational definitions of shareholder value as the highest ethic imaginable. In short, ordinary organizations have capabilities for power that would have been but a dream for a Honecker or a Ford, running a state or a production plant. The trajectory of power has spiraled out from a political economy of the body, has transcended the moral economy of the soul, and now is lodged everywhere and nowhere in a multiplicity of scanning and simulation.

> Hundreds of thousands of workers in both government and private industry are subjected to drug tests, have their prior work records scanned, are diagnosed for general health, intelligence, loyalty, family values, economic and psychological stability (through matches generated in searches of other databases), fitted to job profiles, placed on career tracks – or unemployment tracks – all in addition to routine, rigorous monitoring on the job ... The virtual scene of work is one where the end of work – who the worker *will have been*, what the worker *will have produced*, what path his or her career *will have taken* – governs the entire process before it begins. (Bogard 1996: 117)

Such information is not confined to the gathering of data from the physical spaces controlled, nor is it premised on the crude forms of spying characteristic of the Ford Sociological Department and the Stasi. 'Increasingly virtual realities, artificial intelligence, expert systems, sever us from older forms of control and project that control – refashioned, smoothed and streamlined – onto the plane of simulation ... The god of surveillance is a virtual reality technician's cyborg dream' (1996: 77, 57).

It is not only the security apparatuses and the legislative assemblies that multiply dreams within which identities that are constructs of the profiler, the psychological tester, and the human resources manager become crucial. All large organizations, equipped with the foresight of simulation, can screen out potential deviance from the organization as easily as the society at large. It is the reality of how, increasingly, organizations use informatics' virtual worlds as they construct identities within which our lives will be lived. Our identity, more than ever, will be a social construction, but not necessarily one made under conditions of our own choosing. Organizations will increasingly adopt bio-surveillance technologies, such as retina, fingerprint, and face scanning, and use these to monitor, restrict and govern access. Such data, together with those identities that are coded from market-based information, credit records, credit cards, and other forms of transactions, will ensure that some elements of identity become less negotiable. Given the likely direction and speed of development of genetics, organizational capabilities will increasingly be prefigurative rather than retrospective; as Bogard puts it, 'genetic technology offers the fantastic possibilities of pre-identification, i.e., identities assigned in advance, profiles that we have seen can be used to target bodies for all kinds of future interventions and diversions' (1996: 9). Potential pathologies for organizations – such as prediction of earlier than required executive demise due to genetic codes or lifestyle triggers – can be problems eliminated in advance. Normalization will no longer be remedial or therapeutic, will no longer require the counseling interview as its major device, but will be anticipatory. Bio-psychological screening is becoming ever more closely intertwined with genetic and security screening. Organizational elites will be able not only to reproduce themselves biologically but also to clone themselves socially, with ever more precise simulations.[9]

Expanding identities filling space

If the previous section has presented a pessimistic view of identity politics, the technological dystopian view, there is a more optimistic scenario. Much of the politics that surrounded debates about power in the recent past centered on issues of interests and identity, as we saw in Chapter 8. These politics focused on the indetermination of both interests and identities. However, these debates were only possible in both a theory and a practice informed by postmodernism (Castells 1997) in which a switch occurred from a society that articulated around relations of productive and domestic labor to one whose center of gravity was increasingly relations of consumption. Identities founded in the spheres of work and the traditional family and household became unsettled, rendering the idea of objective interests problematic.

In theory, it was postmodernism that deconstructed the stable identities provided by the great cleavages inherent to the master nineteenth-century narrative of class, which articulated around the relations of production, and the late-twentieth-century narrative of feminism, which centered on the relations of gender. Laclau and Mouffe (1985) made a considerable difference to the saliency of these debates with their theoretical intervention, analytically sidestepping all the orthodoxies that wanted to ascribe real interests to others on the basis of big-T theory, whether Marxism, feminism, or whatever.

The theoretical moves were in part a result of reflection on changing realities as well as changing priorities. In the political theory sphere, Laclau and Mouffe could proclaim as they did, in a Lacanian move, that there was no such thing as society because there is no transcendent signified subject; what we take to be reality is a discursive construct (see Roudinesco (1999) for an introduction to Lacan). In the sphere of political practice Prime Minister Thatcher could and did say the same thing, albeit that she meant it in a different way. For her, as with her close colleague in arms President Reagan, there should be only real individuals exercising their freedoms as sovereign consumers. They were remarkably successful in constructing this as a model of society that was widely emulated in the West. The governmental projects inspired by Thatcher and Reagan clearly valued efficiency and economy over civility and society.

One theoretical response to these changing politics was that an excessively ego-tistical and narcissistic subjectivity became celebrated as postmodern, as a possibility tied into consumption rather than production. In many respects it was the material environment of Reaganomics and Thatcherism that framed these late 1980s debates (Gamble 1988) as much as debates in poststructuralism and feminism, although it is evident that they were in fact interdependent, as leftist intellectuals struggled to come to terms with the new neoliberal conditions of existence. The debates had effects that trickled into the analysis of organizations, as for example in Clegg's (1989) work, largely in terms of a critique of the notion that there are unambiguous identities that possess real, if unknown, unarticulated, or repressed interests. While the main thrust of critique was in terms of a stress on the fragmentation and ambiguity of identities, the frame of reference was very much that of the sophisticated employee in organizations in the advanced sectors of the advanced economies: immaterial labor producing immaterial goods such as a service or a cultural or symbolic product (Hardt and Negri 2000). Integral to this immateriality is the production of new identities – creative knowledge workers and symbolic analysts – for whom work is essentially tied up with their identity and the successful positioning of their identity as a presence in the competitive market of enterprising subjects. Like workers of old they sell themselves, their time, but the point of sale occurs through the successful presentation of their identity as a presence that makes a difference.

Often, these notions of identity are glossed as postmodern, to signify the fluidity and lack of structural determination by relations of production which are taken to be a hallmark of modern identities. The modern was seen to be passing away and the postmodern coming to be. Thus, when Clegg (1989) wrote *Frameworks of power*, much as nearly everyone else, he did not dwell on the possibility that conceptions of identity, based neither on modern relations of production nor on post modern relations of consumption, but instead on fundamental assumptions about the nature of men, women and their relation to a transcendent God, would sprout in the midst of modernity.[10] We now know that this was a peculiar blindness.[11]

After 9/11

From a risk society to a state of insecurity

For a while, until at least the attack of February 26, 1993 on the World Trade Center, it might have seemed as if the old matters of identity were hardly of any concern. After the second more successful attack of 9/11 few could think that was still the case.[12] Islamic claims to identity were serving as circuit-breakers to existing power relations.

What emerged from the Middle East was not so much a reassertion of pre-modern identities but a positioning of a contemporary identity. It is one that expresses a version of Islam as politically grounded within modern frameworks. Religious thoughts are used as political weapons, alongside modern instruments such as the Internet and video, and with a sophisticated grasp of mass media spectacle. What was evident about the actions of the terrorists who commandeered the planes was their intersection with, and irruption into, the global circuits of power that are centered practically, symbolically, and emotionally on New York and Washington. Practically, New York is the media HQ of the world; the Twin Towers were the emblem of global capitalism; and the Pentagon is the symbol of American imperial might. If you want the whole world to watch a spectacle, what other venues would be better to stage it in than New York? The choice of the Pentagon as a target (and the White House, the presumed target of the fourth plane that was crash-landed in the countryside) made the meaning of the attack quite transparent. The primetime crews were right on hand at the center of global distribution networks. The whole world really could be watching what was achieved, very quickly. What was innovative about what the terrorists did was to bring the damage of war to the US mainland in a way that no other adversary ever had achieved, while simultaneously bringing it to the attention of the whole world.

If you want to disrupt circuits of power then you need to determine what the necessary nodal points are that you need to shut down and what the new ones are that you want to create. It is better not to dissipate the effort too much with too many events, for the simultaneity of many different things can never compete for the attention as effectively as a carefully choreographed spectacle. Living to terrorize again is not a paramount value for those who live and die for the politics of the deed, especially where there is the justification of a personally annihilatory but symbolically transcending target. Emotionally, the deaths of thousands of people in a single spectacular caught in the gaze of the whole television-viewing world in a replayable series of instances weigh far heavier as lives in the balance than the infinitely numerically weightier accumulation of deaths that have resulted from US foreign policy over the years. Mostly these were unseen; often they were unreported; and they were not, on the whole, spectacular. Nor, and not to put too fine a point on it, did they engage with the emotions of most people in that most self-centered of nations in which the identity other to that of American is that of 'alien', as US immigration control so nicely puts it.

Of course, that the US has in the past invariably been both politically discriminate and ethically indiscriminate in its choice of friends and enemies is no excuse for the awfulness of what happened on 9/11, but it does put it into some kind of context. Choices involve responsibilities, in foreign relations just as much as any other. And sometimes others will configure and constitute these choices in ways that their progenitors could never have imagined in the past, by disturbing the architecture of politics, meaning, and war utterly. And this seems to be what has happened. The whole world watched the events of 9/11 in New York and Washington over and over again in replay; we can conclude that its designers had a sophisticated grasp of the *realpolitik* of power and its circuitry. They knew how to use fear and terror to try and reconfigure the circuitry of international relations, as well as to destroy lives. With absolutely no resource dependencies to speak of, with hardly any resources in fact, they were able to symbolically overwhelm, circuit-break, and reposition the entire architecture of power that has made the US so comfortable at home, so secure in its projections of power abroad and so despised by those who regard their causes and peoples as its victims.

The explanation of 9/11 that developed from the bin Laden videos makes it evident that fundamentalisms were flourishing through which *pre-modern* claims to identity were paramount. The claims of and for a religiously fundamental identity have found realization and ruthless repression alike in different parts of the Middle East and Muslim Asia.[13] Nor did their impact start and stop there. They also produced resonances amongst the broader Muslim diaspora, of whom there over 20 million in Europe alone.

For any diasporic community the central issue is always one of cultural integration, a 'two-sided process of immigrants' adjustment to a new society without loss of what they consider essential to their identity (or self definition, particularly in the sense of their religion or ethnicity) and, simultaneously, of the adoptive society's accommodation of them' (McGown 1999: 43). The notion of difference that is indexed by the notion of ethnicity is usually thought of in terms of a continuum that stretches from a primordial, internal concept to one that is external and structural. Primordially, it is the attachments and relations that one carries with one that define identity; structurally, it is the boundaries determined by the larger society, rather than the lifeworld that the communities construct, that define them. Externally, Isajiw defines an ethnic group as an 'involuntary group of people who share the same culture or ... descendants of such people who identify themselves and/or are identified by others as belonging to the same involuntary social group' (1979: 21–2). In many developed societies, especially where the Muslim population is concerned, external and internal definitions coincide. In the diaspora of British cities, as McGown argues, for specific ethnic communities there is developing

a strong consciousness of identity through religion, in order to place themselves in a
new society that is predominantly non-Muslim, and indeed to assert themselves within
it … [a context in which] the Islamists have acquired a moral leadership beyond the
circle of those willing to identify themselves as such. (1999: 228)[14]

McGown's (1999: 232–3) research into London Somalis establishes that they are
both alienated from and kept at a distance from British society; they are subject to
more systematic racism than Somalis in Canada; and in terms of their internal lifeworld they have become 'generally more religious on migrating into the diaspora'
and more hostile within the British than the Canadian context. For some in diasporic Muslim communities generally, the hostility is such that their identities in
question see nothing that resonates positively in the offerings that the market produces in abundance in the host society. Instead, they see an overly sexualized,
narcissistic and alienating environment. Revolted by what is on offer in the post
modern market – and we in the West are all embraced by this institution now – for
some a retreat to the certainties offered by fundamentalism seems desirable. Here,
as Durkheim would have expected, an excess of social integration can lead to a surplus of altruistic suicide as some people, in some communities, are prepared to kill
and die for their beliefs in the appropriateness of identity.[15]

One consequence is that, today, all major organizations in societies that are seen
as implicated in the intractable problems of the Middle East – the plight of the
Palestinians and militaristic intervention in the 'War on Terror' – face something a
step beyond what Beck (2002) calls a 'risk society'. Beck defines the risk society as
one in which the processes of modernization have introduced systemic risks and
insecurities previously unknown in nature (2002: 21). The risk society is characterized by decisions that are industrially produced and potentially 'politically
reflexive' (2002: 183). Beck's concern is with industrial production and ecological
risk, typified by phenomena such as acid rain, global warming, and Chernobyl, and
with the loss of identity and heightened insecurity associated with more flexible
work patterns (Beck 1999).

Today, we live not only in a risk society but also in a state of insecurity, a condition
that previously characterized societies quite marginal to Western civilization – such
as Sri Lanka (George and Clegg 1997) in which context we first developed the concept of a state of insecurity. Generalized risk is further amplified by floating signifiers
that attract fear and deliver terror. These signifiers can, in reality, be manifest in the
destruction of anyone, irrespective of beliefs, ideologies, or identities. At essence they
are to do with that most fundamental element of liberal political philosophy – the
security of the body of the individual subjects and the security of the body of the
polity as a whole.[16] With these new threats, as they are apparent on the streets, skies
and subways of Western cities, the risk society is transmuting into a state of uncertainty. Whereas the enemy was eternalized with 9/11 into an Islamic fundamentalism
that was situated in failing states supporting network organizations of terrorists, after
Britain's 7/7 it suddenly transpired that the enemy was within as well as without.[17]
After the explosions that rocked London, the day after the city received news that it
had been chosen to host the 2012 Olympics, and in the week immediately following
Live8, there was widespread shock at the revelation that the suicide bombers were not

emissaries from the Middle East but came from inner city Leeds and Dewsbury. They were homegrown, second-generation British Muslims.

Today, given the decline of traditional party loyalties, young people in general are less likely to find their identity in a voluntary political process of voting and politics.[18] Thus, there are significant groups of people – particularly amongst the young – who are not fully political or democratic subjects in the normal senses of the word; the do not participate in the formal political process because its meaning is estranged from their own sensemaking. In terms of the sense they make, the major sources of meaning are to be found, as Berger (1990) argues, in transcendent ideas of religiosity. By the twenty-first century a group of young Muslim people in Western democracies were involved neither in the signifiers of a secular society nor in the positive polyvalence of the market.[19] Yet, they were not just socially disintegrated, anomic, normless, and meaningless subjects.[20] They were not entirely outside of civility but were building on some notions of civil society that had been nurtured from the most fundamentalist strains in contemporary Islamic thought (Ali 2002).[21] In the West, in societies with large Muslim populations (most of the major EU countries), where a degree of political alienation is allied with a more general cultural and economic estrangement, it is hardly surprising if such young people do not become fully aspirational 'normal' economic subjects. Moreover, where they are not greatly involved in consumption – because its narcissism and sexualization are a constant affront to the religious sensibilities they are developing elsewhere – then they will hardly be incorporated as subjects of consumption.

There is an interesting dovetailing of two quite different projects in the estrangement of religious and cultural identities. Throughout the 1980s and into the 1990s the refrain of economic neoliberalism was that there was no such thing as society. Society could be conceived of simply in terms of individuals making economic choices, using price signals as allocative mechanisms. In the terms of the 'no society' project it was postulated that only individuals should be conceptualized as existentially real. As free subjects they were able to exercise choices in markets, such that consumption became the key to identity. An unanticipated side effect of the project is to whittle down the grounds for identity formation. If you are what you shop to become then identity formation becomes highly contingent on participation in the rituals of a market society. Thus, for those who refused the market and its choices and were estranged politically, economically and ideologically, there was little or no identity available that could relate to the central projects of the type of society in which they found themselves.[22] For those Muslims with utopian religious worldviews estranged from the dominant orthodoxies, if what is on offer is a reality constructed on narcissism, consumerism, and individualism, then it is not surprising that it should be seen as constituting a hegemon that affronts their existence, faith, and identity. Where utopian ideals turn present-day life into a dystopia, it is hardly surprising if some responses are dysfunctional for the social reality that normalcy constructs.

Where utopian ideology exists in communities that barely interact outside the confines of chosen urban patterns of residence, which for all the usual reasons are highly concentrated, then dystopian beliefs about identity, the world, and one's place in it as a member of the broader community can more easily flourish, especially where everything that is needed is found there – food, religion, spouses, culture, and appropriate garb – so there is little need to go outside.[23] Within the embrace of utopianism all faiths develop dystopian groups little involved in the everyday life of a broader society in which they cannot find themselves, where disaffected young people are drawn to radical cliques largely devoid of pluralism, discursively and religiously, because the central role is played by a literalist interpretation of a key text. In such a situation all interpretive politics become condensed into one game of hermeneutics in which those interpretations that seem 'purest' will always attract alienated and anomic individuals.

Finally, as a result of digitalization, individuals have the choice not to be involved in the cultural life of the place where they live, in the larger sense, but to participate more vividly in the cultural life of the diasporic community through Al Jazeera and other media, and thus live a reality that, while it is real, is hardly shared at all with the broader context of everyday life. When this reality is treated on the BBC, CNN or France2, let alone FoxNews, it is rarely a personalized but mostly a dehumanized reality – 26 people were blown up in three suicide attacks in Baghdad on the day that we wrote these words – as opposed to the continuing focus on the people who were destroyed in the bombings on one day in London (7/7/2005) or New York (9/11/2001) or Bali (10/12/2002). These others are constituted as *our* brothers and sisters. We feel their pain, we know their faces, we read about their families, and we share their distress and devastation on the nightly news and in the pages of the newspapers in a way that we do not when we hear statistics from the Middle East. Iraqi people are also brothers and sisters, sons and daughters, mothers and fathers, but their humanity is denied us, because of these others we know nothing. They are just a statistic. If we knew better these other people in places such as Sharm el-Sheikh (23/7/2005), if we knew these people who are not like us, and if in other places, such as Baghdad (25/7/2005), we less routinely expected the statistics, [24] there might be more understanding and a few more heartfelt tears shed for the losses incurred.

Some young people will be drawn to a dystopian view of reality through a utopian view of religion. In countries in which their very presence is reflected as the selves they see in the looking glass of the others through the frame of difference – different color, different ethnicity, different language, different food, different clothes, different lives, and different suburbs, all centered on different religion – this will be especially the case. If, in such circumstances, they might feel their difference existentially, that should hardly be surprising. Especially, that is, when the difference that *you* represent seems to be one on which the other has declared war, via an abstraction of a terror whose sense signifies attack on 'people like us'. If, at the same time, the opportunities for human growth afforded one are rarely posed in terms other than those that are heavily circumscribed for the deeply devout and orthodox, we should not be surprised if a few people take seriously both their future perfect utopia and their present imperfect dystopia.[25]

Elites in a shrinking space and an expanding state of insecurity

Who then, are the elites? They are those who are generated by dominant relations as the authorities governing various circuits of power. They control the nodal points through which legitimacy flows. Some node occupants are born; others are made; and some succeed on merit. Origins are of diminishing importance in a society of flows that are ever more fluid.

In the circumstances we have sketched, we don't expect to see the elites disappearing too quickly. Their circulation might speed up as they fail to deal with the new threats that the risk society and the heightened state of insecurity offer, but circulatory elites have always been essential to power.[26] Existing power holders have a bright future in a world where an ideology of threat and uncertainty pervades the whole social and organizational sphere as a space of heightened risk, together with powers of simulation with which to anticipate, pre-identify and impression manage these risks. The need to organize risk provides unexpected resources with which to perpetuate social relations of increasingly legitimate domination. Among these resources, the paradoxical power of political powerlessness plays a crucial role. It shapes a curious social world where leading elites are both more and more remote from the grassroots and delivering a compelling discourse about common overwhelming constraints weighing unobtrusively from the top to the basement of the social strata. Consequently, there is a widening gap of social hierarchies, an increasingly oligarchic character to political societies, all oriented to managing overarching threats and constraints upon the whole social body. And in the midst of that landscape there is, in parallel, the growing political apathy of the masses, which tends to privilege individual fates over any sort of collective good, and the growing alienation and estrangement of those elements of them that find fundamental meaning in literal interpretations of ancient texts, whether Koran, Torah, or Bible. The Durkheimian 'nightmare' of a vanishing solidarity seems to have taken material form to roam around our lives and worlds.

Contra Beck (2002), risk and individualization do not exhibit their unity as dimensions of the 'reflexive modernization of industrial society', when pre-modern identities are corporeally incorporated yet not culturally intermediated. Under such circumstances, individuals are not freed from their unselfconscious immersion in traditional group determinations and are not challenged to come to terms with and reflect on their unmediated relation to society. The dimensions of insecurity and its associated risks cannot be apprehended as problems that are formally constituted in scientific terms. They are not amenable to rational analysis and solution yet they are a new source of conflict and social formation (2002: 99). Obviously, the emergence of a discourse concerning corporate social responsibility and the importance that many organizations now give to sustainability, and the potential that these have to empower new stakeholders, are one way of registering the changing power effects of the risk society (see Benn and Dunphy (2004) for a discussion of democratic scenarios).

The futures of power are indisputably related to the respective influence of the public and private spheres of action over the large array of political circuits we have delineated in this book, including discourses, organizational forms, political regimes, forms of elite fragmentation and cohesion, and the nature of the political performance that future leaders will strive for. All are now oriented to a legitimate need to increase control, tighten power, and restrict access because of the general, non-specific but existentially real risks posed to organizations by the free-floating signifier of terror.

Contemporary conditions largely shape the futures of power. Power as a concept is 'exploding' in numerous social meanings; power as a resource is disseminated and concentrated; political agendas are dividing into innocuous local decisions and cardinal centers of power. Agency and sovereignty are progressively modeled in a rejuvenated combination. Political life is founded both on claims to establish sovereign centers of power and decision and on scattered and agonistic agencies, whose mediation demands organization.

That soft power now coexists with enhanced harder power arose in response to heightened security threats as the influence of remote and unknown people and collectives increasingly threatened. The most decisive ingredients of political decisions now come from nowhere, or from globally disseminated bodies, from hardly delineated competitors, hardly defined networks, hardly graspable claims arousing in distant places – even from places few have ever heard of previously, such as Kandahar. To get the gist of power futures, we must accept the growing dispersion, first, of systems of meanings and, second, of systems of production of meanings among germane actors. Consequently, one of the most fascinating facets of contemporary and future systems of power is how these dispersions are organized. In addition to the need to incorporate both risk society and the state of uncertainty, the power of contestation, conflict and behind-the-scenes concepts of consciousness and resistance, as well as the media of power, require rethinking.

Frameworks with which to think about the futures of power

The importance of the macro-political developments and their likely effect on the futures of power in organizations is that the futures of power will be largely dependent on the magnitude of the changes that are affecting and will affect the organizational world over the next few decades. In this book we have constantly put forward the socio-historical dimension of the genesis and of the dynamics of power as a concept and as a sociological and political condition of everybody's life in contemporary organizations. Put differently, whether the agenda for change will be minimalist, redistributive, developmental or even structuralist, to take March and Olsen's four (1995) conceptions of the political agenda at the level of societies, the nature and culture of power will be durably affected. Minimalist power is relatively indifferent to substantive outcomes and the construction of identities; it is more used to minimize the costs of political battles. Redistributive power is used to limit inequalities in both the polity and the power of the elite. Developmental power is used to generate shared cultures and educate the people in so far as it constitutes a political community. Structural power is used in the engineering of specific institutions aiming to shape and control the demands of the polity (1995: 242–5). In Table 13.1 we sketch what this might imply for the concept and use of power.

Power is likely to be increasingly institutionalized in the organizational world as the futures of power in organizations revolve around two major issues:

Table 13.1 A framework with which to think about the institutional futures of power

	Minimalist agenda	Redistributive agenda	Developmental agenda	Structuralist agenda
Types of change	Individualistic forms of 'intrapreneurship'	Morally oriented conception and design of organizations	Shaping a true political community Organizations as polities	Creating organizations as powerful political subjects
Outcomes of political actions	Individual consent Voluntary contracts	Human and public welfare	Influencing the values, beliefs and identities of individuals	Institutional and constitutional engineering
Nature of power	Private interactions Power as game	Regulating power resources Establishing a 'balance of power'	Educational Power as virtue	Power as structure
Culture of power	Markets and possessive individualism	Consumer sovereignty	Letting better-informed buyers beware	Increasing institutionalization of regulation by standards rather than the state
Political performance	Organizing, bargaining and exchange Managing coalitions	Offsetting inequalities	Establishing agreements on collective purposes	Inventing institutions

- How will organizations preserve and enhance individual freedom and initiative while relentlessly engineering new managerial institutions that strengthen narrow circles of powerful individuals monitoring the organization from the top? How will they combine a structural and a minimalist agenda?
- How are organizational leaders going to embody the growing societal and political dimensions of their activity? Put differently, the transformation of leadership from a set of managerial practices and rules to a set of institutional capacities implies that we think about power in organizations as a means to educate, to socialize individuals, to create and sustain identities – and to consider the role of elites as governing institutions instead of merely managing organizations.

We can also draw from the works of four major figures of this book, Weber, Simmel, Durkheim, and Foucault, not only to highlight different perspectives, which has already been done in the previous chapters, but to envisage a possible combination of their views to think through the conceptual futures of power, as shown in Table 13.2.

Given the stakes of the present period and the analysis that we have made of them, it goes without saying that we argue that organization studies should not merely shift from an efficiency-oriented perspective to one that is explicitly politically oriented. To comply with a managerial directive is to accede to a moral or political agenda that one does not necessarily share. The role of political power is to invent and engineer powerful institutions that create the necessary obedience-generative constraints and legitimacies inside organizations and societies. One of the most pressing questions posed by a perspective based on a political agenda is that of moral disagreement. The dispersion of individuals and values around the globe in the present context of global 'organizational sprawling' emphasizes the discrepancies between decisions made in some circles of power and the perceptions and interpretations of individuals; put another way, the question of how to manage the common affairs of people who disagree about moral and non-moral matters but live together in the same society/organization should be stressed. The urgent research question posed by the current growingly important 'social agenda' of organizations involves a series of topics. What will be the ways of binding the changing political commitment of individuals to new demands of power and of political communities in organizations that both colonize an increasing amount of their lifeworld and offer a diminishing sense of security? What will be the power of moral 'things' in the design of political structures and in the production of political leaders for organizations in the future? What will be the new balance between directive and soft power? How will organizations act as increasingly political subjects in a world where the changing relations between states and markets increasingly empower non-state actors and disempower individual consumers bewildered by the confusions of alleged choice?

Resistance, political apathy, and transfers of power

One can agree with the idea that the traditional elements of the old European order, resting on kinship, social class, religion, local communities, monarchy (Nisbet 1993), were scrambled by the forces of democracy. No longer as sharp and clear, they form an omelet; in some countries the monarchy has been removed from the mix, in

Table 13.2 The conceptual futures of power

	Weber	Simmel	Foucault	Future power
Political structure of organizations	Regimes of domination	Forms of subordination	Systems of surveillance	Reflexive oligarchies
Power production	Forms of legitimacy and their possible combinations	Forms of relationships between individuals and between individuals and principles (power is *interactive*)	Disciplinary practices and instruments of control	Interactions between 'political niches' (collegial niches) and emergence of 'organizational activists'
Political performance	Social fabric of efficiency	Social fabric of political communities	Pervasiveness of control and the embodiment of control	Fusing political and moral power
Obedience production	Obtrusive and rational production of obedience by readable rules	Production of commitment through the quality of relationships	Production of allegiance through the embodiment of norms	Reflexive authority producing obedience through soft constraints and the power of morality
Concept of power	Organizational power	Relational power	Conventional power	Politically soft power

others the church has been separated from the state, and so on. Traditions live on in some places like a nightmare in the brain of the living, as Marx once put it. One might think of the noble titles, for instance, which decorate the boards of business organizations. But they are tangled up in new circuits of celebrity, where porn stars are indistinguishable from heiresses and heiresses from porn stars, where celebrity is an end in itself, where people are famous for being famous.

The ideological signification of democracy in the organizational world is not only related to a kind of moral utterance. It is also the work of power, since democracy in economic institutions is antagonistic to oligarchic and bureaucratic practices and values. It is not only power in the mechanical sense of 'force applied to a people by external government in the pursuit of its own objectives, but power regarded as arising from the people, transmitted by libertarian, egalitarian and rationalist ends so that it becomes, in effect, not power but only the exercise of the people's own will' (Nisbet 1993: 40). The question arising from this quotation concerns not merely how far organizations can be truly democratic but the peculiar interconnections between democracy, power and morality. As Nisbet (1993) puts it, power without morality is despotism, while morality without power is sterile. Scholars must therefore think through the combination of democracy, power and morality. So far, we have barely begun to do this in the contemporary practices of organizations. How can we reconcile the parameters of a Habermasian ideal speech situation as the form of democracy that respects the humanity of people with the functional necessities of divided, specialized labor and centralized administration? Can the political imagination usher in changes correlative with the new distributed forms of technology that are now available? The pen and the typewriter gave us bureaucracy; can virtuality give us democracy?

We think that future regimes of power will be deeply characterized by their capacity to build credible combinations between these three elements. This is why we consider resistance as an outdated topic in the study of power. The tensions and competition between different combinations of identity are much more interesting than the never-ending description of the always possible or potential resistance of actors, imagined as if they were puppets waiting the old scripts of solidarity to animate them, forever cast in their workerist identities. Today, the solidarities are more likely to be ethically nationalistic or religiously fundamental or both, and the consequences not so much liberatory but terrible. If nineteenth- and twentieth-century organizations might have had many occasions to fear their employees *qua* workers – because of the power of organized labor – the twenty-first century has more to fear from the anonymous terrorist or the barely recognized ethnic and religious tensions that simmer in their remote branch plant's or supply chain's hinterland, brought into the organization by those whom they employ or subcontract.

Contemporary conditions of political action in organizations lead us not so much to consider questions of solidaristic consciousness as to emphasize the question of transfers of power. What is relevant is to study pivotal moments in the life of organizations and individuals, dates that are durably resilient in organizations' and individuals' memories. For instance, power scholars could be inspired by studies on regime changes (Linz 1978) to identify the existence of common patterns in the process leading to changes in political structures, not only in states but also in organizations more generally. Studying the prerequisites for political stability is an all the more important topic in so far as, today, we are experiencing a brutal shift from postwar optimism about the durability of democratic regimes to a more pragmatic and short-term regional perspective on political stability. We do not mean that the period of *coup d'état* is vanishing in states, as the emergence of democratic or quasi-democratic regimes becomes more and more pervasive. In the past, such regime changes have been at the center of political analysis.

As far as organizations are concerned, the study of radical changes of the social and political structure is unlikely to shape the core of the power agenda for organizational analysts, in terms of the macro-impact of state change. However, in terms of the more immediate effects of often hostile takeovers within commercial organizations, when we see the violent end of top management team careers associated with particular organizations, there is great scope for research. Contemporary violence is no longer essentially political but is shifting to the realm of interpersonal and hierarchical relations, especially as they are contingent on stock-market raids and coups.

Within organizations, it is particularly interesting to decipher the signification of the supposed increase in psychological and moral forms of harassment as contemporary figures of obtrusive forms of oppression. The question is whether the threshold of tolerance (the 'zone of indifference') for direct oppressive forms of power is decreasing, while the threshold of tolerance for remote, implicit and soft forms of power and domination is increasing. From this perspective political apathy implies that the perception of political violence in contemporary organizations would be founded on a shared acceptance of the social division existing between elites and non-elites. As Michels (1962) prophesied, the fate of organizations is largely dependent on the fragmentation between competent governors and those who are pragmatically and obediently governed. Such a political division of work implies that the governors establish new forms of control and surveillance on a more and more remote and indifferent polity. That is where the combination between soft forms of power and the political centralization of organizations is worth studying, for instance through the emergence of 'soft bureaucracies' (Courpasson 2000). Power will be shaped in the complex intricacies between the 'absence' of readable power mechanisms (the soft part of the structure) and the constant 'presence' of the organizational machinery (its instruments, ratios and overwhelming 'pressure-generating' systems of control).

When a member of an organization faces a novel and morally charged situation s/he does more than merely apply a formulaic model or process, the organizational machinery, in order to decide on a course of action. In practice there will always be room for interpretation as various ethical models and calculations are used in relation to the activities of organizing and managing. Thus, organizational members have to make choices to apply, interpret and make sense of various competing models of practice (including ethical ones) in specific situations. Such ethical work does not suggest a total 'free play' but implies that moral choice proposes an oscillation between possibilities, where these possibilities are determined situationally

(Derrida 1988). Ethics are *at stake* when norms, rules or systems of ethics clash, and no third meta-rule can be applied to resolve the dilemma. We cannot avoid being moral beings that make choices 'with the knowledge (or at least a suspicion in case efforts are made to suppress or deny that knowledge) that they are but choices. Society engraves the pattern of ethics upon the raw and pliable stuff of morality. Ethics is a social product because morality is not' (Bauman, in Bauman and Tester 2001: 45). And if ethics cannot be articulated, it is invariably because power arbitrates on, overrules, and otherwise struggles to fix meanings.

Ethical codes, norms and models have important implications for organizational members. They are resources that skilful and knowledgeable members use freely in everyday management. As Foucault suggests, 'what is ethics, if not the practice of freedom, the conscious practice of freedom?' (1997: 284). The moral agent, from a power perspective, is one who enacts agency rather than one whose actions are considered to be wholly determined structurally (see Lukes 1974; 2005). One may agree or disagree with particular ethical dictates, but it is what one does in relation to them that determines the practice of ethics.

A concrete example, at the heart of debates about power, and one that we have addressed earlier, makes the point clearly. Despite sustained claims regarding the unjust treatment of women in the workforce, and their relative lack of access to relations that are powerful, equal employment opportunity (EEO) legislation has not been sufficient to gain women equal status in organizations (Blackburn et al. 2000). A simplistic view would suggest that this should not have been the case; the rules should be implemented and complied with so as to produce the desired effects, including the realization of a more ethical and just state of affairs. In practice, discrimination remains enacted through the tacit cultural micro-practices of everyday organizational life (see Martin and Meyerson 1998; Meyerson and Fletcher 2003). Such practices emerge from the relation between explicit EEO pronouncements, the enactment of gender in organizations, and the power and agency of those many people who interact in order to produce gender inequality.

When formal systems of ethics such as codes of conduct are present, following Meyer and Rowan (1977), they can be expected to function as ceremonially adopted myths used to gain legitimacy, resources, and stability, and to enhance survival prospects. The practice of the system far exceeds its explicit statements. Thus, to maintain ceremonial conformity, 'organizations that reflect institutional rules tend to buffer their formal structures from the uncertainties of technical activities by becoming loosely coupled, building gaps between their formal structures and actual work activities' (1977: 340). In their search for legitimacy, organizations use codes of conduct as standards to justify what they do (Brunsson et al. 2000) as well as to fulfill a narcissistic obsession with looking 'good' (Roberts 2003). In this sense, codes of conduct become a 'public relations exercise' (Munro 1992: 98). Goffman (1961: 30) had their meaning nailed when he wrote about the partial reversal of transformation rules in encounters where 'minor courtesies' are displayed to 'women and children in our society' by men, honoring the youngest or weakest 'as a ceremonial reversal of ordinary practice'. The point he makes is that codes of conduct are not constructed out of a sense of esteeming and identifying with another who is like you but are instead an impersonal and productive convenience to secure selfish aims.

Take the example of Enron, a company that won prizes for its 'ethics program', a program designed more for impression management than ethical thoughtfulness (Sims and Brinkmann 2003). Such impression management practices might contribute to organizational legitimacy (Suchmann 1995) but not necessarily to the form of deliberation, decision, and exercise of freedom that characterizes ethically charged organizational problems. Should we analyze organizations in terms of what they say they do in their formal documentation or should we study what they actually do? Clearly, we should do both, while acknowledging that rhetoric has its own practice and it is the relations between the practices, the situations in which they occur, and the audiences they invite, that are important (Corbett and Connors 1999; Cheney et al. 2004; Suddaby and Greenwood 2005).

What needs to be investigated is how people adhere to, violate, ignore or creatively interpret formally ethical precepts. Organizational members engage with such formulations as a potential instrument of power that can be used to legitimize and delegitimize standpoints in power relations. As we saw in Chapter 6, with the cases of the total institutions, compliance can lead to ethically questionable outcomes. If there were guarantees of the ethics produced by following rules then the Eichmann defense would not have the notoriety that it has (Arendt 1994). Therefore, interpreting and adapting rules and maxims according to local circumstances, including sometimes even contravening them, might be deemed ethically sound. Rules are resources to legitimize and to negotiate organizational realities and their application will always be an occurrence of power/knowledge relations. Different versions of these generate conflicting visions of society.

Conflicting visions of society: the emergence of internal 'social movements'?

Organization theory in the broadest sense of the term is very well suited to construct a convincing political theory of contemporary corporations. Actually, an extensive body of literature for decades has been analyzing the conditions of embeddedness of organizational politics in the social structure of corporations (Useem 1984; Ocasio 1994; Gouldner 1956). In Chapter 12 we stressed that the corporate elite is neither as parochial nor as fragmented as pluralist theories suppose, nor is it as unified and cohesive as elitist theories suppose (Davis and Thompson 1994). Rather, a social movement perspective can help to better grasp the current and forthcoming dynamics of power generation and maintenance in organizations. The existence of conflicting visions of organizations and society is likely to be the cornerstone of many studies of organizational dynamics, as current events suggest that collective forms of action and mobilization do not derive from a simple calculus of incentive, but rather depend on a number of uncertain and always questionable organized alliances and coalitions between actors.

Once again, we argue here that one of the most prominent questions for power scholars will continue to be that of who comes to dominate power relations. The main approach to this never-ending issue has, for a long time, been an exchange-based perspective (Pfeffer and Salancik 1978). Based on a presumption of managerial control, internal power struggles, conditioned by specific environmental factors, determine who controls the resources that bestow the power to govern. Yet, one cannot assume that managerial control is still the rule.

Class-based perspectives (Zeitlin 1974), premised on a view of corporate owners and managers living in a relative harmony of interests, do not say much about the effects on this harmony of recent hostile takeovers, of the corporate upheavals of the 1980s, and of the subsequent political maneuverings by corporate managers, let alone are able to address the irruption of the pre-modern world in the post-modern society. Drawing from social movement analysis may enable one to interpret which processes and which common values future collective actors are likely to design as the political face of organizations. How actors translate shared interests into common values is at the heart of current stakes in organizations (Tilly 1978). One of the most germane insights of these studies is that collective mobilization does not derive mostly from a certain level of grievances; an effective social organization among actors is more explicative of potential social movements and organizational turmoil than a given level of incentive, as Mann's (1986) notion of organizational outflanking recommends. One fascinating issue would be to analyze how far current social agendas for organizational leaders (corporate social responsibility and sustainability issues, in particular) will challenge the actual decision-making processes and power distribution, by including new experts in the political process of decision making, and by enhancing the rise of unexpected challengers whose interests are not presently considered in the political structure.

How far do incumbent leaders have an interest in bringing morality back into business discourses and practices, and what risk do they take in doing so of facilitating the emergence of new collective actors? The underlying question is that of the dynamics of corporate elites as a genuinely efficient social movement. If we accept the framework of Tilly (1978), pertaining to the politics of control, we can infer that, with regard to:

- *Group interests*, numerous studies suggest that corporate elites act as a relatively cohesive network through permanent interactions. Interlocks, for instance, can serve as platforms for social action.
- *Social infrastructure*, numerous studies, not least those of Bourdieu, remark that the degree of common identities and social backgrounds linking corporate elite members remains high.
- *Mobilization*, the 'process by which a group acquires collective control over resources needed for collective action' (Davis and Thompson 1994: 156), seems to be a relational skill that is still frequently exercised. Most corporate upheavals and changes are a demonstration of the capacity of corporate elites to gather individuals, skills, expertise and money to achieve a given purpose.
- *Political opportunity structure*, the probability of successful political 'insurgencies' (McAdam 1982), continues to arise out of periods of instability and incumbent elites' challenges.

If we analyze political action as a combination of these four components, we suggest it might be of utmost interest to investigate the potential dynamics encompassed in two contemporary phenomena:

- The current changes of corporate elite (see Chapter 12), as for instance the way internal competition between would-be leaders diminishes the chances of elites acting as a true 'ruling class' or, put differently, how the cut-throat struggles for scarce positions of power affect elite and subelite cohesion.
- The current emergence of new corporate professional actors, such as new types of professions (project managers, business unit managers, the profession of middle management as a whole). Here the investigation could focus on how power structures might be endangered and modified by a collegial type of collective action enhanced by the generation of a kind of 'insurgent consciousness' within the professional niches of the corporation (McAdam 1982: 49).

It remains an open question as to whether potential new political actors might influence structural power (i.e. the rules of the game), or 'only' wrest open redistributive and minimalist forms of power. We put forward the hypothesis that the future power structures of organizations will be largely shaped by the capacity of ruling corporate elites to rejuvenate the pillars of their legitimacy, and by the simultaneous capacity of professional subelites both to be allegiant and to influence the governance of departmental and local subunits. These subelites might act as 'organizational activists' so to speak, working to engineer a new structural differentiation between the center and the periphery.

The specter of 'lost power'

As Tocqueville put it a long time ago:

> In our days, men see that the constituted powers are crumbling down on every side; they see all ancient authority dying out, all ancient barriers tottering to their fall, and the judgment of the wisest is troubled at the sight ... If they look at the final consequences of this revolution, their fears would perhaps assume a different shape. For myself, I confess that I put no trust in the spirit of freedom which appears to animate my contemporaries. I see well enough that the nations of this age are turbulent, but I do not clearly perceive that they are liberal; and I fear lest, at the close of those perturbations, which rock the base of thrones, the dominion of sovereigns may prove more powerful than it was ever. (1945: 314)

A similar statement could have been uttered by any analyst of our days. We have argued on numerous occasions in this book that new types of power, more encompassing and penetrating than ever before in history, are emerging out of the ashes of modern institutions. Power will be less and less submerged in the ethos of well-delineated communities, where the power of the elite could seem to the governed little different from the power exercised by familiar and sometimes reassuring figures such as the father, the priest, or the master. Power is no longer an 'undifferentiated aspect of the social order' (Nisbet 1993: 108). The fragmentation and terror of the risk society as the essence of the postmodern condition are only the most heightened aspects of this state of affairs.

Nisbet explains compellingly that when individuals become separated from institutions, 'there arises ... the specter of lost authority' (1993: 108). One might hypothesize that, in the organizational realm, given the ceaseless fragmentation and individualization of the social body, what is likely is a form of disintegration of the idea of power and, in parallel, a magnification of political power vested (nevertheless) precariously in remote and uncontrollable entities and principles (ethics, the environment, the pension funds, etc.). The increasing looseness of most institutions in our times, and the diffusion of a 'culture of precariousness' amidst the state of insecurity, seem to require a growing concentration of political action, aimed at withstanding the current dislocation of the social foundations of organizations by all the shock troops of the global world, including for instance not only jihad but also fierce competitiveness as new arenas, such as China and India, enter the global scene, as well as increasing insecurity about the impact of the ecology on organizational action and of organizational action on the ecology.

We need to remember the seminal distinction between social authority and political power, the realm of rationality and centralization. Today's organizations are characterized by the fact that power is, so to speak, *not* fused in the wider society. Deference is no longer shown to or expected by elders and betters. Organizations cannot simply rely on staffing their command with high-status males and expecting the subaltern ranks to obey unquestioningly. The social order is no longer mediated by clear-cut figures and organizational institutions supporting masculinity, authority, or religious or ethnic supremacy. It is wavering from one individual to another, from endogenous actors and groups to external constraints, and thus power is not generating individual security and beliefs in the relative unity of organizations as centers of power. Simultaneously, while the idea of power is dislocated, organizations relentlessly produce alternative managerial instrumentations of, and discourses about, performance, that play the role of political devices of control, mediating the invisible power of the invisible center, reshaping the body politic. Following Tocqueville once again, the contemporary evolution of power can be sketched as moving from a situation where the power of a small number of persons prevailed to one where there is the 'weakness of the whole community', which now is being superseded by the antagonistic powers of dispersed and fragmented communities. Order in organizations, as our forebears knew it, even as late as the 1970s and 1980s, can no longer rely on the multiplier effect of an ordered society where ethnicities, genders, age cohorts, and classes knew – and kept – their place. All the past's seeming social solidity has melted into air, and where once there was the illusion of an order that few questioned, now we can see only the effects of repressive tolerance; as long as the elites were mimicked, obeyed and reproduced in the masses' behavior they would be tolerated. Acceptance was contingent on obedience.

There have been attempts by leaders, elites and others positioned as celebrities in the media circuits of power to remake a center that can hold, such as G8 and Live8. The current endeavor of organizational leaders and their delegates to seize upon ethical and environmental topics can be interpreted as an attempt to combine political and moral power in a single figure. Put differently, if the idea of power is dislocating, it is doing so in a period particularly suited for fusing into a single institution (the business corporation) the two faces of power: the rational and centralized, the power-generating performance; and the traditional and diffuse, the power-generating legitimacy, and normative obedience. The joint dynamic of the two forces is all the more interesting and striking in that it contradicts the dynamics Weber foresaw, namely the antagonism between the moral objective of democracy, rule by the people, and the rational side of this objective, bureaucracy.

Behind the endless discourses on corporate social responsibility, one can see the politicization of moral values providing power with a new consistency, which was proposed by Durkheim. Power *is* moral life, because it is through 'the practice of moral values we develop the capacity to govern' (Durkheim 1961: 46). But power is also plural, by definition, according to Durkheim; it is manifested in the diverse spheres of social life, communities, webs of kinship, professions, school, unions, etc. Organizations endeavor to restore the consistency of a powerful social group, by gripping more firmly the individuals, by generating constantly new reasons to bind them to the corporate future, to make them believe they act for the sake of a socially useful and fruitful entity, to give a greater significance to individual actions, as Durkheim put it. Of course, twentieth-century neo-Durkheimians, such as Mayo, were well aware of this function of organic solidarity, a form of corporatism writ small.

Durkheim expected anomie where the social bonds did not cohere. In the nineteenth century anomic suicide was the favored escape attempt. One might interpret today's striking consumption of soft drugs in the workplace as the twenty-first century's substitute for suicide. The causes are partly the same: social atomization, moral emptiness, uncertainty and the specter of 'lost power'. The combined dynamics of the political and moral sides of the business and organizational realm might be likely to supply the 'social substance' now lacking in fragmented individual lives. As Nisbet puts it wittily, 'new forms of social organization must be devised to escape the contradiction involved presently in a horde of individuals whose lives are regulated but not really ruled by the distant, remote, and impersonal state' (1993: 156). Business corporations, because they are *de facto* intrusive, must be potent, to avoid the Durkheimian prophecy of governance:

> [I]nflated and hypertrophied in order to obtain a firm enough grip upon individuals, but without succeeding, the latter, without mutual relationships, tumble over one another like so many liquid molecules, encountering no central energy to retain, fix and organize them. (1951: 389)

The possible peculiarity of present times is that, as we suggested earlier through the idea of 'organizational activism', the overwhelming hypertrophy of the business world in today's societies does not necessarily go hand in hand with the atrophy of other identity-generative kinds of social groups. The current moral wave might be carrying the promises of a joint development. But still, it is out of the agonistic tensions between these forces that a new consistent social order will arise.

From subordination to new forms of oppression?

The question posed by the current plethora of political discourse about the environment, society, sustainability, and responsibility might resemble the kind of emerging political identities that Laclau and Mouffe identified in their landmark *Hegemony and socialist strategy* (1985). We suggest that the current period might be favorable to the emergence of new social movements from the post-Enlightenment space, championing issues of environment, ethics, and even, to some extent, a return-to-simple-life discourse and values.[27] Such movements are intriguing for several reasons.

The political identities emerging from this movement are far from being clear; nobody really knows who are the active behind-the-scene 'messengers' and what are the political struggles and coalitions maneuvering to bring these ideas to the front of the scene. A fuzzy community of politicians, humanitarian activists, journalists, intellectuals, and so on has generated a common agenda to which corporate leaders have more or less recently turned to legitimate new sources of performance.

We think that the type of 'democratic revolution', using Tocqueville's expression, which is represented by these new mass forms of mobilization around specific issues, is likely to produce a slight shift in the name of a newly designed common good, that of the planet and other generalities. In this sphere it is the nongovernmental organizations, such as Greenpeace and World Vision, moral organizations staffed by moral actors, which are decisive. Organizational leaders have already seized upon some of the arguments emanating from these organizations to help them turn some new tricks in their repertoire of corporate discourse, such as the 'triple bottom line'.

One could draw from Laclau's idea that all hegemonically constructed order entails 'ethical investments'; 'hegemony entails the unending interplay of "contingent decisions" between the "ethical" ("ought") and the "normative" ("is")' (Townshend 2004: 277). Current attempts to construct a new democratic and ethical order, which occur in nearly every business discourse or media utterance concerning business, can be analyzed as democratic attempts constituting 'the only form of hegemony that permanently shows the contingency of its own foundations' (Laclau 1990: 86, quoted by Townshend 2004: 277). It remains to be seen how far these pro-democratic and pro-ethics movements are anti-capitalist – and thus true to their origins. What is relatively clear is that the debate is located not inside the capitalist world and the organizational realm, but on its fringe. At the same time what is particularly striking is that organizations, while seizing upon the societal political discourse, do not allow the formation of other types of forces likely to become other hegemonies, without striving to control them. In particular, this is the case with ethical movements, as they pertain to one of the major pillars of the organizational political structure. The legitimacy of corporate elites, and specifically that of their right to act in the name of a common good which is supposed to be a common will, is exemplified by Bill Gates appearing with Bono and Bob Geldof on stage at Live8. Adorned with new 'ethical outfits', the corporate elite is prone to build a new discourse of performance that is all the more decisive as it concerns making organizations true political subjects.

Extending organization power

Power was always a reciprocal matter – not only of its relations and its exercise but also of its anticipation and normative shaping on the part of those subject to it. Today it is a much more instrumentally mediated relationship than one of face-to-face imperative coordination. If the calculus of power continues to be the model for face-to-face organization, and immediate imperative coordination, then power will increasingly seem to be missing in action. Yet, its traces are more pervasive the more mediated they become, and the more the mediations enchant, charm and captivate us; as we have been at pains to argue, seduction may be sensual but is still a form of power. The aspirants to the corporate elites in thrall to their BlackBerries are as mediated in being effects of power as is any lowly checkout worker monitored by the speed of her or his transactions. Of course, the one form of mediation is experienced more seductively and pleasurably than the other. Yet, in either case, the captive checkout operative in less than a square meter of space, or the executive globally roaming, both are held in mediated power relations.

One of the behind-the-scene ideas encompassed in the notion of 'power dispersion' is that in the large and sprawling structures (physical and non-physical) of contemporary organizations, power operates (mostly) indirectly, without face-to-face interactions, in activity systems outside the boundaries of a face-to-face setting. As Goffman (1972) suggests, multisituated game-like activities, such as the 'newspaper game' or the 'banking game', involving occupational communities with motives and positions generated and realizable within the community, can also be analyzed in these terms.

Within the organizations that these games compose and recompose, according to contemporary consulting practice, hierarchies are supposed to flatten and the chains of command are constantly stretching out their tentacles further. While policies are elaborated by a small number of 'informed' power and knowledge holders, their implementation will be carried out by a number of people many levels below. Societal and organizational dynamics are possible because invisible and anonymous people act, react and incorporate their effects and aftermaths. Of course, organizational theorists have long recognized and analyzed the way power extends through hierarchical systems; they have long written about 'determinate hierarchy' (Simon 1976: 22) or declared that 'everyone must be subordinate to someone' (Barnard 1938: 176). Today, nevertheless, the nature of this extension is different.

The 'iconic' dyadic approach to power relations long restricted organization theorists to reciprocal intervention of A and B (Dahl 1957: 202–3; Lukes 1974: 34), as if a connection between the two was a necessary condition for any power relation; but what was left unspecified was how to analyze 'power beyond adjacencies', or 'power at a distance', to use Willer's (2003: 97) expressions. Indeed, taking their cue from the community power debate many theorists would follow Dahl (1957) in insisting that there can be no power at a distance (see the discussion in Clegg 1989: Chapter 2).

We have argued in this book that the development of substructures of power is one of the most likely transformations of the political structures of organizations, if the latter are to extend and refine their democratic side. Strong power substructures are the condition of the development of democratic, polyarchic kinds of organizations. To know whether such arrangements are a desirable objective is another matter, a matter of judgment, of value. But the Weberian distinction between 'feudal hierarchies' and what we have termed 'polyarchic hierarchies' still requires investigation, especially as to how internal 'social movements' are likely to emerge in polyarchic settings, and how far the extension of power relations facilitates or discourages the generation of strong endogenous substructures of power.

We should not forget those who are squeezed by flatter structures – the excluded, or at least diminished, middle. Middle managers occupy highly uncertain and threatening positions, which, while organizationally 'superordinate' in Simmelian terms, 'are squeezed between high power superiors and a subordinate not weakened by exclusion' (Willer 2003: 1324). One can imagine that the subleaders of political substructures will strive to develop alternative means for achieving their goals and imposing their views other than classical dyadic interaction, for instance by using parallel networks of influence, or gatekeeper's positions. The current development of corporate professions through parallel 'private–public' personal endeavors by certain individuals might be seen as part of these attempts to generate power outside of the softly locked power circles of the organization.

Once again, the constant contemporary mobilization of ethical and environmental rhetoric is merely an extension of political ordering, seeking external arguments and faraway actors as determining, at least partially, the internal decision-making systems. New stakeholders have their uses. Furthermore, in the investigation of power at a distance, while it analyzes the effects of new political conditions on elite stability and legitimacy, it is highly likely that the extension of political webs will imply greater legitimacy from, and for, power holders; in that sense, the pillars of legitimacy, since they are no longer essentially founded on face-to-face interactions and 'on the spot' legitimization processes, are shifting to the complex combination outlined in Chapter 11 between meritocratic and hereditary aspects of elite stability. We summarize these reflections in Figure 13.1.

We have suggested in this book that, through the use of social movement theory, newly emerging dynamics entail that contestation is clearly considered as a possible political action. The creation of strong substructures, as well as the mobilization of exogenous rhetorical opportunities, act as a trigger for collective action inside the organization. That is where the never-ending apparent contradiction between the hard power of contestation patterns and authoritarian settings (if we admit organizations are authoritarian settings, not in the sense of dictatorial and totalitarian regimes, but in the sense of non-democratic decision-making systems) and the soft power of governmental rationalities takes on a new sense.

Soft and hard power

The debate over the respective merits and mechanisms of hard and soft forms of power is centuries old. We find it behind the scenes in the fundamental opposition between Hobbesian and Machiavellian versions of politics as the struggle against adversaries, as the vision of sovereignty and the social construction of strategies

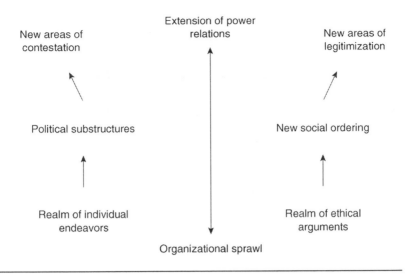

Figure 13.1   New dynamics entailed by the extension of power relations

are at the heart of these versions (see Clegg 1989). At first sight, in the sovereign version there is no need to struggle, as there are neither credible nor powerful enough adversaries; in the strategic version diverse ingredients have to be mobilized to vanquish mobile and hardly controllable adversaries. Put differently, soft and hard versions of power might well be the most structuring conceptual and empirical antagonism in the study and understanding of power.

The debate has intensified recently, perhaps as a result of 9/11. The field of international politics enables us better to grasp the futures of political dynamics in the organizational realm, because it has to deal with the same types of turmoil and political violence (notwithstanding the effects in terms of casualties). On one side, certain thinkers and politicians are constantly declaring soft power irrelevant, as the battle against enemies (of the US in this case) supposes that the only possible response to terror is to engage in coercive strategies, unleash overwhelming violence in tactics of shock and awe, and not to attract and seduce individuals and groups (the terrorists) who, by definition, are repelled by the symbols and sovereign power of America, and the Western world in general. On the other side, another fringe of political scientists, led by Joseph Nye in particular, in the US, claim that it is when hatred is at its peak that soft power should be used. The language of attraction and diplomacy should replace the language of coercion.

Soft power is the ability to get what you want by persuading others to adopt your goals. We are right in the middle of the Lukesian third dimension of power and those positive visions of power familiar from Follett, Luhmann, Parsons, Arendt, or Foucault, power that grows out of a political community and a political culture strong enough to avoid using force and coercion. We recall the old distinction, of which Aron (1972) reminds us, between actual power and potential power. The

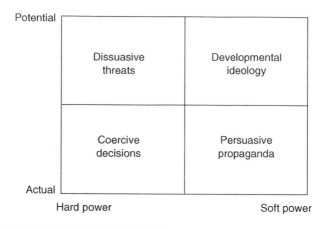

Figure 13.2   Four archetypes of power

power of leaders derives from shrewd articulation between concrete actions (of power) and uncertain potentialities of exercising power. In Figure 13.2 we elaborate a grid with which to analyze the emergence of specific forms of power in organizations. At the crossroads between a soft/hard and an actual/potential continuum of forms of power we suggest there are four major forms interacting to produce the actual mechanisms of power in organizations.

In both archetypes founded on hard power, power holders are clearly definable. Actions and threats come from a specific and clear-cut source. One can assume that power holders know what they are doing when they decide (in a first-dimensional kind of approach) to use political resources to overcome resistance or to force allegiance. In both archetypes founded on soft power, matters are blurred. The persuasive propagandists believe they know what they are doing; they are composed of different sets of actors and instruments (media, technology, discourses) among which the inner circle is barely definable. The idea of developmental ideology is even more complex. It is a form of power defining the nature of exchange and promises, creating an implicit social pact between governors and governed. Moreover, it is a form of power implicitly shaping situations in which actors will be enshrined, in the name of a well-structured and well-defined common good (which, for instance, takes the shape of ethics and societal responsibility). From the common good it is supposed that allegiance will stem. But the common good can never be captured in a mode of domination, in a vision imposed on the others, in a claim based on any pretext of managerial fiat or real ownership over and above those of the managed and non-owning:

> The 'human essence' lying forever in the future, the pool of human possibilities remaining forever unexhausted, and the future itself being unknown and unknowable, impossible to adumbrate ('the absolute other' in Levinas' vocabulary). Such a view of human modality breathes tolerance, offers the benefit of the doubt, teaches modesty and self-restraint.

> If you know exactly what the good society is like, any cruelty you commit in its name is justified and absolved. But we can be good to each other and abstain from cruelty only when we are unsure of our wisdom and admit a possibility of error. (Bauman, in Bauman and Tester 2001: 47)

The peculiarity of the developmental archetype that sees leaders leading those whom they dominate, however softly, however benevolently, is twofold. First, it assumes that there are no fundamental disagreements between leaders and led about the pathways to the future. Both sides of the political hierarchy share a similar awareness of the stakes and the hurdles to overcome in order to manage to build up a common future, 'together'. A common pragmatism might lead to the disappearance of divergences, building a constrained political community in Arendt's terms. Leaders do not exist on the fringes of the organization but are necessarily nested inside a community which is itself hierarchically structured. Second, this pragmatic common shaping of a political community does not mask the unawareness of both sides, leaders and led, of the underlying structure of power constructing, *de facto*, the conditions of political action.

The developmental ideology archetype is a way of combining and fusing the two major political dynamics that we have suggested characterize contemporary organizations: the political community move, and the turn to organizational activism. Between these apparently opposite dynamics (one driving integration, the other driving resistance and fragmentation), new developmental forms of power are acting to fuse the subsequent effects of these dynamics. The supreme exercise of power would be to make organizational activists work for the establishment and maintenance of a true political community, while being unaware that they are being used that way, and thus not really paying attention to it. Needless to say, as far as the fundamentalisms are concerned, the prospects for achieving this seem remote indeed.

Contestation in soft authoritarian organizations and value-based leadership

As we have already suggested earlier in the book, organizations are not an easy place to develop and implement democratic principles and practices. Organizations, and specifically business organizations, are among the least democratic institutions of modern times. Their attachment to hierarchy as an organizing principle is remarkable, as we have suggested. Such proclivities do not mean that most organizations are coercion-based regimes but assert that they are not designed to distribute power equally among members, that power holders are not elected by members, that crucial decisions will be made in small circles of power without necessarily seeking members' opinions, and so forth. Even at their best they are oligarchies based, sometimes, on some notions of merit.

The question of contestation takes interesting shape if we view contemporary organizations as soft authoritarian systems (Courpasson 2006). Following Tilly (1978), we suggest that two general paths are likely to drive forms of contestation: political opportunity and threat. Opportunity will be defined as 'the likelihood that challengers will enhance their interests or external existing benefits if they act collectively ... threat denotes the probability that existing benefits will be taken away or new harms inflicted if challenging groups fail to act collectively' (Almeida 2003: 347). The question of what might drive collective action within organizational settings that are softly coercive invites several answers; for a start we would nominate a collective fear of losing rights and safety, such as holiday entitlements and safety and penalty clauses in workplace agreements; the expansion and extension of new demands designed to preserve old powers, such as enhanced share options for senior management teams; and fear of the unanticipated consequences of those strategies of self-preservation that elites routinely enact, such as the inflation of book-based stock values in the here-and-now through systematic under-investment in the future. Of course, these are not just dysfunctions of private sector organizations; they are only too evident in government and public sector organizations, especially where they are wedded to the neoliberalism of new public sector management, and accounting mechanisms that insist on year-end balanced budgets. It is always easy to balance today's budget if you do not spend for tomorrow's needs. It is also highly irresponsible; today's managers are custodians of tomorrow's life chances. Where they manage as if they were Vikings, pillaging the future, they betray those whose inheritance they have created.

It is by no means sure that subgroups have a chance to enhance their interests and to gain advantage by acting collectively. If, as we contend, organizations are still based on strong central structures of power, the formation of challenging sub-structures requires important cognitive attributions, clearly defined shared interests and organizational resources. For instance, the mobilization of specific internal networks will be required. As Almeida (2003) puts it, in any authoritarian and non-democratic environment, organizational infrastructures are necessary for any actor to link previously unconnected communities.

Following Tilly (1978), once again, three different forms of threat are likely to have an impact on power structures:

1   Economic tensions, which can be attributed either to environmental factors or, more locally, to management causes rather than those that are generalized and generic.
2   The erosion of the rights of organizational members, which means, in the organizational context, that the growing distance between individuals and decision-taking arenas makes people feel as if they are working in less trust-worthy environments.
3   Organization repression and violence, action which might generate sufficiently significant moral shocks and collectively shared emotions to boost group protest activities (on the 'too much is too much' mode). The articulations of this with the perceived threats that emanate from the state of insecurity will be significant; the violence may come from either the state or private sector organizations.

We suggest a specific conjunction of these three elements is at hand in contemporary organizations. If the existence of fuzzily attributable economic difficulties is not sufficient to account for the emergence of contention and contestation, the conjunction of the erosion of rights and the sophistication of coercive methods in organizations (especially through new digital technologies of surveillance and the concertative discipline of teams) is likely to foster, within the organizational polity, new forms of protest and expression. The point is to decipher the reciprocal influences of the public organizational and private spheres in framing individual decisions to contest. What is at issue here is the future of legitimacy.

The future of legitimacy

Many contemporary questions surround the future of legitimacy, but they are not the classic questions derived from the Marxist canon of collective consciousness challenging system legitimation (Habermas 1976). An example of the kind of contemporary challenge to legitimacy is given by the massive emotional gatherings that occurred in France following the death of Pope John Paul II. While the existing circles of elites (both political and intellectual) were discussing the legitimacy of flying the national flag at half-mast, thousands of people, particularly the young, were heading to Paris in specially chartered trains and coaches, while other gatherings occurred in scattered places in France to share common meetings, create spontaneous communities, and reflect on the significance of the event. Whatever one thinks the significance of these events to be, the point is that on this occasion, the elites had lost control of the people's wills and preferences. And that is probably why these elites so harshly and somewhat uselessly focused their critique on the tricolor and the role of the state in that affair, as something whose separation seemed questioned by this undisciplining of civil society. A similar spectacle was observed at the funeral of Princess Diana (see Clegg 2000). A further example would be the defeat of the elite-sponsored referendum in favor of affirming the European constitution that occurred in France on May 27, 2005. The masses did not do as the elites would prefer.

Spectaculars may be the only means capable of mobilizing sufficient energy and social vibrations to foster collective social dynamics in future. The power of private emotions in the triggering of contest waves in organizations or in social and emotional collective action is a long way from the dyadic nature of power and microsocial approaches to power and obedience. As Satow (1975) has long suggested, completing the Weberian types of authority might prove more necessary than ever. If, as we have clearly argued, contestation might arise from unexpected events, the power of value-rational forms of social action *à la* Weber is worth exploring, to shed light on the still absent value-rational forms of leadership. To go back to the question of organizational social movements, we suggest one of the missing links between the ethical and environmental realms of legitimization and the subsequent potential transformation of political structures resides in the absence of a coherent model of leadership. Following Willer, a value-based model of leadership would be founded on 'faith in the absolute value of a rationalized set of norms' (1967: 235). Obedience (of the governors as well as the governed) may be due to an ideology proffering legitimacy such that those in dominant relations of power derive their mandate directly from their exemplary relationship to the goals of that ideology.

The problem with the theory of the ideal type of legitimacy is that value-based leaders are expected to take decisions, regardless of the consequences of those decisions on the organization, from the moment when the decisions are 'aligned' with the goals of the ideology. It is naturally not the case in business organizations, except if we accept the hypothesis of the emergence of global corporate elites, taking decisions in remote circles of power, defending first and foremost the interests of the global corporate village, regardless of the consequences of these decisions on more parochial aspects and subleaders. An uncertain political regime, defending otherworldly objectives, but monitoring simultaneously the necessary adaptations of the concrete organizations in order to survive, would emerge where such events occur.[28]

Conclusion

In the past, in organization theory, it was customary to think of organizations as, by definition, authority systems, characterized by legitimacy, thus precluding analysis of their actual power relations. Calling them by the name of authority already effectively settled the matter, foreclosing debate and enquiry. In the future, as the aim was stated in our opening chapter, after reading this book no one should make that error again. It is an open and contingent matter as to the shapes and forms that power relations assume, which is the major reason that the analysis of total institutions was placed at the heart of this book. It stands as an awful warning of what can happen when authority is unchallenged. Polyphony is not a problem that organizations and their managers have to defeat with managerial imperative, strong culture or centralized decision making; it is what can make them human, rather than inhumane, beings, and better managers and custodians of all those futures they are charged with.

Whosoever says organization must imply power, but there is huge variability and creativity in how the relations implied may be socially constructed. As we have argued in Chapter 5 of this book, if we deconstruct the normal ways in which organization theorists have reflected on power, then eventually we reach a point where we have to address how it is embedded in relations of domination that invariably, almost naturally, seem to be expressed hierarchically. We have been at pains to demonstrate that what might at first glance appear natural may seem somewhat less so on further reflection and deconstruction.

Power cannot *not be*, even if it is expunged, overthrown, dismembered, democratized, flattened, reformed, reframed, enchanted, legitimated, delegitimated, relegitimated, negotiated, renegotiated, made moral, made less ethical, or any other permutations that creativity allows. Relations between people are unthinkable without power because all social relations are relations of various shades of domination, seduction, manipulation, coercion, authority, and so on. Power is; power always will be, and can never not be. Now, we do not say by this that specific relations, forms, practices, processes, structures, identities, and meanings of power will not change. Of course they will. Power may be eternal but its forms are not essential.

Power as a concept and power as a real phenomenon of social relations are affected by contemporary political challenges and strategies. For instance, the French and Dutch people have just rejected the creation of a super-organizational European state as we write, for a complex number of reasons, but among them is clearly a feeling of alienation. Unlike in the fundamentalism encountered earlier in the chapter, the despair is not terminal, nor is it derived from some utopia; on the contrary, it is an alienation from culturally inchoate abstractions as well as the rejection of autonomous entities to which people, in their cultural embeddedness, feel little responsibility.[29] The question today is to know whether organizations are likely to influence regulations and laws and/or to design and institutionalize internal forms of regulations and laws, irrespective of the opinions and acceptance of the states.[30] And will they do so in ways that draw on all the old ideas, in which hierarchical domination, tricked out as managerial authority, prevails, or will they demonstrate a little learning? Most approaches to corporate social responsibility, for instance, do not address the political power dynamics governing the principles of conduct in the relationship between organizations' interests and the interests of communities.

Learning is impossible when the outcomes are already known and assert that only elites, existing structures, and old myths have validity. To learn, we have to let go of old understandings. We need to understand the grip that hierarchy has had on human imagination and try systematically to articulate alternative visions of organization. Through plurality and diversity, the crippling effect on innovation of assuming that hierarchies and their elites necessarily have all the answers may fade away. Of course, there will be no revolution producing a great overthrowing, a break with history. There never is, nor can there ever be. Accommodation will have to be made, organizationally, with hierarchy, if only because of its deep entrenchment as *the* way of doing things.

Looking back, for the last time, let us propose how Weber, Simmel or Durkheim might address contemporary issues such as those we have outlined in this conclusion. They would have suggested the following, we believe. First, the internal dynamics of the corporate elite 'class' are, in large part, independent of the type of political agenda corporations and societies are establishing. The agenda is merely the vehicle through which an interest in elite survival and reproduction is speculated. Whether corporate political action can emerge as something different, as fundamentally changed by the ways power is designed, is the central question.

For Weber and other major thinkers of politics it seems unlikely that fundamental structures of power will be profoundly affected by current changes, whether in the sphere of corporate ethics or in the generalization of a state of insecurity. On the contrary, these would simply be expected to provide new types of arguments, energies, and resources for those inscribed in the inner circles of corporate power. The most powerful power of all for renewing these arguments, energies and resources, of course, is seduction. History is full of ragged trousered philanthropists, bright and principled, who have cast the liabilities and loyalties of birth aside in pursuit of the realities of power and all the pleasures that seduction can bring.[31]

Realists, unlike utopians who expect reward in the hereafter, while they may still bank on the future, always hedge their bets in the here-and-now by pursuing the most reliable means to ensure whatever bliss is desired, accomplished through social relations that deliver power, wealth, and any conceivable pleasure that a healthy body and mind might enjoy, in a society where virtually everything is for sale at a price. And for that which cannot be bought directly, such as security from those others whom one offends by one's existence, then sufficient isolation, distance and space can be bought that serve as a practical surrogate. Welcome to the modern, gated, hypersurveillanced world of power's outer limits.

Classical theorists such as Weber regarded organizations as having a rationalizing mission, best seen as condensed in the responsibilities of the state for the rules of the overall organization game. He would have thought that corporate leaders should be concerned to reduce poverty and discrimination within their own organizations in order to be legitimate enough to demand the same outside their organizational borders, as a part of this rationalization. If corporate leaders failed in such rationalization then we would expect that, while no doubt corporations might be better places if they were to be democratic, democracy is not necessary to enhance profitable interactions with the rest of society. Thus, they can hardly be expected to shift out of necessity, but only out of the courage and insistence of various forms of leadership in these organizations and their societies more generally. In other terms, organizations can't be expected to play an active 'governmental' role in specific countries without leadership, and the poverty and inequalities embedded in existing hierarchies are unlikely to be reduced by those organizations they serve. But, in the neoliberal world, it is hardly likely that governments will address these issues systematically instead.

Increasingly the neoliberal governmental agenda is being delivered by the private sector, acting either alone or through public–private partnerships. Corporate and not-for-profit organizations are now expanding their powers and capacities to occupy the role previously played by the state, which has now become, if not merely a night watchman, an increasingly alert security apparatus with many watchful eyes on those borders threatening its own conceptions of civility. In this scenario, especially as borders are breached by aliens or where, like cuckoos in the nest, aliens have bred within their confines, the old notions of the citizenship state (Marshall and Bottomore 1992) are overtaken by the state as facilitator and underwriter of markets, with varying consumer rights of access, increasingly minimized by exclusion of those considered inadmissible as citizens, mediated by location in the hierarchies of employing organizations. But once again, with power issues in mind, new forms of resistance and activism might arise out of the ashes of local communities and corporate subgroups, around the emergence of new forms of domination – based on non-economic fundamentalisms – with their attendant 'truths'.

One thing that characterized Weber as a classical sociologist and founder of the sociology of organizations was a capacity to see the big picture (which, by and large, is today absent from much contemporary organization and management theory). The big picture was one framed by the broader civilizing process evident in the currents with which reality is socially constructed, the great world religions (Berger and Luckman 1967; Elias 1982). The classical sociologists, such as Weber, Simmel and Durkheim, were all big picture theorists. As such, they would agree that scholars should never forget that, related to any new social agenda, there will be new discourses of truth that might obscure the power dynamics actually shaping the political forms and structures that govern organizations and delimit the forms of possible social relations that members might use to shape the conduct of themselves and of others.

The classical theorists are closer to Foucault than one might imagine. Not for them the notion of truth as a static entity; they see it as something emergent, contingent, a social fact, a configuration, a social action, something over which battles are fought. Unexpected battles will surely shape the futures of power, and the futures of knowledge, battles absolutely necessary to any reflexive understanding of the societies whose truths we have considered and contested in this book. We cannot avoid power relations – and it would be dangerously utopian to assume that we can – but we can exercise freedom in choosing, resisting, rejecting, undermining, accepting, imposing, extending, beguiling, and questioning power. Power is an irreducible element of any imaginable form of life. Thereof, one should speak of power, write about power, and contest power – *often* – and never concede its analytic defeat by abstractions such as efficiency, if only because these abstractions are, as it were, already instruments of power. False dichotomies make for poor science.

Notes

1 The end of history was a thesis advanced by Frances Fukuyama (1992), who saw the demise of the Soviet Union as the ultimate triumph of liberal democracy which, having vanquished fascism, had now done the same for communism. After the fall of the Berlin Wall and the collapse of the Soviet empire, he suggested, the future looked assured and safe for market economies. The thesis was subject to criticism by Huntington (1997) who foresaw a clash of civilizations as the future, rather than a benign global economy. It was a thesis that secured some celebrity after 9/11. The account he proposed was equally flawed but for different reasons: he lumped together, as singular civilizational blocs, societies and beliefs that were far more fissiparous and contested than he allowed. Moreover, Huntington failed to acknowledge the extent to which the 'clashes' in the twentieth century were largely shaped by the rivalry between the respective US and Soviet empires, and their support for whatever corrupt regime, wherever their administration's sense of national interest determined it, that sufficed to guarantee what they defined as their interests. These interests were overwhelmingly strategic, as defined by economic, security and cultural imperatives. The clash of civilizations, in other words, was played out through the mirror of respective imperial interests. Clearly, the demise of the Soviet Union leaves the US as the sole shaper of these global relations – relations within whose context all other inter-organization relations need to be viewed. The start to such an endeavor would be through comparative institutional analysis of local, national elites, their formation and their orientations. Such an endeavor has yet to be systematically undertaken.

2 Eurocommunism (Carrillo 1977) was initiated by the leading Western European communist parties as an electoral project in the 1970s designed to try and attain office through the ballot box, by forming alliances with a broader constituency, including the new middle class – seen through the lens of proletarianization and deskilling – and green and feminist issues and concerns. It failed both to differentiate itself sufficiently from what the social democrat parties were doing and to signal clearly how it differed from what the Soviet empire had to offer.

3 We note that 'postmodern' refers both to the idea that there might be empirical tendencies in the world that are 'post' in the sense of being after modernity and not necessarily a constitutive part of it; and to the idea that there might be such things as postmodernism or postmodern theories.

4 By the end of the twentieth century the Internet had enabled the vertically integrated multinational corporation, under unified ownership, to be replaced by networks of externalized relationships between associated but often autonomous firms. This wider separation of networks which link locations in East Asia with the US and Europe is typified by the operations of electronics companies such as Texas Instruments which distributes research and development between Austin, Texas and Taipei. Smooth operation relies upon a synchronized corporate database physically replicated on identical hardware at each end using a high-capacity data link. The notion of 'networked enterprise' promoted by Castells (1996b) as a means of geographically and temporally constrained collaboration in order to enter and shape specific markets has, however, already been superseded by more durable modes of operation. Companies such as ARM Holdings (http://www.arm.com/) produce high-value intellectual property utilized by global corporations that rely, in turn, upon third-party manufacturing facilities such as those provided by Flextronics (http://www.flextronics.com/). The actors located at each node of the network have a range of geographical locations available to them across which to distribute intellectual property and physical processes – the furthest development of ICT dependent reconfiguration. Computerization within commercial and administrative organizations initially represented an extension of earlier office technologies designed to address internal efficiency. As the potential of computers to manage supply chains and customer relationships became apparent, organizational effectiveness became a primary objective. Finally, as the innovations in business models and inter-firm relationships permitted by the synergies of networking became apparent, inter-organizational management of the production and value chain became the focus of both local and global systems.

5 See http://www.mmm.merseyside.org/cd.htm and http://www.mmm.merseyside.org/project.htm.

6 The second dispute is archived at http://mua.org.au/war/ and is discussed in Clegg (1999).

7 See http://mua.org.au/war/cloak.html and http://www.ilwu19.com/global/wharfie/update65.htm.

8 Despite the relative inadequacy of current wireless application protocol (WAP) mobile telephony, the combination of low earth orbit (LEO) satellites with global positioning systems (GPS) allows location-sensitive services to be delivered to individuals and groups on the move.

9 In the movie Gattaca (Nicoll 1997), the main character, Vincent, notes, ironically in the context of the corporate organization Gattaca, that 'We now have discrimination down to a science.' It is a science that attempts to ensure that one is what one is coded as being, irrespective of what or who one might want to be recognized as being or becoming. The movie demonstrates that resistance is possible, in so far as, as its tagline has it, 'There is no Gene for the Human Spirit.' In the film, human endeavor is exemplified by a self-disciplined subject who overcomes the fact of being someone with invalid genes, and aspires to and achieves what he desires in a journey that is plotted quite consciously as one of redemption through resistance.

10 We make no distinction between fundamentalisms in this regard. In the US abortionists have been shot, and a government building, and the people in it, have been blown up by a truck bomb. Such actions, sociologically, have to be thought through the same terms as those other fundamentalisms that receive more attention in the present conjuncture.

11 It was not just an academic error. The bitter harvest of 9/11 was in large part, if not sown, then at least nourished and fertilized by political decisions made by successive US administrations. A notable case is the Carter–Brzezinski administration, in office at the time that the US first provided aid and advice to the anti-Soviet opposition in Afghanistan in mid 1979, before the Soviet invasion. The immediate end of miring the Soviet Union in its own Vietnam was certainly achieved; however, one cannot think that the outcome of training, supporting and empowering jihadists who would later turn on their erstwhile sponsors was a desired outcome. (On these matters it is instructive to read Tariq Ali's (2002) The clash of fundamentalisms.) There is an analytic point to this small piece of tragic history. One reason why the episodic approach to power is flawed is because to focus on the episode often means not attending to the unanticipated consequences of the social actions that were initiated in the episode in question.

12   While the World Trade Center attack of 9/11 seared itself into the global consciousness, a
      previous terrorist attack by US citizens, on US citizens, should have been sufficient to raise the
      possibility that some identities, *in that country rather than from outside it*, were being shaped
      in fundamentally different ways to the norms of overall social formation. It was a different
      kind of fundamentalism, rooted in anti-statism and the defense of a notion of liberty, nour-
      ished by fervent religiosity, that lay behind an earlier terrorist attack on US soil – the April 19,
      1995 Oklahoma City bombing. This was itself allegedly related to the events that occurred in
      Waco, Texas, on April 19, 1993, when, after 51 days of a blockade of the Branch Davidians
      compound by federal government agents from the United States Bureau of Alcohol, Tobacco
      and Firearms (BATF), supported by the US Army, 74 people died, including many children.
      The interpretation of the events that led up to and occurred on each of these April 19s
      remains highly contested. The analytical point is one of sociological agnosticism: it is not just
      one kind of fundamentalism that can lead to disastrous consequences.
13   It should be clear that the claims made by Islamist fundamentalists are just one of many polit-
      ical positions that find expression within Muslim belief systems. These politics are as complex
      and deep as politics anywhere usually are; again, Tariq Ali (2002) is an excellent guide.
14   McGown (1999) is writing specifically about Somalis in London, whom she contrasts with the
      community in Toronto, where a more formal multiculturalism leads to different outcomes: 'it
      is in large part the political culture of the adoptive society that will determine the quality of
      the connection between Western Muslims and their non-Muslim compatriots' (1999: 231).
      Adding credence to this important point is research by Ghorashi (2004) which looked at the
      identities of Iranians in Orange County, California, after 9/11. Ghorashi finds a situation that
      seems closer to that of Somalis in Ottawa than in London: instead of a binary bilateral posi-
      tioning she finds instead a far more multilayered, multiconnected sense of identity being
      constructed in which the terms are hybrid rather than binary. Her data are drawn from
      people mobilizing through a Network of Iranian–American Professionals in Orange County
      (NIPOC), establishing an identity that is neither binary nor between cultures but which draws
      on plural and fragmented experiences, coded in terms of more than just signifiers of religion
      or ethnicity, although drawing on common experience. A new imaginary which rethinks ways
      of being American is invoked and, after the crisis of 9/11, reinstated as a form of identity posi-
      tioning in which the major difference is established not between the adoptive home and that
      left behind, but between the adoptive identity and those other identities that are being
      inscribed – and risk being ascribed – which are premised on the dominant host society's read-
      ing of Islamic otherness. NIPOC as a form of ethnic network organization becomes a valuable
      resource in countering such ascription and maintaining a claim to difference from the identi-
      ties being ascribed. Given the cultural hybridity of all major cities in modern nations, the real
      claims to pre-modern identity are those, from either side of the imagined binary, which assume
      identity simply 'is' or is 'not'. It is the denial of hybridity that is pre-modern.
15   In the latter case one is dealing with the phenomenon of suicide bombing, which has spread
      from its development by the Tamil Tigers in Sri Lanka to be widely used in violent, politically
      motivated attacks, carried out in a deliberate state of awareness by someone willing to blow
      themselves up in pursuit of what they define as a greater good. In Weberian terms, suicide
      bombers and those organizations that support them are practicing a blend of value and
      instrumental rationality. There is an underlying value ethic which, in the case of Islamic fun-
      damentalisms, has a religious basis, but there is also an instrumental purpose. Suicide bomb-
      ing is a low-cost strategy for achieving high-impact results, due to its 'spectacular' dimension,
      which ensures that the images and accounts are obsessively retailed in the media to such an
      extent that they sear themselves into the consciousness and attitudes of those people who are
      affected in their everyday life, reflected in polls, reflected in pressure on national politicians.
      In this sense the strategy is a rational and strategic choice, at least in territorial politics such
      as those of Palestine: when applied in the context of territorial struggles it can position those
      organizations that sponsor it as potential players in more conventional politics, once their
      dominance has been asserted through the strategy. However, in locations such as Western

cities, where the issue is not territory but the perceived wrongs being done to a faith-based community, then the politics are more gestural and theatrical, more a spectacle, in an echo of what Kropotkin (1898) once advocated as the propaganda of the deed.

16   Irrespective of one's views of the legitimacy, or otherwise, of the US-led Coalition in its occupation of Iraq, it is in that poor benighted country that the political insecurity of the body corporeal and politic seems presently to be most severe. For a balanced view of the human rights excesses on all sides the reader may wish to consult the Amnesty International report on Iraq. It can be accessed at http://www.amnestyusa.org/countries/iraq/document.do?id=ar& yr= 2005.

17   Only some failing states took their place in the front line. Notably absent was Pakistan.

18   Where voting is not voluntary, as in Australia, it at least holds out the possibility of the 'pillarization' of ethnic groups, and thus some form of incorporation or debate about incorporation into the polity and society through a formal project of multiculturalism. It should be stressed, however, that this is no necessary inoculation against fundamentalism.

19   In this respect they had much in common with coreligionist youth in many of the major centers of Muslim population, where neither states nor markets work very effectively, other than to support the venality of the ruling elites and where the most effective institution is often the military, used occasionally to put down popular protests against this venality. Again, one would recommend Ali (2002).

20   Thus, the conceptions subscribed to did not refer to the cleavages between the respectable and the unrespectable poor – with which this book began its journey in the promise of utilitarianism. It is not that these cleavages do not exist anymore, for, while they were extremely relevant in a polyglot society where the centrality of productive relations is secure, they are of far less moment where conventional work no longer occupies the central space for many people on its margins, and where interpretive norms are less easy to legislate and more open to local community interpretations. These are not necessarily religious in character, as can be seen most evidently in the entrepreneurialism of street-level drug culture, where the disrespectable urban poor can aspire to a path out of their present circumstances, using deviant means to pursue legitimate goals of wealth, status and power.

21   Especially the strains of Indian subcontinental Deobandist or Gulf Wahhabist Islam. The strength of these strains has been greatly aided by direct US support of the Pakistan military, the Saudi regime, and Israel. The latter two provide the lever which Al-Quaeda manipulates ideologically to recruit the resentful, while Pakistan provides the US with limited and compromised counter-leverage on the ground. The compromise is due to the penetration of Pakistan's military elites by the very same Islamist ideology that the regime of President Musharraf seeks to oppose. The instruments with which the opposition might be mounted are already riddled with that which the regime ostensibly opposes (Ali 2002).

22   The positive aspects of multiculturalism would hardly do as a basis for identity formation where these were strongly contested by significant strata in the host society, such as the various white supremacist parties and defenders of the faith of the old ways of being, before the empire struck back. The affirmative version of multiculturalism, a positive and inclusive project, and its critique, were routinely hijacked by politicians for their own ends.

23   Hence there is both too much social integration of such youth in community and urban space and insufficient integration with the broader embedment of 'British', 'American', 'French' or whatever society (see Durkheim (2002) for the basic concepts of social integration).

24   From the *International Herald Tribune* (http://www.iht.com/articles/2005/07/25/news/iraq. php) of Monday July 25, 2005: 'A suicide truck bomb rammed into barricades at a police station here in the middle of a raging sandstorm on Sunday, killing at least 25 people and wounding at least 33 others, Iraqi officials said. The American military said at least 40 people died.' No names, no human interest, in effect, no human beings – just statistics.

25   Understanding why something might happen is not equivalent to condoning it, nor is it evident that this understanding necessarily translates into appropriate action. When the causes of a phenomenon – contemporary Islamist terrorism – are so deeply rooted in the dysfunctions of

specific societies in the Muslim world, in the history of their relations with the Christian world and of both with the Jewish world, as well as in the condensation of all these relations in the internal politics of Islamic belief systems, it should be evident that a problem so complex will hardly admit of a simple answer, or be amenable to just one type of pressure applied liberally through force of arms intended, unsuccessfully, to shock and awe. On no side does the rhetoric suggest that a great deal of rational understanding of the other is in evidence. In fact, it appears to be a situation where the rhetorical points of reference are so immanent to their own systems of meaning, and consequently so far apart, that any rational dialog is precluded. Those of us concerned about the security of the body – both corporeal and political – have every reason to be anxious. The state of insecurity stretches out ahead of us as far as the mind can envision. Its organizational implications are not incidental, given existing tendencies to hypersurveillance.

26   The Spanish general election of 2005 might be seen as a case in point.

27   All of these are post-Enlightenment spaces because they are premised on a fundamental – and expanded – sense of respect for the other, rather than emerging from a fundamentalism with which the humanity of the other is barely visible. Concern for the environment, ethics, and the planet generally is a concern with all those others who are yet to come and inhabit the space we presently besmirch. Although the concern may be for nature, it is for nature conceived as the crucible within which we are able to express our humanity. At its furthest, it expands to a respect for all others that might conceivably be the same as our selves – where the nature of self is defined not so much in terms of a speaking subject but in terms of one that possesses a central nervous system. From this position the other includes all animals as well as humans as a particular type of animal.

28   This idea is close to the notion of 'formal ideological group' developed by Nahirny (1962) for groups committed to the maintenance of both organizational structure and ideology.

29   The 'No' vote is, in many ways, as Žižek (2005b) suggests, an expression of hope. It holds out the possibility of a third way between American civilization, based today on the strong market and the state of terror, and the authoritarian state capitalism of China, as modes of organizing the global economy.

30   The history of power and organizations is full of stories showing how organizational leaders may have worked to diminish the influence of the state on the business realm (Perrow 2002). Allowing corporate development while avoiding the intervention of the state was a move made in the name of 'prosperity and growth; and in general for the freedom to externalize costs' (2002: 45). But nowadays, some would argue, a completely different view of political and social relations is to be found in the emergence of a social perspective on corporate activity, one that goes beyond the mere idea that 'ethics pay' and that corporate leaders lobby on social responsibility issues to ease their conscience, while keeping on acting in a self-serving kind of ideology. Maybe, as Margolis and Walsh (2003) argue, the development of social initiatives and strategies from business corporations challenges economic theory. Or maybe the only purpose of such strategies is to enhance a sort of enlightened self-interest?

31   The reference is to the famous early-twentieth-century dramatic work by Robert Tressell (1969[1914]), *The ragged trousered philanthropists.*

References

Abel, E. L. (1980). *Marihuana: the first twelve thousand years*. New York: Plenum.

Abercrombie, N., Hill, S., & Turner, B. S. (1980). *The dominant ideology thesis*. London: Allen & Unwin.

Abrahamson, E. (1997). The emergence and prevalence of employee management rhetorics: the effects of long waves, labour unions, and turnover, 1875 to 1992. *The Academy of Management Journal, 40*(3), 491–533.

Abrahamsson, B. (1980). *The rights of labor*. London: Sage.

Acker, J., & Van Houten, D. (1974). Differential recruitment and control: the sex structuring of organizations. *Administrative Science Quarterly, 19*, 152–163.

Ackles, D. (1969). *Subway to the country*. New York: Electra EKS-74060.

Ackoff, R. L. (1994). *The democratic corporation*. New York: Oxford University Press.

Adams, G. B., & Balfour, D. (2001). The mask of administrative evil: remembering the past, forgetting the present. In J. K. Roth & E. Maxwell (Eds.), *Remembering for the future: the Holocaust in an age of genocides*. London: Palgrave-Macmillan.

Adler, P. S. (1993). Time-and-motion regained. *Harvard Business Review, 71*(1), January–February, 97–108.

Adler, P. S. (2001). Market, hierarchy, and trust: the knowledge economy and the future of capitalism. *Organization Science, 12*(2), 215–234.

Adorno, T., Frenkel-Brunswik, E., & Levinson, D. J. (1968). *The authoritarian personality*. New York: Norton.

Agger, B. (1991). Critical theory, poststructuralism, postmodernism. *Annual Review of Sociology, 17*, 105–131.

Ainsworth, S., & Hardy, C. (2004). Discourse and identities. In D. Grant, C. Hardy, C. Oswick & L. Putnam (Eds.), *Handbook of organizational discourse* (pp. 151–173). London: Sage.

Aitken, H. G. J. (1960). *Scientific management in action: Taylorism at Watertown Arsenal, 1908–1915*. Cambridge, MA: Harvard University Press.

Albert, S., & Whetten, D. (1985). Organizational identity. In L. Cummings & B. Staw (Eds.), *Research in organizational behavior* (Vol. 7, pp. 263–295). Greenwich, CT: JAI Press.

Albrow, M. (1970). *Bureaucracy*. London: Macmillan.

Albrow, M. (1997). *Do organizations have feelings?* London: Routledge.

Aldrich, H. (1999). *Organizations evolving*. London: Sage.

Ali, T. (2002). *The clash of fundamentalisms: crusades, jihads and modernity*. London: Verso.

Ali, T. (2005a). Violence begets violence and so the horrors continue. *Sydney Morning Herald*, July 11.

Ali, T. (2005b). *Street-fighting years: an autobiography of the sixties*. London: Verso.

Allen, J. (2003). *Lost geographies of power*. Oxford: Blackwell.

Almeida, P. D. (2003). Opportunity organizations and threat-induced contention: protest waves in authoritarian settings. *American Journal of Sociology, 109*, 345–400.

Althusser, L. (1971). *For Marx*. London: New Left Books.

Alvesson, M. (1995). *Management of knowledge intensive companies*. Berlin: De Gruyter.

Alvesson, M., & Billing, Y. (1992). Gender and organization: towards a differential understanding. *Organization Studies, 13*, 73–103.

Alvesson, M., & Kärreman, D. (2000). Taking the linguistic turn in organizational research: challenges, responses, consequences. *Journal of Applied Behavioral Science, 36*(2), 136–158.

Alvesson, M., & Willmott, H. (1992a). Critical theory and management studies: an introduction. In M. Alvesson & H. Willmott (Eds.), *Critical Management Studies*. London: Sage.

Alvesson, M., & Willmott, H. (1992b). On the idea of emancipation in management and organization studies. *Academy of Management Review, 17*(3), 432–464.

Alvesson, M., & Willmott, H. (2002). Identity regulation as organizational control: producing the appropriate individual. *Journal of Management Studies, 39*(5), 619–644.

Amar, J. (1920). *The physiology of industrial organisation and the re-employment of the disabled* (Trans. B. Miall). London: Routledge.

Anderson, P. (1974). *Transitions from feudalism to capitalism*. London: New Left Books.

Antaki, C., and Widdicombe, S. (1998). *Identities in talk*. London: Sage.

Appelrouth, S. (2005). Body and soul: jazz in the 1920s. *American Behavioral Scientist, 48*(11), 1496–1509.

Appiah, K. (1991). Is the post in postmodernism the post in postcolonial? *Critical Inquiry, 17*, 336–357.

Arendt, H. (1969). A special supplement: reflections on violence. *New York Review of Books, 12*(4).

Arendt, H. (1970). *On violence*. New York: Harcourt Brace.

Arendt, H. (1993). *Between past and future: eight exercises in political thought*. Harmondsworth: Penguin.

Arendt, H. (1994). *Eichmann in Jerusalem: a report on the banality of evil* (rev. and enl. ed.). New York: Penguin.

Armbrüster, T., & Gebert, D. (2002). Uncharted territories of organizational research: the case of Karl Popper's open society and its enemies. *Organization Studies, 23*, 169–188.

Aron, R. (1972). *Etudes politiques*. Paris: Gallimard.

Ashcraft, K. L. (2001). Organized dissonance: feminist bureaucracy as hybrid form. *Academy of Management Journal, 44*(6), 1301–1322.

Ashcraft, K. L. (2004). Gender, discourse and organization: framing a shifting relationship. In D. Grant, C. Hardy, C. Oswick & L. Putnam (Eds.), *Handbook of organizational discourse* (pp. 275–298). London: Sage.

Ashcraft, K. L., & Flores, L. (2003). 'Slaves with white collars': persistent performances of masculinity in crisis. *Text and Performance Quarterly, 23*, 1–29.

Austen, J. (1813/1982). *Pride and prejudice*. London: Macmillan.

Baak, D., & Prasch, T. (1997). The death of the subject and the life of the organization: implications of new approaches to subjectivity for organizational analysis. *Journal of Management Inquiry, 6*(2), 131–141.

Bachmann, R. (2001). Trust, power and control in trans-organizational relations. *Organization Studies, 22*(2), 337–365.

Bachrach, P., & Baratz, M. S. (1962). Two faces of power. *American Political Science Review, 56*, 947–952.

Bachrach, P., & Baratz, M. S. (1963). Decisions and non-decisions: an analytical framework. *American Political Science Review, 57*, 641–651.

Bachrach, P., & Baratz, M. S. (1970). *Power and poverty: theory and practice*. New York: Oxford University Press.

Bahnisch, M. (2000). Embodied work, divided labour: subjectivity and the scientific management of the body in Frederick W. Taylor's 1907 'Lecture on management'. *Body and Society, 6*(1), 51–68.

Bailey, F. G. (1977). *Morality and expediency: the folklore of academic politics*. Oxford: Blackwell.

Bakhtin, M. M. (1984). *Rabelais and his world*. Bloomington, IN: Indiana University Press.

Ball, T. (1975). Models of power: past and present. *Journal of the History of the Behavioral Sciences*, July, 211–222.

Banerjee, S. (2000). Whose land is it anyway? National interest, indigenous stakeholders, and colonial discourses: the case of the Jabiluka Uranium Mine. *Organization & Environment, 13*(1), 3–39.

Banerjee, S. (2003). The practice of stakeholder colonialism: national interest and colonial discourses in the management of indigenous stakeholders. In A. Prasad (Ed.), *Postcolonial theory and organizational analysis: a critical engagement* (pp. 255–279). New York: Palgrave Macmillan.

Banerjee, S., & Linstead, S. (2001). Globalization, multiculturalism and other fictions: colonialism for the new millennium? *Organization*, 9(4), 683–722.

Banta, M. (1993). *Taylored lives: narrative productions in the age of Taylor, Veblen, and Ford.* Chicago: University of Chicago Press.

Barbalet, J. M. (1987). Power, structural resources and agency. *Perspectives in Social Theory*, 8, 1–24.

Baritz, L. (1974). *The servants of power: a history of the use of social science in American industry.* Westport, CT: Greenwood.

Barker, F., Hulme, P., & Iversen, M. (Eds.). (1994). *Colonial discourse/postcolonial theory.* Manchester: Manchester University Press.

Barker, J. R. (1993). Tightening the iron cage: concertive control in self-managing teams. *Administrative Science Quarterly*, 38, 408–437.

Barnard, C. I. (1938). *Functions of the executive.* Cambridge, MA: Harvard University Press.

Barnes, B. (1988). *The nature of power.* Cambridge: Polity.

Baron, J. N., Dobbin, F., & Jennings, P. D. (1986). War and peace: the evolution of modern personnel administration in the US industry. *American Journal of Sociology*, 92 (September), 350–383.

Barthes, R. (1984). *Mythologies* (Trans. Annette Lavers). New York: Hill and Wang.

Bartos, O. J., & Wehr, P. E. (2002). *Using conflict theory.* Cambridge: Cambridge University Press.

Bass, B., & Avolio, B. (1994). Shatter the glass ceiling: women may make better managers. *Human Resource Management*, 33, 549–560.

Bathelt, H. (2002). The re-emergence of a media industry cluster in Leipzig. *European Planning Studies*, 10(5), 583–611.

Bathelt, H., & Taylor, M. (2002). Clusters, power and place: inequality and local growth in time space. *Geografiska Annaler: Series B, Human Geography*, 84(2), 93–109.

Bauman, J. (1986). *Winter in the afternoon: the recollections of the life of a young girl in the Warsaw ghetto.* London: Virago.

Bauman, J. (1988). *A dream of belonging.* London: Virago.

Bauman, J. (2002). Memory and imagination: truth in autobiography. *Thesis Eleven*, 70(1), 26–35.

Bauman, Z. (1976). *Towards a critical sociology: an essay on common-sense and emancipation.* London: Routledge & Kegan Paul.

Bauman, Z. (1989). *Modernity and the Holocaust.* Cambridge: Polity.

Bauman, Z. (1997). *Postmodernity and its discontents.* Cambridge: Polity.

Bauman, Z., & Tester, K. (2001). *Conversations with Zygmunt Bauman.* Cambridge: Polity.

Baumeister, R. (2002). Yielding to temptation: self-control failure, impulsive purchasing and consumer behavior. *Journal of Consumer Research*, 28(3), 670–676.

Bavelas, A., & Lewin, K. (1942). Training in democratic leadership. *Journal of Abnormal and Social Psychology*, 52(1), 163–176.

Baverez, N. (1998). Étrange capitalisme à la française. *Sociétal*, 17, 30–31.

Beck, U. (1999). *World risk society.* Malden, MA: Polity.

Beck, U. (2002). *Risk society: towards a new modernity* (Trans. Mark Ritter). London: Sage.

Behrendt, L. (2003). *Achieving social justice: indigenous rights and Australia's future.* Annandale, NSW: Federation.

Belk, R. W., Ger, G., & Askegaard, S. (2003). The fire of desire: a multisited inquiry into consumer passion. *Journal of Consumer Research*, 30(12), 326–351.

Bell, G., & Kaye, J. (2002). Designing technology for domestic spaces: a kitchen manifesto. *Gastronomica*, Spring, 46–62.

Bendix, R. (1977). *Max Weber: an intellectual portrait.* Berkeley, CA: University of California Press.

Benello, G. (1969). Wasteland culture. In H. P. Dreitzel (Ed.), *Recent Sociology*, no. 1, pp. 263–291. London: MacMillan.

Benfari, R. C., Wilkinson, H. E., & Orth, C. D. (1986). The effective use of power. *Business Horizons*, *29*(3), 12–16.

Benjamin, W. (1982). *Illuminations*. London: Fontana/Collins.

Benn, S., & Dunphy, D. (2004). Can democracy handle corporate sustainability: constructing a path forward. *Corporate Sustainability*, special issue on 'Governance, innovation strategy, development and methods', *6*(2), 141–155.

Bennis, W. (1978). *On becoming a leader*. Boston: Addison-Wesley.

Bennis, W. G., Berkowitz, N., Affinito, M., & Malone, M. (1958). Authority, power, and the ability to influence. *Human Relations*, *11*(2), 143–155.

Bentham, J. (Ed.). (1843). *The works of Jeremy Bentham* (Vol. 8). Edinburgh: Tait.

Benton, T. (1981). 'Objective' interests and the sociology of power. *Sociology*, *15*(2), 61–184.

Berdayes, V. (2002). Traditional management theory as panoptic discourse: language and the constitution of somatic flows. *Culture and Organization*, *8*(1), 35–49.

Berger, P. (1990). *The sacred canopy: elements of a sociological theory of religion*. New York: Anchor.

Berger, P. L., & Luckmann, T. (1967). *The social construction of reality: a treatise in the sociology of knowledge*. Harmondsworth: Penguin.

Berlin, I. (2003). *The proper study of mankind: an anthology of essays*. London: Chatto and Windus.

Besson, D. (2000). France in the 1950s: Taylorian modernity brought about by postmodern organizers? *Journal of Organizational Change Management*, *13*(5), 423–438.

Bhabha, H. (1994). *The location of culture*. London: Routledge.

Blackburn, R., Jarman, J., & Brooks, B. (2000). The puzzle of gender segregation and inequality: a cross-national analysis. *European Sociological Review*, *16*, 119–135.

Blackler, F. (1995). Knowledge, knowledge work and organizations: an overview and interpretation. *Organization Studies*, *16*(6), 1021–1046.

Blais, A. (1974). Power and causality. *Quality and Quantity*, *8*, 45–64.

Blau, P. M. (1957). Formal organization: dimensions of analysis. *American Journal of Sociology*, *63*, 58–69.

Blau, P. M. (1964). *Exchange and power in social life*. New York: Wiley.

Blau, P. M., & Meyer, M. W. (1971). *Bureaucracy in modern society* (2nd ed.). New York: Random.

Blau, P. M., & Scott, W. (1963). *Formal organizations: a comparative approach*. London: Routledge & Kegan Paul.

Blum, A. F., & McHugh, P. (1971). The social ascription of motives. *American Sociological Review*, *36*, 98–109.

Bobbitt, P. (2002). *The shield of Achilles: war, peace, and the course of history* (1st ed.). New York: Knopf.

Boden, D. (1994). *The business of talk: organizations in action*. Cambridge: Polity.

Boden, D., & Zimmerman, D. (Eds.). (1991). *Talk and social structure: studies in ethnomethodology and conversation analysis*. Berkeley, CA: University of California Press.

Bogard, W. (1996). *The simulation of surveillance: hypercontrol in telematic societies*. Cambridge: Cambridge University Press.

Boje, D. M., & Rosile, G. A. (2001). Where's the power in empowerment? Answers from Follett and Clegg. *Journal of Applied Behavioral Science*, *37*(1), 90–117.

Borkin, J. (1978). *The crime and punishment of I. G. Farben*. New York: Free.

Bourdieu, P. (1977). *Outline of a theory of practice*. Cambridge: Cambridge University Press.

Bourdieu, P. (1984). *Distinction: a social critique of the judgement of taste*. London: Routledge & Kegan Paul.

Bourdieu, P. (1986). The forms of capital. In J. G. Richardson (Ed.), *Handbook of theory and research for the sociology of education* (pp. 241–258). New York: Greenwood.

Bourdieu, P. (1996). *The state nobility: elite schools in the field of power*. Cambridge: Polity.

Bourdieu, P. (2002). *Counterfire: against the tyranny of the market* (Trans. C. Turner). London: Verso.

Bourke, H. (1982). Industrial unrest as social pathology: the Australian writings of Elton Mayo. *Historical Studies*, 217–233.

Bower, T. (1997). *Nazi gold: the full story of the fifty-year Swiss–Nazi conspiracy to steal billions from Europe's Jews and Holocaust survivors.* New York: Harper Collins.

Bowlby, J. (1951). *Maternal care and mental health.* Geneva: World Health Organization.

Bradbury, H., & Lichtenstein, B. (2000). Relationality in organizational research: exploring the space between. *Organization Science, 11,* 551–564.

Brandeis, L. D. (1914) *Other people's money,* available at http://library.louisville.edu/law/brandeis/opm-toc.html

Braverman, H. (1974). *Labor and monopoly capital: the degradation of work in the twentieth century.* New York: Monthly Review Press.

Brezis, E. S., & Crouzet, F. (2002). Changes in the recruitment and education of upper elites in twentieth century western countries. In *Economic History Congress XIII,* Buenos Aires.

Brontë, C. (1847/2000). *Jane Eyre* (Introduction and notes by Sally Shuttleworth, based on the original Smith, Elder & Co. Cornhill 1847 ed.). Oxford: Oxford University Press.

Brown, J. A. C. (1954). *The social psychology of industry: human relations in the factory.* Harmondsworth: Penguin.

Brown, J. S., & Duguid, P. (1991). Organisational learning and communities of practice: toward a unified view of working learning and innovation. *Organisation Science, 2,* 40–57.

Brown, J. S., & Duguid, P. (2000). *The social life of information.* Boston: Harvard Business School Press.

Brunsson, N., Jacobsson, B., & associates (2000). *A world of standards.* New York: Oxford University Press.

Bryman, A. (1992). *Charisma and leadership in organizations.* London: Sage.

Burawoy, M. (1979). *Manufacturing consent: changes in the labor process under monopoly capitalism.* Chicago: University of Chicago Press.

Burawoy, M. (1985). *The politics of production.* London: Verso.

Burchell, G., Gordon, C., & Miller, P. M. (1991). *The Foucault effect: studies in governmentality, with two lectures by and an interview with Michel Foucault.* London: Harvester Wheatsheaf.

Burman, E., & Parker, I. (1993). Against discursive imperialism, empiricism and constructionism: thirty-two problems with discourse analysis. In E. Burman & I. Parker (Eds.), *Discourse analytic research: repertoires and readings of texts in action* (pp. 155–172). London: Routledge.

Burnham, P. (1941). *The managerial revolution.* New York: Day.

Burrell, G. (1988). Modernism, post modernism and organizational analysis 2: the contribution of Michel Foucault. *Organization Studies, 9,* 221–235.

Burrell, G. (1994). Modernism, postmodernism and organizational analysis 4: the contribution of Jurgen Habermas. *Organization Studies, 15*(1), 1–19.

Burrell, G. (1997). *Pandemonium: towards a retro-organization theory.* London: Sage.

Burrell, G., & Morgan, G. (1979). *Sociological paradigms and organisational analysis: elements of the sociology of corporate life.* London: Heinemann Educational.

Burt, R. S. (1992). *Structural holes: the social structure of competition.* Cambridge, MA: Harvard University Press.

Buti, T. (1995). They took the children away. *Alternative Law Journal, 20*(1).

Butler, J. (1990). *Gender trouble: feminism and the subversion of identity.* New York: Routledge.

Calás, M., & Smircich, L. (1996). From a women's point of view: feminist approaches to organization studies. In S. Clegg, C. Hardy & W. Nord (Eds.), *Handbook of organization studies* (pp. 218–257). Thousand Oaks, CA: Sage.

Calás, M., & Smircich, L. (1999). Past postmodernism? Reflections and tentative directions. *Academy of Management Review, 24*(4), 649–671.

Callon, M. (1986). Some elements of a sociology of translation: domestication of the scallops and the fishermen of St Brieuc Bay. In J. Law (Ed.), *Power, action and belief* (pp. 132–161). London: Routledge.

Callon, M. (1991). Techno-economic networks and irreversibility. In J. Law (Ed.), *A sociology of monsters: essays on power, technology and domination* (pp. 132–161). London and New York: Routledge.

Callon, M. (1998). *The laws of the markets.* Oxford: Blackwell/The Sociological Review.

Callon, M. (1999). Actor network theory. In J. Law & J. Hassard (Eds.), *Actor network theory and after.* Oxford: Blackwell.

Cameron, D. (Ed.). (1990). *The feminist critique of language.* London: Routledge.

Cameron, D. (1992). *Feminism and linguistic theory* (2nd ed.). London: Macmillan.

Canguilhem, G. (1992). Machine and organism. In J. Crary & S. Kwinter (Eds.), *Incorporations* (pp. 45–69). New York: Zone.

Cappelli, P. (1999). Career jobs are dead. *California Management Review, 42*(1), 146–167.

Cappelli, P., & Hamori, M. (2004). *The path to the top: changes in the attributes and careers of corporate executives, 1980–2001.* NBER Working Paper no. W10507.

Cappelli, P., & Hamori, M. (2005). The new road to the top. *Harvard Business Review,* January, 25–32.

Carey, A. (1967). The Hawthorne studies: a radical criticism. *American Sociological Review, 32,* 403–416.

Carey, A. (2002). The Hawthorne studies: a radical criticism. In S. R. Clegg (Ed.), *Central currents in organization studies I: frameworks and applications* (Vol. 1, pp. 314–322). London: Sage. Originally published in *American Sociological Review,* 1967, *32,* 403–416.

Carlsen, A. (2005). *Acts of becoming: on the dialogic imagination of practice in organizations.* Unpublished PhD thesis, Norwegian University of Science and Technology, Norway.

Caro, R. (1974). *The power broker: Robert Moses and the fall of New York.* New York: Alfred A. Knopf.

Carr, A. (2000). Critical theory and the management of change in organizations. *Journal of Organizational Change Management, 13*(3), 208–220.

Carrillo, S. (1977). *Eurocommunism and the state.* London: Lawrence and Wishart.

Carter, C., Clegg, S. R., Hogan, J., & Kornberger, M. (2003). The polyphonic spree: the case of the Liverpool dockers. *Industrial Relations Journal, 34*(4), 290–304.

Cartwright, D., & Zander, A. (1953). *Group dynamics: research and theory.* London: Tavistock.

Cassis, Y. (1997). *Big business: the European experience in the twentieth century.* Oxford: Oxford University Press.

Castells, M. (1996a). *The rise of the network society.* Oxford: Blackwell.

Castells, M. (1996b). *The information age: economy, society and culture.* Oxford: Blackwell.

Castells, M. (1997). *The information age: economy, society, and culture. Vol. 2: The power of identity.* Oxford: Blackwell.

Castoriadis, C. (1988). *Los dominios del hombre: las encrucijadas del laberinto.* Barcelona: Gedisa.

Caton, H. P. (1976). Politics and political science. *Politics, XI*(2), 149–155.

CBS (Writer). (1999). The Magdalene laundry. Sixty Minutes. http://www.cbsnews.com/stories/2003/08/08/sunday/main567365.shtml, retrieved February 20, 2005.

Cerny, P. G. (1994). The dynamics of financial globalization: technology, market structure, and policy responses. *Policy Sciences, 27*(4), 319–342.

Chandler, A. D. (1962). *Strategy and structure: chapters in the history of American enterprise.* Cambridge, MA: MIT Press.

Cheney, G., Christensen, L. T., Conrad, C., & Lair, D. J. (2004). Corporate rhetoric in organizational discourse. In D. Grant, C. Oswick, C. Hardy & L. Putnam (Eds.), *Handbook of organizational discourse* (pp. 79–103). London: Sage.

Chia, R. K. G. (1996). *Organizational analysis as deconstructive practice.* Berlin: de Gruyter.

Chia, R. (2000). Discourse analysis as organizational analysis. *Organization, 7*(3), 513–518.

Child, J. (1969). *British management thought.* London: Allen & Unwin.

Child, J. (1972). Organizational structures, environment and performance: the role of strategic choice. *Sociology, 6,* 2–22.

Chouliaraki, L., & Fairclough, N. (1999). *Discourse in late modernity.* Edinburgh: Edinburgh University Press.

Clarke, J., & Newman, J. (1997). *The managerial state: power, politics and ideology in the remaking of the welfare state.* London: Sage.

Clarke, T., & Clegg, S. R. (1998). *Changing paradigms: the transformation of management for the 21st Century.* London: Harper Collins.

Clegg, S. R. (1975). *Power, rule and domination: a critical and empirical understanding of power in sociological theory and organizational life.* London: Routledge.

Clegg, S. R. (1979). *The theory of power and organization.* London: Routledge & Kegan Paul.

Clegg, S. R. (1989). *Frameworks of power.* London: Sage.

Clegg, S. R. (1990). *Modern organizations: organization studies in the postmodern world.* London: Sage.

Clegg, S. R. (1992). Review article. How to become an internationally famous British social theorist. *The Sociological Review, 40*(3), 576–598.

Clegg, S. R. (1994). Power and institutionalism in the theory of organizations. In M. Parker & J. Hassard (Eds.), *Towards a new theory of organizations* (pp. 24–52). London: Routledge.

Clegg, S. R. (1995). Of values and occasional irony: Max Weber in the context of the sociology of organizations. In S. B. Bachrach, P. Gagliardi & B. Munde (Eds.), *Research in the sociology of organizations: studies of organizations in the European tradition* (pp. 1–46). Greenwich, CT: JAI.

Clegg, S. R. (1996). The rhythm of the saints. *Electronic Journal of Radical Organization Theory, 1*(1), 1–6.

Clegg, S. R. (1999). Globalizing the intelligent organization: learning organizations, smart workers, (not so) clever countries and the sociological imagination. *Management Learning, 30*(3), 259–280.

Clegg, S. R. (2000). Power and authority: resistance and legitimacy. In H. Goverde, P. G. Cerny, M. Haugaard & H. Lentner (Eds.), *Power in contemporary politics: theories, practice, globalizations* (pp. 77–92). London: Sage.

Clegg, S. R. (2002). Lives in the balance: a comment on Professors Hinings' and Greenwood's disconnects and consequences in organization theory. *Administrative Science Quarterly, 47*(3), 428–441.

Clegg, S. R. (2003). Managing organization futures in a changing world of power/knowledge. In H. Tsoukas & C. Knudsen (Eds.), *The Oxford handbook of organization theory* (pp. 536–567). New York: Oxford University Press.

Clegg, S. R., Boreham, P., & Dow, G. (1983). *Class, politics and the economy.* London: Routledge & Kegan Paul.

Clegg, S. R., Carter, C., & Kornberger, M. (2004). Get up, I feel like being a strategy machine. *European Management Review, 1*(1), 21–28.

Clegg, S. R., & Courpasson, D. (2004). Political hybrids: Tocquevillean views on project organizations. *Journal of Management Studies, 41*(4), 525–547.

Clegg, S. R., & Dunkerley, D. (Eds.). (1977). *Critical issues in organizations.* London: Routledge & Kegan Paul.

Clegg, S. R., & Dunkerley, D. (1980). *Organization, class and control.* London: Routledge & Kegan Paul.

Clegg, S. R., Hardy, C., & Nord, W. R. (1996). *Handbook of organization studies.* London: Sage.

Clegg, S. R., & Kornberger, M. (2003). Modernism, postmodernism, management and organization theory. In E. Locke (Ed.), *Postmodernism in organizational thought: pros, cons and the alternative* (pp. 57–89). Amsterdam: Elsevier.

Clegg, S. R., Kornberger, M., & Pitsis, T. (2005). *Managing and organizations: an introduction to theory and practice.* London: Sage.

Clegg, S. R., Linstead, S., & Sewell, G. (2000). Only penguins: a polemic on organization theory from the edge of the world. *Organization Studies, 21,* 103–117.

Clegg, S. R., Pitsis, T., Rura-Polley, T., & Marosszeky, M. (2002). Governmentality matters: designing an alliance culture of inter-organizational collaboration for managing projects. *Organization Studies, 23*(3), 317–337.

Clegg, S. R., & Ray, T. (2003). Power, rules of the game and the limits to knowledge management: lessons from Japan and Anglo-Saxon alarms. *Prometheus, 21*(1), 23–40.

Coase, R. H. (1937). The nature of the firm. *Economica,* n.s. *4,* 386–405.

Cohen, J., Hazelrigg, L., & Pope, W. (1975a). De-Parsonizing Weber: a critique of Parsons' interpretation of Weber's sociology. *American Sociological Review, 40*(S), 229–241.

Cohen, J., Hazelrigg, L., & Pope, W. (1975b). Reply to Parsons. *American Sociological Review, 40*(S), 670–674.

Cohen, S. (1972). *Folk devils and moral panics.* London: Routledge.

Cohen, S., & Taylor, L. (1976). *Escape attempts: the theory and practice of resistance to everyday life.* London: Allen Lane.

Coleman, J. S. (1988). Properties of rational organisations. In S. M. Lindenberg & H. Schreuder (Eds.), *Interdisciplinary perspectives on organisation studies* (pp. 79–90). Oxford: Oxford University Press.

Colignon, R. (1997). *Power plays: critical events in the institutionalization of the Tennessee Valley Authority.* Albany, NY: State University of New York Press.

Collinson, D. (1994). Strategies as resistance: power, knowledge and subjectivity. In J. M. Jermier, W. R. Nord & D. Knights (Eds.), *Resistance and power in organizations: agency, subjectivity and the labour process* (pp. 25–68). London: Routledge.

Colville, I., Waterman, R. H., & Weick, K. E. (1999). Organizing and the search for excellence: making sense of the times in theory and practice. *Organization, 6,* 129–148.

Conrad, C., & Poole, M. S. (1998). *Strategic organizational communication.* New York: Harcourt Brace.

Conrad, J. (1998[1902]). *Heart of darkness: an authoritative text, backgrounds and sources, criticism.* New York: Norton.

Cooke, B. (2003). The denial of slavery in management studies. *Journal of Management Studies, 40*(8), 1895–1918.

Cooper, D. (1994). Productive, relational and everywhere? Conceptualising power and resistance within Foucauldian feminism. *Sociology, 28,* 435–454.

Cooper, D., & Hopper, T. (1988). *Debating coal closures: economic calculation in the coal dispute 1984–85.* Cambridge: Cambridge University Press.

Cooper, R. (1990). Organization/disorganization. In J. Hassard & D. Pym (Eds.), *The theory and philosophy of organizations: critical issues and new perspectives* (pp. 167–197). London: Routledge.

Cooper, R., & Fox, S. (1990). The texture of organizing. *Journal of Management Studies, 27,* 575–582.

Cooper, R., & Law, J. (1995). Organization: distal and proximal views. In P. G. Bacharach & B. M. S. Bacharach (Eds.), *Studies of organization: the European tradition* (pp. 237–274). Greenwich, CT: JAI.

Coopey, J., Keegan, O., & Emler, N. (1997). Managers' innovations as 'sense-making'. *British Journal of Management, 8*(4), 301–315.

Coppola, F. (Director). (2002). *Apocalypse now redux.* USA: Universal.

Corbett, E. P. J., & Connors, R. J. (1999). *Classical rhetoric for the modern student.* Oxford: Oxford University Press.

Courpasson, D. (2000). Managerial strategies of domination: power in soft bureaucracies. *Organization Studies, 21,* 141–162.

Courpasson, D. (2006). *Soft constraint: liberal organizations and domination.* Copenhagen: Copenhagen Business Press/Liber.

Court, W. H. B. (1962). *A concise economic history of Britain.* Cambridge: Cambridge University Press.

Crick, B. (1982). *In defence of politics.* Harmondsworth: Penguin.

Crossley, N. (1996). Body–subject/body–power: agency, inscription and control in Foucault and Merleau-Ponty. *Body and Society, 2*(2), 99–116.

Crozier, M. (1964). *The bureaucratic phenomenon.* Chicago: University of Chicago Press.

Crozier, M., & Friedberg, E. (1980). *Actors and systems.* Chicago: University of Chicago.

Cutler, T. (1978). The romance of labour. *Economy and Society, 7*(1), 74–95.

Cyert, R. M., & March, J. G. (1963). *A behavioral theory of the firm.* Englewood Cliffs, NJ: Prentice-Hall.

Czarniawska, B. (1998). *A narrative approach to organization studies.* Thousand Oaks, CA: Sage.

Czarniawska, B., & Sevon, G. (Eds.). (2003). *The Northern Lights: organization theory in Scandinavia.* Stockholm/Copenhagen: Liber/Copenhagen Business School Press.

Dahl, R. A. (1957). The concept of power. *Behavioral Science, 20,* 201–215.

Dahl, R. A. (1958). A critique of the ruling elite model. *American Political Science Review, 52*(June), 563–569.

Dahl, R. A. (1961). *Who governs?* New Haven, CT: Yale University Press.

Dahl, R. A. (1967). *Pluralist democracy in the United States: conflict and consent.* Chicago: Rand McNally.

Dahl, R. A. (1971). *Polyarchy: participation and opposition.* New Haven, CT: Yale University Press.

Dahrendorf, R. (1959). *Class and class conflict in industrial society.* New York: Free.

Dale, K. (2001). *Anatomising embodiment and organization theory.* London: Palgrave.

D'Amico, R. (1982). What is discourse? *Humanities in Society, 5*(3/4), 201–212.

Dandeker, C. (1990). *Surveillance, power and modernity: bureaucracy and discipline from 1700 to the present day.* Cambridge: Polity.

Davenport, S., & Leitch, S. (2005). Circuits of power in practice: strategic ambiguity as delegation of authority. *Organization Studies, 26,* in press.

Davis, G. F., & Mizruchi, M. S. (1999). The money centre cannot hold: banks in the US system of governance. *Administrative Science Quarterly, 44,* 215–239.

Davis, G. F., & Thompson, T. A. (1994). A social movement perspective on corporate control. *Administrative Science Quarterly, 39,* 141–173.

Davis, G. F., Yoo, M., & Baker, W. E. (2003). The small world of the American corporate elite, 1982–2001. *Strategic Organization, 1*(3), 301–326.

Dean, M. (1991). *The constitution of poverty: towards a genealogy of liberal governance.* London: Routledge.

Dean, M. (1992). A genealogy of the government of poverty. *Economy and Society, 21*(3), 215–251.

de Beauvoir, S. (1953). *The second sex* (Trans. H. M. Parshley). New York: Knopf.

de Boer, M., van den Bosch, F. A. J., & Volberda, H. W. (1999). Managing organisational knowledge integration in the emerging multimedia complex. *Journal of Management Studies, 36*(3), 379–398.

Deetz, S. (1992). *Democracy in the age of corporate colonization: developments in communication and the politics of everyday life.* Albany, NY: State University of New York.

Deetz, S. (2003). Reclaiming the legacy of the linguistic turn. *Organization, 10*(3), 421–429.

Deleuze, G. (1988). *Foucault.* Minneapolis: University of Minnesota Press.

Deleuze, G. (1989). What is a dispositif? In T. J. Armstrong (Ed.), *Michel Foucault philosopher* (pp. 159–168). London: Routledge.

Deleuze, G. (1992). Postscript on the societies of control. *October, 59*(Winter), 3–7.

Deleuze, G. (1994). *Difference and repetition.* New York: Columbia University Press.

Deleuze, G., & Guattari, F. (1983). *Anti-Oedipus: capitalism and schizophrenia* (Trans. R. Hurley, M. Seem & H. R. Lane, Preface Michel Foucault). Minneapolis: University of Minnesota Press.

Demsetz, H. (1991). The theory of the firm revisited. In O. E. Williamson & S. Winter (Eds.), *The nature of the firm* (pp. 159 –178). New York: Oxford University Press.

Derickson, A. (1994). Physiological science and scientific management in the progressive era: Frederic S. Lee and the Committee on Industrial Fatigue. *Business History Review, 68*(4), 483–514.

Derrida, J. (1986). Interview. *Domus,* no. 671 (April).

Derrida, J. (1988). Structure, sign and play in the discourse of the human sciences. In David Lodge (Ed.), *Modern criticism and theory.* London: Longman.

Derrida, J. (1992). Force of law: the mystical foundation of authority. In D. Cornell, M. Rosenfeld & D. Carlson (Eds.), *Deconstruction and the possibility of justice* (pp. 3–67). London: Routledge.

Desmarez, P. (1986). *La sociologie industrielle aux États-Unis.* Paris: Armand Colin.

Deveaux, M. (1994). Feminism and empowerment: a critical reading of Foucault. *Feminist Studies, 20,* 223.

Diamond, J. (1998). *Guns, germs and steel: a short history of everybody for the last 13,000 years.* New York: Vintage.

Dick, P. K. (1968). *Do androids dream of electric sheep?* New York: Ballantine.

Digesser, P. (1992). The fourth face of power. *Journal of Politics, 54*(4), 977–1007.

DiMaggio, P. J., & Powell, W. W. (1983). The iron cage revisited: institutional isomorphism and collective rationality in organizational fields. *American Sociological Review, 48*, 147–160.

Domhoff, W. G. (1967). *Who rules America?* Englewood Cliffs, NJ: Prentice-Hall.

Donaldson, L. (1985). *In defence of organization theory: a reply to the critics.* Cambridge: Cambridge University Press.

Donaldson, L. (1995). *American anti-management theories of organization: a critique of paradigm proliferation.* Cambridge: Cambridge University Press.

Donaldson, L. (1996). *For positivist organization theory.* London: Sage.

Doors, The (1967). Light my fire. Los Angeles: Elektra Records.

Dreyfuss, C. (1938). *Occupation and ideology of the salaried employee* (Trans. Eva Abramovitch). New York.

Dubin, R. (1957). Power and union–management relations. *Administrative Science Quarterly, 2*, 60–81.

du Gay, P. (1999). Is Bauman's bureau Weber's bureau? A comment. *British Journal of Sociology, 50*, 575–587.

du Gay, P. (2000a). Enterprise and its futures: a response to Fournier and Grey. *Organization, 7*(1), 165–183.

du Gay, P. (2000b). *In praise of bureaucracy: Weber, organization, ethics.* London: Sage.

Dumm, T. L. (1996). *Michel Foucault and the politics of freedom.* Thousand Oaks, CA: Sage.

Durkheim, E. (1951). *Suicide: a study in sociology* (Trans. John A. Spaulding & George Simpson). New York: Free.

Durkheim, E. (1961). *Moral education: a study in the theory and application of the sociology of education.* New York: Free.

Durkheim, E. (1983). *Pragmatism and sociology.* Cambridge: University of Cambridge Press.

Durkheim, E. (2002). *Suicide: a study in sociology* (Trans. John A. Spaulding & George Simpson, Introduction George Simpson). London: Routledge.

Durrell, L. (1968). *The Alexandria quartet: Justine; Balthazar; Mountolive; Clea.* London: Faber and Faber.

Dussel, E. (1995). *The invention of the Americas: eclipse of 'the other' and the myth of modernity* (Trans. M. D. Barber). New York: Continuum.

Dwork, D., & Van Pelt, R. J. (1996). *Auschwitz: 1270 to the present.* New York: Norton.

Dyer, J. H., & Nobeoka, K. (2000). Creating and managing a high-performance knowledge-sharing network: the Toyota case. *Strategic Management Journal, 21*, 345–367.

Dylan, B. (1964). Chimes of freedom flashing. On *Another side of Bob Dylan.* New York: CBS.

Dylan, B. (1965). It's alright ma, I'm only bleedin'. On *Bringing it all back home.* New York: CBS.

Dylan, B. (1974). Tangled up in blue. On *Blood on the tracks.* New York: CBS.

Eckstein, H. (1969). Authority relations and governmental performance: a theoretical framework. *Comparative Political Studies,* January, 269–325.

Eden, R. (1983). *Political leadership and nihilism: a study of Weber and Nietzsche.* Tampa: University of South Florida Press.

Edwards, C., & Read, P. (1989). *The lost children: thirteen Australians taken from their Aboriginal families tell of the struggle to find their natural parents.* Sydney: Doubleday.

Edwards, R. (1979). *Contested terrain.* New York: Basic.

Eisenberg, E. (1984). Ambiguity as a strategy in organizational communication. *Communication Monographs, 51*, 227–242.

Eisenhardt, K. M., & Bourgeois, L. J. (1988). Politics of strategic decision making in high-velocity environments: toward a midrange theory. *Academy of Management Journal, 31*, 737–770.

Elias, N. (1982). *The civilizing process. Vol. 2: Power and civility.* New York: Pantheon.

Emerson, R. M. (1962). Power–dependence relations. *American Sociological Review, 27*(1), 31–41.

Emmet, D. (1953). The concept of power. *Aristotelian Society Proceedings, 54*, 1–26.

Emmet, D. (1958). *Function, purpose and powers: some concepts in the study of individuals and societies.* London: St Martin's.

Enz, C. A. (1988). The role of value congruity in intraorganizational power. *Administrative Science Quarterly, 33,* 284–304.

Eribon, D. (1991). *Michel Foucault* (Trans. B. Wing). Cambridge, MA: Harvard University Press.

Escobar, A. (1984/5). Discourse and power in development: Michel Foucault and the relevance of his work to the Third World. *Alternatives, X,* 35.

Escobar, A. (1992). Culture, economics, and politics in Latin American social movements: theory and research. In A. Escobar & S. Alvarez (Eds.), *The making of social movements in Latin America: identity, strategy and democracy.* New York: Westview.

Escobar, A. (1995). *Encountering development: the making and unmaking of the Third World.* Princeton, NJ: Princeton University Press.

Etzioni, A. (1961). *A comparative analysis of complex organizations: on power, involvement, and their correlates.* New York: Free.

Etzioni-Halevy, E. (1987). *National broadcasting under siege: a comparative study of Australia, Britain, Israel, and West.* New York: St Martin's.

Etzioni-Halevy, E. (1993). *The elite connection: problems and potential of western democracy.* Cambridge: Polity.

Ewen, S. (1976). *Captains of consciousness: advertising and the social roots of the consumer culture.* New York: McGraw-Hill.

Fairclough, N. (1992). *Discourse and social change.* Cambridge: Polity.

Fairclough, N. (1993). Critical discourse analysis and the marketization of public discourse: the universities. *Discourse and Society, 4,* 133–168.

Fairclough, N. (2003). *Analyzing discourse: textual analysis for social research.* London: Routledge.

Fairclough, N. (2005). Discourse analysis in organization studies: the case for critical realism. *Organization Studies, 26*(6), 915–939.

Fairclough, N., & Wodak, R. (1997). Critical discourse analysis. In T. van Dijk (Ed.), *Discourse studies. Vol. 2: Discourse as social interaction* (pp. 258–284). Sage: London.

Fairtlough, G. (1994). *Creative compartments: a design for future organization.* London: Greenwood.

Fairtlough, G. (2005). *The three ways of getting things done: hierarchy, heterarchy and responsible autonomy in organizations.* Greenways, Dorset: Triarchy.

Falzon, C. (1998). *Foucault and social dialogue.* London: Routledge.

Faulkner, A. S. (1921). Does jazz put the sin in syncopation? *Ladies Home Journal, 38,* 16–34.

Fayol, H. (1949). *General and industrial management.* London: Pitman.

Fehér, F., Heller, A., & Márkus, G. (1983). *Dictatorship over needs: an analysis of Soviet societies.* Oxford: Blackwell.

Feingold, H. (1983). How unique is the Holocaust? In A. Grobman & D. Landes (Eds.), *Genocide: critical issues of the Holocaust* (pp. 397–401). Los Angeles: Simon Wiesenthal Center. Also accessible at http://motlc.wiesenthal.com/resources/books/genocide/chap10.html#2.

Fleischmann, E. (1964). De Weber à Nietzsche. *Archives Européennes de Sociologie, 5,* 190–238.

Fligstein, D. (1985). The spread of the multidivisional form among large firms, 1919–1979. *American Sociological Review,* June, 377–391.

Flyvbjerg, B. (1998). *Rationality and power: democracy in practice.* Chicago: University of Chicago Press.

Flyvbjerg, B. (2001). *Making social science matter.* Cambridge: University of Cambridge Press.

Folger, J. P., Poole, M. S., & Stutman, R. K. (1997). *Working through conflict: strategies for relationships, groups, and organizations* (3rd ed.). New York: Longman.

Follett, M. P. (1918). *The new state: group organization, the solution for popular government.* New York: Longman, Green.

Follett, M. P. (1924). *Creative experience.* New York: Longman, Green.

Follett, M. P. (1995). *Mary Parker Follett – prophet of management: a celebration of writings from the 1920s.* Cambridge: Cambridge University Press.

Ford, J. D., Ford, L. W., & McNamara, R. T. (2002). Resistance and the background conversations of change. *Journal of Organizational Change Management, 5*(2), 105–121.

Forman, M. (Director). (1975). *One flew over the cuckoo's nest.* USA: United Artists.

Foucault, M. (1965). *Madness and civilization: a history of insanity in the age of reason.* New York: Vintage.

Foucault, M. (1972). *The archaeology of knowledge.* London: Tavistock.

Foucault, M. (1977). *Discipline and punish: the birth of the prison* (Ed. A. Sheridan). London: Allen & Lane.

Foucault, M. (1979). Governmentality. *Ideology and Consciousness, 6,* 5–21.

Foucault, M. (1980). *Power/knowledge* (Ed. C. Gordon). New York: Pantheon.

Foucault, M. (1982). The subject and power. In H. L. Dreyfus & P. Rabinow, *Michel Foucault: beyond structuralism and hermeneutics.* Chicago: University of Chicago Press.

Foucault, M. (1984). Polemics, politics, and problematization. In P. Rabinow (Ed.), *The Foucault reader.* New York: Southern.

Foucault, M. (1988a). *Politics, philosophy, culture: interviews and other writings, 1977–1984* (Trans. A. Sheridan, Ed. L. D. Kritzman). London: Routledge.

Foucault, M. (1988b). The care of the self as a practice of freedom. In J. Berbauer & D. Rasmussen (Eds.), *The final Foucault* (pp. 1–20). Cambridge, MA: MIT Press.

Foucault, M. (1990). *The history of sexuality.* London: Penguin.

Foucault, M. (1997). *Ethics: subjectivity and truth* (Ed. P. Rabinow). New York: New.

Foucault, M. (2003a). *Society must be defended* (Trans. D. Macey). Harmondsworth: Penguin.

Foucault, M. (2003b). The birth of biopolitics. In P. Rabinow & N. Rose (Eds.), *The essential Foucault* (pp. 202–207). New York: New.

Fournier, V., & Grey, C. (2000). At the critical moment: conditions and prospects for critical management studies. *Human Relations, 53*(1), 7–32.

Fox, A. (1974). *Beyond contract: work, power and trust relations.* London: Faber.

Fraser, N. (1981). Foucault on modern power: empirical insights and normative confusions. *Praxis International, 1*(3), 272–287.

Fraser, N. (1989). *Unruly practices: power, discourse, and gender in contemporary social theory.* Cambridge: Polity.

Freidson, E. (1986). *Professional powers: a study of the institutionalization of formal knowledge.* Chicago: University of Chicago Press.

French, J. R. P., & Raven, B. (1968). The bases of social power. In D. Cartwright & A. Zander (Eds.), *Group dynamics.* New York: Harper & Row.

Friedan, B. (1965). *The feminine mystique.* Harmondsworth: Penguin.

Friedman, A. (1977). *Industry and labour.* London: Macmillan.

Friedmann, G. (1946). *Problèmes humaines du machinisme industriel.* Paris: Gallimard.

Friedrich, C. J. (1937). *Constitutional government and democracy.* New York: Gipp.

Frost, P. (1980). Toward a radical framework for practicing organization science. *Academy of Management Review, 5,* 501–508.

Fukuyama, F. (1992). *The end of history and the last man.* London: Hamish Hamilton.

Fulop, L., & Linstead, S. (1999). Power and politics in organizations. In L. Fulop & S. Linstead (Eds.), *Management: a critical text* (pp. 182–209). Basingstoke: Macmillan.

Funder, A. (2002). *Stasiland.* Sydney: Text.

Gadamer, H.-G. (1989). *Truth and method* (2nd ed.) (Trans. J. Marshall). New York: Continuum.

Gamble, A. (1988). *The free economy and the strong state: the politics of Thatcherism.* London: Macmillan.

Game, A., & Pringle, R. (1979). Sexuality and the suburban dream. *Australian and New Zealand Journal of Sociology, 15*(2), 4–15.

Gandz, J., & Murray, V. V. (1980). The experience of workplace politics. *Academy of Management Journal, 23*(2), 237–251.

Garfinkel, H. (1967). *Studies in ethnomethodology.* Englewood Cliffs, NJ: Prentice-Hall.

Garrick, J., & Clegg, S. R. (2000). Organizational Gothic: transfusing vitality and transforming the corporate body through work-based learning. In C. Symes & J. McIntyre (Eds.), *Working knowledge: the new vocationalism and higher education* (pp. 153–171). Buckingham: Society for Research into Higher Education and Open University Press.

Gaventa, J. (1980). *Power and powerlessness: quiescence and rebellion in an Appalachian valley.* Oxford: Clarendon.

Geertz, C. (1973). *The interpretation of cultures: selected essays.* New York: Basic.

Geertz, C. (1995). *After the fact: two countries, four decades, one anthropologist.* Cambridge, MA: Harvard University Press.

George, R., & Clegg, S. R. (1997). An inside story: tales from the field – doing organizational research in a state of uncertainty. *Organization Studies, 18*(6), 1015–1023.

Gephart, R. (1978). Status degradation and organizational succession: an ethnomethodological approach. *Administrative Science Quarterly, 23*(4), 553–582.

Gergen, K. (1999). *An invitation to social construction.* London: Sage.

Gherardi, S. (1999). Learning as problem-driven or learning in the face of mystery? *Organization Studies, 20*(1), 101–124.

Ghorashi, H. (2004). How dual is transnational identity? A debate about dual positioning of diaspora organizations. *Culture and Organization, 10*(4), 329–340.

Gibson, Q. (1971). Power. *Philosophy of the Social Sciences,* 101–102.

Giddens, A. (1968). 'Power' in the recent writings of Talcott Parsons. *Sociology, 2,* 257–272.

Giddens, A. (1976). *New rules of sociological method.* London: Hutchinson.

Giddens, A. (1977). *Studies in social and political theory.* London: Hutchinson.

Giddens, A. (1979). *Central problems in social theory.* London: Macmillan.

Giddens, A. (1981). *A contemporary critique of historical materialism.* London: Macmillan.

Giddens, A. (1984). *The constitution of society.* Cambridge: Polity.

Giddens, A. (1990). *The consequences of modernity.* Cambridge: Polity.

Gilbreth, F. B. (1972). *Motion study: a method for increasing the efficiency of the workman* (Introduction Robert Thurston Kent). Easton, PA: Hive.

Gilbreth, F. B., & Gilbreth, L. (1916). *Fatigue study: the elimination of humanity's greatest waste. A first step in motion study.* New York: Sturgis & Walton.

Gillespie, R. (1993). *Manufacturing knowledge: a history of the Hawthorne experiments.* Cambridge, MA: Cambridge University Press.

Goethe, J. W. von (2005). *Elective affinities* (Trans. J. Hollingdale). Harmondsworth: Penguin.

Goffman, E. (1956). *The presentation of self in everyday life.* Harmondsworth: Penguin.

Goffman, E. (1961). *Asylums.* Harmondsworth: Penguin.

Goffman, E. (1963). *Stigma: notes on the management of spoiled identity.* Englewood Cliffs, NJ: Prentice-Hall.

Goffman, E. (1972). *Encounters: two studies in the sociology of interaction.* London: Allen Lane.

Goffman, E. (1976). *Gender advertisements.* London: Macmillan.

Goldberg, C. A. (2001). Social citizenship and a reconstructed Tocqueville. *American Sociological Review, 66*(April), 289–315.

Goldhagen, D. J. (1996). *Hitler's willing executioners: ordinary Germans and the Holocaust.* New York: Knopf.

Goldthorpe, D., Lockwood, D., Bechoffer, F., & Platt, J. (1969). *The affluent worker in the class structure.* Cambridge: Cambridge University Press.

Goldthorpe, J. E. (1996). *The sociology of post-colonial societies: economic disparity, cultural diversity and development.* New York: Cambridge University Press.

Gopal, A., Willis, R., & Gopal, Y. (2003). From the colonial enterprise to enterprise systems: parallels between colonization and globalization. In A. Prasad (Ed.), *Postcolonial theory and organizational analysis: a critical engagement* (pp. 233–254). New York: Palgrave Macmillan.

Gordon, R. D. (2002). Conceptualizing leadership with respect to its historical-contextual antecedents to power. *The Leadership Quarterly, 13*(2), 151–167.

Gouldner, A. W. (1954). *Patterns of industrial bureaucracy.* New York: Free.

Gouldner, A. W. (1955). Metaphysical pathos and the theory of bureaucracy. *American Political Science Review, 49,* 496–507.

Gouldner, A. W. (1956). Explorations in applied social science. *Social Problems, 3*(3), 169–181.

Gouldner, A. W. (1971). *The coming crisis of western sociology.* London: Heinemann.

Graham, L. (1998). *Managing on her own: Dr. Lillian Gilbreth and women's work in the interwar era.* Norcross, GA: Engineering & Management Press.

Gramsci, A. (1971). *From the prison notebooks.* London: Lawrence and Wishart.

Grant, D., & Hardy, C. (2004). Introduction: struggles with organizational discourse. *Organization Studies, 25*(1), 5–13.

Grant, D., Hardy, C., Oswick, C., & Putnam, L. (2004). *Handbook of organizational discourse.* London: Sage.

Grant, D., Keenoy, T., & Oswick, C. (1998). *Discourse and organization.* London: Sage.

Grant, R. M. (1996a). Prospering in dynamically competitive environments: organisational capability as knowledge integration. *Organisational Science, 7*(4), 375–387.

Grant, R. M. (1996b). Toward a knowledge-based theory of the firm. *Strategic Management Journal, 17*, 109–122.

Gray, B., & Ariss, S. D. (1985). Politics and strategic change across organizational life cycles. *Academy of Management Review, 10*(4), 707–723.

Greenberg, K. J., & Dratel, J. L. (2005). *The torture papers: the road to Abu Ghraib.* Cambridge: Cambridge University Press.

Greenwood, R., & Hinings, C. R. (1996). Understanding radical organizational change: bringing together the old and the new institutionalism. *Academy of Management Review, 22*, 1022–1054.

Greenwood, R., & Hinings, C. R. (2002). Disconnects and consequences in organization theory. *Administrative Science Quarterly, 47*, 411–421.

Greenwood, R., Hinings, C. R., & Brown, J. (1990). 'P 2-form' strategic management: corporate practices in professional partnerships. *Academy of Management Journal, 33*(4), 725–755.

Greer, G. (1970). *The female eunuch.* London: MacGibbon & Kee.

Grenier, G. (1988). *Inhuman relations: quality circles and anti-unionism in American industry.* Philadelphia: Temple University Press.

Grey, C. (2005). *A very short, fairly interesting and reasonably cheap book about studying organizations.* London: Sage.

Grey, C., & Willmott, H. (2002). Contexts of CMS. *Organization, 9*(3), 411–418.

Grice, S., & Humphries, M. (1997). Critical management studies in postmodernity: oxymorons in outer space? *Journal of Organizational Change Management, 10*(5), 412–425.

Gronow, J. (1988). The element of irrationality: Max Weber's diagnosis of modern culture. *Acta Sociologica, 31*, 327–329.

Gudykunst, W. B. (1998). *Bridging differences: effective intergroup communication.* Thousand Oaks, CA: Sage.

Habermas, J. (1971). *Knowledge and human interests* (Trans. Jeremy J. Shapiro). Boston: Beacon.

Habermas, J. (1976). The analytic theory of science and dialectic. In T. Adorno et al. (Eds.), *The positivist dispute in German sociology.* London: Heinemann.

Habermas, J. (1979). *Communication and the evolution of society* (Trans. and Introduction Thomas McCarthy). Boston: Beacon.

Habermas, J. (1986). The genealogical writing of history: on some aporias in Foucault's theory of power (Trans. Gregory Ostrander). *Canadian Journal of Political and Social Theory, 10*, 1–2.

Habermas, J. (1987a). Some questions concerning the theory of power: Foucault again. In J. Habermas (Ed.), *The philosophical discourse of humanity* (pp. 266–293). Cambridge, MA: MIT Press.

Habermas, J. (1987b). *The theory of communicative action* (Trans. T. McCarthy). Cambridge: Polity.

Hacking, I. (1991). How should we do the history of statistics? In G. Burchell, C. Gordon & P. Miller (Eds.), *The Foucault effect: studies in governmentality* (pp. 181–196). London: University of Chicago Press.

Hacking, I. (2004). Between Michel Foucault and Erving Goffman: between discourse in the abstract and face-to-face interaction. *Economy and Society, 33*(3), 277–302.

Hägerstrand, T. (1970). What about people in regional science? *Regional Science Association Papers, XXIV*, 7–21.

Hall, P. (1989). *The political power of economic ideas.* Princeton, NJ: Princeton University Press.

Hall, S. (2001). Foucault: power, knowledge, and discourse. In M. Wetherell, S. Taylor & S. J. Yates (Eds.), *Discourse theory and practice: a reader* (pp. 72–81). London: Sage.

Hallsworth, A., & Taylor, M. (1996). Buying power: interpreting retail change in a circuits of power framework. *Environment and Planning A, 28,* 2125–2137.

Hallsworth, A., Taylor, M., Jones, K., & Muncaster, R. (1997). The US food discounter's invasion of Canada and Britain: a power perspective. *Agribusiness, 13*(2), 227–235.

Hancock, P., & Tyler, M. (2004). MoT your life: critical management studies and the management of everyday life. *Human Relations, 57*(5), 619–645.

Haney, C., Banks, C., & Zimbardo, P. (1973). Interpersonal dynamics in a simulated prison. *International Journal of Criminology and Psychology, 1,* 69–97.

Hannah, M. (1997). Imperfect panopticism: envisioning the construction of perfect lives. In G. Benko & U. Stohmayer (Eds.), *Space and social theory: interpreting modernity and postmodernity* (pp. 344–359). Oxford: Blackwell.

Hannan, M. T., & Freeman, J. H. (1977). The population ecology of organizations. *American Journal of Sociology, 82,* 929–940.

Hannan, M. T., & Freeman, J. H. (1984). Structural inertia and organizational change. *American Sociological Review, 49,* 159–164.

Hardt, M., & Negri, A. (2000). *Empire.* Cambridge, MA: Harvard University Press.

Hardy, C. (1996). Understanding power: bringing about strategic change. *British Journal of Management,* S3–S16.

Hardy, C., & Clegg, S. R. (1996). Some dare call it power. In S. R. Clegg, C. Hardy & W. R. Nord (Eds.), *Handbook of organization studies* (pp. 622–641). London: Sage.

Hardy, C., & Leiba-O'Sullivan, S. (1998). The power behind empowerment: implications for research and practice. *Human Relations, 51*(4), 451–483.

Hardy, C., Palmer, I., & Phillips, N. (2000). Discourse as a strategic resource. *Human Relations, 53*(9), 1227–1248.

Hardy, C., & Phillips, N. (1999). No joking matter: discursive struggle in the Canadian refugee system. *Organization Studies, 20*(1), 1–24.

Hardy, C., & Phillips, N. (2004). Discourse and power. In D. Grant, C. Hardy, C. Oswick & L. Putnam (Eds.), *Handbook of organizational discourse* (pp. 299–317). London: Sage.

Harker, R., Mahar, C., & Wilkes, C. (Eds.). (1990). *An introduction to the work of Pierre Bourdieu.* London: Macmillan.

Harré, R. (1995). Discursive psychology. In J. A. Smith, R. Harré & L. van Langenhove (Eds.), *Rethinking psychology* (pp. 143–159). Thousand Oaks, CA: Sage.

Harré, R., & Madden, E. H. (1975). *Causal powers.* Oxford: Blackwell.

Harstock, N. (1987). The feminist standpoint. In S. Harding (Ed.), *Feminism and methodology* (pp. 157–180). Bloomington, IN: Indiana University Press.

Harstock, N. (1990). Foucault on power: a theory for women? In L. J. Nicholson (Ed.), *Feminism/postmodernism* (pp. 157–175). New York: Routledge.

Hatch, M. J. (1997). *Organization theory: modern, symbolic, and postmodern perspectives.* Oxford: Oxford University Press.

Haugaard, M. (1997). *The constitution of power.* Manchester: Manchester University Press.

Haugaard, M. (2000). Power, ideology and legitimacy. In H. Goverde, P. G. Cerny, M. Haugaard & H. Lentner (Eds.), *Power in contemporary politics: theories, practice, globalizations* (pp. 59–76). London: Sage.

Haugaard, M. (Ed.). (2002a). *Power: a reader.* Manchester: Manchester University Press.

Haugaard, M. (2002b). Nationalism and modernity. In S. Maleševi & M. Haugaard (Eds.), *Making sense of collectivity: ethnicity, nationalism and globalism* (pp. 122–137). London: Pluto.

Haugaard, M. (2003). Reflections on seven ways of creating power. *European Journal of Social Theory, 61*(1), 87–113.

Hayes, P. (Ed.). (1991). *Lessons and legacies: the meaning of the Holocaust in a changing world.* Evanston, IL: Northwestern University Press.

Heckscher, C. (1994). Defining the post-bureaucratic type. In C. Heckscher & A. Donnellon (Eds.), *The post-bureaucratic organization* (pp. 14–62). Thousand Oaks, CA: Sage.

Hegel, G. F. W. (1998). *The Hegel reader* (Ed. Stephen Houlgate). Oxford: Blackwell.

Heidegger, M. (1977). *Basic writings*. New York: Harper & Row.

Heiskala, R. (2001). Theorizing power: Weber, Parsons, Foucault and neostructuralism. *Social Science Information, 40*(2), 241–264.

Hekman, S. (1996). *Feminist interpretations of Foucault*. University Park, PA: Pennsylvania State University Press.

Held, D. (1980). *Introduction to critical theory: Horkheimer to Habermas*. Cambridge: Polity.

Henderson, L. J. (1935). *Pareto's general sociology: a physiologist's interpretation*. Cambridge, MA: Harvard University Press.

Henderson, L. J., Whitehead, N. T., & Mayo, E. (1937). The effects of social environment. In L. Gulick & L. Urwick (Eds.), *Papers on the science of administration*. New York: Institute of Public Administration, Columbia University.

Hennis, W. (1988). The traces of Nietzsche in the work of Max Weber (Trans. K. Tribe). In *Max Weber: essays in reconstruction* (pp. 146–162). London: Allen & Unwin.

Hernes, T., & Bakken, T. (2003). Implications of self-reference: Niklas Luhmann's autopoiesis and organization theory. *Organization Studies, 24*, 1511–1535.

Hetrick, W. P., & Boje, D. M. (1992). Organization and the body: post-Fordist dimensions. *Journal of Organizational Change Management, 5*(1), 48–57.

Heyl, B. S. (2002). The Harvard 'Pareto Circle'. In S. R. Clegg (Ed.), *Central currents in organization studies II: contemporary trends* (Vol. 2, pp. 3–23). London: Sage. Originally published in *Journal of the History of the Behavioural Sciences*, 1968, *4*, 316–334.

Hickson, D. J. (1966). A convergence in organization theory. *Administrative Science Quarterly, 11*, 224–237.

Hickson, D. J., Butler, R. J., Cray, D., Mallory, G. R., & Wilson, D. C. (1986). *Top decisions: strategic decision-making in organizations*. San Francisco: Jossey-Bass.

Hickson, D. J., Hinings, C. R., Lee, C. A., Schneck, R. E., & Pennings, J. M. (1971). A strategic contingencies theory of intraorganizational power. *Administrative Science Quarterly, 16*(2), 216–229.

Hickson, D. J., Hinings, C. R., Lee, C. A., Schneck, R. E., & Pennings, J. M. (2002). A strategic contingencies theory of intraorganizational power. In S. R. Clegg (Ed.), *Central currents in organization studies II: contemporary trends* (Vol. 5, pp. 3–19). London: Sage.

Higgins, W. (2004). *Journey into darkness*. Blackheath, NSW: Brandl & Schlesinger.

Hindess, B. (1996). *Discourses of power: from Hobbes to Foucault*. Oxford: Blackwell.

Hinings, C. R., Hickson, D. J., Pennings, D. J., & Schneck, R. E. (1974). Structural conditions of intraorganisational power. *Administrative Science Quarterly, 12*, 22–44.

Hinings, C. R., & Mauws, M. (2004). Organizational morality. http://www.bc.edu/church21/meta-elements/pdf/hinings.pdf.

Hirschman, A. O. (1970). *Exit, voice, and loyalty: responses to decline in firms, organizations, and states*. Cambridge, MA: Harvard University Press.

Hitler, A. (1924). *Mein Kampf*. http://www.hitler.org/writings/Mein_Kampf/.

Hobbes, T. (1651). *Leviathan* (Ed. A. D. Lindsay 1914). New York: Dutton.

Hocker, J., & Wilmot, W. (1991). *Interpersonal conflict*. Dubuque, IA: Brown.

Hodge, R., & Kress, G. (1988). *Social semiotics*. Ithaca, NY: Cornell University Press.

Hogan, J., & Green, A.M. (2002). E-collectivism: on-line action and on-line mobilisation. In L. Holmes, D. M. Hosking & M. Grieco (Eds.), *Organising in the Information Age: distributed technology, distributed leadership, distributed identity, distributed discourse*. Aldershot: Ashgate.

Holmer-Nadeson, M. (1996). Organizational identity and space of action. *Organization Studies, 17*, 49–81.

Holmstrom, J., & Stalder, F. (2001). Drifting technologies and multi-purpose networks: the case of the Swedish cash card. *Information and Organisation, 11*, 187–206.

Holt, D. B. (1995). How consumers consume: toward a typology of consumption practices. *Journal of Consumer Research, 22*(6), 1–25.

Homans, G. C., & Curtis, C. P. Jr (1934). *An introduction to Pareto: his sociology.* New York: Knopf.
Hopwood, A. G., & Miller, P. (Eds.). (1994). *Accounting as social and institutional practice.* Cambridge: Cambridge University Press.
Horkheimer, M. (1993). *Between philosophy and social science: selected early writings* (Trans. G. Frederick Hunter, Matthew S. Kramer & John Torpey, Introduction G. Frederick Hunter). Cambridge, MA: MIT Press.
Hoskin, K., & Macve, R. (1988). The genesis of accountability: the West Point connections. *Accounting, Organizations and Society, 13*(1), 37–73.
Howe, A. (2001). Habermas, history and social evolution: moral learning and the trial of Louis XVI. *Sociology, 35*(1), 177–194.
Hoy, D. C. (Ed.). (1986). *Foucault: a critical reader.* Oxford: Blackwell.
HREOC (1997). *Bringing them home.* Canberra: Human Rights and Equal Opportunity Commission.
Hughes, R. (1987). *The fatal shore: a history of the transportation of convicts to Australia, 1787–1868.* London: Collins Harvill.
Hume, D. (1902). *An enquiry concerning human understanding.* Oxford: Clarendon.
Humphries, S. (Director). (1998). *Sex in a cold climate.* Bristol: Testimony Films for Channel 4.
Hunter, I. (1993). Subjectivity and government. *Economy and Society, 22*(1), 123–134.
Huntington, S. (1973). Transnational organizations in world politics. *World Politics, 25*(3), 333–368.
Huntington, S. (1997). *The clash of civilizations and the remaking of world order.* Harmondsworth: Penguin.
Husserl, E. (1962). *Ideas: general introduction to phenomenology* (Trans. W. Gibson). London: Collier Macmillan.
Ibarra-Colado, E. (1999). Los saberes sobre la organización: etapas, enfoques y dilemas. In C. A. Castillo (Ed.), *Economía, organización y trabajo: un enfoque sociológico* (pp. 95–154). Madrid: Pirámide.
Ibarra-Colado, E. (2001a). Foucault, gubernamentalidad y organización: una lectura de la triple problematización del sujeto. *Iztapalapa, 21*(50), 321–358.
Ibarra-Colado, E. (2001b). *La universidad en México hoy: gubernamentalidad y modernización.* México: DGEP-UNAM/FCPyS-UNAM/UAM-I/ANUIES.
Ibarra-Colado, E. (2004). Globalisation disputes: markets attack ethics ... ethics break in markets. Paper presented at the symposium 'What Is To Be Done About Management Ethics?', Australian Research Council Special Project Learned Academies Scheme. University of Technology, Sydney, 16–17 December.
Ibarra-Colado, E. (2005). Latin America's organization studies challenges in the 21st century: moving from the centre toward the margins. Paper presented at the Academy of Management Annual Meeting, Honolulu, Hawaii, USA.
Ignatieff, M. (1978). *A just measure of pain: the penitentiary in the industrial revolution, 1750–1850.* New York: Pantheon.
Ikenberry, J., & Kupchan, C. (1990). Socialisation and hegemonic power. *International Organization, 44*(3), 283–315.
Isaac, J. C. (1987). *Power and Marxist theory: a realist view.* Ithaca, NY: Cornell University Press.
Isajiw, W. W. (1979). *Definitions of ethnicity.* Toronto: Multicultural History Society of Ontario.
Jackson, N., & Carter, P. (1998). Labour as dressage. In A. McKinlay & K. Starkey (Eds.), *Foucault, management, and organization theory: from panopticon to technologies of self* (pp. 49–64). London: Sage.
Jacoby, S. (1997). *Modern manors: welfare capitalism since the new deal.* Princeton, NJ: Princeton University Press.
Jacoby, S. (1999). Are career jobs headed for extinction? *California Management Review, 42*(1), 123–145.
Jacoby, S. (2005). *The embedded corporation: corporate governance and employment relations in Japan and the United States.* Princeton, NJ: Princeton University Press.
Jacques, R. (1996). *Manufacturing the employee: management knowledge from the 19th to 21st centuries.* Thousand Oaks, CA: Sage.

Jacques, R. (1999). Developing a tactical approach to engaging with 'strategic' HRM. *Organization*, 6(2), 199–222.

Jagger, M., & Richards, K. (1968). Street fighting man. On *Beggars banquet*. London: London Records.

James, B. J. (1964). The issue of power. *Public Administration Review*, 24(1), 47–51.

Janouch, G. (1971). *Conversations with Kafka*. London: Deutsch.

Jaques, E. (1967). *Equitable payment*. New York: Pelican.

Jay, M. (1996). *The dialectical imagination: a history of the Frankfurt School and the Institute of Social Research 1923–1950*. Berkeley, CA: University of California.

Jaya, P. (2001). Do we really 'know' and 'profess'? Decolonizing management knowledge. *Organization*, 8(2), 227–233.

Jehn, K. A. (1997). A qualitative analysis of conflict types and dimensions in organizational groups. *Administrative Science Quarterly*, 42, 530–557.

Jehn, K. A., Northcraft, G. B., & Neale, M. A. (1999). Why differences make a difference: a field study of diversity, conflict and performance in workgroups. *Administrative Science Quarterly*, 44, 741–763.

Jermier, J. (1985). 'When the sleeper wakes': a short story extending themes in radical organization theory. *Journal of Management History*, 11(2), 67–80.

Jermier, J. M., Nord, W. R., & Knights, D. (Eds.). (1995). *Resistance and power in organizations: agency, subjectivity and the labor process*. London: Routledge.

Jewett, R., & Lawrence, J. S. (1988). *The American monomyth*. Lanham, MD: University Press of America.

Johnson, D., & Johnson, F. (1982). *Joining together*. Englewood Cliffs, NJ: Prentice-Hall.

Johnston, P. (2004). Outflanking power, reframing unionism: the basic strike of 1999–2001. *Labor Studies Journal*, 28(4), 1–24.

Jones, C., & O'Doherty, D. (Eds.). (2005). *Manifestos for the business school of tomorrow*. Åbo: Dvalin.

Jordan, J. M. (1994). *Machine-age ideology: social engineering and American liberalism, 1911–1939*. Chapel Hill, NC: University of North Carolina Press.

Joslyn, K. S., & Taussig, F. W. (1932). *American business leaders*. New York: Macmillan.

Joyce, P. (1980). *Work, society and politics: the culture of the factory in later Victorian England*. New Brunswick, NJ: Rutgers University Press.

Kaesler, D. (2004). From academic outsider to sociological mastermind: the fashioning of the sociological 'classic' Max Weber. *Bangladesh e-Journal of Sociology*, 1(1). http://www.bangladesh sociology.org/Content.htm, retrieved January 7, 2005.

Kaiser, A., & Muller, A. (2003). Foreword. In A. Muller & A. Kieser (Eds.), *Communication in organizations* (pp. 7–17). Frankfurt-am-Main: Lang.

Kalberg, S. (1980). Max Weber's types of rationality: cornerstones for the analysis of rationalization processes in history. *American Journal of Sociology*, 85, 1145–1179.

Kallinikos, J., & Cooper, R. (1996). Writing, rationality and organization: an introduction. *Scandinavian Journal of Management*, 12(1), 1–16.

Kalyvas, A. (2005). Popular sovereignty, democracy, and the constituent power. *Constellation*, 12(2), 155–291.

Kanigel, R. (1997). *The one best way: Frederick Winslow Taylor and the enigma of efficiency*. New York: Viking.

Kanter, R. M. (1977). *Men and women of the corporation*. New York: Basic.

Kanter, R. M. (1990). *When giants learn to dance*. London: Unwin Hyman.

Kaplan, A. (1964). Power in perspective. In R. L. Kahn & E. Boulding (Eds.), *Power and conflict in organizations* (pp. 11–23). London: Tavistock.

Kaufmann, S. (1993). *The origins of order: self-organization and selection in evolution*. New York: Oxford University Press.

Keiser, A. (2002). From asceticism to administration of wealth: mediaeval monasteries and the pitfalls of rationalization. In S. R. Clegg (Ed.), *Central currents in organization studies I: frameworks and applications* (Vol. 1, pp. 120–140). London: Sage. Originally published in *Organization Studies*, 1987, 8(2), 103–124.

Kelly, M. (Ed.). (1994). *Critique and power: recasting the Foucault/Habermas debate.* Cambridge, MA: MIT Press.

Kelly, P. (1992). Special treatment. On *Hidden things.* Melbourne: Mushroom.

Kelman, H. C. (1973). Violence without moral restraint: reflections on the dehumanization of victims and victimizers. *Journal of Social Issues, 29*(4), 25–61.

Kendall, G., & Wickham, G. (1999). *Using Foucault's methods.* London: Sage.

Kent, S. A. (1983). Weber, Goethe, and the Nietzschean allusion: capturing the source of the 'iron cage' metaphor. *Sociological Analysis, 44,* 297–319.

Kesey, K. (1973). *One flew over the cuckoo's nest.* London: Pan.

Klein, N. (2001). *No space, no choice, no jobs, no logo: taking aim at the brand bullies.* New York: Picador.

Knights, D., Noble, F., Vurdubakis, T., & Willmott, H. (2001). Chasing shadows: control, virtuality and the production of trust. *Organization Science, 22*(2), 311–336.

Knights, D., & Vurdubakis, T. (1994). Power, resistance and all that. In J. M. Jermier, D. Knights & W. R. Nord (Eds.), *Resistance and power in organizations* (pp. 167–198). London: Routledge.

Knights, D., & Willmott, H. (1987). Power and subjectivity at work: from degradation to subjugation. *Sociology, 23*(4), 475–483.

Kogut, B., & Zander, U. (1996). What do firms do? Coordination, identity and learning. *Organisation Science, 7,* 502–518.

Kolb, D. (1986). *The critique of pure modernity: Hegel, Heidegger and after.* Chicago: University of Chicago Press.

Kondo, D. (1990). *Crafting selves: power, gender, and discourses of identity in a Japanese workplace.* Chicago: University of Chicago Press.

Kornberger, M., Carter, C., & Clegg, S.R. (2005). Rethinking the polyphonic organization: managing as discursive practice. *Scandinavian Journal of Management.*

Kotz, D. (1978). *Bank control of large corporations in the United States.* Berkeley, CA: University of California Press.

Krackhardt, D. (1990). Assessing the the political landscape: structure, cognition, and power in organizations. *Administrative Science Quarterly, 35,* 342–369.

Kramarae, C., Thorne, B., & Henley, N. (1983). Sex similarities and differences in language, speech and nonverbal communications: an annotated bibliography. In B. Thorne, C. Kramarae & M. Ebben (Eds.), *Language, gender and society.* Rowley, MA: Newbury House.

Kramer, R. M., & Gavrielli, D. A. (2005). Power. In N. Nicholson, P. G. Audia & M. M. Pillutla (Eds.), *The Blackwell encyclopedia of management* (2nd ed.). Organizational behaviour (pp. 321–324). Oxford: Blackwell.

Kropotkin, P. (1898). *Anarchism: its philosophy and ideal.* San Francisco, CA: Free Society.

Kuhn, T. S. (1962). *The structure of scientific revolutions.* Chicago: University of Chicago Press.

Kunda, G. (1992). *Engineering culture.* Cambridge, MA: MIT Press.

Labov, W., & Fanshel, D. (1977). *Therapeutic discourse: psychotherapy as conversation.* New York: Academic.

Laclau, E. (1990). *Reflections on the revolution of our time.* London: Verso.

Laclau, E., & Mouffe, C. (1985). *Hegemony and socialist strategy.* London: Verso.

Lagendijk, A., & Cornford, J. R. (2000). Regional institutions and knowledge: tracking new forms of regional development policy. *Geoforum, 31,* 209–218.

Lakoff, G., & Johnson, M. (1980). *Metaphors we live by.* Chicago: University of Chicago Press.

Lakoff, G., & Johnson, M. (1999). *Philosophy in the flesh: the embodied mind and its challenge in Western thought.* New York: Basic.

Landau, D. (1972). *Political science and political theory.* New York: Macmillan.

Landsberger, H. A. (1958). *Hawthorne revisited: management and the worker, its critics and developments in human relations in Industry.* Ithaca, NY: Cornell University Press.

Lanzmann, C. (Director). (1985). *Shoah.* France: New Yorker Films Video.

Lasch, C. (1991). *The culture of narcissism: American life in an age of diminishing expectations.* New York: Norton.

Lash, S., & Urry, J. (1987). *The end of organized capitalism.* Cambridge: Polity.

Lasswell, T. E. (1965). *Class and stratum: an introduction to concepts and research.* Boston, MA: Houghton Mifflin.

Latimer, J. (2004). Commanding materials: (re)legitimating authority in the context of multi-disciplinary work. *Sociology, 38*(4), 757–775.

Latour, B. (1983). Give me a laboratory and I will raise the world. In K. D. Knorr-Cetina & M. Mulkay (Eds.), *Science observed: perspectives on the social study of science.* London: Sage.

Latour, B. (1987). *Science in action: how to follow scientists and engineers through society.* Cambridge, MA: Harvard University Press.

Latour, B. (1996). *Aramis, or, the love of technology.* Cambridge, MA: Harvard University Press.

Law, J. (1996). Organising accountabilities: ontology and the mode of accounting. In R. Munro & J. Mouritsen (Eds.), *Acccountability: power, ethos and technologies of managing.* London: Thomson.

Law, J. (1999). After ANT: complexity, naming and topology. In J. Law & J. Hassard (Eds.), *Actor network theory and after.* Oxford: Blackwell/The Sociological Review.

Law, J., & Hassard, J. (1999). *Actor network theory and after.* Oxford: Blackwell/The Sociological Review.

Layton, E. T. Jr (1986). *The revolt of the engineers: social responsibility and the American engineering profession.* Baltimore: Johns Hopkins University Press.

Lazega, E. (2000). *The collegial phenomenon.* Oxford: Oxford University Press.

Lee, A. (1980). *Henry Ford and the Jews.* New York: Stein & Day.

Leiser, S., & Backhouse, J. (2003). The circuits-of-power framework for studying power in institutionalization of information systems. *Journal of the Association for Information Systems, 4,* online.

Leventhal, R. S. (1995). Information and technology in the Holocaust. http://jefferson.village.virginia.edu/holocaust/infotech.html.

Levi, P. *Collected poems* (Trans. Ruth Feldman & Brian Swann). London: Faber.

Levin, I. (1999). *The last deposit: Swiss banks and Holocaust victims' accounts* (Trans. N. Dornberg). Westport, CT: Praeger.

Lewin, K. (1950). The consequences of authoritarian and democratic leadership. In A. W. Gouldner (Ed.), *Studies in leadership: leadership and democratic action* (pp. 409–417). New York: Harper.

Linstead, S. (1985). Jokers wild: the importance of humour in the maintenance of organizational culture. *Sociological Review, 33,* 741–767.

Linstead, S., Fulop, L., & Lilley, S. (Eds.). (2004). *Management and organization: a critical text.* London: Palgrave.

Linz, J. J. (1978). Crisis, breakdown and reequilibration. In J. J. Linz & A. C. Stepan (Eds.), *The breakdown of democratic regimes.* Baltimore: Johns Hopkins University Press.

Linz, J. J., & Stepan, A. C. (Eds.). (1978). *The breakdown of democratic regimes.* Baltimore: Johns Hopkins University Press.

Lipset, S. M., Trow, M. A., & Coleman, J. S. (1956). *Union democracy: the internal politics of the International Typographical Union.* Glencoe, IL: Free.

Litterer, J. A. (1959). *The emergence of systematic management as shown by the literature of management from 1870 to 1900.* New York: Garland.

Little, S. E., & Clegg, S. R. (2005). Recovering experience, confirming identity, voicing resistance: the Braceros, the Internet and counter-coordination. *Critical Perspectives on International Business,* special issue on 'The globalisation of labour: counter-coordination and unionism on the Internet', *1*(2/3), 123–136.

Littler, C. R. (1982). *The development of the labour process in capitalist societies: a comparative study of the transformation of work organization in Britain, Japan and the USA.* Aldershot: Gower.

Litwak, E. (1961). Models of organization which permit conflict. *American Journal of Sociology, 67*(September), 177–184.

Locke, J. (1976). *An essay concerning human understanding.* London: Dent.

Loomba, A. (1998). *Colonialism/postcolonialism.* London: Routledge.

Lopes, P. (2005). Signifying deviance and transgression: jazz in the popular imagination. *American Behavioral Scientist, 48*(11), 1468–1481.

Lorraine, K. (2003). The Magdalene Sisters. http://reviewedmovies.com/review.php?reviewID=937, retrieved February 20, 2005.

Lounsbury, M., & Carberry, E. (2004). From king to court jester: Weber's fall from grace in organizational theory. http://64.233.161.104/search?q=cache:o5alMyH9eN8J:www.economyandsociety.org/publications/wp18_Lounsbury-Carberry_04.pdf+Parsons,+ASQ+1956&hl=en&client=firefox-a, retrieved February 20, 2005.

Lucio, M. M. (2000). European works councils and flexible regulation: the politics of intervention. *European Journal of Industrial Relations, 6*(2), 203–216.

Luhmann, N. (1979). *Trust and power: two works by Niklas Luhmann* (Introduction Gianfranco Poggi). London: Wiley.

Luhmann, N. (1986). The autopoiesis of social systems. In F. Geyer & J. van der Zouwen (Eds.), *Sociocybernetic paradoxes* (pp. 172–192). London: Sage.

Luhmann, N. (1995). *Social systems.* Stanford, CA: Stanford University Press.

Lukacs, G. (1968). *History and class consciousness* (Trans. R. Livingstone). London: Merlin.

Lukes, S. (1974). *Power: a radical view.* London: Macmillan.

Lukes, S. (1977). *Essays in social theory.* London: Macmillan.

Lukes, S. (1986). *Power.* Oxford: Blackwell.

Lukes, S. (2005). *Power: a radical view* (2nd ed.). London: Macmillan.

Lycett, M. P., & Paul, R. J. (1999). Information systems development: a perspective on the challenge of evolutionary complexity. *European Journal of Information Systems, 8*(2), 127–135.

Lynch, M. (1982). Technical work and critical inquiry: investigations in a scientific laboratory. *Social Studies of Science, 12,* 499–534.

Lynch, R. A. (1998). Is power all there is? Michel Foucault and the 'omnipresence' of power relations. *Philosophy Today, 42*(1/4), 65.

Lyotard, J. F. (1984). *The postmodern condition: a report on knowledge* (Trans. Geoff Bennington & Brian Massumi). Minneapolis: University of Minnesota Press.

Macherey, P. (1978). *A theory of literary production* (Trans. G. Wall). London: Routledge.

MacIntyre, A. (1971). *Against the self images of the age.* London: Duckworth.

Macintyre, S., & Clark, A. (Eds.). (2003). *The history wars.* Carlton, Vic.: Melbourne University Press.

MacMillan, I. C. (1978). *Strategy formulation: political concepts.* St Paul, MN: West.

Macpherson, C. B. (1962). *The political theory of possessive individualism: Hobbes to Locke.* Oxford: Clarendon.

Madsen, B., & Willert, S. (1996). *Survival in the organization: Gunnar Hjelholt looks back at the concentration camp from an organizational perspective.* Aarhus: Aarhus University Press.

Maguire, S., Phillips, N., & Hardy, C. (2001). When silence = death, keep talking: trust, control and the discursive construction of identity in the Canadian HIV/AIDS treatment domain. *Organisation Studies, 22*(2), 285–310.

Maier, C. S. (1970). Between Taylorism and technocracy: European ideologies and the vision of industrial productivity in the 1920s. *Journal of Contemporary History, 5,* 27–61.

Malarek, V. (2003). *The Natashas: the new global sex trade.* Toronto: Viking.

Malone, T. (2004). *The future of work: how the new order of business will shape your organization, your management style, and your life.* Boston: Harvard Business School Press.

Mandel, M. (1989). *Making good time: Scientific management; The Gilbreths; Photography and motion; Futurism.* Riverside: California Museum of Photography.

Mann, M. (1986). *The sources of social power. Vol. I: A history of power from the beginning to AD 1760.* Cambridge: Cambridge University Press.

Mann, M. (1993). *The sources of social power. Vol. II: The rise of classes and nation states from 1760 to 1914.* Cambridge: Cambridge University Press.

Mant, A. D. (1983). *Leaders we deserve.* Oxford: Robertson.

March, J. G. (1955). An introduction to the theory and measurement of influence. *American Political Science Review, 49,* 431–451.

March, J. G., & Olsen, J. P. (1995). *Democratic governance*. New York: Free.

March, J. G., & Simon, H. A. (1958). *Organizations*. New York: Wiley.

Marcus, A., & Segal, H. P. (1989). *Technology in America*. New York: Harcourt Brace Jovanovich.

Marcuse, H. (1964). *One dimensional man*. Boston, MA: Beacon.

Margolis, J. D., and Walsh, J. P. (2003). Misery loves companies: rethinking social initiatives by business. *Administrative Science Quarterly, 48*, 268–305.

Marks, J. (2000). Foucault, Franks, Gauls: Il faut défendre la société. The 1976 lectures at the Collège de France. *Theory, Culture and Society, 17*(5), 127–147.

Marshall, N., & Rollinson, J. (2004). Maybe Bacon had a point: the politics of interpretation in collective sensemaking. *British Journal of Management, 15*(1), 71–86.

Marshall, T. H., & Bottomore, T. (1992). *Citizenship and social class*. London: Pluto.

Martin, J., & Meyerson, D. (1998). Women and power: conformity, resistance, and disorganized co-action. In R. Kramer & M. Neale (Eds.), *Power and influence in organizations* (pp. 311–348). Thousand Oaks, CA: Sage.

Marx, K. (1976[1887]). *Capital*. Harmondsworth: New Left/Penguin.

Marx, K., & Engels, F. (1998[1847]). *The German ideology: including Theses on Feuerbach and Introduction to the critique of political economy*. Amherst, NY: Prometheus.

Maslow, A. (1962). *Toward a psychology of being*. Princeton, NJ: Van Nostrand.

Maslow, A. H. (1978). A theory of human motivation. In V. H. Vroom & E. L. Deci (Eds.), *Management and motivation* (pp. 27–41). Harmondsworth: Penguin.

Mason, J. (Ed.). (1993). *Child welfare policy: critical Australian perspectives*. Sydney: Hale & Iremonger.

Maturana, H. R., & Varela, F. J. (1980). *Autopoiesis and cognition: the realization of the living* (Preface Sir Stafford Beer). Dordrecht: Reidel.

Maurice, M., Sorge, A., & Warner, M. (1980). Societal differences in organizing manufacturing units: a comparison of France, West Germany and Great Britain. *Organization Studies, 1*, 59–86.

May, J. D. (1965). Democracy, organization, Michels. *The American Political Science Review, 59*(2), 417–429.

May, T. (2001). Power, knowledge and organizational transformation: administration as depoliticization. *Social Epistemology, 15*(3), 171–185.

Mayes, B. T., & Allen, R. W. (1977). Toward a definition of organizational politics. *Academy of Management Review, 2*, 674–678.

Mayo, E. (1922). Industrial unrest and nervous breakdowns. *Industrial Australian and Mining Standard*, 63–64.

Mayo, E. (1933). *The human problems of an industrial civilization*. Cambridge, MA: Harvard University Press.

Mayo, E. (1975). *The social problems of an industrial civilization*. London: Routledge & Kegan Paul.

Mayo, E. (1985). *The psychology of Pierre Janet*. Westport, CT: Greenwood.

McAdam, D. (1982). *Political process and the development of black insurgency, 1930–1970*. Chicago: University of Chicago Press.

McCarthy, T. (1989). *The critical theory of Jürgen Habermas*. Cambridge, MA: MIT Press.

McEwan, I. (2005). *Saturday*. London: Cape.

McFarland, A. (1969). *Power and leadership in pluralist systems*. Stanford, CA: Stanford University Press.

McFate, M. (2005). Anthropology and counterinsurgency: the strange story of their curious relationship. *Military Review*, March–April, 24–38.

McGown, B. R. (1999). *Muslims in the diaspora: the Somali communities of London and Toronto*. Toronto: University of Toronto Press.

McHugh, P. (1968). *Defining the situation: the organization of meaning in social interaction*. Indianapolis: Bobbs-Merrill.

McKinley, A., & Starkey, K. (1997). *Foucault, management and organization theory: from panopticon to technologies of self*. London: Sage.

McNeil, K. (1978). Understanding organizational power: building on the Weberian legacy. *Administrative Science Quarterly, 23*, 66–87.

Mead, G. H. (1934). *Mind, self and society: from the standpoint of a social behaviorist* (Ed. with Introduction Charles W. Morris). Chicago: University of Chicago Press.

Mead, G. H. (1938). *The philosophy of the act* (Ed. Charles W. Morris with J. M. Brewster, A. M. Dunham & D. L. Miller. Chicago: University of Chicago Press.

Mechanic, D. (1962). Sources of power of lower participants in complex organizations. *Administrative Science Quarterly, 7*(3), 349–364.

Meisel, J. H. (1962). *The myth of the ruling class: Gaetano Mosca and the elite.* Ann Arbor, MI: University of Michigan Press.

Merkle, J. (1980). *Management and ideology.* Berkeley, CA: University of California Press.

Merton, R. K., Gray, A., Hockey, B., & Selvin, H. (Eds.). (1952). *Reader in bureaucracy.* New York: Free Press.

Meyer, J. W., & Rowan, B. (1977). Institutionalized organizations: formal structure as myth and ceremony. *American Journal of Sociology, 83,* 340–363.

Meyer, S. (1981). *The five dollar day: labor management and social control in the Ford Motor Company, 1908–1921.* Albany, NY: State University of New York.

Meyerson, D., & Fletcher, J. (2003). A modest manifesto for shattering the glass ceiling. In R. Ely, E. Foldy & M. Scully (Eds.), *Reader in gender, work, and organization* (pp. 230–241). Oxford: Blackwell.

Michels, R. (1915). *Political parties: a sociological study of the oligarchical tendencies of modern democracy.* New York: Free.

Michels, R. (1962). *Political parties: a sociological study of the oligarchical tendencies of modern democracy* (Trans. E. Paul Eden & C. P. Paul, Introduction Seymour Martin Lipset). New York: Collier.

Milgram, S. (1967). The small-world problem. *Psychology Today, 1,* 61–67.

Milgram, S. (1971). *The individual in a social world.* Reading, MA: Addison-Wesley.

Milgram, S. (1974). *Obedience to authority.* New York: Harper-Collins.

Miliband, R. (1969). *The state in capitalist society.* New York: Basic.

Miller, J. (1993). Foucault's politics in biographical perspective. *Salmagundi, 97,* 30–44.

Miller, P. (1987). *Domination and power.* London: Routledge.

Miller, P. (1992). Accounting and objectivity: the invention of calculating selves and calculable spaces. *Annals of Scholarship, 9*(1/2), 61–86.

Mills, A., & Tancred-Sheriff, P. (1992). *Gendering organizational analysis.* Newbury Park, CA: Sage.

Mills, C. W. (1957). *The power elite.* New York: Oxford University Press.

Mills, C. W. (1967). *Power, politics & people: the collected essays of C. Wright Mills.* New York: Oxford University Press.

Mintzberg, H. (1983). *Power in and around organizations.* Englewood Cliffs, NJ: Prentice-Hall.

Mintzberg, H. (1984). Power and organizational life cycles. *Academy of Management Review, 9*(2), 207–224.

Mizruchi, M. S. (1992). *The structure of corporate political action: interfirm relations and their consequences.* Cambridge, MA: Harvard University Press.

Mizruchi, M. S. (1996). What do interlocks do? An analysis, critique and assessment of research on interlocking directorates. *Annual Review of Sociology, 22,* 271–302.

Mizruchi, M. S., & Fein, C. (1999). The social construction of organizational knowledge: a study of the uses of coercive, mimetic, and normative isomorphism. *Administrative Science Quarterly, 44,* 653–683.

Mol, A. (1999). Ontological politics: a word and some questions. In L. J. Hassard & J. Hassard (Eds.), *Actor network theory and after* (pp. 75–89). Oxford: Blackwell.

Molotch, H., & Boden, D. (1985). Talking social structure: discourse, dominance and the Watergate hearings. *American Sociological Review, 50,* 273–288.

Monbiot, G. (2000). *Captive state: the corporate takeover of Britain.* London: Macmillan.

Montesquieu, C. (1989). *The spirit of the laws.* Cambridge: Cambridge University Press.

Moore, M. (Director). (1989/2003). *Roger and me.* Hollywood: Warner Home Video (cinema 1989, DVD 2003).

Morgan, G., & Sturdy, A. (2000). *Beyond organizational change: structure, discourse and power in UK financial services.* London: Macmillan.

Morriss, P. (2002). *Power: a philosophical analysis.* Manchester: Manchester University Press.

Morrow, R. (1994). *Critical theory and methodology.* Thousand Oaks, CA: Sage.

Mosca, G. (1939). *The ruling class: elements of political science* (1896). New York: McGraw-Hill.

Moscovici, S., & Faucheux, C. (1972). Social influence, conformity bias, and the study of active minorities. In L. Berkowitz (Ed.), *Advances in experimental social psychology* (Vol. 6, pp. 149–202). New York: Academic.

Mosse, G. (1978). *Toward the final solution.* London: Dent.

Mouffe, C. (2000). *The democratic paradox.* New York: Verso.

Muir, J. (2004). Public participation in area-based urban regeneration programmes. *Housing Studies, 19*(6), 947–966.

Mullan, P. (Director). (2004). *The Magdalene sisters.* London: PFP Films.

Mumby, D. K. (1992). Two discourses on communication, power, and the subject: Jurgen Habermas and Michel Foucault. In G. Levine (Ed.), *Constructions of the self* (pp. 81–104). New Brunswick, NJ: Rutgers University Press.

Mumby, D. (2001). Power and politics. In F. Jablin & L. Putnam (Eds.), *The new handbook of organizational communication* (pp. 585–623). Thousand Oaks, CA: Sage.

Mumby, D. (2004). Discourse, power and ideology: unpacking the critical approach. In D. Grant, C. Hardy, C. Oswick & L. Putnam (Eds.), *Handbook of organizational discourse* (pp. 237–258). London: Sage.

Mumby, D., & Clair, R. (1997). Organizational discourse. In T. A. van Dijk (Ed.), *Discourse studies. Vol. 2: Discourse as social interaction* (pp. 180–205). London: Sage.

Munro, I. (1992). Codes of ethics: some uses and abuses. In P. Davies (Ed.), *Current issues in business ethics* (pp. 97–106). London: Routledge.

Munro, R. (1999). Power and discretion: membership work in the time of technology. *Organization, 7*(3), 429–450.

Münsterberg, H. (1913). *Psychology and industrial efficiency.* Boston, MA: Houghton Mifflin.

Nafziger, E. (1988). *Inequality in Africa: political elites, proletariat, peasants and the poor.* Cambridge: Cambridge University Press.

Nahapiet, J., & Ghoshal, S. (1998). Social capital, intellectual capital and the organisation advantage. *Academy of Management Review, 23*(2), 2–266.

Nahirny, V. C. (1962). Some observations on ideological groups. *American Journal of Sociology, 67,* 397–405.

Namaste, K. (1996). The politics of inside/out: queer theory, post-structuralism and a sociological approach to sexuality. In S. Seidman (Ed.), *Queer theory/sociology.* Oxford: Blackwell.

Narayanan, V. K., & Fahey, L. (1982). The micro-politics of strategy formulation. *Academy of Management Review, 7*(1), 25–34.

Nelson, D. (1975). *Managers and workers: origins of the new factory system in the United States, 1880–1920.* Madison, WI: University of Wisconsin Press.

Nelson, D. (1980). *Frederick W. Taylor and the rise of scientific management.* Madison, WI: University of Wisconsin Press.

Nelson, D., & Campbell, S. (1972). Taylorism versus welfare work in American industry: H. L. Gantt and the Bancrofts. *Business History Review, 46*(1), 1–16.

Nelson, R. R., & Winter, S. G. (1982). *An evolutionary theory of economic change.* Cambridge, MA: Harvard University Press, Belknap Press.

Neu, D. (2003). Accounting for the banal: financial techniques as softwares of colonialism. In A. Prasad (Ed.), *Postcolonial theory and organizational analysis: a critical engagement* (pp. 193–212). New York: Palgrave Macmillan.

Newton, T. (1996). Agency and discourse: recruiting consultants in a life insurance company. *Sociology, 30*(4).

Nicoll, A. (Director). (1997). *Gattaca.* USA: Sony.

Nietzsche, F. W. (1967). *On the genealogy of morals* (Trans. W. Kaufmann & R. J. Hollingdale). New York: Vintage.

Nietzsche, F. W. (1968). *The will to power.* London: Weidenfeld & Nicolson.

Nietzsche, F. W. (1973). *Beyond good and evil* (Trans. R. J. Hollingdale). Harmondsworth: Penguin.

Nisbet, R. A. (1993). *The sociological tradition.* New Brunswick, NJ: Transaction.

Nonaka, I., & Takeuchi, H. (1995). *The knowledge creating company.* Oxford: Oxford University Press.

Nugent, P. (2004). *Africa since independence: a comparative history.* London: Palgrave.

Nyl, C. (1995). Taylorism and hours of work. *Journal of Management History, 1*(2), 8–25.

Ocasio, W. (1994). Political dynamics and the circulation of power: CEO succession in US industrial corporations 1960–1990. *Administrative Science Quarterly, 39,* 285–312.

Ocasio, W., & Kim, H. (1999). The circulation of corporate control: selection of functional backgrounds of new CEOs in large U.S. manufacturing firms, 1981–1992. *Administrative Science Quarterly, 44,* 532–562.

O'Connor, E. S. (1999). The politics of management thought: a case study of Harvard Business School and the Human Relations School. *Academy of Management Review, 24*(1), 117–131.

Ogilvy, J. (1977). *Many dimensional man: decentralizing self, society and the sacred.* Oxford: Oxford University Press.

O'Neill, J. (1986). The disciplinary society: from Weber to Foucault. *British Journal of Sociology, 37*(1), 42–61.

Orly, B., & Goclaw, R. (2005). Narrating the power of non-standard employment: the case of the Israeli public sector. *Journal of Management Studies, 42*(4), 737–760.

Orssatto, R. J., & Clegg, S. R. (1999). The political ecology of organizations: toward a framework for analyzing business–environment relations. *Organization and Environment, 12,* 263–279.

Orssatto, R., den Hond, F., & Clegg, S. R. (2002). The political ecology of automobile recycling in Europe. *Organization Studies, 23*(4), 639–666.

Osborne, D., & Gaebler, T. (1992). *Reinventing government: how the entrepreneurial spirit is transforming the public sector.* Reading, MA: Addison-Wesley.

O'Shea, A. (2002). Desiring desire: how desire makes us human, all too human. *Sociology, 26*(11), 925–940.

Oswick, C., & Richards, D. (2004). Talk in organizations: local conversations, wider perspectives. *Culture and Organization, 10*(2), 107–123.

O'Toole, P. (1997). Treating networks seriously: practical and research-based agendas in public administration. *Public Administration Review, 57*(1), 45–52.

Palmer, B. (1975). Class, conception and conflict: the thrust for efficiency, managerial views of labor and the working class rebellion, 1903–22. *Review of Radical Political Economics, 7*(2), 31–49.

Palmer, D., & Barber, N. (2001). Challengers, elites, and owning families: a social class theory of corporate acquisitions in the 1960s. *Administrative Science Quarterly, 46*(1), 87–120.

Pareto, V. (1916). *Trattato di sociologia generale.* Florence: Barbèra.

Pareto, V. (1935). *The mind and society* (Trans. A. Bongiomo). New York: Harcourt, Brace.

Pareto, V. (1971). *Manual of political economy* (Trans. A. S. Schwier). New York: Kelley.

Parker, I. (1992). *Discourse dynamics.* London: Routledge.

Parker, M. (2002). Queering management and organization. *Gender, Work and Organization, 9*(2), 146–166.

Parsons, T. (1937). *The structure of social action: a study in social theory with special reference to a group of recent European writers.* New York: Free.

Parsons, T. (1950). *The social system.* New York: Free.

Parsons, T. (1956). Suggestions for a sociological approach to the theory of organizations I, II. *Administrative Science Quarterly, 1,* 63–85, 223–239. Reprinted in S. R. Clegg (Ed.) (2002), *Central currents in organization studies I: frameworks and applications* (Vol. 1, pp. 24–64). London: Sage.

Parsons, T. (1963). On the concept of influence. *Public Opinion Quarterly, 27*(1), 37.

Parsons, T. (1964). *Essays in sociological theory*. New York: Free.

Parsons, T. (1975). On 'de-Parsonizing' Weber (comment on Cohen et al.). *American Sociological Review, 40*, 666–670.

Peaucelle, J. L. (2000). From Taylorism to post-Taylorism: simultaneously pursuing several management objectives. *Journal of Organizational Change Management, 13*(5), 452–467.

Peltonen, T., & Tikkanen, H. (2005). Productive power, organized markets and actor-network theory. In B. Czarniawska & T. Hernes (Eds.), *Actor network theory and organizing* (pp. 268–284). Oslo/Copenhagen: Liber and Copenhagen Business School Press.

Pennings, H., Hickson, D. J., Hinings, C. R., Lee, C. A., & Schneck, R. E. (1969). Uncertainty and power in organizations: a strategic contingencies model of sub-unit functioning. *Mens en Maatscappij, 23*.

Perez, C. (1983). Structural change and assimilation of new technologies in the economic and social systems. *Futures*, October, 357–375.

Perrow, C. (1986a). *Complex organizations: a critical essay*. Glenview, IL: Scott, Foresman.

Perrow, C. (1986b). Economic theories of organization. *Theory and Society, 15*, 11–45.

Perrow, C. (2002). *Organizing America: wealth, power, and the origins of corporate capitalism*. Princeton: Princeton University Press.

Perrucci, P., & Pilisuk, M. (1970). Leaders and ruling elites: the interorganizational bases of community power. *American Sociological Review, 35*, 1040–1057.

Peters, T. (1987). *Thriving on chaos: handbook for a management revolution*. New York: Knopf.

Peters, T. (1992). *Liberation management: necessary disorganization for the nanosecond nineties*. London: Macmillan.

Peters, T., & Waterman, R. (1982). *In search of excellence*. New York: Harper & Row.

Pettigrew, A. M. (1973). *The politics of organizational decision making*. London: Tavistock.

Pettigrew, A. M. (1985). *The awakening giant: continuity and change in imperial chemical industries*. Oxford: Blackwell.

Pettigrew, A. M. (1992). On studying managerial elites. *Strategic Management Journal, 13*, 163–182.

Pettigrew, A. M. (2002). Strategy formulation as a political process. In S. R. Clegg (Ed.), *Central currents in organization studies II: contemporary trends* (Vol. 5, pp. 43–49). London: Sage.

Pfeffer, J. (1981). *Power in organizations*. Marshfield, MA: Pitman.

Pfeffer, J. (1992). Understanding power in organizations. *California Management Review, 35*, 29–50.

Pfeffer, J. (1993). Barriers to the advance of organizational science: paradigm development as a dependent variable. *Academy of Management Review, 18*, 599–620.

Pfeffer, J. (1995). Mortality, reproducibility, and the persistence of styles of theory. *Organization Science, 13*, 681–686.

Pfeffer, J., & Salancik, G. (1974). Organizational decision making as a political process. *Administrative Science Quarterly, 19*, 135–151.

Pfeffer, J., & Salancik, G. (1978). *The external control of organisations: a resource dependence perspective*. New York: Harper & Row.

Pfeffer, J., & Salancik, G. (2002). The bases and uses of power in organizational decision making: the case of a university. In S. R. Clegg (Ed.), *Central currents in organization studies II: contemporary trends* (Vol. 5, pp. 21–42). London: Sage.

Phillips, N. (1995). Telling organizational tales: on the role of narrative fiction in organizational analysis. *Organization Studies, 16*(4), 625–649.

Phillips, N., & Brown, J. (1993). Analyzing communication in and around organizations: a critical hermeneutic approach. *The Academy of Management Journal, 36*(6), 1547–1576.

Phillips, N., & Hardy, C. (1997). Managing multiple identities: discourse, legitimacy and resources in the UK refugee system. *Organization, 4*(2), 159–186.

Phillips, N., & Hardy, C. (2002). *Understanding discourse analysis*. Thousand Oaks, CA: Sage.

Pilger, J. (1999). *Hidden agendas*. New York: Vintage.

Pitkin, H. F. (1972). *Wittgenstein and justice: on the significance of Ludwig Wittgenstein for social and political thought*. Berkeley, CA: University of California Press.

Pitsis, T., Clegg, S. R., Marosszeky, M., & Rura-Polley, T. (2003). Constructing the Olympic dream: managing innovation through the future perfect. *Organization Science, 14*(5), 574–590.

Plamenatz, J. (1949). *Mills' utilitarianism.* Oxford: Blackwell.

Poovey, M. (1995). *Making a social body.* Chicago: University of Chicago Press.

Popper, K. R. (1965). *Conjectures and refutations: the growth of scientific knowledge.* New York: Basic.

Porter, E. (2002). *What is this thing called jazz? African American musicians as artists, critics, and activists.* Berkeley, CA: University of California Press.

Potter, J., & Wetherell, M. (1987). *Discourse and social psychology: beyond attitudes and behaviour.* London: Sage.

Poulantzas, N. (1973). *Political power and social classes* (Trans. T. O'Hagan). London: NLB.

Poulantzas, N. (1978). *State, power, socialism* (Trans. P. Camiller). London: NLB.

Power, M. (1997). *The audit society: rituals of verification.* Oxford: Oxford University Press.

Prasad, A. (Ed.). (2003). *Postcolonial theory and organizational analysis: a critical engagement.* New York: Palgrave Macmillan.

Prasad, P., & Eylon, D. (2001). Narrating past traditions of participation and inclusion: historical perspectives on workplace empowerment. *The Journal of Applied Behavioral Science, 37*, 5–14.

Pred, A. (1977). The choreography of existence: comments on Hagerstrand's time geography and its usefulness. *Economic Geography, 53*, 207–221.

Price, B. (1992). Frank and Lillian Gilbreth and the motion study controversy, 1907–1930. In D. Nelson (Ed.), *A mental revolution: scientific management since Taylor* (pp. 58–76). Columbus, OH: Ohio State University Press.

Probyn, E. (2005). Sex and power: capillaries, capabilities and capacities. In C. Calhoun, C. Rojeck & B. S. Turner (Eds.), *The Sage handbook of sociology* (pp. 516–529). Thousand Oaks, CA: Sage.

Przeworski, A. (1985). *Capitalism and social democracy.* New York: Cambridge University Press.

Psathas, G. (1995). *Conversation analysis.* Thousand Oaks, CA: Sage.

Pugh, D. S. (Ed.). (1971). *Organization theory: selected readings.* Harmondsworth: Penguin.

Pugh, D. S., & Hickson, D. J. (Eds.). (1976). *Organizational structure in its context: the Aston Programme 1.* London: Saxon.

Pugh, D. S., Hickson, D. J., & Hinings, C. R. (1971). *Writers on organizations.* Harmondsworth: Penguin.

Putnam, L., & Fairhurst, G. (2001). Discourse analysis in organizations: issues and concerns. In F. M. Jablin & L. Putnam (Eds.), *The new handbook of organizational communication: advances in theory, research and methods* (pp. 235–268). Newbury Park, CA: Sage.

Putnam, R. D. (1976). *The comparative study of political elites.* Englewood Cliffs, NJ: Prentice-Hall.

Putnam, R. D. (1993). The prosperous community: social capital and public life. *American Prospect, 13*, 35–42.

Putnam, R. D. (1995). Bowling alone: America's declining social capital. *Journal of Democracy, 6*, 65–78.

Raab, J. (2003). More than just a metaphor: the network concept and its potential in Holocaust research. In G. D. Feldman & W. Seibel (Eds.), *Networks of Nazi persecution: division of labor in implementing the Holocaust.* London: Berghahn.

Rabinow, P. (Ed.). (1984). *The Foucault reader.* Hamondsworth: Penguin.

Ransom, S., & Stewart, J. (1994). *Management for the public domain: enabling the learning society.* New York: St Martin's.

Reed, M. (1985). *Redirections in organizational analysis.* London: Tavistock.

Reed, M. (1998). Organizational analysis as discourse analysis: a critique. In T. Grant & C. Oswick (Eds.), *Discourse and organization* (pp. 193–213). London: Sage.

Reed, M. (2001). Organization, trust and control: a realist analysis. *Organization Studies, 22*(2), 201–228.

Reed, M. (2004). Getting real about organizational discourse. In D. Grant, C. Hardy, C. Oswick, & L. Putnam (Eds.), *Handbook of organizational discourse.* London: Sage.

Rees, S., & Rodley, G. (1995). *The human costs of managerialism: advocating the recovery of humanity.* Leichhardt: Pluto.

Reynolds, H. (1990). *The other side of the frontier: Aboriginal resistance to the European invasion of Australia* (Foreword C.D. Rowley). Ringwood, Vic.: Penguin.

Rhodes, C. (2001). D'oh: The Simpsons, popular culture and the organizational carnival. *Journal of Management Inquiry, 10*(4), 374–383.

Ritzer, G. (1992). *Sociological theory.* New York: McGraw-Hill.

Ritzer, G. (1993). *The McDonaldization of society.* Thousand Oaks, CA: Pine Forge.

Ritzer, G. (2004). *The globalization of nothing.* Thousand Oaks, CA: Pine Forge.

Robbins, S. P., & De Cenzo, D. A. (2005). *Fundamentals of management.* New York: Prentice-Hall.

Roberts, J. (2003). The manufacture of corporate social responsibility: constructing corporate sensibility. *Organization, 10*(2), 249–265.

Rodrigues, S., & Child, J. (2003). Co-evolution in an institutionalized environment. *Journal of Management Studies, 40*(8), 21–37.

Roe, M. J. (1994). *Strong managers, weak owners: the political roots of American corporate finance.* Princeton, NJ: Princeton University Press.

Roethlisberger, F. J., & Dickson, W. J. (1939). *Management and the worker: an account of a research program conducted by the Western Electric Company, Hawthorne Works, Chicago* (assistance and collaboration H. A. Wright). Cambridge, MA: Harvard University Press.

Roman, C., Juhasz, S., & Miller, C. (Eds.). (1994). *The women and language debate: a sourcebook.* New Brunswick, NJ: Rutgers University Press.

Rook, D. (1987). The buying impulse. *Journal of Consumer Research, 14*(9), 189–199.

Roper, L. (1994). *Oedipus and the devil: witchcraft, sexuality, and religion in early modern Europe.* London: Routledge.

Rose, A. M. (1967). *The power structure,* New York: Oxford University Press.

Rose, N. (1989). *Governing the soul.* London: Routledge.

Rose, N. (1991). Governing by numbers: figuring out democracy. *Accounting, Organizations and Society, 16*(7), 673–697.

Rose, N. (1996). *Inventing our selves: psychology, power, and personhood.* Cambridge: Cambridge University Press.

Rose, N. (1999). *Powers of freedom.* Cambridge: Cambridge University Press.

Rosen, M., Orlikowski, W. J., & Schmahmann, K. S. (1990). Building buildings and living lives: a critique of bureaucracy, ideology and concrete artifacts. In P. Gagliardi (Ed.), *Symbols and artifacts: views of the corporate landscape* (pp. 69–84). Berlin: de Gruyter.

Rosenfeld, P., Giacolone, R. A., & Riordan, C. A. (1995). *Impression management in organizations: theory, measurement, practice.* London: Routledge.

Rothschild-Whitt, J. (1979). Collectivist organization: alternative to rational-bureaucratic models. *American Sociological Review, 44,* 509–527.

Roudinesco, E. (1999). *Jacques Lacan* (Trans. Barbara Bray). New York: Columbia University Press.

Roy, D. (1958). Banana time: job satisfaction and informal interaction. *Human Organization, 18,* 158–168.

Ryan, K. (2004). *Social exclusion and the politics of order in modern Ireland: from panopticism to inclusive governance.* Unpublished PhD, Department of Political Science and Sociology, National University of Ireland, Galway.

Sacks, H. (1972). An initial investigation of the usability of conversational data for doing sociology. In D. Sudnow (Ed.), *Studies in social interaction* (pp. 31–74). New York: Free.

Sacks, H. (1992). *Lectures on conversations* (Vol. 1). Oxford: Blackwell.

Said, E. W. (1979). *Orientalism.* New York: Vintage.

Said, E. W. (1993). *Culture and imperialism.* London: Chatto & Windus.

Salancik, G., & Pfeffer, J. (1974). The bases and use of power in organizational decision making. *Administrative Science Quarterly, 19,* 453–473.

Salzer-Morling, M. (1998). As God created the earth: a saga that makes sense? In D. Grant, T. Keenoy & C. Oswick (Eds.), *Discourse and organization* (pp. 104–118). London: Sage.

Satow, R. L. (1975). Value-rational authority and professional organizations: Weber's missing type. *Administrative Science Quarterly, 20,* 526–531.

Sawaki, J. (1991). *Disciplining Foucault: feminism, power, and the body*. New York: Routledge.

Sayer, D. (1991). *Capitalism and modernity: an excursus on Marx and Weber*. London: Routledge.

Scarborough, H., & Burrell, G. (1996). The axeman cometh: the changing roles and knowledges of middle managers. In S. R. Clegg & G. Palmer (Eds.), *The politics of management knowledge* (pp. 173–189). London: Sage.

Schattschneider, E. E. (1960). *The semi-sovereign people: a realist's view of democracy in America*. New York: Holt, Rinehart & Winston.

Schils, E. A. (1956). *The torment of secrecy*. London: Heinemann.

Schlosser, E. (2001). *Fast food nation: what the all-American meal is doing to the world*. Harmondsworth: Penguin.

Schreurs, P. (2000). *Enchanting rationality: an analysis of rationality in the Anglo-American discourse on public organization*. Delft: Uitgereverji Eburon.

Schroeder, R. (1987). Nietzsche and Weber: two 'prophets' of the modern world. In S. Lash & S. Whimster (Eds.), *Max Weber, rationality and modernity* (pp. 207–221). London: Allen & Unwin.

Schudson, M. (1984). *Advertising: the uneasy persuasion*. New York: Basic.

Schutz, A. (1967). *The phenomenology of the social world*. Evanston, IL: Northwestern University Press.

Schwenk, C. R. (1989). Linking cognitive, organizational and political factors in explaining strategic change. *Journal of Management Studies, 26*(2), 177–188.

Scott, J. (1990). *Domination and the arts of resistance: hidden transcripts*. New Haven, CT: Yale University Press.

Scott, J. (Ed.). (1994). *Power: critical concepts*. London: Routledge.

Scott, R. (Director). (1982). *Blade runner*. United States: Warner.

Scott, W. D. (1911). *Increasing human efficiency in business: a contribution to the psychology of business*. New York: Macmillan.

Scott, W. R. (1987a). *Organizations: rational, natural, and open systems*. Englewood Cliffs, NJ: Prentice-Hall.

Scott, W. R. (1987b). The adolescence of institutional theory. *Administrative Science Quarterly, 32*, 493–511.

Sedgwick, E. K. (1994). *Tendencies*. London: Routledge.

Seibel, W. (2002). The strength of perpetrators: the Holocaust in Western Europe, 1940–1944. *Governance, 15*(2), 211–240.

Selznick, P. (1949). *TVA and the grass roots: a study in the sociology of formal organization*. Berkeley, CA: University of California Press.

Selznick, P. (1957). *Leadership in administration: a sociological interpretation*. Evanston, IL: Harper & Row.

Selznick, P. (1992). *The moral commonwealth: social theory and the promise of community*. Berkeley, CA: University of California Press.

Sewell, G. (1998). The discipline of teams: the control of team-based industrial work through electronic and peer surveillance. *Administrative Science Quarterly, 43*, 397–428.

Shenhav, Y. (1999). *Manufacturing rationality: the engineering foundations of the managerial revolution*. Oxford: Oxford University Press.

Sica, A. (1988). *Weber, irrationality, and social order*. Berkeley, CA: University of California Press.

Silverman, D. (1970). *The theory of organization*. London: Heinemann.

Silverman, D. (1974). Accounts of organizations. In J. McKinlay (Ed.), *Processing people*. New York: Holt, Rinehart, Winston.

Silverman, D. (1993). *Interpreting qualitative data*. London: Sage.

Simmel, G. (1950). *The sociology of Georg Simmel* (Trans. & Ed. Kurt H. Wolff). Glencoe, IL: Free.

Simmel, G. (1964). *Conflict and the web of group affiliations* (Trans. K. H. Wolff & R. Bendix). New York: Free.

Simmel, G. (1971). *On individuality and social forms: selected writings*. Chicago: University of Chicago Press.

Simon, H. A. (1957). *Models of man.* New York: Wiley.

Simon, H. A. (1976). *Administrative behavior: a study of decision-making processes in administrative organization* (3rd ed.) (Foreword Chester I. Barnard). New York: Free.

Sims, R., & Brinkmann, J. (2003). Enron ethics (or: Culture matters more than codes). *Journal of Business Ethics, 45,* 243–256.

Sinclair, J., & Coulthard, M. (1975). *Towards an analysis of discourse: the English used by teachers and pupils.* Oxford: Oxford University.

Sinclair, U. (1906). *The jungle.* New York: Doubleday, Page.

Smith, M. (2002). The 'ethical' space of the abattoir: on the (in)human(e) slaughter of other animals. *Human Ecology Forum, 9*(2), 49–58.

Solzhenitsyn, A. I., & Parker, R. (1963). *One day in the life of Ivan Denisovich.* Harmondsworth: Penguin.

Solzhenitsyn, A. I., & Whitney, T. P. (1995). *The Gulag archipelago, 1918–1956: an experiment in literary investigation.* London: Harvill.

Sorenson, O. (2005). Complexity theory. In N. Nicholson, P. G. Audia & M. M. Pillutla (Eds.), *The Blackwell encyclopedia of management* (2nd ed.). Organizational behaviour (pp. 56–57). Oxford: Blackwell.

Sorge, A. (1991). Fit and the societal effect: interpreting cross-national comparisons of technology, organization and human resources. *Organization Studies, 12,* 161–190.

Sorokin, P. (1925). American millionaires and multimillionaires: a comparative statistical study. *Journal of Social Forces, 3*(4), 627–640.

Spender, D. (1980). *Man made language.* London: Routledge & Kegan Paul.

Spender, J. C., & Kijne, H. J. (Eds.). (1996). *Scientific management: Frederick Winslow Taylor's gift to the world?* Boston: Kluwer.

Spielberg, S. (Director). (1993). *Schindler's list.* United States: Universal.

Sprague, R. H., & McNurlin, B. C. (1986). *Information systems management in practice* (2nd ed.). London: Prentice-Hall.

Sprague, R. H., & McNurlin, B. C. (1997). *Information systems management in practice* (4th ed.). London: Prentice-Hall.

Spybey, T. (1984). Traditional and professional frames of meaning in management. *Sociology, 18,* 550–562.

Stark, D. (2002). Class struggle and the transformation of the labour process: a relational approach. In S. R. Clegg (Ed.), *Central currents in organization studies I: frameworks and applications* (Vol. 1, pp. 84–119). London: Sage. Originally published in *Theory and Society,* 1980, *9*(2), 89–130.

Starkey, K., & McKinlay, A. (1998). *Foucault, management and organization theory: from panopticon to technologies of self.* London: Sage.

Steffy, B., & Grimes, A. (1986). A critical theory of organizational science. *Academy of Management Review, 11*(2), 322–336.

Stokes, J., & Clegg, S. R. (2002). Once upon a time in a bureaucracy. *Organization, 9*(2), 225–448.

Suchman, M. (1995). Managing legitimacy: strategic and institutional approaches. *Academy of Management Review, 20*(3), 571–610.

Suddaby, R., & Greenwood, R. (2005). Rhetorical strategies of legitimacy. *Administrative Science Quarterly, 50,* 35–67.

Sudnow, D. (1972). *Studies in social interaction.* New York: Free.

Swedberg, R. (1998). *Max Weber and the idea of economic sociology.* Princeton, NJ: Princeton University Press.

Szakolczai, A. (1998). *Max Weber and Michel Foucault: parallel life-works.* London: Routledge.

Tannen, D. (1990). *You just don't understand: women and men in conversation.* New York: Morrow.

Tannen, D. (1994). *Talking from 9 to 5: how women's and men's conversational styles affect who gets heard, who gets credit, and what gets done at work.* New York: Morrow.

Tantoush, T., Clegg, S. R., & Wilson, F. (2001). CADCAM integration and the practical politics of technological change. *Journal of Organizational Change Management, 14*(1), 9–27.

Taylor, F. W. (1911). *Principles of scientific management*. New York: Harper.

Taylor, M., & Hallsworth, A. (2000). Power relations and market transformation in the transport sector: the example of the courier services industry. *Journal of Transport Geography, 8*, 237–247.

Teece, D. J., Pisano, G., & Shuen, A. (1997). Dynamic capabilities and strategic management. *Strategic Management Journal, 18*(7), 509–533.

Temin, P. (1999). The American business elite in historical perspective. In E. S. Brezis & P. Temin (Eds.), *Elites, minorities and economic growth* (pp. 19–40). New York: Elsevier, North Holland.

Therborn, G. (1976). *Science, class and society*. London: NLB.

Thomas, P. (2003). The recontextualization of management: a discourse-based approach to analysing the development of management thinking. *Journal of Management Studies, 40*(4), 775–799.

Thomas, W. I. (1923). *The unadjusted girl*. Boston: Little, Brown.

Thompson, E. P. (1967). Time, work-discipline, and industrial capitalism. *Past and Present, 38*, 56–97.

Thompson, E. P. (1968). *The making of the English working class* (rev. ed.). Harmondsworth: Penguin.

Thompson, E. P. (1970). *Warwick University Ltd: industry, management and the universities*. Harmondsworth: Penguin.

Thompson, J. D. (1956a). On building an administrative science. *Administrative Science Quarterly, 1*, 102–111.

Thompson, J. D. (1956b). Authority and power in identical organizations. *American Journal of Sociology, 62*, 290–301.

Thompson, J. D. (1967). *Organizations in action: social science bases of administrative theory*. New York: McGraw-Hill.

Thompson, P. (1990). Crawling from the wreckage: the labour process and the politics of production. In D. Knights & H. Willmott (Eds.), *Labour process theory*. London: Macmillan.

Thompson, P. (1993). Postmodernism: fatal distraction. In J. Hassard & M. Parker (Eds.), *Postmodernism and Organizations*. London: Sage.

Thompson, P. (2005). Brands, boundaries, and bandwagons: a critical reflection on critical management studies. In C. Grey & H. Willmott (Eds.), *Critical management studies: a reader*. Oxford: Oxford University.

Thompson, P., & Ackroyd, S. (1995). All quiet on the workplace front? A critique of recent trends in British industrial sociology. *Sociology, 59*(4), 615–633.

Thompson, P., & Ackroyd, S. (1999). *Organizational misbehaviour*. London: Sage.

Thompson, P., & McHugh, D. (2002). *Work organisations* (3rd ed.). London: Palgrave.

Thompson, P., & Warhurst, C. (Eds.). (1998). *Workplaces of the future*. London: Macmillan.

Thorne, B., Kramarae, C., & Ebben, M. (1983). *Language, gender and society*. Rowley, MA: Newbury House.

Thorne, L., & Saunders, S. B. (2002). The socio-cultural embeddedness of individuals' ethical reasoning in organizations. *California Management Review, 44*(3), 37–54.

Tilly, C. (1978). *From mobilization to revolution*. New York: Random.

Tilly, C. (1991). Domination, resistance, compliance ... discourse. *Sociological Forum, 6*(3), 593–602.

Ting-Toomey, S. (1985). Toward a theory of conflict and culture. In W. Gudykynst, L. P. Stewart & S. Ting-Toomey (Eds.), *Communication and culture* (pp. 71–85). Beverley Hills, CA: Sage.

Tinker, T. (Ed.). (1985). *Paper prophets*. New York: Holt, Rinehart & Winston.

Tocqueville, A. (1945). *Democracy in America* (1835) (Ed. P. Bradley, Trans. H. Reeve). New York: Knopf.

Tocqueville, A. (2000). *Democracy in America* (Trans. Harvey C. Mansfield & Delba Winthrop). Chicago: University of Chicago Press.

Townley, B. (1994). *Reframing human resource management: power, ethics and the subject at work*. London: Sage.

Townley, B. (1998). Beyond good and evil: depth and division in the management of human resources. In A. McKinlay & K. Starkey (Eds.), *Foucault, management and organization theory: from panopticon to technologies of self* (pp. 191–210). London: Sage.

Townshend, J. (2004). Laclau and Mouffe's hegemonic project: the story so far. *Political Studies*, *52*(2), 269–288.

Trahair, R. (2001). George Elton Mayo. In *Biographical dictionary of management* (p. 326). Bristol: Thoemmes.

Tressel, R. (1969[1914]). *The ragged trousered philanthropists*. London: Lawrence & Wishart.

Tribe, K. (1983). Prussian agriculture – German politics: Max Weber 1892–97. *Economy and Society*, *12*, 181–226.

Turner, B. S. (1984). *The body and social theory*. Oxford: Blackwell.

Turner, R. (1960). Sponsored and contest mobility and the school system. *American Sociological Review*, *25*, 855–867.

Üsdiken, B., & Pasadeos, Y. (1995). Organizational analysis in North America and Europe: a comparison of co-citation networks. *Organization Studies*, *16*, 503–526.

Useem, M. (1984). *The inner circle: large corporations and the rise of business political activity in the US and UK*. New York: Oxford University Press.

Vaara, E., Kleymann, B., & Serist, H. (2004). Strategies as discursive constructions: the case of airline alliances. *Journal of Management Studies*, *41*(1), 1–35.

Vaara, E., Tienari, J., Piekkari, R., & Santti, R. (2005). Language and the circuits of power in a merging multinational corporation. *Journal of Management Studies*, *42*(3), 595–623.

Vallas, S. P. (1991). Workers, firms, and the dominant ideology: hegemony and consciousness in the monopoly core. *Sociological Quarterly*, *32*, 61–83.

van Krieken, R. (1990). The organisation of the soul: Elias and Foucault on discipline and the self. *Archives Europeénes de Sociologie*, *31*(2), 353–371.

van Krieken, R. (1992). *Children and the state: social control and the formation of Australian child welfare*. Sydney: Allen & Unwin.

van Krieken, R. (1996). Proto-governmentalization and the historical formation of organizational subjectivity. *Economy and Society*, *25*(2), 195–221.

van Maanen, J. (1995). Fear and loathing in organization studies. *Organization Science*, *6*, 687–692.

Vincent, I. (1997). *Hitler's silent partners: Swiss banks, Nazi gold, and the pursuit of justice*. New York: Morrow.

Wacquant, L. J. D. (1993). Bourdieu in America: notes on the transatlantic importation of social theory. In C. Calhoun, E. LiPuma & M. Postone (Eds.), *Bourdieu: critical perspectives* (pp. 235–262). Cambridge: Polity.

Waters, M. (1989). Collegiality, bureaucratization and professionalization: a Weberian analysis. *American Journal of Sociology*, *3*, 271–278.

Waters, M. (1993). Alternative organizational formations: a neo Weberian typology of polycratic administrative systems. *The Sociological Review*, 54–81.

Watson, T. J. (1982). Group ideologies and organizational change. *Journal of Management Studies*, *19*(3), 259–275.

Watson, T. J., & Bargiela-Chiappina, F. (1998). Managerial sensemaking and occupational identities in Britain and Italy: the role of management magazines in the process of discursive construction. *Journal of Management Studies*, *35*(3), 285–301.

Watts, D. J. (1999). 'Networks, Dynamics, and the Small-World Phenomenon. *American Journal of Sociology*, *105*(2), 493–527.

Watts, S. L. (1991). *Order against chaos: business culture and labor ideology in America 1880–1915*. New York: Greenwood.

Weber, M. (1919a/1948). *Wissenschaft als Beruf*. Berlin: Dunker & Humblot.

Weber, M. (1919b/1948). *Politik als Beruf*. http://www.mynetcologne.de/~nc-clasenhe/soz/lk/beruf.htm.

Weber, M. (1921). *Gesammelte politische Schriften*. München: Duncker & Humboldt.

Weber, M. (1922a). *Gesammelte Aufsätze zur Wissenschaftslehre*. Tübingen: Mohr.

Weber, M. (1922b). *Wirtschaft und Gesellschaft: Grundriß der verstehenden Soziologie Studienausgabe*. Köln/Berlin: Kiepenheuer & Witsch.

Weber, M. (1924a). *Gesammelte Aufsätze zur Sozial- und Wirtschaftsgeschichte*. Tübingen: Mohr.

Weber, M. (1924b). *Gesammelte Aufsätze zur Soziologie und Sozialpolitik*. Tübingen: Mohr.

Weber, M. (1930). *The Protestant ethic and the spirit of capitalism* (Trans. T. Parsons). London: Allen & Unwin.

Weber, M. (1946). *From Max Weber: essays in sociology*. New York: Oxford University Press.

Weber, M. (1947). *The theory of social and economic organization* (Trans. A. M. Henderson & T. Parsons). New York: Harper & Row.

Weber, M. (1949). *The methodology of the social sciences*. New York: Free.

Weber, M. (1954). *Max Weber on law in economy and society*. Cambridge, MA: Harvard University Press.

Weber, M. (1962). *Basic concepts in sociology*. Secaucus, NJ: Citadel.

Weber, M. (1965). *The sociology of religion*. London: Methuen.

Weber, M. (1970). *Max Weber: the interpretation of social reality*. London: Joseph.

Weber, M. (1974). *Max Weber on universities: the power of the state and the dignity of the academic calling in Imperial Germany*. Chicago: University of Chicago Press.

Weber, M. (1976). *The protestant ethic and the spirit of capitalism* (2nd ed.). London: Allen & Unwin.

Weber, M. (1978). *Economy and society: an outline of interpretive sociology*. Berkeley, CA: University of California Press.

Weedon, C. (1987). *Feminist practice and poststructural theory*, Oxford: Blackwell.

Weick, K. E. (1969). *The social psychology of organizing*. Reading, MA: Addison-Wesley.

Weick, K. E. (1995). *Sensemaking in organizations*. Thousand Oaks, CA: Sage.

Weintraub, J. (1979). *Virtue, community, and the sociology of liberty: the notion of republican virtue and its impact on modern western social thought*. Phd Dissertation, Department of Sociology, University of California, Berkeley, CA.

Weiss, R. M. (2000). Taking science out of organization science: how would postmodernism reconstruct the analysis of organizations? *Organization Science, 11*(6), 702–731.

West, C., Lazar, M., & Kramarae, C. (1997). Gender in discourse. In T. van Dijk (Ed.), *Discourse studies. Vol. 2: Discourse as social interaction* (pp. 119–143). Sage: London.

West, C., & Zimmerman, D. (1987). Doing gender. *Gender & Society, 1*, 125–151.

Westergaard, J., & Ressler, H. (1975). *Class in a capitalist society: a study of contemporary Britain*. London: Heinemann Educational.

Westwood, R., & Linstead, S. (Eds.). (2001). *The language of organizations*. London: Sage.

Whitehead, A. N. (1925). *Science and the modern world*. London: Macmillan.

Whitley, R. (1994). The internationalization of firms and markets: its significance and institutional structuring. *Organization, 1*, 101–124.

Whitlock, G. (2000). *The intimate empire*. London: Cassell.

Whyte, W. (1960). *The organization man*. Harmondsworth: Penguin.

Wilde, A. W. (1978). Conversations among gentlemen: oligarchical democracy in Colombia. In Juan J. Linz & Alfred Stepan (Eds.), *The breakdown of democratic regimes: crisis, breakdown and reequilibrium*. Baltimore: Johns Hopkins University Press.

Wilkins, B., & Andersen, P. (1991). Gender differences and similarities in management communication. *Management Communication Quarterly, 5*, 6–35.

Willer, D. (1967). *Scientific sociology: theory and method*. Englewood Cliffs, NJ: Prentice-Hall.

Willer, D. (2003). Power-at-a-distance. *Social Forces, 81*(4), 1295–1334.

Williams, K., Haslam, C., & Williams, J. (1992). Ford versus 'Fordism': the beginning of mass production? *Work, Employment & Society, 6*, 517–555.

Williams, P., & Chrisman, L. (Eds.). (1993). *Colonial discourse and postcolonial theory: a reader*. Hemel Hempstead: Harvester Wheatsheaf.

Williamson, O. E. (1981). The economics of organizations: the transaction cost approach. *American Journal of Sociology, 87*, 548–577.

Willis, P. (1974). *Learning to labour: how working class kids get working class jobs*. Westmead: Saxon.

Willmott, H. (1997). *Rethinking management and managerial work: capitalism, control and subjectivity.* London: Sage.

Wilson, F. (2003). *Organizational behaviour and gender* (2nd ed.). London: Ashgate.

Winch, P. (1958). *The idea of a social science.* London: Routledge & Kegan Paul.

Windschuttle, K. (2002). *The fabrication of Aboriginal history. Vol. 1: Van Diemen's Land 1803–1847.* Paddington, NSW: Macleay.

Winner, L. (1995). Who will we be in cyberspace? http://polaris.gseis.ucla.edu/pagre/tno/september-1995.html, retrieved 4 January, 2005.

Wittgenstein, L. (1967[1953]). *Philosophical investigations.* Oxford: Blackwell.

Wittgenstein, L. (1972[1953]). *Philosophical investigations* (3rd ed.). Oxford: Blackwell.

Wolin, S. S. (1960). *Politics and vision.* Boston, MA: Little Brown.

Wood, L. A., & Kroger, R. O. (2000). *Doing discourse analysis: methods for studying action in talk and text.* Thousand Oaks, CA: Sage.

Wrege, C. D. (1995). F. W. Taylor's lecture on management, 4 June 1907, an introduction. *Journal of Management History, 1*(1), 4–7.

Wrege, C. D., & Greenwood, R. G. (1991). *Frederick W. Taylor – the father of scientific management: myth and reality.* New York: Irwin.

Wrege, C. D., & Hodgetts, R. M. (2000). Frederick W. Taylor's 1899 pig iron observations: examining fact, fiction, and lessons for the new millennium. *Academy of Management Journal, 43*(6), 1284–1291.

Yates, J. (1989). *Control through communication: the rise of system in American management.* Baltimore: Johns Hopkins University Press.

Young, R. (2001). *Postcolonialism: an historical introduction.* Oxford: Blackwell.

Zald, M. (2002). Spinning disciplines: critical management studies in the context of the transformation of management education. *Organization, 9*(3), 365–385.

Zeitlin, M. (1974). Corporate ownership and control: the large corporation and the capitalist class. *American Journal of Sociology, 79*, 1073–1119.

Zeraffa, M. (1976). *Fictions: the novel and social reality.* Harmondsworth: Penguin.

Zimmerman, D. H. (1971). The practicalities of rule-use. In J. D. Douglas (Ed.), *Understanding everyday life: toward the reconstruction of sociological knowledge.* London: Routledge & Kegan Paul.

Žižek, S. (2005a). Beyond discourse analysis. In *Interrogating the real* (pp. 271–284). London: Continuum.

Žižek, S. (2005b). The constitution is dead: long live proper politics. *The Guardian.* http://politics.guardian.co.uk/eu/comment/0,9236,1499088,00.html.

Index

Please note that references to non-textual information such as tables are in *italic* print, while notes are denoted by the letter 'n' and note number following the page number. American spellings are used.

Printed in the United States
133287LV00005B/17/P